Germany since 1789

Germany since 1789

A Nation Forged and Renewed

2nd edition

David G. Williamson

macmillan education   palgrave

First published 2005
This edition published 2016 by
PALGRAVE

Palgrave in the UK is an imprint of Macmillan Publishers Limited, registered in England, company number 785998, of 4 Crinan Street, London, N1 9XW.

Palgrave Macmillan in the US is a division of St. Martin's Press LLC, 175 Fifth Avenue, New York, NY 10010.

Palgrave is a global imprint of the above companies and is represented throughout the world.

Palgrave® and Macmillan® are registered trademarks in the United States, the United Kingdom, Europe and other countries.

ISBN 978–1–137–35004–6 hardback
ISBN 978–1–137–35005–3 paperback

This book is printed on paper suitable for recycling and made from fully managed and sustained forest sources. Logging, pulping and manufacturing processes are expected to conform to the environmental regulations of the country of origin.

A catalogue record for this book is available from the British Library.

Library of Congress Cataloging-in-Publication Data
Names: Williamson, D. G.
Title: Germany since 1789 : a nation forged and renewed / David G. Williamson.
Other titles: Germany since 1815
Description: 2nd edition. | New York, NY : Palgrave Macmillan, 2016. | Original edition published under title: Germany since 1815. New York, N.Y. : Palgrave Macmillan, 2005. | Includes index.
Identifiers: LCCN 2015039868| ISBN 9781137350046 (hardback) | ISBN 9781137350053 (pbk.)
Subjects: LCSH: Germany – History – 1789-1900. | Germany – History – 20th century.
Classification: LCC DD203 .W48 2016 | DDC 943 – dc23
LC record available at http://lccn.loc.gov/2015039868

Printed and bound by CPI Group (UK) Ltd, Croydon, CR0 4YY

To Sue, a loyal, loving and very patient friend and partner

Contents

List of Illustrations

List of Maps

Preface

This book is aimed at both academic students of history studying courses on modern German history and the general reader, who wishes to know more about the turbulent course of German history since 1789. A knowledge of German history is vital for anybody wishing to understand the evolution of modern Europe. Germany has, after all, had a profound impact on European, American and world history in the 20th century. Today that is still so: Germany is seen, even by her old enemies, as the 'benign hegemon' of the EU. Historians debate whether or not Germany caused the First World War, but what is undeniable is that Germany played a key role in the defeat of the Russian Empire, and so by default the birth of the USSR. The Second World War accelerated the dissolution of the European colonial Empires and the vacuum that the defeat of Hitler created in central Europe led to the long Cold War and the division of the European continent until 1990. Both the threat of Soviet expansion and the need to contain a revived (albeit for the time being only a West) German state also led to western European integration with its immense, and as yet unfinished, consequences for the traditional structure of Europe's nation states. It is not surprising then that historians have paid so much attention to the 'course of German history' in the 19th and 20th centuries.

The object of this book is to provide for all who are interested in this period, a concise, readable and up-to-date study of German history since 1789, which combines the key facts of the period with analysis and wider reference to crucial historical debates. Once cognizant of these, readers will be in a position to understand and value recent trends in German historiography, which often explore the significance, for example, of memory, regional and 'everyday history' (*Alltagsgeschichte*).

The book is divided into four main chronological parts: 1789–1870, 1871–1918, 1918–1945 and 1945–1990, but the later section also includes an extended section analysing the first decades of the new Berlin Republic. Each chapter starts with an introduction outlining the major problems, issues and questions that arise from the events covered in it. The purpose of this is to focus readers' attention on the often paradoxical and complex nature of German history. This approach is further developed in the assessment in the final section of the book. Focus boxes and notes in the margin help elucidate points made in the text by providing background information or summaries of historiographical debates, while a timeline at the beginning of each chapter provides a guide to the key dates of the relevant material covered in the chapter. The text is comprehensively cross-referenced so that readers can explore the origins and consequences of events they are studying, as well as being reminded of the remarkable longevity of some issues in German history. In Part Six of the book there is a collection of documents, which both provides a basis for further discussion and helps readers understand more fully issues dealt with in the main text. Where the documents are relevant to the text, the relevant document number is indicated in the page margin. At the end of the book there is a critical bibliography of books in English on the period of German history covered by this book. It is divided into chronological sections so that readers can readily explore issues raised in this study in greater depth. There is also a glossary explaining the technical terms used in the text.

As the main focus of this book is on the German state or 'Germany', domestic Austrian politics are only touched upon where they are relevant to this history.

DAVID G. WILLIAMSON

Acknowledgements

The author and publishers wish to thank the following for permission to use copyright material.

Bundesbildstelle Berlin, for the post-1945 photographs © copyright Bundesbildstelle Berlin.

The Imperial War Museum, for a French cartoon commenting on Bismarck's attempts to keep France and Russia apart in the 1880s (ref: Q81754). The image is reproduced with permission of the trustees of the Imperial War Museum, London.

I would also like to thank Rachel Bridgewater at Palgrave for her encouragement and help, Mr Gogulanathan Bactavachalane for his kindness and patience, and Sue Morrow for putting up with an author and his proofs.

Maps

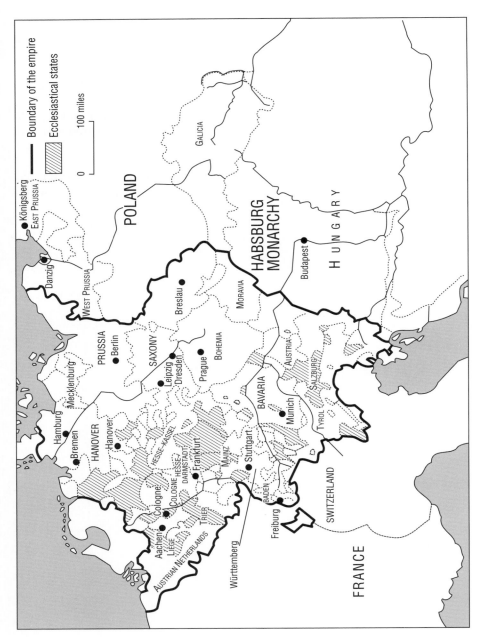

Map I Germany in 1789 (from Brendan Simms, *The Struggle for Mastery in Germany, 1779–1850,* Macmillan, 1998, p. ix)

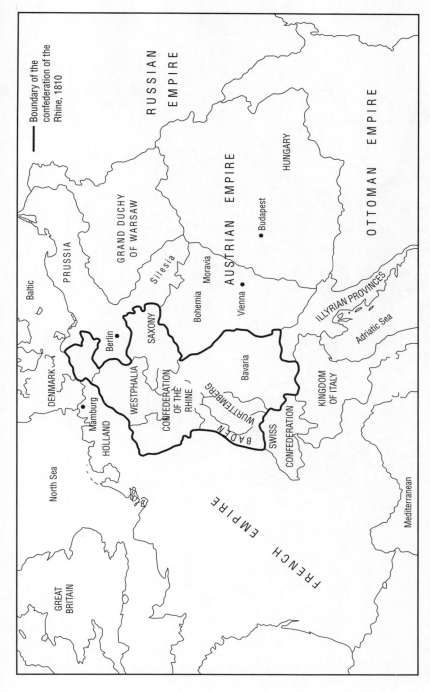

Map 2 Germany in 1810: the impact of Napoleon

Boundary of the confederation of the Rhine, 1810

GREAT BRITAIN

North Sea

Baltic

DENMARK

Hamburg

HOLLAND

PRUSSIA

Berlin

GRAND DUCHY OF WARSAW

RUSSIAN EMPIRE

Silesia

SAXONY

WESTPHALIA

CONFEDERATION OF THE RHINE

Bohemia

Moravia

AUSTRIAN EMPIRE

Vienna

HUNGARY

Budapest

Bavaria

WÜRTTEMBERG

BADEN

SWISS CONFEDERATION

KINGDOM OF ITALY

ILLYRIAN PROVINCES

Adriatic Sea

FRENCH EMPIRE

Mediterranean

OTTOMAN EMPIRE

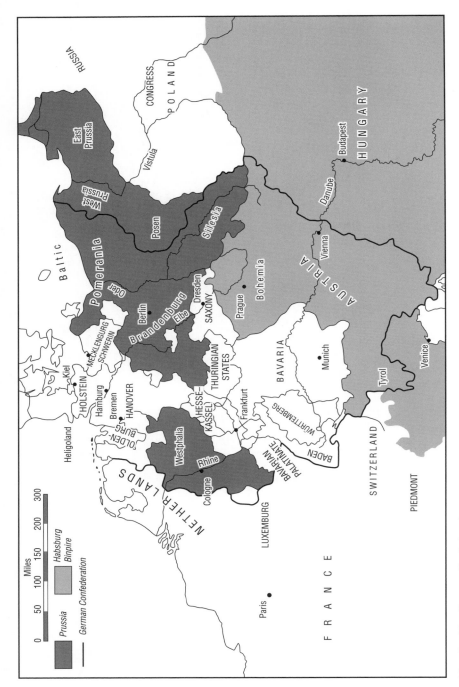

Map 3   The German Confederation

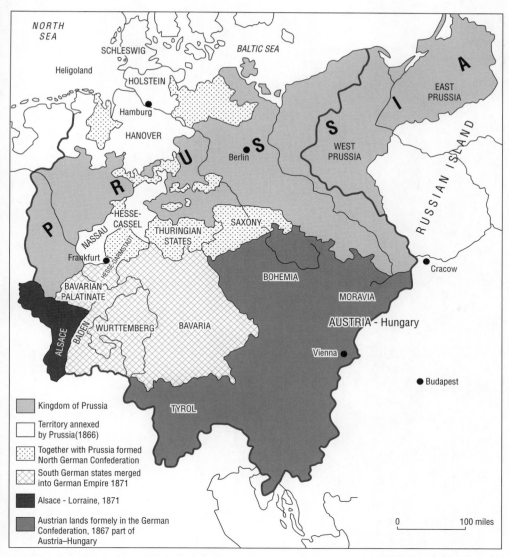

Map 4 The unification of *Kleindeutschland*

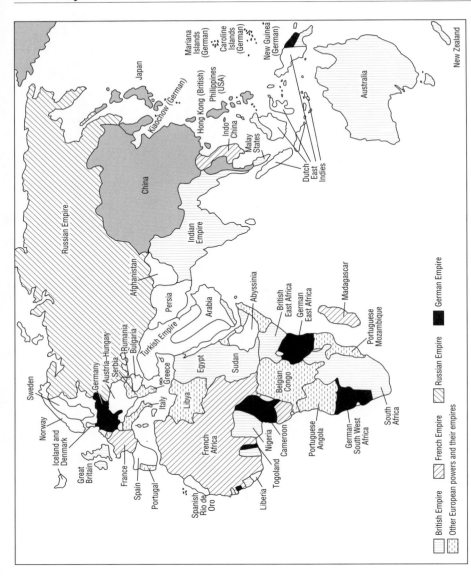

Map 5 Germany's colonial empire in Africa and Asia, 1913

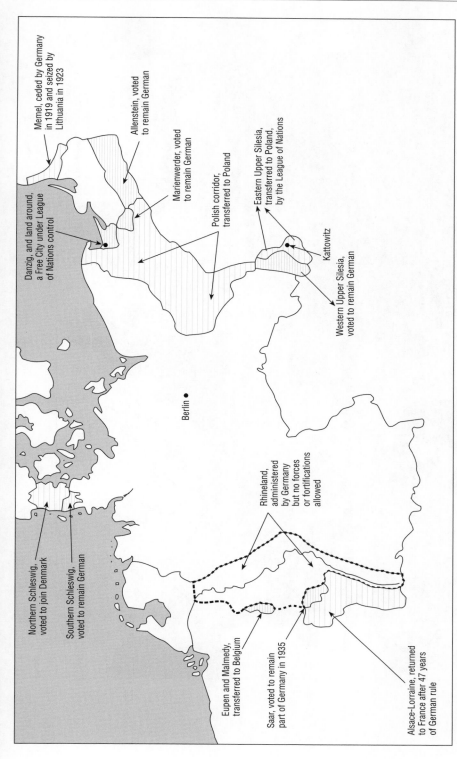

Memel, ceded by Germany in 1919 and seized by Lithuania in 1923

Allenstein, voted to remain German

Marienwerder, voted to remain German

Polish corridor, transferred to Poland

Eastern Upper Silesia, transferred to Poland, by the League of Nations

Kattowitz

Western Upper Silesia, voted to remain German

Danzig, and land around, a Free City under League of Nations control

Berlin

Rhineland, administered by Germany but no forces or fortifications allowed

Northern Schleswig, voted to join Denmark

Southern Schleswig, voted to remain German

Eupen and Malmedy, transferred to Belgium

Saar, voted to remain part of Germany in 1935

Alsace-Lorraine, returned to France after 47 years of German rule

Map 6 Germany's territorial losses, 1919 (adapted from map in *New Perspective*, vol. 5, no. 2, December 1999 Sempringham – www.ehistory.org.uk)

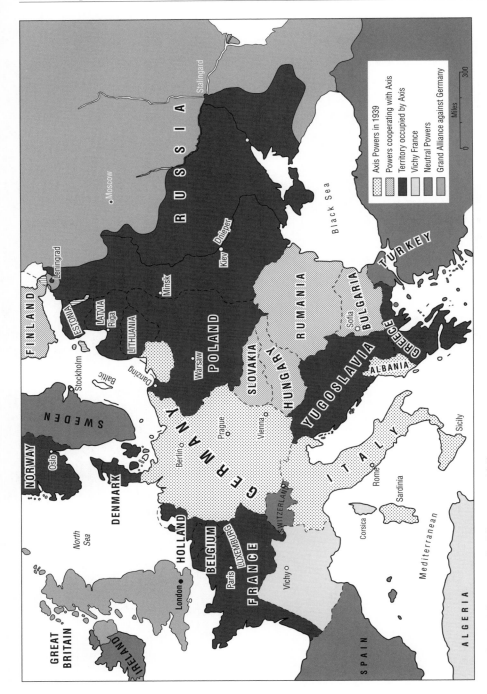

Map 7   Nazi Germany at its fullest extent, 1942

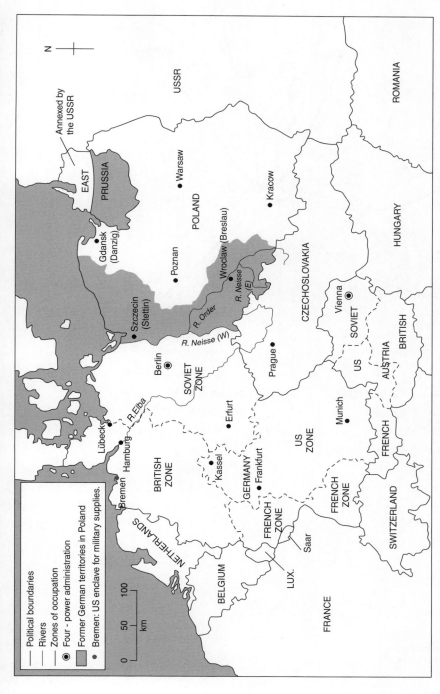

Map 8   Germany, 1945–1949 in which year the FRG was formed from merging the three western zones and the GDR from the Soviet zone. In 1990 the GDR merged with the FRG to form a united Germany.

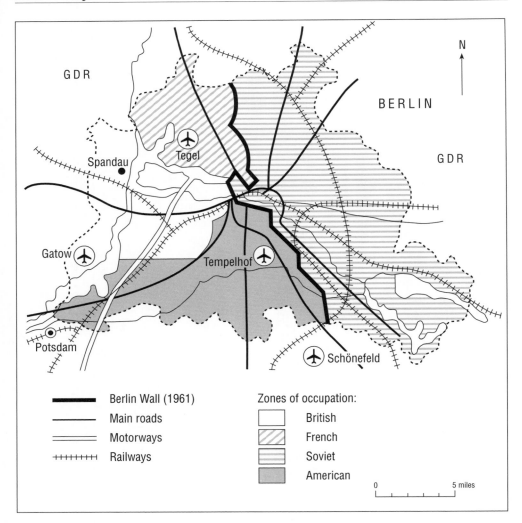

Map 9   Berlin, 1945–1990

Part One

Germany Unified, 1789–1871

1 Germany Recast: The French Revolutionary Wars and the Vienna Settlement, 1789–1815

Introduction: problems, issues and questions

Like Poland, Germany, to use Norman Davies' apt description, was also a country 'on wheels',[1] which frequently changed its frontiers. What was the real Germany, if such an unhistorical question can be asked? The Holy Roman Empire of the German Nation, the Rhineland Confederation or the Confederation of 1815, or were the two confederations merely transit stages to the Bismarckian Empire? The seismic events of the French Revolution and the establishment of the Napoleonic Empire reshaped Germany. Napoleon is often seen as the midwife of modern Germany. Thomas Nipperdey, for instance, begins his magisterial history of Germany with the words 'In the beginning was Napoleon',[2] but was Napoleon the sole architect of the new German territorial settlement or did the German princes themselves seize the chance to be liberated from the 'dead hand' of the Empire? On the other hand it can also be argued that the Empire was far from 'dead'. Its loose federalism provided a viable structure for the German-speaking peoples of central Europe until it was abolished by Napoleon. Indeed it is arguable that its presence is still missed today by federally and European minded Germans.

Military defeat was the catalyst to the Prussian reform movement, but how accurate is the term 'defensive modernization', which is often used to describe the Prussian reforms? Do these reforms, as Hans-Ulrich Wehler argues, mark the point at which Prussia began to diverge from western Europe, as they only partially modernized Prussia by leaving the traditional authorities still in place? Increasingly, as we shall see, historians are rejecting or modifying this somewhat simplistic interpretation of Prussian historical development.[3] The French occupation certainly led to the growth of a German political nationalism, particularly in Prussia, but did this in reality amount to much? Had the new nationalists any idea of what sort of Germany they wanted, or was their nationalism essentially a romantic and often blood-curdling backlash against the French? Was the creation of the German Confederation a 'betrayal' of German nationalism or, as modern historians argue, was it in fact an institution shaped by the Holy Roman Empire's legacy of federalism and a product of its times?[4]

Germany on the eve of the French Revolution

On the eve of the French Revolution German Europe consisted of some 687,000 square kilometres and 29 million inhabitants and was potentially the largest political entity in Europe, but it was fractured into 1800 different territories varying in size from the Kingdom of Prussia and the Austrian German, Bohemian and Moravian territories of the Hapsburg Empire to small territories of barely a few square kilometres. Many of these were further subdivided by internal ecclesiastical, legal and fiscal boundaries. Up to a point these fragmented states found a degree of political expression in the Holy Roman Empire of the German Nation. Its aim, as James Sheehan has succinctly put it, was 'not to clarify and dominate but rather to order and balance fragmented institutions and multiple loyalties'.[5]

The Holy Roman Empire

The origins of the Holy Roman Empire of the German Nation lay in Charlemagne's subjugation of the Germanic tribes in the last third of the 8th century. Crowned Holy Roman Emperor on Christmas Day 800, Charlemagne's ambition was to reconstruct the western part of the old Roman Empire. He was to succeed only briefly and some 40 years later the Empire was partitioned, with the western section ultimately becoming France, while the eastern section eventually became the Holy Roman Empire of the German Nation and was to survive until its abolition by Napoleon in 1806. For much of its history the Empire was characterized by its lack of centralization, its diversity and by an elected head of state, the Holy Roman Emperor. For most of the 19th and 20th centuries this very diversity led German and Anglophone historians to dismiss the Empire, at least for its last century and a half, as a sclerotic anachronism preventing the emergence of a German national state. In retrospect the future seemed to belong to Prussia, which possessed the necessary military and economic force to unify Germany and propel her into 'modernity'. This 'Borussian' or Prusso-centric view was epitomized by the works of Heinrich von Treitschke (1834–1896), the nationalist historian, who was appointed Professor of History at Berlin University (see p. 116) and was drummed into generations of German school children. Even defeat in 1945 and the dissolution of Prussia (see p. 295) failed initially to alter the perception of the Empire as a hopelessly failed institution. Indeed historians, seeking to explain the disastrous turn of German history in the first part of the 20th century, blamed the Empire for delaying the emergence of a German unitary state and so causing the catastrophic divergence of its history from its neighbours in western Europe. In other words it was one of the key reasons responsible for its so-called **Sonderweg**, a term that will frequently be referred to in this work. This view did not go unchallenged. As early as 1967 Karl von Aretin in a seminal study began the process of looking at the Empire on its own terms. He and later historians have shown that it was 'far from moribund'.[6] Indeed the development of the European Union has led some historians to see it as a forerunner of European integration. Johannes Burkhardt, for instance, observed that it 'had already ... solved the constitutional issues, which others are beginning to discuss in the twenty-first century'.[7]

    In fact comparisons with the EU are exaggerated. Whereas the EU seeks by centralization to establish itself as a major political power, the Empire on the other hand attempted to protect the *status quo* and the independence of the smaller states. In the words of the Swiss Jurist, Johannes von Müller, it made Germany 'free through fragmentation'.[8] To what extent did it in reality achieve this? Was the Empire a viable political organization, which in retrospect could have offered the German peoples an alternative to the state, which Bismarck created? Essentially, an effective state must enjoy credibility in the eyes of its subjects. To retain this it has to be able to defend its inhabitants militarily and, through an effective judicial system, guarantee their freedom to pursue their business free from intimidation and violence. To accomplish this the state must be able to raise the necessary funds through taxation, ensure that sufficient armed forces are raised through conscription and be able to guarantee an independent legal system. In fact as Peter Wilson has emphasized, imperial military and fiscal institutions did offer for much of its history 'collective security for the entire Reich'.[9] The *Reichstag* allotted to each territory of the Empire a sum of money and men to be raised, which enabled it in 1735, for instance, to mobilize some 85,000 troops. The Reich's legal system, overseen by the Supreme Court, the *Reichskammergericht* (Imperial Cameral Court), provided an invaluable framework for solving disputes between the states. Throughout the 18th century it dealt with an average of 230–250 cases a year.

Sonderweg: Literally special path. Scholars such as Hans-Ulrich Wehler, using Britain and France as models, have argued that industrialization in Germany was not accompanied by social and political 'modernization' or democratization. Hence Germany took its 'special path'. This is disputed, particularly by D. Blackbourn and G. Eley.

The head of the Empire, the Emperor, was elected by the college of electors (see below). Each new emperor had to sign an 'electoral capitulation', an agreement which committed him not to violate the laws and customs of the Reich. The Emperor's political powers could be divided into two categories: his royal prerogatives, which empowered him to reassign the minor estates (fiefs) when they fell vacant, and to bestow honours on the nobility. More importantly he had the right to appoint a number of judges in the imperial courts and set the order of the agenda in the *Reichstag*. Although the Emperor's prerogatives were increasingly limited, he nevertheless retained considerable influence through his powers of patronage and by the fact that as 'his powers were never listed completely, they remained theoretically unlimited enabling him to derive new rights in response to changed circumstances'.[10]

The *Reichstag* was divided into three colleges or curia to use the Latin term: the College of Electors, which by 1777 consisted of the Archbishops of Mainz, Trier and Cologne and the rulers of Bohemia, the Palatinate, Saxony, Brandenburg and Hanover, the College of Princes and the College of Cities. Did the *Reichstag* together with the **Kreis** assemblies constitute a 'proto parliamentary' system in that together they possessed some of the characteristics of representative institutions?[11] The *Reichstag* took few decisions of principle. By the late 18th century its main role was to discuss and legitimate actions taken either singularly or collectively by the princes and to strive for consensus. The ten *Kreis* assemblies had been established in the 16th century and played an important regional role not only in implementing decisions by the *Reichstag* and the verdicts of the courts but also in ensuring that the interests of the lesser territories would be taken into account by the larger German states.

Kreis: Literally circle, an administrative subdivision.

Austria and Prussia

There were two rival centres of potential hegemony in the Reich: Austria and Prussia. Neither was a compact nation state and both had territory outside the Empire. Austria was a large disparate empire, the territories of which included the Archduchy of Austria, Styria, Carinthia and Carniola, the Bohemian and Hungarian crown lands, as well as the Austrian Netherlands, Lombardy, Mantua and Galicia. By 1720 the territories controlled by the Habsburgs were greater than those of the entire Reich. Inevitably this made the Reich of less importance to Austria, even though the imperial title of Emperor, which remained with the Habsburg dynasty except for a brief interlude from 1742 to 1745, still afforded the dynasty considerable prestige, influence and scope for patronage.

From 1640 to 1786 Prussia was ruled by the Hohenzollern dynasty, which produced three monarchs of exceptional calibre. Thanks to their military, fiscal and administrative policies, Prussia was able to raise and finance a disproportionately large army. Territorially Prussia's emergence in the 18th century as a great German power occurred in three stages. It acquired a strong central European core during the 17th century and between 1702 and 1745 added further territories, the most important of which was Silesia. To this it added the land gained from the three partitions of Poland in 1772–1795. Its opportunities to expand were also greatly assisted by its closeness to Poland and Sweden, which were powers in decline, rather than to a powerful France in the west.

As it was ultimately Prussia that was to create a Prussian-dominated *Kleindeutschland* in the 19th century, its rise to the status of a great German power by 1772 is the subject of considerable debate. To Borussian nationalist historians, such as Treitschke and Gustav Freytag (1816–1895), Prussia's rise from 'the sand box'[12] of the Reich to a great power was little short of miraculous, while others see it more rationally as a result of the Hohenzollern's acquisition of east Prussia in 1618–1648 and Upper Silesia in 1741 and its lucky survival in the Seven Years War.

In 1740 Frederick II exploited the death of the Emperor Charles VI and the accession of the young inexperienced Maria Theresa to seize the wealthy province of Silesia. By 1742 Austria was on the verge of collapse. For the first time the newly elected Emperor was a Bavarian-Wittelsbach, rather than a Hapsburg. With French help he hoped to mobilize the resources of the Empire and annex Austria and Bohemia. His subsequent defeat saved Austria but weakened the Empire. The Emperor was seen as a mere pawn of the French and Prussians, and the *Reichstag* refused to grant help to either side on the grounds that this was not an imperial war. When Charles VII died in 1745, Maria Theresa's husband, Francis, Duke of Lorraine, was elected Emperor, but the title was no longer so important to Vienna as it had once been. The refusal of the German states to rally to the Hapsburgs lessened the significance of the Empire in the eyes of Vienna, while the states increasingly perceived Austria and its dependent territories to be following interests which were diverging from the rest of the Empire.

As a consequence of the War of the Austrian Succession, Prussia now became Austria's main enemy. In 1756 the Seven Years War broke out when Prussia launched a pre-emptive attack against Saxony. This led in effect to a German civil war within a European and global war. Prussia backed by Britain dominated north Germany, while the southern German states allied with Austria, Russia and France, which was also engaged in a worldwide conflict with Britain. Prussia decisively defeated the French and their imperial allies at Rossbach in 1757 (see p. 11), but by 1761 was surrounded by its enemies and faced imminent defeat. Only the death of Czarina Elizabeth in January 1762 and the accession of Peter III, who immediately ended hostilities, enabled Prussia to survive and make peace with an exhausted Austria in February 1763 that left Silesia in Prussian hands.

The 'Third Germany'

German history in the 18th century is often seen through the lens of Prusso-Austrian dualism, which is regarded as the precursor to the war of 1866 (see p. 92), but this is to ignore the other territories of the Empire, the so-called 'Third Germany', composed of such medium-sized states (*Mittelstaaten*) as Bavaria, Saxony and Hanover as well as the numerous city states and smaller territories, which wanted neither Prussian nor Austrian domination. For them the Empire remained an important element of stability in central Europe, and there was no shortage of political and legal theorists who were ready to defend its existence and propose new reforms. Even though the Empire was abolished by Napoleon in 1806, its federalist legacy was to influence the subsequent reorganizations of Germany in the 19th century.

See Map 1

In 1785 the medium-sized states set up the League of Princes (*Fürstenbund*) specifically to reform the imperial constitution and provide protection against the growing power of Prussia and Austria. However, neither Prussia nor Austria wanted to destroy the Empire. The imperial title still had some political importance for Austria, and Prussia saw the Empire as a way of blocking Hapsburg plans. Prussia in fact took over the League of Princes to thwart Austrian plans for exchanging the Netherlands for Bavaria.

The economy of the Empire

Economic integration within the EU and the introduction of the euro in 2001 have led to a more sympathetic reassessment of the Empire's economy. Economically, as politically, the Empire was fragmented. However the *Reichstag* did attempt to regulate some key aspects of the economy, such as trade embargoes on hostile powers, quarantine arrangements during epidemics, road construction and currency questions, relying on the *Kreis* assemblies to implement its decisions. There was no uniform commercial code, and the mass of tolls and tariffs certainly impeded inter-German trade. Yet in the opinion of Peter Wilson 'the Reich mitigated the adverse impact of German territorial fragmentation'.[13] The structure of the Reich facilitated inter-regional cooperation and encouraged internal movement of labour. Economic activity was predominantly of local or regional character, and there was no single, unified imperial market. There existed, however, by 1800 several distinct trade networks linking up the south-eastern regions of the Reich to the Adriatic and the northern and western territories to the Baltic and North Sea.

Although the Reich had no common currency, in the 16th century two basic currency systems were in existence: the silver Thaler in the north and the gold florin in the south. All other types of coins, of which there were 1200 in circulation in 1692, were valued against these according to their gold or silver content. Initially the *Kreis* assemblies attempted to regulate inter-regional rates through regular meetings. Gradually in the 18th century this system collapsed as the larger states ignored the official rate of exchange and began to devalue the florin or Thaler. Austro-Prussian rivalry exacerbated the problem and prevented any solution.

Industry and agriculture

In comparison to Britain, at the end of the 18th century German industry was still backward. Textiles and timber production formed the basis of the largest industries, but some 800,000 tons of coal a year were mined as well as one million tons of iron ore. Large-scale factory production did not become common until the 1830s (see p. 55). Production was still carried out in small rural based workshops, which were supplied locally with wool, linen, wood and other raw materials. This 'putting-out system' (*Verlagswesen*) arguably retarded the development of the factory system as it allowed entrepreneurs to make large profits without the expense of supervising employees and the introduction of expensive modern machinery. This system helps explain why under half the population worked on the land for their main livelihood, even though the over-whelming majority lived in the countryside. The predominance of small, inefficient farms, which had little spare produce to sell, led to the enclo-sure of woodlands and commons to produce more effective units of pro-duction in both east and west Germany.

Life in the Empire

As elsewhere in Europe, life in the German states for the great mass of the people was hard and precarious, and usually only half a particular genera-tion reached their late twenties. The majority of Germans died before they reached the age of four. If males survived childhood, they could look forward to a life expectancy of some 50 years, while women were lucky to reach their mid-thirties. Altogether well over a third of Germans were dependent on good harvests for survival.

Throughout the Empire society was organized into 'orders' or 'estates' rather than classes: nobles, clergy, burghers and peasants. These estates were all subject to different laws and regulations. Most of the German population worked or lived on the land and was still legally subject to an old-established lordship or *Herrschaft*, the privileges and powers of which might be exercised by the landed nobility, the Catholic Church, the local territorial ruler or perhaps just a tenant farmer leasing land from the church. In the west and south, labour services had often been commuted into cash payment, although the lordships remained the legal owners of the land and still enjoyed the hunting rights. Traditionally, historians have contrasted this with the situation in the Prussian lands east of the Elbe in Prussia, where the lord of the manor, or **Junker**, exercised direct control over his peasants who, in exchange for the land they cultivated, had to offer labour services in cash or kind. In fact recent research by William Hagen among others has shown this model to be exaggerated and that in reality the two systems had more similarities than differences. In a detailed study of Brandenburg Hagen has shown that the old stereotype of autocratic *Junkers* and passive peasants, which has often been used to justify arguments about the failure of democracy and

The term **Junker** comes from the German *Jungherr*, which applied to sons of the Prussian landed gentry serving as officer cadets. Later the term came to describe the Prussian landown-ers with large estates east of the Elbe, many of whom served in the Prussian bureaucracy or army.

liberalism in Germany in the 19th and 20th centuries, is inaccurate. On the contrary, Hagen's study shows how tenant farmers used both the existing seignorial courts and new legislation introduced by Frederick II to contest their lordships' decisions.[14]

Compared to the rest of Europe, the Empire had a greater density of towns. By 1800 some 26 per cent of the population lived in towns, the majority of which had a population of less than 10,000. Many of the burghers owned land outside the town and cultivated it. The towns, were organized into a corporate structure under which their population was divided into the 'patriciate' (the ruling mercantile elite) and burghers, the majority of whom were master craftsmen, small-scale businessmen and shopkeepers, who were mostly organized into craft guilds. Beneath them were the urban poor consisting of mainly unskilled workers, migrants and servants.

By 1800 this old corporate structure of society was in the process of change as a new middle class or bourgeoisie began to emerge. It was stronger in the larger cities where economic expansion gave opportunities to new entrepreneurs, and it was supplemented by a growing bureaucracy and intellectual elite.

Women toiled in the fields at harvest times or when male labour was short. They also played a prominent role at home in the cottage industries which grew up as a result of the putting-out system (see above). Here wives were economically equal partners of their husbands. In the households of the more prosperous burghers and the new bourgeoisie it was increasingly accepted that the woman's unique task was to preside over the 'private sphere' and create an oasis of peace for her family. Legally criminal law treated both sexes as equally liable, but in civil law, particularly cases dealing with property, women were represented by male relatives, unless they were widows.

The Empire and national identity

To what extent did the Germans feel themselves to be a people? A. J. P. Taylor argued sweepingly that the German people had 'been for more than a thousand years, unmistakably a people'.[15] This was the view of the German philosopher and theologian, Johann Gottfried Herder (1774–1803). He argued that in practice there was a German fatherland, which was defined not territorially but by the idea of a German **Volk**, a community formed by language, culture, law and common institutions.

Volk: people sharing a common ethnic origin, language and culture, but not necessarily belonging to the same state.

The new Romantic Movement sought to define Germany on the basis of language and ethnicity and some intellectuals such as the writer and philosopher, Thomas Abbt (1738–1766) began to use the word 'nation'. Certainly the Germans were united by a common language, although they spoke this in many different dialects, which were not always comprehensible to other Germans. By the last quarter of the 18th century there was a real German literary culture facilitated by networks of publishers, the new periodicals, reading societies and libraries. The printed word and personal connections linked people right across German-speaking Europe, from Strasburg to Riga and Hamburg to Vienna. This did, however, involve only a small, educated elite in Germany and did not touch the great majority of Germans, whose culture was still primarily local and traditionally based on their villages, churches and market towns. In practice the Empire afforded the Germans an acceptable framework in which to reconcile their local patriotism to the overall imperial structure.

The traditional Borussian view represented, for example, by H. A. Winkler, is that German nationhood was blocked by the Empire until Bismarck unified Germany in 1866–1871, and consequently was left with 'the "consolation prize" of being only a "cultural nation"'. Yet more recently this view is challenged by 'federalist' historians such as Georg Schmidt, Maiken Umbach and Joachim Whaley. Schmidt indeed argues that the Empire was a distinct entity with its own 'federal nationalism'.[16] Foreigners often referred to the Empire as 'Germany'. While the wars against the Turks, the Swedish and above all the French to a certain extent led to the Empire being perceived in the 18th century by the German peoples as a 'German Fatherland', this approach can exaggerate the loyalty felt to the Empire. Prussia, after the Seven Years War, formed a new focus of loyalty. Frederick II's defeat of the French at the Battle of Rossbach was welcomed as a blow against French cultural hegemony. One musician and man of letters, Christian Daniel Schubert (1739–1791), in his weekly, *Deutsche Chronik*, observed in 1774 that the Germans had both an emperor and a king to be proud of, but it was the king (Frederick II) who was singled out for especial praise as 'the cynosure of the world, the great original of present and future heroes'.[17]

The impact of the French Revolution

German intellectuals greeted the news of the French Revolution with enthusiasm, but most felt no need to emulate it in their own states where the principles of **enlightened absolutism** had already achieved much. The princes were seen by the bureaucrats and the bourgeoisie as allies against the reactionary forces. Not surprisingly, the princes, too, did not feel threatened by the events in France. Joseph II of Austria, for instance, was convinced that the initial reforms of the new French government were in fact mere copies of his own. The minor uprisings that occurred in the Rhineland and in Saxony in 1789–1790 were easily contained.

Enlightened absolutism: the term used to describe the modernizing reforms carried out by many European 18th-century monarchs. These were inspired by the Enlightenment (see p.15), but had no intention of widening political participation.

The Convention of Reichenbach and the Austro-Prussian war against France, 1790–1795

In 1789 yet another conflict between Prussia and Austria seemed imminent. In February 1788 Austria had joined Russia in an attack on the Ottoman Empire. Fearing that this could lead to the partition of Turkish territory and a dramatic increase in Austrian power, the new Prussian monarch, Frederick William II, prepared for war. He fermented revolts in Hungary, the Austrian Netherlands and Galicia, but in July 1790 both sides pulled back from the brink and negotiated the Convention of Reichenbach. Arguably, as Brendan Simms has pointed out, this was 'the real revolution in German politics'.[18] The two great German powers, which had been locked in confrontation since 1740, were now allies and had the potential to remodel Germany. However, it was against France, which appeared to be paralysed by revolution that they eventually decided to move. When it became clear that the decision of the French Assembly to abolish the **feudal privileges** of the nobility and the diocesan rights of the bishops was to be extended to Alsace, Austria and Prussia, motivated not least by the prospect of annexations in the west at France's cost, issued the Declaration of Pillnitz in 1791. This committed the two states to defending the principle of hereditary monarchy against revolutionary threats. In the subsequent alliance negotiated in February 1792, provisional plans were drawn up for the future of Alsace. Austria would retain a part of it, while the rest would be handed over to the Elector Palatine as compensation for the Prussian annexation of Jülich and Berg (both of which were part of the Palatinate). In April 1792 France responded by declaring war on the two powers. After the decisive defeat of Prussia at Valmy in September 1792, it was the French who occupied the Rhineland. In response the western *Kreise* of the Reich mobilized troops and the Empire declared war on France a year later. Although the French were forced to retreat, the allies suffered a further severe defeat at Fleurus in Flanders in June 1794, and in the following year the French reoccupied the Rhineland.

By 1796 the French were in possession of most of southern Germany, which was to have profound consequences for the future of the Empire. Prussia, facing an insurrection in its **Polish territories**, which it had acquired in 1793, lacked the strength and the financial clout to fight on two fronts and dropped out of the war in 1795, to be followed soon by Baden, Württemberg and Bavaria. In the subsequent Treaty of Basel with France, Prussia in a secret codicil accepted the French occupation of the left bank of the Rhine. In return the French recognized the establishment of a Prussian-dominated neutral zone in northern Germany and promised Prussia compensation on the right bank of the Rhine. Here a precedent was set for linking French annexations with compensation at the expense of the Holy Roman Empire.

French-occupied Rhineland, 1792–1801

In October 1792, as we have noted above, the French briefly occupied the southern section of the Rhineland. The French hoped to exploit peasant unrest with the slogan 'peace on the cottages, war on the palaces', but they rapidly found that this discontent was not revolutionary. Local Jacobins, who had fled the Rhineland in 1789, returned in the baggage train of the French army intent on applying the principle of the French

---

These **feudal privileges** derived from the medieval manorial system whereby a peasant held land from his lord in exchange for services both in cash and kind.

See Document 1

Polish territories: Prussia received most of West Prussia from the first partition of Poland in 1772. In 1793 Prussia gained some 2716 kilometres of Polish territory from the second partition of Poland. The defeat of the Polish uprising in 1795 led to the third partition of Poland between Russia, Prussia and Austria.

Revolution to the Rhineland. They formed Jacobin clubs and with French backing set up a short-lived revolutionary republic in Mainz in March 1793. It failed to win any significant public support and collapsed in July when the French were forced to retreat. In 1794 the French returned and a large French army occupied the whole of the west bank of the Rhine. The Rhineland was then ruthlessly exploited in the interests of the French war effort, but where possible the French army now worked through local officials and the existing administrative structure. Although the Holy Roman Emperor, Francis II, specifically criticized 'persons lacking German [sic] spirit and heart ...', it was understood that it was better for the local officials to cooperate temporarily with the French occupying power rather than risk the administration falling into the hands of German revolutionaries.[19] With the formal annexation of the left bank of the Rhine territories legalized by the Treaty of Lunéville (see below), French rule gained, at least on paper, a legitimacy it had previously lacked.

Treaty of Lunéville

After the Treaty of Basel, Austria and the imperial armies continued the increasingly unsuccessful war against revolutionary France and in 1797 had little option but to negotiate the Peace of Campo Formio. Austria unofficially accepted the French occupation of the Rhineland in return for the Archbishopric of Salzburg, which set a precedent for the secularization of the lands and cities held by the imperial church. However, before this agreement could be implemented war broke out again in 1799 when Austria, bowing to British and Russian pressure, resumed hostilities against France. Napoleon's subsequent victory at Marengo in 1800 (achieved seven months after becoming First Consul in France) opened up the way for the French invasion of the Austrian Empire. Faced with this threat Francis II made peace with Napoleon at Lunéville, which confirmed the French annexation of the Rhineland. The German rulers who lost territory there would be compensated by land taken from the Imperial Church. It was left to the Imperial Delegation (*Reichsdeputations-hauptschluss*), which had been set up by the *Reichstag*, to work out the practical details of this territorial redistribution. Its decisions, however, were pre-empted by the princes who, with French support, seized neighbouring imperial cities and church lands to strengthen their own territories. Those who gained most were the middle-sized states of Bavaria, Württemberg and Baden, which were given the basic shape they were to possess until their incorporation into the Bismarckian Empire in 1866–1871. Their consolidation was achieved at the expense of the imperial cities and the ecclesiastical territories, which were drastically reduced in number 'in a single destructive sweep'[20]; the imperial cities were reduced to just six and the ecclesiastical territories to just three.

Was the Empire now 'as good as dead'? Peter Wilson argues that it still, even then, had the potential to survive. The settlement was more than a 'fig leaf of legitimacy'[21]: the rulers who benefited from the reorganization took over responsibility for the debts of the annexed territories, and the clergy, who lost their benefices, were compensated with pensions. Also the fact that the reorganization had promoted a large number of counts to the status of princes led to hopes that a revived empire might serve as a balance to the power of Austria and Prussia.

The dissolution of the Holy Roman Empire, 1806

It was, however, Napoleon who finally destroyed the Reich. In March 1803 the French occupied Hanover and, in a series of provocative incidents, increasingly violated Imperial territory. The Austrians responded by joining the Anglo-Russian alliance and declared war on France in July 1805. Prussia, tempted by Napoleon's offer of Hanover, remained neutral, while Bavaria, Baden and Württemberg allied with France, perceiving the French to be a more effective guarantee of their own independence. In the three months between October and December an entire Austrian army was forced to surrender at Ulm, Vienna was occupied and a Russo-Austrian force routed at Austerlitz.

These developments threatened the very existence of the Empire, and its western states began to look to Paris for leadership. In the spring of 1806 the Elector of Regensburg Aschaffenburg, Archbishop Karl von Dalberg (1744–1817), tried to persuade Napoleon to accept the imperial crown, arguing that the southern and western states would be better off linked to France than in an empire controlled by Austria and Prussia. Napoleon rejected this idea and, instead, dissolved the Empire and set up the **Confederation** of the Rhine in July 1806 as a buffer between France and its potential enemies in eastern Europe. Francis, who had already proclaimed himself Emperor of Austria, accepted this and abdicated as Holy Roman Emperor. The Empire was now 'history', but its legacy was still to play a role in shaping the German state in the future.

Confederation: a form of union of individual states in which the independence of each state is preserved. It contrasts with a **federation**, which insists on the supremacy of a common government.

The defeat of Prussia

The Napoleonic victories confronted Prussia with the stark choice of either becoming a French satellite or else belatedly fighting for its independence. Prussia declared war on France in August 1806 only to have its armies destroyed at Jena and Auerstädt in October. Within two weeks Napoleon entered Berlin and Frederick William and his government fled to Memel. Once Napoleon had defeated the Russians at Friedland the following June, Prussia, deprived of its ally, had little alternative but to sign the Treaty of Tilsit and accept Napoleon's plans for recasting central Europe.

Reconstruction and reform, 1807–1812

In the catastrophic period after the French victories of 1806–1807, France was the puppet master of Germany. Not only did Napoleon determine its organization, but the German states had to accept French economic policy and actively participate in the economic blockade of Britain. The historic Holy Roman Empire had been replaced by a new 'tripartite arrangement'.[22]

- The area on the left bank of the Rhine was annexed outright by France.
- Napoleon's allies in what can be called the 'third Germany' formed the Confederation of the Rhine. In return for their loyalty and willingness to provide troops and money for the French war effort, they were granted autonomy within the Confederation, while the electors of Bavaria and Württemberg were made kings and the ruler of Baden was made a grand duke. Initially the Confederation numbered 16 German states, but by 1811 a further 23 territories had joined the Confederation.
- The two great German powers, Austria and especially Prussia, were gravely weakened, but retained their sovereignty, although in practice Prussia was virtually a French satellite (see below).

A consequence of French domination was the radical reform and modernization of both rump Prussia and the states within the Confederation. The French Revolution had destroyed the old Empire, which was 'the overarching constitutional structure'[23] within which Germany, in all its diversity and fragmentation, had existed for centuries. The surviving German states now needed to come to terms with this new reality.

See Map 2

Prussia

The terms of the Treaty of Tilsit were punitive: Prussia lost the eastern territories, which it had acquired from the three partitions of Poland (see p. 7) and was reduced to a rump of four provinces, which were occupied by French troops. It was also forced to pay a large war indemnity, while its army was reduced to a mere 42,000 men. Altogether Prussia lost 49 per cent of its territory and 46 per cent of its population. Contemplating the destruction which the war and the subsequent French occupation had wrought, **General Carl von Clausewitz** feared that what had been achieved in Prussia 'throughout the centuries ... will now be destroyed in perhaps a decade'.[24]

In this situation Frederick William turned to the reformers in Prussia, grouped around Barons Hardenberg and Karl vom und zum Stein. All were convinced that only a complete political transformation would enable Prussia to regain its strength and defeat the French. To survive, Prussia would have to base itself, in the words of one of the military reformers, Neithardt von Gneisenau, on 'the triple alliance of arms, science and constitution'. Between them Stein and Hardenberg were responsible for the implementation of a programme, which has variously been described as 'offensive' (Brendan Simms) or 'defensive' (Hans-Ulrich Wehler) modernization.[25]

Up to a point the reforms were a mixture of both in that they aimed to protect Prussia from revolution from below, as well as preparing it for an eventual victorious confrontation with France. On the other hand they were also inspired by the **Enlightenment**, the liberal economic theories

General Carl von Clausewitz (1770–1831): Prussian general and military theorist, who in his book *On War* stressed the importance of military and psychological factors in war.

Enlightenment: an intellectual movement, the purpose of which was to reform society using reason and science.

Key political figures in Prussia, 1807–1815

Karl August von Hardenberg (1750–1822), who came from a wealthy landowning family in Hanover, joined the Prussian civil service and was foreign minister in the Prussian government, 1804–1806, but was dismissed on Napoleon's orders in 1807 because he supported an alliance with Britain. He was replaced by **Heinrich vom und zum Stein** (1757–1831) as the king's chief minister. Stein descended from a family of imperial knights owning estates in the Rhineland. He had joined the Prussian civil service in 1780 and in 1804 was Minister of Economic Affairs. He remained in power for little more than a year as he too was forced out of office after French spies discovered evidence that he favoured a German national uprising against Napoleon. He fled to Russia where he became the adviser on German issues to the Russian government. After a caretaker government run by two civil servants, Hardenberg returned to power in the position of State Chancellor in 1810. His reforms were aimed at the restoration of Prussia as a great power. **General August von Gneisenau** (1760–1831) became a cult figure after his brilliant defence of Kolberg against the French and used his prestige to support the cause of military reform.

---

of the British economist, Adam Smith (1723–1790), and, indeed, by the new nationalism unleashed by the French Revolution.

Stein began his ministry with his famous October Edict, which announced that after '11 November 1810 there will be only free people' in Prussia. In a series of reforms, which were implemented by Hardenberg in 1810–1811, all restrictions on landownership were lifted and the serfs officially became free peasants. However, they were still not liberated from their compulsory labour obligations until 1821 (see p. 53).

To create a structured and rational administration to replace arbitrary rule by royal cronies, Stein in November 1808 persuaded the king to set up a central ministry (*Staatsministerium*) run by five ministers, each of whom would be responsible for a separate department. This then opened up the way for a series of important administrative reforms that went far to recast Prussia's administrative system for the next century. The country was divided up into administrative districts, the *Regierungsbezirke*, and in 1812 the lower-tier organizations, the *Kreise*. The *Regierungsbezirke* were organized on a collegiate basis under a president, who was 'first among equals' and consequently reached decisions through discussion and consensus.

The *Kreise* were put firmly under state control. Their directors were appointed by the state and given power over all the local authorities. The director was assisted by six deputies chosen by an electoral college composed equally of peasants, townsmen and landowners. However, *Junker* opposition was to force the government to suspend this reform in 1814. It was in the towns that Stein's plans for reform were the most successful: by the Municipal Ordinance of 19 November 1808, the towns were given a system of municipal self-government, which enabled them, through elected councils, to determine taxes and expenditure. With the failure of the *Kreis* reforms in the countryside, the cities became, in 19th-century Prussia, beacons of reform. Stein also intended to convene a Prussian parliament to strengthen the government in its dealings with the French, but after his ejection from office the plans were delayed until Hardenberg called a provisional 'Assembly of Notables' in February 1811. This was replaced by an 'interim' National Representative Assembly in 1812, which he optimistically hoped would support his reforms, but, instead, it concentrated its energies on successfully blocking the *Kreis* reforms. It was dissolved in July 1815.

When Hardenberg returned to power in 1810 Prussia was facing a crippling financial crisis caused by the state's debts and French demands for reparations. If Prussia defaulted on reparation payments, the French had the legal right to reoccupy Prussia. Hardenberg thus had little option but to increase taxation. He also attempted to improve the supply side of the economy by creating a freer labour market and a competitive economic climate by abolishing the restrictive practices of the guilds. The right to practice a trade was now open to anybody. By the emancipation edict of 1812 Prussia partially emancipated its Jews: in return for the freedom to own property, travel and marry at will, the Jews were to integrate by adopting German names and giving up their distinctive beards and kaftans. To improve efficiency, to forge unity and to create better educated citizens, the state also accepted the need to supervise the education of teachers and to inspect both elementary and grammar schools and the universities. Education was, in the view of the Prussian education minister, Wilhelm von Humboldt, a 'practical need of the state'. In the 19th century the Prussian education system was to become a model for the developed world.

Of crucial importance for the future were, of course, the military reforms. To survive, Prussia had to emulate the French and create a nation in arms. The key to military reform was universal conscription, but, to avoid French military intervention, this could only be introduced once Prussia joined the war against Napoleon in February 1813. The regular army was drastically overhauled. A large number of its officers were dismissed, and from now on commissions could only be gained on merit. In March 1813 the concept of a 'people in arms' became a reality when the *Landwehr* was formed. This was a reserve army or militia organized by district committees, which could select educated citizens as officers. In the eyes of the military reformers it represented a fusion of the *Volk* and the Prussian army. The rest of the male population between 15 and 60, who had not been mobilized, was liable to be conscripted to the *Landsturm*, which was essentially a home guard and potential guerrilla force with no proper uniform, and it also elected its officers. In response to the fears that the *Landsturm* was potentially a revolutionary force, it was subjected to tight control by the state and in July 1813 ordered to adhere to the conventional rules of war.

The Rhineland Confederation

Many contemporaries looked upon the Confederation as a new edition of the old Empire; others even saw it as the model for a new Germany. There were plans for a diet (assembly) to draw up and define its collective powers, but it never met. German, and indeed most European, historians between the 1870s and the 1950s, on the other hand, tended to view the Confederation with its creation of several key, middle-sized German states as part of the long-drawn-out process of building a united Germany. In fact, as James Sheehan has pointed out, the opposite can be argued as 'the creation of several medium sized, relatively well integrated states, ready and willing to preserve their identity states, did not make the formation of a nation state any easier'.[26]

See Map 2

Like Prussia, the states within the Confederation were faced with similar tasks of reorganization. The Grand Duchy of Berg, the Kingdom of Westphalia and the **Grand Duchy of Frankfurt** were deliberately intended by Napoleon to be model states constructed along the lines of Napoleonic France, each practising French law as enshrined in the Code Napoleon, which would inspire central Europe to emulate their example. Under Napoleon's brother, Jerome, Westphalia was given a constitution, a parliament elected on a narrow franchise, civil equality and religious liberty, yet in reality what counted was French military power and bureaucratic control. Westphalia was virtually stripped bare to provide the French empire with money and mercenaries. However, Saxony and the two Mecklenburg states in the north were able to retain their independence. For strategic reasons Napoleon made Saxony a kingdom and its monarch the titular head of the newly created grand Duchy of Warsaw, as well as awarding it with lands seized from Prussia.

Grand Duchy of Frankfurt: created by Napoleon in 1810; dissolved October 1813.

In south Germany, Baden, Bavaria and Württemberg sought to integrate the land ceded to them by Napoleon into their core territory. Baden quadrupled in size, Württemberg doubled, while Bavaria had to absorb 80 territories, which had previously been independent within the old Empire. This expansion inevitably changed the nature of these three states and forced their governments to adopt radical reforms over the next five years, which were both animated by the spirit of the enlightened absolutism of the late 18th century and tempered by the ideas of the French Revolution. These reforms by no means achieved what they promised, but they at least laid the foundations for unified and effective administrations and collectively strengthened the south German states and the potential of the 'third Germany'. In Baden Grand Duke Frederick followed the advice of Sigismund von Reitzenstein (1766–1847), his senior minister, and introduced the Code Napoleon and organized the state into ten *Kreise* each under the control of the local director. In Bavaria Count Montgelas (1759–1838) swept away the old administration and replaced it with four (later increased to five) ministries. Similar reforms also took place in Württemberg, Hesse-Darmstadt and Nassau. These centralizing policies met determined resistance from many of the former imperial cities and the nobility who feared the threatened removal of their privileges. In fact the nobility lost their political powers, but retained most of their lands and wealth at the expense of the peasantry. In Bavaria, for instance, Montgelas abolished serfdom but, as the majority of peasants could not afford to compensate their landowners for the loss of their feudal privileges, it was only in 1848 that emancipation became a reality.[27]

The annexed territories

The French annexation of the territories on the left or west bank of the Rhine was legalized by the Treaty of Lunéville (see pp. 13–14). The area was absorbed into metropolitan France and, unlike the rest of Germany, experienced the full rigours of Napoleonic government. Up to 1945 its history was disputed by historians and politicians on both sides of the border. The French 'congratulated themselves for having elevated the Rhineland out of the middle ages' while the Germans described French rule as 'alien and oppressive' and painted Prussia as the liberating power.[28] After 1945 the focus shifted to the confrontation between 'Jacobins' and 'aristocrats', with historians from the German Democratic Republic (GDR) paying immense interest to the former. Referring to the considerable volume of research on these Jacobins, Blanning ironically observed that 'rarely has so much attention been lavished by so many on so few'.[29]

Traditionally, the territorially fragmented states of the Rhineland had looked to the Reich for protection of their autonomy. Consequently, there was considerable support for the Austrian Habsburgs, as the family which had traditionally provided the candidate for the imperial throne. In 1805, when war broke out between Austria and France, there was widespread opposition to conscription into the French army and the mobilization of the National Guard. Yet with Austria's defeat, the opposition subsided. In 1810 Napoleon's marriage with the Austrian princess, Archduchess Marie Louise, was met with considerable enthusiasm.

The balance sheet of Napoleonic rule in the Rhineland is inevitably mixed. As part of France the Rhinelanders were subjected to 'big government', high taxes and liability to conscription. On the other hand, Napoleon staffed the governments of the new departments with local officials, and the new gendarmerie restored law and order. Economically the French Continental System and the British blockade created both winners and losers. Merchants, unable to import goods from Britain, lost out, while the textile industry was faced with high duties on imported cotton, yet Rhenish manufacturers had the big advantage of access to the large internal market of the French Empire. The manufacturers of the newly created Grand Duchy of Berg (see above) actually petitioned Napoleon to become a French province in 1811. However, with the tightening of the **Continental System** in 1810, a much harsher economic regime was introduced. To mitigate it, smuggling increased, which 'eventually developed into a sophisticated industry', replete with its own insurance service and with credit and distribution networks covering a large part of Europe. This both undermined respect for Napoleon's rule and led to a so-called 'customs terror' by the French authorities.[30]

In an attempt to tighten the economic war against Britain in 1810, Napoleon annexed a whole swathe of states from the mouth of the Rhine

Continental System: In 1806, in response to the British blockade of France, Napoleon introduced the Continental System, which prohibited trade with Britain.

to Lübeck in the east, reaching down as far south as Münster, Osnabrück and Luneburg. These states experienced the harsher side of Napoleonic rule. The old Hansa ports of Bremen, Lübeck and Hamburg lost their traditional institutions and were barred from full access to the French economy.

The emergence of German nationalism

German nationalism before 1789 was predominantly a cultural phenomenon (see pp. 10–11), but the destruction of the Holy Roman Empire and the triumph of Napoleon created the preconditions for the emergence of a new German nationalism, which not surprisingly had an anti-French focus. German nationalism did, however, remain ambivalent. What sort of Germany did it embrace? Did it hark back to the Empire or did it anticipate the formation of a nation state?

The collapse of the Empire had created an institutional void, which the governments of the surviving states in Germany attempted to fill by creating new institutions that would inspire the loyalty of their citizens and create a new political community. This was certainly the case in the south German states and in Prussia. Both Stein and Hardenberg frequently invoked the nation, but as Matthew Levinger has observed 'for all of the Prussian reformers' enthusiasm about the prospects of national awakening, they studiously avoided one political question of crucial importance: was the nation Prussia or Germany?'.[31]

The Prussian government attempted to exploit nationalism to strengthen both the state and loyalty of its subjects to the Crown, but it soon discovered that nationalism was a powerful, indeed potentially revolutionary, ideology that claimed that the authority of the nation had greater legitimacy than the Crown and the traditional established order. Early German nationalism was heavily influenced both by the Romantic Movement (see p. 10) and German Protestantism, particularly **Pietism**.

For the most part its proponents were members of the educated middle classes, who, as a result of the lack of opportunities in the academic and administrative professions, were often forced to accept work as tutors or apprentices. The new nationalist ideology was expressed with dramatic effect by the philosopher, Johann Gottfried Fichte (1762–1814), in his electrifying series of lectures entitled *Reden an die deutsche Nation* (*Addresses to the German Nation*), which he delivered to the Berlin Academy in the winter of 1807–1808, and by the publicist Ernst Moritz Arndt (1769–1860). Both men elevated nationalism into a new religion. Fichte stressed Germany's unique racial and cultural strengths and argued that in fighting against French domination it was carrying out an historic mission. Arndt was even more forthright when he appealed to the Germans 'to let hatred of the French be your religion, let freedom and fatherland be your saints to whom you pray'.[32]

Two years later more active efforts were made to spread the ideology of nationalism. It was given more definite shape in November 1810. Two

Pietism: emerged in the late seventeenth and early eighteenth centuries. Pietists believed passionately in the importance of the relationship between the individual and God.

See Documents 1 and 2

teachers, Friedrich Friesen (1784–1814) and Friedrich Jahn (1778–1852), set up the *Deutsche Bund* (German League) with the aim of eventually unifying 'our scattered, divided and separated *Volk*'. Another group was the *Tugendbund* or 'Society for the Practice of Public Virtue' whose main achievement was to smuggle out Prussian officers across the frontier to serve with the Russian army when Franco-Russian relations deteriorated. The latter two organizations had a small membership, but in 1811 Jahn founded a more influential organization, the *Turngesellschaft* (Gymnastic Society). Through gymnastics, night marches and paramilitary manoeuvres it aimed to inspire patriotism in high school and university students, although as the movement spread, artisans participated in it as well. It played a key role in politicizing contemporary students and familiarizing them with such concepts as 'Germany', 'Fatherland' and '*Volk*'. Again what exactly the 'Fatherland' was remained unclear. Jahn himself initiated an inconclusive debate within the movement about whether the future German constitution should be based on the 'traditional' German institutions or designed along more democratic lines. What is clear, however, is that the nationalist movement 'played an important role in constituting a politicized public sphere in Prussia and the other German states during the early nineteenth century',[33] which increasingly challenged the monopoly over public life claimed by the Crown. The wars of liberation of 1813–1814 were to test the strength of the new nationalist ideology (see below).

The defeat of Austria, 1809

Austerlitz, the defeat of Prussia and the *approchement* between Russia and France after Tilsit isolated Austria and made institutional reform essential if it were to survive. Yet the government was divided both on what measures to take and on what foreign policy to follow. Count Sinsendorf, the Minister of the Interior, advocated greater centralization of the administration and, for the time being anyway, cooperation with Napoleon. The foreign minister, Count Philip Stadion (1763–1824), and Archduke Charles (1771–1847) the Emperor's brother, were convinced that peace was impossible with France and hoped to appeal to Austrian patriotism and indeed German nationalism to defeat Napoleon. It was the uprising against the French intervention in Spain that ultimately convinced Stadion, Metternich (see p. 24) then ambassador in Paris, and finally the Emperor that there was no option but war. They argued that the very failure of the Spanish monarchy to resist Napoleon had triggered a popular revolt and the downfall of the monarchy.

The Austrian army was expanded and a trained militia (*Landwehr*) was formed. Stadion launched a propaganda programme which aimed 'to make Austrians consciously identify themselves with the state and its individual provinces, so they would willingly fight and sacrifice for God, Emperor and country'.[34] The intention of this campaign was ultimately to strengthen the monarchy and had little in common with the popular nationalism of Jahn and Friesen.

In April 1809, taking advantage of the French military involvement in Spain, Austria declared war on France in the hope that both Prussia and Russia would come to her assistance and that nationalism would set Germany ablaze. In fact Austria was rapidly defeated. Neither Russia nor Prussia intervened and the Confederation states fought as allies of Napoleon. Apart from a rebellion in the Tyrol, which was primarily directed against the modernizing effects of Bavarian rule, riots in the Sarre department of the Rhineland in protest against French conscription and a few small-scale raids by Prussian units acting without any higher authority, there were no nationalist insurrections.[35]

Although Prussia's inactivity infuriated the Prussian officer corps and ultimately led to what amounted to mutiny at Tauroggen in 1813 (see below) the Austrian defeat merely confirmed Frederick William's and Hardenberg's assessment that without an alliance with Russia war against France was futile. Austria's humiliating defeat at Wagram led to Metternich's conclusion that only an alliance with France would ensure Austria's existence.

Napoleon's defeat

Not only did Frederick William and his advisers mistrust the whole concept of a popular nationalist uprising against the French, but the international situation was in reality deeply unfavourable to the dreams of the patriots. Austria refused to join another coalition against France, while Britain could offer little assistance. Even Russia assumed that when war came again, Prussia would be overrun by the French and that the crucial struggle with France would eventually take place in Poland.

In 1812 Napoleon was at the height of his power, yet until he had finally eliminated Russian power, his position was not secure. In preparation for the coming conflict he forced Frederick William to conclude a humiliating offensive alliance in February 1812 with France, which not only committed Prussia to fight Russia but also to quarter and supply the Grand Army in preparation for the invasion. In May Napoleon ordered his German allies to attend a congress of princes in Dresden as a preliminary to the invasion of Russia. As Karen Hageman observes 'the 1812 alliance with France was tantamount to a total surrender by Prussia. It imposed heavy burdens on the population and because of requisitions and pillaging reminded people of the French occupation of 1806–1808'.[36]

On 24–25 June the Grand Army, a third of which was made up of Germans, crossed the Niemen. Its destruction through disease and the skilful tactics of the Russians forced Napoleon to retreat. In December 1812, when Tsar Alexander I decided to turn the hitherto defensive war into a struggle for the liberation of Europe, the commander of the Prussian corps, General Yorck von Wartenburg, defied the orders of the king and concluded an unauthorized armistice at Tauroggen with the Russians. Meanwhile, in East Prussia, Stein, who had earlier fled to Russia, set

up a provincial assembly which conscripted troops to reinforce Yorck. Both Frederick William and Hardenberg initially hesitated to break with Napoleon, but under pressure from the war party in Prussia and confronted by the reality of Napoleon's defeat in Russia, agreed to the Treaty of Kalisch of 27–28 February. This cemented the new Russo-Prussian alliance and a month later the Proclamation of Kalisch announced that the aim of the allies was the 'restoration of the German constitution alone by the German princes and people and in accordance with the original spirit of the German people'. What this in reality meant is hard to say. Perhaps H. W. Koch is right to observe that it was a 'careful contradictory formulation out of which everyone could take just what he desired'.[37]

In Prussia at any rate the subsequent war had some characteristics of a popular uprising. Conscription was made obligatory and special units of volunteers, the *Freikorps*, were formed with the aim of appealing to pan-German nationalism. Some 6 per cent of the total population were mobilized, some 27,000 of these being volunteers, of which students, intellectuals and artisans formed over half. Mobilization was accompanied by a massive propaganda campaign. The Protestant clergy was instructed to deliver patriotic sermons, while some of the writings of Ernst Moritz Arndt, who was Stein's secretary during the war, enjoyed large print runs, which enabled them to trickle down to the rank and file of the Prussian army. The government also appealed specifically to women to raise funds and a series of organizations such as the Patriotic Women's League (*Vaterländischer Frauenverein*) were set up.[38]

In retrospect the *Freikorps* and the war of liberation became a powerful myth, which inspired later generations of nationalists right up to 1945. A mass of memoirs, stories, histories, pageants and paintings all portrayed the war of liberation as a seminal experience in German nationalism and claimed that it was a people's war. This was an exaggeration. While many students, teachers and intellectuals can well be seen as early German nationalists who were inspired by the concept of German nationalism, research points to 'a correlation between the degree of voluntary mobilization and the damage inflicted by French requisitioning'.[39] The over-representation of artisan volunteers is, for example, a result of material suffering caused by the French occupation, rather than an ardent nationalism. Frederick William, despite the Proclamation of Kalisch, was interested primarily in Prussian rather than German patriotism. As Sheehan has pointed out the '*Volk*'s role in its own "liberation" was, at best, a minor one. Napoleon was defeated by regular armies, not patriotic poets and quaintly attired gymnasts'.[40] Thus to a great extent 'this "birth myth" of the German nation was an artificial construct of nationalist ideology'.[41]

The states of the Confederation of the Rhine viewed with considerable trepidation the advance of Prussian and Russian troops into central Germany. The Proclamation of Kalisch threatened their rulers with 'destruction through strength of public opinion and the power of righteous arms' unless they cooperated. With the exception of the two Mecklenburgs, the states ignored the Russo-Prussian alliance and looked to Austria for protection from annexations by a revengeful and victorious Prussia. Indeed after Napoleon's two minor victories of Lützen and Bautzen in May 1813, which led to a temporary armistice, their rulers dropped negotiations with the Austrians and rallied to Napoleon.

By the end of June, with Wellington's victories in Spain, the military balance was tilting away from France. Metternich still hoped that he would be able to mediate a compromise peace between Napoleon and the coalition, but when this failed Austria declared war on France in August. The war had an ambiguous note. For the patriots it was a war of the people for emancipation and freedom, while for Frederick William and Metternich it was primarily a struggle for dynastic rights and claims, balance of power and restoration. On 16 October French hegemony in Germany and indeed in Europe was finally broken at the battle of Leipzig. By the end of November Napoleon had retreated across the Rhine, to be followed on 31 December by the coalition forces, which reached Paris at the end of March. On 6 April Napoleon abdicated and was exiled to Elba. On 30 May the Treaty of Paris ended the Napoleonic wars.

Prince Klemens Wenzel von Metternich, (1773–1859)

Klemens von Metternich's family owned land in the Rhineland and Bohemia. His father was a diplomat who at the time of his birth was Austrian ambassador at Trier, Koblenz and Mainz. Klemens also became an Austrian diplomat, eventually becoming Austrian ambassador in Paris. In 1809 he was appointed Austrian foreign minister after Austria's defeat by Napoleon. Initially he had no option but to come to terms with Napoleon so as to avoid the dismemberment of the Austrian Empire. In 1813 he joined the alliance against France and a year later presided brilliantly over the Congress of Vienna (1814–1815), where he witnessed the triumph of his conservative policies of monarchical restoration and defensive alliances against aggression and revolution. He became Austrian chancellor in 1821 and, until forced to resign in 1848 (see p. 64), used his formidable skills to defend the 1815 settlement.

The German question

With the defeat of Napoleon the whole German question re-emerged:

- How were the German territories to be reorganized?
- What would be the fate of Napoleon's German allies and the Rhineland Confederation?
- Could the old Empire be resurrected?
- Could Austria and Prussia remain allies or would they revert to being rivals?

Stein, Arndt and the German nationalists envisaged a united Germany. Stein was even ready to see Prussia dissolved. In December 1812 he remarked that 'you may do with Prussia what you like ...',[42] but once

Prussia and Austria entered the war it became clear that unification was a utopian idea. Both these powers were determined to preserve their independence and freedom of action. Prussia and Austria agreed to dissolve the Rhenish Confederation, but disagreed on the future role of its members. Hardenberg hoped for major Prussian territorial gains in northern and eastern Germany, while Metternich hoped to preserve the smaller states as a buffer between France and Russia. Metternich scored a diplomatic success in October 1813 when he negotiated the Treaty of Ried, by which Bavaria agreed to join the coalition on the condition that its sovereignty and territorial possessions were guaranteed. In November and December similar treaties were signed with Württemberg, Hesse-Darmstadt, Baden, Nassau, Saxe-Coburg and Hesse-Kassel. This ensured essentially that the Napoleonic reorganization of southern Germany would remain intact and that no united national Germany in the guise of the old Empire would emerge.

The Central Administration of the Rhineland

The Central Administration was set up by Prussia and Austria under Stein in March 1813 to administer the liberated territories. Stein and his two key assistants, Johann Sack (1733–1859) and Justus Grüner (1777–1820), intended that their administration would inspire the population to take part in a nationalist crusade against Napoleon, which would provide the necessary stimulus for the creation of a united Germany. In this they were assisted by nationalist intellectuals, of whom the most vociferous was Joseph Görres (1776–1848). In January 1814 he launched the *Rheinische Merkur*, which called for a united Germany under joint Austro-Prussian leadership. Metternich viewed Stein's efforts to galvanize the Rhinelanders with nationalism with suspicion and dismissed him and his advisers as 'Prussian Jacobins'. In May 1814 the Central Administration was dissolved and, until a final settlement was reached at the Congress of Vienna, Prussia took over the administration of the Lower and Middle Rhine while a joint Austrian–Bavarian Commission administered the area south of the Mosel. Predictably the latter did everything it could to counter 'Prussian Jacobinism', while in the Prussian Zone attempts to instil a sense of German nationalism still continued under Johann Sack, who was now in charge. Sack's efforts were not popular with the Rhinelanders, relatively few of whom had joined the local *Landwehr* voluntarily in the winter of 1812–1813 or during the 'Hundred Days' in 1815 (see p. 27). According to Michael Rowe 'Rhinelanders already felt themselves to be German. It was not something they needed to demonstrate, and especially not to the Prussians'.[43]

The Vienna Settlement

In 1814 the five great powers of 1789 still dominated post-war Europe: Russia, Britain, France, Austria and Prussia. In France the Bourbon monarchy was restored and the Treaty of Paris recognized her frontiers of

1792. The other questions involving Poland, the Italian and German states and the former Austrian Netherlands were to be settled at a congress to be held in Vienna. Peace did not witness the return of the competitive international politics of the 18th century when war rather than diplomacy was the norm. Twenty-five years of warfare had produced, to quote Paul Schroeder, a 'transformation' in international affairs.[44] However, imperfectly, at Vienna the great powers sought through painful compromise to produce a viable international system that reconciled their demands with the security needs of the smaller powers. At least until 1848, they were largely successful. They were motivated above all by the fear of renewed revolution in France once again creating havoc in Europe.

When the allied powers assembled at Vienna in the autumn of 1814, the settlement of German Europe was one of the most complex problems confronting them. Their statesmen had not only to define the boundaries of the surviving German states but also to achieve a balance between interstate cooperation and independence. Should there, for instance, be a federation, a confederation or a straight Prusso-Austrian hegemony? Stein, as early as the autumn of 1813, had made radical proposals for amalgamating the Rhineland Confederation states into a 'third Germany', which would be linked to Austria and Prussia. These ideas were then worked on by Wilhelm von Humboldt (1767–1835), the Prussian ambassador in Vienna. Hoping that a federal Germany would eventually evolve, he proposed first of all a voluntary confederation in which the states would create a joint defence force and then gradually coordinate their domestic policies. The essential precondition of success would be close Austro-Prussian cooperation. Hardenberg, in his 41 Articles, put forward a draft constitution for an 'Eternal Confederation' which would be run by a committee of the larger German states under the joint direction of Austria and Prussia. He was in effect proposing joint Austro-Prussian control over the German states in return for Austria's acceptance of Prussia as an equal partner within the Confederation. Initially Metternich and Emperor Francis, as well as Britain, Russia and France were inclined to accept the Prussian plan, despite bitter opposition from the *Mittelstaaten*. In the end it was the eruption of the Saxon–Polish dispute, which divided Prussia and Austria, that saved the *Mittelstaaten* from this plan. The German Committee was suspended and, although negotiations on the future of Germany continued, by the end of February the chance of a breakthrough seemed remote.

The situation was, however, dramatically changed by Napoleon's escape from Elba in March. It was now essential to agree on a German settlement before the monarchs and statesmen left Vienna to fight a new war against Napoleon. It powerfully concentrated the minds of the German princes on the need to reach a compromise on the German question.

The Saxon–Polish Issue

In 1806 Napoleon strengthened his influence in Saxony by turning it into a kingdom and appointing its new king the absentee ruler of Poland. When the French were driven from Germany, Prussia hoped to annex Saxony as compensation for her former Polish territory, which she was ready to cede to Russia, except for Posen and the Kulm district. Initially both Metternich and Castlereagh, the British foreign minister, appeared to agree to the Prussian annexation of Saxony, provided Prussia withdrew her backing for Russian ambitions in Poland. In response to furious complaints from Tsar Alexander, Austria had rapidly to back-pedal and withdraw the offer of Saxony, but this met with equally outraged opposition from Prussia. Hardenberg initially escalated the crisis when he threatened that Prussia would turn its temporary occupation of Saxony into a permanent one, while general Boyen and Gneisenau were ready to fight Austria. This led to a brief war scare and on 3 January 1815 a secret alliance between Britain, France and Austria against the unlikely possibility of a Russo-Prussian attack. By early February a compromise was reached whereby the tsar received most of the Napoleonic Duchy of Warsaw, and Prussia was given only the northern half of Saxony and territories in the Rhineland and Westphalia as compensation.

Details of the territorial and political settlement in Germany were rapidly agreed on in May. Metternich, using all his diplomatic skills, managed to persuade both Prussia and the *Mittelstaaten* to agree on the formation of the German Confederation, which was confirmed, together with territorial changes in Italy, Holland and elsewhere, in the Vienna Final Act of 8 May 1815. He particularly reassured Bavaria by inserting in Article 1 a specific guarantee of the sovereignty of the individual states. 'What emerged in June 1815 by luck and compromise more than artful design was a loose confederation based upon an informal dualism. Austria leading the Confederation as a whole, while in practice conceding Prussian hegemony in north Germany'.[45]

See Map 3

The Hundred Days

Napoleon's defeat at Waterloo temporarily raised hopes among the Prussian patriots of a revised settlement. In the armistice and occupation negotiations after Waterloo, Blücher (1742–1819), the commander of the Prussian army, and Gneisenau in defiance of Hardenberg, demanded massive reparations and indemnities, which would have involved the surrender of Alsace-Lorraine, the Saar and Luxemburg. Castlereagh (1769–1822), the British representative, Metternich and the tsar came to the conclusion that the Prussian army was a potentially revolutionary force ready to turn against its own government, but ultimately all Prussia managed to achieve in the second Treaty of Paris were a few minor boundary changes on the Belgian frontier and the transfer of the fortresses of Landau and Saarlouis to the German Confederation.

The creation of the German Confederation

The defeat of Napoleon and the failure of Prussia to reopen the German question left plans for creating the Rhineland Confederation intact. The Confederation, together with the absorption of Belgium by the Netherlands and the Italian settlement, which placed the Italian states under Austrian hegemony, were all part of what Sperber calls the 'structure of containment', of France and indeed of the potentially destabilizing power of Russia.[46]

The Rhineland Confederation consisted of the 39 states which had survived the wrecks of the Holy Roman Empire and the Rhineland Confederation. Besides the territories of Austria and Prussia, which had previously been included in the Empire, the most important members were the kingdoms of Saxony, Bavaria, Hanover and Württemberg, and the Grand Duchies of Hessen and Baden. The great majority of members, including the four free cities of Lübeck, Frankfurt, Bremen and Hamburg, were small territorial units. Twenty-one member states had populations of under 100,000 and the smallest, Liechtenstein, had a population of barely more than 5000. Prussia emerged as the main beneficiary after absorbing northern Saxony, former Polish territory around Danzig, Swedish Pomerania and considerable territories in the Rhineland and Westphalia. Hanover, which kept its dynastic links to Britain, became a kingdom, while Bavaria received Ansbach, Bayreuth, Würzburg and Aschaffenburg. Baden and Württemberg gained little but survived the post-Napoleonic reorganization intact. Austria annexed no German territory. Her main aim was the consolidation of her dynastic territories and new position in Italy. Within Germany itself, Metternich's policy was to rely on diplomacy rather than force in order to maintain Austrian hegemony. He intended to exploit the role allotted to Austria of President of the Diet to ensure that the Confederation did not evolve into a federal state.

The Vienna Final Act in June 1815 created only 'the skeleton of the German Confederation',[47] as its constitution was still to be developed. Although it represented a decisive break with the old Empire, it still bore a passing resemblance to it. Austria provided its permanent presidency. Like the Empire, it was also a defensive league of independent states and free cities intended to block any one power, be it France or Russia, from dominating central Europe.[48] According to Article 11 of the Confederation Treaty (*Bundesakt*), members were permitted to make alliances with other states as long as these were not aimed against the Confederation or any of its members. In the event of the Confederation going to war, the individual states would supply money and troops, and renounce the negotiation of any independent peace treaties, which only the Confederation could conclude.

It possessed only one statutory institution, the Diet, in which, as formerly in the old Reich, the individual states were represented by ambassadors rather than elected representatives. This was to meet in plenary sessions only when there were important matters to consider, such as constitutional changes, which affected the whole Confederation. Any change in the constitution required unanimity and consequently even the smallest state enjoyed an effective veto. Normally it was envisaged that the Diet would meet in the Smaller Council (*Engerer Rat*) in which 17 votes were distributed among the 39 members. The larger states – Austria, Prussia, Bavaria, Saxony, Hanover and Württemberg, Baden, Electoral Hesse, the Grand Duchy of Hesse, Denmark whose king was the Duke of Holstein and the Netherlands – had one vote each, while the remaining votes were distributed among the other states.

See Document 3

Conclusion

The Germany of 1815 was very different from that of 1789. The old Holy Roman Empire contained over 1800 different states, cities and territories, while the new German Confederation had just 39. The dynamics of the Empire had been dominated for most of the 18th century by Austro-Prussian rivalry. The German Confederation, on the other hand, was based on close Austro-Prussian political cooperation, which more or less survived until 1848. The 'third Germany' was strengthened by Metternich's acceptance of the Napoleonic settlement in southern Germany. In retrospect, the Prussian–German or Borussian school of historians saw Napoleon as the midwife of a united Germany and his destruction of the Empire as acting as a catalyst for the emergence of German nationalism under Prussian leadership, which eventually resulted in the unification of Germany in 1871. Revisionist historians writing after 1945 have, however, reacted to this Prusso-centric approach and argued that both the Empire and the Confederation had the potential to survive as viable solutions, which respected German diversity, while affording the individual states some degree of collective protection.

2 The Post-war Era 1815–1846: Restoration and Change

Introduction: problems, issues and questions

Like the Holy Roman Empire, the German Confederation was relegated to the 'historical lumber room'[1] by the Borussian school of historians, as it had little relevance for either nationalism or liberalism, the two most powerful ideologies in Germany in the second half of the 19th century. Seen from the perspective of German unification in 1871, it appeared to be an entirely negative political structure, which merely retarded the apparently inevitable move to unification under Prussia. Is this, however, an accurate assessment? If the history of the Confederation and its member states is analysed more sympathetically within the context of its times rather than through the distorting lenses of the Bismarckian Empire, can it be argued that the Confederation was, to quote Paul Schroeder, an 'intermediary body', which had at least the potential to balance the ambitions of the major German powers with the smaller states' need for security and protection?[2] Within the shell of the Confederation a considerable degree of 'modernization' took place: the *Zollverein* was formed, although Austria did not join, and industrialization accelerated. Given that there was no unified Germany with a parliamentary constitution, did this development mark the beginning of what

Hans-Ulrich Wehler calls Germany's 'Double Revolution'[3] whereby Germany eventually became an industrial giant lacking an effective liberal or democratic constitution – the so-called *Sonderweg*?

See Document 3

The German Confederation

The historian of the German Confederation, Wolf Gruner, pointedly stresses that the 'Confederation could and did not intend to become a unified national state'. Instead, its task was to create a structure which would give some common expression to the territories, which had survived the collapse of the Empire, while at the same time preserving their traditions and independence. The Confederation also had a key role to play as Europe's '*Zentralstaat*' in the European balance of power: it had to be strong enough to deter Russia and France from threatening central Europe, while also shielding its smaller members from the ambitions of Austria and Prussia.[4]

The formative years, 1816–1829

After Napoleon's final defeat in June 1815 the task confronting the Confederation's diet (assembly) was to 'fill out the skeleton'[5] created by the Vienna Final Act. Important questions to address concerned defence, inner German trade and transport, civil rights and political representation. Delayed by territorial disputes between Bavaria and Austria the diet did not meet until November 1816. Inevitably its members were divided not only on these questions but also on the whole future direction of the Confederation. Prussian reformers, like Wilhelm von Humboldt, the Prussian representative in the diet, hoped that it would develop into a federal state in which Prussia would play a key role, a view not shared by the smaller states for whom it was a way of protecting their independence, while to Metternich it was essentially a piece in the jigsaw of his overall European policy, constructed to protect not only the interests of the Habsburg monarchy, but also prevent war and revolution.

Initially, however, Austria and Prussia were able to work together effectively. Both saw the value of the Confederation as a protection against Russian and French influence and even Metternich ready initially to advocate constitutional reform within Austria. The two powers also showed a statesman-like restraint in claiming fewer votes in the diet's two councils than their size in fact merited. Obstruction within the diet came rather from the medium states (*Mittelstaaten*), which were determined to prevent the Confederation from intervening in their domestic affairs. They consequently rejected any attempt by the Confederation to regulate the complex legacy of **mediatization**. Initial plans for facilitating inter-German trade also foundered for fear that a customs union would impinge on the independence of the smaller German states. Metternich also failed to persuade the south German states to introduce conservative estate-based constitutions (see p. 33). Instead, the rulers of

Mediatization: effectively the annexation of a state or free city, which had been under the direct authority of the Holy Roman Emperor, by another state. The deposed princes and knights were left with some rights and privileges, but no political power.

Baden, Bavaria and Württemberg opted for elected assemblies with a limited representation, which could more effectively integrate their new populations. Later these were to become a training ground for the German liberals.

Growing protests

The lack of constitutional reform in Prussia and the majority of the other states, as well as the failure of the Confederation to develop into a federal entity, led to growing agitation. Joseph Görres, both in the *Rheinische Merkur* (see p. 25) and in his Koblenz Address of 1818, pressed for the introduction of a Prussian constitution. The *Rheinische Merkur* was banned in Baden, Württemberg and Bavaria as its support for German unity threatened these states' independence. Vociferous protests were also made by the students and intellectuals in the new *Burschenschaften* (fraternities) movement, which was pledged to work for a united Germany (see p. 50). In October 1817 the *Burschenschaften* organized a nationalist festival at the **Wartburg**, which was attended by some 500 students, to celebrate both the tercentenary of the German Reformation and the defeat of Napoleon at Leipzig in 1813.

In March 1819, August von Kotzebue (1761–1819), playwright, conservative publicist and a political agent, who was employed by the Russian legation in Mannheim, was assassinated by Karl Sand, a theology student, and *Burschenschaft* member. This murder and then its partial justification by Wilhelm de Wette (1780–1849), a theology professor at the University of Berlin – who argued that while the assassination was a crime it was 'to some extent absolved by steadfastness and sincerity of conviction'[6] – alarmed both the King of Prussia and his fellow rulers. While historians have tended to belittle their fears, they were uncomfortably aware that the French Revolution had begun with demands for reform of the French state.

Wartburg had symbolic meaning for German Protestants since it was there that Martin Luther translated the New Testament into German in 1521– 1522.

See Documents 4 and 5

Karlsbad Decrees and the Vienna Final Accords

Metternich skilfully exploited the alarm created by the incident to strengthen the conservative forces within the Confederation. Conferring with Frederick William at Teplitz in August 1819 he secured his backing for a series of repressive laws aimed at the universities and the press. These were then approved by the representatives of ten members of the Confederation at a special conference at Karlsbad, and presented as a *fait accompli* to the diet, which met at Frankfurt in late September.

The Karlsbad Decrees strengthened the repressive nature of the Confederation. The University Law dictated a code of conduct for both students and staff which undermined the traditional autonomy of the universities and was to be enforced by the individual state governments. This code ensured the expulsion of nationalist professors and the dissolution of the *Burschenschaften*. Similarly the Press Law compelled the states to reintroduce censorship and made their governments ultimately responsible for all published material that appeared within their frontiers. Prussia had originally wanted a special federal tribunal, which would both have investigated and passed sentence on political radicals. However, Frederick William was persuaded by Metternich to accept a Central Federal Investigation Office at Mainz, which would eventually communicate its findings to the Diet, and so prompt the individual state governments to take action. Metternich, who was hardly a convinced federalist, did, however, make the 'astonishing concession'[7] that in a real emergency he would agree to setting up a federal court. Finally the Confederation was given the legal powers to intervene if one of the member states refused to carry out instructions for implementing the decrees.

The Karlsbad Decrees gave Metternich the opportunity to strengthen the hand of the Prussian conservatives, stifle demands by Humboldt and his fellow reformers for a federal constitution and cement Austro-Prussian cooperation. This new axis enabled Austria and Prussia to create a dualistic hegemony and dictate the agenda at the ministerial conferences held in Vienna 1819–1820, which determined the final shape of the Confederation. After 6 months of negotiation, the diet was presented with a revised constitution for the Confederation, the Vienna Final Accords (Wiener *Schlussakte*), which it had to accept without debate. The 65 articles of the accords, finally confirmed the conservative nature of the Confederation. In many ways the Confederation now became, as Sheehan has argued, 'a kind of counter-revolutionary holding company through which Metternich could coordinate governmental action against his political enemies'.[8]

| See Document 6 |

All mention of Jewish emancipation and religious freedom was dropped. Article 58 vetoed any acceptance by the princes of a constitution 'that would limit or hinder them in fulfilment of their duties to the Confederation'. Article 54 committed each member of the Confederation to setting up a 'constitutionally guaranteed assembly of the estates', but neither Prussia nor Austria had any intention of doing this, while the south German states had already set up their own parliaments (see above). Although there was no supreme federal court, the Confederation did have the legal powers to adjudicate between states. Article 29 of the accords stressed that every German should have access to justice and was instrumental in gradually forcing the German states to set up their own supreme courts. While power remained firmly with the existing sovereigns, the Confederation was nevertheless invested with potentially far-ranging powers. Article 26, for instance, gave it the right to intervene in the affairs of the member states to maintain order. Militarily a similar balance was struck between the independence of the individual states and the needs of the Confederation. The War Constitution of 1821 made provision for the formation of a single, federal army in wartime under one commander, who would be chosen by the (Smaller Council) *Engerer Rat*, although in peace these forces would remain under the command of their own rulers. The federal army (*Bundeswehr*) was to consist of ten corps, of which Prussia and Austria would each provide three, Bavaria one and the remaining states another three. Over the next decade the Confederation gradually became what Metternich had intended. The weak and incompetent Austrian ambassador, Count von Buol-Schauenstein (1797–1865), was replaced in 1822 by the more formidable Count von Münch-Bellinghausen (1797–1865), whose purpose, as the British ambassador wrote, was to establish 'the sole and exclusive supremacy'[9] of Austria. Under his watchful eye, the debates and spontaneity of the earlier assembly sessions were curtailed. The diet remained a congress of ambassadors and the publication of its minutes were kept to the barest minimum. His task was made much easier when, in May 1823, Metternich insisted that the liberally-inclined ambassadors of Hesse-Darmstadt, Hesse-Kassel and Württemberg be dismissed for criticizing the reactionary policies of the three eastern powers – Russia, Austria and Prussia.

The impact of the revolutions of 1830–1831

In July 1830 economic and political discontent in France led to the overthrow of Charles X and his replacement by 'the citizen king' Louis Philippe (1773–1850). The revolution was a catalyst for political change not only in France, but it led to revolts in Belgium, Poland and in the Papal States in Italy. It triggered a series of crises and war scares, which threatened to embroil the Confederation in war with France. There was a particularly tense 'standoff' in 1831 when in response to the Austrian repression of revolts in the Papal city of Bologna, France sent in troops to Ancona. Within the Confederation the revolutions prompted demands for constitutional reform, which ultimately led to an increase in the number of constitutional states. For the first time, democratic and socialist groups also emerged 'on the fringe of German politics'.[10]

The Confederation and the international crisis

Metternich's first reaction to the French Revolution of 1830 was to call for military intervention, but the weak state of the Confederation's armies ensured that this was only bluff. The situation became more serious when the revolts spread to Belgium and Luxemburg, which were both part of the United Netherlands, created in 1815 by the Congress of Vienna. As Luxemburg was a member of the Confederation, the Dutch king appealed to it for help. Austria, distracted by revolts in its satellite states in Italy and weakened by financial problems (see p. 46), was unable to give a decisive lead to the Confederation. Prussia, on the other hand, reacted more vigorously. Not only did it force the diet to discuss the Luxemburg issue, but it committed itself to raising 160,000 troops in the event of war. In fact conflict was avoided through great-power cooperation and Luxemburg was eventually in 1839 recognized as a sovereign state within the Confederation in personal union with the Dutch king.

The domestic impact

The French revolution also had considerable repercussions within the Confederation. Exacerbated by poor harvests, unrest broke out in Hanover, Saxony, Brunswick and Hesse-Kassel, which forced the rulers in all four states to grant political constitutions. In the assemblies, especially in the south-west German states, the liberals became more assertive, and there was a flood of political pamphlets. In the Palatinate, the journalist Johann Wirth (1798–1848) set up the *Presseverein* (Press Union) as a pressure group to campaign for liberal ideals throughout German-speaking Europe. In May it organized a large-scale 'political festival' in the ruins of the old castle near Hambach, where dramatic and radical demands for a united, liberal and democratic Germany were made (see p. 48).

These ideas alarmed both Metternich and Frederick William. As in 1819, Austria and Prussia first of all reached agreement on a list of measures, the Six Articles, and only then were the other states consulted. These increased the power of the princes and the Confederation to muzzle liberal dissidents in the *Landtage*. A few days later a further tranche of measures, the Ten Articles, were announced, which banned political meetings and reminded the state governments to enforce the existing Karlsbad Decrees.

The abortive attack in Frankfurt in early 1833 by a small group of students, university lecturers and Polish refugees on the guardhouse of the local police gave the Confederation another chance to intervene in the internal affairs of a member state (see p. 50). It sanctioned the occupation of the city by federal troops under the command of an Austrian general and brushed off British and French criticism by rejecting the right of foreign powers to interfere in the internal affairs of the German Confederation.

See Document 7

For the rest of the decade Metternich continued his offensive against what he perceived to be the revolutionary threat. In June 1833 the Confederation created a centralized Bureau of Political Investigation, which could set up tribunals to examine dissidents, and security measures were further tightened up in the so-called Sixty Articles of June 1834. Although the articles were secret and were never discussed by the diet, the German states were committed by Article 60 of these decrees to implementing them, as if they were a federal decree. Further decrees were issued between 1835 and 1836, aimed at curbing threats from revolutionary students and travelling journeymen and banning the circulation of works written by the authors of 'Young Germany', a group of young writers, who rebelled against traditional morality and religion.

Travelling journeymen: skilled craftsmen, who would travel in search of work

By 1835 George Werner argues that it was 'increasingly difficult to visualize the diet serving as a vehicle for German unification',[11] but then was German unity a practical proposition in the 1830s? It is, as Christopher Clark reminds us, 'important not to overestimate the power and homogeneity of German nationalism as a political force during this period'.[12] More serious criticisms of the confederation were its evident military weakness in the crises of 1830–1831 and 1840, and its failure to devise an effective customs union, both of which are explored below.

Tensions and rivalries within the Confederation

Interstate politics within the Confederation were dominated by the dual hegemony of Austria and Prussia. As long as these two states cooperated, their power could not be effectively challenged. The medium-sized southern states, Bavaria, Württemberg and Baden did intermittently consider between 1817 and 1829 the creation of an independent third force within the Confederation, the so-called **German Trias**, but the inherent rivalries between these three states effectively prevented any possibility of a 'triadic federation' being formed.

German Trias: the three medium-sized German states of Bavaria, Württemberg and Baden

Austro-Prussian dual hegemony was only workable as long as Austria could stop the Confederation from becoming a federal state, and Prussia had no ambitions to seize the leadership of Germany. In the longer term, however, conflict between the two states seemed inevitable. Brendan Simms has argued that 'the new geopolitical configuration of central Europe after 1815 almost predetermined Prussia's victory in the struggle for mastery in Germany'.[13] Through her territorial gains in 1815 (see p. 28) Prussia's influence in Germany was strengthened, while Austria was increasingly distracted by her possessions in Italy and the Balkans, and was consequently unable effectively to protect the smaller states in southern and western Germany from the threat of French aggression. Prussia, in contrast, had no ambitions outside Germany, and had a vital interest in defending the Rhine frontier and in creating a German customs union, which would knit together its eastern and western territories. In both these areas Prussian interests increasingly converged not only with those of German nationalism, but also with the security concerns and economic interests of the south German states.

See Map 3

Customs union: a free-trade area where no customs duties are levied

The Bernstorff initiative

Austria's weakness and Prussia's more vigorous response during the Belgian crisis of 1830–1831 made military cooperation with Prussia increasingly attractive for the 'Trias'. Bavaria wanted an alliance with Prussia that would provide protection against France on the Rhine, but at the same time constrain Austria from plunging the Confederation into war with France in defence of her Italian possessions. Württemberg cautiously supported this approach, while Baden was ready to go further still and encourage Prussia to take the lead in turning the Confederation into a more cohesive federation which would be able to harness German nationalism. In August 1831 Count Christian von Bernstorff (1769–1835), the Prussian foreign minister, arguing that Prussia, 'as the state that would have to bear the greatest burden in the event of federal war' should 'seize the initiative in all areas where successful leadership will lead to greater preparedness and security', invited the south German states to send representatives to Berlin to begin negotiations on a military alliance. Two years later he even argued that Prussia's mission was to encourage 'the union of all German governments'.[14] However, under pressure from Metternich, Frederick William agreed to drop these potentially revolutionary ideas and replace Bernstorff with the more conservative Friedrich Ancillon (1767–1837), and for the time being the Prussian–Austrian special relationship was restored. In the final analysis Prussia was not yet ready or willing to challenge Austria.

The *Zollverein*: an economic Confederation?

Yet the strongest challenge to Austria mounted by Prussia was the creation of the German *Zollverein*. In 1815 interstate trade in Germany was crippled by the lack of a customs union. Each state levied its own tariffs and excise duties. Merchants trading, for instance, between Berlin and Switzerland had to cope with ten sets of customs tariffs and transit dues. The negotiation of a German customs union should have been one of the first tasks of the Confederation. Article 19 of its constitution actually committed the diet to deliberating 'upon the manner of regulating the commerce and navigation from one state to another'. Essentially, however, **political particularism** and the widely divergent economies of the different states all ensured that no progress was made.

The only other alternative was for small groups of states to negotiate regional customs unions. Prussia was the first German state to begin this process. Since its western provinces were separated from its core territory in the east and it had a 7500 km customs boundary studded with small enclaves belonging to other states, Prussia had a vital interest in negotiating a larger free-trade area. In 1818 the Prussian government accordingly introduced a new and strictly enforced customs law, which was aimed at creating an integrated Prussian customs system and compelling the small states surrounded by Prussian territory to join. In 1819 Schwarzburg-Sonderhausen entered the Prussian customs system and set a precedent by which the other small enclaves joined over the next 12 years. By the mid-1820s, influential Prussian officials like Albrecht Eichhorn (1779–1856), the head of German and customs affairs in the Foreign Ministry, and Friedrich von Motz (1775–1830), the finance minister, were urging the creation of what could be called a 'separate confederation with regard to customs policy',[15] at least as far as northern and central Germany went. To achieve this, Prussia pursued a complex policy of pressure and concession towards her smaller neighbours. Its greatest success, which, in the words of Heinrich Treitschke, the nationalist historian and National Liberal politician, reverberated around the German states 'like a bombshell',[16] was to establish a bridgehead on the

Zollverein: customs union – an area of free trade between the German states

Political particularism: the principle that each state should have the maximum independence within the German Confederation

See Document 9

other side of the Main by persuading Hesse-Darmstadt in 1828 with some remarkably generous concessions to join the Prussian customs union. The adhesion of Hesse-Darmstadt to the Prussian customs system made the new Bavarian-Württemberg union, which had been negotiated in January 1828, less viable and moved the King of Württemberg to remark that 'sooner or later we shall be forced to follow [Hesse-Darmstadt's] example'.[17]

See Map 3

To block the further expansion of both the Bavarian and Prussian customs unions, Hanover, Hesse-Kassel, Nassau, Saxony and some of the Thuringian states as well as Brunswick and Bremen, formed with encouragement from Austria the Middle German Commercial Union (MGCU) in December 1828. Members had specifically to commit themselves not to join a rival union. Heavy transit dues on goods passing through MGCU from non-member states were levied, with the express intention of interrupting trade between the eastern and western provinces of Prussia. However, this had little impact on Prussia, as Motz first managed to negotiate both the opening up of two trade routes between north and south Germany outside the control of the MGCU and in May 1829 a commercial treaty with the Bavarian-Württemberg union. The final blow to the viability of the MGCU was delivered by the defection of Hesse-Kassel in 1831, which at last enabled Prussia to link up her western and eastern provinces. In March 1833 Prussia negotiated a joint customs union with the Bavarian and Württemberg Union, which was joined almost immediately by Saxony. On New Year's Eve 1833, all toll restrictions within the union were dropped and the German *Zollverein* came into being. In 1835–1836 Frankfurt, Nassau and Baden joined, followed in 1841–1842 by Brunswick and Luxemburg, leaving only 11 states outside the union.

See Document 10 and 11

The customs union has 'long played an almost mythical role in explanations of Prussia's eventual rise to political and economic supremacy in Germany'.[18] Treitschke saw it as heralding the ultimate conflict between Austria and Prussia, which ended on the field of Königgrätz, while Wilhelm Roscher, a professor in political theory at Göttingen, was convinced in the late 1860s that it was 'not only the most beneficial, but also the greatest event in German history between Waterloo and Königgrätz'. The view was largely echoed by post-1945 West German historians such as Helmut Böhme, who saw it as the economic blueprint for a united Germany.[19]

Current research is more sceptical about its long-term political and economic consequences (see pp. 55–56). Yet, even so, there is a danger of underplaying its importance. Nipperdey argues that between 1814 and 1848 it was 'the single outstanding event in all German politics'.[20] It did strengthen Prussian influence over the other German states, and contemporaries were certainly aware of its potential impact on Austro-Prussian relations, as it isolated Austria economically within the Confederation, but politically it did not forge a united Germany (see p. 92). Indeed, at this stage Prussia had no intention of doing so.

The functioning of the *Zollverein*

The main organ of the *Zollverein* was the General Council, which met annually each time in a different member state, and was the body where the key decisions on customs tariffs were made. Each full member state had one vote (the Thuringian states had one vote between them, and Nassau and Frankfurt also shared a vote) and was represented by its own envoy, who was bound by instructions from his home government. Decisions could only be made through unanimity. Trade and shipping treaties with non-member states were in practice negotiated by Prussia on behalf of all the *Zollverein*'s members.

The individual states implemented the decisions taken by the General Council. Each state levied the agreed tariffs at their frontiers, but the sharing out of these funds between the member states was the responsibility of the Central Treasury of the *Zollverein* in Berlin, and was calculated on an annual basis. This revenue was welcomed by the state governments as it was independent of any parliamentary control. To check that its members were carrying out the instructions from the General Conference correctly, officials from one state would monitor their colleagues in another. Constitutionally these officials were employees of their own states, but gradually they evolved a loyalty to the *Zollverein*. Huber has called this 'a vivid example of institutional change, which inevitably takes place in a group of states tied together [economically]'.[21]

Austrian reaction

Metternich viewed these events with consternation. When the *Zollverein* Treaty was signed in 1833, he could only stand on the sidelines and warn the Emperor that 'within the large federal union' (*sic*) there was being created 'a smaller rival confederation ... which all too quickly will become accustomed to following its own objectives with its own means'.[22] In 1841 he even urged Austria's entry into the *Zollverein*, but fear of Prussian economic competition and the divisive effects of excluding those Habsburg territories from entry which were not part of the Confederation ensured that nothing came of this initiative. Lacking the economic strength to counter the *Zollverein*, Metternich could only assert Austrian influence within the Confederation by defending those German rulers, who faced revolutionary and liberal challenges. In this, Metternich was joined by Prussia, whose actions, particularly during the Hanoverian constitutional crisis helped reassure the conservative rulers of the smaller states of Prussia's own conservative credentials, whilst gradually winning them over to joining the *Zollverein*.

The Hanoverian constitutional crisis 1837–1841

In 1837 on the death of the British king, William IV, his brother, Ernst August, the **Duke of Cumberland**, became the Elector of Hanover. He immediately incensed liberal opinion by abrogating the 1830 constitution and replacing it with a more reactionary one. As a consequence seven Göttingen University professors including the historian Friederich

Duke of Cumberland: The accession of Queen Victoria to the British throne led to the end of the personal union between Britain and Hanover. As a consequence of the Salic law banning the female succession, the Hanoverian Crown was inherited by Ernst August, the Duke of Cumberland.

Dahlmann (1785–1860) and the philologists Wilhelm (1786–1859) and Jakob Grimm (1785–1863) refused to obey the oath of allegiance, which Ernst August demanded from all state employees, and were promptly suspended from their duties. In Gruner's words their stand 'became the symbol for the battle for liberal reform in the states of the German Confederation and marked an important escalation in the German constitutional movement'.[23] As the Vienna Final Accords (see p. 28) had laid down specifically that state assemblies could only be dissolved constitutionally, Bavaria, Baden, Württemberg and Saxony attempted to refer the matter to the diet of the Confederation hoping that it would declare Ernst August's action illegal, but under pressure from Austria and Prussia, the diet declared in 1839 that it lacked the necessary power to involve itself in that 'internal state affair'.[24]

The Rhine Crisis of 1840

In 1840 events in France again appeared to threaten the Confederation. When the French government was forced by the other European powers to give up its support for the occupation of Syria by Mehemet Ali, the Pasha of Egypt, and ally of France, the French government perceived this to be an intolerable humiliation. In the subsequent explosion of frustrated nationalism, French public opinion demanded as compensation the annexation of the left bank of the Rhine. Although the Austrian ambassador in the diet urged the German states to ensure that their armies were ready for war, it was once again shown that only under Prussian direction would the Confederation be able to defend itself. In reality Metternich was determined not to provoke France, but Prussia actually went as far as mobilizing 200,000 troops and made great efforts to put the western fortresses on a war footing.

The threat of a revisionist France on the Rhine unleashed a surge of nationalist feeling throughout Germany, which looked to Prussia for leadership. The spirit of this new nationalism inspired Nikolaus Becker's Rhineland song, *Der deutsche Rhein*, which became in effect a popular German national anthem. The crisis soon abated with the resignation of the French prime minister, Adolphe Thiers, but it had seriously weakened the idea of an independent 'third Germany', and began the slow and often interrupted process of convergence of the south German states on Berlin.[25]

Prussia and the Confederation

The accession of Frederick William IV in 1840 did not mark a dramatic change in Austro-Prussian relations. The new king was undoubtedly a German patriot, but his vision of Germany's future seemed to be a resurrection of the old Empire under Austrian leadership rather than a dynamic national state under Prussian leadership. This vision was not, however, shared by some of the King's close advisers: General Karl von Radowitz (1797–1853), the Prussian military plenipotentiary at the diet in Frankfurt, who was also the king's confident; Karl von Canitz (1783–1852), the Prussian ambassador in Vienna; and Christian von Bunsen (1791–1860), the ambassador in London. Radowitz argued that Prussia, as it was already doing in the *Zollverein*, should establish a moral and political hegemony in Germany, which would eventually enable it to challenge Austria. Ultimately this would entail creating some sort of liberal constitution, which would give Prussia the moral leadership of Germany and enable it to harness German nationalism.

Radowitz at first concentrated on a drastic overhaul of the federal military constitution. He overcame the squabbling of the Trias to gain agreement on the construction of fortifications at Ulm and Rastatt, and also in 1843 persuaded them to take steps to improve their armed forces. In 1847 he gained Frederick William's support for a reform programme aimed at strengthening the Confederation through liberalizing it from above rather than awaiting more radical revolution from below, but this move was overtaken by the revolts of 1848 (see Chapter 3).[26]

Domestic politics in the German states

Despite their historic names, many of the German states in 1814 were virtually new constructions. Their governments were thus faced with the problem of both integrating often extensive new territories and establishing legitimacy for the new regimes sanctioned by the Vienna Conference. Only through the intervention of the state could their populations be assimilated and a new loyalty created. The state stood above the individual interest and could weld both the former free cities and the dispossessed ruling classes, which had previously enjoyed independence in the now defunct Holy Roman Empire, into a cohesive whole. Thus everywhere the state had by necessity to become more bureaucratic, and increasingly it was civil servants rather than the nobility or princes who in effect ran the states and began to impose a uniform pattern on society. As Thomas Nipperdey observed, the state 'now burdened the citizen with three of the great obligations of the modern man: the universal obligation to pay taxes, compulsory school attendance, and obligatory military service'.[27]

Prussia

In 1815 Prussia was, in all but name, a new state. It was divided into ten provinces (later reduced to eight) and consisted of an uneasy union of the old territories with a very disparate group of lands, comprising the Rhineland, Westphalia, Saxony, Swedish Pomerania and the

See Map 3

province of Posen, all of which had diverse political, legal and social constitutions. How was this somewhat random collection of territories to be welded together into a whole? Too much stress on the unity of the Prussian 'nation' would alienate both the Rhinelanders and the Poles in Posen, who had no loyalty to Prussia. Possibly a new constitution and a representative assembly might help unify the state, but this was a controversial matter. In January 1815 a constitutional commission was set up, and in April actually got as far as recommending the creation of a representative assembly, but could not agree on its powers. Hardenberg wanted it to have some control over the state's finances and powers to amend legislation, while the king and the conservatives argued that it should be merely a consultative assembly. In May the king actually promised a constitution and a state representative assembly (*Landtag*), but he was, no doubt deliberately, ambiguous about whether it was to be a 'representation of the people' or an 'assembly of representatives of the Prussian provinces'.[28]

With the final defeat of Napoleon and the conclusion of the Vienna settlement, the king's support for a constitution declined. The Prussian conservatives were further strengthened by the unrest which led to Kotzebue's murder in 1819 (see p. 32). When Frederick William, Metternich and Hardenberg met at Teplitz in August, Prussia declared that it would 'establish no general popular representation', but rather a 'central committee of representatives of the land'.[29] By December 1820 even this watered-down proposal was dropped. As a consequence of the liberal revolts in Spain, Portugal and Naples in 1820, which led temporarily to the creation of constitutional monarchies in these states, the king shelved the whole constitutional question. Instead, as an alternative to a central Prussian parliament, the government set up in 1823–1824 assemblies in the ten provinces, in which representatives of the nobility, the burghers (townsmen) and the peasantry were represented. Longterm ownership of land was a key qualification for election. The assemblies were only empowered to make decisions on a few minor matters, and increasingly the representatives of both the burghers and nobility began to demand a greater political role. For instance the Rhineland assembly, which was first convened in 1826, regularly debated such issues as Church-state relations, local government reform and Jewish emancipation.[30] The diets also regularly, but unsuccessfully, petitioned Frederick William to allow the minutes of these debates to be published. There were, too, frequent requests to the Crown to give the whole Prussian state a representative constitution.

Prussia is often described as a state wearing a 'Janus face', which faced both ways. On the one hand it was a modern administrative state, humanely and efficiently run, and committed to free trade and economic and educational reform. It possessed a uniform education system with elementary schools for the majority of children and grammar schools (*Gymnasien*) for those heading towards universities, which was the envy of the civilized world.[31] It had an efficient and often enlightened civil service. Its provinces were run by the ***Oberpräsidenten***, who were granted by the government a considerable degree of independence, while the actual administration was carried out at district level by the ***Regierungspräsidenten***, who exercised their power on a collegiate basis. The same principle functioned right at the centre of government. After Hardenberg's death in 1822, the ***Staatsministerium*** also became a collegiate body, which made decisions collectively. The ***Staatsrat*** which was composed of the royal princes, ministers and senior civil servants, was able critically to discuss drafts of new laws and in many ways played a role similar to a senate or a revising chamber.

On the other hand, Prussia was also 'the classic state of the restoration'[32], lacking a parliamentary constitution. Indeed it is argued by some historians that 'the project of absolute monarchy was fulfilled in Prussia not during the era of Frederick the Great but only in the aftermath of the Napoleonic wars'.[33] In the aftermath of the Karlsbad Decrees the influence of the conservatives steadily strengthened. Reform-minded civil servants were neutralized and in core Prussia, east of the Elbe, the special status and privileges of the Junkers were restored. In the new provincial assemblies half the representation was reserved for the owners of the landed estates. They retained their tax privileges and were still able to appoint the local ***Landrat***. The conservatives were also able to exploit the reaction caused by Kotzebue's murder to weaken the *Landwehr* (see p. 17) and strengthen the regular army, on whose royalist loyalties the Crown could safely rely.

> **Oberpräsidenten:** heads of provincial administration;
> **Regierungspräsident:** chief administrators of the governmental districts;
> **Staatsministerium:** central ministry;
> **Staatsrat:** privy council.

> **Landrat:** head of the district administration

Problems of integration

Both Posen and the Rhenish provinces were Catholic. The Rhineland was, of course, German but very far from Prussian. It looked rather to the Habsburgs than the Hohenzollerns. Its great cities, Aachen and Cologne, had been Free Imperial City States under the Holy Roman Empire. As part of the Rhineland Confederation it had also enjoyed the benefits of the *Code Napoleon*, which made all citizens equal before the law. The Province of Posen on the other hand was Polish, but unlike the Rhineland it had been briefly part of Prussia from 1793 to 1806 as a consequence of the third Polish partition. However, like the Rhineland it also briefly came under Napoleonic control, in 1806 and then became part of the Grand Duchy of Warsaw where it was subject to the *Code Napoleon*.

The Rhineland

On 5 April 1815 the newly formed Rhenish province, the Grand Duchy of the Lower Rhine and Cleve, Berg and Geldern with a population of two million, were incorporated into the Prussian state. Their inhabitants were promised that Prussia would respect their religious rights, enforce justice and grant a constitution. Two very different and contradictory systems had now to coexist within the Prussian state. Not only was the overwhelming majority of the population of the Rhenish provinces Catholic, whereas core Prussia was Protestant, but the political and social culture of the Rhineland was very different from Prussia. The Rhenish cities of Aachen and Cologne had a strong tradition of local autonomy, which Napoleonic rule had not destroyed, while the introduction of Napoleonic law gave the provinces a more modern and egalitarian legal system than the Prussian *Allgemeines Landrecht.* Consequently it is hardly surprising that there was so little enthusiasm in the Rhineland for Prussia. The supporter of the German nationalist cause, the physicist Johann Friedrich Benzenberg (1777–1846), aptly observed that Rhinelanders might accept rule from Berlin in order to remain German, but refused to become Prussian.[34]

> **Allgemeines Landrecht:**
> General State Law introduced into Prussia in 1794

The Rhineland was annexed at a time when Hardenberg's proposals for reform were still being debated. To conservatives its French institutions contained the 'poison' of liberalism and nationalism.[35] Their prejudices seemed to be confirmed both by Görres' petitioning campaign of 1817 agitating for a constitution and the unrest throughout the Rhineland culminating in the murder of Kotzebue (see p. 32). The Karlsbad Decrees led to a crackdown on alleged revolutionaries in the Rhineland. Arndt, for instance, was suspended from his professorship at Bonn University in November 1820 after the police had conducted a dawn raid on his house.

The triumph of the Prussian conservatives in 1820 effectively ruled out the creation of a Prussian national parliament. Instead the Rhinelanders were given a provincial assembly comprising four estates, which gave 'undue political weight to the insignificant nobility' much to the anger of the citizens of Aachen and Cologne, whose own delegates represented 120 times more constituents and 35 times more tax revenue than their aristocratic colleagues in the Second Estate. It is no wonder that the population dismissed the assembly as an 'assembly of fools' or '*Narrentag*'.[36]

In the absence of a more representative body at both national and provincial levels the Napoleonic legal codes served as a 'substitute constitution'.[37] These guaranteed the principle of equal citizenship and trial by jury. Although the conservatives in the Prussian administration feared that French law would 'contaminate' the rest of Prussia, Hardenberg agreed to its continuation in the Rhineland until such a time as the whole legal system in Prussia was revised.

However, for the majority of the population it was the Catholic Church that served as the principal 'focus'[38] of an alternative allegiance, which over time was to create considerable friction with Berlin leading to the *Kulturkampf* of the 1870s (see p. 126). Initially the Catholic hierarchy enjoyed good relations with the Prussian government, but a major problem was created by the extension to the Rhineland of the Prussian mixed marriage law, whereby all children with Protestant fathers would automatically be christened Protestants. Opposition to this led in 1837 to the arrest of the Archbishop of Cologne, which aggravated relations between the Catholics and the Berlin government not only in the Rhineland but throughout Prussia.

Grand Duchy of Posen

In the east, Prussia acquired the Grand Duchy of Posen, whose population of nearly a million was predominantly Polish and Catholic. Their right to autonomy was guaranteed by the Vienna Final Act. Initially this was honoured by the Prussian government. The oath of allegiance given by the Polish nobility to the Prussian Crown specifically described the Prussian monarch as 'the King of that part of Poland under Prussian rule'. Polish remained the official language in the law courts, schools and local government and the local diet was elected by the Polish nobility. Poles were also appointed as *Landräte* and the head of the province, or *Statthalter*, was Prince Anton Radziwill (1775–1833), a local Polish magnate.

At the Prussian universities several nationalist societies were founded by Polish students, which, like their German counterparts, faced repression and closure. In 1830 an uprising in the Russian-controlled Grand Duchy of Warsaw broke out, which was only repressed after large-scale fighting. Posen remained calm, but some 2500 Poles from Posen crossed the frontier to help their compatriots. In the aftermath of the fighting thousands of Polish refugees fled both to Paris and the German cities, where they were welcomed by German liberals, who at that stage sympathized with the Polish struggle for independence. In Posen, however, the 1830 revolt led to the Prussian government reversing its former tolerant policies. The post of *Statthalter* was abolished and the new Prussian *Oberpräsident*, Edward Flotwell, began to replace Polish officials with Prussians, rein back the influence of the Catholic Church and curtail the use of Polish as an official language. With the accession of Frederick William IV in 1840 these policies were relaxed, as they had proved counter-productive and had failed to eliminate Polish nationalism.

Austria

The Austria of Metternich dominated the German Confederation, and it was still taken for granted that Austria was a German power. Its ruling dynasty, capital city and senior civil servants were all German, and German was also the language of the army and the bureaucracy. Within the Habsburg Empire, as Sperber had commented, 'the political trends in the neighbouring German and Italian states were echoed but rather more feebly'.[39] There were small political associations in Vienna and the larger cities, and, as in the German states to the north, nationalism was a key demand of liberalism. The crucial difference, however, between Austria and the rest of Germany was that there was no one nationalist movement, but instead a mass of mutually contradictory and hostile movements such as, for example, German and Czech nationalism in Bohemia and Hungarian and Croatian in Hungarian Croatia. These divisions made it easier for Austria to control its empire through a policy of divide and rule, but they effectively ensured that it could never put itself at the head of German nationalism, a role which was open for Prussia to seize.

Austrian influence in Germany was also eroded both by financial weakness and its failure, in contrast to Prussia, to modernize the bureaucracy and the institutions of the state. The determination of Hungary to defend its fiscal privileges prevented the government from ever getting to grips with the Empire's finances. Some 30 per cent of its revenue, for example, went on simply servicing its loans, while the cost of mobilizing its army against France in 1831 exhausted the financial reserves the government had been accumulating through increases in direct taxation.[40]

The other German states: the 'Third Germany'

In contrast to Prussia, Baden, Bavaria and Württemberg introduced constitutions to integrate their recently acquired territories and win the loyalty of their new citizens. In 1815 Baden was on the brink of dissolution, and power appeared to be devolving back into the hands of the magistrates, burghers and traditional noble estates. To weld the state together, the grand duke was persuaded by a group of reforming civil servants to accept the most 'modern' or liberal constitution in Germany. The upper house of its assembly was still dominated by the nobility, but its lower house, composed of 63 members, was elected by individuals who met the necessary property and tax qualifications. This was unique in Germany because the link between possession of the vote and class was broken, and it had the potential to 'overturn social and political arrangements on all levels of society'.[41] It also contained a bill of rights which gave the population the fundamental rights of equality of taxation, religious freedom and equality before the law.

The Bavarian and Württemberg monarchies also came to the conclusion that limited parliamentary constitutions would help integrate their new territories and populations. The Bavarian constitution, which was introduced in 1818, included a bill of rights, which promised its citizens equality before the law, even though the nobility were still guaranteed certain privileges. The chamber of deputies was still chosen according to the old estate-based principles, in that there were five separate categories of voter, but it was also made clear that its duty was to represent the state as a whole rather than individual classes. In Württemberg, too, a constitution was used to buttress the power of the Crown and weaken the embittered **mediatized nobility** by creating an elected chamber in which they would be in a minority.

The **mediatized nobility** were the former imperial knights of the Holy Roman Empire, who lost their land, but not their titles, when the Empire was abolished in 1806.

The power of the new south German parliaments was, of course, very limited. The Crown still controlled the composition of the executive ministries and was solely responsible for foreign and military affairs. Yet the elected chambers had to give their consent to new taxes and fiscal bills, and became increasingly skilled in opposing ministers who broke the constitution. In 1832, for instance, the Bavarian assembly forced the king to dismiss his minister of the interior and withdraw a censorship decree. South Germany became an important testing ground for German liberalism as a whole and gave liberal deputies valuable experience in parliamentary opposition.

In the smaller central and north German states, which had not gained new territories, there was a greater continuity with the past. The four 'free cities' of Hamburg, Bremen, Lübeck and Frankfurt all re-established their former estate-based constitutions. Similarly, in both Mecklenburgs, Saxony and Hanover, the old estate-based constitution remained in place, while Hesse-Kassel returned to its pre-revolutionary system of absolutism. In Schleswig-Holstein the nobility attempted to defend themselves against the centralizing policies of the King of Denmark by demanding a constitution along **estate-based** lines. The king rejected this, but did temporarily ease up on his attempts to integrate the two duchies into Denmark (see p. 61).

Estate-based constitutions: constitutions based on the three traditional estates

The growing national context of the political debate

In an introductory essay in the first edition of the *Staatslexikon* (State Encyclopaedia) in 1834, Theodor Welcker (1790–1869), the liberal academic and politician in the Baden assembly argued that politics dominated people's thoughts and actions in a way that had not occurred before.[42] His perception was correct. There had been rapid growth in the publication of lexicons, periodicals and newspapers, as well as lectures and the foundation of social, literary and learned institutions, all of which extended the **'public sphere'**. The legacy of the French revolution and the Napoleonic wars as well as the growth in the power of the state as tax collector, organizer of education and economic regulator had sharpened political awareness, and the new provincial assemblies in Prussia and parliaments in south Germany provided for a forum where grand political concepts could be discussed. The 1830s and 1840s witnessed not only the growing debate between nationalists, liberals and democrats on the one side and conservatives and reactionaries on the other, but also the emergence of socialism and political Catholicism.

Public sphere: an area in social life where individuals can meet, perhaps in clubs or discussion groups, to discuss social and political problems

Liberalism

German liberalism was 'a multiform, almost protean movement with conflicting tendencies and blurred boundaries'.[43] Its origins lay in the 18th century Enlightenment, the ideas of the British classical economists such as Adam Smith (1723–1790) and the complex checks and balances of the Holy Roman Empire (see pp. 4–6). It only emerged as a political movement in reaction to the 'restorative paralysis'[44] of 1815. The term liberal became generally used in 1830. Its core demands were the establishment of:

- the rule of law
- a constitutional monarchy
- freedom of association, the press and of belief
- representative government with an elected parliament
- faith in the ability of the state to implement reform
- a belief in 'progress', but not in revolution
- German unity.

The origins of liberalism: Liberalism was essentially about self-government and the freedom of the individual. It was thus opposed to both the old feudal, corporate society and the authoritarian state. The term can also be applied to the economic and social spheres where many liberals wanted the minimum controls on individuals, business and industry.

How these objectives were to be reached and what precisely they entailed was a matter for debate. Certainly for the liberals, representative government most definitely did not mean universal suffrage. They distrusted the masses, and believed that it would result in 'rule by those without assets'.[45] They also emphatically rejected female suffrage, as they saw civil society as being composed of male heads of households. For most liberals it was the middle class or *Mittelstand* that was the political core of the population.

The bureaucratic reforms, which were carried out by what has been called 'the liberal civil service' working under Stein and Hardenberg (see pp. 15–17) in Prussia and also by their colleagues in the south German states created what Langwiesche has called 'the prerequisites' for constitutional liberalism.[46] Initially liberalism was strongest in south Germany, where parliaments gave liberal politicians a platform for their views, but liberal deputies were not directly involved in political decisions, and they could only hope that the government could be influenced by their views. In the Rhineland liberalism managed to exploit the old traditions of civil liberty going back to the Holy Roman Empire and argued that these traditions would be strengthened by a constitution. The Karlsbad Decrees (see p. 32) effectively put an end to the influence of the 'liberal wing' of the civil service and this early period of 'German liberalism'.

The French revolution of 1830 strengthened liberalism in the Confederation. In Brunswick, Hesse-Kassel, Saxony and Hanover, liberals exploited the riots and fear of revolution to persuade the rulers to grant constitutions. In the Palatinate, the journalist, Johann Wirth, set up the *Presseverein* as a pressure group to campaign for liberal ideals throughout German-speaking Europe. By 1832 it already had 5000 members, and well over a hundred branches in Bavaria. In the Palatinate the *Mittelstand* (lower middle classes) made up some 65 per cent of its membership. Elsewhere its branches were dominated by the educated middle classes, who also supplied its leadership. In May the *Presseverein* held a large-scale 'political festival' in the ruins of the old castle near Hambach, which inspired a series of similar meetings throughout Germany. Its organizers called for a united, liberal Germany, but rejected revolution and violence. Radical proposals to create a revolutionary committee to work towards unification were rejected as being too utopian (see p. 35).

Although Metternich was able to restore order within the Confederation the events of 1830–1833 went some way to turning liberalism into a national movement. A mass of liberal periodicals and books, such as Rotteck's *Staastslexikon*, kept political debate at a fever pitch. The significance of the creation of the *Zollverein* and its subsequent development was also closely watched by the liberals. In the Rhineland liberals like Ludolf Camphausen (1803–1890) and Gustav Mevissen (1815–1899) began to see the *Zollverein* as a 'gravitational force',[47] which through the creation of a 'Customs Parliament' would lead to the unification of Germany. The Hanoverian constitutional crisis (see pp. 39–40) led to liberals throughout Germany rallying to the support of the 'Göttingen Seven'. By

1840 liberalism was becoming a national movement drawing support from the wave of nationalism inspired by the Rhineland crisis (see p. 51). It was helped by the growing economic and cultural integration of Germany, although links with Austria remained weak. Its division into a left and right wing was also becoming discernible. Its left wing was increasingly pressing for a strong parliamentary system in which the state would of necessity bow to parliament, while right-wing liberals were more pragmatic and looked to the state as a potential ally against too disruptive a pace of economic and social change.

The democrats and socialists

To the left of the liberals there emerged in the 1840s both the radical democrats and the early socialists. The radicals, led by members of the intelligentsia, such as Johann Jacoby, a physician from Königsberg, drew their strength from 'the little people',[48] that is the dependent and exploited. In September 1847 the radical wing of the Baden opposition met with similar groups from the neighbouring states in Offenburg and agreed on a programme which called for a people's militia, equal voting rights, educational opportunities for the poor, and an end to the 'disparity between the rich and poor'.

The first socialist organization, the 'League of the Just', was formed in 1836–1837 largely as a result of the efforts of Karl Schapper (1812–1870), a former student and *Burschenschaft* member at Giessen University, and Wilhelm Weitling (1808–1871), who had been a journeyman tailor. Their targets were the impoverished craftsmen (see p. 57) rather than the industrial workers, but they envisaged revolution and the creation of a new regime of equality. This pre-industrial socialism was bitterly criticized by Karl Marx, who, by drawing on the philosophy of **Feuerbach** and the Young Hegelians, produced a blueprint for revolution, which called upon the industrial proletariat to rise up and revolt. His Communist Manifesto of 1848 was, however, way in advance of its times, as industrialization in Germany was still in its infancy and his supporters consisted mainly of intellectuals rather than workers.

See Document 12

The philosopher, **Ludwig Feuerbach**, freed Hegelianism from its spiritual dimension and thus opened the way for applying Hegel's theories to the material world. The implication of this was that man himself could create the ideal world on earth rather than waiting for the afterlife.

Nationalism

Early 19th-century German nationalism like liberalism was a similarly protean movement. What was the nation? Was it Prussia as the Prussian reformers seemed to indicate (see p. 20) or was it an object of 'quasi religious devotion'[49] embracing the whole of German-speaking Europe as the romantic nationalists believed? Was this 'Germany' to be defined by its institutions and culture or its race? Friedrich Jahn the founder of the gymnastic societies and the *Burschenschaften* (fraternities), for instance, believed that 'Germany' should include Switzerland, Denmark and the Low Countries.

After the War of Liberation, 1813–1814, and the disappointments of the Vienna Settlement, the hopes and ambitions of the romantic

Pan-German: all-German, stretching right across all the German states

nationalists were represented principally by the gymnastic societies and the *Burschenschaften*. These aimed to create a new **pan-German** ethos of friendship and honour and influenced the thinking of a whole generation of university students. In some ways they were the prototype of a modern political party and pioneered rallies and mass public meetings as a new form of public event. On 18–19 October 1817 the *Burschenschaften* held a rally at the Wartburg (see p. 32), which was attended by 500 students, and a year later the *Allgemeine Deutsche Burschenschaft* (the General German Fraternity) was set up as a pan-German student organization. Within the *Burschenschaften*, a radical wing led by Karl Follen a lecturer at Giessen University, emerged which aimed to create a united republican Germany, by force if necessary.

See Documents 4 and 5

This first phase of nationalist agitation was brought to an end by the Karlsbad Decrees (see p. 32). The *Burschenschaften* and other nationalist organizations were banned, but they continued to exist secretly, particularly in southern Germany where the repression was less severe. The decrees also disciplined the 'liberal wing' of the Prussian civil service with the consequence that the concept of the 'Prussian nation' unlike that of the 'German nation' rapidly became an anachronism. Increasingly the task of defining what the German nation would consist of was left to the bourgeois liberal activists, many of whom had been members of the *Burschenschaften*. Nationalism, as Hans-Ulrich Wehler observed, now came to belong with liberalism 'like a pair together'.[50] The German liberals aimed to combine liberation from external control with internal self-government. Undoubtedly nationalism was a 'modernizing force' that aimed to sweep away the restrictions of the restoration era but the liberals were divided about what sort of a united Germany they envisaged and the role the individual states would play in it. Only later did the creation of the Prussian-dominated *Zollverein* lead some to see Prussia as 'the champion and defender of the new Germany'.[51]

The revolutionary events in France and Belgium of 1830 both strengthened liberalism in Germany and also encouraged a brief revival of romantic nationalism. Students and academics were well represented at the Hambacher *Fest* in May 1832 (see p. 35). In April 1833 a small group of Heidelberg *Burschenschaft* members, academics and Polish exiles inspired by the Paris revolution 3 years earlier launched an abortive coup in Frankfurt (see p. 35), the capital of the German Confederation, with the intention of creating a German republic. The Six Articles and the defeat of the Frankfurt 'insurrection' once again forced the nationalists to camouflage their activities. Choirs, scientific, historical and philological societies now became the main medium for the nationalist message. Choral groups would meet regularly at large regional festivals where nationalist songs were sung with great enthusiasm.

German nationalism was part of a powerful pan-European and even American movement. It was inspired and strengthened by both the example of the Greek uprising against the Turks in the 1820s and the revolt of 1830 in Russian Poland. The imagined threat of a French invasion of the Rhineland in 1840 (see p. 40) triggered, as we have seen a large-scale nationalist reaction, the spirit of which was caught by Nikolaus Becker's Rhineland song, *Der deutsche Rhein*, which was sung to over two hundred different tunes throughout Germany. Similarly, the ongoing intention of the Danish Crown to integrate the Duchy of Schleswig into the Danish state (see p. 61) caused growing concern among the German nationalists. In July 1844 some 12,000 people flocked to the Schleswig-Holstein singing festival and the 'battle hymn', *Schleswig-Holstein meerumschlungen* (sea encircled), became as popular as the Rhineland song.

By the 1840s the German national movement had acquired 'a broad social base'.[52] The majority of its members were liberals, but a significant minority were 'democratic republicans'.[53] The liberal nationalist elites were in close and regular touch with each other right across Germany and attracted support from the younger generation and the commercial middle classes. In the meantime **the gymnastic and singing societies associations** had developed from elitist to popular organizations where journeymen and master craftsmen dominated. The former was increasingly sympathetic to democratic aims. By 1848 about 250,000 Germans were organized in various nationalist organizations. Thanks to the improvement in communications, the press and the ever more frequent inter-regional festivals, nationalism's tentacles had spread throughout Germany.

Gymnastic societies: In 1842 were again legalized in Prussia and much of central and southern Germany,

The emergence of a national culture

Although there was no political consensus among the poets and writers during this period, the Young German Movement, whose two most gifted writers were Heinrich Heine (1897–1856) and Georg Büchner (1813–1837), believed passionately in a united liberal German state. Even after the intensified surveillance and censorship introduced by the Six Articles in 1832 (see p. 35), which drove Heine into exile, their works continued to be circulated clandestinely. Patriotic songs dominated choir festivals, but music and opera also assumed an increasingly national character, as can be seen, for example, in Richard Wagner's (1813–1883) operas, *Rienzi* and *Tannhäuser*, composed in 1841 and 1845 respectively. It is also possible to see the beginning of the 'nationalization of culture', which became much more pronounced in the 1860s. The new subject of German philology, which was pioneered by Jacob Grimm, and the growing interest in German medieval history and the rediscovery of Germany's ancient legal traditions all reflected this. Monumental new architecture, memorials to great German heroes and museums also increasingly expressed the idea of a German national and cultural identity.

Conservatism

The roots of German and European conservatism lay in the opposition to the enlightened absolutism of the 18th century, the principles of the French Revolution and the emerging liberalism of the post-war era.

Initially it appeared that conservatism was doomed to remain a reactionary, anti-modernist movement totally opposed to the development of the modern state. Thanks, however, to the work of the right-wing philosopher, Friedrich von Stahl (1802–1861), a workable synthesis between traditional, estate-based, conservative ideas and the need to come to terms with the reality of the contemporary state was devised in the 1840s. On the one hand, Stahl stressed the existence in society of a 'preordained order beyond human will' and a close relationship between church and state. On the other hand, he recognized the need for a constitution and an elected parliament, but it would be a monarchical constitution, in which the Crown would determine policy, while parliament would be the legislature and guarantor of both the constitution and the legal rights of the subjects. This formula enabled the conservatives to escape from the cul-de-sac of total opposition to the modern state. Traditionally the conservatives had been opposed to nationalism. Yet there were now signs that these two enemies were drawing closer to each other. Joseph von Radowitz (see pp. 41 and 76), the councillor and confidant of Frederick William IV of Prussia, was beginning to argue that, to survive, the Prussian monarchy and state needed to accept the 'idea of nationality [which] was the most powerful force of the present time'.[54] Other thinkers, like the German social reformer Victor Huber (1800–1869), were putting forward programmes for social conservatism, which involved a state-controlled welfare policy and the setting up of cooperatives, which would give workers a chance of gaining property and running their own businesses.

Political Catholicism

After the French Revolution, the Catholic Church became a fierce critic of the claims of the modern state and liberal individualism. As early as the 1830s, small groups of Catholic delegates began to join forces in the south German assemblies, but it was the arrest of the Archbishop of Cologne in 1838 by the Prussian authorities for opposing regulations on mixed marriages between Protestants and Catholics that acted as a catalyst for the development of Catholicism as a political force (see p. 44). Political Catholicism was in itself a coalition of forces. On the one hand, there were the conservatives, whose politics were a mixture of romanticism and conservatism. They regarded unquestioning faith in the institutions of the Catholic Church as the key to opposing the secular and reformist evils of the time. On the other hand, there were Catholics, mainly in the Rhineland who supported liberal demands for individual freedom and a constitution, while there was also a growth in social Catholicism, which urged controls on *laissez-faire* capitalism, limits on property ownership and the guarantee of full employment by the state. There was considerable tension between Catholicism and nationalism. The Catholic paper, *Historische-politische Blätter*, observed that there was 'a vastly more profound bond' between a Catholic German and a Catholic

Laissez-faire
capitalism: belief in a completely free economy and working conditions uncontrolled by the state

African than between the former and a German atheist.[55] The Catholics also distrusted Prussia and instinctively looked to Catholic Vienna rather than to Protestant Berlin to take the lead in German affairs.

A Catholic faction was formed in the Prussian *Landtag* in 1852, but it was not until 13 December 1870 that the Catholic Centre party was founded as a national party (see p. 125).

Economic and social developments

Although the outlines of the old regime remained intact, in reality German society was 'shaken up and rearranged in the decades before 1848',[56] but the pace and impact of modernization was uneven. Large-scale capitalist landowners lived next to subsistence farmers, while, in the Rhineland, modern factories sprang up in areas where traditional crafts-men continued to sell their wares exclusively within their own villages.

Agriculture

In 1815 Germany was an overwhelmingly rural society with three-quarters of its population living in the countryside. The poor were still vulnerable to harvest failures, which, as in 1816–1817 and 1845–1846, intensified mass poverty and ultimately starvation. At the same time the slow and uneven process of peasant emancipation led to major social and economic changes. In Prussia, the peasant emancipation law of 1821 eliminated personal servitude and removed restrictions on the sale of rural property. However, according to the edict of 1816, only those peas-ants who had the resources to support a team of horses or oxen were eligible to buy their property. This effectively reduced the smaller peas-antry to the position of landless labourers who worked on the Junkers' estates in return for a cottage and a garden. The landed elite were the main beneficiaries of the reform in Prussia. Overall as a class they acquired some four million **Morgens** of land from the peasantry and some were able to turn them into modern, capitalist concerns. The eco-nomic climate did not, however, favour the Junkers. In the early 19th century, land values collapsed as did grain prices as a result of the intro-duction of the British **Corn Laws**. The consequence of this was that many individual landowners had to mortgage their properties and a consider-able number were bankrupted, their estates often being purchased by members of the commercial bourgeoisie.[57]

Corn Laws: tariffs aimed at protecting cereal producers in the UK and Ireland from foreign competi-tion, 1815–1846 **One Morgen** was equivalent to 0.5 to 2.5 acres (0.2 to 1 hectare).

Elsewhere, emancipation developed differently. In some areas like Mecklenburg, Hesse-Darmstadt and Hesse- Kassel and Hanover, progress towards emancipation was much slower than Prussia, while in Schleswig-Holstein and on the left bank of the Rhine, emancipation led to more favourable conditions for the peasantry. The enclosure of common lands hit the poorer peasantry throughout Germany a devastating blow, as it deprived them of their customary rights of free grazing for their animals and collection of fuel. This combined with the increase in rural popula-tion led to seasonal migration within Germany and also emigration to Brazil and especially the USA.

Despite the damage done to the German grain trade by the Corn Laws, the productivity of German agriculture doubled between 1800 and 1850. Thanks to the steady improvement in agricultural implements, and the application of applied science to agriculture, which led to the development of artificial fertilizers, modern intensive farming gradually replaced the old medieval **three-field system** throughout most of Germany, and arable land increased by 20 per cent as common and waste land was increasing brought under the plough. By the time the Corn Laws were repealed by the British Parliament in 1846, agriculture, particularly on the large estates in Prussia, was potentially well placed both to export to Britain and to support the growing domestic population.

Three-field system: the traditional medieval system of farming whereby farmers allowed one field to lie fallow for a season in order to rest it

Industry

The industrial revolution and its consequences determined the fate of the whole period covered by this book. It revolutionized production and the economy, and irrevocably changed German society, although, compared to Britain, the full impact on the German states of the industrial revolution was felt later. Germany did not yet form a single market and lacked the abundant capital which Britain could draw on from her colonial trade, yet it did possess many of the essential preconditions for industrialization. There were a large number of skilled workers, a strong professional middle class and a social discipline reinforced by Christianity. The reforms introduced by Napoleon in the Rhineland Confederation and by Stein and Hardenberg in Prussia, as well as the emancipation of the peasantry, began to create a society more orientated towards personal liberty, property and social mobility. The Vienna Settlement also went some way towards simplifying the German political map.

In 1815 Britain was an economic colossus that dominated the world, and the German market was flooded with cheap British goods, which initially came near to throttling local industries. Yet this experience was not entirely negative. In the medium term it facilitated industrialization through the delivery of cheap, half-finished goods, and goaded the Germans into copying and eventually competing with British industrial techniques. Although the British government did everything it could to stop 'industrial espionage' and the export of modern machinery, thousands of Germans went to Britain to learn the secrets of industrialization. Gradually, the combination of British ideas and German skills laid the foundations of the German industrial revolution. The governments of the German states assisted in creating the basic conditions for industrialization by improving the communications network – roads, canals, railways and the *Zollverein*. Reform-minded civil servants also attempted to inculcate the 'entrepreneurial spirit' in the population by arranging trips abroad for up-and-coming technicians, organizing industrial exhibitions and generally encouraging a more *laissez-faire* economic climate by setting up chambers of commerce and industry.

How was the early industrial revolution financed?

Although Germany was not as short of capital as historians originally believed, capital backing for industrial projects was much harder to secure than in either France or Britain. **Joint-stock companies** were formed to finance shipping and railway companies, but initially industrial projects were largely financed by capital from the entrepreneurs themselves and their families. It was only with the foundation of the first credit banks, the *Schaffhausen Bankverein* in 1848 and the *Diskonto-Gesellschaft* in 1851, that credit became more easily available to industrialists.

Unlike Britain, it was not the textile industry in Germany that led the industrial revolution. Although most of the cotton industry was powered by steam by the 1830s, the wool industry was much slower to adapt, and in 1850 only 50 per cent of its production was steam-driven, while the linen industry remained a pre-industrial cottage industry that was almost destroyed by British competition. Mechanization did not, however, halt the growth in the number of hand weavers. In 1800, for instance, there were about 315,000 weavers in Germany, while 50 years later this total had risen by nearly 70 per cent. The reason for this was largely because the abundance of cheap labour made cottage industries still just about economically viable.

> **Joint-stock companies:** companies formed on the basis of capital which is jointly owned by a number of people

The iron and coal industries began the process of technological modernization. First the **puddling process** for producing wrought iron was imported from England, and then in the 1830s rolling mills and coke-fired blast furnaces appeared. These innovations, which required a ready access to coal supplies, ensured that successful foundries had to move to the coal mining regions of the Ruhr or Upper Silesia, or else to areas with good transport connections. This in turn stimulated the development of the coal industry. The construction of the railways enormously boosted production in both these two industries. The first 6-km stretch of railway was built between Nuremberg and Fürth in 1834. By 1840, 468 km of railway track had been laid in the German states and 473 in Austria. Ten years later this had risen to 5859 in the former area and only 1357 in the latter. The rapid pace of railway construction ensured that there was a growing demand for engines, tracks, iron and coal, even though at first much of the equipment was imported from England. Railways also meant that ore and coal would now potentially be available to factories anywhere in Germany. The railways increased the mobility of labour and enabled its concentration in large-scale plants.

> **Puddling process:** the making of bar iron with coal rather than charcoal furnaces

The economic impact of the *Zollverein*

The economic impact of the customs union is as controversial as is its alleged contribution to German unity. Following Friedrich List's argument that without a protective tariff the Germans would be reduced to being economically dependent on Britain, a long tradition of historians (more recently, for example, Walther G. Hoffmann and Hans Mottek) have argued that the creation of the *Zollverein* was a turning point in German economic history because it created a tariff wall behind which German industry could modernize itself. The actual economic benefits of the customs union are, however, more difficult to quantify. Wehler stresses that it created a market of 30 million and enabled the infant German industries to enjoy the economies of scale, but he is somewhat vague as to whether the German industries actually did take advantage of this during the period 1840–1860.[58] It is of course true that Germany's economic position did improve between those years. Yet, as Henderson has observed, 'it is easy to see a connection between the two. But it is a dangerous half-truth – an over simplification of a highly complicated situation – to say the one caused the other'.[59] Hans-Joachim Voth argues that Prussia's economy 'derived little benefit from it',[60] and points out that, while the potential for economic growth in Germany was high, in practice both its investment and **GDP** were disappointing. Between 1840 and 1860, for instance, its growth in GDP averaged 1.6 per cent, compared to 2.1 in Britain and 4.7 in the USA. He also stresses that the customs union generated inter-German trade, at the cost of exports. Nevertheless, the argument over the economic impact of the *Zollverein* is inconclusive. Even Voth is uncertain about whether the *Zollverein* really did provide economies of scale which compensated for the other short comings of the German economy. Probably, as Sheehan has remarked, 'the best that can be said is that the *Zollverein*, especially in combination with other phenomena, such as railroad construction, helped to promote growth'.[61]

GDP: gross domestic product

German society between old and new

Although superficially the years 1814–1847 appeared to be a period of restoration, in reality they were a period of change. Despite the preservation of the monarchical principle and with it the whole apparatus of the courts and the nobility, a radical-social economic transformation was taking place. In Prussia the Junkers only remained a strong force as long as they could modernize their estates. In southern Germany the nobility were strictly subject to the laws of the bureaucratic state, and while they were represented in the upper chambers of the new assemblies, they lost many of their original privileges. In Baden, for instance, they lost both their exemption from taxation and their legal privileges. In Bavaria (but also in Prussia) the traditional aristocracy was infiltrated by rich merchants, middle-class landowners and Jewish bankers.

A new bourgeois society was struggling painfully to be born. The emerging bourgeois elite was, however, very diverse. Businessmen and industrialists were divided by regional, social and economic differences. To the bourgeoisie also belonged the *Bildungsbürgertum*, composed of civil servants, the intelligentsia and Protestant clergy. The civil servants, selected on the new meritocratic principle of educational achievement

Bildungs-bürgertum: educated bourgeoisie

Biedermeier culture and the role of women

The term *Biedermeier* was coined in the 1850s to describe the developing bourgeois culture in the post-war period of 1815–1848. The home was no longer a workshop but rather a refuge from the world. The father of the family, perhaps a civil servant, teacher or businessman, worked away from home, while the mother presided over the domestic scene. For the middle classes the decline of the home as a production unit, where the women's contribution had been vital, had the consequence of narrowing the range of the bourgeois woman's sphere of activities and of limiting her to the role of homemaker. For the wives of peasants and artisans, the situation was, of course, different, as they continued to play a vital economic role in their husbands' businesses. For bourgeois women wishing to escape from 'the private sphere', there were chances of voluntary work in welfare organizations or as nurses trained, for example, by the Rhenish-Westfalian Association of Deaconesses. Very few women, such as Fanny Lewald (1811–1889) or Louise Aston (1814–1871), for example, who were both from prosperous, professional backgrounds, even had the courage to reject the marriage plans of their parents or divorce their husbands and earn their own living and pursue their own interests.[62] Several high-powered salons were also hosted by wealthy and intellectually well-connected women, such as Dorothea Veit (1763–1839) and Caroline Schlegel Schelling (1763–1809), which attracted leading members of the German intelligentsia.

rather than birth, were in many ways the shock troops of the new order, yet ironically they too had evolved into an estate which extracted privileges from the governments they served.

The new bourgeois society was a society of individuals rather than estates and corporate bodies. The old control exercised by the feudal lords in the countryside and the guilds in the town was breaking down under the dual pressures of a market-driven society and the **demographic revolution**. Some of the surplus population was able to find work in the new factories, migrate to the cities or emigrate, while others had no option but to work for lower rates in the traditional craft industries. By the 1830s mass poverty had become a major social problem, which contemporaries, using the English word, called *Pauperismus*. A large underclass had emerged, which could no longer be sustained by the traditional structures of society.

Demographic revolution: the immense changes caused by greater longevity of life and the increase in the population

See Document 12

By the early 1840s, German society was becoming increasingly atomized and the individual alienated. How was it to be given a new basis of cohesion? Gradually, abstract ideas like the nation or the ideologies of political liberty and social equality as represented by liberalism or socialism became the focus for new loyalties. New types of organization, such as political and cultural clubs and associations, filled the gap left by the collapse of the old society. In the countryside, however, despite the inroads made by modern capitalist agriculture, the peasantry remained a potentially conservative force, increasingly hostile towards the cities, bureaucracy and liberal individualism. After 1848 it was there that the forces of anti-modernism – the conservatives, particularists, Catholics and royalists – were to find their chief support.

Conclusion

Historians have had particular difficulty in attempting to characterize the years between 1814 and 1848. Some refer to it as a period of restoration; others by using the term *Vormärz*, see it primarily as a mere interim period leading to the 1848 revolts.

The years 1814–1848 were only in a very limited sense a period of restoration. The German Confederation based on the cooperation of Prussia and Austria was a very different structure from the old Holy Roman Empire, and the major German states had gone through a political and territorial transformation. To describe the years 1815–1848 as the *Vormärz* period focuses attention on the growth of nationalism and the social discontents that fused together to cause the 1848 revolts, and thus runs the risk of distorting the history of the period. It was, as David Blackbourn has stressed, a period 'of transition, marked by ambiguous conflicting elements'.[63] Modern industry coexisted with the traditional craft industries and developing parliamentary politics in southern Germany. Liberal and nationalist demonstrations or 'festivals' coexisted with the survival of the traditional estates, the autocratic rule of the princes and the revival of a strong anti-modernist Catholicism. The largest popular demonstration in Germany was the pilgrimage of over a million Catholics from all over Germany to Trier in 1844 to see what they believed to be the Holy Robe of Christ. As Heinrich Heine observed, Germany had turned into a 'hybrid creature ... [t]hat is neither fish nor fowl'.[64]

> **Vormärz:** literally pre-March 1848 (the month the revolutions broke out in Germany), usually referring to the years 1830–1848

3 *Revolution and Reaction, 1847–1858*

TIMELINE

1846	*July*	Christian VIII's 'open letter' triggered Schleswig-Holstein crisis
1847	*April*	Combined meeting of the Prussian provincial assemblies in Berlin
	November	Swiss civil war
1848	*25 February*	Declaration of French Republic
	27 February	Mannheim Rally
	5 March	Heidelberg Assembly demanded a national parliament
	13 March	Outbreak of revolution in Vienna
	18 March	Uprising in Berlin
	29–30 March	Camphausen-Hansemann ministry established in Berlin
	30 March–3 April	Pre-parliament in session in Frankfurt
	12 April	Outbreak of revolution in Baden
	1 May	Elections to Constituent National Parliament in Frankfurt
	16 May	Emperor Ferdinand fled to Innsbruck
	18 May	National Assembly met at Frankfurt
	16 June	Prague fell to Windischgrätz
	20 June	Resignation of Camphausen government
	29 June	Archduke John elected Regent and head of provisional German government
	26 August	Armistice of Malmö
	6–31 October	Uprising in Vienna
	5 December	Imposition of new Prussian constitution
1849	*4 March*	Dissolution of Austrian parliament
	3 April	Frederick William rejected imperial crown
	5 April	Austria recalled delegates from Frankfurt Assembly
	3 May	Outbreak of Saxon revolution
	7 May	Prussia rejected imperial constitution
	14 May	Prussian delegates recalled from Frankfurt
	31 May	Rump (Frankfurt) Assembly moved to Stuttgart
	18 June	Rump dissolved by Württemberg troops
1850	*March*	Erfurt parliament
	November	Proclamation of Olmütz
1851		Confederation restored
1853		*Zollverein* renewed for 12 years
1854–1856		Crimean War
1859		Franco-Piedmontese war against Austria

Introduction: problems, issues and questions

See Document 13

The key question about 1848 is whether it marks a terminal defeat for German liberalism, which set Germany on its authoritarian *Sonderweg*. This line was emphatically taken by A. J. P. Taylor, who observed in 1945 that '1848 was the decisive year of German, and so of European, history',[1] implying that the failure of the liberals in 1848–1849 to unify Germany opened the way to the establishment of an authoritarian state under Bismarck in 1871 and eventually the Third Reich. After 1871 historians contrasted Bismarck's successful policy of blood and iron with the efforts of the theoretical chatterers in the Frankfurt National Assembly to unify Germany. At the very least, the events of 1848 were seen as a mere stage to 1871 and not worth study for their own sake. However, in 1919 the black, red and gold flag of the revolutionaries became the new flag of the Weimar Republic, while Theodor Heuss (1884–1963), a leading liberal and, later, President of the *Bundesrepublik* in 1949 advocated making the Frankfurt constitution the model for the new West German constitution (see pp. 306–307). Nevertheless, the majority of contemporary German historians continued to view the revolutions of 1848 with a hostility reinforced by their own experiences of the turmoil of November–December 1918 (see pp. 188–190). It was significant, for instance, that Veit Valentin's classic history of the 1848 revolutions met with hostility from established scholars and its publication was delayed until 1930.[2] During the Third Reich the revolutions were interpreted as the first proper national uprising in German history, but one that, thanks to the intervention of foreign powers and the corroding influence of democracy and constitutionalism, was ignominiously aborted.

After 1949 the two successor states to the German Reich laid claims to the legacy of 1848. The FRG stressed the constitutional achievements of the revolution, while the GDR was primarily interested in the role of the peasants and workers. Slowly in the 1960s and 1970s, under the influence of the social sciences, West German historians began to synthesize all the diverse themes of the 1848–1849 revolutions and put them into their European context. Increasingly the revolts are seen more as a complex crisis of modernization which witnessed the emergence of modern politics and attempts to forge a German nation.[3]

The coming of the revolution

Although the speed with which the 1848 revolutions swept across Europe took some contemporaries by surprise, it had been clear for several years that the *ancien régime* was facing an imminent and possibly terminal crisis. Gustav Freytag (1816–1895), the writer and historian, later recalled 'how we lived then like people who feel under their feet the pressures of the earthquake'.[4] Explaining why the revolutions occurred on the scale they did inevitably runs the risk of simplifying a highly complex set of events. Yet there are certain common patterns to the events: they were more than just a delayed reaction to the agrarian crisis or a liberal backlash against the Prussian government or the Metternich regime. They constituted, in effect, a crisis of modernization where institutional, economic, social and political crises all converged.

Growing demands for German unity and constitutional change, 1846–1848

Throughout German-speaking Europe there was a growing desire among the educated and propertied classes for increased political representation and power. The political experience they had gained through clubs, associations and town councils put them in a strong position to exploit the fiscal crisis facing the governments of the German states in 1847–1848 to demand political reform. In 1847 the Prussian government decided to build a railway linking its eastern and western provinces for both strategic and economic reasons. Unable to raise the money privately, Frederick William IV rashly summoned a combined meeting of the Prussian provincial assemblies to authorize loans. Inevitably, as Metternich had foreseen, this fuelled the liberals' demands for a Prussian parliament and gave them an opportunity to seize initiatives, which were progressively to undermine absolute government until it collapsed the following year. They refused point-blank to grant any loans until an elected parliament had been convened in Berlin, a demand which the Crown rejected. They also attempted to push the government into extending the anti-discriminatory Jewish legislation of 1812 to the whole kingdom as a symbolic act of liberalism.

Similarly in Baden, the liberals used the government's need to increase the military budget to extract political concessions, while, in Austria, Metternich was ultimately driven to calling an **estates-general** to gain sanction for new loans and taxes on 12 March 1848, a day before the outbreak of the revolution. As in France in 1789, the *ancien régime* in Germany had already been fatally weakened by the fiscal crisis before the political revolution broke.

Estates-general: a meeting of representatives of the estates or orders

In the autumn of 1847, left-wing liberals and democrats in Baden and the neighbouring states met in Offenburg and insisted that Germans should have 'a fatherland and a voice in its affairs'. A few weeks later a group of more moderate liberals convened in Heppenheim and urged that the *Zollverein* should be given representative institutions so that it 'would become irresistibly attractive to other German states, and finally lead to the inclusion of the Austrian lands within the Confederation and thus found a true German power'.[5] These resolutions were fully reported in the pages of the newly founded liberal *Deutsche Zeitung*, which was printed in Heidelberg and read by liberals in both north and south Germany.

The impact of the Schleswig-Holstein and Swiss crises

In July 1846 Christian VIII of Denmark triggered a major crisis when he announced that he was determined that Denmark should annex Schleswig where the Germans constituted only about half the population (Holstein was wholly German). This would mean ignoring the Treaty of Ripen of 1460 that guaranteed the 'eternal' unity of both Schleswig and Holstein. The two duchies were nominally ruled by the King of Denmark, but enjoyed autonomy under their own constitutions. This threat to Schleswig, as William Carr observed, made 1846 'a vintage year for German nationalism'. In the resulting uproar, according to the Prussian General von Radowitz, 'legitimists, liberals, radicals, Catholics, Protestants, dogmatists, rationalists, pantheists, Austrians, Prussians, Saxons, Franks, Swabians, all rose as one man'[6] in protest to defend the independence of the ethnic Germans in the duchies. In March 1848 Christian's successor, Frederick VII, in an act that was to lead to war proclaimed the annexation of Schleswig by Denmark.

A year later the Swiss civil war erupted in November 1847. Since 1830 Switzerland had been split between the reactionary, ultra-Catholic *Sonderbund* (Special Alliance) and a predominantly Protestant liberal alliance. By the summer of 1847 the liberals were in the majority in the Swiss Diet and demanded a modern liberal constitution and freedom of the press. The *Sonderbund's* intransigence led to a brief civil war, which the liberals won. The defeat of the *Sonderbund* without any intervention from Austria and the subsequent setting up of a liberal federation in 1848 was seen as evidence by liberals throughout Europe that the repressive system of 1815 could be overturned.

The agrarian and social-economic crises

From 1845 to the autumn of 1847, the German states, like the rest of Europe, suffered a series of bad harvests and were faced with what Hans-Ulrich Wehler called the last of the agrarian crises of 'the old type', as they were still predominantly pre-industrial societies, which were dependent on the food they grew. Food shortages caused prices to rise and by May 1847, when they reached their peak, the cost of food had risen between 90 and 130 per cent. The price of a bushel of rye, for instance, rose from 51 silver pennies in 1845 to 87 in 1847, while over the same period a bushel of wheat rose from 65 to 110.[7] The food shortages were exacerbated by speculators and the continuing export of wheat and use of scarce supplies of grain and potatoes for brandy and schnapps. This intensified the sufferings of the urban and rural poor, especially the hand-workers desperately attempting to survive on low wages in overcrowded and fiercely competitive trades, and in turn depressed consumer demand and led to the contraction of industry. Domestic depression coincided with a global financial crisis, which spread to Germany from Britain and America. By the end of 1847 the whole of the German banking and credit structure was in crisis. In most cities about 30 per cent of the population was only able to survive thanks to charity. Malnutrition also made the population vulnerable to typhus. In Silesia 50,000 people died, while in East Prussia the total reached 40,000. From 1844 onwards an increasing number of popular protests, which took the form of riots or attacks on food convoys, took place. With the good harvest of late summer 1847 the agrarian crisis began to abate, but by exposing the incompetence of the local authorities it reinforced the desire for change and reform.

Bushel: a measure of capacity for corn, etc., equivalent to 36.4 litres

See Document 12

The outbreak of the revolution

The European context

The depth of the economic crisis, the apparent inability of the authorities and the growing power and organization of the opposition to the *ancien régime* created the context for the 1848 revolutions. The revolts first started in Sicily and then spread to Naples where King Ferdinand was forced to establish a constitutional monarchy. However, the spark that ignited the revolts in central Europe and indeed most of continental Europe was the Paris revolution of 24 February, which brought about the downfall of King Louis Philippe and the subsequent proclamation of the French Republic. The news of it quickly crossed the Rhine and then spread through German Europe. Holland, Belgium and the Scandinavian powers were also affected. The only areas to escape revolution were Britain, the Iberian states and Russia.[8]

The German states

Wolfram Siemann has described the German revolution as presenting 'an image of a chain of local rebellions, all rapidly following and coinciding with one another'.[9] Its rapid spread was facilitated by the infectious optimism that a new era was dawning, the power of rumour, the belated lifting of press controls by the Confederation Diet on 3 March, and above all by the new railways.

The unrest began in Mannheim, fanned out to the north and east and then paralysed Vienna and Berlin. On 27 February the storm broke with the Mannheim rally, which anticipated many similar gatherings throughout Germany. A petition, drawn up by the republican Gustav von Struve (1805–1870), was handed to the government in Karlsruhe. Its call for a people's army with elected officers, complete freedom of the press, trial by jury and the immediate summoning of a German parliament rapidly became known throughout Germany as the 'March Demands'. Similar demands were made in Hesse-Darmstadt, Nassau, Hanover, Württemberg, Bavaria, Saxony, Oldenburg and Brunswick, as well as in the Prussian provinces of the Rhineland and Silesia. In Munich the armoury was stormed, while in Cologne on 3 March a rally of 5000 inhabitants led by Andreas Gottschalk (1815–1849), a doctor and leading local radical, demanded the arming of the population and the guarantee of work and welfare, but it was quickly broken up by Prussian troops. Simultaneously a series of peasant revolts broke out in the impoverished and overpopulated areas of the Black Forest and the Bavarian Odenwald. The peasants were primarily interested in terminating the last of their feudal obligations, and the remaining rights of the mediatized princes and former imperial knights (see pp. 18–19), who still controlled about a third of the state's territory. Once these were granted, they had no more interest in revolution and became an essentially conservative anti-revolutionary force over the next 18 months.

See Document 14

Initially the princes of the smaller German states hoped that Prussia and Austria would intervene to crush the revolts, but revolutions in both Vienna and Berlin made this impossible. Riots forced Metternich to resign on 13 March and 2 days later compelled the Emperor to promise a constitution. In Berlin, mobs had been gathering and making demands similar to those advocated by Struve and Gottschalk. On 17 March Frederick William agreed to recall the United provincial assemblies, which had met in Berlin in 1847, and grant a constitution. The following day, however, when troops fired into a peaceful crowd in front of the royal palace, a revolt broke out, which persuaded the king to order the army to withdraw from Berlin and appoint a transitional ministry composed of aristocratic and *grossbürgerlich* (upper middle-class) liberals led by the banker, Ludolf Camphausen.

See Document 15

March ministries: the governments set up as a result of the revolutions in March

With the appointment of the **March ministries** in Prussia, Austria and the other German states, the moderate liberals believed that the revolution was over, and that the time had come to consolidate their gains by drafting new constitutions at both state and national level, which would inhibit a further escalation of revolutionary violence but it was not possible simply to turn off popular unrest like a tap. There was still hunger and poverty in both the large towns and the countryside and a volatile public mood, which led to continued agitation and the formation of pressure groups and political leagues. Inevitably a split began to develop between the moderate liberals and the democrats. In Saxony the two groups organized rival leagues, which rapidly came to symbolize the deep social, institutional and ideological cleavages throughout the German Confederation. In Württemberg the left was contemptuous of the new government's call for peace and order so that the future constitution could be decided with 'reason and moderation'. One radical journalist observed that 'we no more want to be ruled by the liberal **plutocrats** than we did by the old reactionary system'.[10]

Plutocrats: members of the wealthy elite

In Baden increasing tension developed between the moderates and radical democrats. When the radical journalist, Josef Fickler (1808–1865), was arrested on 8 April, an uprising broke out among the peasants, journeymen, day-labourers and students in southern Baden, which became a test of strength between the radicals and the moderate liberals. The government appealed for military help from the Confederation, which sent a force of some 30,000 men. Friedrich Hecker (1811–1881) and Gustav Struve, the leaders of the revolt, hoped to arm the population and persuade the federal troops to mutiny, but their decisive defeat at the Battle of Kandern on 20 April showed that this was an illusion, and indicated the limits to the power of the revolutionaries. In these revolutions women played a noticeable part. Some were killed on the barricades and many participated in the demonstrations and as observers in the democratic clubs. They also collected money for the purchase of weapons and ammunition

The reaction of the German Confederation: the committee of 17

As early as 10 March the German Confederation set up the Committee of 17, which was composed of prominent moderate liberals such as Max von Gagern (1810–1889), and Friedrich Dahlmann, one of the 'Göttingen

Seven' (see pp. 39–40) to revise its constitution 'in keeping with the times'. It recommended the expansion of the Confederation to include Posen and Schleswig, and the creation of a federal German constitution, which would have sufficient power to ensure that the new nation state would operate as a military, economic and political unit, despite the continuing 'independence of the individual German states'.[11] It was to have a hereditary emperor and a bicameral *Reichstag* in which representatives of the states and the ruling princes would sit. This initiative failed firstly because it did not enjoy the support of the rulers of Hanover, Bavaria, Austria and Prussia, and secondly because it was impossible to build a German nation state 'without reference to the revolutionary movement'.[12]

The pre-parliament

Of vital importance for the course of the revolution was the meeting of 51 leading liberals and democrats from south-west Germany, which was held on 5 March at Heidelberg. Despite profound differences, they agreed to set up a committee of seven to summon 'a more complete assembly of trusted men from all German peoples', which met at Frankfurt between 31 March and 3 April.

This 'pre-parliament' regarded itself as the leading voice of the nation, even though it had not been officially sanctioned by either the states or the Confederation. The radical wing, led by Struve, attempted to transform the pre-parliament immediately into a revolutionary convention, which would claim legislative power and create a republic on American lines, but to the moderate majority these ideas were unacceptable. There was, however, agreement that there should be elections to a future constituent assembly, which would agree on the new German constitution. Theoretically the elections were to be held on the basis of universal manhood suffrage, but there were no instructions as to whether these elections were to be direct or indirect, and 'inexplicably'[13] – probably intentionally – the demand had found its way into print that only 'mature, independent' citizens could vote.

The Frankfurt National Assembly

Each state interpreted the Frankfurt electoral guidelines as it wished. The majority of the German states set up a system in which the final choice of candidate was made by a college of electors. In some states there was a secret ballot, but in others it was public. Similarly, the term 'mature, independent' citizen was used by others to exclude men whose income was too low to be taxable. By law the number of elected members was to be 649, but as the Czech inhabitants of Bohemia and Moravia boycotted the elections only some 585 delegates were elected. Over the course of the 13 months of its existence, 18 May 1848–18 June 1849, as a result of frequent changes in personnel due to illness, retirement, and so on, a total of some 812 deputies, the overwhelming majority of whom were from the professional classes, sat for varying periods in the assembly. The single biggest group (436) were employed by the state governments as administrators, judicial officials or teachers and university lecturers. There were only 56 members representing the commercial middle classes, while only three small-scale farmers and four craftsmen were elected.

Parties and associations were to develop over the year, but in May such groupings were only tentative and incoherent. The political nation still consisted of 'loose and informal groups of local notables, social and cultural organizations with latent political objectives, and a small, imperfectly defined national élite whose prominence rested on their reputation as publicists or state parliamentarians'.[14] Although an overwhelming majority of the delegates could generally be called liberals and were determined to create a united constitutional German state, there were, even at this early stage of the revolution, a number of problems that would ultimately undermine the authority of the Frankfurt Assembly:

- There was no consistent majority in Frankfurt that could achieve unanimity on key issues.
- The individual states, especially Prussia and Austria, were competing centres of power, which could challenge any decision taken in Frankfurt.
- The Assembly had no power to raise taxation.
- It was not clear where the boundaries of the new Germany should lie.
- Any unification of Germany would require international consent.

I The introduction of Archduke John of Austria as Imperial Administrator in the Frankfurt Assembly in the Paulskirche, Frankfurt, 12 July 1848

Leipzige Illustrierte

Parliamentary organization

The Assembly convened in the Paulskirche, which was cramped and lacked adequate facilities. Initially the delegates were divided up into 15 sections, each responsible for a particular administrative task, such as electing a committee. Within the first few weeks, the majority of deputies joined factions, which took the names of the restaurants or cafés where, in the absence of committee rooms in the **Paulskirche**, they met to discuss pressing issues. The groups were often fluid and at least a hundred delegates refused to identify with any of them, but gradually parties did emerge, as it became obvious that like-thinking men needed to combine in support of their views. In the final analysis this enabled the assembly to operate, despite the verbose tendency of so many of their members. The left-wing groups were the most effective in relating to their voters. Through a series of congresses and popular mass organizations (see pp. 71–72) they began to construct solid bases of support in German society. Some deputies wrote reports on their activities for their constituents or articles for local newspapers, while voters bombarded their representatives with petitions, declarations, and so on. Clearly, huge strides were made towards creating a modern parliament, but poor communications, the continued existence of the independent states and the ambiguity of the Frankfurt Assembly's powers ensured that institutionally it remained weak and uncertain.

> **Paulskirche:** St Paul's Protestant Church in Frankfurt, built in 1833. Second to the Cathedral the largest building in the city.

'The Provisional Central Power' May–October 1848

Before creating a national executive, the Frankfurt Assembly had to establish its claim to superiority over the individual state assemblies. Inevitably this met with some hostility both from state governments which wished to safeguard their own particularist powers and from the conservative factions, particularly the *Café Milani* and *Landsberg* groups. On 19 May Franz Raveaux (1810–1851), a left-wing democrat, failed to win a majority for a motion asserting Frankfurt's superiority over the

---

Party groupings in the Frankfurt National Assembly

Parties		Approximate percentage of members
Café Milani	(right wing/conservative)	6
Casino, Landsberg and Augsburger Hof	(centre-right/Constitutional liberals)	34
Württemberger Hof and Westendhall	(centre-left/parliamentary liberals)	13
Deutscher Hof and Donnersberg	(left/ democratic)	15
Non-aligned		32

Source: W. Siemann, *Die Frankfurter Nationalversammlung 1848/9 zwischen democratischem Liberalismus und konservativer Reform*, Frankfurt, Lang, 1976, p. 27.

Prussian assembly, but he did secure a compromise resolution which stated that 'all regulations of individual parliaments which are not in agreement with its yet to be determined constitution will be considered valid only with reference to the latter regardless of current validity'.[15] This at least opened up the way for the creation of some sort of central government, but there was disagreement between the right and left about the form that this was to take. The former wanted the participation of the Austrian and Prussian Crowns, while the latter argued for a republican executive committee. The Assembly's chairman Heinrich von Gagern (1799–1880), a former Liberal deputy in the Hesse-Darmstadt assembly, carried the day with a compromise proposing the Austrian Archduke John (1782–1859) as *Reichsverweser* or Imperial Regent, who would be elected by the assembly, but who would then appoint an independent executive. On 28 June 'the Provisional Central Power' was accordingly set up in the form of a small cabinet consisting of a minister-president and ministers of foreign affairs, the interior, finance, justice, trade and war. The Confederation diet had little option but to accept this and shortly after declared that its 'present activity' was 'concluded', giving the somewhat ambiguous impression that it was suspended rather than dissolved, so leaving open the option that the states could at some stage reactivate it.[16]

How much power did this central authority really have? It had no means of raising taxation and was dependent on financial handouts from the individual states. It also lacked a civil service and above all an army. In an attempt to remedy this latter deficiency, the war minister, a former Prussian general, tried to insist that the armies of the individual states should pay homage to the regent and wear the colours of the new German Empire. The smaller states were ready to accept this but it was rejected by Prussia, Austria, Bavaria and Hanover.

The Constitutional Committee

Devising a constitution for a united Germany proved a lengthy business. The Frankfurt Assembly elected on 24 May the Constitutional Committee which took the fateful decision to start with the question of fundamental rights rather than with the complex task of drafting a constitution. The Frankfurt deputies have traditionally been accused of letting time slip away while discussing the abstruse principles of fundamental rights. It was, for instance, not until October 1848 that the committee began to grapple with the key questions of whether Austria should be an integral part of the new German state and who should be the head of that state. On the other hand, the decision to begin with the question of fundamental rights can be defended. They were, after all, to quote Thomas Nipperdey, 'an elementary, emotional and popular reality; they were like the articles of the civilian faith and represented the very meaning of the constitutional state'.[17] In a sense they were the symbol of the revolution and would override the rights of the individual states. To start here was also a political decision because the question of fundamental rights represented an area of potential agreement between the factions in the assembly. Those who wished to exclude Austria from a united Germany felt that they needed time before they could win majority backing for their ideas. Similarly there was also hope that a declaration of fundamental rights would go some way to appease the radicals, who were pushing for far-reaching social changes.

The dominant group on the constitutional committees responsible for drafting these rights was the centre-right Cassino constitutional Liberals, but it also included two key left-wingers, Robert Blum (1807–1848) and Franz Wigard (1807–1885), from the *Deutscher Hof*. The final version contained 12 articles. Freedom of speech, the freedom to publish and the right to assemble and form organizations were guaranteed, as was religious freedom subject only to the state's general laws. Parliament would deliberate in public. In an attempt to create civil equality aristocratic privilege was abolished, equality in appointment to public office announced and full equality was granted to all religious groups including the Jews. Free basic education was guaranteed under state provision. State protection was to be extended to every 'German citizen', but, as will be seen below, in a state with no clearly defined frontiers this was a somewhat ambiguous clause.

The German question

One of the most controversial issues debated at Frankfurt concerned what constituted the 'German nation'. Opinion was roughly divided between those who believed in self-determination and saw nationalism as an ideology of liberation for Germans and non-Germans alike, and those who primarily saw it in terms of the assertion of German self-interest and power. The general assumption of most of the deputies was that the territory of the German Confederation would serve as a basis for the new Germany, but this of course, as Wolfram Siemann has pointed out, 'was based on a pre-national construct which as a loose federation of princes and city republics, had incorporated constitutional hybrid relationships which ran counter to the nationality principle'.[18] The northern, eastern and southern borders of the Confederation followed the former frontiers of the Holy Roman Empire and did not mark a clear-cut ethnic divide. Germans were mixed up with Danes, Poles, Czechs, Slovaks, Slovenes, Croats, Italians and Dutch. So inevitably the process of creating a new German state would cause acute international and ethnic tension, as can be seen by the reaction of the Frankfurt Assembly to the complex questions of nationality and territory.

See Map 3

Posen

In the pre-parliament a majority had voted for the re-creation of the Polish state, but in practice when confronted in May 1848 with a nationalist uprising in the Prussian province of Posen where the population was predominantly Polish (see p. 45), parliament supported the military measures taken against the rebels by the Prussian government. The *Realpolitik* of many liberals was given expression by Wilhelm Jordan (1819–1904), a radical deputy from Prussia, who advocated a 'healthy national egoism' in the Polish question. He dismissed the views of the pro-Polish party as mere 'cosmopolitan liberalism' and argued that Germany's claims in Poland rested on its strength and the rights of conquest.

See Document 16

South Tyrol

Lombardy: In April 1848, Piedmontese and other Italian forces had invaded Lombardy to assist the rebels against Austria. They were defeated in July 1848

Logically the assembly should have supported a motion in June put forward by five of the deputies requesting that the districts of Trent and Rovereto, which were settled mainly by Italians, should be separated from the German Confederation. The democrats supported this idea, but shortly before the debate took place the Austrians reconquered **Lombardy**. The majority now rejected the motion and totally ignored the principle of national determination, which they so vehemently supported in Schleswig-Holstein, and agreed with the crude argument of an Austrian deputy: 'we own South Tyrol and we will keep it'.[19]

Bohemia and Moravia

Prague uprising: After 6 days of street fighting, 12–18 June, Czech students and workers were defeated in Prague, and the Czech National Committee was dissolved.

Here, too, the overwhelming majority in the Paulskirche assumed that both these provinces would belong to a future German state, despite the fact that 48 out of the 68 Bohemian deputies refused even to send their deputies to Frankfurt. While the majority were in favour of protecting the large Slav minorities in these provinces, there was a point-blank refusal to countenance the setting up of an independent Czech nation, and consequently Prince Windischgrätz's (1787–1862) defeat of the **Prague uprising** in June 1848 was welcomed by the majority in Frankfurt, even though there were fears about the consequences of that victory for the liberal cause within Germany.

Limburg and Schleswig-Holstein

In both Limburg and Schleswig-Holstein, nation-making ran up against international reality. Limburg was a Dutch province and, in response to nationalist claims from Frankfurt, Britain, France and Russia, made clear their support for the status quo. In March 1848 the German movement in Schleswig-Holstein countered the Danish annexation of Schleswig (see p. 62), by declaring an emergency and setting up a provisional state government. The Schleswig-Holstein issue had an explosive force that could unite both constitutional liberals and democrats and potentially radicalize the revolution. On 12 April the Frankfurt Assembly declared war on Denmark and sent in a force under the supreme command of the Prussian General Count von Wrangel (1784–1877) which advanced as far as Jutland, but the Danish fleet was able to inflict considerable economic damage by blockading the Prussian coast. The Provisional Central Power at Frankfurt took over the direction of the war and in the Assembly increasing demands were made for the construction of a German fleet as it was claimed that Germany was now a great power.

The conflict became a test case for the international standing of the new central government at Frankfurt. It could have led to a European war, in which conceivably German unity might have been forged, when Russia and Britain, who were the guarantors of Schleswig-Holstein under international law, vetoed the absorption of Schleswig into a united Germany. On 26 August the weakness of the central power in Frankfurt was painfully revealed when the Prussian government, partly as a result of Anglo-Russian pressure and partly as a consequence of the Danish blockade, unilaterally signed the Truce of Malmö with Denmark. Lacking an army, Frankfurt could not intervene and had little option but to accept the truce. This unleashed a storm of criticism, and the government under Karl von Leiningen (1814–1856) was forced to resign when the assembly voted by 238 to 221 to reject it. A new cabinet led by Friedrich Dahlmann, which was supported by the opponents of **the Malmö Truce**, was appointed, only to fall apart when it became clear that even a shared hatred of the truce could not in practice bridge the fundamental political differences between the democrats and moderate liberals. Another cabinet under the Austrian Anton von Schmerling (1805–1893) was formed, and in the end the Assembly had no option but to vote in favour of the truce on 16 September. This triggered renewed popular unrest right across Germany, including riots in Frankfurt itself, the so-called September Revolution, which shattered the fragile national unity created by the Schleswig-Holstein crisis.

Malmö provided for the withdrawal of both Prussian and Danish troops and the temporary administration of Schleswig-Holstein by a Prusso-Danish commission.

Popular politics, spring–autumn 1848

The revolution of March 1848 unleashed political forces, which led not only to the founding of parties in Frankfurt, but to the emergence at local level of a number of political associations representing a wide range of political views. A whole hierarchy of regional and district committees and congresses evolved with the ultimate aim of creating nationally-based parties and pressure groups. For instance, a congress of craftsmen's and tradesmen's representatives from all over Germany met in Frankfurt in July and set up an organization to lobby the assembly for protective measures against the economic consequences of modern capitalism. A month later the Workers' Congress in Berlin decided to set up the General German Workers' Brotherhood, which by the spring of 1849 had approximately 15,000 members. This attempted unsuccessfully to focus the attention of the assembly on the key questions of health insurance and the right to work. To the left of these groups was the Communist League, which attempted ineffectually to coordinate the emerging workers' societies into a national movement. There were, too, a large number of democratic and constitutional associations. In June the Democratic Association and Workers' Society of Marburg organized a congress in Frankfurt, which was attended by representatives from 89 other associations, to draft a programme for a national democratic party. It then went on to set up in Berlin the first central party office in Germany. The Constitutional Liberals attempted to follow suit by forming the National Association in Kassel in September. The Catholic associations followed the same pattern. Pius Associations, which took their name from Pope Pius IX, were founded throughout Catholic Germany and, at a congress in Mainz in early October, their representatives came together to create a national organization. Even the Prussian Conservatives were forced to organize on an all-Prussian basis to defend the Crown and to strengthen their campaign to return to the *status quo ante* of 1847. In July 1848 Ernst Ludwig von Gerlach (1790–1861), a member of the conservative **Camarilla** at the Prussian court, created the Association for King and Fatherland, which was the first conservative central party organization in Germany.

In response to the defeat of the revolutions in Vienna and Berlin and the subsequent execution of Robert Blum by an Austrian firing squad in November 1848 the deputies of the three left wing factions, *Donnesberg, Deutscher Hof* and *Westendall* formed the Central March Organization to defend what had been achieved by the revolution. Throughout Germany it issued press releases, organized rallies and demonstrations. By March 1849 it had about 950 local associations and 500,000 members.

Women were often permitted to attend meetings of political organizations, even those of conservative and Catholic groups, but were usually not allowed actively to participate. Women's groups, however, were founded where members made speeches, read newspapers to each other and discussed political events. Louise Otto (1819–1895) and Louise Dittmar (1807–1895) took on a more active role by lecturing and founding newspapers, which concentrated on feminist issues, that were to be taken up later in the century, such as the right to vote, reform of the marriage law and access to higher education.

Camarilla: a group of reactionary politicians at the Prussian court

Political developments in Austria and Prussia

During 1848 the actual pace of political developments in each state varied, but the real nerve centres of the revolution were in Berlin and Vienna, and it was here that the fate of the revolutions in central Europe would ultimately be determined.

See Document 17

Austria

In the spring of 1848 the Habsburg Empire seemed to be on the brink of disintegration. The government's attempts to appease both the non-German nationalities and the liberals met with failure. On 11 May, rioting by armed students and workers forced the government to extend the suffrage, and the emperor fled to Innsbruck for safety. At this stage, nationalism and liberalism seemed to be in the ascendant throughout the Empire. Yet over the next 2 months the *ancien régime* began to recover. First the Czech nationalists were defeated in Prague by General Windischgrätz in June (see above), and then in July the Habsburg possessions in Italy were saved by General Radetzky's (1786–1858) victory at Custoza. In October, however, a second revolution broke out in Vienna, when troops stationed there mutinied and refused to move against the Hungarians. Their defeat by General Windischgrätz was the decisive turning point of the revolutions in central Europe and opened up the way for a new government in Austria, headed by the former diplomat Prinz Felix zu Schwarzenberg (1800–1852), to restore the independence and power of the Habsburg Empire as an alternative to a united *Grossdeutschland*. Parliament was removed to Kremsier in Moravia and in March a new Austrian constitution was announced.

Prussia

In the course of the summer of 1848, as the newly elected Prussian *Landtag* debated the future of Prussia's constitution, the political forces of the right started to recover. At court Leopold von Gerlach and the Camarilla began to turn the king against the revolution, while leading conservative landowners, including Otto von Bismarck, formed the League for the Protection of Landed Property. By the time the new constitution was drafted, the king, backed by the army and the conservatives, was in a position to stage a coup. On 2 November he dismissed the von Pfuel ministry, which was attempting to forge a compromise between the court and parliament, and appointed Count Brandenburg (1792–1850), a reliable, conservative soldier, as minister-president. A week later, General von Wrangel occupied Berlin with 13,000 troops and ordered parliament to dissolve itself. A new constitution was decreed and elections took place in late January/early February 1849. The new constitution was 'a surprisingly liberal document'[20] until revised in May (see p. 78). The upper house was chosen by restricted franchise, but the lower house was elected by virtually all adult males, and the cabinet was ultimately responsible to parliament. The king, however, retained his direct authority over the army.

Frankfurt and the German constitution

It was against the background of these events that the Frankfurt Assembly began to consider the intricate question of a German constitution in October. It was clear that a united Germany would have to be a federal state. Its federal nature was a historic reality, but how in practice was the balance between Prussia, Austria and the rest of the states to be secured? Could the small states be amalgamated as was to occur later in 1947 (see p. 295)? Alternatively could Prussia be weakened by turning it into a loosely knit structure of provinces? And then there was the major question of the role of Austria and its non-German territories.

Initially a clear majority of delegates in Frankfurt assumed that German Austria together with Bohemia would belong to the new German federal state, while the non-German parts of the Habsburg Empire (see Map 3) would be connected to the Reich by personal union. If the Austrian Empire had disintegrated, a **grossdeutsch** solution might have been possible, but once it was clear that it would survive, it was increasingly appreciated that Austria could not logically remain a major power if one half of it was part of another major power – *Grossdeutschland*. In November Schwarzenberg in the Kremsier declaration signalled that he wished to see the whole Austrian Empire represented in a restored German Confederation rather than in a *grossdeutsch* state. This led to the resignation in December of Schmerling, who was a vigorous proponent of the *grossdeutsch* solution, and his replacement by Heinrich von Gagern as prime minister.

By early January the Constitutional Committee had drafted plans for a federal empire. Responsibility for the army, foreign relations, customs, coinage and postal services would all belong to the imperial government. There was, however, still no consensus on how universal the franchise should be, the powers of the Crown, or indeed the place of Austria in the new state. On 13 January von Gagern managed to gain support in the assembly for a **kleindeutsch** Germany ruled by the royal house of Prussia but 'joined in a special relationship to a unified Habsburg Reich'. Ten days later this compromise solution fell apart when a coalition of *grossdeutsch* supporters and left-wingers defeated a motion to create a hereditary monarchy. In March 1849 Schwarzenberg announced a new constitution for the Austrian Empire, which effectively ruled out any participation in a *Grossdeutschland*. This marked the point when the majority of the deputies in the national assembly and indeed 'most commentators and much of public opinion'[21] came to accept that the exclusion of Austria from a united Germany was inevitable. The moderate liberal *kleindeutsch* supporters now had little option but to agree to a wider franchise bill and a stricter control on the Crown's powers of veto to secure enough democratic support on 28 March to win a majority of 42 in favour of offering the position of hereditary emperor of the new German Empire to Frederick William of Prussia. The constitution consisted of a directly elected chamber or '*Volkshaus*' and an upper house or *Staatenhaus* where representatives of the states would sit. These proposals gained the backing of 28 states but were rejected by Austria, Prussia, Hanover, Saxony, Bavaria and Württemberg. Frederick William viewed the offer of the Crown as a 'dog collar, with which they wish to lash me to the revolution of 1848'.[22]

The **grossdeutsch** (greater German) solution would have included the German-speaking parts of the Habsburg monarchy. The **kleindeutsch** (small German) solution involved the exclusion of Austria and the creation of a predominantly Protestant, Prussian-dominated Germany – as was to happen in 1871 (see Ch. 4).

See Document 18

Kremsier declaration, November 1848

Although there would be no directly elected parliament, Schwarzenberg proposed an assembly attended by delegates from the individual state parliaments. The number of delegates each state could send would be calculated on the basis of its population, which would favour Austria with its total population of 38 million, as opposed to 32 million in the rest of the German states. While it could be argued that this proposal would ensure German hegemony in central south-east Europe, it was in the end rejected because the majority at Frankfurt wanted a German national state.

The defeat of the revolution

By a small majority (190:180) the National Assembly decided to press on and set the date for elections to the new national parliament for 15 July. If Prussia refused to participate, the ruler of the next largest state represented in the new German upper chamber, the *Staatenhaus*, would be invited to become the imperial governor. This attempt by the assembly to speak over the heads of the state governments, directly to the people, was bitterly opposed by the *Reichsverweser*, Archduke John (see p. 68), on the grounds that it was both unconstitutional and would lead to civil war. In protest at his intervention, Heinrich von Gagern resigned and the Archduke then appointed a right-wing cabinet, which was almost immediately rejected by a damaging vote of no confidence. Increasingly the national assembly pursued a more radical line, and called on the people to defend the new constitution. Prussia, Austria, Hanover and Baden retaliated by recalling their deputies. When the Prussian *Landtag* in Berlin recommended the acceptance of the new constitution, it was immediately dissolved. By 27 May only 103 left-of-centre delegates remained at Frankfurt. Three days later they moved to Stuttgart, where they announced the dismissal of Archduke John, and the appointment of a new government, but on 16 June the Stuttgart assembly was dissolved at bayonet point by Württemberg troops.

The governments of the states which had rejected the constitution were now faced with uprisings coordinated by the Central March Association. Uprisings took place in Silesia and the Rhineland, but these were easily crushed. In Saxony, Württemberg, the Bavarian Palatinate and Baden revolutionary forces were strong enough to force the governments on to the defensive. Compared, however, to March 1848, the revolutionaries were in a weak position. There was no supporting action from the peasantry, many of the middle classes were fearful of the new radicalism and the Prussian army was able to intervene first in Saxony and then in the Palatinate and Baden to defeat the revolutionaries. The fighting came to an end when the fortress of Rastatt in Baden surrendered to the Prussians.

Even though the 1848 revolts and the Frankfurt Assembly proved to be an invaluable school of politics for the German people, they had nevertheless failed to create a unified, liberal, federal Germany. The reasons for this are complex and overlapping:

- The initial easy successes of the revolts bred an over-confidence among the revolutionaries.
- The revolutionaries themselves were divided.
- The polycentric nature of Germany made it more difficult for the Frankfurt regime to establish its ascendancy.
- The attempt to forge a *Grossdeutschland* wasted valuable time, as it was impractical to assume that a great power like Austria would in fact dismember itself to enter a purely German union.
- The rulers of the German states were much stronger than they initially looked and enjoyed the support of their armed forces and bureaucracy.

On the other hand it is important to put the 1848 revolts in Germany into their European context. In central Italy and the Kingdom of Naples the revolts of 1848–1849 were likewise defeated, and in France the coup d'état of December 1851 led to the replacement of the liberal republic by a plebiscitary dictatorship under Louis Napoleon. So the failure of the revolution in Germany was part of a European-wide phenomenon rather than something uniquely German.

The struggle to restore the Confederation

Paradoxically, as Prussia took the lead in defeating attempts to create a liberal *Kleindeutschland*, Prussian diplomats were, behind the scenes, attempting to persuade the rulers of the German states to adopt a Prussian version of the plan. The author of this initiative was the courtier and close friend of Frederick William, Joseph von Radowitz, Prussian military representative to the Confederation, 1836–1848 (see p. 41). Although a conservative and Catholic deputy in the Frankfurt Assembly, he had supported Gagern's *kleindeutsch* solution. When the king rejected it, he persuaded him to accept what became known as the Radowitz Plan: the creation from above of a conservative, *kleindeutsch*, national Germany – the so-called Prussian Union. In May 1849, while Austria was still involved in military operations in Hungary and Italy, Prussia, Saxony, Hanover, Württemberg and Bavaria met to consider Radowitz's Plan. The two southern states pulled out, but Hanover and Saxony both supported the Prussian initiative. On 28 May the constitution for the proposed new German union was issued. It was modelled on the Frankfurt constitution of 28 March but there were significant changes: universal manhood suffrage was replaced by an indirect, class-based suffrage and the 'chief executive', the King of Prussia, had an absolute rather than **suspensive veto** over legislation. In June, Prussia, Hanover and Saxony proposed elections throughout Germany for a national parliament. Twenty-six German states participated in the elections for the parliament, which convened in Erfurt in March 1850, while ten opted to remain outside the

Suspensive veto: a veto that can suspend legislation until it is reconsidered by parliament. If re-passed by a majority, it becomes law.

union. The parliament was boycotted by the democratic left on the grounds that it was a mere camouflage for Prussian absolutism, but many of the Constitutional Liberals supported it in the hope that it would ultimately lead to German unity.

In Vienna Schwarzenberg viewed the union as a direct challenge to Austrian interests in Germany. Once the **Hungarian revolt** had been defeated in August 1849, he was able to organize an increasingly effective counter-offensive against it by appealing to the states' fear of Prussian domination. Saxony and Hanover withdrew from the union and joined Bavaria, Württemberg and Austria to announce their support for a reconstituted Confederation in February 1850. Germany was now effectively divided into two increasingly hostile blocs.

> **Hungary** had declared itself independent of Austria in April 1849, but, with help from Russia, Austria had forced it to capitulate at Világos on 13 August 1849.

The Hesse-Kassel incident and the Proclamation of Olmütz

In the autumn the constitutional crisis in Hesse-Kassel threatened to plunge Germany into civil war. The ruler, Duke Frederick William, had replaced a liberal ministry with an ultra-reactionary government. He dissolved the assembly when it opposed the new government's budget and started to levy taxes illegally. He attempted to quell the resulting uproar by appealing to Schwarzenberg for help. Austria and its allies, diplomatically supported by Russia, were only too ready to intervene, as Hesse-Kassel was a strategically important state dominating Prussia's civilian and military roads to the west. In early November 1850, Prussian and Austrian armies began to mobilize and converge on Hesse-Kassel. The Austrians were strengthened with units from Bavaria and Württemberg. Shots were actually exchanged between Prussian and Bavarian troops on 8 November. The Prussians, however, facing the prospect of a war against Austria, the south German alliance and Russia, backed down, and agreed to the joint Austro-Prussian Proclamation of Olmütz on 29 November. By this, Prussia consented to demobilize its army, dissolve the Erfurt Union and discuss plans for reforming the Confederation at a conference to be held at Dresden in December.

> See Map 3

> See Document 19

Prussia had certainly suffered a serious diplomatic and political defeat at Olmütz, but not everything went Austria's way at Dresden. Prussia was able to block Schwarzenberg's proposals for integrating Austria's non-German territories into the Confederation, and, instead, the old Confederation of 1815, which had been moribund since the spring of 1848, was revived. Commenting on this resurrection Schwarzenberg observed, 'a threadbare and worn coat is still better than no coat at all'![23]

> **Louis Napoleon,** the nephew of Napoleon I, like Bismarck later (see p. 96), introduced universal manhood suffrage. Until the late 1860s the French Chamber had little power, and Napoleon consolidated his regime by appealing to the bourgeoisie, exploiting nationalism and appeasing the working classes with welfare reforms (see Document 20).

Reaction and restoration? German domestic politics, 1850–1858

The 1850s were certainly a time of reaction, but paradoxically governments, like the Bonapartist regime, which was established in France by **Louis Napoleon** in December 1851, often used strikingly modern policies to bolster their regimes. The great majority of the German states retained their constitutions, albeit heavily revised, which ultimately kept open the option for change. Many governments, particularly the Prussian government, displayed a new element of social realism, by which through judicious reforms and appeasement of each social class they attempted to gain a broadly based consent or at least toleration of their quasi-authoritarian regimes.

Although the exact course of reaction differed in each state, the German Confederation attempted to direct and guide it by setting up a special coordinating committee. The states were ordered to reverse the constitutional changes that had occurred in 1848 and to ensure that parliamentary procedure, the military oath of loyalty, the behaviour of the press and the voting system did not conflict with the monarchical principle. The Confederation sent out a constant stream of directives to the state governments and even dispatched commissioners to intervene directly in the domestic politics of Bremen and Frankfurt. Although in 1854 the Confederation promulgated a Press and Association Law binding for each member state, its preferred tactics were to manoeuvre the individual state governments into revoking the constitutional settlements of 1848–1849, so that the subsequent opprobrium would fall on them. In this it was largely successful. The individual state governments rolled back the constitutional achievements of 1848 through the imposition of new voting systems based on the Prussian model, and at election times did not hesitate to intervene directly to influence the electorate. Workers' associations were suppressed, the civil service purged and the emphasis on teaching in schools was shifted to obedience and religion, while teacher training was carefully monitored.

In April 1849 Frederick William dissolved the Prussian assembly, when it voted to accept the new *kleindeutsch* constitution, which had just been drawn up in Frankfurt (see above), and a month later imposed the three-class voting system. After elections, which were boycotted by the left, he promulgated a new constitution, which survived until 1918. The Crown was strengthened through the right of veto and the power to issue emergency decrees as well as to declare martial law. Its ties with the army were strengthened by the creation of a royal military cabinet, which was responsible directly to the king. In 1854 the upper house was reorganized so that effectively the majority of its members were hereditary members of the nobility. As in the other German states, the press was muzzled, the civil service purged of liberals and educational policies exercised along conservative lines. Yet in many areas government policy pursued a Bonapartist rather than reactionary line. There were attempts to reconcile the different classes to the loss of political liberty. The complete liberation of the peasants was confirmed, efforts were made to protect the craftsmen from hostile economic trends by restoring the authority of the guilds, and factory inspectors were appointed to enforce the implementation of health and security legislation.

The three-class voting system remained in place until 1918. The voters were not divided by estate or class, but by the amount of taxes they paid. In 1849, 4.7 per cent belonged to the first category, 12.6 to the second and 82.7 to the third. Each class accounted for a third of the electors, who in turn chose the actual delegates. The voting system did not necessarily guarantee a conservative majority. In the 1860s liberal majorities were regularly returned.

The cushion of economic growth

The 1850s and 1860s were a period of accelerating economic growth throughout the confederation, which gradually created employment and a rising standard of living for the expanding population. Economic growth also enabled the 'restoration' governments to balance their repressive political policies with more enlightened social reforms. The breakthrough of German industrialization occurred in the 1850s and 1860s. The Austrian economist, Carl von Czoernig, observed that the pace of change had been so rapid that 'conditions in 1847 seem much closer to 1758 than 1858'.[24] The volume of trade in both the *Zollverein* and Austria nearly doubled between 1851 and 1857. The creation of joint-stock companies, albeit not on a large scale, and the formation of modern investment banks helped sustain the momentum of economic growth up to the worldwide depression of 1857–1859. This hit the Austrian economy severely, but the rest of German Europe escaped relatively lightly, and growth resumed again in 1860–1861. The war of 1859 with France and Piedmont (see below) further weakened Austria economically and left her heavily in debt.

Overall, the record of growth in the 1850s and 1860s for the *Zollverein* economic zone was impressive, and by the 1860s it had the largest railway network on the continent. The use of steam power in factories was becoming universal and pioneering steps were being taken towards mechanizing production. At the world exhibition of 1862, German machine tools were at least as good as their British competitors. Similarly, the output of the German textile industry, and coal and steel industries, increased dramatically over the period 1850 to 1865. Nevertheless the *Zollverein* economy still lagged behind Britain, the USA, France and Belgium. In 1860, Prussia's share of world manufacturing was only 5 per cent, as compared to Britain's 20 per cent and France's 8 per cent.[25] However, in the longer term the fact that Germany's most dynamic economic region, the Ruhr, lay within Prussian territory was to have, as James Sheehan has put it, 'profound political consequences'.[26]

See Document 21

Austro-Prussian relations

The ultra-conservatives in Berlin, such as Ernst von Gerlach (1795–1877) and his brother Leopold, assumed that the re-establishment of the Confederation would lead to the re-establishment of the close cooperation that had existed between Prussia and Austria between 1815 and 1848. In fact cooperation between the two great German powers became increasingly difficult to maintain, as both, in the dramatic words of Bismarck who was now the Prussian representative to the Confederation in Frankfurt, were breathing 'the air out of each other's mouths; one must yield or be "yielded" to'.[27] By this he meant that Austria needed to dominate the Confederation to protect its position as a great power, which would inevitably prevent Prussia from gaining its full potential as leader of a *kleindeutsch* union. Although Frederick William and his advisers in Berlin did not share Bismarck's apocalyptic assessment of Austro-Prussian relations and were more wary of the Bonapartist government in France, the latent antagonism between the two states became increasingly obvious in the negotiations to renew the *Zollverein* and the discussions on the foreign policy of the Confederation during the Crimean War and Franco-Piedmontese struggle against Austria in 1859.

See Document 22

When the *Zollverein* Treaty came up for renewal in 1853, the Austrians proposed its replacement by a new, central European, free-trade zone. The prospect was attractive to the south German states and Saxony, but opposed fiercely by Prussia, which did not want to forfeit its leadership of the *Zollverein*. Thanks to the efforts of Rudolf von Delbrück (1817–1903), the director of the foreign trade section in the Ministry of Commerce, Prussia managed to strengthen its position within the *Zollverein* by offering Hanover and Oldenburg entry on very favourable terms. At first, as a means of putting pressure on Berlin, the pro-Austrian states threatened to form an independent customs union with Austria, but ultimately the pull of the Prussian economy was too powerful for them to resist. The Austrians were marginalized and had no option but to sign a 12-year trade agreement with Prussia and agreed not to raise the question of entry into the *Zollverein* until 1860.

The Crimean War, 1854–1856, was fought by Britain, Turkey, France and Piedmont against Russia to prevent the implementation of Russian plans for the partition of the Turkish Empire.

The outbreak of the **Crimean War** led to further friction between the two powers. Austria, fearing Russian influence in the Balkans, refused to assist the Russian Empire against Britain and France, even though Russia had supported her against Prussia in 1849–1850. In early 1854 Prussia reluctantly signed a defensive treaty with Austria, but was not ready to be dragged into war by her. When the Austrians proposed to mobilize the Confederation's forces under Austrian supreme command in the case of a Russian invasion of the Balkans, Prussia in common with the other members of the Confederation voted against the proposal. At Frankfurt Bismarck ably exploited the fears of the smaller states that this would lead to war and the subsequent break-up of the Confederation to the great advantage of the French, by declaring that the Confederation would fight only to defend its own neutrality. He was thus able to imply that Prussia, unlike Austria, was a purely German state whose security interests were identical with the great majority of the states of the Confederation.

Franco-Piedmont alliance: To drive Austria out of Italy, Napoleon and Cavour, the prime minister of Piedmont, had secretly planned at Plombières in 1858 to provoke Austria into an attack on Lombardy.

When war broke out between Austria and the **Franco-Piedmont alliance** in April 1859, Prussia again initially tried to remain neutral, but with the defeat of Austrian forces at Magenta and Solferino, Berlin abandoned this position and prepared to drive a hard bargain with Vienna. In exchange for military assistance, Prussia now insisted on equality with Austria within the Confederation, supreme command of forces on the Rhine and military and political **hegemony** in northern Germany. Austria, believing that the Confederation would inevitably be drawn into the struggle, was unwilling to make these concessions, but the matter was never put to the test. On 11 July France and Austria ended the war with the Armistice of Villafranca. Austria had suffered a heavy defeat in Italy and the loss of Lombardy, but had nevertheless prevented Prussia from strengthening its position within the Confederation.

Hegemony: leadership by one state over others

Conclusion

Was the 1848 Revolution the 'turning point that did not turn'? Certainly no united, liberal Germany was created and the final stages of the revolt were crushed on a scale and with a ruthlessness not seen since the Peasants' Revolt in 1525. On the other hand, the triumph of the conservatives did not lead to a return to the *status quo*. Even if they had not ultimately been successful, the 1848 revolts had given birth to a new politics. The liberals, the democrats and the conservatives had all organized on a national scale. The more far-sighted conservatives, who included Radowitz and eventually the young Otto von Bismarck, also realized that future governments of the right would have to harness nationalism together with liberalism and compensate both the masses and the bourgeoisie for the absence of political liberty by social reforms and economic prosperity. Thus it was no surprise that the 1850s witnessed the most determined intervention by the state in the social question until Bismarck's welfare reforms in the 1880s (see p. 129).

The economic, political and international climate in the 1850s was very different from that of the previous decades. The 1848 revolts had not led to the dramatic creation of a liberal Germany, but they had revealed the strength of nationalism and the potential for popular participation in politics, as well as confirming that a Prussian-led *Kleindeutschland* was the most likely, if not yet inevitable, formula for the united Germany of the future. The revolts also led to the introduction of a parliamentary constitution into Prussia, albeit one with a three-class franchise that grossly distorted the political power of the property-owning classes, but, as elections later in the decade were to show (see p. 83), did not rule out the possibility of liberal majorities and the potential for political change. Within the Confederation the events of 1849–1850 also irreparably damaged the Austro-Prussian partnership which had dominated Germany since 1815. Although Prussia did return, to quote Marx, 'as a rueful sinner into the fold of the reconstituted diet of the Confederation', its aims increasingly diverged from those of Austria.[28]

4 The Unification of Germany, 1858–1871

Introduction: problems, issues and questions

The 13 years between 1858 and 1871 are a major watershed in both German, and European history. The Confederation was swept away. First Austria and then France were decisively defeated, and a *Kleindeutschland* emerged under Prussian leadership to become a major European power. The dream of the *kleindeutsch* Frankfurt liberals seemed at last to be realized. This really was a turning point that turned! German unification in the form that it took can all too easily be portrayed as 'a marvellous march of events in which each stage seems to slip into its appointed place'.[1] Undoubtedly 'powerful structural factors'[2] were pushing the German states towards unity, but in the early 1860s it was by no means clear what form that would take. There was certainly 'nothing inevitable' about the emergence of a Prussian-dominated *Kleindeutschland* but then neither was 'the actual outcome ... an accident'.[3]

The international background

Bismarck's successes can only be understood within the context of the dramatic shifts in the balance of power which had occurred in Europe in the 1850s. In France the new **plebiscitary regime** under Napoleon III, which was seen by the German conservatives as a successor of the 1848 revolutions,[4] was a destabilizing force. France played a major role in causing both the Crimean and Italian wars of 1859 (see p. 80). The Crimean War ruptured the Austro-Russian axis, which had been of decisive importance in restoring Austria's position in Germany in 1850, while Austria was further weakened by her defeat by France and Piedmont and the subsequent loss of Lombardy in 1859. British and Russian distrust of French ambitions ensured that both were ready to tolerate the prospect of German unity under Prussia.

> **Plebiscitary regime:** a regime basing its legitimacy on plebiscites or referenda

The Renaissance of liberalism: the 'new era'

At the end of the 1850s the conservatives were in retreat in every major German state. In Bavaria King Maximilian cooperated with the liberals to introduce a series of reforms including the completion of the legal emancipation of the Jews. In Württemberg the liberal Lamey-Roggenbach (1825–1907) cabinet took office and its reforms 'became a field of domestic political experimentation, on which German liberalism was able to test out and prove its ability to govern'.[5] In Austria, too, a reforming government under Count Rechberg (1806–1899) was appointed, and in 1861 the February Patent announced the introduction of a bicameral chamber with an elected lower house.

There were also significant changes in Prussia. In October 1858 Crown Prince William was appointed regent when his brother was incapacitated by a severe stroke. Politically this was good news for the liberals. William had supported the Radowitz Plan and opposed Olmütz (see p. 77). He ignored the plans of his stricken brother to abolish the constitution and appointed a new cabinet of a moderately liberal persuasion. The reactionary Camarilla lost its authority, and, as the elections to the lower house of the Prussian assembly in 1858 were no longer influenced by the government, the liberals were able to win a majority.

By 1860 liberalism, despite its many divisions, dominated the political debate throughout the German states. It set the tone in the Protestant churches, education, in much of the press, local government and business associations. 'It was almost a foregone conclusion that science and literature, students and all young people were liberals'.[6] Throughout Germany, wherever there were free elections, the liberals won majorities. However, these successes were deceptive. Liberalism was not a mass movement, and it failed to reach out to the peasantry, the urban lower classes and the great majority of the Catholics. It was led by elites, and only became the dominant force in Prussian politics at a point when the masses were not yet mobilized.

The constitutional conflict in Prussia

In Prussia the liberals seriously misinterpreted William's own politics. Their honeymoon with him was essentially based on illusory hopes and misunderstanding, as was to be shown in the bitter conflict that broke out over the reform of the army. The liberals believed passionately in integrating the army into society and making it subject to parliament, while the main thrust of the government's army reforms went in the opposite direction, and was intended to strengthen the grip of the professional officer corps and downgrade the role of the part-time *Landwehr*, or reserve army (see p. 17). This threatened the fundamental conception of a 'civilianized army' as represented by the *Landwehr*, which was as important to the liberals as 'the rights of man'.[7]

Initially the liberal leaders in the assembly attempted to find a compromise, but von Roon (1803–1879), the war minister, supported by the ultra-conservative, General Edwin von Manteuffel (1809–1885), Chief of the Military cabinet, who was hoping to persuade the regent to abolish the constitution, and if necessary launch a conservative counter-revolution, ruthlessly exploited the liberals' willingness to make provisional financial grants and pressed on with the military reorganization. With the foundation of the Progressive Party in June 1861, the left-wing liberals were able to mount a much more effective opposition against the Crown and widened the conflict by calling for a drastic reform of the constitution. After the election of December 1861, in which the progressives emerged as the largest group with 109 seats, the opposition began to subject the military budget to a painstaking analysis, so that it could draw attention to the funds illegally being transferred to the war ministry from other government departments. William retaliated by dismissing the 'New Era' government and appointing a much more conservative administration led by Prince Adolf zu Hohenlohe (1797–1873), but the subsequent elections in March 1862 again produced an overwhelming liberal majority. After further attempts to compromise were rejected by William, who, on the death of his brother, Frederick William IV, had now become king, the liberals were determined not only to reject the budget but also to force the king to appoint a liberal ministry.

Otto von Bismarck's appointment as Prussian minister-president

At first William was ready to abdicate rather than accept their demands, but, as a last throw, he turned to Bismarck who, in anticipation of this move, had been summoned to Berlin by von Roon. Bismarck was the only alternative between abject surrender to the liberals or the appointment of the conservative hard liner General Edwin von Mantuefel. Bismarck, as we have seen, had already made a name for himself as a pugnacious defender of Prussian interests at Frankfurt (see p. 79). In 1859 William moved him as ambassador to St Petersburg in an attempt to improve relations with Austria and 3 years later, very briefly to Paris.

The details of the army bill

As a soldier, William wanted to modernize and expand the Prussian army. For 50 years the size of the Prussian army had not increased at all and only about a third of those eligible to serve were called up. When they had completed their service with the colours, they became reservists to the regular army for 2 years and thereafter joined the *Landwehr* for a further 7 years. The officer corps was, however, both scornful of the part-time civilian officers of the *Landwehr* and suspicious of their political reliability. The war minister, Albrecht von Roon, consequently worked out the following plan for reform:

- The size of the standing army would virtually be doubled.
- The number of new recruits would be increased annually from 40,000 to 63,000.
- The period of active service would be set at 3 years.
- The *Landwehr* and the reserves would also be reorganized. The regular army would now be responsible for the first 5 years of the reserve service of the former conscripts, while the *Landwehr* would be allocated the remaining 4 years. The *Landwehr* would be deployed only at home and behind the front, and its officers would also gradually be replaced by professionals from the regular army.

Bismarck was born in 1815 into an old-established Junker family from Mark Brandenburg, but thanks to the social connections of his mother, Wilhelmina Mencken, whose father had been secretary to the royal cabinet, he was, as a boy, a frequent visitor to the Prussian royal household. After studying at Göttingen University, he entered the Prussian civil service, but soon resigned to return to farm the family estates at Schönhausen. He had been a member of the combined provincial assemblies, which met in Berlin in 1847 (see p. 61), and during the revolutions of 1848 had made a reputation for himself as an ultra-conservative Junker, royalist and counter-revolutionary. His appointment as Prussian minister at Frankfurt was a reward for this staunch support. However, at Frankfurt he no longer indulged in 'the ultra-conservative illusion that despite all that happened the restoration of the past was both desirable and feasible'.[8] Instead he sought to deal with the world as it was and to mobilize German nationalism behind Prussia's efforts to seize the leadership of Germany. Bismarck was to dominate German politics and diplomacy for nearly three decades. He has been both praised by historians as a 'world historical figure' and depicted as the evil genius who set Germany on the road to the horrors of the Third Reich. What is beyond doubt is that he is a towering figure in German history and was 'that rare creature, "a real political genius"'.[9]

Conflict with the liberals

For all his political genius, however, Bismarck initially underestimated the problems facing him. He hoped to resolve the constitutional crisis quickly before it impaired his freedom of action in foreign policy. He withdrew the budget proposals for 1863 and established contact with the more moderate wing of the Progressive Liberals, to whom he held out the prospect that he would be able to a persuade the king to compromise on the length of compulsory military service. Within days, however, he succeeded in polarizing the political situation still further with his notorious 'Blood and Iron speech' to the budget committee of the assembly. The liberals jumped to the conclusion that he was threatening them with a *coup d'état*, when in reality this was a crude attempt to unite the assembly behind a revisionist policy aimed at creating a *Kleindeutschland*. When the king stubbornly refused all compromise, Bismarck had no alternative, if he were to remain in power, but to bypass the assembly. Consequently he encouraged the upper house to reject the amendments to the 1862 budget, and when the liberals protested, the assembly was **prorogued**. Bismarck argued that this action was constitutionally defensible as a deadlock between the two houses created a 'constitutional hiatus', which the government had every duty to fill. The battle between Bismarck and the liberals resumed when parliament met again in January 1863 and for the next 6 months Bismarck was involved in a desperate fight for political survival, but by late summer he had established with the support of the Crown a virtual dictatorship. The civil service was purged, the press censored and municipal councils were banned from discussing politically sensitive subjects. Following the example of Napoleon III (see p. 77), Bismarck also played with the idea of advising the king to agree to a *coup d'état* and then holding a **plebiscitary election** based on universal franchise, which would mobilize the masses against the liberals. In May he held exploratory talks with Ferdinand Lassalle (1825–1864), the leader of the General Workers' Association, and put before the cabinet a series of schemes for social reforms, which, if necessary, would enable him to draw up a programme designed to attract a mass electorate. However, on reflection, he decided to draw out the crisis until support for the liberals began to ebb away. Although it had a large majority in the *Landtag*, the liberal opposition was in reality much weaker than it seemed. It was composed of factions, which found it difficult to work together, while the executive enjoyed the loyalty of the army, controlled the civil service and was able to collect taxes, whose yield increased thanks to the booming economy.

Nevertheless, despite the bitter conflict over the army bill, there was potentially considerable common ground between Bismarck and the liberals. His economic policy met with their overwhelming support. His exclusion of Austria from the *Zollverein* and the free-trade treaties with Britain, Belgium, France and Italy for example, were all welcomed, as was the Mining Law of 24 June 1865, which established the freedom of exploration and exploitation. Similarly, the successful conclusion of the war against Denmark (see p. 90) also impressed many of the moderate and right-wing liberals. Yet, as William still refused to recognize parliament's powers over the military budget, the constitutional conflict dragged on into the summer of 1866, and Bismarck remained unable to reconcile the bulk of the liberals.

See Document 23

Prorogue: to suspend an assembly for a time without dissolving it and holding fresh elections

Plebiscitary election: one based on a single issue – endorsement of Bismarck and the Crown

See Document 21

The German question, 1859–1863

Public opinion and German unity: the *Nationalverein* and the *Reformverein*

The relative political freedom of the 'new era' encouraged between 1858 and 1863 the formation of *kleindeutsch* pressure groups, such as the *Kongress deutscher Volkswirte* (Congress of German Economists), the *Deutscher Handelstag* (German Trade Association) and the *Nationalverein* (the German National Society).[10] These formed an interlocking network of organizations throughout Prussia and the other German states, and together with the liberal press did much to revive the debate on the German question. Their membership was composed of elite, university-educated and largely Protestant middle-class professionals. The most effective of these groups was undoubtedly the *Nationalverein* which was founded in 1859 by Rudolf von Bennigsen (1824–1902), a liberal deputy in the Hanover assembly, Viktor von Unruh (1806–1886), the former president of the Prussian Assembly of 1848 and the democrat Hermann Schulze-Delitzsch (1808–1883). It was inspired by the Italian **National Society** and its members wanted an 'Italian-type solution' to German unity, which would involve the creation of a united Germany under Prussian leadership and the restoration of the *kleindeutsch* constitution of 1849 (see p. 74). The society shrugged off arguments that its policies would lead to the Prussianization of Germany because it believed that the very process of unification would liberalize Prussia. At its peak it had a membership of 25,000, but once Bismarck came to power in Prussia, these arguments became increasingly difficult to sustain, and it rapidly lost support.

> **The National Society** was founded in Piedmont in 1856 and its aim was to raise support for a united Italy under the leadership of Piedmont –'the Italian Prussia'.

The *kleindeutsch* policies advocated by the *Nationalverein* and its allied pressure groups were opposed by a cross section of Catholics, anti-Prussians, **particularists**, *grossdeutsch* liberals and democrats on the grounds that they would lead to the division of Germany through the exclusion of Austria. Their support came mainly from Bavaria, Württemberg, Hesse-Kassel, Hesse-Darmstadt and Hanover. In 1862 the German Reform Society (*Deutscher Reformverein*)[11] was set up by the originally *kleindeutsch* supporter Heinrich von Gagern (see p. 75), the economist Moritz Möhl (1802–1888) and the democrat Julius Fröbel (1805–1892) to campaign for a united *Grossdeutschland*, but it was split between those who wanted only to maintain the status quo of the Confederation and those who wanted a genuine *grossdeutsch* parliament, which would be dominated neither by Austria or Prussia. The *grossdeutsch* cause certainly benefited from a general mistrust of Prussia in southern Germany, but initially *grossdeutsch* liberals, such as Gagern, also optimistically hoped that the constitutional changes in Austria, which had resulted in the creation of an elected parliament in 1861 (see p.83), might lead to Austria adopting a more liberal attitude towards the reform of the Confederation. While the debate on the future of Germany was dominated by the elites, to the more politically aware workers organized in the Cooperative Movement or

> **Particularists:** those believing that each state should have its own laws and pursue its own interests.

Ferdinand Lassalle's German Workers' Association it was axiomatic that unity was an essential framework in which social and political reforms could be implemented, but like the liberals they were divided on the merits of a *grossdeutsch* or *kleindeutsch* union.

Austro-Prussian rivalry and the reform of the Confederation

In both Berlin and Vienna, policies for the reform of the German Confederation were 'a confusion of plans, actions and counter actions, irritations and fluctuations'.[12] Nevertheless in 1861, broadly three main approaches can be identified:

1 An Austro-Prussia dualistic hegemony with Austria, with the presidency of the Confederation alternating between Vienna and Berlin. In return for a free hand north of the Main, Prussia would guarantee Austria's last possession in Italy – Venetia.
2 Vienna was tempted by this solution and its diplomacy fluctuated between confrontation and cooperation but in the final analysis it wanted to perpetuate its leading role in the Confederation. It mistrusted Prussia and feared that compromise would only lead to further demands from Berlin.
3 The south German states, distrusting both Austria and Prussia, wanted to strengthen the authority of the Confederation without creating a Prussian–Austrian hegemony, by setting up a diet composed of delegates from the state assemblies.

When it became clear by the summer of 1861 that no Austro-Prussian agreement was possible, the Prussian foreign minister, Albrecht von Bernstorff (1808–1873), began to consider reviving the Radowitz Plan (see p. 76), the threat of which brought the medium-sized states, who dreaded Prussian domination, closer to Austria. In July 1863 Austria made one last attempt to seize the initiative in Germany and produced a complex plan for reform of the Confederation, which involved creating a directorate of ministers from the five largest states, an assembly of princes and a federal parliament elected from the state parliaments. The Austrians attempted to neutralize Bismarck's opposition by inviting the princes to a conference without first holding a ministerial meeting to prepare the agenda. Bismarck persuaded William to boycott the meeting and then played the nationalist card by proposing a central parliament elected by the 'entire [German] nation'. This would inevitably maximize Prussian, as opposed to Austrian, influence within the Confederation, as only little more than a third of Austria's population was ethnically German. The Prussian boycott of the conference effectively torpedoed the Austrian initiative, as reform of the Confederation was meaningless without Prussian participation. The eruption of the Schleswig-Holstein crisis in the winter of 1863–1864 prevented for the time being any further Austrian initiative.

The Danish war and the Schleswig-Holstein question, 1863–1865

After the brief Confederate–Danish war ended in the Truce of Malmö in 1848 (see p. 71) the great powers in the Treaty of London of 1852 confirmed that Schleswig and Holstein, while remaining under the Danish crown, would continue to enjoy constitutional autonomy. They also decided that as Frederick VII of Denmark was childless, the succession of the female line would also apply to both Denmark and the duchies, which up to this point could only be inherited through the male line. The Duke of Augustenburg, the candidate of the male line, was persuaded through financial compensation to give up his claims, and so clear the way for the eventual succession of Christian IX. However, the Treaty of London satisfied neither the Danes nor the Germans, and Schleswig-Holstein continued to be an issue that enflamed nationalist passions on both sides. In March 1863 Frederick VII with the support of Sweden, decided to exploit the growing tension between Prussia and Austria and integrate Schleswig into a unitary Danish constitution. After his unexpected death in November, his successor, Christian IX, (1818–1906) immediately confirmed the new constitution. This open violation of the London Treaty prompted the Duke of Augustenburg's son, Frederick (1829–1880), to claim the duchies and insist on their separation from Denmark. Augustenburg was backed throughout Germany by liberals and nationalists, whether *gross* or *kleindeutsch*. Within the Confederation the medium-sized states championed his claims as they welcomed the prospect of an independent Schleswig-Holstein joining the Confederation as a further counterweight to Austria and Prussia. Indeed Bavaria hoped that their championing of Augustenburg would lead to a more central role of the *Mittelstaaten* (see p. 31) in a reconstructed Germany.[13]

Bismarck, however, had consistently argued that, unless the territories could be annexed by Prussia outright, Danish possession was preferable to their independence under Augustenburg, who would probably oppose Prussian interests in the Confederation. He was also wary of provoking Anglo-Russian intervention, as had occurred in 1848 (see p. 71). Inevitably this refusal to support Augustenburg made Bismarck even more unpopular with the liberals, but to the Austrians it was a welcome sign that Bismarck was apparently no longer seeking to exploit German nationalism. At first both Austria and Prussia attempted to moderate the Confederation's determination to support Augustenburg. They argued that the Danish violation of the treaty rather than his claims were the basis for military action. On that basis the two powers agreed to the temporary occupation of Holstein by Confederate troops – Saxons and Hanoverians – in December. In January, however, when Augustenburg set up court unofficially at Kiel, the Prussian Field Marshall von Wrangel was put in command of all the federal forces in order to pre-empt unilateral action by confederate troops. The Austro-Prussian alliance of 16 January 1864, which effectively sidelined the Confederation, committed both states to

See Map 4

The Battle of Düppel or Dybbol, February 1864: The Danes had evacuated the *Dannenvirke* defence line in the night of 5–6 February to Düppel in eastern Jutland. In the ensuing battle for Düppel the new professionalism of the Prussian army was seen for the first time. Prussia had a clear organizational and numerical superiority over the Danes. The recently acquired Dreyse rifles and artillery also proved their worth. Düppel finally fell on 18 April after a 6-hour bombardment, the ferocity of which was not to be rivalled until the spring of 1915.

determining the future of the duchies by joint agreement. Austria hoped that this would prevent Prussia from annexing them. On 31 January when the Danes refused to withdraw from Schleswig, Prussian and Austrian forces crossed the frontier.

Bismarck's immediate aim was to avoid great-power intervention until Denmark had been decisively defeated. In March, when Britain proposed an international conference in London, he was able skilfully to delay its meeting until Prussian forces had decisively defeated the Danes at **Düppel** on 8 April. When the conference met 2 weeks later, the Danes, believing that they had the backing of the great powers, again refused to restore the autonomy of Schleswig. In response Austria and Prussia repudiated the London Treaty, but left open the possibility of continuing dynastic ties with the Danish throne. Neither France, Russia nor Britain were willing to intervene and the Danes were left isolated. When the armistice, which had halted the fighting during the conference, expired on 26 June, the Danes were defeated within days, and by the Treaty of Vienna, which was signed on 30 October, the Danish government handed over Holstein, Schleswig and Lauenburg to Prussia and Austria. For the time being, these territories were then put under joint Austro-Prussian military occupation. Austria and Prussia agreed privately that they would decide on the future of the duchies without consulting the Confederation.

Denmark's defeat confronted Austria with a difficult dilemma: should it do a deal with Berlin after all and recognize Prussian hegemony in North Germany in return for a guarantee of its possession of Venetia? In Schönbrunn in August 1864 this alternative was discussed by Bismarck and the Austrian foreign minister, Count Rechberg (1806–1899). Provisional agreement was even reached that Prussia should receive the duchies in return for guaranteeing Venetia and helping with the reconquest of Lombardy. How genuine Bismarck was in offering this is hard to say. It may be that he was attempting to secure continued Austrian cooperation by 'dangling once more, as so often in the past, the enticing possibility of such a bargain'.[14] The settlement was however rejected by both Emperor Franz Joseph who refused outright to cede the duchies to Prussia, and by William, who at that stage was still reluctant to ignore the legality of Augustenburg's claims.

Throughout the winter of 1864–1865 the future of Schleswig-Holstein remained undecided. To thwart Prussian ambitions in the duchies, Austria now advocated handing over the administration to Augustenburg, while Bismarck increasingly pushed for their annexation by Prussia. By the summer of 1865 it seemed that only force would decide their future. The king, who was now won over to the idea of annexation, and the Prussian Crown Council were ready to go to war to annex the duchies. With the help of the Jewish financier, Gerson von Bleichröder (1822–1893), Bismarck, despite the refusal of the Prussian assembly to vote funds, was able to raise sufficient sums of money for a 1-year military campaign,[15] but he still held back because he was uncertain as to how the great powers, especially France, would react, and he also needed more time to win over public opinion at home.

In August, responding to an Austrian initiative, he accepted, after talks at Bad Gastein, a compromise solution. Lauenburg was to be purchased by Prussia and the administration of the Duchies to be divided: Schleswig was to be administered by Prussia and Holstein by Austria, although legally **joint sovereignty** would remain intact. The Gastein Agreement, as Bismarck himself said, 'papered over the cracks' and bought time either for a lasting solution or war.

> **Joint sovereignty:** joint power and control

Renewal of the *Zollverein*: Austria's economic Königgrätz?

Parallel to the Austro-Prussian diplomatic struggle over the future of the duchies ran the battle for economic control of the *Zollverein*. In 1853 further discussions on Austria's entry had been postponed for a 7-year period (see p. 80), but by 1860 it was already clear that any attempts by Austria to enter the *Zollverein* would once again meet with implacable Prussian hostility. The following year Prussia began negotiations for a free-trade treaty with France. Such an agreement would certainly be economically beneficial, but it would also serve an important political purpose, since it would effectively block Austria from joining the *Zollverein* because its industry was too weak to compete without protection against French imports. Despite intense pro-Austrian lobbying from the 'third Germany', Prussia and France signed the treaty in 1862.

When the *Zollverein*'s treaties came up for renewal in 1865, Austria demanded that the free-trade treaty should be scrapped, so that it could join the union. Again the 'third Germany' rallied to Austria, but in the final analysis it realized that the *Zollverein* was indispensable to its economic interests. Bismarck insisted that each member state would have to accept the Prussian–French Treaty *before* the *Zollverein* treaties could be renegotiated. The *kleindeutsch* liberals, the *Nationalverein*, the Congress of German Economists and the German Trade Association all put intense pressure on the governments of the German states to accept Prussia's demands. It was clear that realistically, as Lothar Gall has put it, the *Zollverein* already constituted 'so solid a network of interests that breaking out of it or dissolving it in favour of further combinations scarcely seemed a serious possibility any more'.[16] By October all the small and medium states had capitulated and on 16 May 1865 the *Zollverein* was renewed for a further 15 years. Ludwig II of Bavaria reluctantly conceded in August 1984 that his government had no option but to renew the treaty as the South 'would be compelled through powerful interests sooner or later to join up with the rest of Germany'.[17]

Had Prussia inflicted an 'economic Königgrätz' (see below) on Austria? Thomas Nipperdey describes it as a 'preliminary round in the resolution of the German question'.[18] In itself, Austria's rebuff was not decisive.

'Economic preponderance', as Pflanze has stressed, 'did not lead necessarily to political domination'.[19] However, to contemporaries, even if they distrusted Bismarck, Prussia's victory in the *Zollverein* indicated that over the longer term there appeared to be no real economic and political alternative to Prussian leadership in Germany.[20]

The defeat of Austria

Bad Gastein, not surprisingly, failed to improve Austro-Prussian relations. Throughout the winter of 1865–1866 relations between Prussia and Austria continued to deteriorate. In Schleswig the Prussians systematically attempted to stamp out support for Augustenburg, while the Austrians pursued the opposite course in Holstein. By February 1866 the Prussian Crown Council agreed that war was inevitable. On 8 April, Bismarck, by holding out the promise of **Austrian Venetia**, concluded an offensive alliance with Italy for a period of 3 months. On the following day he challenged Austria head-on by proposing the reform of the German Confederation: the federal assembly would now become a proper national parliament for which every male German citizen would have the vote. This would, of course, effectively marginalize Austria with her much smaller ethnic German population, while enabling Prussia to appeal to German nationalism, but in fact this transparent manoeuvre merely alienated not only the medium-sized states that did not want Austria humiliated, but also many liberals who feared universal franchise and did not trust Bismarck an inch.

Throughout April and May the Austrian and Prussian armies began to mobilize, but still at this stage Bismarck did not totally close off all options for a settlement with Austria. He appeared to take seriously a proposal, which was made by the **von der Gablenz brothers** to divide Germany into Austrian and Prussian spheres of influence. He even had a plan drawn up which attempted to square the circle of an Austro-Prussian division of Germany along the Main and the election of a national parliament. Austria rejected this at the end of May, and then on 1 June unilaterally broke the Austro-Prussian Treaty of January 1864 (see p. 89) by referring the whole Schleswig-Holstein issue to the Confederation. Prussia retaliated by invading Holstein and proposing a reform of the Confederation along *kleindeutsch* lines which would irrevocably exclude Austria. The Austrians appealed to the other members of the Confederation for support and secured French neutrality through a promise to cede Venetia to Italy. Despite their acceptance of Prussian leadership within the *Zollverein*, Baden, Bavaria, Württemberg, Hesse-Kassel and Hesse-Darmstadt, Saxony and Hanover all rallied to Austria, while only the small states and enclaves in northern Germany supported Prussia. Bismarck declared the Confederation dissolved and Prussian troops immediately occupied Saxony, Hanover and the Hesse-Kassel.

Austrian Venetia: Venetia had been awarded to Austria in 1815 and its annexation was demanded by the new Italy created in 1860.

The von der Gablenz brothers: one, Anton, was a Prussian assembly deputy, the other, Ludwig, was the Austrian commissioner in Holstein.

Napoleon's attitude towards the German question

The opportunist policies of France remained a constant threat to Bismarck. Napoleon had two overriding aims: he wanted to complete the unification of Italy by handing Venetia to the Italians and to placate French nationalism in the event of a Prussian victory in Germany by gaining some concessions in the Rhineland, such as a buffer state under French protection, border changes along the Palatinate or even the outright annexation of the Saar. Clearly Napoleon did not want an Austro-Prussian understanding as that would have stymied his plans for Venetia and reorganizing central Europe. He therefore rather clumsily attempted to play Prussia off against Austria. Bismarck did not need a French alliance but French neutrality was indispensable. Both sides therefore attempted to exploit the situation: Bismarck hoped to escape paying a price for French neutrality but skilfully hinted, when he met Napoleon at Biarritz in October 1865, at the prospect of compensation in Luxemburg. Napoleon was careful to keep his options open between Austria and Prussia, even though he had persuaded the Italians to negotiate an agreement with Prussia. The diplomatic situation therefore remained fluid right up to the eve of war. Napoleon proposed a European conference to settle the German and Italian questions, but, luckily for Bismarck, the other great powers distrusted Napoleon's motives. Then finally on 12 June France and Austria signed a secret agreement. Austria would surrender Venetia even if it defeated Prussia, and the balance of power in the Confederation would be tilted against Prussia, probably by creating an independent Rhineland state.

The Seven Weeks' War

On the face of it, Bismarck seemed to be taking an enormous risk. Neither the liberals nor the conservatives supported the war. The former deeply distrusted Bismarck, while the latter disapproved of the humiliation of Austria and feared the consequences of revolutionary nationalism. To contemporaries a prolonged war risking foreign intervention and ultimately leading to an Austrian victory seemed the most likely outcome. The Berlin Stock Exchange was even speculating on an Austrian victory! However, although intervention from the opportunist Napoleon III could not be ruled out, Austro-Russian cooperation, which had been of decisive importance in restoring Austria's position in Germany in 1850 no longer existed (see p. 80).

To force a rapid conclusion, Bismarck was ready to bring pressure to bear on Austria by mobilizing the nationalism of the non-German peoples of the Habsburg Empire. Hungarian and Italian 'legions' were positioned in Silesia, and Garibaldi (1807–1882), the Italian veteran of the wars of unification, was promised Prussian support to wage guerrilla war in Dalmatia. Plans were also drawn up to promise the Czechs an independent state. Yet none of these strategies was necessary. The war lasted 7 weeks and ended in an overwhelming Prussian victory. By 29 June the armies of Hanover and Hesse-Kassel had been eliminated, and on 3 July the Austrians themselves were defeated at Königgrätz (Sadowa). By 18 July Prussian troops were only 19 km from Vienna.

In many ways Königgrätz was a victory of a modern army equipped by a rapidly industrializing state over a more backward power, which lacked the funds to modernize its armed forces. Although the Austrian artillery had been reorganized after the defeat of 1859 (see p. 80), its troops lacked sufficient training, and the organizational and command structure of the army was still inadequate. The armies of the medium sized states were uncoordinated and concerned with their own strategic interests. The Bavarians, for instance, did not come to the help of the Austrians in Bohemia. In contrast, the Prussian army was well trained and equipped. General Helmuth von Moltke (1800–1891), the Prussian chief of staff, was a soldier of genius, whose campaigns were based on rational and thorough planning. After the Danish war he had created a railroad section in the General Staff and established district commands based on the railways. In 1866 Prussia could use six trunk lines for mobilizing its troops, but Austria had only one. The Prussian army had also been fully equipped with the breech-loading needle gun, while the Austrians still used the old muzzle-loading rifles. On the other hand 'contrary to patriotic legend'[21] Königgrätz was not entirely a model of military planning and leadership. Of the three Prussian armies that were to converge on Austrian forces, the second army advanced so slowly that the Austrians could have defeated it, had they been better led. As it was, the bulk of the Austrian army managed to escape intact across cross the Danube.[22]

The diplomatic and political settlement

Nevertheless the Prussian victory proved to be decisive, and Austria appealed to Napoleon to mediate. Bismarck now realized that he would have to end the war quickly or else face the danger of French intervention. With considerable difficulty he persuaded the king, who wanted the ultimate triumph of occupying Vienna, to accept French proposals for an armistice and agreed on 26 July to the conclusion of the Preliminary Peace of Nikolsburg. In early August, somewhat belatedly responding to pressure from his advisers, Napoleon demanded the whole of the left bank of the Rhine up to Mainz. The scale of these demands destroyed his credibility as protector of south German independence, and made it easier for Bismarck to negotiate military treaties with the south German states, which agreed to place their armies firmly under the control of Berlin in wartime. Bismarck was then able to threaten Napoleon with the prospect of a nationalist war waged by the German nation under arms and forced him to climb down.

On 23 August the provisional treaty was confirmed at Prague. Austria was excluded from Germany and the old German Confederation was dissolved. North of the river Main, Prussia would have a free hand to form a new association of states – the North German Confederation, while to the south the states would preserve their independence, but would be free to form a southern confederation if they so wished.

On 20 September 1866 Prussia annexed Schleswig-Holstein, Hanover, Hesse-Kassel, Nassau and the city of Frankfurt. As a result of French pressure, Saxony escaped this fate, although it had to join the North German Confederation. In the autumn Bismarck also insisted that negotiations on the reform of the *Zollverein* should begin.

See Document 24

The North German Confederation

The Austrian defeat was a major turning point in German and European history. It eliminated all possibility of a *grossdeutsch* solution and expelled Austria from the German political community after a period of nearly a thousand years. In 1866 the former German Confederation was divided into not just two but three parts: the North German Confederation, the southern states and Austria. The **Main line** had, however, been breached by the military alliances between the North German Confederation and the southern states and of course by the *Zollverein*, which was in the process of reorganization. Bismarck, even if he had wanted to, could now no longer turn away from the German question. He had allied Prussia with the dynamic forces of nationalism and, until German *kleindeutsch* unification was completed, the situation in Germany would remain potentially unstable.

See Map 4

Main line: the north-south divide formed by the river Main

The indemnity bill

The war also drastically changed the internal political situation in Prussia. In the Prussian assembly elections, which were held on the day of Königgrätz, the liberals suffered heavily from rejecting Bismarck's war-expenditure programme and the conservatives made large gains. When the assembly met in August 1866, the constitutional conflict was still unresolved, but, contrary to the wishes of the conservative diehards, Bismarck did not scrap the constitution. In fact he persuaded the king to put before assembly an indemnity bill which would give retrospective approval to the government's expenditure on the armed forces over the previous four years. The bill caused an agonizing debate on both the right and left, but in the end it was carried by an overwhelming majority of moderate conservatives and liberals on 3 September. In the course of the winter these divisions crystallized into two new political groupings: the Free Conservatives and the National Liberals, which were both ready to cooperate with Bismarck in creating a new Germany.

The constitution

The constitution, like almost everything Bismarck achieved, has never ceased to be the subject of considerable controversy. Was it, as Sir Charles Grant Robertson called it in 1918, 'the Königgrätz of liberalism in Germany' or did it in practice, as the controversial lover of paradoxes,

A. J. P. Taylor, remarked some 50 years later, make North Germany 'a constitutional country'.[23] In the longer term it challenged the German liberals by creating a democratic *Reichstag* (lower house), which certainly facilitated the eventual rise of the SPD (German Social Democratic Party).

The key features of the constitution, which was in essence to be unchanged until 1918, were:

1 The *Praesidium*, or presidency, which was a post created for the King of Prussia. Nominally he was responsible for foreign affairs, the declaration of war and the dismissal of confederate officials. He was also supreme commander of the armed forces.

2 Initially Bismarck envisaged that a professional diplomat would be chancellor of the North German Confederation, whose main task would be to chair the *Bundesrat* (upper chamber). He would receive instructions from Bismarck as minister-president of Prussia, but once its potential importance became clear, Bismarck filled the post himself, whils still remaining minister-president in Prussia.

3 The *Bundesrat* was composed of representatives nominated by the governments of the member states who voted strictly according to their instructions. While all legislation had to be approved by both houses, constitutional changes needed a two-thirds majority which was impossible to secure without Prussian consent. To secure Prussia's position, Bismarck had allotted it a total of 17 out of 43 seats. This was reached by combining the votes possessed by Prussia and those of the states which it had annexed in the former Confederation Diet.

4 The *Reichstag*, as Pflanze has stressed, emphasized 'the fundamental dilemma of [Bismarck's] constitutional thinking'.[24] He wanted to use it as a potential check on the Crown, the federal states, the bureaucracy and the liberals without creating parliamentary government. He therefore took the key decision to introduce **universal male franchise**. Potentially, he hoped, this would enable him, like Napoleon III, to appeal over the heads of parliament to the people, but to discourage the formation of popular workers' and peasants' parties, there was to be no payment of parliamentary deputies. Initially there were also to be no annual budget provisions for parliamentary control of military expenditure or rights of interpellation. However, once the constituent assembly was elected on 12 February 1867, in which the National Liberals emerged as the largest party, Bismarck made several important concessions: legal immunity to deputies during parliamentary sessions; the right to **interpellate**; voting by secret ballot in general elections; and the crucial commitment to hold elections 60 days after the dissolution of parliament. Reluctantly Bismarck also gave the *Reichstag* the power to approve the annual budget, but this did not give parliament complete control over the Confederation's finances. Most of its expenditure was earmarked for the military or 'iron' budget, as it was called. Initially Bismarck refused to make this dependent on a parliamentary vote, but in April when a complete deadlock had been reached with the *Reichstag*, which threatened the whole constitutional settlement, he did

Universal male franchise: In practice the secret ballot did not become effective until proper ballot envelopes and voting booths were introduced in 1902.

Interpellate: Subjecting ministers to parliamentary questioning

agree to a compromise that was facilitated by the war scare over Luxemburg (see below). The size of the army was fixed until 31 December 1871. Thereafter any further expansion bringing with it an increase in the budget would have to be approved by the *Reichstag*.

The constitution was approved by the *Reichstag* on 16 April 1867. Up to a point, as Steinberg has argued, it was a constitution that was constructed to suit Bismarck and safeguard 'an arrangement in which a strong chancellor bullies a weak king'.[25] Bismarck had managed to protect both the Crown's and Prussia's power within the North German Confederation, whils ensuring that his own position was almost impregnable. On the other hand in many ways the constitution also reflected the realities of German politics in 1867 and was a compromise between the forces of liberalism, nationalism, democracy and Prussian conservatism. Lothar Gall has argued that it was 'much more a consumption of something for which the time was ripe than the manipulative creation of an individual'.[26]

Bismarck and southern Germany, 1867–1870

There was little support in Bavaria and Württemberg for a southern confederation. Prince Hohenlohe-Schillingfürst (1819–1901), the prime minister of Bavaria in the autumn of 1867, drew up a draft for the 'united states of southern Germany', but it was rejected by both his colleagues in the cabinet and the Württemberg government on the grounds that it would only facilitate the eventual absorption of the southern states by the North German Confederation. It was exactly for this reason that Bismarck had supported Prince Hohenlohe's proposal. He observed to the pro-union government of Baden that 'if what exists is breached, even though it be through a south-German confederation, a healthy national life will grow by itself out of the ruins'.[27]

Bismarck was acutely aware of the dangers of the power vacuum in the south, particularly after the Luxemburg crisis (see below). He developed a whole web of policies for gradually integrating the south by attempting to tighten its economic, military and political links with the north in such a way that an irresistible momentum towards national unity would be set up. The armies of the southern states were reorganized along Prussian lines and the *Zollverein* Treaty was renegotiated. Its General Council and the right of any member to veto a policy (see p. 39) were scrapped and replaced with a new council firmly under Prussian control and a popularly elected *Zollverein* parliament. In these elections Bismarck had expected that the National Liberals and their allies would sweep the board in the southern states, but a large majority of the southern deputies was implacably hostile to any attempt to turn the economic union into a political one. The Democratic People's Party in Württemberg warned, for example, that entry into the North German Confederation would involve excessive taxation, conscription and 'keeping your mouth shut',[28] while in

---

The Luxemburg crisis

This crisis has been described by George Mosse as 'the dress rehearsal for the crisis of 1870'.[29] Having failed to gain any concessions on the Rhine in August 1866, Napoleon put out feelers to buy Luxemburg. The duchy was linked to Holland in that it was in personal union with the Dutch crown (see p. 34), but it had been part of the German Confederation and had been garrisoned by Prussian troops since 1814. Bismarck's reaction to the French initiative appears to have been opportunist. At first he seemed to encourage it but, when the news of the Franco-Dutch talks became public in March 1867, he turned against it. The French were convinced that he had led them into a trap, and the crisis intensified their distrust of Bismarck's foreign policy. Although the crisis helped him achieve a settlement over the iron budget with the National Liberals (see above) Bismarck did not at that point wish to risk war with France. Bismarck indicated that he would accept the mediation of the great powers and a compromise was eventually arranged whereby the Prussian garrison withdrew and the duchy was neutralized under great-power guarantee, but the Dutch King remained as Grand Duke.

---

the Bavarian elections in November 1869 the [Bavarian] Patriot party won the majority of seats. The evolutionary approach to German unity seemed to have failed completely.

War and unification

By early 1869 Bismarck was coming under increasing pressure in the *Reichstag* to complete unification. Yet, given the resistance of the southern states, how was this to be achieved? One possible solution was to provoke a major crisis with France, perhaps even a war, which would overcome south German objections by appealing to a common German nationalism.

The Hohenzollern candidature and the Ems Telegram

'Complications': Until the capture of German diplomatic documents in 1945 the exact degree of Bismarck's role in the Hohenzollern candidature affair was a secret. In the aftermath of the Versailles treaty, which was justified by accusations of German war guilt (see p. 192), it was vital for the German government to keep the history of Bismarck's machinations secret. The documents were published in 1957.

The domestic crisis in Spain caused by the overthrow of Queen Isabella of Spain by a junta of generals in September 1868 provided Bismarck with an opportunity to provoke France. To replace Isabella, the Spanish approached Prince Leopold, a member of the south German and Catholic branch of the Hohenzollerns. In June 1870, after Bismarck had exerted considerable pressure on him, and despite reservations on the part of William I, he accepted. Bismarck, as he told his agent in Madrid, Major Max von Versen, was undoubtedly looking for **'complications'**[30] with the French, although these 'complications' did not necessarily entail an actual war – a major diplomatic crisis would probably suffice.

Bismarck had hoped that the Spanish parliament would ratify the agreement quickly, so that the French would be confronted with a *fait accompli*. However a mistake by a cypher clerk in the Prussian embassy in Madrid caused an unscheduled delay, during which the news reached Paris. The explosion of anger in the press and the French Chamber prompted William to persuade Leopold to stand down. The French had achieved a resounding success, and Bismarck, convinced that Prussia had suffered a humiliation worse than Olmütz (see p. 77), actually thought of resigning, but he was saved by the French foreign minister's failure to recognize the extent of his victory, and his determination to force William to give written guarantees against a renewal of Leopold's candidacy. William, who was holidaying in his palace in Ems, refused the imperious demands of the ambassador, even though there was no question of Leopold changing his mind again, and sent Bismarck an account of his interview (the so-called Ems Telegram). After checking with Moltke whether the army was ready to fight, Bismarck edited the telegram to give it a more aggressive 'spin', and released it to the press. In Paris it so infuriated the war party at court, in parliament and in the cabinet that Napoleon was driven to declare war on 19 July. Bismarck had certainly done much to provoke the war, but the French could have avoided it – at that point anyway – because the substance of their demands had already been offered. As William Halperin observed, the responsibility for war 'rests not on one side or the other but squarely on both'.[31]

The Franco-Prussian War

With the declaration of war, there was an upsurge of nationalist feeling throughout Germany comparable in many ways to that experienced in August 1914. This was fully shared by many women particularly those in the upper and middle classes, who volunteered as nurses, administrators and created work opportunities for soldiers' wives and widows during the winter of 1870–1871. Emperor William I later observed that they had created German unity through their actions in the humanitarian sphere before political unity had become a reality.[32]

As did Austria in 1866, France looked the more formidable adversary, but the Prussian army again triumphed, although the war lasted longer than Bismarck had expected. Once again, Moltke's organization and logistics were far superior to those of his opponents. He was able to move and sustain 700,000 to 800,000 troops over many hundreds of square miles. While the Prussians had superior artillery, the French army had better rifles and the *mitrailleuse*, a machine gun which fired 150 rounds a minute, but its troops were poorly led and organized. Thus the Prussians were able to inflict major defeats on the French at Sedan in September and Metz in October, and Paris itself was put under siege by the end of September.[33]

The international situation again favoured Prussia and her south German allies. Napoleon had failed to create a triple alliance with Austria and Italy, despite a draft agreement in 1869, because the Italians refused to cooperate with the French until the French garrison, which had been protecting the Papacy in Rome since the revolt of 1849, had been withdrawn. The Austrians, fearing an Italian attack on Trieste and Dalmatia, would not ally themselves with France until Italy was a committed member of the alliance.

Bismarck also did all he could to localize the conflict. For instance, he skilfully defused the international crisis triggered by Russia's unilateral repudiation of the clauses in the 1856 Paris treaty, which enforced the neutralization of the Black Sea after the end of the Crimean War (see p. 80). If that crisis had erupted into war, it would almost certainly have coalesced with the Franco-Prussian conflict. He was able to avoid this by proposing an international conference in London where a face-saving compromise for both Britain and Russia was devised, and he stopped France from raising the issue of the war by securing agreement from the other powers to leave it off the agenda in return for his services as mediator. Yet, despite these military and diplomatic advantages, the war dragged on longer than Bismarck wished. Although Napoleon's regime collapsed after Sedan, the new republican government continued to fight. By December 1870 'the prestige of Sedan was dribbling away and with it all hope of securing a peace as cheap and successful as that which followed Sadowa'.[34]

The Treaty of Frankfurt

As soon as Paris fell in January, Bismarck seized the chance to end the fighting. On 25 January 1871 a 3-week armistice was signed, which a month later was confirmed as a preliminary peace. The Germans extracted severe terms: Alsace and Lorraine, including the fortress of Metz, were annexed to provide a vital strategic barrier against any future French attempts to invade Germany, and an indemnity was to be paid over 4 years, after which an army of occupation in the eastern provinces would be withdrawn. These terms were confirmed at the Treaty of Frankfurt in May 1871. The annexation of Alsace and Lorraine were to become the symbol of France's defeat and fuelled her desire for revenge. Lothar Gall was to call this annexation 'a miscalculation of great consequence'.[35]

The unification of Germany

The initial wave of nationalism unleashed by the war provided Bismarck in Theodore Hamerow's words with 'a sudden blessed opportunity'[36] to complete the unification of Germany. Baden, Hesse-Darmstadt and Württemberg recognized that union with the North German Confederation was becoming inevitable, and even Bavaria agreed in principle that the *status quo* in Germany could no longer be preserved, but it wished to dissolve the existing North German Confederation and replace it with a much more loosely structured organization.

In October the southern states sent delegations to Versailles to negotiate the terms of a German union with Bismarck. In separate negotiations with the southern states he was able to play them off against each other, and by threatening Bavaria with economic and political isolation, he forced its government to adopt a more flexible policy. Nevertheless he had to make considerable concessions, which strengthened the power of the states in the *Bundesrat*:

- Before declaring war or taking action against a recalcitrant member state, the federal government now had to gain the approval of the *Bundesrat*.
- A vote of 14, rather than, as originally, two-thirds of the *Bundesrat*, could now block any constitutional amendment.
- Concessions were also made, authorizing local taxation and administration of the postal and telegraph systems, while Bavaria and Württemberg were permitted to maintain their own armies in peace time.

The negotiations were successfully concluded by the end of November and King Ludwig of Bavaria was bribed by Bismarck to invite William to accept the title of emperor. By January 1871 the necessary enabling legislation had passed through both the north German *Reichstag* and the assemblies of the southern states and on 18 January 1871 the German Empire was proclaimed in the Hall of Mirrors at Versailles. The consequences of this for both Europe and the German peoples were to be momentous.

See Document 25

Conclusion

The decade of 1860–1870 was one of the most significant in the history of Germany and indeed Europe. It witnessed the final defeat of Austrian claims to dominate the German Confederation and the unification of *Kleindeutschland* under Prussian leadership. As long as the member states of the German Confederation accepted her leadership, Austria could control the German Confederation, but her power was increasingly eroded over the years up to 1866. After 1815, thanks to her possession of the Ruhr coal fields and her pivotal position as the first line of defence against France, Prussia emerged as the strongest German power. Although the Frankfurt Assembly of 1848–1849 failed to unite Germany, Austria's refusal to participate in a *grossdeutsch* union, effectively made the *kleindeutsch* solution the only viable option for German unity. Her failure to assist Russia in the Crimean war also crucially deprived her of Russian support in the event of war against Prussia. Even so unity was by no means inevitable. Bismarck's skill and determination were of course key factors but he was assisted by the misjudgements of his opponents in Vienna and Paris, by the fluid diplomatic situation, which enabled both the Austrian and French wars to be fought in isolation and finally by the superior skills of the Prussian army, aided, of course by luck and the mistakes of their opponents.

Part Two

The Second Empire,
1871–1918

5 *Economic, Social and Cultural Transformation*

TIMELINE

1871–1873	Boom fuelled by the French indemnity and currency reform
1873	The Stock Exchange crash and beginning of the Great Depression
	The May Laws
1875	Foundation of the *Reichsbank*
1876	The Central Association of German Industrialists and League for Tax and Economic Reform founded
1878	Anti-Socialist Law
1879	General Protective Tariff introduced
1880	Industrial production sinks to the levels of 1872–1873
1884	Accident Insurance Act
1889	Old-age pensions introduced
1890	Anti-Socialist Laws lapse
1892	Hauptmann's *Die Weber* performed
1893	Agrarian League formed as a response to cuts in the grain tariffs
1894	German Women's Association set up
1895	Great Depression ends
	Wilhelm Röntgen discovers X-rays
1898	Secessionists quit the German General Art Association
1908	Women given right to attend political meetings

Introduction: problems, issues and questions

The economic transformation of modern Germany between 1870 and 1914 was both rapid and impressive. Between 1890 and 1914 the population increased from 50 to nearly 68 million people. Within a generation 'Germany passed from being Britain's favourite market to Britain's major industrial competitor'.[1] Germany developed many of the characteristics of an advanced, modern industrial society: the norms of bourgeois culture became universally accepted, except by a few *avant-garde* artists and intellectuals, women slowly started to acquire equality, and the largest labour movement in Europe, the German Social democratic Party (SPD), which was founded in 1875, began the gradual process of integrating the new working classes into German society. Yet strong pre-industrial features still survived (as indeed they did in Britain): the aristocracy – particularly the Prussian, a large rural sector and a sizeable remnant of the traditional *Mittelstand*.

The crucial question to consider is what the impact of this breakneck industrialization and urbanization on the German people was, and who were the winners and losers of this process? In the 1960s historians such as Fritz Stern, Ralph Dahrendorf and George Mosse argued that the psychological trauma of rapid industrialization led to a backlash against industrialization and the creation of the anti-modernist and anti-Semitic

völkisch: its ideology preached the creation and preservation of a traditional Germanic, national and above all racial community.

völkisch movement, which was to have a formative effect on Nazi ideology. The danger of this view is that it looks at German society and culture in the 30 years before 1914 through the lens of the Third Reich rather than studying them within the context of their times. Today cultural historians are, for instance, equally interested in the development of popular culture in Germany during this period and its influence on society.[2]

Economic developments, 1871–1913

The boom years of 1871–1873

Currency reform: Until 1871 the German states had six independent currencies. Between 1871 and 1873 the Reich introduced the new mark currency, which was based on the gold standard.

The unification of Germany triggered a short-term speculative boom. Until 1873 the economy grew at a rate of nearly 5 per cent per annum, while as many ironworks and machine manufacturing companies were set up in the period 1871–1875 as in the preceding 70 years. This spectacular expansion was facilitated by the generous credit policies of the banks, the prompt payment of the French indemnity, which was used to finance public works and above all by the inflationary effects of the **currency reform** of 1871, which added some 762,000,000 marks to the amount of free capital in the economy.

In 1872 in Prussia alone, 49 new banks were formed, among which were the two giants of the future, the *Dresdner Bank* and the *Deutsche Bank*. These channelled funds into the new **joint-stock companies**, the formation of which had been made easier by the law passed by the *Reichstag* in June 1870, but many of them lacked adequate financial backing and gambled on amassing short-term profits that would help them to build up adequate capital reserves. The easy availability of credit led to the setting up of large numbers of unsound companies, most of which went bankrupt when the Berlin stock market collapsed in the autumn of 1873 as a consequence of the financial crisis in America and the dramatic crash on the Viennese stock market.

Joint-stock companies: 1871: 207 new joint-stock companies were floated for 758 million marks

1872: 479 for 1.5 billion marks

1873: 242 for 544 million marks

The Great Depression 1873–1896

At first a backlog of railroad projects kept the economy afloat, but by 1876 falling demand hit both the textile and the engineering industries. The engineering firm, Borsig, for instance, produced 166 locomotives in 1875, but only 80 in 1876. There followed a long period of retarded or, at best, intermittent growth. It was not until 1880 that production achieved the levels of 1872–1873, but it began to falter again between 1882 and 1886. Between the autumn of 1886 and the end of 1889 there was a strong recovery when net domestic product rose on average by 4 per cent per year, but in 1890 it again went into sharp decline. It was only in 1894 that the economy at last began to experience a prolonged upturn, which continued, apart from brief recessions in 1900–1901 and in 1909, until 1913.

Although the severity of the Great Depression can be exaggerated, its economic impact was nevertheless considerable. Initially production was cut back, profits declined, the workforce was laid off, particularly in the engineering industries, and wages fell. In Berlin in 1879, for instance, 25 per cent of the industrial workers were unemployed. Only after 1880 did wages begin to creep upwards again. Inevitably once the boom broke, crisis management became the priority of the banks and industry. While before 1873 entrepreneurs were ready at least to pay lip-service to *laissez-faire* economics, the slump made them more than ready to seek protection from vicious competition in a contracting market. **Cartels**, or trusts, were founded, which fixed prices, working conditions and production, so that members would not undermine each other. In 1875 there had been only eight cartels; by 1895 this number had increased to 143 (see below).

Hans Rosenberg (1904–1988) argued that the depression helped to shift 'the centre of gravity of political agitation ... from issues of ... national unification and constitutional reconstruction ... to a crude emphasis on economic objectives'.[3] According to this view, which was to influence historians such as Hans-Ulrich Wehler and Volker Berghahn, it provided the context for German politics right up to 1914 by encouraging the emergence of interest groups, anti-Semitism and **social imperialism**. Modern economic historians are wary of attributing too much importance to the depression on the grounds that its severity was much exaggerated, but at the very least it did accelerate the creation of cartels and pressure groups and delivered a severe blow to *laissez-faire* economics.[4]

Both the industrialists and the great east Elbian estate-owners, who were facing severe competition from cheap foreign imports, founded highly effective pressure groups, which increasingly began to win the economic argument for the introduction of **tariffs**, and were an important factor in Bismarck's decision to abandon free trade in 1879 (see p. 128). Protective tariffs shielded the land owning aristocracy and German agriculture from the destructive effects of economic competition. The perceived failure of liberal *laissez-faire* economics also helped weaken political liberalism, which became associated by its critics with the excesses of free trade and **Manchesterism**. The depression galvanized the right and led to the creation of a more popularly-based conservative party, while it also played a part in bringing together the parties of the left to form the Social Democratic party (SPD) in 1875.

Cartel: a manufacturer's group set up to control and regulate production and prices

Social imperialism: a term developed in the 1960s to describe efforts by Bismarck and his successors to unite a socially divided Germany by pursuing an imperialistic foreign policy which would appeal to all Germans as nationalists

Tariffs: duties placed on imports to protect local industries and products

Manchesterism: *laissez-faire* practices as in 19th-century Britain

The Years of Prosperity, 1896–1913

The German economy emerged from the depression both transformed and strengthened. In 1873 the consumer industry had still played the dominant role, but by the mid-1890s it was heavy industry which called the tune. Organized into cartels, closely linked to the banks and with its domestic markets protected by tariffs, it had survived the recession and was far stronger in 1895 than it had been in 1873. It was able to undercut its rivals abroad by selling at 40 per cent below the prices in the domestic market.

Germany also made remarkable progress in developing the chemical, electrical and engineering industries, which were in the forefront of the second industrial revolution. At the turn of the century Germany's share in dyes accounted for 90 per cent of the world's production, while by the early 1900s it had also established a virtual world monopoly in chemicals, electrical goods and precision instruments. By 1910 the German mercantile fleet was the second largest in the world, and Germany had become the third largest creditor nation in the world. Sixty per cent of its exports went to Britain, France and Russia, and the German economic penetration of Latin America, South Africa and the Ottoman Empire created what amounted to an informal empire. In 1872 Germany's exports totalled 2,492,000,000 marks; by 1913 this had grown to 10,097,000 marks. In the dangerously polarized world of 1914 this was to make German world trade a hostage to international events.

This impressive growth was facilitated by a number of factors. The observation by the British economist Maynard Keynes that the German Empire was built more truly on coal and iron than on blood and iron certainly highlights the value of the Ruhr and Silesian coal mines and the iron ore deposits in Lorraine, the Saar and the Rhineland to the German economy. Growth was also assisted by a good transport system, the stimulation of massive urban expansion (see below), access to loans from the City of London, which together with the German banks financed the commercial development of new inventions, and not least by the new technical universities and vocational schools.

Corporate capitalism and government intervention, 1900–1914

The trend towards concentration and cartelization continued right up to the war and beyond. For instance, by 1900 the ten largest coalmining companies produced 59 per cent of Germany's coal, while the five biggest dyestuff companies were responsible for 90 per cent of Germany's total output, and by 1905 there were 350 cartels, which attempted to guarantee economic stability for their members so that businesses could rely on secure profits. In the years before 1914 the state became increasingly involved in economic policy. Here Hans-Ulrich Wehler sees 'the birth of a phenomenon of our own times' where 'under the prevailing system of state regulated capitalism political authority is chiefly legitimized by the government's concern to correct disturbances to economic growth so as to preserve the continuing stability of the economy and society'.[5] With the mark tied to the gold standard, the government could not devalue to help exports, but it could assist through tariffs, and it was also able to subsidize shipping lines and reduce freight rates for export.

Pressure groups and cooperatives

Pressure group: a group or association set up to further a particular interest by influencing government policy

A characteristic that all advanced economies shared in the years before 1914 was the emergence of pressure groups, which enjoyed close contacts with the government and the political parties. In Germany this development was particularly marked. The largest **pressure group** was the Agrarian League (see p. 133), and one of the most powerful was the heavy industrial Central Association, which was formed in 1876 to campaign for the introduction of tariffs. When this was achieved in 1879, it widened its brief to address other political and economic matters of interest to industrialists. These two organizations by no means enjoyed a monopoly of influence. The Confederation of Industrialists represented the smaller firms, while the *Hansabund* was formed in 1909 as a union of commercial, exporting and shipping interests. Interest groups representing a wide spread of commercial and white-collar interests sprang up, which in 1911 were united under an umbrella organization, the Imperial German Middle Class [*Mittelstand*] Confederation. In a period where economic issues were of increasing importance, these interest groups were able to influence public opinion, and make their views felt in the *Reichstag* through representatives in the parties closest to them or indeed directly at government level (see p. 133).

The cooperative movement

The cooperative movement also became a major economic and social force in rural Germany. In the late 1850s Hermann Schulze-Delitzsch (1808–1883) launched the cooperative movement in an attempt to turn the industrial proletariat into self-employed small entrepreneurs. This failed, but under Friedrich Raiffeisen (1818–1888) and Wilhelm Haas (1839–1913) the movement took on a fresh lease of life and by 1914 some 80 per cent of German peasant landowners were members of agricultural cooperatives. These both lent money through peasant banks and supplied the peasants with fertilizers, animal feed and modern agricultural machinery. By 1900 the cooperatives were increasingly forming regional or state organizations, which, in the words of one agricultural journalist, were strong enough to 'be a power with which other economic groups must reckon'.[6]

Social change

Rapid economic growth transformed life and conditions for the majority of the German people. Not only did the German population increase by 60 per cent between 1870 and 1914, but by 1910 roughly two-thirds of the German population lived in urban areas. Berlin and the great cities of western and central Germany acted as magnets for migrants from the rural east and south. Accelerating industrialization and urbanization created new classes, demands for equality, female emancipation and explosive pressures that threatened the Bismarckian political compromise.

Women: inequality and progress towards emancipation

Before the industrial revolution, the majority of women had worked in **cottage industries**, small workshops or on the land very much as the equals of men. Industrialization, however, did trigger an important change. It created many more jobs that did not require specific skills.

Cottage industries: businesses and carried on at home

These were for the most part given to women, who were paid less than men and whose promotion prospects remained very low indeed. Similarly, in offices and the new department stores women entered as secretaries or shop assistants with relatively restricted career prospects. Women also began to find employment in the public sector – as telephone operators, for example.[7] The large expansion in the size of the bourgeoisie and the managerial middle classes also created a great demand for female servants. Altogether in 1907 roughly 30 per cent of the total workforce was female.

The majority of women among the middle classes stayed at home in the 'private sphere', although in the case of artisans and shopkeepers, for example, wives might sometimes work behind the counter or do the accounts. The chief task of the wives of the bourgeoisie, however, was to run comparatively large households, supervise the servants and entertain for their husbands. Their domestic world was in the words of Volker Berghahn 'a world set apart from the virile ambiance of men, who engaged in business, gathered in clubs and smoke rooms, and occasionally even challenged each other to a duel'.[8]

See Document 26.2

It remained the norm for the majority of middle-class girls to prepare themselves for becoming young ladies and, eventually, wives and mothers, rather than embarking upon professional careers. Nevertheless, the big expansion in state education did open the doors to single women who wished to enter the teaching profession. By 1911 there were 24,000 women teachers, although they were paid far less than their male colleagues. Gradually, however, after 1890 an increasing but still small number of women began to sit the all-important *Abitur*, which was the basic qualification for university entrance. Saxony and Bavaria had allowed women to attend lectures even before the Empire had been founded. Only in the 1890s did the Prussian universities follow, and by 1905 some 1669 women were registered as 'auditors'. It was the south German universities, too, that first opened their doors to women as properly enrolled students. It was not until 1909 that the Prussian universities admitted women, but already by 1914 women made up 7 per cent of the total number of their students.

Right up to 1918 women were very much second-class citizens in Germany. Married women's rights to inherit property and decide the future of their children were strictly controlled by law, and in the event of divorce they lost most of their property. Neither could they vote in national elections, although in some states women with the right property qualifications were able to vote in local elections. Women were even banned from attending political meetings until 1908 despite ore perhaps even because of the precedents set in 1848 (see p. 64). This did not, however, mean that they had no collective voice in German life. The General German Association of Women had been founded before the unification of Germany and was committed to the cause of educating women. Specific professional associations for women teachers and commercial employees were founded, such as the Association of White-collar Women Workers. In 1894 the German Women's Association (BDF) was set up, which acted as an umbrella organization for 70,000 members and 137 associations. Under the leadership of Marie Stritt (1855–1928), the BDF became more radical and feminist. Not only did it demand the vote, but it also claimed full legal equality for women within marriage, equal pay, educational opportunities and abortion on demand.

In 1908 the Reich Law of Association at last gave women the right to attend political meetings and campaign politically. Paradoxically, after this concession a large number of traditionally-minded women joined the BDF. The German Evangelical Women's League, for instance, became affiliated to it, and immediately began a campaign against demands for legal abortion. Similarly, the female suffrage movement, which had originally been close to the SPD, moved closer to the National Liberals. By 1912 the BDF leadership adopted the argument that women were uniquely equipped to heal the bitter social divisions in Germany, and unite the nation into a national racial community – an attitude that was later to lead to a qualified acceptance of the Nazi regime in 1933.

The working class

The urban working class was not monolithic. Besides being composed of Germans from all over the Empire as well as immigrant Poles (see p. 114), there were also divisions between skilled and unskilled workers, and Catholics and Protestants, and, of course, men and women. Nevertheless, the great majority shared the same formative experiences of urban life. They lived in overcrowded flats and rooms in working-class ghettos in the cities; most had experienced unemployment and continued to live under the shadow of sudden redundancy. The introduction of social insurance by Bismarck in the 1880s (see p. 129), and the gradual extension of its provisions over the ensuing decades, the boom conditions for most of the period after 1895 and the slow but steady rise in wages gradually created more tolerable conditions. There was also the prospect of upward mobility. Labourers had the opportunity to become skilled workers, whose children in due course often managed to move into the lower middle classes and become white-collar workers.

The trade unions and the SPD played an increasing role in creating a working-class consciousness in Germany. Blackbourn has called the labour movement 'a fixed point in a turning world, fostering a common identity and providing – through party press, unions, cooperatives – an opportunity for working men to exercise responsibility'.[9] By 1914 there were three million trade unionists, 85 per cent of whom were members of the left-wing, free-trade unions. The SPD, the largest socialist party in the world, had nearly a million members to whom it was both an inspiration and a reassurance. In many ways the labour movement was a substitute religion and a way of life with its own socialist system of moral values, its choral societies, cycling clubs, drama groups and so on, while also offering chances of improvement through educational courses and access to lending libraries.

See Document 26.1

The old and the new *Mittelstand*

The concerns and politics of the *Mittelstand* are of great interest to historians because allegedly this was the class that provided mass support for the Nazi Party in the years 1930–1933. Many historians see the 1890s as the crucial decade in which the *Mittelstand* began to move to the right and ended up succumbing to 'Hitler's promises of social prestige and economic prosperity'.[10] This interpretation can by no means be discounted but it suffers, as James Retallack has pointed out from the use of imprecise and blanket terms, which lump the *Mittelstand* together as one monolithic class.[11]

The industrial revolution created a new middle class of white-collar employees in industry and commerce composed of foremen, clerks and petty officials. Between 1882 and 1887 their share of the workforce rose from 4.7 to 10.7 per cent. On the one hand they distanced themselves from the working classes and saw the monthly payment of their salaries and separate insurance schemes as signs of social superiority, but on the other they were critical of the apparent self-assumed superiority of the bourgeoisie and their claim to represent the nation.

The old *Mittelstand* or petty-bourgeois was essentially pre-industrial. Although the **craft trades** suffered in the depression, many managed to survive, and by 1907 the number of firms employing between one and five people still accounted for 31.2 per cent of those involved in manufacturing. Up to a point, industrialization created opportunities for small business to concentrate on specialized services. In the cutlery industry in Solingen, for instance, small workshops produced high-quality cutlery. Others, however, were not so lucky. Tailors, shoemakers, many small shopkeepers, and so on, all had difficulties in making ends meet, and were faced with the constant threat of proletarianization. Competition from larger enterprises produced a 'widespread demoralization'[12] among the old *Mittelstand* at the turn of the century, and numerous sectional organizations were set up to protect the rights of small businesses. Small businessmen and self-employed craftsmen were instinctively hostile to liberalism, which they frequently equated with 'Manchesterism', or cut throat competition, and 'Jewish capital', and had an ingrained belief that the state should support them in preserving their status.

> **Craft trades:** traditional pre-industrial trades such as weaving, baking, shoe making, carpentry, pottery, etc.

The bourgeoisie

In Wilhelmine Germany this class ran big business and staffed the professions, and its culture permeated society as a whole. It has been accused by a whole school of historians in both Germany and abroad of lacking 'a developed civic spirit',[13] of becoming feudalized and in effect through its spinelessness and failure to dominate politics, of allowing Germany by default to take its fatal *Sonderweg*. Usually these accusations are accompanied by comparisons with Britain. Yet, as British social historians have shown, the political role of the bourgeoisie in Britain, where the nobility remained influential for so long, can be exaggerated, and David Blackbourn and Geoff Eley have argued that the German bourgeoisie cannot so easily be branded as the guilty men of German history. There was, of course, intermarriage between the Prussian nobility and the grander bourgeoisie and a move by the more prosperous businessmen to buy estates from bankrupt Junkers, but this did not necessarily lead to their feudalization. After all, this pattern of intermarriage had been observable in England for centuries. The bourgeoisie in Germany certainly had a deep respect for the army and the reserve officer corps, and liked professional and academic titles and medals, but this did not, however, erode its core bourgeois philosophy: its belief in property, achievement, law and order, the importance of family and rules of conduct governing personal behaviour. In fact, important bastions of former aristocratic power like the officer corps in the army, the consular corps in the diplomatic service and the Reich and Prussian bureaucracies were gradually being taken over by the bourgeoisie.

Culturally the bourgeoisie dominated Germany. The rule of law, which enmeshed artisans, aristocrats, peasants, princes and workers, reflected bourgeois values. Zoos, museums, libraries and galleries, which were all open to the public, as well as spa resorts, the grand hotels, formal fashions, like evening dress, and fashionable restaurants were all part of the 'public sphere' created by the bourgeoisie. Blackbourn has even argued that 'the very success of a dynamic capitalist economy and a buoyant bourgeois society in Germany made political dominance in one sense less necessary'.[14]

Junkers and peasants

'Until recently German peasants and rural workers were the two most forgotten components of rural society'.[15] The same, however, could not be said about the east Elbian landowners or Junkers, who for long have been seen as undemocratic manipulators of the political process and cosseted by tariffs. They certainly exercised a power and influence far in excess of their numbers. The 1902 tariff laws protected their staple crops of rye and potatoes, while the law on entailed estates (*Fideikommis*) prevented the break-up of their family estates. In theory the three-class voting system in Prussia enabled the estate-owners in the rural districts to maximize their strength (see p. 78). However, more recent studies by James Retallack and Geoff Eley emphasize the independence of the peasantry and show that the Junkers in reality were often unable to manipulate them politically.[16] Neither do historians now treat the 'Junkers' as a monolithic class. Nipperdey makes distinctions between 'reactionary' Junkers, 'liberal conservative' Junkers, 'cabbage' Junkers and 'capitalist' Junkers, and so on.[17]

The controversial role of the Junkers in German history should not, however, divert attention from the other much larger sector of the German agrarian economy. Unlike its counterpart in Britain, German agriculture remained a powerful industry. In 1907 some 35 per cent of the economically active population still worked on the land. Almost three-quarters of the total cultivated area was in the hands of working farmers who owned anything between 25 and 50 acres. Up to a point it is possible to argue that the Junkers were supported at the expense of the rest of German agriculture in that grain tariffs hit dairy, poultry and pig farmers, who needed cheap, imported feed grain and fodder. Yet a large number of smaller farmers also benefited from protective duties, which shielded them, for example, from the economic competition of imported wine and livestock.

Superficially, German agriculture continued to prosper in the period 1870–1914. Overall food production doubled between 1870 and 1913. Agricultural colleges produced a new class of scientifically trained farm managers and farmers, which led directly to the introduction of improved seeds, crops and animal breeding, while the large east Elbian estates were becoming increasingly mechanized. Nevertheless, farmers were facing growing **structural problems**. Labour costs rose as millions quitted the land to work in heavy industry and the cities (see p. 109), and the contribution of agriculture to GNP declined from 41 to 23 per cent between 1870 and 1913. German farming enjoyed an Indian summer of prosperity, but both at home and abroad the balance was shifting against it.

Structural problems: fundamental problems which affected the very structure of the agricultural industry

The minorities

In the late 19th century, tolerance of racial or cultural minorities was not a characteristic which the fiercely nationalist nations of Europe cultivated. Thanks to the social imperialism of Bismarck and his successors, German unity was forged by reference to both external enemies and the ethnic and culturally alien 'enemy within'.

Into this category, of course, fell the Catholics, whose position in Germany and the *Kulturkampf* is dealt with in the next chapter.

Poles, Danes and Alsatians

Nationalists perceived the Poles to be the main threat to the cohesion of the German state. According to the 1910 census there was a Polish population of over three million in Prussia's four eastern provinces (see p. 12), while nearly half a million Poles lived and worked in the Ruhr. The Ruhr coal companies sent agents to recruit Polish workers and gradually a chain migration pattern developed in which women and children followed the men. In 1905, nearly 600,000 'foreigners', the majority of whom were Poles from the eastern provinces, worked in the Ruhr, the northern ports and the mines in Lorraine and central Germany. Their living conditions and treatment by employees was generally harsh. They were often housed in barracks and treated with hostility by their fellow German workers. Inevitably this pattern of east–west migration left the great estates in the east short of labour, which was remedied by recruiting seasonal labour from Russian and Austrian Poland.

Under Bismarck the Prussian government began a programme for Germanizing the eastern provinces. In 1886 the Royal Prussian Colonization Commission was set up to buy up bankrupt estates and settle German peasants on them. Over the next few years Polish was eliminated as a language of instruction in all primary schools, and state officials and conscripts of Polish origin were posted to western Germany where they could learn 'the blessings of German civilization'.[18] Bismarck and his successors underestimated the determination of the Poles to preserve their identity. The Poles, for instance, set up a Land Bank in 1889 to assist Polish farmers to buy land and pay their debts. By 1914 it was clear that Bismarck's policies had failed to change the ethnic character of the border populations in the east. Both 'nationalities were deadlocked in their competition for landowning primacy, neither one clearly winning or losing'.[19]

> In 1815 the fourth partition of Poland took place between Austria, Prussia and Russia.

The other Slavic minorities in Germany had a less developed national consciousness. The Masurians, located mostly along the southern border of East Prussia, spoke a Polish dialect, but were Protestant and loyal to the Prussian state, while the Kashubians in West Prussia were Catholics, but not ethnic Poles and had little interest in self-determination. There were, also, nearly 70,000 Slavic Sorbs in the Lausitz area between the Elbe and Oder and 121,345 Lithuanians in West Prussia (see Map 4).

In Northern Schleswig there was a population of 139,400 Danes. As with the Polish areas in eastern Germany attempts were made to Germanize the province by insisting on the teaching in schools being conducted in German. The Danish minority fought back by publishing their own papers and setting up their own cultural organizations, rather as the Poles had done in the Ruhr. Gradually, however, the majority of Danish nationalists were absorbed in the mainstream parties, particularly the SPD. In the 1912 election the Nationalists polled a mere 5.5 per cent of the votes. In Alsace-Lorraine a similar process of Germanization took place, assisted by the emigration of many French speakers over the border into France. In 1875, 77 per cent of the population still spoke French, but by 1910 the total of German speakers had risen to 87 per cent.

The Jews

In 1815 the majority of Jews in Germany were pedlars, small traders and home-workers in cottage industries. A few were also dealers and money-lenders, and an even smaller number were *Hofjuden* (court Jews) like the Rothschilds. Yet by 1871, thanks to the continuing extension of civil rights and the increasing liberation of the economy from the guilds and restrictive practices, the Jews were able to become active in trade and industry and move into the professions. Increasingly important areas for middle-class Jewish employment were trade, catering, transport, insurance and textiles, while in the professions Jews made up 6 per cent of all doctors and 15 per cent of all lawyers in Germany. In 1895, 10 per cent of all university students were Jews, yet they had considerable difficulties in gaining posts in the civil service or university teaching. Not all German Jews, however, were middle class. There was still a significant minority, composed largely of immigrants from eastern Europe – in 1910 about 20,000 – who worked in mining, construction and manufacturing.

Although some Jews merged into the German population by intermarriage, religious conversion and changing their names, the majority of German Jews wished to assimilate without giving up their religion, and increasingly saw themselves as 'German citizens of the Jewish faith'. Like most of their fellow Germans, they saw religion and civic life as two distinct areas. Yet, despite their desire to embrace German culture, anti-Semitism became increasingly more strident in the Empire. The reasons for this were an explosive cocktail of economic jealousy, extreme nationalism and the emergence of the new *völkisch* anti-modernist conservatism.

The Stock Exchange crash of 1873, by putting the spotlight on prominent Jewish bankers like the Rothschilds and Bleichröder, initially did much to fuel anti-Semitism. In 1878 the Jews were the subject of a more concentrated onslaught from Adolf Stoecker (1835–1909), a Lutheran pastor and court chaplain, whose Christian Social Party became openly hostile to the Jews and accused them of being a 'people within a people'. Throughout the 1880s there were further attacks from pamphleteers like Wilhelm Marr (1819–1904) and Otto Böckel (1859–1923). In the 1890s, immigration of eastern European Jews, whom Treitschke, the high-profile Berlin history professor (see p. 5), characterized as 'the multitudes of assiduous trouser selling youths from the inexhaustible cradle of Poland',[20] caused considerable concern and was one of the reasons why the anti-Semitic parties managed to win 16 seats in the *Reichstag* in the 1893 elections.

The tide of anti-Semitism did begin to ebb in the first decade of the new century, and the number of anti-Semitic deputies fell to seven in 1912, but the combination of racism and eugenics gave it a new twist. The popularizer of these ideas was the Anglo-German Houston Stewart **Chamberlain**, who, in his two-volume *Foundations of the Nineteenth Century*, equated the 'superiority' of the German race to their racial purity. His arguments that the real threat to this 'superiority' came from the Jews were to be employed by the Nazis later.

Chamberlain, 1855–1927, was the son of a British admiral. He became a German citizen and a great admirer of the composer, Wagner, whose daughter he married.

The emancipation of the Jews in Germany 1815–1869

In 1820 there were 270,000 Jews living in what later became the German Empire and a further 85,000 in the Austrian territories of the Confederation. By 1871 the former figures had increased to 512,000, and the latter to 200,000. It was only after 1850 that migration into the cities began. In Berlin, for instance, the Jewish population rose from 5645 in 1837 to 36,000 in 1866. Under the impact of the French occupation the Jews were emancipated in Westphalia and Hesse in 1808 and Frankfurt in 1811. Prussia followed suit in 1812 (see p. 17). Elsewhere emancipation was a long, drawn-out process and finally completed in the 1860s. Jews received legal equality in Bavaria in 1861, Württemberg in 1861–1864, Baden in 1862, Austria in 1867 and the North German Confederation in 1869.

Imperial Germany differed fundamentally from the Third Reich. It ultimately accepted that the Jews were German citizens. During the anti-Semitic riots in Neustettin (1881), Xanten (1891) and Constance (1900) the state authorities did not hesitate to use troops to restore order and hand out stiff punishments to rioters. The young Jewish businessman and polymath, Walter Rathenau (1867–1922), argued with some exaggeration that the Jews 'as an alien secluded race in the middle of German life' were only saved from destruction by the power of the law 'holding in check all natural violence'.[21]

The Sinti and Roma

The **Sinti** and **Roma** (see p. 261), who numbered a mere 2000 in 1900, were the smallest of the ethnic groups in Germany. Their traditional pre-industrial customs and itinerant life both alienated and alarmed the settled majority and state authorities, who frequently referred to the 'gypsy plague'. They were subjected to harassment by philanthropic organizations, such as the 'Mission for South East Europe' and put under pressure by the state to abandon their nomadic life. It was, for instance, made obligatory for traveller's children to attend school in 1899. Also, great efforts were made to expel foreign travellers, who frequently crossed over the Austrian and Russian frontiers into the Empire.

See Document 27

Sinti and **Roma:** travellers who first came to Germany from the Punjab in the 15th century

Cultural developments

The great events of 1870 were not immediately mirrored in the work of contemporary artists, writers and composers. Gordon Craig, for instance, has pointed out that as 'the infrastructure of the new Reich was being laid, German artists were writing about times infinitely remote, or filling their canvasses with tritons and nereids (sea nymphs) and Greek columns'. Even the contemporary work of Richard Wagner, the composer, whose work is so often seen as expressing the new German nationalism, seemed to have 'only the remotest connection with the society in which he lived'.[22] Yet the demand for official portraits of German worthies and the depiction of great historical scenes inevitably created a lucrative market for artists. Anton von Werner's (1843–1915) paintings of battles and ceremonies were particularly popular, and when he was made Director of the Royal Institute of Fine Arts in Berlin, he became the most influential artist in Germany. Conventional sculpture also enjoyed immense popularity, especially after 1890, as there was an insatiable demand for monuments celebrating the unification of Germany and statues of Bismarck, the 'Iron Chancellor'.

For the most part German fiction in the Bismarckian period also intended to be morally 'uplifting' and avoided contentious subjects, although a few writers like Theodor Fontane (1819–1898), Wilhelm Raabe (1831–1916) and Max Kretzer (1854–1941) did explore more profound

See Document 28

issues. Historical novels were popular, as were novels and short stories set predominantly in Germany's rural backwaters. Theodor Storm (1817–1888), who lived most of his life in Husum on the North Sea coast, was one of the leading writers of this genre with his tales set in north-west Germany.

By the early 1890s, however, German and indeed European culture had reached a turning point. What the cultural historian Peter Gay has called a revolution 'transformed culture in all its branches. It utterly changed painting, sculpture and music ... A very troop of masters compelled Western civilization to alter its angle of vision, and to adopt a new aesthetic sensibility, new philosophical style, a new mode of understanding social life and human nature'.[23] In Germany the manifestations of these changes soon became clear. The *Free Stage* theatre company, directed by Otto Brahm (1856–1912), and supported by iconoclastic intellectuals like Theodor Wolff and Maximilian Harden (1861–1946), began to produce a series of naturalist plays such as Gerhardt Hauptmann's (1862–1946) *Before Sunrise*, which dealt with alcoholism, immorality and cupidity, and *The Weavers*, a dramatized account of the sufferings of the handloom weavers in Silesia in 1844. A few years later Frank Wedekind (1864–1918) was able to deal on the stage with hitherto taboo questions such as murder, masturbation, homosexuality and prostitution.

See Document 12

The art scene also experienced dramatic upheaval. Both in Berlin and Munich artists rebelled against the conservative art establishment and seceded from the Association of German Artists. In Berlin in 1898 a group of the modernists, including Max Liebermann (1847–1936), Max Slevogt (1868–1932), Lovis Corinth (1856–1925) and Käthe Kollwitz (1867–1945), challenged the Association by holding an independent exhibition of art. In due course the Secessionists, as they called themselves, broke into rival groups, the most famous of which were the *Blaue Reiter* and *Die Brücke*.

Literature and poetry ceased to give a uniform message. Some poets and writers like Stefan George (1868–1933) advocated the retreat to the inner self, while others, like Thomas Mann (1875–1955) in *Buddenbrooks*, explored the fragility of the bourgeois world, or else like his brother, Heinrich Mann (1871–1951), Carl Sternheim (1878–1942) and Ludwig Thoma (1867–1941), the hypocrisy of Wilhelmine Germany. This message of increasing diversity and uncertainty was reinforced by contemporary science. The work of Heinrich Hertz (1857–1894) on electric waves, Wihelm Röntgen (1845–1923) on X-rays and Einstein's potentially revolutionary idea that radiation consisted of totally independent particles of energy destroyed the old ideas of a static universe and led to questioning whether there were actually any laws of nature. Like the writers and artists, scientists were coming to the conclusion that everything was relative.

See Document 28

These literary and artistic experiments were not widely understood by the general public. William II who showed great interests in modern developments in science and engineering, lost few opportunities to denounce modern art as 'loathsome'[24] or un-German, and the authorities at his instigation attempted to stop the Secessionists' work being exhibited at the 1904 World Fair in St Louis, USA. The Kaiser and the traditionalists were, however, fighting a losing battle. The *Reichstag* condemned his meddling, and in the words of the SPD deputy, Paul Singer, (1844–1911) declined 'to have a republic of the arts with William II at its head'.[25] Above all, two factors combined to defeat efforts by the artistic establishment to suppress the modernist movement: the federal nature of Germany ensured that if pressure on an artist or director of an art gallery in Berlin, for example, became too intimidating, Munich, Stuttgart or Dresden might well be more accommodating and, similarly, playwrights could circumvent a ban on their work by having it performed privately.

Critics from the right

The fiercest critics of Imperial Germany came from the right. By far the greatest, although most misunderstood, of these was the philosopher Friedrich Nietzsche (1844–1900). In his brilliant, colourful and pithy style he mocked the pretensions of Imperial Germany. As early as 1873 he warned that the consequences of the military victories of 1870–1871 were 'capable of converting our victory into a complete defeat: the defeat, even the death of German culture for the benefit of the German empire'.[26] He bitterly denounced the philistinism of Germany and the soulless process of mass education. Although Nietzsche himself was not a nationalist or anti-Semite, in the 1890s he became a cult figure of the new anti-modernist, *völkisch* ideology and was celebrated for his anti-modernism and cult of the heroic individual.

The most influential member of this new ideology was Paul de Lagarde (1827–1891), who focused his attack on both the materialism and the creeping liberalism of the Bismarckian Reich. He argued that German society could only be revived by purging it of the Jews and liberalism, and by creating a new conservative nobility. Simultaneously he advocated German domination of central Europe. The anti-modernist message was further developed by Julius Langbehn (1851–1907) in his book *Rembrandt Als Erzieher* (*Rembrandt as Educator*). Rembrandt was depicted as an ideal figure of a golden era, whose values would serve as a model for the new Germany. Fritz Stern argues strongly that these critics developed an ideology, which not only 'resembled National Socialism but which the National Socialists themselves acknowledged as an essential part of their legacy'.[27]

Collectively these romantic anti-modernist critics helped spread the sort of mystical and exaggerated nationalism which Hitler was later to exploit. However, how widespread was the philosophy of what Stern calls 'cultural despair'? It certainly had a profound impact on the German youth movement, the **Wandervögel**, and on contemporary *Gymnasien* and university students. David Blackbourn suggests that, not surprisingly,

Wandervögel
('birds of passage'):
German youth
movement
composed mainly
of Gymnasien
students who
sought to escape
from the discipline
of school and dull-
ness of city life by
walking and
camping in the
remote German
countryside. For a
time they even
called their founder,
Karl Fischer, the
Führer and greeted
him with cries of
'*Heil*!'

it was more strongly shared by the intellectuals and university educated upper middle classes than by businessmen, engineers and scientists, although Walther Rathenau (see above), a dynamic financier and busi-nessman also fancied himself as a prophet of despair. Among the German bourgeoisie a much milder version of this dramatic cosmic despair was the apprehensive reaction, which could also be found among their British counterparts, to the rapid urbanization of Germany and a corresponding tendency to romanticize rural life. This did not, of course, prevent pride in the great achievements of German science and industry – the very symbols of modernity.[28]

Conclusion

The Empire is a paradoxical period in German history. In so many areas it witnessed the breakthrough to modernity. From being a late developer in the first industrial revolution, Germany became a pioneer of the second industrial revolution. Similarly, its artists, writers and scientists were busy setting the intellectual agenda for most of the rest of the 20th century, while its workers had organized the largest and most effective socialist party in Europe. Bismarck had also laid the foundations for a welfare state, which other nations were to emulate years later. All these factors made it the most modern state in Europe, yet, as is explored in the next chapter, many historians argue that these achievements were to a great extent nullified by what Wolfgang Mommsen called the 'basic mis-match between economic change on the one hand and developments in the political sphere on the other.'[29]

6 Domestic Politics from Bismarck to Bethmann Hollweg

Introduction: problems, issues and questions

It is not surprising that the Second Empire is analysed so intensely by modern historians to see whether it was during those years that the seeds of the Nazi takeover in 1933 were sown. Hitler, of course, claimed to be the heir of Bismarck, but he was critical of his failure to deal with the 'Jewish problem' and the moderation of his foreign policy after 1871. The Nazi era and defeat in 1945 inevitably encouraged a reappraisal of Bismarck's record. The venerable German historian Meinecke (1862–1954) questioned 'whether the germs of later evil (Nazism) were not already present in the Bismarckian Reich',[1] but with the exception of Erich Eyck, whose biography of Bismarck was published in Switzerland during the Second World War, most of his colleagues agreed with S. A. Kaehler in 1946 that any attempt to link Bismarck with Hitler was 'legend and propaganda', but foreign historians were not so convinced. Otto Pflanze, the later author of an authoritative three-volume study of Bismarck, argued for instance in 1955 that, there is 'a line of development from Bismarck through Ludendorff to Hitler'.[2] It was, however, Fritz Fischer's seminal study of German war aims (see p. 164) and the emergence of the **structuralists** of the **Bielefeld School** that led to a radical reappraisal of the Second Empire. The doyen of the Bielefeld historians, Hans-Ulrich Wehler,[3] argues that Bismarck's deliberate decision to stop Germany from developing into a constitutional state through his skilful manipulation of the political parties, social imperialism, plebiscitary elections and negative integration tactics set Germany on the *Sonderweg* that led ultimately to the Third Reich. If this is true, Bismarck bears a particularly heavy responsibility for the course of subsequent German history. These arguments have not gone unchallenged. Detailed research into local German history by British historians, Richard Evans, David Blackbourne and Geoff Eley, and the American Margaret Anderson, considerably modifies the picture of a passive people ruthlessly manipulated by Bismarck and the Prusso-German elites. Blackbourne points out that the bourgeoisie 'in practice … occupied a dominant position' in the Second Empire (see p. 113). Eley also questions the *Sonderweg* theory by arguing that the 'very modernity' of the Second Empire with its universal male franchise for elections to the *Reichstag* and first class welfare, local administrative and educational systems made further democratization for the time being unnecessary.[4] Arguably, however, the Empire's root problem was structural. Its government was not responsible to parliament and its ministers were appointed by the Kaiser and not elected. Therein lay the cause of much of the political difficulties confronting the Empire after 1890.

Structuralists: historians, who apply a structural analysis to history. This plays down the role of the individual and places more emphasis on the influence of the economy and other factors such as the political structure of the state.

Bielefeld school of historiography: This school, based at Bielefeld University, where H.-J. Wehler was professor of history (1971–1996), is one of the leading structuralist centres in Germany.

See Document 20

The constitutional context

It took time for the new Germany to develop into a national state. When the German Empire was formed, the North German Confederation was merely adapted to absorb the south German states. It continued, in Wolfgang Mommsen's words to be a 'system of skirted decisions',[5] which protected the predominance of Prussia, while temporarily, at least, satisfying the National Liberals and appeasing the south German states. Jonathan Steinberg has observed that 'the entire period from 1866 to 1890 is one long institutional tinkering'.[6] The Empire contained many of the characteristics of a parliamentary regime. It was a constitutional state with a parliament elected by universal franchise and vigorous political parties. On the other hand, 'such outward liberalism was … deceptive, the document upon which the whole legal framework rested was not a constitution in the normal sense of the word, but rather took the form of a treaty of 25 sovereign states for the ordering of their common affairs'.[7] This accounted for the structure of its upper house, the *Bundesrat* or federal council, where the federal states were represented by diplomats rather than politicians, as they had been in the Confederation. A considerable amount of legislation was delegated to the state governments, whose existing and often conservative constitutions were not affected by unification. The constitution could theoretically still be abrogated by the sovereigns of the German states and consequently the recurring threats of a *coup d'état* made by Bismarck or William II were in the final analysis quite possible and hung like the 'sword of Damocles over German political life'.[8]

> **Skirted decisions:** decisions that avoid the main problems

Bismarck disliked the idea of collective government and consequently no proper Reich cabinet existed. In 1867 he had set up the chancellor's office which, over the next decade, he expanded into eight separate imperial departments: the Foreign Office, the Treasury, the Interior Office, the Admiralty, Posts and Telegraphs, and the offices for Alsace-Lorraine, the railways and judicial affairs. These departments, however, never met as a cabinet, but were coordinated by an imperial Chancellery, headed by Rudolf Delbrück through which Bismarck communicated his instructions to all departments except for the Foreign Office, which reported directly to him. The real expression of German unity was the *Reichstag*, which represented the whole nation. It had the right to veto legislation and could even propose legislation, but it could not dissolve itself or force the chancellor to resign. Bismarck held the view that the *Reichstag* was a body which should react to events rather than initiate them. In other words, as he observed in 1884, 'it should ... prevent bad laws from being passed ... and the waste of public money; but it cannot govern'.[9] In practice, however, the power of the *Reichstag* turned out to be greater than Bismarck had envisaged. With the emergence of mass parties like the Catholic Centre party and the SPD, he became increasingly afraid that it would develop into the dominant organ in the constitution. In 1867 the Pomeranian Junker, Alexander von Below, had warned him about the unpredictability of democratically elected parliaments by pointing out that 'it's impossible to win a battle of Königgrätz before every election'![10]

Although Prussia controlled only 19 out of the 58 seats in the *Bundesrat*, and could theoretically be outvoted by a combination of the southern states, in reality its size, wealth and power placed it in a category of its own. It controlled 65 per cent of the territory of the Empire and 62 per cent of the population. The historian, Arthur Rosenberg, described the *Bundesrat* 'as the constitutional fig leaf of Prussian rule over the Empire',[11] as it disguised the reality of Prussian power in the Reich:

- The chancellor, as the Prussian minister-president, presided over the *Bundesrat*.
- Prussia provided most of the officials who worked in the new central agencies under Delbrück, which further strengthened its position within the Empire.
- The Reich was also dependent on Prussia financially since the central government had very limited powers of taxation and relied on grants from the federal states.

- Militarily Prussian hegemony was absolute; the Prussian General Staff took over the role of strategic planning for the German land forces and the Prussian minister of war was also the Reich minister for war.

The head of the nation and president of the federation of German princes was the *Deutscher Kaiser* (German emperor), the King of Prussia, whose formal powers remained considerable. He was theoretically in control of the nation's foreign policy. He appointed the chancellor and the members of the Reich civil and foreign services, and he was also supreme commander of the armies of all the German states, except Bavaria, Saxony and Württemberg although in wartime their army also came under Prussian control. Both the civil and military cabinets were responsible to him rather than parliament.[12]

In essence the new Reich could only function effectively if there was close cooperation between the Prussian and Reich administrations. In 1872 Bismarck briefly resigned his post as Prussian minister-president, but he quickly discovered that this led to such friction between the Reich and Prussia that he resumed it after only 5 months. As long as Bismarck remained chancellor, he was able to hold the federal structure of the Empire together, but the danger remained that a future German chancellor would be confronted by the conflicting pressures of a conservative Prussia where the three-class voting system ensured after 1878 thanks to the decline of the liberals a large conservative majority in the *Landtag*, and a more left-wing *Reichstag* voted in on universal franchise.

The Liberal era, 1871–1878

A. J. P. Taylor observed that it was hard to judge whether between 1871 and 1877 'Bismarck or the National Liberals determined the character of German policy'.[13] Both they and to a lesser extent the Progressives were his natural allies and worked closely with him in the task of creating the necessary administrative and legal infrastructure for the new Empire. The Conservatives believed that Bismarck had become 'the lackey of Liberalism',[14] but in fact the limits of the Liberals' influence were shown whenever Bismarck's intentions diverged from their own. For instance they failed to defeat an authoritarian press law which gave the government the power to imprison newspaper editors for publishing sensitive information and agreed to a septennial (*Septennat*) rather than an annual military budget.

The *Kulturkampf*

In 1871, some 36 per cent of the population of the Empire was Catholic. In Bavaria, Baden, Alsace-Lorraine, the Rhineland as well as in West Prussia, Silesia and Posen they were in the majority. In the latter three provinces the vast majority of Catholics were also part of an ethnic minority – the Poles. Catholics were underrepresented in the professions, the higher ranks of the army and bureaucracy in the new Empire, but overrepresented among the small self-employed rural and urban artisans. The Protestants dominated the Empire as a whole. The whole tradition of German liberalism was also essentially anti-Catholic and many of the leading liberals were sons of Protestant priests. In Margaret Anderson's words: 'the historiography they learned at their mothers' knees depicted Luther as a national and liberal as well as a religious hero'.[15]

Initially in 1870 German Catholics had welcomed the defeat of France and the unification of Germany, but to protect Catholic cultural and religious interests in a context of strident Protestant-dominated nationalism they founded the Catholic Centre Party in December 1870, which was led by the formidable Ludwig Windthorst (1812–1891), the former Minister of Justice in Hanover. To the Liberals the Catholic Centre Party was a Trojan horse in the new and predominantly Protestant Germany, as it attracted those who remained sceptical about Prussian-led *Kleindeutschland* – the potential or actual *Reichsfeinde*, especially the Poles and the Alsatians.

Already in the 1860s a *Kulturkampf* had broken out in Baden with the Catholic Church over the control of elementary education. The Papacy had also contributed to the growing polarization between Protestants and Catholics by promulgating first in 1864 the *Syllabus Errorum*, which condemned the very doctrines liberals believed essential for a free society, and then in 1870, the doctrine of **Papal infallibility**. Tension between liberal nationalism and Catholicism was intensified by the **occupation of Rome** and its annexation by Italy in September 1870. The Pope bitterly rejected any offers of compensation from the Italian state and forbade devout Catholics from playing any official role in the state. The battle lines between liberalism and Catholicism had now been drawn. In France, Italy, Germany, Austria and any country where there was a substantial Catholic population a domestic *Kulturkampf* was waged over what Steinberg calls the 'apparatus of daily life', that is education, the organization of hospitals (should, for instance, the nurses be nuns?), divorce and marriage laws and the whole charitable status of churches, convents and monasteries.[16]

The image of the Centre Party as an 'international agent' of Catholicism appeared to be confirmed in the eyes of Liberals and Conservatives when the party asked the emperor in February 1871 to restore the temporal power of the papacy in Rome, a request which was rejected. The strength of anti-Catholicism in Germany was revealed when in early April a Centre motion to include the basic civil rights of freedom of speech, of assembly, of the press and of belief and scientific research, all of which were in fact tenets of liberalism in the new imperial constitution, was rejected by an overwhelming majority of 223 to 59 composed for the most part of liberals.

To what extent did Bismarck genuinely share the fears and anti-Catholic prejudices of his fellow Protestants? In the autumn of 1870 when Italian troops had occupied Rome, he had considered briefly the

Reichsfeinde: literally enemies of the Reich, that is those Germans who were sceptical about the social and political structure of Bismarckian Germany

Kulturkampf: a struggle between cultures. A term used to describe Bismarck's conflict with the Catholic Church, 1871–1887.

Papal infallibility: the doctrine that the Pope when acting in his role as the leader of the Catholic Church, is prevented by God from any chance of theological error

Occupation of Rome: Until 1870 Rome was independent of the Italian state and ruled by the Pope.

See Document 29

diplomatic advantages of offering the Pope refuge in Germany,[17] but a year later he gave government support to the waging of a bitter *Kulturkampf* in Prussia. Why was this? The Bielefeld school of historiography argues that this was a classic example of Bismarck's technique of negative integration, whereby he hoped to unite the Protestant majority in Germany against the Catholic 'enemy' within, while deflecting the Liberals from pursuing awkward questions about the liberty of the individual and constitutional reform. Bismarck certainly exploited the political advantages of the *Kulturkampf*, but this underestimates both his very real concern that the Centre Party would rally the *Reichsfeinde* and his hatred of Ludwig Windthorst, its leader and the former Minister of Justice in Hanover.

Recusant: those who refuse to comply with a law or regulation

As education and religious affairs were the responsibilities of the states rather than of the Reich, the *Kulturkampf* was waged principally by the Prussian, Baden and Hesse-Darmstadt governments. The most important elements in the Prussian *Kulturkampf* were the two May Laws of 1873 and 1874. In Prussia the May Law of 1873 extended state control over Catholic theological colleges, set up a Royal Tribunal for Ecclesiastical Affairs and allowed provincial governors to veto the appointment of parish priests. A year later further legislation sanctioned the confiscation of church properties and the imprisonment of **recusant** bishops. The Catholic lawyer and writer, Julius Bachem (1858–1945), admittedly with some exaggeration, compared the *Kulturkampf* to the **'Diocletian Persecution'** of the early Christians.[18] Nevertheless for the Catholics the May Laws of 1873 turned Prussia into a police state until they were repealed in the late 1880s. In the first 4 months of 1875, for instance, 241 clergy and 136 newspaper editors were fined or jailed.

Diocletian Persecution: Bachem is referring to the persecutions carried out during the reign of Roman Emperor, Diocletian, AD 284–385.

See Document 29

While these laws strengthened liberal support for the government, Bismarck failed to destroy the Centre Party. Windthorst successfully encouraged the Catholic voters to make the election 'a great plebiscite' against the *Kulturkampf*, and in 1874 won 91 seats. The growth of the party was visible evidence that Bismarck had suffered the first significant defeat of his political career.

The change of course

Between 1874 and 1878 Bismarck's government faced mounting challenges both at home and abroad. Politically he had failed to defeat the Centre Party, and his apparent dependence on the National Liberals was alienating the Prussian conservatives and indeed the emperor, on whom ultimately Bismarck was dependent for power. Even his relationship with the National Liberals was bedevilled by what Lothar Gall calls 'subliminal mistrust'.[19] Under the influence of Eduard Lasker (1829–1884) the National Liberals were moving leftwards, and had opposed both Bismarck's Press law of 1874 and attempted unsuccessfully to give the *Reichstag* the power to vote annually on a military budget.

The stock exchange crash of 1873 and the subsequent depression (see p. 106) also began to transform the political situation. As the Liberals were closely identified with *laissez-faire*, free trade and industrialization, they were made 'to bear responsibility', as James Sheehan has observed, 'for what various groups did not like about the contemporary world'.[20] In the election of 1877 the National Liberals lost 27 seats, while the new German Conservative Party which supported the introduction of tariffs nearly doubled its seats from 22 to 40.

The depression caused a crisis in the Reich's finances. The decline in industrial production led to a steep fall in tax receipts, which the central government received from the individual states. Bismarck initially hoped to open up new sources of revenue by nationalizing the highly profitable railway companies, but this was opposed by Bavaria, Saxony and Würt-temberg. Similarly, an increase in indirect taxation on tobacco, sugar and brandy was opposed by the Liberal parties as it would entail a lessening of parliamentary control over the budget.

By the end of 1877 the intensification of the Balkan crisis risked a Russo-Austria war, which would force Germany to choose between Russia and Austria (see p. 146), while at home Bismarck had failed to persuade the Emperor to sack a potential rival Albrecht von Stosch (1818–1896), the head of the newly created German Admiralty. The gov-ernment appeared to be increasingly 'boxed in' by problems,[21] and it even seemed that the end of the Bismarck era was approaching. Bismarck explored several possibilities to strengthen his government. Initially he attempted to win over the more moderate National Liberals by offering their leader, Rudolf von Bennigsen (1824–1902), the position of Prussian minister of the interior with the intention of forcing them to share responsibility for the government of the Empire. The manoeuvre failed when the National Liberals demanded two further seats in the cabinet, a request which, given Williams' suspicions of the Liberals, was out of the question.

A more radical alternative was opened up on the death of Pope Pius IX in early February. His successor, Leo XIII (1810–1903), was anxious to end the *Kulturkampf*, which opened up to Bismarck the possibility of a new political alignment in which the Centre and Conservatives instead of the Liberals became the government's allies. Shortly after Leo had made diplomatic contact with the Emperor, Bismarck announced in the *Reichsrat* the creation of a government tobacco monopoly, a policy bit-terly opposed by the Liberal free traders, but supported by the Centre. Bismarck also made it clear that this was a first step towards the introduc-tion of tariffs, which would place the Empire's finances on much sounder foundations.

To ensure the passage of a tariff bill through the *Reichstag* Bismarck needed drastically to weaken the National Liberals, while building up an alliance with the Centre – if at all possible – and the Conservatives. His opportunity came when on 11 May 1878 there was an attempted assassi-nation of the emperor, which was at first thought to be a socialist plot.

Assassination attempts: the first was carried out by a mentally ill plumber's apprentice; the second one was attempted by Doctor Karl Nobiling (1848–1878), an expert on soil and crop production, whose chief aim was self-publicity.

See Document 30 for the Anti-Socialist Law

Bismarck immediately introduced an anti-socialist bill into the *Reichstag* with the intention of not only weakening the Social Democratic Party but also of creating tension between the left and right wings of the National Liberal Party, but it was overwhelmingly defeated. Then on 2 June another **assassination attempt** on William provided Bismarck with the opportunity to call a crisis election, which enabled the Conservatives to make considerable gains at the expense of the Liberals. In return for limiting the initial period of the proposed anti-socialist law, which would ban socialist meetings and publications and empower the authorities to imprison or fine socialist 'agitators' the National Liberals, despite considerable reservations, were prepared to join the Conservatives in voting for the bill.

The introduction of tariffs

In the spring of 1879 Bismarck then asked the *Reichstag* to approve legislation for levying tariffs on iron, iron goods and grain, and indirect taxes on salt, coffee, tobacco and selected luxury goods. The National Liberals were now prepared to support the bill only if the *Reichstag* could determine the salt tax and coffee duties annually, but Bismarck rejected this outright, as it would have entailed strengthening parliamentary control over the Empire's finances. He therefore had little option but to renew negotiations with the Centre. In the interests of the farming lobby in his own party, Windthorst was ready to back protection, but he was under pressure to indicate that this did not entail general support for Bismarck, the hated perpetrator of the *Kulturkampf*. Nor indeed did he wish to make the government more independent financially of the federal states. Bismarck, therefore, had no option but to accept a proposal which strengthened German federalism, from the Bavarian Centre deputy, Georg von Frankenstein (1825–1890). According to this only a fixed percentage of the income from the new duties would be allocated to the Empire, while the rest would go to the states, which would continue to make their annual budgetary contributions to the Empire. Consequently in July 1879 a Conservative–Centre majority, joined by 15 right-wing National Liberals, approved the bill. Ironically the Centre, as Windthorst remarked, had become the liquidator of the 'bankruptcy of the liberal Economy'.[22]

The 'second founding' of the Reich

To historians like Helmut Böhme, who view Bismarck's policies 'through the lens of economic interest',[23] 1879 is a more important turning point than 1871. Bismarck had in effect refounded the Empire, and set it on a conservative course. He had gained, as the French ambassador observed, 'one of the most substantial triumphs of his career'[24] and the long-term consequences of this were to influence the Empire until 1918. The new tariff policy marked a real shift to the right and brought together the alliance of 'iron and grain' that was to play a key role in German politics.

Bismarck had, however, failed to make the Empire financially independent of the German states, and, despite the temporary majority for tariffs, he had also lost control of the *Reichstag* until 1887. Bismarck's calculation that the National Liberals would split and that the majority would rally behind the government did not immediately work out. In 1880 the party did indeed split but in the 1881 election the breakaway group under Lasker, the Secessionists, won almost as many seats as the National Liberal Party itself. Inevitably, the political realignments of 1878–1880 strengthened the position of the Centre in the *Reichstag*, but Bismarck was not able to end the *Kulturkampf* immediately and turn the Centre into an ally. He attempted to make concessions on the May Laws but in July 1880 the Conservatives and National Liberals deleted key provisions, which would have allowed the Prussian government to pardon exiled bishops. Windthorst also skilfully blocked attempts by Bismarck to appeal to the right wing of his party by annually submitting to the *Landtag* a proposal for exempting the administration of the sacraments from criminal prosecution, which would have made the May Laws unenforceable. In the election of 1881 Bismarck suffered a major defeat, when over three-quarters of the newly-elected *Reichstag* were opposed to the government. For the next 5 years all Bismarck's bluster and threats could not hide the fact that he had lost control of the *Reichstag*. The American historian, Enno Kraehe, observed that Bismarck's predicament reminded him 'less of an Iron Age Chancellor than [the then American President] George Bush facing a Democratic Congress on the defense budget'.[25]

Defending the fragile structure of the Empire from corrosive change became a 'labour of Sisyphus',[26] which increasingly involved escalating attacks against the Social Democrats, **'Bonapartist' plebiscitary elections**, imperialist diversions in Africa and attempts to weaken the *Reichstag*. Bismarck sought to neutralize the Social Democrats both by renewing the Anti-Socialist Law, and by seeking to integrate the workers into what Otto Pflanze called a 'German national consensus based on the Prussian–German establishment'[27] through his pioneering welfare measures. Of course these welfare reforms were 'of limited value', as Lynn Abrams has argued.[28] For instance only 10 per cent of sickness and accident claims were successful. Yet Bismarck's welfare measures gave Germany the 'first modern social welfare service in the world' and by any assessment was 'a significant achievement'.[29] The Accident Insurance Bill of 1881 was closely based on proposals made by August Bebel, the leader of the SPD, in 1879. Initially Bismarck intended that the employers should pay two-thirds of the premiums and the employees a third, while the state would also make a considerable contribution. The state subsidy was of particular importance for he hoped to win over the working class with it. In the *Reichstag*, however, it was opposed by both the Centre and the National Liberals who voted against the state contribution, and the SPD itself, which was reluctant to accept reforms from the

See Document 20

'Bonapartist' plebiscitary elections: 'single issue' elections based on the precedent set by Napoleon III's plebiscites

See Document 20

Corporatism:
the process of integrating both workers and employers, organized in groups, into the administration and government of the state

hated Bismarck. In 1883–1884 the *Reichstag* did approve both a health insurance bill and an amended accident insurance bill, which had no state subsidies. Into the administration of both schemes Bismarck introduced an element of **corporatism**: health insurance was to be administered by local health committees which were elected by employers and workers, while the accident insurance scheme was organized by the employers, divided into groups according to industries. Bismarck hoped that these novel corporate associations would create the basis for a future body that could eventually replace the *Reichstag*, even if this had to be carried out by a *coup d'état*.[30] In 1889 Bismarck completed his welfare legislation with the introduction of the old-age pension. Here there is clear evidence that Bismarck had been influenced by Napoleon III, as he told the *Reichstag* 'that the attachment of most Frenchmen to the government ... is mainly connected with the fact that most Frenchmen are state pensioners'.[31]

Despite these measures Bismarck failed signally to prevent the steady rise of the SPD. In the 1884 election it managed to increase its seats to 24, which entitled it to regular representation on the *Reichstag* committees, and by 1890, 30 SPD delegates sat in the *Reichstag*. On the other hand, this did encourage the National Liberals to cooperate more closely with Bismarck and the Conservatives. In 1884 the south German National Liberals at a congress in Heidelberg unequivocally accepted Bismarck's welfare and tariff policies, and in the election of that year the Progressive vote markedly declined. Bismarck's expansionary policy in Africa and South East Asia (see pp. 149–150) also attracted the National Liberals and led to their close cooperation on the colonial question.

Nevertheless, even though the underlying trend of the 1884 election was favourable, Bismarck still faced an unmanageable *Reichstag*, and by 1886 he was ready to seize any opportunity to dissolve it at an opportune moment. His chance came with the potentially dangerous combination of the Bulgarian crisis and the rise of Boulanger in France (see p. 150). Bismarck immediately brought forward the *Septennat* and demanded a 10 per cent increase in the size of the army. When the Progressives and the Centre tried to reduce the period covered by the grant, Bismarck contemptuously dismissed their efforts to compromise and dissolved the *Reichstag* in January 1887. During the subsequent election campaign he did all he could to create an atmosphere of crisis, and his machinations were rewarded by the election of a parliament in which the pro government *Kartell* (bloc) composed of Free Conservatives, Conservatives and National Liberals won a clear majority, enabling him to pass the *Septennat*. However, within the *Kartell* there were tensions between the National Liberals and Conservatives over tariffs. Neither did the National Liberals give up their attempts to push Bismarck into making further constitutional concessions. In 1889 Bennigsen proposed the appointment of a Reich minister of finance responsible to the *Reichstag*. As a possible future alternative to the *Kartell*, Bismarck worked for a rapprochement with the Centre, which became possible once the **second 'peace bill'** in April 1887 effectively ended the *Kulturkampf*.

The second 'peace bill', which extended the concessions granted by the first 'peace bill' of 1885, allowed several bishoprics to reopen seminaries, although the Polish bishoprics of Ermland, Kulm and Gnesen-Posen were excluded. It also allowed the readmission into Prussia of the contemplative, charitable and pastoral orders at the discretion of the Prussian cultural ministry.

The accession of William II and Bismarck's downfall

In March 1888 the old Emperor died. If his heir, Crown Prince Frederick, had survived, Bismarck would eventually have been replaced by a more liberal chancellor, although this would not have been easy, as Bismarck would have fought every inch of the way and would have skilfully rallied public opinion against Frederick. The Crown Prince was seen as an Anglophile hen-pecked husband dominated by his English wife, Victoria, who apparently wished to convert the Empire to Gladstonian liberalism. Bismarck had already skilfully turned Frederick's son, William, against his father. By the time Frederick came to the throne, he was suffering from terminal cancer and died 3 months later.

The accession of William II was a turning point in the history of the Empire. William was an unstable and neurotic figure, who suffered from rapid mood swings and at times may even have been mentally ill.[32] His complex love–hate relationship with his English mother and Great Britain was to create considerable political problems. Partly to spite his parents he had closely allied himself with Bismarck, but when he came to the throne in 1888, he was determined to rule Germany in reality. According to the Crown Prince of Austria, his political opinions were the same as 'a dyed-in-the-wool Junker and reactionary' although initially this did not seem to be the case.

See Document 31

Bismarck assumed that his advice would in the final analysis be accepted, but he rapidly found himself in serious disagreement with the young emperor (or, to use the German, Kaiser, as he is more commonly known to English-speaking readers) over several major issues. The Kaiser was suspicious of ending the *Kulturkampf* and wished to see the existing *Kartell* with the National Liberals and Conservatives maintained. Above all William intended to ease Bismarck out of power and then appoint a man of his own choice. To enhance his independence of the 'reactionary' Bismarck, he set out to establish himself as a progressive monarch, who could win over the workers. He received, for example, a delegation of striking miners from Ruhr coalfields in 1889.

Bismarck responded to these challenges to his power by attempting to conjure up a crisis that would make himself indispensable to the Crown. In October 1889, a few months before the next election, he introduced into the *Reichstag* a new anti-socialist bill, which would not have to be renewed at regular intervals, as in the past, but would be permanent. When the opposition of the National Liberals to this threatened the unity of the *Kartell*, he rejected all requests from the Kaiser to accept a compromise. He calculated that the collapse of the *Kartell* would lead to an increase in the Social Democratic vote in the election, and that then the chastened National Liberals and propertied classes would turn to him for leadership. When, as predicted, the elections led to a strengthening of the Centre, the **Freisinnige Partei** (formerly the Progressive Liberals), and the SPD, Bismarck, intent on provoking a major crisis that would frighten the Kaiser into sanctioning a coup, planned to present the new *Reichstag* with the anti-socialist bill and a greatly increased military budget.

Freisinnige Partei: this split in 1893 and in 1910 reunited as Progressive People's Party.

As he waited for this crisis to mature, he took steps to tighten his grip on the Prussian cabinet by reviving the old Prussian cabinet order of 1852, which forbade ministers from being received by the Crown without the consent of the prime minister. This threatened the Kaiser with the prospect of being politically isolated and led directly to him presenting Bismarck with the choice of either withdrawing the order or resigning. Bismarck, lacking majority support in the *Reichstag*, resigned on 18 March 1890 and was replaced by General von Caprivi.

Bismarck in retirement

Initially the country was glad to see Bismarck go. The German writer, Theodor Fontane observed optimistically 'It is fortunate that we are rid of him, and many, many questions will now be handled better, more honourably, more clearly than before'.[33] Within a year Bismarck began to write articles bitterly critical of his successor, and in 1891 even become a member of the National Liberal Parliamentary Party, although he never took up his seat. However, by the time he died the 'historical Bismarck' had been eclipsed by the 'superhuman Bismarck, who from the Meuse to the Memel decorated market places and rural resorts in stone and bronze'.[34]

Germany after Bismarck

Bismarck had dominated the Empire since its creation. His towering presence gave domestic politics a continuity, which they lacked after 1890. The growth of popular pressure groups, the emergence of the SPD as the largest party in the *Reichstag*, the attempts by the Kaiser to make 'personal rule' a reality, the abandoning of Bismarck's belief that Germany was a saturated power with no territorial ambitions, as well as the accelerating industrialization, makes the nature of Wilhelmine Germany hard to grasp. Did, as the Bielefeld school argue, its strident imperialism, authoritarian structures and the growing popularity of *völkisch* thought prepare the way for Nazism? Or was it an infinitely more complex, pluralistic society grappling with the powerful forces of modernity and change?

The new politics, 1890–1914

The 1890s witnessed the emergence of mass politics in Germany. Major issues such as imperialism, commercial and fiscal policies and the social question all helped mobilize large numbers of the peasantry and the working and middle classes, who had previously not participated in politics. The most dramatic evidence of growing mass participation in politics was the growth of the SPD which by 1912 represented a third of the electorate. It was an effectively organized and centrally controlled 'people's party', which by 1914 also attracted bourgeois and secular

Catholic voters. Its success was accompanied by a massive expansion of the free-trade unions, which were affiliated to the SPD, to nearly three million members by 1913.

The nature of the other parties also changed. During the Bismarck era they were dominated by the local elites, who formed loose organizations to fight particular elections. A tight party central organization was almost non-existent and mass campaigning almost unknown. This began to change in the 1890s. Fee-paying mass membership increased, permanent officials were employed and a whole range of new techniques were used to mobilize voters at elections. Thomas Nipperdey describes the 1890s as a 'major moment of flux', in which the old largely liberal dominated politics of the Bismarck era gave way to 'a more complex and fragmented array of forces'.[35]

On the right, as a result of the growing crisis in the countryside (see p. 114), peasant radicalism was finding expression in the emergence of peasant leagues and the rise of anti-Semitic parties (see p. 116), which promised to rid the countryside of 'Junkers and Jews'. In 1893 the Agrarian League was founded ostensibly to oppose Caprivi's tariff policies, but it was also an attempt by the east Elbian aristocracy to channel and control popular agitation so that it did not challenge their own position. It was not, however, just a Junker pressure group; it was also 'a pressure group of a new kind'[36] that appealed to rural populism. In 1898 the league had enrolled 157,000 smallholders and 28,500 middle-sized farmers, as compared to just 1500 large landowners. By 1913 it had a membership of 300,000 farmers.

In the 1890s nationalist opinion was mobilized by a number of associations such as the Pan-German League, which in 1912 played a key role in launching the Defence League to campaign for a rapid expansion of the army, the Society for the Eastern Marches, and above all the Navy League. As pressure groups, their aims were usually far in advance of the government's. The Pan-Germans wished, for instance, to incorporate Holland and Austria into Germany. These leagues sometimes cooperated with the government but were not controlled by them. Effectively they evolved into a strident nationalist opposition and helped create among their members a feeling of disillusionment with the government's policies. See Document 32

The mushroom growth of these associations marked a growing politicization of ever larger sections of the German people, but how much direct influence did they in fact exert over the government? The Agrarian League with its links with the Conservative Party and a firm base in rural Germany played a key role in returning protectionist deputies, who by 1907 made up a third of the *Reichstag*. The Navy League played a major role in creating the political climate in which the *Reichstag* passed successive naval bills, although it was frequently critical of what it perceived to be the government's timidity. Active in its membership were representatives of heavy industry, ship building, the export trade and a broad spectrum from the Free Conservatives to the National Liberals as well as a wide cross section of the middle classes.

General Leo von Caprivi and the New Course, 1890–1894

While the pressure groups were mobilizing public opinion from below, the constitution of 1867–1871 remained unchanged. It had worked most effectively when the National Liberals had been the largest party in the *Reichstag* and had cooperated with Bismarck in the 1870s, and when William I had given his chancellor virtually a free hand. By 1890 these important preconditions for success had changed. Not only was the party composition of the *Reichstag* very different, but the new Kaiser was determined to take over the powers the constitution still ascribed to the Crown (see p. 124). At times William attempted, to quote Wehler, to be 'both Emperor and Chancellor in one'.[37] William held a deep belief in the 'sacral role' of the Crown as an appointed mediator between God and his subjects. Clark argues that he wanted to enlarge the 'neutral middle ground in German politics' and unite the natural patriotic anti-socialist and anti-particularist majority in support of a modern and powerful Germany.[38]

William's choice as Bismarck's successor caused widespread surprise. Leo von Caprivi, the son of a judge (1831–1899), was a distinguished soldier and staff officer, who not surprisingly lacked political experience. Of course the successor to Bismarck would under any conditions have faced a difficult task, but his task was made even more challenging by Bismarck's implacable hostility and William's constant intervention in politics. After the divisiveness of the long Bismarck era, Caprivi, with the political naivety of the professional soldier, was determined to seek a political consensus. His concept of consensus, however, was to differ from his master.

On 26 April at Bremen, in a speech laced with nautical allusions, William announced that Germany was now launched on a 'new course'. As far as Caprivi was concerned, this involved policies which would attract a broad coalition of support from all groups who put country before party. In his first speech to the Prussian assembly he announced that he would 'take the good from wherever and from whomsoever it may come'.[39] To ease the confrontational political climate which Bismarck had created, Caprivi tried to create a more collegiate style of government and encourage ministers and state secretaries to take on more responsibility and act on their own initiative. In practice far from creating harmony this merely gave ministers added freedom to intrigue against Caprivi.

He also made efforts to appease the Centre Party, the ethnic minorities and the SPD. In Alsace-Lorraine compulsory passport restrictions were dropped and in the eastern provinces the absolute ban on the use of Polish in schools was lifted. Similarly he hoped to win the goodwill of the working classes by enacting a series of safety laws regulating conditions in the workplace and prohibiting Sunday employment. More controversially in 1891 he embarked on a programme to cut the tariffs on grain imports from 50 to 30 per cent, which provided cheap food for the urban classes at the expense of agriculture. These measures failed to win Caprivi's government any lasting support, as his policy of standing above the parties prevented him from building up an effective electoral alliance.

The SPD pressed for further reforms, while the Centre demanded the realization of the concessions already promised. Above all his tariff policy met with implacable opposition from the right wing of the Conservative Party, and led to the foundation of the Agrarian League (see above) and the radicalization of the Conservative Party.

In early 1892 Caprivi attempted to gain support from the Centre to strengthen his position in the *Reichstag* by proposing a new Prussian school bill, which would restore Catholic confessional schools in Prussia. William reluctantly accepted the school bill when Caprivi threatened to resign, but his government dropped it in the face of opposition from the National Liberals, the left liberals, Bismarck and even the SPD. In response to this defeat Caprivi resigned as Prussian minister, and the position was taken by Count Botho zu Eulenburg (1831–1912), an ultra-conservative, who used every opportunity to oppose Caprivi's policies.

Over the next 2 years Caprivi's position became increasingly untenable. The success of the SPD vote in the elections of 1893, which increased by some 300,000 votes, alarmed the Kaiser and the Conservatives. The termination of the Reinsurance Treaty and the failure to negotiate an Anglo-German alliance (see p. 153) also emphasized Germany's growing isolation in Europe and led to the generals demanding an increase in the military budget and the size of the army by 77,500 men. Caprivi obtained parliamentary consent for this, but only after making concessions that infuriated William. He managed to persuade the *Reichstag* to agree to the bill by cutting conscription from 3 to 2 years and by conceding its right to debate the military budget every 5 rather than 7 years. This struggle to get the army bill through parliament led William to contemplate the possible formation of a National Liberal–Centre–Conservative bloc and a new anti-Socialist bill. If that failed as a last resort, he was ready to consider radical changes in the constitution brought about if necessary by a *coup d'état*.

In the spring of 1894 William, irritated by Caprivi's refusal to become a mere tool of the Crown, considered replacing him with Botho zu Eulenburg. Worried by the increase in the SPD vote and the assassination of the French President, Sadi Carnot (1837–1894), by an anarchist, William was persuaded to back Eulenburg's proposal to put a draconian bill aimed more at combating 'revolutionary tendencies' in the SPD and trade unions than dealing with anarchism before the *Reichstag*. Like Bismarck earlier, Eulenburg hoped that its rejection would give William the necessary excuse to suspend the constitution. In the end, in the face of stubborn opposition from Caprivi to Eulenburg's plans for a coup and the fear of the consequences such a coup would have for the unity of the Reich, the Kaiser backed down. Caprivi could probably have hung onto office for some time longer, but, in the face of unremitting attacks from the right, he decided to resign in October. Eulenburg, confronted with opposition from Caprivi's allies within the Foreign Office, Marschall von Bieberstein (1842–1912) and Friedrich von Holstein (1837–1909), also resigned at the same time.

Who was now to become the new chancellor? Any candidate acceptable to William would have to be a man without strong opinions, who would implement faithfully the constantly changing policy of his master. On the advice of his close adviser and cousin to the former Prussian Minister-President, the diplomat Count Philipp zu Eulenburg-Hertefeld (1857–1921), he appointed the 75-year-old Hohenlohe, the former Bavarian prime minister and governor of Alsace-Lorraine as a 'respectable figure head',[40] who would be easier to manipulate than his predecessors.

William's 'personal rule' and Prince Chlodwig zu Hohenlohe-Schillingsfürst, 1894–1900

The degree of William's influence on the Reich government is the subject of considerable historical debate. Wolfgang Mommsen regards the term 'personal rule' as an exaggeration and argues that eventually it amounted to little more than 'muddling through with the existing system, while trying as far as possible to patch up cracks and weaknesses within the governing elite'. On the other hand, John Röhl, Isabel Hull and Katherine Lerman[41] have shown that William did manage to create a political system which revolved around him and was responsive to his personal wishes. 'Personal rule' did not, however, imply an outright dictatorship by the Kaiser. His advisers, particularly Philipp zu Eulenburg, who formed the so-called **Liebenberg Circle** were wary of his mercurial temperament and feared the consequences of a *coup d'état*, particularly as it might lead to the southern German states seceding from the union. Eulenburg observed, for instance: 'When William appears as an actual ruler, that is only his perfect right. The only question is whether the consequence can be endured in the long run'.[42] Personal rule in reality meant that the key departments in the Empire and Prussia were in the hands of men appointed by the Kaiser to carry out his wishes. This involved both promoting his policies and blocking those that he disapproved of. However, in reality, as we can see from the defeat of the anti-socialist bill 'there was a gap between William's absolutist rhetoric and the constrained position he occupied in reality'.[43]

The Liebenberg Circle

The Liebenberg Circle was the name given to a group of the Kaiser's confidants and friends, the most influential of whom were Philipp zu Eulenburg (1857–1921), Kuno von Moltke, (1847–1923), Axel von Varnbüler and Karl von Dornberg. They were cultured, deeply conservative, homoerotic and interested in spiritualism. The journalist, Maximilian Harden (1861–1927) was convinced that they formed a secret and even occult camarilla and that their advice to William actively harmed Germany. In 1907–1908 Harden destroyed the group's influence when he accused Eulenburg and Moltke of homosexuality in highly publicized trials, which led to their dismissal by William.

Although his government had constantly to contend with the *Reichstag*, which blocked and mauled legislation, the Kaiser's will was the main force behind the Hohenlohe government. Virtually on every issue the Kaiser intervened and had his own agenda. William was the driving force behind the government's efforts to weaken the SPD. Although Hohenlohe had no sympathy for the SPD, he refused to go along with his demands for a coup, arguing that this would only lead 'to conflict with the federal states, civil war and the dissolution of the Reich'.[44] Nevertheless, he did resurrect parts of Botho zu Eulenburg's anti-socialist bill (see above) in December 1894, but the new bill was rejected by the *Reichstag*. A law designed to restrict trade union activities met a similar fate in August 1899.

William suffered a further defeat over the Prussian War Ministry's proposal in the spring of 1895 to modernize the Military Legal Code of 1845 by allowing courts martial to be held in public. William was implacably opposed to this measure, despite the fact that such procedure was the norm in many other European states and that Hohenlohe himself had introduced a similar law in Bavaria in 1869. In the autumn Ernst von Köller (1841–1928), the Prussian Minister of Interior, an avid opponent of the war ministry's reform plans, was caught leaking ministerial minutes on the military justice question, in an attempt to weaken the support of his colleagues for the bill. William was immediately forced to dismiss Köller by Hohenlohe, who was backed by an outraged and united cabinet, which also for good measure rejected the candidates put forward by the Kaiser to replace him. This appeared indeed to be a victory 'for the principal of collegiate government over the capricious interventionism of William's II'.[45] In reality, however, the cabinet was in no position to exploit its victory. Its unity was only temporary, and in the final analysis ministers were dependent on the Kaiser for their authority. Unlike their contemporaries in Britain they were not members of a party, which could command a majority in the parliament.

In January 1896 Hohenlohe confided in a friend that 'despite all failings'[46] the Kaiser still considered him to be the best chancellor in the circumstances. Behind the scenes, however, Philipp zu Eulenburg and William were determined to restore the authority of the Crown. Eulenburg was grooming Bernhard von Bülow (1849–1929) to take over the chancellorship. Bülow had assured him that he would regard himself as the executive tool of his majesty and that with him 'personal rule in the good sense would begin'.[47] Over the next 18 months ministers who had opposed William were dismissed. Both the Prussian War Minister, General Walther Bronsart von Schellendorff (1833–1914), and the Empire's Foreign Minister, Marschall von Bieberstein, were sacked in 1897. The latter's departure opened the way up for the appointment of Bülow to the Foreign Office to launch a new era of **Weltpolitik** and of Admiral von Tirpitz (1849–1930) to the Naval Office with a remit to build up a powerful German navy. Both projects enjoyed the backing of the Kaiser. Hohenlohe remained chancellor until he was at last replaced by Bülow in

Weltpolitik: literally world policy or, in other words, a policy aimed at acquiring a worldwide colonial empire

October 1900, but, excluded from policymaking and secretly dependent on financial handouts from the Crown, he cut a sorry figure. Nevertheless despite this purge, in December 1898, as a result of persistent pressure from the Centre, the SPD and the left liberals, the reforms to the Prussian military code were at last implemented, despite William's opposition.

Bernhard von Bülow

Apart from Bismarck, Bülow (1849–1929) was the ablest of William's chancellors. He was an experienced diplomat, who had served in most European capitals and from 1893 to 1897 had been German ambassador in Rome. He headed a government in which the key departments were headed by men loyal to the Kaiser. Bülow himself claimed that he regarded himself as 'the executive instrument of His Majesty, so to speak his political Chief of Staff'.[48] Does this then amount to what J. C. Röhl calls 'institutionalized personal rule'.[49] Clark is rather more sceptical. He argues that Bülow was perfectly capable of pursuing his own policy by flattering and manipulating the monarch.

The key to political success, Bülow believed, was to create an alliance between the agrarian and industrial interests, which was given the name of *Sammlungspolitik* (policy of concentration), and then 'reconcile, pacify, rally [and] unite' the population through a successful foreign policy. This was reinforced by the construction of a major battle fleet, which proved so popular that the government sought to exploit it in the words of Wolfgang Mommsen, 'as a principle means of **secondary integration**'.[50] However, the passions unleashed by *Weltpolitik* (see p. 155) and the fleet could not so easily be controlled from above. The nationalist pressure groups were frequently bitterly critical of Bülow's relative moderation and dismissed his *Sammlungspolitik* as the 'feeble minded dogmatism of party life' which obstructed true nationalist consciousness.[51] They wanted a more radical approach to naval construction regardless of its dangers.

Initially Bülow enjoyed considerable political success and won the Kaiser's trust. He avoided confrontation in the Prussian assembly and the *Reichstag*, and used the press effectively to communicate the aims and achievement of his government. To appease the agrarians and heavy industrialists, Bülow avoided tackling such divisive subjects as tax reform and, after prolonged negotiations, increased the tariffs on grain and iron, while allowing most raw materials with the exception of timber to be imported freely. Nationally the tariff policy, which significantly increased the price of food, was unpopular, and in the election of 1903 Conservative losses and SPD gains led to a significant change in the party balance in the *Reichstag*, which resulted in the Centre enjoying a dominant position. Bülow had little option but to conciliate the party. He lifted the ban on the entry of Jesuits into Germany and during 1904–1905 managed to win Centre support for financial reform, trade treaties, the army bill and canal bill, which in the face of Conservative opposition approved the construction of

Secondary integration: attempts to mobilize the population in support of the state through such diversionary tactics as imperialism and expansion of the navy

a canal linking the Rhine and the Elbe. By both the Liberals and Conservatives he increasingly became criticized as the 'Centre Party Chancellor'.

Up to the summer of 1905 Bülow, through his conciliatory policy in parliament and careful cultivation of the mercurial Kaiser, had created at least the semblance of political stability. In recognition of this the Kaiser made him a prince. In the early summer of 1905 the popularity of his government was dramatically increased by the initial success of his Moroccan policy (see p. 156), which led to the fall of the French foreign minister, Delcassé. Yet within a few weeks the Bülow's system entered a protracted period of crisis, which ended in his dismissal in 1909. The success in Morocco was short-lived and ended in a humiliating diplomatic defeat for Germany, which severely shook the government. The government was increasingly harried by attacks by the left wing of the Centre Party, supported by the SPD, on the German colonial administration in South West Africa (see p. 150), which was accused of brutality, corruption and incompetence. Ominously for Bülow the Kaiser also began to lose confidence in him. In August 1906 he even sounded out Graf Monts (1852–1930), the German ambassador in Rome, as to whether he would replace Bülow. Possibly in the belief that the Kaiser's confidant, Philipp zu Eulenburg, was actively working against him, Bülow failed to alert the Kaiser of Harden's press campaign against the Liebenberg Circle in the *Zukunft* (see above), and he may even have passed him some incriminating information. Eulenburg's destruction as a public figure in the subsequent libel trials certainly eliminated a key influence on William and a potential rival to Bülow, but this came at the cost of deepening estrangement between chancellor and Kaiser.

If Bülow was to remain in power, he needed to reassert his influence in the *Reichstag* and free himself from dependence on the Centre Party. His chance came when the *Reichstag* budget committee rejected the colonial estimates in December 1906. Bülow immediately seized the opportunity to dissolve the *Reichstag*. His fortunes momentarily revived when he fought a brilliant election, in which he persuaded the Liberal parties to cooperate with the Conservatives so that the domination of the *Reichstag* by an SPD–Centre 'Red–black' alliance could be avoided. Aided by considerable funds from finance and industry and with the support of the Pan-German and Navy Leagues, he fought a brilliant campaign, which appealed to patriotism but studiously avoided reference to thorny domestic problems. Potentially this election marked a significant move towards a more democratic government as it indicated, to quote Katherine Lerman, that 'the Kaiser's confidence alone was not sufficient to permit his remaining in office'.[52]

The *Daily Telegraph* affair

Bülow's success was short-lived and the new Conservative–Liberal bloc began rapidly to unravel when the Liberals attempted to exploit his dependence on them to demand reform of the Prussian franchise. The

Conservatives in their turn ignored the financial plight of the Reich, which had witnessed a near doubling of the national debt since 1900, and again decided to vote against any form of income or property tax and even began to consider cooperation with the Centre Party. It was, however, Bülow's handling of the *Daily Telegraph* affair in November 1908 which finally undermined his position with the Kaiser. The Kaiser had rashly agreed to have a conversation, which had taken place with Colonel Stuart Wortley after his state visit to Windsor, published in the *Daily Telegraph* at the height of the Bosnian crisis (see p. 157). He had claimed, for instance, that he had thought up the military plan for defeating the Boers in the Anglo-Boer South African War of 1899–1902. Whils conceding that German public opinion was hostile to Britain, he painted himself as Britain's true friend. Bülow was actually sent a draft of the interview, which he could have amended, but he probably failed to read it. When it was published, it unleashed a storm of ridicule and anger in Germany, and momentarily united the parties in the *Reichstag* in demanding constitutional reform, which would diminish the royal prerogative. Briefly there was an opportunity to force the Kaiser to become a constitutional monarch, but the chance was lost, when the parties failed to keep a united front in the *Reichstag*. Instead, Bülow was able to get away with making the Kaiser promise to abide by the *existing* constitution. William deeply resented the chancellor's failure to spring to his defence and, once it was clear that Bülow was unable to get his bill for reforming the Empire's finances through the *Reichstag*, he had little

See Document 33

option but to resign in June 1909.

The *Daily Telegraph* affair, the Moltke–Eulenburg scandals and Bülow's resignation effectively ended the Kaiser's personal rule as far as the domestic affairs of the Empire went, although from time to time he would still make controversial speeches. In foreign and military affairs, however, he jealously guarded his powers and continued to make decisive interventions.

Theobald von Bethmann Hollweg

William's initial choices for successor ranged from General von der Goltz (1843–1916), who was the military adviser to the Sultan of Turkey, to Botho zu Eulenburg, the former Prussian minister-president, but in the end he was persuaded by Bülow himself to appoint Bethmann Hollweg (1856–1921), the Reich Secretary of State for the Interior. Bethmann had served in the Prussian civil service, later becoming Prussian minister of the interior (1905–1907). His approach to government was essentially one of damage limitation rather than of attempting to find root-and-branch solutions. If necessary he was willing to adopt a strong line with the Kaiser to block harmful interventions. He also hoped to bring together the Liberals, Conservatives and the Centre to alleviate the main tensions in contemporary Germany, but this was not to be an easy task. His cautious attempts to remove the worst abuses from the Prussian voting system (see p. 78) were regarded as too radical by the Conservatives and insufficiently radical by the National Liberals, and had to be dropped by his government in May 1910. Similarly, his efforts to reconcile the Poles met with violent opposition from the Conservatives and the Society of the Eastern Marches. Bethmann's policy during the Second Moroccan Crisis (see pp. 158–159) not only led to a storm of criticism from the nationalist associations but in the *Reichstag* debate of 9 November 1911 the traditional pro-government parties, the Conservatives, Free Conservatives and National Liberals united to attack his government's foreign policy.

The election results of January 1912, in which the SPD became the single largest party in the *Reichstag* with 110 seats, exacerbated Bethmann's problems. On the right, fear of the growing strength of socialism led to closer links between the Conservatives, Free Conservatives and the Nationalist Associations. It was possible to see the emergence of what one journalist called a 'Bloc of the Right'. Far from being a front for traditional east Elbian conservatism, its radical nationalism involved in Geoff Eley's words, 'a systematic appeal to the people not just as a formality of public opinion, but as a constructive ideological assault on the old order, its parliamentary practices and forms of legitimacy'.[53]

The elections of 1912 produced a progressive majority in the *Reichstag*. In theory the SPD together with the liberals and the smaller parties representing the Poles and the other nationalities could dominate the *Reichstag*, but neither the right wing of the National Liberals nor the left wing of the SPD would in reality tolerate such a combination. This produced a complete deadlock in the *Reichstag*. Bethmann Hollweg thus attempted where possible to bypass the *Reichstag* and to stress that he stood above the quarrelling parties, and when this was impossible all he could do was to work towards 'creating majorities from issue to issue'.[54] His greatest success in conjuring up a temporary majority was the passing of the army bill in 1912. He was certainly helped by the Balkan crisis (see p. 159) and the newly founded Defence League, which did much to win public support for a larger army, but crucially the government also agreed to a Reich property tax, which persuaded the SPD to support the bill.

Impediments to SPD–Liberal cooperation

How possible was an alliance between the SPD and the Liberal parties in 1912? The SPD was an uneasy alliance between moderates or 'revisionists', who sought change constitutionally, and radicals, who were, theoretically at least, ready to wage a revolutionary struggle and thus opposed cooperation with the bourgeois parties. These two contradictory views were up to a point reconciled by (1) the Erfurt Programme of 1891, which combined an orthodox Marxist criticism of society with a set of moderate demands, which did not entail a revolution to implement, and (2) Karl Kautsky, who argued that as capitalism was doomed and would inevitably collapse, a revolution as such was not needed. The moderates were greatly strengthened by the growth in the free-trade unions (see p. 111), which in 1905 and 1906 persuaded the party to stop agitating for a political general strike. On communal health, housing and unemployment boards, town councils and provincial assemblies, as well as in the Baden assembly, there were examples of cooperation between the SPD and the Liberal parties, but nationally it was possible only to achieve a fleeting cooperation. In 1912, for instance, the SPD voted with the National Liberals for measures which were intended to finance an expansion of the army because this would introduce the principle of taxing profits made from the increase in land value, but key groups in the National Liberals feared that they would have to pay for collaboration by agreeing to radical social reform and thus this cooperation remained exceptional.

The Zabern affair

See Document 34

The stalemate in the *Reichstag* made Bethmann more dependent on the Kaiser and the opinions of the bureaucrats, courtiers and generals who were close to him. Bethmann's weakness was illustrated by the crisis which blew up in the autumn of 1913, when a young lieutenant's insults to Alsatian recruits led to demonstrations in the town of Zabern in Alsace. The army overreacted and arrested the ringleaders. Privately Bethmann disapproved of its high-handedness, but, as the Kaiser in his role as supreme commander or war lord supported the army and insisted that it was an internal matter, Bethmann was forced to defend it in the *Reichstag*, and met with an overwhelming vote of no confidence. In a sense the Zabern affair was a 'lightning flash',[55] which suddenly illuminated the state of German politics on the eve of the Great War. It showed the fragility of Bethmann's government: it had no backing in the *Reichstag* and was dependent on an emperor, who was surrounded by a conservative military entourage which exaggerated the threat from the SPD and was preoccupied by Germany's increasing international isolation. It also highlighted the unique position of the army within the Bismarckian constitution as 'an extra-parliamentary, institutional legacy of absolutism within an otherwise constitutional Rechtstaat'.[56]

Rechtstaat:
a constitutional state governed according to the rule of law

Conclusion: the house that Bismarck built

Initially the Bismarckian constitution represented a viable compromise, between the conflicting demands of Prussia, the liberals and the individual states. However, after Bismarck's rejection of the National Liberal demand for three seats in the cabinet in 1878 (see p. 127) it increasingly became a straitjacket that distorted the constitutional development of Germany. As long as the Bismarck–William I axis survived, the German constitution was just about workable, but after his dismissal the attempts by William II to implement personal rule, introduced a new tension into the constitution. William took an active interest in policy formulation and in asserting his right to control all appointments to the government, bureaucracy, the diplomatic corps and the armed forces. It was therefore vital for key figures in the armed forces and both the Prussian and imperial governments to have direct access to the Kaiser. Inevitably this intensified personal and departmental rivalry and led to what Wehler has called 'a polyocracy of rival centres of power'.[57] Bismarck's constitutional legacy was thus more one of chaos rather than of authoritarianism. This chaos was compounded by the inability of the government of the day to control the *Reichstag*.

In a lecture at the end of 1918 Max Weber (1864–1920), the eminent German sociologist, observed that Bismarck 'left a nation totally without political education ... totally bereft of political will, accustomed to expect that a great man at the top would provide their politics for them'.[58] Weber, of course, made these remarks after the German defeat and the emergence of the charismatic authority of Hindenburg and Ludendorff in 1916 (see p. 172), but how accurate an assessment are they of pre-war Wilhelmine Germany?

The brief analysis of German politics given in this chapter indicates that the *Reichstag* was a powerful legislature, despite its inability to choose the government. It did not hesitate to criticize the Kaiser, the army and his ministers or reject or amend legislation. Universal manhood suffrage for the *Reichstag* elections, the development of mass parties and popular pressure groups inevitably educated the German population in at least some of the practice of democracy. Germany therefore was hardly a nation 'totally without political education'! Again, in these pre-war years did Germany yearn for a great man any more than any other contemporary nation did? The restraints of Bismarck's constitution and the nervous, impetuous figure of the Kaiser prevented the emergence of a democratically elected government under a chancellor, who could appeal to the nation. In that context the emergence of a 'great man' who could break through the deadlock of contemporary politics was naturally tempting to the Germans. No less a man than the businessman Walther Rathenau (see p. 170), who was both a liberal and a *völkisch* romantic, perceptively warned Bethmann Hollweg in 1912 that political reform would either 'come as the consequence of unfortunate events or "heroically" at a time of prosperity and introduced by a new Hardenberg'.[59] Could Germany have evolved peacefully into a parliamentary state without the traumatic experiences of a lost war? Manfred Rauh is surely right to argue that by 1914 the Empire was subject to a gradual but slow process of parliamentarization. Margaret Anderson puts forward the interesting idea that without the war the Bismarckian system would in the end have evolved into a parliamentary regime: 'the jump need not have been violent. Perhaps the death of the Kaiser at eighty-three would have speeded a regime change – in 1941 – analogous to Spain's at the death of Franco at the same age in 1975'.[60] That is, however, 'virtual history'! War in fact did intervene and German history took a different course. Even so, could Germany really have waited until 1941?!

7 German Foreign Policy, 1871–1914

Introduction: problems, issues and questions

It is a paradox that Bismarck, the diplomat, after 1871 is seen by some historians as a great force for peace, who presided with such moderation and flexibility over Germany's new position in Europe that he deserves, at the very least, the posthumous grant of the Nobel Peace Prize. Whereas Bismarck, the politician, is pilloried as the man who launched Germany on its unhappy *Sonderweg*. William Langer, in his classic book, *European Alliances and Alignments, 1871–1890*, which was first published in 1931, argues that 'no other statesman of his standing had ever before shown the same great moderation and sound political sense of the possible and desirable'. Yet was Bismarck, the diplomat, really such a paragon of virtue after 1871? Bruce Waller, for instance, has pointed out that Langer's views on German foreign policy 'were strongly coloured by the effort to take a fair-minded view after the excesses of wartime propaganda'. He argues on the contrary that

Bismarck 'created and preserved tension' by encouraging rivalry in the colonies and the Balkans and that at times 'Bismarck's actions would have led to war had it not been for the good sense of other European statesmen.'[1]

By 1914 Germany had alienated Britain, France and Russia. Was this Bismarck's legacy or a consequence of the clumsiness of his successors? The changes in the global balance of power – particularly Russia's defeat by Japan, the spectacular development of the German economy and the strength of popular nationalism throughout Europe, as well as the Kaiser's determination to drive forward colonial expansion and the construction of a battle fleet aimed at Britain, made it very difficult to revert to a policy of Bismarckian 'balance'. The crucial question in the second half of this chapter is therefore to ask to what extent German foreign policy was responsible for the outbreak of war in 1914 or did the nations, as David Lloyd George was later to argue 'slither' into war.

> See Document 35

The new Bismarckian foreign policy, 1871–1879

The year 1871 was a major turning point in Bismarck's foreign policy: between 1862 and 1871 Bismarck had created what amounted to a new Europe, and now, like Metternich in 1815, he needed peace to preserve it. The unification of Germany had marked a decisive shift in the balance of power in Europe. In Britain, Disraeli went so far as to argue in the House of Commons: 'This war represents the German revolution, a greater political event than the French revolution of the last century.'[2] Although the military and diplomatic balance had shifted from Paris to Berlin, the new German Empire was still a fragile compromise, which, or so Bismarck feared, could be destroyed by a hostile European coalition. Bismarck's priority was therefore to convince the great powers that Germany was a satiated power with no further territorial ambitions. As Christopher Clark has pointed out, this policy 'exacted a cost. It required that Germany always to punch under its weight'.[3]

Bismarck's aims remained constant even though the diplomatic situation changed. He wished to give priority to domestic consolidation, while maintaining Germany's dominant position in Europe. It was of overriding importance to avoid the creation of a hostile alliance against the Empire. In Europe he needed therefore to isolate France, which had been humiliated by defeat and the loss of Alsace-Lorraine, and appease it in areas, such as Africa where its policy represented no threat to Germany. He wished to see **Austria** survive as a great power and act as a bulwark against Russian expansion into the Balkans, but good relations with Russia were of crucial importance as it was both a potential ally of France and also the main rival of Austria in the Balkans.

Austria: After 1867 and the new settlement with the Hungarians (*Ausgleich*), officially Austria became Austria–Hungary, but in most books is still referred to as Austria.

The League of the Three Emperors

The **League of the Three Emperors** is often seen as a deliberate attempt by Bismarck to isolate France, but it was initially a way of defusing mutual

Austro-Russian distrust. The tsar was determined to prevent Austria from exploiting its increasingly good relations with Berlin to the detriment of Russia, and Bismarck was able skilfully to paper over the differences between the two powers in talks which culminated in the League of the Three Emperors in 1873. It is true that it was 'an empty frame',[4] but for the time being it enabled Bismarck to avoid making a choice between Russia and Austria. Indeed Jonathan Steinberg calls it 'a foreign policy construction, which remained a set and fixed element of Bismarck's foreign policy to the moment of his resignation'.[5]

The league's inadequacies were quickly revealed by a sudden crisis which blew up with France in 1875. Bismarck had become sufficiently concerned by France's economic and military recovery to make a serious diplomatic misjudgement. He inspired a bellicose leader in the *Berliner Post*, on 8 April, entitled *Is War in Sight?*, which seemed to indicate that Germany was about to attack France. This impression was further strengthened when the German ambassador at St Petersburg began publicly to defend the idea of a preventive war against France. Bismarck was probably bluffing, but the reaction of Britain and Russia indicated the underlying changes in the European balance of power brought about by German unification. Both powers made it clear to Bismarck that they did not want to see the destruction of France. Bismarck rapidly managed to reassure them that he had no aggressive intentions and the crisis blew over, but the incident underlined the potential weakness of Germany's position in Europe and showed that the threat of further German expansion in Europe at the expense of France would eventually create the hostile coalition which Bismarck feared so much.[6]

> **League of Three Emperors** was negotiated on 6 June 1873 at Schönbrunn when the emperors of Germany, Austria–Hungary and Russia agreed to 'consult together' in the event of a crisis and 'to impose the maintenance of peace in Europe against all attempts to destroy it from whatever quarter they come'. If joint military action were needed, a fresh agreement would have to be concluded.

The Eastern Crisis, 1875–1878

The league was subjected to a more testing challenge when Turkish power in the Balkans was undermined by a chain of events, which started in July 1875 with uprisings in Bosnia and Herzegovina. This threatened to create a power vacuum that both Austria and Russia would compete to fill. Bismarck attempted to mediate between Russia and Austria, while avoiding giving Russia the decisive backing the tsar requested. Initially this seemed to work, and Russia and Austria drew up plans for the peaceful partition of the Balkans. At Budapest in March 1877 Austria actually agreed to Russian military intervention at the price of acquiring Bosnia and Herzegovina, but once the Russians reached Constantinople 8 months later the Russian government unilaterally negotiated at San Stefano a settlement with the Turks, which ignored the Budapest treaty. Britain reacted by sending a naval force to the Straits, and, in an attempt to defuse what had become a dangerous international crisis, the powers appealed to Bismarck to summon a congress in Berlin to devise a compromise.

> In Bosnia and Herzegovina a predominantly Christian peasantry, many of whom were still serfs, were oppressively controlled by Muslim landowners. Thus social divisions coincided with religious and ethnic ones.

Bismarck in his role as 'honest broker' dominated the Berlin negotiations. Yet, however hard he tried to be neutral, the very fact that he presided over a congress that stripped Russia of many of its gains from the Turkish war made the Russians bitterly resentful of Germany's 'false friendship'.[7] Under Bismarck's skilful chairmanship, the congress managed to find at least temporary solutions to some of the intractable problems of the Eastern question. The large Bulgaria, which the Russians arbitrarily recognized at San Stefano, was broken up into three parts in an effort to minimize Russian influence, while Austria was given the right to occupy, but not annex, Bosnia and Herzegovina. Although the Russians did make some gains, the congress was described by the tsar as 'a European coalition against Russia under the leadership of Prince Bismarck'.[8]

Bismarck's alliance system

The Austro-German Dual Alliance, 1879

One consequence of the Berlin Congress was the dissolution of the Three Emperors' League. Initially Bismarck attempted to revive it, but Russia's resentment at his chairmanship of the congress made this impossible, and he began in November 1878 to work towards a defensive alliance with Austria–Hungary. Despite William's reservations the Austrian alliance was signed on 7 October 1879. It was initially to last 5 years but could be renewed. Its terms were:

- Should one power be attacked by Russia, the other would come to its rescue with 'the whole war strength' of its empire.
- If either empire was attacked by a third power, the other would adopt a neutral but friendly attitude.
- The alliance was secret but in the event of another major crisis with Russia its details would be leaked to the tsar to discourage him from taking any further action.

The Dual Alliance was a 'landmark in European History'.[9] In 1854 Bismarck had accused the Prussian government of 'tying the trim ... Prussian frigate to the worm eaten old Austrian galleon'. Had he in fact done exactly this in 1879? Helmut Böhme and Lothar Gall argue that Bismarck intended to create a large central European bloc (*Mitteleuropa*) which would be able to compete with the Russian and British empires.[10] Bismarck was convinced that it was in Germany's interests for Austria to survive as a great power to block Russian expansion in the Balkans. Up to a point the Dual Alliance tied Germany to Vienna, but it also gave Berlin considerable influence over Austrian foreign policy, which would in a real crisis enable Bismarck to ensure that the Austrians did not provoke an unnecessary war with Russia.

The Alliance of the Three Emperors

Even while Bismarck was concluding the Austrian alliance, he was putting out diplomatic feelers to St Petersburg. By the autumn of 1879 the tsar accepted that he had little alternative but to improve Russo-German relations, and sent a mission to Berlin to discuss a possible agreement.

This was a diplomatic victory for Bismarck, as it vindicated his argument that an Austro-German alliance would force Russia to adopt a more flexible policy. Bismarck hoped to revive the Three Emperors' League, which would open up the way to better relations between Vienna and St Petersburg and continue to keep France isolated. Little progress could be made until Austria was ready to give up the prospect of cooperation with Britain against Russia, but once the British Liberals won the general election of April 1880, British foreign policy became less hawkish and the prospect of an Anglo-Austrian agreement receded. Bismarck was now able to exert pressure on Vienna to respond to Russian demands less negatively, but, to square the circle, he also had to mislead the Russians into believing that the Dual Alliance did not automatically guarantee Germany's defence of Austria in the event of a Russian attack. The Three Emperors' Alliance was signed on 18 June 1881. The treaty was in the first instance to last 3 years. The three powers agreed that:

- The Straits should be closed to the warships of all nations, which would stop Britain threatening to send its navy into the Black Sea to threaten Russia.
- Austria conceded the eventual reunification of Bulgaria, while Russia agreed that at some time in the future Austria should annex Bosnia and Herzegovina.
- If a member of the League went to war with a fourth power, unless it was the Ottoman Empire, the other two powers would remain neutral.
- There were to be no territorial changes to the Ottoman Empire without the agreement of the three signatory powers.

The Triple Alliance, 1882

In retrospect the Alliance of the Three Emperors was 'little more than an armistice',[11] as it provided no long-term solution to Austro-Russian rivalry in the Balkans. Russian foreign policy remained unpredictable. The new tsar, Alexander III, received conflicting advice from the professional diplomats on the one side, who wanted good relations with Germany, and the leading Pan-Slavs, on the other side, who argued that a struggle between the German and Slav races led by Russia was inevitable. Bismarck, alarmed that the **Pan-Slavs** were beginning to establish contact with Russian sympathizers in the French army and press, attempted to strengthen the Dual Alliance, so that it would deter even the most fanatical Pan-Slav without, discouraging the pro-German party in Russia. Consequently, when Italy, alarmed by the French occupation of Tunis which it regarded as its own sphere of interest, sought in 1882 an alliance with Austria, Bismarck immediately suggested expanding it to a triple alliance. Both the Central Powers agreed to support Italy in the remote chance of an attack from France, while Italy would assist them only if they were attacked by two other powers (effectively France and Russia).

The **Pan-Slav** movement was formed in 1858 and saw Turkey, Austria and increasingly Germany as Russia's main enemies.

The real gain for Germany was that Austria was now freed from the threat of an Italian attack on her southern flank should war break out with Russia. Austria's position was further buttressed first by the Serbian alliance in June 1881 and then by the Romanian alliance in 1883, which Germany also joined, thereby turning it into 'a clear defensive alliance against Russia'.[12] Despite this anti-Russian front, Bismarck also successfully persuaded the tsar to renew the Three Emperors' Treaty both by refusing demands at home for further tariff increases on Russian grain imports, and by encouraging German banks to subscribe to Russian loans.

Bismarck's foray into imperialism, 1884–1885

In 1884–1885 Germany acquired a colonial empire five times the size of the German Empire. This has puzzled historians, since Bismarck had always scornfully dismissed colonies as an expensive luxury for a newly formed state like Germany comparable to 'a poverty stricken Polish nobleman providing himself with silks and sables when he needed shirts'.[13] Bismarck did not however hide his motives. In essence he wanted to reach an understanding with France by encouraging her colonial ambitions. He remarked to the French ambassador in 1880: 'I want you to turn your eyes from Metz and Strasburg by helping you elsewhere.'[14] A Franco-German rapprochement would pay dividends in Europe for Bismarck, and show both Britain and Russia that the mutual hostility of the two countries was not necessarily permanent. He was in fact anticipating the *Weltpolitik* of the Wilhelmine era, when he observed to the French ambassador in 1884 that the concept of a European balance of power was now obsolete and replaced by a new 'oceanic balance' or global balance of power.[15]

See Map 5

This was undoubtedly his main motive, but Bismarck was not unresponsive to the cries for help from the North German colonial traders. P. M. Kennedy, for instance, argues that Bismarck's policy was a calculated response to the pressure on German trade in South West Africa and the South Seas.[16] Alternatively, there are the arguments that Bismarck's foray into imperialism was determined by domestic politics: he could use the colonial issue to divide the Liberals, as the National Liberal Party and the newly founded *Kolonialverein* (Colonial League) were pressing for colonies, while the left liberals opposed them. This assessment is given powerful backing by the Foreign Office official, Friedrich von Holstein, who observed that Bismarck's colonialism 'was scarcely more than an election stunt'.[17] Another domestic advantage of colonialism was that it could be exploited to provide an immediate quarrel with the British, once Crown Prince Frederick came to the throne (see p. 131). Bismarck, like other European leaders, also realized that an exciting colonial policy with easy conquests could unite the German people behind him and 'legitimize the status quo' of his government, a policy which H.-U. Wehler has called 'manipulated social imperialism'.[18]

Document 20

In the spring of 1884 the German government granted formal protection to German trading stations in South West Africa, the Cameroons, Togoland and New Guinea to forestall British claims to the area (see Map 5). Bismarck took the obvious step of distracting the British by exploiting Anglo-French differences in Egypt, but he also needed French support to ensure that Germany's interests were protected in the Congo and West Africa. Suspicious that the British were using Portugal's weakness to increase their own influence in the Congo, he refused to recognize the Anglo-Portuguese Treaty of February 1884, and with French assistance pushed the Portuguese into proposing an international conference, which was held in Berlin in November 1884. The decision taken there to set up the Congo Free State, the frontiers of which were to remain open to international commerce, forced Britain to abandon its plans to control the Congo Basin indirectly through Portugal.

The foundation of Germany's colonial empire

Bismarck hoped that the trading companies themselves would be responsible for administering the new colonies, while the Reich would simply provide external protection. In fact, once having intervened in Africa, Bismarck found that he could not run Germany's colonial empire on the cheap. In West and East Africa the chartered companies proved so incompetent that the government was landed with responsibility for both internal administration and defence. For instance, the East African Company drove the African population into open revolt in 1888, and was only saved by the dispatch of German troops, while the South West African Company was so inefficient that an imperial commissioner was dispatched to take control. In 1889 the New Guinea Company also went bankrupt.

The Bismarckian alliance system under pressure

By the spring of 1885 Bismarck's attentions were once more concentrated on Europe. In France the ultra-nationalist General Boulanger (1837–1891) had just been appointed war minister, while the eruption of the Bulgarian crisis again plunged the Balkans into turmoil. The crisis, which destroyed the Three Emperors' League and brought Europe close to war, was caused by the unification of Bulgaria with **Eastern Rumelia** in September 1885 under Prince Alexander, who was determined to liberate the state from Russian influence. The Russians retaliated by strengthening their influence in Bulgaria and forcing Alexander to abdicate. Inevitably this revived British and Austrian fears of a Russian occupation of Bulgaria, and the Alliance of the Three Emperors collapsed.

Eastern Rumelia: created at the Congress of Berlin in 1878 in order to prevent the emergence of a 'big' Bulgaria.

Both Austria and Britain now looked to Berlin to take the lead against Russia, but Bismarck was determined not to be pushed into confrontation at the very time that Boulanger was urging a war of revenge against Germany. He therefore urged Austria and Russia, whom he described as 'two savage dogs', to divide the Balkans into spheres of influence, while

2   French cartoon commenting on Bismarck's attempts to keep France and Russia apart in the 1880s

Imperial War Museum, no. Q81754

behind the scenes making it clear to Vienna that Germany would not be dragged into war against Russia as a result of Bulgaria. Instead he persuaded Britain, Italy and Austria to negotiate the first Mediterranean Agreement in February 1887 with the aim of containing Russia in the Balkans and the Straits. At the same time he ensured the isolation of France in western Europe by renewing the Triple Alliance in February 1887 and encouraging an Italian–Spanish agreement, which was aimed at preventing French colonial expansion in North Africa.

The Reinsurance Treaty, 18 June 1887

Any improvement in Germany's relations with Russia depended on the outcome of the struggle to influence the tsar, which was bitterly waged between the Pan-Slavs and the traditionally pro-German Russian Foreign Office. Although in March 1887 the tsar rejected Pan-Slav demands for a total break with Germany, he still refused to renew the Three Emperors' Treaty, and instead negotiated a new 3-year agreement with Berlin-the Reinsurance Treaty, which was signed on 18 June 1887. Its terms were:

- Both empires were pledged to be neutral in a war fought against a third power unless Germany attacked France, or Russia attacked Austria.
- Germany recognized the rights 'historically acquired' by Russia in the Balkans – particularly in Bulgaria.
- Turkey was not to allow the navy of a power hostile to Russia to pass through the Straits. If it did, both Germany and Russia would regard it as an act hostile towards themselves.

The Reinsurance Treaty failed to calm the tension in the Balkans. When Prince Ferdinand of Coburg, who had been born in Vienna and had served with the Austrian army, was appointed to the Bulgarian throne by the country's parliament in July 1887, the Pan-Slavs whipped up a vitriolic press campaign against Germany, which was accused of secretly supporting Austria. In the autumn it seemed that Russia was about to invade Bulgaria. To stop this, Bismarck applied financial pressure by ordering the *Reichsbank* not to accept Russian bonds as collateral security for loans raised in Germany. This led to a sudden collapse of confidence in Russian credit, and so discouraged Russia from occupying Bulgaria and risking war with Austria. In December Bismarck, again quite contrary to the spirit of the Reinsurance Treaty, further strengthened the position of Austria by persuading Britain and Italy to negotiate

Historians and the Reinsurance Treaty

Arguably, to quote Otto Pflanze, 'no treaty concluded by Bismarck has been subjected to greater scrutiny and more controversy.'[19] Ever since the publication of the treaty in 1919, historians have disagreed about whether it contradicted the Dual Alliance with Austria by recognizing Russia's 'right historically acquired' in the Balkans. Pflanze, A. J. P. Taylor and William Langer insist that it did not, as Bismarck had often suggested dividing the Balkans into Austrian and Russian spheres of influence. Yet C. J. Lowe stresses that it 'conflicted with the spirit, if not the letter, of the Dual Alliance of 1879'.[20] In Gall's opinion, 'had it come to the notice of the other side [Austria or Britain] it would have shattered the credibility of German policy, almost certainly brought about the collapse of Bismarck's intricate system of alliances and left Germany largely isolated'.[21] It contradicted the Mediterranean Agreement, the point of which was to deter Russia from expanding into the Balkans. Admittedly Germany did not sign this agreement, but Bismarck had encouraged its negotiation. Historians also argue about the significance of the treaty. To Langer it signified the completion of an 'intricate system of checks and balances which was intended to preserve the peace of Europe' but Taylor regarded it 'at best' as a temporary and not very effective means for dealing with the crisis of 1885–1887, a view which is essentially shared by Gall.[22]

a second Mediterranean Agreement aimed at keeping Russia out of Bulgaria and Turkey.

Although these measures deterred the tsar from sending troops into Bulgaria, the Russians did not stop their efforts to undermine Ferdinand. They also looked to Paris for the loans which Berlin was no longer ready to raise. Inevitably this strengthened Franco-Russian relations, but neither side was as yet ready for an alliance. When William II came to the throne in June 1888 (see p. 131), and began to urge on Bismarck a British alliance, the tsar belatedly offered to renew the Reinsurance Treaty permanently, but Bismarck was dismissed in March 1890 before negotiations could begin.

Bismarck's diplomatic legacy

By 1890 Bismarck had constructed a web of alliances of almost Heath Robinson-like proportions. His foreign policy has been described as a 'conjuring trick' (Taylor) 'crisis management' (Gall), 'expediency rather than creativity' (Craig) or 'a system of "stop gaps"' (Hildebrand).[23] It was based, as Gall has pointed out, on a system that 'that permitted the Reich to intervene in a regulatory fashion in the ever more precarious balance of power and thus maintain the status quo in a manner favourable to its existing system'.[24] In the final analysis it was aimed at preserving the peace in Europe, but it was becoming increasingly outdated as the traditional European system was evolving into a global political system.

The 'New Course' in foreign policy

After Bismarck's dismissal, it was not surprising that German Foreign Office officials advised his successor, General Leo von Caprivi, not to renew the Reinsurance Treaty with Russia. They feared that if details of the treaty leaked out, Russia would blackmail Germany by threatening to reveal its contradictions to Britain and Austria. Caprivi agreed and began to work for a new alliance system or 'New Course', which eventually would ally Britain with the Triple Alliance, and so hold in check both Russia and France. He was sure that Germany was now strong enough to renounce Bismarck's complicated system of checks and balances and to ally more closely with states with which it seemed to have a common interest. The lapsing of the Reinsurance Treaty brought to an end the Bismarckian diplomatic system of complex checks and balances and ultimately led to the Franco-Russian Alliance of 1894, an alliance which he had always sought to avoid.

Even before the Reinsurance Treaty had officially terminated, the German government had already approached the British government with a proposal to settle any outstanding colonial disagreements. The British drove a hard bargain. In return for Germany giving up its claims to Zanzibar and extensive areas of East Africa, they ceded Heligoland, a strategically important island which dominated the mouths of the Elbe

See Maps 4 and 5

and the Weser rivers. Had this agreement led to Britain joining the Triple Alliance, it would have been a considerable achievement of German foreign policy, but neither this brief *entente coloniale* nor the subsequent Franco-Russian alliance of January 1894 persuaded the British government to abandon its policy of isolation. The foreign policy of the New Course had failed, but both Caprivi and the foreign secretary, Marschall von Bieberstein, still believed that if only the British could be convinced of the fragility of their position, they could still be persuaded to join the Triple Alliance. Consequently in a series of colonial disputes involving the possession of the Samoan islands, the legality of the Anglo-Congolese Treaty of 1894, the boundaries of the Sudan and the Transvaal both Caprivi and then Hohenlohe took a strongly anti-British position in the hope that the British would draw the conclusion that it was better to have Germany as a friend than an enemy. Ironically in January 1894 the British Prime Minister, Lord Roseberry, in response to Austrian fears of an imminent Russian attack on the Turkish straits showed a readiness to assist Austria provided the Triple Alliance kept France in check. Caprivi did not explore this offer as he was now attempting to weaken the Franco-Russian rapprochement by negotiating a new trade agreement with Russia.

In the Transvaal Germany's anti-British policy was to have lasting repercussions on Anglo-German relations. The Transvaal was effectively a British satellite state, but its economy was dominated by Germans who controlled the National Bank, held the whisky and dynamite monopolies, and supplied the state's water. Consequently, when Cecil Rhodes, the Prime Minister of Cape Colony, on his own initiative launched a badly planned and unsuccessful attempt to overthrow Paul Krüger, the President of the Transvaal, the so-called 'Jameson Raid', the Kaiser at first wanted to declare the Transvaal a German protectorate, send military aid to Krüger and then summon a congress in Berlin, which would redraw the map of South Africa. In the end he was persuaded that, because of British sea power, these were just empty threats, and instead he sent a telegram to Krüger, which congratulated him on having maintained the independence of the Transvaal. However illegal the raid had been, this telegram was a diplomatic blunder. It may have been intended as Marschall told *The Times* journalist, Valentine Chirol, as 'a lesson to England that she could not with impunity play fast and loose with Germany's friendship', but in this it failed and did much to turn British public opinion against Germany.

See Document 36

Neither did it win any support from either France or Russia.

Imperialism and navalism: the Bülow period, 1897–1909

The press, the Colonial League and the Pan-Germans had all enthusiastically endorsed the government's policy towards the Transvaal. There was an ideological consensus in Germany which supported colonial expansion and a more vigorous assertion of German power. Economically by

1900 Germany was already a world power, but German industry, with the partial exception of heavy industry, was not so much interested in colonies but rather in export opportunities in Europe, the Balkans, South America and South Africa. German imperialism was primarily an ideological and political policy. It was, like British and French imperialism, a product of the popular belief in social Darwinism – the struggle for survival between nations. The German elites for the most part shared this view and believed that Germany should play a greater role in world affairs. The Kaiser, particularly, was an enthusiastic supporter of *Weltpolitik*. With Bülow's appointment as state secretary for foreign affairs and Tirpitz's appointment to the Navy Office he had two men in power, whom he hoped would make Germany a greater force in the world.

As a politician of his time, Bülow was an imperialist, but he also understood that imperialism was politically popular, and that it enjoyed the Kaiser's support. Bülow was convinced that he could exploit the rivalries in Asia and Africa between the British Empire on the one hand and the French and Russian on the other to gain colonial concessions. Thus it was not surprising that German colonial policy was erratic and provocative. The government missed no opportunities 'to obtain territorial trophies that they could present as successes to the German public'.[25] Through its opportunism Germany contrived, at one time or another, to alienate all the great powers, yet as soon as the situation threatened to escalate into a major international incident Germany usually retreated. The total sum of its efforts by 1907 were **Kiao-Chow**, Britain's share of **Samoa** and several of the former Spanish islands in the Pacific.

> See Map 5
>
> The Germans seized **Kiao-Chow** in November 1897; in December 1899 Britain renounced to Germany all its rights over Western **Samoa**.

Ultimately the successful development of *Weltpolitik* was dependent on the construction of the German navy, which was seen as a visible symbol of Germany's great power status and a guarantee that it would not suffer further humiliation at Britain's hands. Structuralist historians[26] argue that the naval programme was essentially an attempt to appease leaders of heavy industry and rally the conservative and nationalist forces against the SPD in the election of 1898. It was certainly popular with heavy industry, but the Conservatives and the agrarians were more sceptical, as they feared that it would ultimately strengthen German industry at the expense of agriculture. The structuralist approach also ignores the personalities of both the Kaiser and Admiral Tirpitz. William was an ardent supporter of the fleet, and appointed Tirpitz, an advocate of battleship construction, Secretary of State for the German Imperial Naval Office specifically to build up Germany's naval forces. Tirpitz, a Social Darwinist, was convinced that if Germany did not possess a strong navy, it would be strangled by Britain. In his dramatic expansion of the German fleet he consistently enjoyed the Kaiser's support, despite mounting criticism of his policy in the years immediately before 1914.

The launching of the German naval programme in 1898 led to growing tension and an arms race with Britain, which by 1912, in the words of the Austrian foreign minister, had become the 'dominant element of the international situation'.[27] The German government planned to build within 20 years a fleet of 60 battleships, which was intended for action against the British in the North Sea. When completed, Tirpitz calculated that this would keep the British in check and also force them to make major colonial concessions to Germany, but this tactic failed once Britain responded by increasing the size of its own fleet and building the dreadnought battleships.

See Document 38

Germany's hopes of extracting concessions from an isolated and vulnerable British Empire received a severe setback during the years 1904–1907. In 1904 what was initially seen in London as a colonial entente was successfully negotiated with France, the centrepiece of which was French agreement not to block British plans for financial reform in Egypt, provided Britain recognized France's right to maintain law and order in Morocco. A year later Russia's defeat in the Russo-Japanese war of 1904–1905 ended the Russian threat to British interests in China and opened the way up to the Anglo-Russian colonial **entente** of 1907.

Entente: understanding or friendship between two states

Concerned that the Entente Cordiale was the first step in an Anglo-French–Russian realignment against Germany, Bülow decided to challenge the French position in Morocco by pursuing what Mark Hewitson calls a strategy of **'brinkmanship'**,[28] which ran the risk of war. Germany had a strong case because, according to the **Madrid Convention** of 1880, it had the right to be consulted about Morocco's future. Bülow was sure that neither Britain nor Russia, which had not only been defeated by the Japanese, but also faced growing internal unrest, would support the French. He was optimistically convinced that both the Dual Alliance and the Anglo-French Entente would be destroyed, that a new Russo-German alliance would emerge and that France would consequently be forced to come to terms with Germany without the risk of war. Thus when in early 1905 the French government ignored all warnings from Berlin and sent a mission to Fez with instructions to start reforming the Moroccan administration, the Germans demanded a conference on the future of Morocco. Initially Berlin gained a significant diplomatic success: the French cabinet agreed and, bowing to massive German pressure, Delcassé (1852–1923), the foreign minister, resigned in June 1905. In July the Kaiser and Tsar Nicholas II met at Björkö and signed a defensive alliance which would operate against any power in Europe. Nicholas was also assured that the Moroccan crisis was a 'stepping stone' to better Franco-German relations.

Brinkmanship: the practice of pushing a crisis to the brink of war to achieve a successful conclusion

The Madrid Convention of 1880 was signed by 14 powers including Germany, Britain, France, the USA, Italy and Austria.

Yet these successes were purely temporary, and by April 1906 Germany had suffered a crushing defeat. Berlin failed to break up the Franco-Russian alliance, as **the Russian government** overruled the tsar, refused to abandon it, and in November 1905 let the Björkö agreement lapse. The Entente was significantly strengthened when the British government came down firmly on the side of the French, and even authorized secret military staff talks between the British and French armies on the subject of sending an expeditionary force to France in the event of war with Germany. When the Moroccan conference, which was attended by most

The Russian government: As a result of the 1905 revolution, Russia had become a semi-constitutional monarchy and the Tsar's authority was weakened.

of the signatories of the Madrid Convention with the addition of Russia, opened at Algeciras in January 1906, Germany secured the backing of only Austria and Morocco. The other nine states agreed that France had a special interest in Morocco, although Germany did win the concession that the powers should enjoy equal economic rights within Morocco. All in all, Berlin suffered a major diplomatic setback. By insisting on a conference and defending the independence of Morocco, the German government had excluded the possibility of negotiating a separate deal with France.

See Document 39

For his last 3 years in power, Bülow continued to pay lip-service to *Weltpolitik*, but he became increasingly anxious to slow down the tempo of naval construction and find some sort of compromise with Britain. The financial burden of naval rearmament weighed ever more heavily on the Reich's finances, but public opinion and the agitation of the Navy League, as well as Tirpitz's determination to press on with the production of at least three battleships a year to counter Britain's new dreadnought 'super' battleships, ensured that no progress could be made. However, concerning Morocco Bülow was more successful when he negotiated an economic agreement with France in February 1909. By this, Germany recognized France's special political interests in Morocco as long as both countries were able to share equally in its economic development. Only in the Bosnian crisis did he win what David Kaiser calls 'a cheap diplomatic success',[29] when he unconditionally supported the Austrian annexation of Bosnia–Herzegovina and forced Russia to back down.

The Bosnian crisis 1908–1909

The Russians proposed a deal with Austria whereby their warships would be able to pass through the Straits while this right would still be denied to the other powers. In exchange, Austria would annex Bosnia and Herzegovina, which it had administered since 1878 (see p. 148). This was agreed to informally in September 1908, although A. P. Izvolsky, the Russian foreign minister, later claimed that it was understood by both parties that the decision would have to be confirmed by a European conference, but this was never put down on paper. The Austrians duly annexed Bosnia–Herzegovina in October, while the Russians found little international support for their plans at the Straits. In both Russia and Serbia, which eventually hoped to make these provinces part of a Greater Serb state, there were strong protests and even demands for war against Austria. Izvolsky proposed a conference of the great powers, but Austria immediately vetoed this proposal, as it feared a repetition of what had happened at Algeciras, where Germany had been heavily outvoted. What made the crisis so dangerous was that Austria, which had the unconditional backing of Germany, was ready to fight Serbia even if she were supported by Russia. Bülow had given Aehrenthal a 'blank cheque', when he informed him on October 30: 'I shall regard whatever decision you come to as the appropriate one.'[30] His intention was to isolate Russia and break up the Franco-Russian alliance. The

Russians received backing from neither the French, who were busy negotiating the Moroccan Agreement with Germany, nor the British. Russian attempts to persuade the Germans to mediate were ruthlessly brushed aside and the Russian government had no option but to accept the annexation, especially as it was not ready to fight a war. The crisis seriously damaged Russia's relations with Germany and Austria, and made cooperation in the Balkans much more difficult, whilst at the same time bringing Russia and Serbia together. D. C. B. Lieven argues that German behaviour during the Bosnian crisis 'exerted a real influence over the way in which the Russian government handled the crisis of July 1914'.[31]

Bethmann Hollweg and the coming of war

Historians have been inclined to play down the significance of Bethmann Hollweg's thinking on foreign policy partly because he rose within the ranks of the Prussian home civil service. Yet he did have strong views on the foreign policy Germany should follow, but these often clashed not only with those of the Kaiser and Tirpitz, but also his Foreign Secretary, von Kiderlen-Wächter, who dismissed the Chancellor as a weak 'earth worm'. Bethmann sought both to improve relations with the members of the Triple Entente and to pursue a more realistic *Weltpolitik* by reverting to the concept of creating a compact German colonial empire in central Africa and Asia Minor. He hoped that he could achieve this through agreement with Britain, but he was going to drive a hard bargain: Germany would only limit the size of its fleet if Britain was prepared to remain neutral in a continental war, a proposal which Britain could not accept as it would open the way to a German hegemony over Europe. With Russia, relations did become more cordial. In September 1910 Tsar Nicholas visited William at Potsdam, but German attempts to persuade the Russian government to declare that it would not support 'a policy hostile to Germany which England might follow' failed.

Any hopes that Bethmann had of lessening the political tension in Europe were interrupted by the outbreak of the Second Moroccan Crisis in 1911. French troops were sent to occupy Fez in May 1911 to protect the Europeans working there from local unrest. It rapidly became obvious that France had every intention of turning Morocco into a protectorate. Inevitably this broke the 1906 and 1909 agreements and enabled Germany to reopen the Moroccan question. Kiderlen-Wächter, acting virtually independently of Bethmann, seized the chance to reverse the humiliation of Algeciras and gain a dramatic diplomatic triumph by warning – in another act of 'brinkmanship' – the French that if they remained in Morocco, Germany would insist on some form of territorial compensation. As France made no response, on July 1 the German government sent the *Panther*, a gunboat, to the south Moroccan port of Agadir. Kiderlen-Wächter was convinced that if enough pressure was exerted on France, it could be persuaded to cede the French Congo to

Berlin, which in turn would enable the German government later to put pressure on Brussels into to surrender much of the Belgian Congo to Germany. When Britain strongly objected to these demands, Kiderlen-Wächter initially advocated war, but there was little support for this in Berlin or indeed in Vienna. The stock market fell sharply; the Kaiser had no stomach for it and Tirpitz did not want to risk his fleet at this juncture. The German government therefore had little option but to draw back and accept a compromise involving an offer of an economically worthless slice of the French Congo.

The Moroccan crisis was 'a decisive caesura'.[32] The nationalist pressure groups and the Conservatives bitterly condemned the government for its weakness and the idea began to take root in German public opinion that without a major war Germany had no chance of achieving her global political ambitions. Yet the option of a major war was becoming increasingly more of a gamble. The General Staff pointed out that the military balance of power was shifting against Germany. It was particularly concerned by the expansion of the Russian army and the construction of strategic railways in the western provinces, and predicted ominously that Russia, contrary to the assumptions of the Schlieffen Plan (see p. 163), would be able to mobilize *before* France could be defeated. Bethmann was pessimistically convinced that 'the future belongs to Russia which grows and grows and weighs upon us like a heavier and heavier nightmare'.[33] These assessments made a rapprochement with Britain all the more important, but the informal negotiations with Lord **Haldane** (1856–1928) in Berlin in February 1912 came to nothing because Tirpitz, with the Kaiser's support, refused to slow down the tempo of naval construction unless Britain committed itself to neutrality in the event of a German–French war.

In the autumn of 1912 the Balkan states, seizing the opportunity of the Italo–Turkish war in Libya, declared war on Turkey, and by December had virtually driven the Turks out of Europe. The sheer speed and scale of their victory created an acute crisis for the great powers. Austria was now faced with a greatly strengthened Serbia, which had occupied part of Albania and enjoyed the support of Russia. Initially the Kaiser himself was inclined to reject Austrian appeals for help, but on Bethmann's advice he came round to seeing that, in the interests of Germany's own position in Europe, Austria could not be weakened. The crisis deepened on 2 December when Bethmann stated in the *Reichstag* that if the Austrians were attacked by Russia, 'then we would fight for the maintenance of our own future and security'.[34] Commenting on this speech 2 days later, Sir Edward Grey (1862–1933), the British foreign minister, reminded the German ambassador that Britain could not stand back and allow France to be defeated. The Kaiser was infuriated by Grey's message and on 8 December convened a 'war council' which was attended by the army and naval chiefs. The conference agreed that war was ultimately unavoidable, but, at Tirpitz's behest, decided to delay it until the Kiel Canal was finished in the summer of 1914. In the meantime, public opinion was to be prepared for the inevitable hostilities.

Haldane negotiations: The German government indicated, through the Anglo-German financier, Sir Ernest Cassel, that it would like to discuss the naval question with a British minister. Haldane, the war minister, who was, anyway, about to visit Germany, was thus sent to begin negotiations.

The 'war council' of 8 December 1912

How important was this conference? John Röhl and Fritz Fischer regard it as a key date on the road to war, although Wolfgang Mommsen and David Kaiser are more sceptical. Kaiser indeed argues that for Tirpitz the fleet became an end in its own right. He calls him 'a true cold war warrior', who 'continually stressed England's supposed threat to Germany's world position to justify the fleet's existence, while pushing the date of any clash further into the future.[35]

As Röhl has commented, 'Historians of all shades of opinion have thus placed themselves in the unusual position of arguing to a certain extent against the sources. For them the evidence … is too sharp, too exact, "too good to be true".[36] Christopher Clark, for instance, argues that Williams's sense of panic rapidly dissipated, and when the **Second Balkan War** broke out in April 1914 he opposed any moves that might lead to war.[37] Nevertheless after the conference, steps were taken to prepare Germany for war, such as the army bill of April 1913, the building up of gold reserves and laying in of food supplies. At the very least it can be argued that the conference 'is best seen not in terms of a German decision for war, but in terms of a decision against long-term peace'.[38]

The Second Balkan War:
Bulgaria, which felt cheated of its just share of territory, attacked Serbia. The Greeks, the Romanians and the Turks all supported Serbia and within a month Bulgaria was defeated. Significantly the subsequent Treaty of Bucharest much to the alarm of Austria increased the territories of Serbia.

The Outbreak of the First World War

On 28 June 1914 Franz Ferdinand, the heir to the Austrian throne, and his wife were assassinated in Sarajevo by Gavrilo Princip who was closely associated with the Serb terrorist group, the Black Hand. The assassination confirmed Austrian suspicions of Serbia, and provided an excuse to eliminate the Serb 'menace'. To succeed, however, Vienna needed German support in case of Russian intervention, and also had to move quickly while the shock of the assassination was still fresh in the minds of the European governments. On 4 July Count Hoyos was sent to Berlin with a letter from the Austrian Emperor, which openly stated that Austrian policy was to eliminate Serbia as 'a political factor in the Balkans'.[39] Initially the Kaiser prevaricated, but under pressure from the Austrian ambassador agreed that action needed to be taken as quickly as possible against Serbia. According to the Austrian ambassador's report of the proceedings the Kaiser remarked that 'he had been prepared for this for years, and if it should come to a war, Germany would stand by our side …'. Optimistically he added that Russia was unprepared for war 'and would certainly think long and hard over whether to issue the call to arms'.[40] Later this advice was endorsed by Bethmann Hollweg and the Foreign Office, while von Falkenhayn, the War Minister, assured the Kaiser that the army was ready for war.

In retrospect this was a major turning point in the crisis. Was the German government deliberately seeking a conflict with the other great powers on what it believed were conditions which favoured Germany? The diary of Kurt Riezler, Bethmann's private secretary, to whom the chancellor confided his intentions and worries, sheds considerable light on Bethmann's intentions.[41] Its entries suggest that Bethmann and von Jagöw, the Foreign Minister, were convinced that if decisive action against Serbia could be kept localized without Russian or French intervention, it was most likely that the south-eastern European states could be realigned behind Germany, the Franco-Russian alliance would collapse and the way to colonial expansion would be opened up with the consent of Britain. If, as was all too possible, a continental war broke out, it was better that it came sooner rather than later while the balance of forces still favoured Germany. This seems to suggest that Germany was ready to unleash a war for its own ends. Yet two of the most recent historians of the causes of the Great War modify this interpretation somewhat.

See Document 40

Margaret MacMillan rejects the view that Germany 'was determined to bring about such a war for its own ends'. On the other hand she concedes that its leaders 'were prepared to accept the possibility of war partly because, if war were going to come, the time was favourable for Germany and partly because Austria–Hungary had to be kept as an ally'.[42] This certainly appears to endorse Konrad Jarausch's arguments that Bethmann Hollweg was taking 'a calculated risk'.[43] Yet Clark adds an argument with a somewhat Jesuitical twist to this interpretation by stating that the 'Germans were not taking risks, but testing for threats'. By this he means that they were testing to see if Russia really intended 'to rebalance the European system through war'.[44]

In dealing with Serbia speed was the essence. An Austrian ultimatum followed by a brief and victorious war would, so Berlin hoped, produce a *fait accompli*, which the great powers would accept. Yet the delays in mobilization caused by so many soldiers being given **'harvest leave'** and the need to consult the Hungarians, ensured that it was not until 23 July that the ultimatum was sent to Belgrade. The crucial part of the ultimatum insisted that Serbia should, under the supervision of Austrian officials, implement a whole series of anti-terrorist measures. In 'a masterpiece of diplomatic equivocation',[45] which gave the impression of reasonableness, Belgrade rejected the Austrian demands on 25 July. Briefly the tone if not the content of the note seemed to indicate that a conflict could be avoided. The Kaiser now reversed his bellicose position and decided that an Austrian diplomatic rather than military triumph over Serbia would be sufficient. On 26 July the British put forward a plan for a conference of ambassadors to meet in London to discuss the crisis. This was welcomed by the Italians and the French. The Germans, by now aware of the threatening scale of the crisis, argued that direct Austro-Russian talks would be more effective, but they did nothing to facilitate these. For Berlin the priority was, as Bethmann told his ambassador in Vienna, 'solely one of finding a way to realise Austria's desired aim, that of cutting the vital chord of Greater Serbia propaganda without it at the same time bringing on a world war, and if the latter cannot be avoided in the end, of improving the conditions under which we have to wage it where possible'.[46]

Harvest leave: Austrian troops were given leave to help gather in the harvest.

Vienna broke off diplomatic relations and on 28 July declared war on Serbia. The following day Austrian gun boats on the river Save had opened fire on Serbian troops. Whether the war could be kept localized was now dependent on the reaction of the great powers. Essentially Russian policy became clear as early as the Russian Council of Ministers' meeting on 24 and 25 July: Austria was regarded as Germany's stalking horse, and the principal adversary. As attempts to conciliate it in previous crises had failed, ministers were sure that war with Germany would eventually occur even if Russia embarked on a policy of further conciliation. Convinced that France stood unambiguously behind Russia, now was as good a moment as any to risk war. On a state visit to St Petersburg the French President Raymond Poincaré had urged Russia to take a firm line against Austria. The crisis of July 1914 'conformed exactly to the Balkan inception scenario that the alliance over many discussions and summit meetings, had come to define in recent years as the optimal *casus belli*'.[47]

Possibly, given more time, war could have been avoided, but in both Germany and Russia the military planners were desperate to mobilize their forces before hostilities broke out. German mobilization, for instance, was, to quote Margaret MacMillan, 'unlike all others'. Once started it was almost impossible to stop: 'it was not a diplomatic tool; it was war itself'.[48] The Russian government issued orders for a partial mobilization of the army on 28 July. Forty-eight hours later this was changed to full mobilization, despite an initial 'wobble' of the tsar and a belated personal appeal from the Kaiser. Given the Schlieffen Plan, which depended on defeating the French *before* the Russian army was fully ready, Germany had no alternative but to act quickly. On 31 July it sent an ultimatum to Russia warning its government that unless mobilization was halted within 12 hours, Germany would fully mobilize its armed forces. At 5 p.m. on 1 August the German army was mobilized and later that evening Germany declared war on Russia.

Given the strength of the SPD in the *Reichstag* and the country as a whole, an important factor in Bethmann's strategy had been to justify Germany's declaration of war as a defensive action against Russia. He had been specifically reassured by the moderate SPD leader, Albert Südekum (1871–1944), that his party would support a defensive war against Russia. The great questions now were what would France and Britain do? German planning was based on the assumption that France would immediately support Russia, *but* if the unexpected happened and France decided to remain neutral, the German ambassador in Paris was instructed on 31 July to issue an 18-hour ultimatum demanding the surrender of the two fortresses of Toul and Verdun to Germany as a pledge of its good faith. At first it seemed that the war just might be confined to the east. On the evening of 31 July the German ambassador reported a proposal from the British Foreign secretary, Sir Edward Grey, that Britain would remain neutral provided that France was not attacked. Initially this news was greeted with relief in Berlin. However,

Schlieffen Plan

In the event of a two-front war involving France and Russia, accepted military thinking in Germany in the decades after 1871 was that initially France would be contained in the west, while Russia was defeated in the east. In 1905 the Schlieffen Plan drawn up by Alfred von Schlieffen, the Chief of the Prussian General Staff, reversed this strategy so that France would be the first to be attacked. Nevertheless the option of initial large-scale action against Russia was kept open right up to April 1913, and so presumably could still have been put into operation only a year later. Seizing on this fact the American historians, Marc Trachtenberg and Dennis Showalter, argue that Germany did in fact have military options in 1914, and was not the prisoner of a strategic timetable. On the other hand, Annika Mombauer argues strongly that the army had no intention of abandoning the Schlieffen Plan, even if that was possible, and in practice the German government was after all the prisoner of a military timetable.[49] On 1 August when there appeared to be a chance of keeping France out of the war (see below) the Kaiser's suggestion to Moltke that he deployed only against Russia met with the response that in that case the army would be reduced to 'a messy heap of disorderly armed men without supplies'. To this the Kaiser answered: 'your uncle [Helmuth, Moltke the older] would have given me a different answer (see p. 94)'.[50]

later in the evening, when it emerged that this proposal had not even been cleared by the British cabinet, Moltke resumed preparations for the invasion of France. On 1 August the French cabinet decided on a general mobilization of the army and at 7 o'clock that evening Germany declared war on Russia.

It was still not clear whether Britain would declare war on Germany. Grey himself argued that Britain could not stand aside and let France be crushed, but at the end of July there was only minority support in the cabinet for intervention. This changed on 2 August when the German ultimatum was sent to Brussels demanding the right of free passage for its troops through Belgian territory. It justified this demand on the grounds that Germany had 'accurate' knowledge that France was planning to occupy Belgium. Paradoxically, as Christopher Clarke argues, it might have been wiser 'simply to break into and across Belgian territory, making one's excuses as one went and dealing with the matter afterwards as a *fait accompli*'.[51] The British cabinet, was resigned to this happening and had repeatedly stressed that it would not regard such an operation as a *casus belli*. However, the firm and dignified rejection of Germany's demand by Belgium publically wrong-footed the Germans, and was a major propaganda victory for the Entente, which enabled them to obscure their own often dubious machinations and paint Germany as the ruthless aggressor. On 3 August the Germans declared war on France, claiming alleged French infringements across the border into Alsace. The following day German troops invaded Belgium, an action which was to bring Britain into the war. An ultimatum demanding an immediate German withdrawal was sent to Berlin at 2 p.m. that afternoon, and when it expired at midnight (German time) Britain was at war with Germany.

Conclusion: the question of German war guilt

The question of war guilt has played a key role in German history. Article 231 of the Treaty of Versailles in 1919 fairly and squarely placed the blame for 'imposing the war' on Germany and her allies. By the 1920s historians not only in Germany but in Britain, the US and even France rejected this as a one-sided assessment. This remained the accepted view until the emergence of the Fischer thesis, which argued in *Griff nach der Welt-macht* (1961) and *Krieg der Illusionen* (1969)[52] that Germany had pursued an aggressive policy to further her expansionist aims. This provoked a furious controversy and accusations from both conservative politicians and historians that Fischer was reverting to the accusations of Article 231. Fischer's emphasis on the influence of domestic policy, the pressure groups and the elites on German foreign policy was developed by Volker Berghahn, Hans-Ulrich Wehler, Jürgen Kocka and Wolfgang Mommsen of the Bielefeld school (see p. 122).

By the 1970s the Fischer thesis had become the 'new orthodoxy', but over the next three decades his arguments were modified by more con-servative historians, such as Egmont Zechlin, Karl Dietrich Erdman and Gregor Schöllgen,[53] who stressed the defensive nature of German foreign policy and argued that Germany in the final analysis was ready to risk war in order to break out of an isolation imposed upon it. In 1998 Niall Ferguson was to argue that fiscal and political constraints, which were a product of the democratically elected *Reichstag* and the decentralized federal system, instilled in German leaders 'a sense of weakness' and made her ready to contemplate a pre-emptive strike, 'while she could more or less still pass the test' to quote Moltke the younger.[54]

The intense debate in Germany triggered by Fischer has also inspired historians to look more carefully at the record of the other belligerent powers, which shows that they too were ready to accept war to remove threats and consolidate their position. Christopher Clark draws the con-clusion from this that it is meaningless to turn a study of the outbreak of war into 'an Agatha Christie drama at the end of which we will discover the culprit standing over a corpse … with a smoking pistol'. He sees the causes of the war, rather, as 'a multilateral process of interaction'.[55]

What, then, in light of these sometimes contradictory arguments, is Germany's responsibility for the outbreak of the war? The emergence of Germany as a great military and economic power was indeed a threat to the more established states like Britain, France and Russia. The war was arguably fought about real international issues of the sort that had in previous centuries led to conflict. Paul Schroeder has even argued that historians should ask 'not why World War I but why not? … World War I was a normal development in international relations …'.[56]

Could Germany have avoided war by deliberately punching below her weight? In the age of popular imperialism and social Darwinism such a policy was scarcely practical. Certainly the growth of the German fleet antagonized Britain, as German support for Austria in the Balkans did Russia. German policy, which Mark Hewitson has described as 'brinkmanship',[57] repeatedly risked war and seemed at times calculated to alienate all its neighbours, as the two Moroccan and Bosnian crises showed. This, of course, strengthened the Triple Entente and made Germany more dependent on its one remaining ally, Austria–Hungary. It was not surprising therefore that within Germany there was a widespread feeling that the military balance was tilting against it. In the final analysis, Bethmann saw the July crisis as a window of opportunity. If it could successfully be resolved to Austria's advantage without the Entente coming to the assistance of Russia, then Germany's position in Europe would be greatly strengthened, the Franco-Russian alliance ruptured, and the way would be open to future colonial expansion. If the Entente stood by Russia, then war was preferable now rather than later. Ironically, in retrospect it can be seen that time was really with, rather than against, Germany. There is no evidence that Germany was actually weakening *vis-à-vis* Russia, and her peaceful economic penetration of Europe, South America and the British Empire was visibly growing. With patience, diplomatic skill and some luck, the Great War could have been avoided without a German 'surrender'.

See Document 38

8 Germany at War, 1914–1918

Introduction: problems, issues and questions

The German defeat in 1918 is often attributed to the bad management of its war economy and the success of the British blockade. Jay Winter, for instance argued that 'in effect the German state dissolved under the pressure of industrial war'.[1] Jürgen Kocka[2] sees its defeat as a consequence of the failure to distribute scarce resources fairly, which ultimately led to the revolution of November 1918. The German war economy is frequently contrasted with the apparent success of the British and French economies, which according to Winter were both 'more equitable and efficient'.[3] However this view is strongly challenged by Neil Ferguson,[4] as it ignores the overwhelming economic advantages enjoyed by the Entente Powers, as well as exaggerating the efficiency of the British and French war economies. Given that Germany came within an ace of winning the war, it can be argued that the German war economy proved a remarkable success. More Maybe more compelling reasons for Germany's defeat can be found in political rather than material factors particularly in the relationship between its civil and military authorities.

The 'spirit of 1914'

The spirit of unity and the great wave of patriotism that engulfed the nation when war broke in August 1914 is legendary, and was nostalgically recalled in the Weimar Republic. All the parties, including the SPD, voted for war credits, and a political truce (*Burgfrieden*) was announced by the Kaiser in the famous words: 'I no longer recognize parties; I recognize only Germans.' However, this spirit of 1914 was not as universal as later myths would have it. Local histories have indicated that it was also accompanied by deep feelings of anxiety, while many in the Labour movement only reluctantly accepted their party's endorsement of the war as a necessary defence against the ultra-reactionary Tsarist Russia.[5] The 'spirit of 1914' was a powerful emotion that temporarily hid the bitter divisions in German society and inevitably meant different things to different classes. To the university educated upper middle classes it was a powerful confirmation that Germany's distinctive constitution and route to modernization was essentially viable, even if it needed some reform. The Conservatives saw the new mood of national unity as a chance to halt the rise of socialism and to defend the privileges of the Junkers and industrialists. Rewards to the German people would not be constitutional reform but Germany hegemony on the European Continent. This view was hardly shared by the working classes themselves; to them 'the spirit of 1914' raised expectations of further political and social reform and a new practical spirit of equality. As the war dragged on, disillusion set in and the hopes that it had raised 'took on an aura of an elusive fantasy, a painful reminder of the idealism that had reigned in the first hour'.[6]

See Document 41

The strategic background, 1914–1915

By the early autumn of 1914 the strategic character of the war had become clear. In the east, as the Battle of Tannenberg had shown, the Russians could be defeated, but their armies still remained in the field and threatened Austria, while in the west the Anglo-French counter-attack across the Marne and the subsequent German retreat to the Aisne marked the beginning of a deadly, static war of attrition, a pattern which persisted until the spring of 1918. This reverse led to the replacement as Chief of the General Staff of von Moltke, who had suffered a nervous breakdown, by General von Falkenhayn (1861–1922). The failure of the Schlieffen Plan left the Germans fighting a war on two fronts, which consumed ever larger numbers of troops, munitions and equipment. Meanwhile British control of the seas ensured that the Royal Navy was able to blockade Germany and that the German colonial possessions in Africa and Asia were quickly seized by Allied forces – it was only in German East Africa (now Tanzania) that the Germans, under the leadership of General von Lettow-Vorbeck (1870–1963), managed to fight a successful guerrilla war against the British right up to November 1918. The Entente and Central Powers both attempted to secure Turkish support through rival offers of concessions. In October 1914 German promises to support Turkish annexation of Russian border territory led to Turkey declaring war on the Entente. During the winter of 1914–1915 Italy remained neutral but joined the Entente in May 1915 when promised the Austrian territories of South Tyrol, Istria and much of the Dalmatian coastline.

The problem of food and raw materials

Germany, like its adversaries, had to adapt its economy and society to the demands of an industrial war, but this was made more difficult by the fragmentation of its administration between federal, state and local institutions. The Prussian Law of Siege, which came into operation at the outbreak of war, gave executive power to local corps commanders, who were directly responsible to the Kaiser, but their districts did not correspond to the borders of the existing state and regional governments. This led to the chaotic proliferation of committees and bureaucracy.

The most immediate challenge to the German war effort came from the British blockade, which threatened to strangle the German economy by intercepting imports of vital raw materials. That this threat was averted was largely the work of Walther Rathenau,[7] under whose initial chairmanship the Prussian War Office set up the War Materials Section (KRA). In cooperation with the industrialists, this office formed war materials corporations, the task of which was to buy or requisition all available raw materials both in Germany and the occupied areas and then distribute them to the war industries. The German war economy developed within what Roger Chickering has called a 'hybrid institutional framework'.[8] The 200 war materials corporations that were eventually created were financed by the government and organized the production of armaments and equipment for the armed forces. Some participants, like Rathenau himself and his colleague, Wichard von Moellendorf (1881–1937), believed that these were creating the basis for a unique German post-war 'national socialism' in which industry and government would cooperate closely. The munitions industry was one of the great triumphs of the German war effort, and right up to October 1918, despite the blockade, the German army never went short of munitions. In blunting the impact of the British blockade, the work of German scientists was crucial. Fritz Haber (1868–1934) and Robert Bosch (1861–1942), for instance, devised a process for **nitrogen fixation** which made German munitions production independent of imported nitrates. Similarly, German chemists also invented synthetic cellulose, which replaced imported cotton in the munitions industry.

Nitrogen fixation: the process whereby nitrogen in the atmosphere is converted into ammonia

The ability of the German government to distribute food was not nearly as effective. While it is true that nobody actually died *directly* of

3 The Kaiser's speech at the opening of the *Reichstag* on 4 August 1914 made the headlines in this Berlin newspaper. The Kaiser made his famous statement that he recognized 'no more political parties – just Germans'

Berliner Lokal-Anzeiger, 4 August 1914, front page

starvation in the Empire during the war, 'undernourishment became a mass phenomenon, a festering source of demoralization, discontent and domestic strife'.[9] The British blockade and the Russian ban on grain exports led to an immediate decline of some 25 per cent in German food production, which was exacerbated by the voracious demands of the army. Responding to the laws of supply and demand, the price of food rose sharply. At first the city governments and the other local authorities attempted to impose price ceilings, but by the end of 1914 it was clear that food would have to be rationed. A start was made with bread when the Imperial Grain Corporation was created, which served as a model for

Walther Rathenau, 1867–1922

Son of Emil Rathenau, the founder of AEG, Walther Rathenau was a polymath, who was not only one of Germany's leading businessmen, but also a prolific writer. He had reported on the situation in German South West Africa in 1907, advised both Bülow and Bethmann Hollweg, and had been considered as a possible Reich secretary of state. After he left the KRA in 1915, thanks partly to his own lecture on the subject, he became a national hero, and for the remainder of the war his books on the future of Germany and of the economy became best-sellers. However, as he advocated a semi-socialist or, perhaps more accurately, a 'national socialist' economic model, he also made many enemies and attracted bitter anti-Semitic attacks. He became known as 'Jesus in morning dress'. By November 1918, since he had urged Germany to fight on in the hope of gaining better peace terms, he was rejected by the SPD, and it was not until 1921 that he entered the Wirth government as minister for reconstruction. Appointed foreign minister in January 1922, he was murdered in June by right-wing assassins (see p. 198).

rationing meats, vegetables, fruits, oils and potatoes. In 1916 the War Food Office was set up, but unlike the KRA it lacked the power to override military and civilian food agencies, while itself creating a maze of baffling red tape.

In parts of Germany rationing and distribution were effective, especially in the smaller towns that enjoyed access to the countryside, but it was the big conurbations that suffered most, where bottlenecks on the railways delayed food distribution. For the first 2 years the good harvests of 1914 and 1915 took the edge off the food shortages, but the cumulative effect of the blockade cannot be exaggerated, as it produced serious shortages in fertilizers, fats and meats, which compounded the shortages of many staple commodities. Although the wealthy and up to a point the skilled workers could supplement their rations through the black market, it was the lower-paid, unskilled workers,[10] the professional classes and the **white-collar** office workers and their families in the big cities who suffered most.

White-collar workers: office workers

The move to total war

Falkenhayn believed that the war could only be concluded satisfactorily by convincing Britain that Germany was invincible. Firstly he hoped that Russia could be persuaded to accept a peace based on moderate terms after defeat on the Eastern Front. In the meantime Germany should destroy Britain's maritime commerce through an unrestricted U-boat campaign, but this strategy rapidly ran into problems. The submarine campaign had to be called off when it threatened in May 1915, after the sinking of the *Lusitania*, to bring the USA into the war. In early 1916

Falkenhayn decided to concentrate on knocking France, which he perceived to be 'England's best sword', out of the war by attacking the historic fortress of Verdun. He aimed to mount a series of limited actions, which would provoke French counter-attacks. Hopefully these would be destroyed by the 'mincing machine' of the German artillery. He calculated that the fall of the fortress and the decimation of the French forces would lead to a collapse in French morale.[11] However, French morale held and the Germans not only failed to take Verdun but suffered some 336,832 casualties.

Together this costly failure at Verdun, the indecisive naval battle of Jutland in June, 1916, which still left the British in control of the seas, the large-scale Allied offensive at the Somme in July and the initially successful Brusilov offensive in the east, confronted Germany with the choice of either attempting to secure a negotiated peace or an even more ruthless mobilization of men and economic resources – total war in fact. Bethmann Hollweg desired the former[12] and used these setbacks to persuade the Kaiser to drop Falkenhayn, and replace him with von Hindenburg, the victor of Tannenberg and his chief of staff, Erich von Ludendorff (see p. 177).

Lusitania: 1198 out of the 2000 passengers carried by the *Lusitania*, a Cunard liner, were drowned. Many of these were Americans.

The Hindenburg Programme, August 1916

Bethmann gambled that Hindenburg's charisma would make a negotiated peace for the German people acceptable. Here, however, he miscalculated, as the new military leaders had no intention of advising the Kaiser to end the war. On the contrary they took immediate steps to prosecute the war more vigorously. Ludendorff proclaimed the total mobilization of the German economy and demanded immense increases in munitions and weapons. The Supreme War office (*Kriegsamt*) under General Groener (1867–1939) was set up to oversee and to organize the whole war economy. The age of conscription was lowered to 18, which had the effect of increasing the number of conscripts for 1917 by 300,000. In November the Auxiliary Service Law came into force: every eligible man in Germany between the ages of 17 and 60 was to be conscripted for war work, if he was not already in the armed forces. Under pressure from the SPD, it also conceded that the unions would take part in the administration of this law and set up conciliation committees to settle disputes.

By the end of 1916 the Germans had lost 1,500,000 men.

The Programme failed to meet its targets. In practice the creation of the Supreme War Office compounded bureaucratic confusion, and its attempts to close down non-essential industries led to a field day for lawyers who were able to question its actions at every level. By early 1917 it was clear the quotas were not being met. Despite desperate efforts to use every bit of scrap iron, German industry was producing less steel in February 1917 than it had in July 1916. Neither did it have much success in mobilizing extra labour, if only because it had already been deployed.

Field Marshal Paul von Hindenburg (1847–1934) and General Erich von Ludendorff (1865–1937)

Hindenburg was the living symbol of the Prussian military class. He had been decorated in the war of 1870 and retired in 1911 as a commander of an army corps. In 1914 he was recalled and given command of the eastern front. His chief of staff, **Erich von Ludendorff**, was a brilliant, bourgeois staff officer, who had been head of the Operations Section of the General Staff and had been the driving force behind the massive expansion in the German army just before the war. After his success in destroying the Liège fortress in August 1914, he was appointed Hindenburg's chief of staff. Together they formed a remarkable team. Ludendorff's organizational skills complemented Hindenburg's enormous popularity. After the epic Battle of Tannenberg, Hindenburg's prestige in Germany was immense, and he became the symbol of German determination to win the war. Already by the end of 1914 a Hindenburg cult had come into existence and everywhere large wooden statues of him were put up. Funds for the war effort were raised by encouraging admirers to purchase nails to hammer into the statue. Hindenburg's fame soon grew to such an extent that the Kaiser himself became jealous. It was the legacy of this fame that he was elected President of the Weimar Republic in 1925 (see p. 223).

Deportations:
Compare this to the much more ambitious labour-deportation programmes carried out in the Second World War. See pp. 281–283.

To meet this shortfall, over 100,000 Belgians were **deported** into Germany and 600,000 Poles were either persuaded or forced to work on German farms. Ultimately the Programme was unsustainable. It was, to quote Gerald Feldman, 'the triumph not of imagination, but of fantasy ... In his pursuit of an ill-conceived total mobilization for the attainment of irrational goals, Ludendorff undermined the strength of the army, promoted economic instability, created administrative chaos, and set loose an orgy of interest politics.'[13]

Financing the war

'Every gun, shell, sandbag, cartridge box, horseshoe, belt buckle and boot nail carried a price tag',[14] which had to be paid for by the federal government, whose budget had increased by the end of the war more than ten times since July 1914. State and local government also had to shoulder the enormous costs involved in supporting the families of soldiers at the front, subsidizing rations for the poor, paying the salaries of the newly expanded army of bureaucrats, while at the same time continuing to pay the salaries of those officials who had been called up. Both central and local government were thus confronted with the urgent problem of how to raise sufficient funds to cover their escalating costs. The options were either to tax or to borrow. The federal government was loath to introduce direct taxation, although the states and communes did in fact levy direct taxes on property and income. Karl Helfferich (1874–1924), the minister for finance, was convinced that direct taxation would be both divisive and bad for morale, and it was not until 1916 that a federal value-added tax, which was aimed at the war profiteers, was introduced, but this was in practice easily evaded. By 1916 taxation only covered about 15 per cent of the direct costs of the war. Economic historians have traditionally criticized Germany for financing the war through inflationary borrowing rather than direct taxation. Yet, as Ferguson has shown, in practice Germany was 'acting no differently from other combatants'.[15] Britain, for instance, paid for only 18.2 per cent of its wartime expenditure out of direct taxation. The crucial difference, however, between the finances of the Entente Powers and Germany was that Germany had no access to the global financial markets and had to raise the necessary funds at home.

A crucial source of money, as it was in all the belligerent states, was the sale of war bonds, which proved to be very popular and were purchased by both individuals and institutions in great numbers. By the end of the war nearly a hundred billion marks had been raised through these bonds. Yet this only covered two-thirds of federal costs and, of course, the interest on the bonds would ultimately still have to be paid. In the event of victory the defeated enemy would be presented with this bill, but in the meantime there was no alternative but to print money. At local level the federal government set up loan *bureaux*, which could lend money to the states and local government agencies, and even to private borrowers, on more generous terms than the banks. They were also allowed to print their own notes, which had the legal status of money. These policies led to escalating inflation, which became one of the defining experiences of the German home front. It resulted in the German people themselves paying for the war and made great inroads into their savings. A war bond, for instance, which was bought in August 1914 at 1000 marks was, 4 years later, worth in current prices a mere 300 marks. Inflation on this scale was inevitably a source of widespread anxiety on the home front. Again, it is important to put this into context. All the belligerent states suffered from inflation between 1914 and 1918, but apart from Russia and Austria, the greatest increase was in Germany, whose money supply increased between these two dates by 285 per cent compared to 110 per cent in Britain.[16]

Winners and losers: the impact of total war on the German people

The war affected every German, but on the home front its impact was diverse and created both winners and losers. It brought about a fundamental restructuring of the German economy. The heavy industries, particularly the chemical industry, underwent immense expansion, while the consumer industries were slimmed down or in some cases even closed, unless they could become contractors or subcontractors for war materials. In Wesel, for instance, by the winter of 1916–1917 about half the small businesses and workshops had to shut down as a result of the Hindenburg Programme. Inevitably then, it was those Germans who worked for or supplied the large war industries who were best placed to survive the war in good shape.

In many ways the war consolidated class divisions in Germany. It weakened the middle classes, enriched the employers in the war industries and made the working classes more cohesive. Workers switched jobs frequently and the differentials between skilled and unskilled workers and male and female workers narrowed. In the war industries, workers' wages steadily increased in relation to the rest of the population, even though this did not exempt them from the effects of inflation and food shortages. The Programme had also extended an embryonic form 'of social partnership'[17] to the unions, which gave them real influence over the drafting of legislation dealing with wages and prices. When the Auxiliary Service Law was submitted to the *Reichstag* (see p. 171), the SPD successfully extracted from the government significant concessions for the trade unions. Their representatives were now to sit on the committees in each district which were to administer labour mobilization, and it was agreed that in all factories of more than 50 workers joint committees of labour and management would deal with disputes over wages and conditions.

Throughout the middle and professional classes inflation created a feeling of deep insecurity. Those who suffered most were the non-unionized white-collar employees, who were on fixed salaries which were steadily eroded by inflation. Towards the end of the war public officials and salaried employees were beginning to organize and even to strike.[18] The professional classes, academics, higher civil servants, journalists and lawyers also experienced a marked decline in their standard of living. The financial destruction of these classes was completed by the hyper-inflation of 1923 (see p. 203), but the origins of this crisis lay in the way the German government had to finance the war.

Women and the family

Traditionally the war has been seen as the real beginning of female emancipation in Germany, as elsewhere in Europe. German women inevitably experienced the war differently from men. The official assumption was still that women belonged in the 'private sphere' and thus were not legally mobilized by the Auxiliary Service Law of 1916. In reality it was only the more prosperous middle-class women who could afford to remain in the 'private sphere'. Working-class women, despite being recipients of public welfare to compensate them for the absence of their husbands at the front, had little option but to seek employment, as they had to take responsibility not just for running the home, but also for earning sufficient money to pay for essentials to enable their families to survive. By October 1918 more than a third of the total workforce was female. Women quitted jobs in domestic service or lower-paid jobs in textiles or food processing for work on the assembly lines in the armaments industries. In Krupp's factories, for instance, women made up over 40 per cent of the workforce. The wage differentials between the sexes narrowed and women became politicized by joining trade unions. In 1918 they formed 25 per cent of the socialist unions' membership. Many middle-class women were compelled to work in clerical or secretarial positions in order that their families might survive financially. Upper middle-class women, whose servants could wait in the food queues on their behalf, gravitated to charitable organizations. Through the voluntary National Women's Service they began to organize soup kitchens, child care centres, organizations for collecting second-hand clothes, and so on, and began to experience real responsibility in the public sphere for the first time.

For the majority of children the war entailed neglect and the long absences of their mothers, who were involved in war work. Large numbers of children grew up in fatherless households. The younger children were often looked after by siblings or in day-care centres. Like the rest of the population they suffered from varying degrees of malnutrition, and, according to one contemporary estimate, nearly 40 per cent suffered from rickets. As a result of the requisitioning of school buildings, the call-up of teachers, the shortage of coal which led to the closing of schools during cold weather in winter, and the employment of children at harvest time, education was interrupted and perfunctory. Hundreds of thousands of older children were also given pre-military training in paramilitary organizations. In their teens most working-class children were already at work fulltime in the factories. The disorientation of German youth led to a dramatic rise in juvenile crime and truancy. In Cologne this increased from 15 to 48 per cent in the first 3 years of the war. Attempts were made to control the behaviour of young workers by imposing curfews, banning them from cinemas and forcing them to deposit the major part of their wages in saving accounts.

For comparison with the even greater disruption to education and family life in the period 1942–1945, see pp. 283–284.

Was there a sexual revolution?

It was an accepted part of war that soldiers, even if they were married, should have access to prostitutes. Their infidelity was considered much less shocking than female promiscuity on the home front. The latter challenged the 'supportive bond that ordered relations between home and the battlefront'.[19] Major transit centres like Düsseldorf saw prostitution develop on a large scale. The degree of promiscuity among middle-class, married women is impossible to determine, but it was the subject of cartoons, jokes and many a serious article in the newspapers and magazines.

War aims and domestic politics, August 1914–August 1916

For the first 2 years of the war Bethmann managed to preserve a rather precarious domestic peace. As part of the *Burgfrieden*, party strife in the *Reichstag* virtually ceased. In a special enabling act it had delegated its legislative powers to the *Bundesrat*, which now assumed the power to promulgate legislation. Although the *Reichstag* still maintained the right to review legislation, its importance was marginalized for the first half of the war.

Bethmann Hollweg's efforts to preserve the *Burgfrieden*

The key to domestic peace was to preserve the *Burgfrieden* and not to allow the potentially divisive issues of post-war domestic reform and war aims to stir up public controversy. It was vital to keep the SPD behind the war effort. It had willingly voted for war credits in August 1914 because it was convinced that Germany was fighting a war of survival and not of conquest. Apart from a few members on the right of the party, it was implacably opposed to annexations. The bourgeois parties on the other hand, including the Centre and the Progressives, initially advocated a policy of annexation. The Pan-Germans, the nationalist pressure groups and the right-wing parties all supported ambitious plans of annexation in both western and eastern Europe and hoped that the realization of these demands would distract the people from demands for domestic reform. Subjected to these conflicting pressures, Bethmann attempted to avoid committing himself publically to a definite programme for as long as possible. Nevertheless his September Programme, drawn up by his secretary Kurz Riezler, showed that in the event of a German victory he had a series of far-reaching demands up his sleeve, which would have resulted in the reduction of Belgium and France to vassal states as well as the creation of a German-dominated **Mitteleuropa** and **Mittelafrika**. In that sense, as Fritz Fischer has argued, he was potentially no less expansionist than the Pan-Germans, although it is important to remember as Bethmann himself stressed that these were not detailed plans but 'only *ad hoc* ideas which could be influenced through changes in the fortune of arms'.[20]

Mitteleuropa: a proposed customs union, the centre of which would be the Austrian and German empires and which would stretch from France to the Near East

Mittelafrika: a proposed area of German territory between German East Africa and German South West Africa including the Belgian Congo and Portuguese Angola

For the first 2 years of the war Bethmann managed to keep the *Burgfrieden* intact. Popular support was still widespread for the war, and, except in the *Reichstag*, censorship prevented any public criticism. Both the Protestant and Catholic churches supported the war effort and the tiny German Peace Society was hounded by the authorities. There was somewhat more opposition to the war among the socialist working classes in such radical bastions as Bremen, Braunschweig Berlin, Düsseldorf and Leipzig. In December 1915, 20 SPD deputies actually voted against war credits, and by the summer of 1916 the *Burgfrieden* was coming under increasing pressure. Labour Day (1 May), was marked by demonstrations in Berlin. When **Karl Liebknecht** (1871–1919), the leader of the left-wing of the SPD, was sentenced by a military court in June to 4 years in jail for his anti-war campaign, a series of strikes broke out in Berlin, Essen and other industrial centres. These were a turning point in the history of the opposition to the war because they were the beginning of the purely political strikes which had the potential to paralyse the war economy. However, the great majority of the SPD continued to support the war, partly out of patriotism and also because it actually promised considerable political gains for the working classes. Victory would, they hoped, end the hostility and discrimination which the labour movement had suffered before the war. The need to win the support of organized labour had enabled trade union and party leaders to force the government to make a number of key concessions, such as the legal recognition of trade unions, the establishment of arbitration boards in the larger factories and a role for the unions in the administration of the Auxiliary Service Law in 1916.

> **Karl Liebknecht:** publicly opposed the war as early as December 1914. In 1916 he began to circulate, together with Rosa Luxemburg, a series of anti-war newsletters, the so-called 'Spartacus letters'. He was jailed for anti-war activities in 1916 and was released in October 1918 (see p. 188).

The dismissal of General von Falkenhayn

The longer the war continued, the greater the political and domestic strains became. As early as December 1914, Falkenhayn had already conceded that Germany could not win the war outright. The consequences to be drawn from this became a matter of bitter dispute between the generals and the civilian leadership. Bethmann was no Bismarck who had curbed the extravagant ambitions of the generals, but then he was hindered by the increasing weakness of the Kaiser, who was rapidly becoming a mere shadow of himself and lacked the will to arbitrate between the armed forces and the civilians. The Kaiser as early as August 1914 had transferred to the Chief of the General Staff the right to make operational decisions in his name. Throughout the war he remained at the German *Grosses Hauptquartier*, a 'prisoner of his generals' in the words of the Austrian ambassador.[21] As the heads of the army and navy were responsible solely to the Supreme War Lord (see p. 124), the Kaiser, there was no war cabinet or institutional forum where service chiefs and ministers could together discuss options and policies. Strategic and political decisions were, therefore, decided in an atmosphere of intrigue and mutual hostility.

By August 1916 Verdun, Jutland, the Somme, Brusilov offensive and finally Romania's declaration of war on 28 August, had so discredited Falkenhayn's strategy that Bethmann was able to persuade the Kaiser to dismiss him a few days later. In his place Hindenburg was appointed to the supreme command, with Ludendorff as his chief of staff and 'first quartermaster', in the optimistic hope that they would support an attempt to negotiate a peace settlement with the Entente Powers on the best possible terms[22] (see pp. 170–171).

The supremacy of Hindenburg and Ludendorff, September 1916–September 1918

From now on the supreme command (OHL), or rather, behind the scenes, Ludendorff, became the dominant force in domestic politics. Essentially Ludendorff believed that civilian politicians, and even the Kaiser, were subordinate to the military. His power was based on the charismatic authority which he enjoyed by virtue of his association with Hindenburg. He was a strong advocate of the advantages of a military dictatorship, but the multipolar nature of power in the federal state of Germany in practice prevented him from creating one, although he became the single most powerful figure in the Empire.

Ludendorff, with Hindenburg's implicit support, dramatically upped the stakes in Germany's war aims. He contemptuously dismissed Bethmann's ambiguities and prevarications, and encouraged the widest fantasies of the nationalists. By forcing the government to announce the creation of an independent Poland in November 1916, he also effectively torpedoed any chance of a negotiated peace with Russia, which considered the Grand Duchy of Warsaw to be an integral part of its empire. Then in January 1917 the high command persuaded the Kaiser to agree to renewing unrestricted submarine warfare against Britain, which, far from resulting in a British defeat, brought the USA into the war on the side of the Entente as an 'allied and associated power'. The constant flood of manifestos from nationalist pressure groups, which, with the full encouragement of the high command, demanded the creation of a German *Mitteleuropa* also contradicted the idea that Germany was fighting a defensive war and polarized the political forces in Germany. Increasingly, the right consolidated behind Ludendorff, while the left began to unite behind the demand for a negotiated peace. Bethmann's promotion of Hindenburg and Ludendorff had been a major political blunder, as he recognized when he confided to his inner circle: 'With Falkenhayn Germany risks losing the war strategically – with Ludendorff politically'.[23] This was indeed to be a prescient view.

The peace resolution and its consequences

The March revolution in Russia had 'an electrifying impact'[24] in Germany, and indeed throughout Europe. It provided a model for the workers of how economic issues could be exploited to bring about both democratic reform and the end of the war. In April 1917, when a cut in the bread rations led to massive strikes in Berlin, Leipzig, Brunswick, Halle and Magdeburg, the strikers consciously echoed the cries in Russia for 'bread, land and peace', and formed workers' councils based on the soviets. Within the *Reichstag*, the dissident socialists who had voted against the war loans and been expelled from the SPD now set up

The USPD survived until 1922, when its more moderate members rejoined the SPD, while those on the left joined the Communists.

their own party, the Independent German Social Democratic Party (**USPD**). In the *Reichstag* they could count on 24 members, while, outside parliament, their strength lay in the Ruhr, Berlin and the other industrial cities.

The very existence of the USPD on its left flank put pressure on the majority SPD (MSPD) to call for a negotiated peace. By 1917 the ideological assumptions of the war had been transformed. Russia, crippled by revolution, was ready to make peace, while democratic America had come into the war on the side of the Entente. To appease the MSPD and head off their opposition to the war, Bethmann managed to persuade the Kaiser to promise in his 'Easter offer' on 7 April 1917 the abolition of the three-class voting system in Prussia (see p. 78) and reform the *Bundesrat* after the war, but the announcement was ambiguous, vague and unconvincing. Neither were there any signs of concessions to the policy of a negotiated peace from Hindenburg and Ludendorff, who, on the contrary, drew up a programme of war aims that was more ambitious than anything hitherto advocated – the so-called **Kreuznach Programme**. Bethmann reluctantly accepted this programme, although he did tell the *Bundesrat* that his aim was a peace with Russia that would exclude 'any idea of rape' and would leave 'no sting, no trace of resentment'.[25] Increasingly it was becoming clear that the debate on war aims was becoming 'inextricably bound up with the debate on Germany's constitutional arrangements'.[26] Those who wanted a negotiated peace had no option but to support demands for constitutional reform which would break the army's grip on power. Conversely those, like the members of the Fatherland's Party (see below) who dismissed Bethmann as a traitor, supported the authoritarian powers of the High Command.

Bethmann's attempts to hold the balance between left and right resulted only in a policy of vacillation and ambiguity that alienated both sides and also shook the confidence of the Centre and Liberal parties in him. In the early to mid summer of 1917 the topics of the Prussian franchise reform and negotiated peace dominated the *Reichstag*. The leader of the left wing of the Centre, Matthias Erzberger (1875–1921), seized the chance to reveal to the Main Commission of the *Reichstag*, when it met in early July to deliberate on war credits, alarming information which he had received from Colonel Bauer (1869–1929), Ludendorff's political link man. Bauer had told him that Austria was in a desperate situation. In the spring of 1917 the Austrian government had informed Berlin that 'the Monarchy was at the end of its endurance',[27] and in March **Emperor Karl Joseph** had secretly made contact with the French with the apparent offer of a **negotiated peace**. The Germans were only informed about this later by the Austrian foreign ministry.

This information as well as mounting evidence that the U-boat war was failing persuaded the Centre party, the MSDP and the Progressives, which formed a majority in the *Reichstag*, to pass the Peace Resolution on

Kreuznach Programme: In eastern Europe Germany would annex Estonia and Lithuania and Poland would become a satellite state. In western Europe Belgium would become a German satellite state and the ore and coal basin of Longwy-Briey would be annexed from France.

Karl Franz Joseph (1887–1922) was grandnephew of Franz Joseph, and was the heir to the Austrian and Hungarian thrones after the assassination of Franz Ferdinand. He became emperor on 21 November 1916.

Negotiated peace: Officially the Austria ruled out a separate peace without Germany, but on 24 March Emperor Karl appeared to offer France support for the return of Alsace-Lorraine and a separate peace. In the end this was rejected by the Entente because it threatened 'Allied unity', as it made no concessions to Italy, which had only entered the war after being offered Austrian territory (see p. 168).

19 July 1917. This challenged the OHL by bluntly stating: 'The *Reichstag* strives for a peace of understanding and permanent reconciliation of peoples. Forced territorial acquisitions and political, economic and financial oppressions are irreconcilable with such a peace'. Although the USPD abstained and argued that this did not go far enough, it was nevertheless an impressive assertion of parliamentary defiance of the OHL, which marked the beginning of a new period of political confrontation and was a major blow to the domestic consensus.

See Document 43

Even while the Peace Resolution was being debated on the floor of the *Reichstag*, Bethmann had managed to persuade the Kaiser on 10 July to make a more definite announcement that the next Prussian *Landtag* would be elected on a new democratic franchise. This together with the issue of the Peace Resolution persuaded Ludendorff and Hindenburg on 11 July to hand in their resignation to the Kaiser on the grounds that they could no longer work with the chancellor. Despite William's initial reluctance to let Bethmann go, lacking any firm support in the *Reichstag* and bitterly opposed by the army, Bethmann had no option but to hand in his own resignation on 13 July. The resignation 'marked a fundamental caesura' in the Kaiser's reign. Power now decisively shifted to 'the Siamese twins' as Williams called Ludendorff and Hindenburg.[28] Bethmann was replaced with the Prussian bureaucrat, Georg Michaelis (1857–1936), whose views were more in tune with those of the generals. At the same time to counter the influence of the USPD the OHL launched an intensive programme of patriotic propaganda among the troops and the civilians at home. Ludendorff also gave his support to the German Fatherland Party, which was led by Tirpitz and the banker Wolfgang Kapp (1858–1922) and supported by the parties of the right and heavy industry. By January 1918 it had become a national movement with nearly a million members. From the left it was by the 'People's League for Freedom and Fatherland' with an equally impressive membership which urged a compromise peace and constitutional reform.

Within the *Reichstag* the supporters of a moderate peace gained in confidence. The *Reichstag*'s budget committee, which continued to meet even when the *Reichstag* was adjourned, now began to acquire the role of a parliamentary executive agency, and discussed vital matters of domestic and foreign policy. The three parties, which had supported the peace resolution, liaised with the National Liberals and established a joint consultative committee, and in October 1917 a parliamentary majority successfully passed another resolution calling for the democratic reform of the Prussian suffrage. The OHL in response to these developments, again intervened and had Michaelis sacked, but this time Ludendorff consulted the party leaders and persuaded the Kaiser in October 1917 to appoint Georg von Hertling (1843–1919), a Bavarian aristocrat aged 74, who was a member of the Centre party and prime minister of Bavaria.

Hertling was by no means a puppet of the OHL. He appeared to back constitutional reform and even included several of the party leaders in the cabinet, but his appointment did not mean that the OHL was beginning to entertain the idea of a negotiated peace. By the end of 1917 the Entente had been shaken by the successive failures of the Nivelle Offensive, the Third Battle of Ypres, the Italian defeat at Caporetto and the October Revolution in Russia, which brought Lenin to power. There seemed, therefore, a window of opportunity to achieve a compromise peace, but this was firmly rejected by Hindenburg and Ludendorff, who seized the chance of the Russian collapse to dictate to the Bolsheviks the harsh, annexationist peace of **Brest–Litovsk**. This led to a renewal of strikes in Berlin and the other industrial centres in January, but the peace itself was ratified in the *Reichstag* by an overwhelming majority, and indicated that Ludendorff's determination to play for the highest stakes could still pay off, if it was possible to exploit the temporary weakness of the Allied and Associated Powers and win a decisive victory in the west.

Brest-Litovsk: March 1918, forced the Russians to surrender Poland, the Baltic provinces, the Ukraine, Finland and the Caucasus.

The collapse of the Ludendorff offensive and military defeat

The spring offensive in March 1918 was the OHL's final gamble, but the odds were heavily against its success; the Allied forces, supported now by American troops, were greater and far better supplied, and were in a position to prolong the war for as long as was necessary. Initially the Ludendorff offensive enjoyed some success. Four separate attacks, thanks to local superiority, surprise and good planning, managed to make significant initial gains. By early June the Germans were just 56 miles from Paris, but then exhaustion, lack of supplies and the superiority of Allied resources soon thwarted all hopes of a decisive breakthrough. The Allied counter-offensive began on 18 July with an attack on the Marne composed of 19 French divisions and four American. Throughout August and September the Allied attacks continued, and by late September the Germans were in full retreat, but this never became a rout. On the contrary in the chilling words of Neill Ferguson 'the Germans continued to be highly effective at killing the enemy'.[29] Nevertheless there were growing signs that German morale was deteriorating. The number of men ready to surrender increased and desertion 'sky rocketed'. In August the German army lost 228,110 men, of whom over 100,000 had deserted.[30] While the Germans were coming under increasing pressure on the Western Front, the Austrian army in Italy after the Italian offensives on the Grappa and Piava had virtually disintegrated. In September the French had also opened up the Salonika front and Bulgaria capitulated on 30 September. The Turkish capital was now threatened by Allied forces in Macedonia.

See Documents 44 and 45

The armistice negotiations and domestic turmoil

On 29 September a sick and exhausted Ludendorff informed both Hindenburg and Hertling that the war was lost and that an immediate appeal should be made to the American President, Woodrow Wilson, for

29. September 1918
Nr. 39
27. Jahrgang

Berliner
Jlluſtrirte Zeitung
Verlag Ullſtein & Co, Berlin SW 68

Einzelpreis einſchließlich Teuerungszuſchlag
15 Pfg.
oder 24 Heller

Deutſcher Panzerwagen mit zwei Mann der Beſatzung im Tankanzug, von denen einer eine Splittermaſke trägt.

4   On the very day when General Erich von Ludendorff informed the German government that the army needed an immediate armistice, the readers of the *Berliner Illustrirte Zeitung* were given the impression that Germany was still invincible. The caption of this picture reads: 'A German tank with its two-man crew in tank uniform, one of whom is wearing a protective splinter mask'

Berliner Illustrirte Zeitung, 29 September 1918, front page

an armistice. It was hoped that his peace programme, summarized in the 14 Points would enable Germany to regain her colonies and retain at the very least the German-speaking sections of Alsace-Lorraine. The German elite embraced the 14 Points 'much like a drowning person reaches for a life-line'.[31] In an effort to make this appeal more persuasive, Ludendorff urged the creation of a more representative regime, which would have a greater impact on Washington than the defeated and discredited OHL and the Hertling government it had put in place. William accepted this advice and on 3 October appointed Prince Max von Baden, who had been recommended by Conrad Haussmann, the leader of the Progressive People's Party, on the assumption that he combined democratic ideas with the necessary social prestige needed to stand up to the army. Once the news of the armistice appeal became public, the demand for peace 'gathered momentum like an avalanche'.[32] When the American replies of 14 and 23 October indicated that President Wilson was in effect demanding the abdication of the Kaiser before negotiations could take place, it became increasingly clear that public opinion would willingly sacrifice the monarch to gain peace.

On 28 October the *Reichstag* approved sweeping measures to prepare the way for the creation of a constitutional parliamentary government. Even at this stage the armed forces showed that they were not ready to subordinate themselves to parliament. On 18 October Hindenburg assured his commanders that the Western Front was now 'secure' and dismissed the 14 Points as unacceptable. A resignation threat from Max von Baden forced William to intervene and confirm the superiority of the civil government over the High Command, which led to Ludendorff's resignation and his flight in disguise to Sweden.

The German navy also attempted to ignore the civil government and on 24 October Admiral Hipper (1863–1932) ordered the fleet to put out for one last desperate battle against the British. This action was to be the catalyst for the revolution. In protest, the sailors at Wilhelmshaven mutinied. When about a thousand of these were arrested, their colleagues organized mass protest meetings, disarmed their officers and formed soviets or councils, which by the evening of 4 November controlled Kiel. In the next few days Workers' and Soldiers' Councils were set up in Hamburg, Bremen, Düsseldorf, Leipzig, Frankfurt and Berlin. Von Baden hoped at first that this tidal wave of protest could be contained and a constitutional monarchy preserved provided the Kaiser and the Crown Prince both abdicated. After failure to secure the Kaiser's agreement, he announced their abdication at noon on 9 November without any authorization. The following day the Kaiser went into exile in Holland.

See Document 46

In the meantime, Ebert demanded that power should be transferred to those who enjoyed the 'full confidence of the people'. On 9 November von Baden handed over power to him. Ebert's initial plan was to form a coalition government based on the Democrats, MSPD, USPD and Progressives, but this met with strong opposition from the Workers' Councils in Berlin. They demanded that the Workers' and Soldiers' should elect an assembly that would then appoint a provisional government. To pre-empt this, Ebert negotiated a direct agreement with the USPD to set up a new provisional government in the form of the Council of People's Representatives, consisting of three MSPD and three USPD delegates Councils which were modelled on the Russian soviets.

The most pressing task facing the new government was to negotiate the armistice. The German delegation, headed by Matthias Erzberger, began negotiations on 6 November, and had little option but to agree to the demands dictated by the Allies, which anticipated the coming peace terms. On the Western Front these involved the immediate cession of Alsace-Lorraine to France, the withdrawal of the German army to a line 30 miles east of the Rhine and the occupation by the Allies of the west bank of the Rhine and of the three bridgeheads of Mainz, Coblenz and Cologne. The Germans were also to surrender large amounts of artillery and heavy equipment as well as the High Seas Fleet and to abrogate the Treaty of Brest–Litovsk.

See Map 6

On 11 November the armistice was signed. The Germans evacuated the occupied areas of France, Belgium and Luxemburg by 26 November and the first Allied troops crossed the German frontier in early December to occupy the Rhineland.

Conclusion

The German people performed prodigious feats during the Great War and managed to keep a much larger coalition of states at bay for over 4 years. The total war economy, the strength of German industry and the *Burgfrieden* were all factors which strengthened the German war effort, yet ultimately Germany was locked into conflict with a coalition which it could not destroy. The intervention of Great Britain cut Germany off from its overseas trade and access to the American money markets. This ensured that the German people suffered the full rigours of the British blockade, and that the costs of the war could not be eased by foreign loans. Direct taxation had its limits and the shortfall in its finances had to be met by printing money, with disastrously inflationary consequences.

The *Burgfrieden* played a key role in uniting the German people and strengthening the legitimacy of the state, but, as the pressures on the home front intensified, divisions re-emerged. The formation of the USPD in April 1917 and then the Peace Resolution in July created the first major cracks in the *Burgfrieden*. The quasi-Bonapartist dictatorship of Hindenburg and Ludendorff, with its fanatical determination to win a total victory, polarized the political situation and prevented the German government from exploring any possibility of a negotiated peace. Yet paradoxically it was also the collapse of Ludendorff's nerve in September 1918 that precipitated Germany's defeat. By October the German retreat was slowing down and Allied generals were reporting a stiffening of resistance It is conceivable that Germany could have resisted for another winter and possibly have achieved better peace terms. What is not debatable is that for Germany and Europe, the Great War was '*the* great seminal catastrophe'[33] of the 20th century. Both its immediate and long-term consequences are the theme of the rest of this book.

Part Three
The Weimar Republic and the Third Reich

9 Revolution and Instability, October 1918–1923

Introduction: problems, issues and questions

Like armchair strategists, who are so quick to spot mistakes made in the midst of 'the fog of war', historians retrospectively reveal the mistaken assumptions or timidity of politicians. In the 1950s, interpretations of the 'abortive revolution' of 1918–1919 were influenced by the Cold War. West German historians, like Karl-Dietrich Erdmann, argued that Ebert and the Majority Socialists (**MSPD**) had little option but to cooperate with the old elites if Germany was to avoid a Communist revolution and create a parliamentary regime. The mirror image of this view was taken by East German historians, who accused the MSPD leaders and the Independent Socialists (USPD) of betraying the revolution. The rise of the New Left in West Germany in the 1960s and 1970s (see p. 354) and the increasing availability of fresh sources made the German workers' movements in the period 1918–1920 a popular topic of research. Revisionist historians, such as Francis Carsten, Eberhard Kolb and Susanne Miller, showed that initially the MSPD and the moderate members of the USPD had a huge majority in the Workers' and Soldiers' Councils, and argued that Ebert should have taken a tougher line with the army, nationalized the mines immediately and implemented the MSPD's programme fully. Only with the failure of Ebert to act more decisively did the radical left gain greater influence from the spring of 1920 onwards.[1] Ebert was, however, in tune with the majority of the German workers, who wanted national elections for a democratic *Reichstag* as soon as possible, and he was able to organize these in early January. Perhaps his mistake was not to harness more effectively the great reservoir of support for democratic and parliamentary socialism in the Soldiers' and Workers' Councils in the last 2 months of 1918. His failure certainly enabled the pre-war elites in the civil service, judiciary and army to survive the defeat, but then without their support could Ebert's moderate revisionary socialism have survived?

MSPD: the SPD split in April 1917 into the USPD and MSPD (see p. 179). The USPD itself split in 1920 and most of its members either joined the KPD or returned to the MSDP in 1922.

Friedrich Ebert, 1871–1925: After 1913 Ebert was co-chairman of the SPD. He led the temporary government during the revolution of 1918–1919, and was then appointed the first president of the Weimar Republic.

An abortive revolution?

Once the Armistice agreement was signed on 11 November and the fighting stopped, the Council of People's Representatives turned to domestic politics. Ebert had hoped to keep open the possibility of preserving a constitutional monarchy, though not of course under William II, but his hand had been forced by his colleague and co-chairman of the MSPD, Philipp Scheidemann (1865–1939), who had without any consultation, announced a republic to a mass demonstration in the *Reichstag* square on the afternoon of 9 November. In fact Ebert and the leaders of the Majority Socialists had already achieved their principal aims with the announcement of the October reforms introducing constitutional government. For them, the November 'revolution' was an unnecessary distraction from the main business of dealing with the problems of demobilization, food distribution and preparing for the peace negotiations, all of which needed the help of the traditional military and bureaucratic elites. Ebert regarded the Council as just a caretaker government until a constituent assembly had been elected. The Spartacist Union, led by Karl Liebknecht and Rosa Luxemburg (see p. 177), and the left wing of the USPD wanted, however, a soviet rather than a parliamentary regime in Germany, the replacement of the army by a workers' militia and the nationalization of all medium-sized and large farms and industries. They hoped that an executive council appointed by an assembly elected by the Berlin Workers' and Soldiers' Committees would in practice act as the real revolutionary government, but their lack of political skills enabled the MSPD and moderate USPD members to outmanoeuvre them on the council. In an effort to put pressure on the moderates, the Spartacists organized demonstrations and strikes, which merely pushed the SPD further to the right and made them more reliant on the traditional authorities in their efforts to dampen down unrest at home.

On 10 November, General Groener (1867–1939), the quartermaster general of the army, pledged his loyalty to the Council of People's Representatives, provided that it supported the officer corps' efforts to maintain discipline. Five days later another important step was taken to pacify the home front when the Central Working Association (*Zentralarbeitsgemeinschaft*) Agreement was negotiated between the trade unions and heavy industry. The employers recognized the unions as the 'authorized representatives of the workers', and agreed to an 8-hour day and the establishment of workers' committees in all firms with a workforce of more than 50. Essentially they were hoping that these concessions would buy off the workers and so avoid the nationalization of their businesses – a calculation that proved correct. They were as Gerald Feldman has stressed 'in effect abandoning their long standing alliance with the Junkers and the authoritarian state for an alliance with organized labour'.[2]

Despite the USPD's frequently repeated mantra of 'all power to the Soviets', there was in reality an overwhelming majority in favour of calling a national assembly. On 29 November the Council of People's Representatives announced a new electoral law introducing proportional representation and full female suffrage. The actual date of 19 January for the election was set by the first Congress of Workers' and Soldiers' Councils which met in Berlin from 16–20 December. Ebert and the moderates had won the most important battle, but the majority of the congress called for the council not to wait for the elections before introducing such key reforms as the socialization of industry and the creation of a people's militia to replace the regular army.

These demands, of course, ran contrary both to Ebert's assurances to Groener and the Central Working Association agreement. His obvious unwillingness to implement them led to the resignation of the Independent Socialists from the council and the Prussian government. The extreme left, which embraced the Spartacus Union and the Bremen left-wing radicals, united to form the Communist Party, and then proceeded to launch the doomed uprising in Berlin on 5 January, which has been called the 'revolution's **battle of the Marne**'.[3] It was ruthlessly repressed by the *Reichswehr* and the newly formed volunteer militia, the *Freikorps*, which on 15 January murdered the Communist leaders, Karl Liebknecht and Rosa Luxemburg.

The uprising created bitter divisions in the labour movement, which lasted until Hitler created a forced unity with the Nazi Labour Front (see p. 238). The leaders of the Majority Socialists tightened their links with the bureaucracy, the army and the bourgeois parties, while the USPD, joined by a considerable number of MSPD defectors,

Freikorps: Gustav Noske (1868–1946) as minister of defence and with Ebert's support, encouraged the recruitment by former officers of volunteer forces. This appealed to the mass of demobilized young officers and NCOs, who could not fit back into civilian life, as well as students and adventurers. The politics of the *Freikorps* was overwhelmingly monarchist and right-wing.

Battle of the Marne: September 1914, which resulted in decisively checking the German advance on Paris

who were sickened by the failure of the Ebert government to achieve any structural reforms, moved to the left. This was the start of the second phase of the revolution. In the Prussian *Landtag* and local elections of the spring of 1919 the MSPD lost considerable support, while the USPD made impressive gains. From January to April there were strikes and uprisings throughout Germany, and soviet republics were set up in Munich, Bremen, Mülheim and Halle. The brutal measures employed by the *Freikorps*, which waged a war of revenge against the workers, led to an increasing polarization in German society.

Reichswehr: the German army, a term used up to 1935

The National Assembly

While the MSPD and USPD dominated the political agenda in Germany in the weeks before the elections to the National Assembly, the parties of the centre and the right attempted to adapt to the new political climate. The former Conservative parties, the small anti-Semitic groups, the Pan-Germans and the right wing of the National Liberals, which was close to heavy industry, united to form the German National People's Party (DNVP). It was, to quote Geoff Eley, 'a highly unstable synthesis'[4] as it combined both the pre-war nationalists, heavy industrialists and representatives of the old Prussian Conservative Party. The Centre Party initially tried to break away from its Catholic image (see p. 125) and adopted the name of the Christian People's Party in an attempt to become more non-denominational, but the new name failed to catch on. In Bavaria, where Catholic opinion was more right-wing and critical of the Republic, the local Centre Party broke away and formed the Bavarian People's Party (BVP). The Progressive Party and the left wing of the National Liberals regrouped under the name of German Democratic Party (DDP), while the rump of the National Liberals founded the German People's Party under Gustav Stresemann (DVP).

The revolution in Munich

The King of Bavaria abdicated on 7 November, and an unstable USPD–SPD coalition government was set up by Kurt Eisner (1867–1919). In the election of January 1919 the USPD lost most of its support. In response to the assassination of Eisner by a Munich university student, Graf Anton von Arco auf Valley (1897–1945), a group of USPD members and anarchists declared a 'Council's Republic'. An attempt to crush it with troops failed on 13 April, but played into the hands of the extremists, who, under the leadership of the Communist Eugen Leviné (1883–1919), a veteran of the Russian 1905 revolution, attempted to introduce a Russian-style Soviet Republic. It lasted just over 2 weeks. It organized a 'red army', but, after bitter fighting which involved atrocities on both sides, it was crushed by *Reichswehr* and *Freikorps* troops. These traumatic events had a lasting impact on public opinion in Bavaria and help explain why it became a bastion of the radical right (see p. 196).

In the elections on 19 January the moderate democratic parties, the SPD, the Centre and the DDP gained a decisive majority. The new National Assembly was convened in Weimar so that its deliberations would not be threatened by the turbulence of Berlin. The SPD, which had gained 38 per cent of the vote, provided both the first president of the Republic, Ebert, and the chancellor, Philipp Scheidemann. The government was based on the SPD, DDP and Centre – the Weimar coalition – and reflected the reality of German politics, in which there was a consensus for a moderate, 'reforming parliamentary democracy'.[5]

Apart from the peace treaty with the Allied and Associated powers (see below) its first task was to end the transitionary political period and draw up the basic structure of the new constitution. Its main institutions, the *Reichstag*, the presidency and the cabinet, as well as a committee to represent the individual states, were confirmed by an interim law, while the assembly set up the Constitutional Committee to work on the details. Hugo Preuss (1860–1925), a former National Liberal and constitutional expert, who had been appointed minister of the interior, presented it with an initial draft, which envisaged a federal Germany with a strong central government, but over the next 6 months this was modified and a compromise was arrived at between the Reich and the states. The constitutional privileges of Saxony, Bavaria and Württemberg (see p. 101) were abolished and the states, whose ruling families had all been swept away in November 1918, were now called the *Länder* (states). The upper house, or the *Reichsrat*, lost its veto and became merely an advisory chamber. The executive was at last made responsible to the *Reichstag*, which was to be elected according to **proportional representation** by universal suffrage. The head of state was the Reich president, who was directly elected by the people for an initial period of 7 years, although there was no limit to the times he could stand for re-election. He was in many ways a substitute emperor, whose powers were designed as a check on the powers of the *Reichstag*. He appointed and then could dismiss the Reich government; he could order a referendum and Article 48 empowered him to proclaim a state of emergency to safeguard public security and order. The constitution also contained a section on individual rights – equality before the law, free speech, equality for women and the right to strike. The MSPD managed to secure articles guaranteeing the socialization of 'suitable' businesses in private hands as well as the establishment of works councils (see p. 215).

After 1945 it was argued that the Weimar constitution had facilitated the rise to power of the Nazi Party. Proportional representation did indeed magnify the influence of the small parties and make the formation of durable coalitions more difficult, while the existence of Article 48 gave wide-ranging powers to the president, which were abused in the period 1930–1933. Similarly, the demand for a referendum could easily be exploited to obstruct the democratic process, as it was by the nationalist right during the debate over the Young Plan in 1929 (see p. 210). All this, however, is to read history backwards. The overriding importance in 1919 for the new constitution was to provide a framework for stability and

Proportional representation: the principle whereby parties are represented in parliament in direct proportion to the number of votes they poll

See Document 47

social peace. It was as Anthony McElligott has pointed out, 'based on class compromise, a sort of refashioned *Burgfrieden*'.[6]

The Versailles '*Diktat*'

From November 1918 up to early May 1919 the Germans were living in what the theologian Ernst Troeltsch (1865–1923) called 'the dreamland of the Armistice period'.[7] The German government initially hoped that by stressing its democratic credentials it would be able to conclude a peace based on the 14 Points. Its overriding aim was to protect the potential of the German economy so that the way was left clear for a renaissance of German economic power. There was no intention of paying the Allies an indemnity, even though it was conceded that the cost of rebuilding the devastated areas of Belgium and France would have to be met. As for territorial concessions, the cession of Alsace-Lorraine to France was accepted, as were limited annexations by the new state of Poland, but these were to be balanced by the inclusion of Austria and the other German-speaking areas of the former Habsburg Empire in the Reich. Finally, it was assumed that the new democratic Republic would play a key role in the League of Nations and would remain a great power.

When the German delegation was summoned to Paris on 7 May to be presented with the draft terms of the treaty, it received a rude shock:

- Basing their demand on Article 231 which declared Germany guilty of unleashing the war, the Allies and the USA demanded that Germany should pay a war indemnity that would compensate them for their losses. The exact amount was to be fixed by the Reparation Commission by May 1921.
- Upper Silesia and most of the provinces of West Prussia and Posen were awarded to Poland; only in Marienwerder was there to be a plebiscite. Danzig was to become a free city, under the protection of the League of Nations, and northern Schleswig was to be returned to Denmark.
- In the west, besides Alsace-Lorraine reverting to France, Eupen and Malmedy were to be ceded to Belgium, while the Saar was to be put under the administration of the League of Nations for 15 years, after which there would be a plebiscite. The Rhineland was to be permanently demilitarized and occupied for a period of 15 years by Allied troops as a guarantee of the execution of the treaty.
- Germany would lose all her colonies and foreign investments, as well as most of her merchant navy.
- The German army was to be cut down to 100,000 men, its navy to a mere 15,000, while the General Staff was to be disbanded. Tanks, aircraft, submarines and poison gas were all forbidden.
- Germany was not invited to join the League of Nations.

The Germans were allowed only 14 days to consider these terms. Initially there was unanimous agreement that they were unacceptable. The Foreign Office attempted to force a revision by arguing that the 14 Points and the German–American exchange of notes in October 1918 had the legal status of a treaty and that Germany was not alone in starting the war. On 16 June, when the German delegation was handed the final version of the treaty, the only appreciable concession which the Allies made was the decision to hold a plebiscite in Upper Silesia. The treaty met with a storm of protest in Germany and triggered a political crisis splitting the cabinet and leading to the resignation of Scheidemann, but, given Germany's military weakness, the new chancellor, Gustav Bauer (1870–1944), had no option but to accept it.

Versailles was a harsh treaty, which directly affected millions of Germans in the Rhineland, Upper Silesia and West Prussia, yet it was not the **Carthaginian peace** that contemporaries accused it of being. Despite reparations, the loss of 13 per cent of its territory and the consequent handing over of six million Germans to alien regimes, Germany's great power potential remained. Given time and skill, as Gustav Stresemann was to show (see pp. 208–210), revision was possible. Nevertheless 'it inflicted too deep an injury on the self-perception of the German public and politicians for even one of its basic clauses to be left in place'.[8] Its rapid destruction after 1933 was to contribute to Hitler's popularity.

> See Map 6

> See Documents
> 50, 51.1, 51.2

> **Carthaginian peace:** the peace of revenge and destruction which the Romans imposed on Carthage

---

The occupied Rhineland

This was broken up into four zones: Belgian, British, American and French. The northern two zones (Belgian and British in 1920) were to be evacuated after 5 years, the central zones (French and American in 1920) after 10 years, although the Americans left in January 1923 and were replaced by French troops, and the third zone (French in 1920) in 1935 after 15 years. By the Rhineland Agreement an inter-allied Rhineland High Commission was set up under a French High Commissioner. It was not an administrative body, but existed solely to protect the occupying troops, but it was empowered to declare martial law if necessary. This gave the army commanders the power to intervene in the German civil administration only after obtaining specific approval from the High Commission. Despite not signing the Treaty of Versailles the US kept some 1000 troops in their zone (Coblenz) until February 1923.

Post-war politics, 1919–1923

The legacy of the war

Few would disagree with Wolfgang Mommsen that 'the seedbed of extremist nationalism and the eventual rise to power of the National Socialists was a set of social and economic factors that had their origins in the Great World War'.[9] The legacy of the war created immense problems for the new Republic. Total war had grossly distorted the German economy. Armament production inflated the heavy industrial sector and accelerated the pre-1914 trend towards, industrial concentration, while the British blockade had ruined the German export trade. All of this led to a massive restructuring of industry to the detriment of the consumer and craft industries. The government was also burdened with a massive public debt of 250.7 billion marks by November 1918, which was exacerbated by welfare payments to war invalids and widows, and reparations. As much of the war expenditure had been financed by loans, bonds and the printing of money, inflation gathered pace. Prices had risen by over 250 per cent during the war, and this was only a taste of what was to come. The war bonds into which many patriotic Germans had poured their savings (see p. 173) were valueless by 1923.

As we have seen (in Chapter 8), the war had polarized society into winners and losers: apart from the owners of the war industries – about a 120,000 people – who made immense fortunes, those who gained most were the skilled workers in the war industries, while the middle classes were the greatest losers. Civil servants, white-collar workers, small businessmen and craftsmen all saw their status eroded, and their savings, which many had invested in war loans, destroyed. Inevitably this increased the sense of bitterness felt about Germany's defeat and the Versailles settlement, and made these groups susceptible to the siren voices of the nationalist right. There was a longing to re-create the exhilarating experience of the 'spirit of 1914', which contrasted so favourably with the divisive politics of the Weimar Republic. The bonarpartism and charisma of Hindenburg and Ludendorff also set a dangerous precedent for a plebiscitary dictatorship imposed undemocratically on Germany.

Threats from within, 1920–1922

The 'stab in the back' myth: This originated in a statement made to the Investigation Committee of the National Assembly on 18 November 1919 by Hindenburg. It was immediately taken up by the right, but also found considerable support across the political spectrum among those who could not come to terms with Germany's military defeat. By 'stab in the back' it was implied that the strikes and mutinies of October–November 1918 had forced the high command into negotiating an armistice.

Successive governments were confronted by a series of political economic and social problems which appeared insoluble. Not only were they under enormous pressure from the French, who were determined to exploit the peace treaty to weaken or even dismember Germany, but the Republic was threatened from within by both the extreme left and the extreme right. By December 1919 the USPD had committed itself to establishing the dictatorship of the proletariat, while in the Ruhr workers were joining syndicalist organizations and were ready to take direct action against the capitalists and the 'class enemy'. In January 1920 labour unrest on the railways and the coalfields, and a mass demonstration culminating in an attack on the *Reichstag* prompted the government to declare a state of emergency, which temporarily brought the situation under control.

The government viewed the left as the major threat to the Republic, yet the strikes and violence 'owed more to the utterly desolate material conditions than to any developed critique of the revolutionary settlement'.[10] In reality the assault from the right was potentially far more dangerous. 1919 had witnessed a polarization which had caused many white-collar

SOUVENIR—XMAS 1919

Photographic house and camera
repairing works

AUG. LANG
Mechanician of precision
COLOGNE
KL. NEUGASSE 9/11
Always bargains in **second-hand** binoculars
Zeiss-Goertz, Voigtländer and Leitz etc.

SAVE
TIME — TROUBLE — MONEY
BY BUYING YOUR
CUTLERY
IN COLOGNE, WE HAVE

RAZORS, POCKET-
KNIVES, SCISSORS,
MANICURE SETS,
KNIVES, FORKS AND
SPOONS, SAFETY-
RAZOR BLADES

AT THE LOWEST PRICES FROM
STOCK IN COLOGNE.

F. ADAMS
GLADBACHERSTRASSE 21

!ARCADIA!
Hohestrasse 79 **COLOGNE** Brückenstr. 5-9

**First-class Confectioners
Shop and Wine Restaurant**

OWN pastry   First-class cooking
Best wines   Beer in decanters
·
ORCHESTRA
·
Tables may be reserved
by telephone A 5444

Officers and civilians only

Christian Krug
COLOGNE
Breitestrasse 52 Telephone A 8882
Theatre wardrobes etc. for
hire. Great choice in gent-
lemen's and ladies dresses.
We buy and hire out.

NÜCHEL & HILLEBRECHT
COLOGNE, Glockengasse, Telephone A 5566
Corner Kreuzgasse   Close Schauspielhaus

**UNIFORM MAKERS
MILITARY OUTFITS**
Manufacture of all Uniforms
for the Army of Occupation.
First-class References.

46

5   German shopkeepers made the best of a bad job and set out to sell to the British
occupying forces by advertising in the British military newspaper, the *Cologne Post*
Cologne Post, Souvenir Number, Christmas 1919, p. 46

workers and members of the *Mittelstand* to move from the centre to the
right. Students too had embraced a new, hard-line, nationalist ethos,
while right-wing papers and pamphlets maintained a constant barrage of
agitation against the 'shameful peace' and the **'stab in the back' myth**.
This attitude was fully shared by many academics, teachers, Protestant
priests and members of the judiciary. The latter, holding posts from
which they could not be constitutionally dismissed, often dispensed a
highly politicized form of justice. Leading Weimar politicians became the
target of constant verbal and sometimes physical abuse.

In July 1919 Ludendorff had together with Wolfgang Kapp, a founder member of the Fatherland Party (see p. 180), and in close contact with General Lüttwitz, the commander of the *Reichswehr* in central and eastern Germany, set up the National Association with the intention of over-throwing the Republic. Their opportunity came when the government, under pressure from the Allies, began to disband the *Freikorps*. Kapp and Lüttwitz seized the chance to exploit their members' alarm at the imminent prospects of unemployment. On 10 March Lüttwitz presented Ebert with demands for his resignation and the retention of the *Freikorps*. When the government dismissed him, the Ehrhardt *Marine Brigade* occupied Berlin and proclaimed Kapp chancellor. General Reinhardt, the *Reichswehr* commander-in-chief, was ready to crush the *putsch*, but, as none of his generals would agree to supply the necessary troops, the government fled first to Dresden and then to Stuttgart. Kapp's bluff was called both by a spontaneous and nationwide general strike by the trade unions and, as Hagen Schulze has pointed out, also by the refusal of the senior civil servants in the Prussian and national governments to cooperate.[11] On 18 March Kapp and Lüttwitz had little option but to flee to Sweden.

The *putsch* was successful only in Bavaria, where the *Reichswehr* commanders were able to force the government to resign, replacing it with a right-wing regime which became a 'focus of order'. Bavaria rapidly became 'an Eldorado for extreme right-wing organizations and the leading personalities of militant right-wing radicalism'.[12] It was there that Hitler, who had been employed by the *Reichswehr* in 1919 to counter the impact of left-wing and pacifist propaganda on the troops, joined the DAP, the German Worker's Party.

See Document 50

The unions hoped that the defeat of the *putsch* would lead to a purge of hostile right-wing elements in the army and administration, an accelerated socialization programme and the formation of a new, more left-wing government, but the Ruhr uprising (see p.197) in April effectively prevented the regime from moving decisively against its enemies. As in January 1919 *Reichswehr* troops were again needed to restore order and to defeat the 'Red Army' in the Ruhr.

In the wake of the defeat of these upheavals, the government brought forward to early June the date of the first election to be held under the new constitution. The results were a disaster for the Weimar coalition. Disillusionment on both the right and the left led to heavy losses for the MSPD and DDP, while the USPD and the right-wing DVP and DNVP chalked up impressive gains. The original Weimar coalition parties could now command only 205 seats out of 459. The immediate prospects for stabilizing the regime were complicated by the MSPD's decision not to participate in the government. After 3 weeks of negotiations a minority DVP–Centre coalition was formed by the Centre politician, Konstantin Fehrenbach. The SPD 'tolerated' the administration but avoided accepting political responsibility for its decisions. Only in May 1921 with the formation of a new Weimar coalition (see p. 200) under Josepf Wirth did the MSPD re-enter government.

See Document 51.2

The Ruhr uprising

Over the winter of 1919–1920 a growing desire for direct action had been developing in the Ruhr. The Kapp *putsch* acted as a catalyst for this. In mid-March 1920 fighting broke out in the eastern Ruhr when workers suspected that *Freikorps* troops were moving to crush the syndicalist movement. 'Overnight', as Wolfgang Mommsen has written, 'the mass strike of Ruhr workers against Kapp and Lüttwitz was transformed into a movement of open insurrection, directed simultaneously against the counter-revolutionary activities of suspect *Reichswehr* units and the policies of the national government, and accompanied by somewhat ill-concerted "wildcat" acts of socialization'.[13] The revolt was supported by about 80,000 men and led by a loosely coordinated group of Workers' Councils. Initially it inflicted some sharp defeats on the *Reichswehr*. Carl Severing, the Prussian minister of the interior, representing the Majority Social Democrats and trade union leaders, managed to divide the insurgents by accepting some of their demands – the so called 'eight points'. In April the rump of the 'Red Army' was ruthlessly crushed and some 5000 insurgents sought refuge in the British Rhineland Zone.

Until 1924 domestic politics were dominated by the problems connected with the execution of the Treaty of Versailles. The bitter wrangles with the Allies over reparation payments gave successive governments every excuse to delay stabilizing the currency. Accelerating inflation made it more difficult for the Reparation Commission to estimate the amount Germany could pay, but this was not the only reason why the Weimar governments did not grasp the nettle of currency stabilization. The explosive internal situation ensured that no party was ready to risk a policy of financial cuts and retrenchment, which would simultaneously increase unemployment and cut welfare benefits. Allowing the currency to inflate also helped exports and prevented rising unemployment. In June 1922 according to a report by the American ambassador, Rathenau (see p. 170), who was now foreign minister, 'declared the choice had been between inflation and revolution, and as between the two he favoured inflation'.[14] The growing strength of the Communist Party, with which the left wing of the USPD had amalgamated in October 1920, was evidence that, despite the defeat of the Ruhr uprising, left-wing militancy was far from dead. In the spring of 1921 insurrections broke out in Merseburg, Halle and Mansfeld, although they were defeated within a few days by paramilitary police.

The protracted struggle with the Allies over the execution of the peace terms (see below) inflamed the radical right. Former members of the *Freikorps* formed Patriotic leagues and secret societies. Some of these developed into terrorist groups which assassinated separatists and informers who had assisted the Allied occupying forces. Others conducted a campaign to eliminate prominent socialists and politicians of the Weimar coalition, who had appeased the Entente Powers. In the summer of 1921 Karl Gareis (1889–1921), the USPD leader, and Matthias

Erzberger were murdered, and in June 1922 Walther Rathenau was assassinated because he was attempting to pursue a policy of cooperation with the Entente in the hope of persuading it to revise the Treaty of Versailles. As a Jew he was in a particularly vulnerable position given the anti-Semitism of the radical right (see p. 218).

Rathenau's murder created an enormous sensation and momentarily rallied support to the Republic. A law for the 'Protection of the Republic' was passed, despite opposition from the DNVP, the BVP and the KPD, which enabled the government to prohibit extremist organizations, but its effectiveness was limited by the reluctance of the judiciary to ban right-wing organizations and by the refusal of the Bavarian government to implement it. Given the political polarization in Germany, the government also decided to delay the elections for the presidency until the summer of 1925. Attempts to strengthen the coalition by bringing in the DVP led, however, to the withdrawal of the SPD, and the subsequent collapse of Wirth's second administration in November 1922. A new and much more right-wing administration was formed by Wilhelm Cuno, the head of the Hamburg–America shipping line, who packed the cabinet with non-party experts.

The struggle for survival: foreign policy, 1919–1922

'The Great War', as Adam Tooze has written, 'may have begun in the eyes of many participants as a clash of empires, a classic great power war, but it ended in something far more morally and politically charged – a crusading victory for a coalition that proclaimed itself the champion of a new world order'.[15] The crusade was led by the US, whose industrial and financial resources so overshadowed those of the European states. President Wilson was determined to use this power to engineer a new liberal world order. For him the new League of Nations would put an end to imperialist rivalry. The tragedy for Europe, and indeed the world, was that the American Congress refused to ratify the Treaty of Versailles, although the US did sign its own peace treaty with Germany, terminating hostilities in 1921. The US consequently never joined the League and only in 1924 began tentatively to play a financial role in Europe in the winter of 1923/24.

Within Europe in the immediate post-war years the leading powers were Britain and France. The main priority of France was permanently to weaken Germany and safeguard herself against any future revival of German ambitions. The new Soviet Russia that emerged from the Russian revolution and subsequent civil war had survived only by the 'skin of its teeth'.[16] Although ideologically it was a threat to central and western Europe in reality it was only a shadow of the power it had been in 1914 or was to become in 1945. The Austrian and Turkish empires had disintegrated and Italy regarded itself as 'a proletarian nation' embittered by the failure of the Entente to honour its promises of 1915 (see p. 168).

Germany's foreign policy aims after the signature of the Treaty of Versailles were summarized by Hermann Müller, the foreign minister, in the *Reichstag* in July 1919: Germany was committed to renouncing the use of military force and reaching an understanding with the Entente Powers and where possible to fulfilling the treaty, but at the same time it would direct all of its energies towards its peaceful revision.

See Document 48

In practice, however, German foreign policy had little room for manoeuvre. The Reich was, in these early post-war years, 'more an object of policy by the *Entente*'[17] than an independent force in its own right. German foreign policy therefore oscillated between despairing opposition and more constructive attempts to modify the treaty. For Germany, given the US reluctance to involve itself in European politics, there consequently appeared to be two main possibilities for achieving treaty revision: one was to exploit Anglo-French differences in the hope that this would weaken the united front of the Entente and lead to concessions to Germany; the other policy, favoured by the army, influential diplomats and some industrialists, was to come to an understanding with the USSR, which would strengthen Berlin's hand against the Entente, but this was a dangerous strategy, which ran the risk of contaminating Germany with Bolshevism.

Those who favoured a Russian alliance were encouraged in August 1920 by dramatic developments in the **Polish–Soviet war**, when the Russian advance on Warsaw threatened to transform the situation in Europe. The prospect of the collapse of Poland and the subsequent option of revising Poland's western frontiers with Soviet backing caused immense excitement in Germany, but the government cautiously declared its strict neutrality. Whether this would have held in the event of a Soviet victory is hard to say, but the Battle of Warsaw on 16 August, where the Russians were routed, effectively blocked the immediate possibility of German–Soviet cooperation and 'preserved for the *Entente* the dominant voice in European stabilization'.[18] Consequently, throughout the winter and spring of 1920–1921 German policy essentially remained dependent on the decisions of the Entente on reparations, the disarmament question and the plebiscite in Upper Silesia.

Polish–Russian war: triggered by the polish invasion of the Ukraine

Of these three, reparation was by far the most crucial. The British aimed to fix the global sum as quickly as possible in the hope that once Germany knew the full sum of its debts, it would be able to raise credit in America and begin payments. The French government was also playing with the idea of coming to an agreement with Berlin, which would effectively turn Germany economically into a junior partner. The upshot of this thinking was the Seydoux Plan, which could have enabled Germany to pay a large part of her reparation bill in industrial equipment and raw material deliveries, but it was rejected by both Britain and Germany at the Brussels Conference at the end of 1920. The German government noted that France had still not given up the right to take sanctions and that no exact figure had been given regarding the total reparations it would have to pay or deliver. Besides, there was also considerable opposition from both German and British industrialists, who feared the French might exploit the treaty to dominate German heavy industry.

At the Paris Conference in January 1921 the Allies at last agreed on a provisional figure of 226,000 billion gold marks to be paid over a period of 42 years. This caused an outcry in Germany and was immediately rejected by the German government, which produced its own figures a month later. These amounted to a modest overall payment of 30 billion gold marks, which was also conditional upon the retention of Upper Silesia. The offer was so obviously inadequate that the Entente occupied Düsseldorf, Duisburg and Ruhrort. As one German official conceded, Berlin had made a 'tremendous mistake in allowing France the opportunity of putting herself in the right'.[19] As a final gamble before the Reparation Commission came up with fresh figures on 1 May, Walther Simons (1861–1937), the German foreign minister, appealed to America and produced a payments plan for 50 billion marks, which, had it been produced earlier, might have been acceptable, but the Americans at this stage still refused to be drawn into the reparation conflict. At the end of April the Reparation Commission finally completed its study of Germany's financial liabilities and fixed the German debt at 132 billion gold marks. The gap between the Allied and German figures seems huge but over 82 billion of this sum consisted of class C bonds, which were likely not to be issued until 1957.[20] Although the figure was considerably less than the amount provisionally fixed in Paris in January, the amount was accepted by the Allied leaders, who on 5 May dispatched an ultimatum to Berlin giving the Germans a week to accept the new payment schedule, after which the Ruhr would be occupied. In Berlin the Fehrenbach government resigned, and a new more broadly based administration led by **Joseph Wirth** was formed on 10 May and accepted the Entente's demands. This did not, however, mean that he would not seek to modify the reparation figure. He made no secret of the fact that 'the goal of our entire policy must be the dismantling of the London ultimatum'.[21] However, he and Walther Rathenau, who was initially minister for reconstruction and then foreign minister hoped to achieve this through negotiation rather than confrontation.

Joseph Wirth, 1879–1956: Wirth had been a mathematics teacher in Baden. He was on the left wing of the Centre Party, and was a passionate democrat and republican. He was chancellor from May 1921– November 1922 and pursued a policy of fulfilment, that is, of attempting to carry out the Treaty of Versailles.

Were reparations set too high?

The debt of 132 billion gold marks was divided into three sets of bonds: A, B and C. The last series was worth 82 billion gold marks, and would not be issued until German exports had made a recovery. Effectively this raised a large question mark over whether in reality they would ever be issued at all, as the British had no wish to see a massive boom in the German export trade. Thus, effectively, the German debt was set at 50 billion gold marks. Was even this sum payable?[22] Given the state of German finances in 1921, it still presented immense problems. The only way Germany could pay in gold equivalent was to purchase foreign currencies, but as the value of the mark declined, this became increasingly expensive. The debt of 50 billion gold marks could, for example, only be raised by selling the sum of

750 billion paper marks on the foreign exchange. However, there were ways of paying this sum. The French were ready to consider the transfer of industrial shares to their ownership, although this was opposed by the British, who did not wish to see the French have an important say in German heavy industry. Many German industrialists and bankers such as the DNVP leader, Helfferich, and the industrialist, Stinnes, argued that reparations were the root cause of inflation, but in fact if the German government had grasped the nettle of stabilizing the currency, increasing taxation and deflating domestic demand, this would theoretically have freed resources for an export drive and made the transfer of reparations funds possible, but how feasible this would have been in a period of acute global recession is open to question. Reversing the social gains of the 1918–1919 revolution by extending working hours and cutting pay, would have made this approach possible, but were bitterly opposed by the MSPD, which was still the largest political party in the *Reichstag*. Tooze argues that the general strike that defeated the Kapp *putsch* 'demonstrated that organized labour had a veto over the politics of the Republic'. Yet it lacked the majority to introduce a wealth levy and 'steep progressive taxation', which was an alternative way to finance reparation payments.[23] On the other hand the lowering of inflation and the stabilization of prices might, as Ferguson has pointed out, have reduced the incentive to strike for higher wages and made organized labour more quiescent.[24]

For the next 6 months the Upper Silesian issue dominated German politics. In the plebiscite in April 1921 a majority in the industrial area and 60 per cent of the total vote had opted for Germany. To pre-empt any move to restore the industrial region to Germany, an armed revolt broke out in the night of 2–3 May, led by the Polish nationalist, Wojciech Korfanty (1873–1939). His forces, covertly supported by the French, quickly established themselves along the so-called Korfanty line some 80 kilometres to the west of Kattowitz. Polish intervention caused outrage in Germany and German **self-defence forces** backed by volunteers then moved into Silesia and attacked the insurgents.

> **Self-defence forces:** Many of the volunteers were members of the *Freikorps* who had gone 'underground' to defy the Allied ban on paramilitary groups.

> See Map 6

Wirth cooperated closely with the British in the hope that prime minister Lloyd George would be able to ensure that Upper Silesia remained German. In August the Upper Silesian question transferred to the League of Nations where the French contrived to secure a decision, which ultimately gave the key industrial triangle to the Poles. The policy of closer cooperation with Britain had failed to save Upper Silesia, and Wirth resigned in protest, although he returned to power 4 days later.

On 31 August 1921 the Wirth government paid the first instalment of reparations punctually, but, as the government, like its predecessors, still shied away from stabilizing the currency, cutting expenditure and imposing new taxes, it was becoming ever clearer that Germany would not be able to pay the second instalment on time. In the short term, Wirth and Rathenau, sought a **moratorium** from the Entente. Both wanted to play for time until America was ready to take part in a general reparation and inter-Allied debt settlement.

> **Moratorium:** a temporary suspension of debt payments

Rathenau also pursued initiatives in both Paris and London, which could, given time, have led to a solution to the reparation crisis. He attempted to revive a version of the Seydoux Plan when he signed the Wiesbaden Accords with Loucheur (1872–1971) on 6 October, which would have increased the amount of reparations delivered in kind and envisaged 'direct Franco–German cooperation as the core of western European reconstruction',[25] but opposition from both French and German industrialists prevented their implementation. The eastern department of the German foreign office favoured an economic agreement with the Soviet Union, while Rathenau preferred a settlement with the Entente Powers.

He was therefore sympathetic to Lloyd George's plan for the formation of a European consortium to rebuild the Russian economy, although he wanted it to involve central and south-eastern Europe too. Yet when the European powers, including the USSR, met to discuss it at Genoa in April 1922, the Soviets were suspicious that the Western powers and Germany would gang up against them, while Germany was apprehensive that they would come to an understanding with Russia, which would permit the Soviet regime to claim reparations and even signal a new anti-German coalition. Rathenau was consequently persuaded by his officials to sign the Treaty of Rapallo unilaterally with the USSR. Both powers mutually renounced any claims to reparations, and agreed to normalize trading relations and enter into full diplomatic relations. This brought the conference to an abrupt end and raised the spectre of a German–Soviet alliance, which according to Lloyd George, posed 'a terrible danger to [the] peace of Europe'.[26] It also intensified mistrust in Paris where Raymond Poincaré, who was convinced that only the threat to occupy the Ruhr would force the Germans to pay reparations, had recently returned to power as prime minister.

Rathenau was assassinated in June before he was able to repair the diplomatic damage caused by the treaty, and the Wirth government resigned in November. The new administration headed by Wilhelm Cuno faced the imminent threat of the French occupation of the Ruhr. In July 1922 the Germans requested a 2-year moratorium on reparation payments, but Poincaré, faced with no financial concessions on French debts from either Britain or America, insisted that the price of a moratorium would have to be the expropriation by the Reparation Commission of the state-owned mines in the Ruhr and the dyestuff industry. Despite British opposition, he seized the chance to implement his policy when, in early January 1923, the Reparation Commission declared Germany to be in default on deliveries of timber and coal. On 9 January French and Belgian engineers, protected by five French and one Belgian division, began to take control of the Ruhr industries.

The Ruhr occupation and hyperinflation, 1923

The immediate impact of the Ruhr occupation was to unite the German nation. For a few months the 'spirit of 1914' seemed to return. The government suspended all reparation payments and instructed the population of the Ruhr to go on strike and refuse to work for the French. In the short term these passive resistance tactics worked. In the first half of 1923 less coal and coke was delivered than in the last 10 days of 1922. Essentially the plan was to convince the French that their policy would fail, but this policy put enormous pressure on the German economy. To subsidize the strikers and compensate for the lost tax revenues from the Ruhr, the government printed ever larger sums of money. The value of the mark continued to sink rapidly, and by August it was worthless. From 4.2 marks to the dollar in July 1914 it had risen to 4,200,000,000,000 by 15 November 1923. In Gordon Craig's expressive comment, 'for millions of Germans these figures created a lunatic world … in which the simplest objects were invested by alchemy with monstrous value'.[27] This completed the impoverishment of the large number of the middle classes dependent on fixed incomes, war bonds and insurance annuities.

See Document 52

By August it was clear that, although France's international position was weakening, Germany could no longer maintain the passive resistance campaign. The Cuno government resigned and a 'grand coalition' of the MSPD, DDP, Centre and DVP was formed, with Stresemann as chancellor. He called off passive resistance on 26 September, but his attempt to gain the necessary powers to get the economy moving again by asking the *Reichstag* to agree to an enabling act was, at first, thwarted by the SPD, which feared that the act would enable the government to extend the working day and roll back of the social and economic gains made in the revolution. This led to the temporary collapse of the Grand Coalition on 3 October, but it was reconstructed once the MSPD was reassured that the 8-hour day would only be extended in exceptional circumstances when the good of the country clearly demanded it. The enabling bill was then approved by the *Reichstag* a week later. In November the minister of finance, Hans Luther, replaced the devalued mark with the new temporary currency, the *Rentenmark*, which was backed by mortgage bonds based on the assets of industry and agriculture, and in August 1924 was succeeded by the new *Reichsmark*.

See Document 47

Gustav Stresemann, 1878–1929

Stresemann was the most prominent liberal politician in the Weimar Republic. He started his business career as a promoter of industrial interests in Saxony and entered the *Reichstag* as a National Liberal member in 1903. During the war he was an ardent supporter of the extreme war aims of the Pan-German League. After the war he founded the DVP, and he voted against the new republican Weimar constitution in 1919. Gradually, however, he came to accept the Republic, and publicly backed it after Rathenau's assassination in 1922. He was chancellor from August to November 1923 and foreign minister continuously from August 1923 until his death in October 1929.

Internally the Reich government was faced with subversive threats from both the extreme left and extreme right. The Communists planned a **'German October'**. In both Saxony and Thuringia the KPD began to

German October: This is a reference to the second Russian revolution of October 1917 when the Bolsheviks seized power.

make military preparations for an uprising, but these were thwarted by vigorous central government intervention. In Thuringia the KPD resigned from the state government and the proletarian defence units were disbanded, while the Saxon government was dismissed, and a state commissioner appointed. Only in Hamburg did an uprising of a few hundred communists take place, but it was speedily crushed.

The right viewed the end of passive resistance as a betrayal and surrender to the French. In October the 'Black *Reichswehr*', a secret reserve army which it had built up in case of war with France mutinied in Küstrin, but was quickly suppressed. The real centre of right-wing resistance was Bavaria where the government was under pressure from patriotic, nationalist and paramilitary associations, which had set up the *Kampfbund* under the patronage of Ludendorff and led by Hitler. The *Kampfbund* planned to emulate Mussolini's march on Rome and stage a coup against the Berlin government. When passive resistance was halted in the Ruhr, the Bavarian government declared a state of emergency and appointed Ritter von Kahr (1862–1934), who was himself a member of the Patriotic Associations, state commissioner. In October local *Reichswehr* troops refused to obey orders coming from the Berlin government. General von Seeckt (1866–1936), the commander-in-chief of the *Reichswehr*, who had been entrusted with full executive power under article 48 'to take all measures necessary for the security of the Reich' declined to intervene, but he did warn Kahr and the local *Reichswehr* commander, von Lossow (1868–1938), not to become involved with the extreme nationalism of the local Patriotic Associations. Ultimately these warnings were heeded when they both refused to join the abortive Hitler–Ludendorff *putsch* of 9 November. The contrast between the *Reichswehr*'s intervention in Saxony and Thuringia and its refusal to take vigorous action in Bavaria led to the resignation of the MSPD on 2 November. The party was bitterly critical of the way Stresemann had allowed *Reichswehr* troops to occupy Dresden and had also deposed Erich Zeigner (1886–1949), the Saxon minister-president, while refusing to take a similarly tough stance against the Bavarians. Three weeks later it combined with the Nationalists to defeat the government in the *Reichstag*. Prophetically, President Ebert told his party: 'The reasons why you have felled the Chancellor will be forgotten in six weeks, but you will feel the effects of your stupidity for the next ten years.'[28]

Kampfbund: Fighting League

After the failure of the Munich *putsch*, the wave of unrest in the Reich subsided, but in the Rhineland and the Ruhr, Germany still faced an acute threat from France. Although the costs of the Ruhr occupation had caused a precipitous decline in the value of the franc and Anglo-American pressure had forced Poincaré on 30 November to agree in principle to the setting up of an experts' committee to review the whole question of reparations, the French were determined to impose their will on the Rhineland and Ruhr before that committee met. They signed short-term agreements with the Ruhr industrialists, which they hoped would form the basis of a more permanent settlement, and discussions took place with Louis Hagen (1855–1932) and Kurt von Schröder (1889–1966), the Cologne bankers, on the possible establishment of a Rhenish currency. Similarly, they gave every encouragement to the Rhineland separatists. The Reich had little option but to 'stick it out'[29] and wait for American intervention. Time was now working against the French. Rhineland separatism had collapsed as a result of local opposition, and in Britain in January 1924 a pro-German Labour government came into power. By January, when the Experts Committee chaired by the American banker, Charles Dawes (1865–1951), began its work, it was clear that the French would ultimately have to leave the Ruhr.

Hitler, the Nazis and the Munich *putsch*

Hitler was the son of an Austrian customs official. Failing to gain a place at the Academy of Fine Arts in Vienna, he became an increasingly impoverished drifter, first in Vienna and then in Munich. In the former city he enthusiastically absorbed contemporary Social Darwinist, *völkisch* and racist thinking. In August 1914 he volunteered to join a Bavarian regiment and was awarded the Iron Cross (First Class). In the summer of 1919 his skills as an agitator were recognized and he was employed to counter the impact of communist, socialist and pacifist propaganda among the troops. He joined the German Workers' Party, which was later renamed the National Socialist German Workers' Party (NSDAP) of which he became chairman in July 1921. Its 25-point programme was nationalist, anti-Semitic and anti-capitalist in character, and committed to the takeover of agricultural land in the national interest. By spring 1923 it had become one of the largest of the extreme right-wing groups in Bavaria. It was a measure of Hitler's standing in right-wing Bavarian circles that in September 1923 he became the political leader of the *Kampfbund*, which had been formed to coordinate tactics against the Republic. The party's paramilitary force, the SA, was integrated into the military wing of the *Bund*, and Hitler was the 'drummer', whose task was to mobilize public opinion to support a *putsch* in Munich, as a preliminary to taking Berlin by force. The new government was to be headed by Ludendorff, although Hitler would also be a member.

To have any chance of success the *Kampfbund* needed the backing of von Kahr and the heads of the Bavarian police and the local *Reichswehr* units, but, after hearing that the *Reichswehr* would not move against the elected government in Berlin, these officials began to have second thoughts. This left Hitler in a dangerous situation. His followers demanded action, but if he delayed too long the right moment would pass. He consequently tried to coerce Kahr by seizing him and his colleagues while they were addressing a public meeting at the *Bürgerbräukeller* on the evening of 8 November. Reluctantly bowing to force, they agreed to support him, but then Hitler, who was called away to deal with a problem involving the seizure of the Engineers' Barracks, left them in charge of Ludendorff. The latter allowed them to go home on receiving their word of honour that they would support Hitler, but the following morning, they ordered the police to break up the planned march into the city centre. A few days later Hitler was arrested. In February 1924 he was given the minimum sentence of 5 years' imprisonment, with a virtual promise that he would be released early on probation. The publicity the *putsch* received and the subsequent trial turned Hitler into a national figure.

Conclusion

From November 1918 to the Ruhr crisis of 1923–1924 Germany lurched from crisis to crisis. Given the enormous economic and social problems that were the legacy of the world war, Wolfgang Mommsen argues that 'the fate of the Weimar Republic was, in a sense, sealed from the start'.[30] Clearly the war accelerated the decline of the middle classes and distorted the German economy as well as bitterly dividing the country and saddling it with a punitive and humiliating peace treaty, but the fact that the Weimar Republic survived the first four turbulent years of its existence shows that its eventual collapse was by no means inevitable. As John Hiden has observed, 'Weimar democracy was more resilient than has often been acknowledged.'[31] It was after all Italy that experienced the first Fascist government in Europe rather than Germany! The Republic was not unique in experiencing domestic crisis and bloodshed. In the years immediately after the ending of the First World War the power vacuum left by the collapse of the Russian, Turkish and Austrian Empires led to civil war and ethnic animosities.[32] Even Britain experienced a large-scale and bloody insurrection in Ireland and violent strikes at home.

10 *Partial Stabilization, 1924–1929*

Introduction: problems, issues and questions

The dominating question concerning the years 1924–1930 are the nature of Germany's recovery and its fragility, the popularity of the Republic, its 'modernity' and the extent to which Stresemann normalized Germany's relations with France and Britain and paved the way for its re-emergence as a great power. Economically Germany was making a recovery, but structurally how strong was this recovery? How hobbled was industry by labour troubles and an expensive welfare state? Domestically, too, the intensity of the quarrels, which at times had bordered on civil war, had abated, but disillusionment with the Republic still ran deep: the victims of hyperinflation and the agrarian crisis felt betrayed, and many felt frightened and threatened by the pace of change. The Weimar Republic was also despised by youth, intellectuals and artists, even when it was so generous with cultural subsidies. To what extent can these weaknesses and reservoirs of unpopularity be seen as the structural cracks in the Republic, which to quote Detlev Peukert, were 'an outward sign of hidden weaknesses that might prove fatal when the structure was next subjected to severe strain'?[1] Modern historians such as Anthony McElligott and Colin Storer, however, question this idea of a 'doomed republic'. Rather they stress its artistic vibrancy, its advanced welfare provision and question the accepted idea that 'German democracy was weak and ineffective'.[2]

Foreign policy

Both before and during the war Stresemann had been a strident German nationalist but Germany's post-war humiliations convinced him that only a policy of rapprochement with France could open the way up to a restoration of German influence in Europe. This conversion was not initially brought about by a fundamental change of attitudes but rather by the pragmatic recognition of Germany's situation.

Essential to the success of Stresemann's plans was the adoption of the Dawes Plan, which the Experts Commission, chaired by Charles Dawes (see p. 205), had produced in April 1924. The plan, which was provisional and was to be renegotiated within 10 years, was accepted by Britain, France, the USA and Germany at the London Conference in August 1924, and provided the economic context in which his policy of détente could be conducted. While it did not alter the final total of reparations fixed in 1921, it recommended that an 800-million-mark loan was to be raised privately, mainly in America. Initially annual reparation payments would be modest, but by 1929 they would rise to their full level. Payments were to be secured by the revenues of the German railways, customs and taxes, and a committee of foreign experts was to sit in Berlin to ensure that the transfer of payments to Allied accounts would occur in a way that did not damage the German economy. In the event of Germany again refusing to pay, a repetition of the unilateral Franco-Belgian occupation of the Ruhr in 1923 would be prevented by America sending a representative to sit on the Reparation Commission, who would be able to act as an effective brake on the French. After the Plan had been approved by the *Reichstag* in August, American capital began to pour into Germany, so enabling an albeit fragile economic recovery. The Dawes Plan set 'the stage for the economic restoration of the post war system [and] defanged the Versailles Treaty'.[3]

Détente: a state of lessened tension or growing relaxation between two or more states

In January 1925 the former wartime allies were committed by Article 429 of the Treaty of Versailles to evacuate the Cologne Zone. The French, however, refused to agree on the grounds that Germany had used the Ruhr crisis to delay its disarmament. To defuse this crisis, Stresemann, with the support of the British ambassador, Lord D'Abernon (1857–1941), put forward an ambitious plan for an international guarantee by the European great powers of the territorial status quo in western Europe. These proposals led to the Locarno Treaties, the key provision of which was a guarantee of the demilitarization of the Rhineland and the existing frontiers between Germany on the one side, and France and Belgium on the other.

The French attempted to extend the guarantees to Germany's eastern borders, but Stresemann agreed only to conclude arbitration treaties with Poland and Czechoslovakia. Viewed in hindsight this was arguably a missed opportunity. The collapse of the Russian and Austrian empires despite the border revisions dictated by the Treaty of Versailles had left Germany stronger in eastern Europe than before the war. Consequently, if Stresemann had dropped the policy of revision and accepted the new

Polish–German frontiers, Germany would have been in a position 'to offer a zone of security and cooperation similar to that created in the West, and would in all likelihood have assumed the informal role of dominant power in the region, thanks primarily to her economic strength.'[4] On the other hand, the renouncement of any attempt to regain the lands lost in the east would have been intensely unpopular with the German nationalists, and would most likely have intensified Soviet suspicions of Locarno.

The USSR regarded Stresemann's Locarno policy with considerable suspicion and, to safeguard its interests, pressed for an agreement committing each side to neutrality if war were to break out with a third power – in reality Poland. Stresemann accepted Soviet demands and after informing the Western powers the Treaty of Berlin was signed with the USSR in April 1926. Stresemann was grappling with what the diplomat Carl von Schubert (1882–1947) called 'the old problem of our foreign policy, to harmonize our interests in the East with those of the West, a problem which is unavoidably forced on us by our central geographical position …'.[5] In a sense it was a return of the Bismarckian policy of the Reinsurance Treaty (see pp. 151–152). The German foreign office saw it as a means of maintaining a balance between east and west Europe and of safeguarding German independence. Both the *Reichswehr* and industry welcomed it as it enabled the former to continue developing weapons banned by the Treaty of Versailles on Soviet soil, while the latter hoped to increase its exports to the USSR.

Despite French reservation about the Soviet–German negotiations, the Cologne Zone was evacuated in January 1926 and Germany joined the League 9 months later. Stresemann hoped that a rapprochement with France would prepare the way for the withdrawal of the Inter-Allied Military Control Commission (**IACC**) from Germany, speed up the evacuation of the Rhineland and possibly facilitate the return of the *Saar*. In 1926 while enjoying a gourmet meal with the French prime minister, Aristide Briand (1862–1932), at Thoiry, he proposed that Germany would pay off a large part of its reparations debts to Belgium and France in exchange for the evacuation of the Rhineland and the return of the Saar, provided the Americans could be persuaded to underwrite this with a loan to Germany. The plan, however, had to be shelved when it became clear that potential American subscribers were not interested.

A dramatic, comprehensive revision of the treaty was thus not practical politics in the short term In January 1927 Stresemann secured agreement for the withdrawal of the IACC, and in 1928 the Müller government (see p. 224) did launch a major initiative to persuade Britain and France to evacuate the Rhineland and to agree to a revision of the Dawes Plan. The American bankers were ready to revise Germany's reparation total downwards, as it was clear that unless this was done, once Berlin had to pay the full annual instalments under the plan, there would be little capital left to service the loans raised since 1924 in America. An independent committee of experts, set up and chaired by the American

See Document 53

The IACC: began work in 1920. During the Ruhr crisis it was unable to operate. Its final report was completed in January 1927. Even when it withdrew military experts attached to the British and French embassies remained until January 1930 to check on the demolition of the eastern fortifications.

banker, Owen Young (1874–1962), recommended that the total overall reparation sum should be reduced from 132 billion gold marks to 112 billion, to be paid over the course of 59 years. If Germany accepted this plan, Britain and France were ready to evacuate the Rhineland in 1930. Stresemann accepted these terms at the Hague Conference in August 1929 and French attempts to set up a new Commission of Verification and Conciliation to monitor the demilitarization of the Rhineland were defeated by joint Anglo-German pressure. Stresemann did not live to see the ratification of the Hague Treaty, but the agreement to evacuate the Rhineland made it more palatable to the German people. Nevertheless, in December the government was forced by the Nazis and nationalist right to hold a referendum, which declared that its signature would be an act of high treason as it perpetuated the 'enslavement' of the German people. This, however, was easily defeated (see below) and the plan became law on 20 January 1930.

With the evacuation of the Rhineland, Germany's restoration as a great European power was virtually complete. Like his successors in the 1950s, Briand came to the conclusion that Germany could only be peacefully contained through some form of European federation. At the tenth meeting of the League of Nations' Assembly in 1929 he outlined a vague scheme for a 'kind of federal link between peoples who are grouped together geographically, like the peoples of Europe'.[6] Stresemann reacted favourably but he was more interested in creating a purely economic union in which Germany could play the key role and bring her economic muscle to play. Nothing, however, was to come of this, as Stresemann's death and the world economic crisis brought the Franco-German rapprochement to a halt.

In the 1950s there were attempts to claim Stresemann as an advocate of European unity and compare his policy to Konrad Adenauer's support for European integration (see p. 312). Stresemann, however, was essentially dealing with the Germany Bismarck united, while Adenauer was the Chancellor of a west German state smaller than the Confederation of the Rhine. Like his contemporaries Stresemann was no 'Euro-idealist'. As his biographer, Jonathan Wright points out, 'he genuinely believed in peaceful revision and close understanding with France on which revision depended. But he also saw himself as a patriotic German in the tradition of Stein and Bismarck, promoting German interests as Briand promoted French interests'.[7]

Economic recovery?

Concentrating on the early years of the Republic, 1919–1923 and then the depression of 1929–1933, historians have largely overlooked the ongoing crisis caused by the stabilization of the mark in November 1923.[8] Inflation, at any rate up to the autumn of 1922, provided an easy formula which enabled employers to pass on the costs of higher wages to the customer in the form of higher prices. Similarly, it allowed the state to finance its greatly expanded welfare policies. Stabilization, however, confronted both the employers and the state with tight restrictions. The only way that workers' demands for higher wages and the greatly increased claims for welfare benefits and pensions could be met was by an 'economic miracle' on the scale of that experienced by the *Bundesrepublik* after 1949 (see p. 334). This did not, however, happen, and the subsequent industrial militancy and bitterness of those who had lost their life savings in the inflation helped destabilize the Republic. Knut Borchardt[9] has calculated that they could only have been adequately compensated if the per capita (per person) national income had increased by about 25 per cent compared to the figure in 1913. In fact, by 1929 it had increased by a mere 6 per cent.

After the stabilization of the mark in November 1923 the government was confronted with demands for compensating the millions of creditors, pensioners and small investors who had seen their savings, annuities and government bonds destroyed by inflation, and reimbursed in useless paper money. The Supreme Court, in an important decision, decided that the narrow legal argument that a mark remained a mark whether before or after stabilization might be correct legally but was wrong morally, and called on the government to have every individual debt revalued by the courts on the basis of the current economic situation of each debtor and creditor. Clearly such a cumbersome procedure was economically unacceptable to the government. A high revaluation would cost millions of marks, which the economy could not afford, and might well once again trigger inflation. Under cover of the enabling act which remained in force from September 1923 until the spring of 1924 (see p. 203), the government issued a decree providing for a 15 per cent revaluation of private debts, with

German industrial production, 1913–1929

Year	Industrial production
1913	100.0
1919	37.0
1922	70.0
1923	46.0
1924	69.0
1927	100.0
1928	103.8
1929	102.8

Source: Adapted from Knut Borchardt, *Perspectives on Modern German Economic History and Policy*, Cambridge, Cambridge University Press, 1991, pp. 171–172.

payment postponed until 1932. When the creditors rejected this, the government, after bitter arguments with their pressure groups, eventually in 1925 agreed to two laws: one set the resettlement of private debts to be paid at between 12.5 and 25 per cent (of the original amount) in 1932, while the other regulated the repayment of public debts (for the most part war bonds) at a mere 12.5 per cent of the original value, to be spread over 30 years. The creditors bitterly resented this and saw it as a deliberate betrayal of them by the Republic, an issue which the Nazis were later electorally to exploit (see p. 231).

Stabilization also led to the collapse of the Central Working Association Agreement of December 1918 and the quasi-corporate agreements between the employers and the unions (see p. 189). Wage disputes became more bitter as employers and workers fought over whether profits should be distributed mainly in the form of higher wages or else reinvested in industry. The presence of the KPD on the left of the SPD (as the MSPD can again be called again in light of the dramatic decline of the USPD in 1924) ensured that the free-trade unions had to fight bitterly to keep the loyalty of their members. Compulsory state arbitration of strikes, which had been introduced in 1919, also paradoxically worsened the situation by allowing both employers and employees to adopt deeply entrenched antagonistic attitudes, as in the final analysis it was the state that was responsible for arbitration. The employers saw state arbitration as essentially biased in the interests of the workers, who, in a series of wage disputes between 1924 and 1928, had made considerable gains. The more modern industries, particularly firms such as Siemens, still attempted to maintain a degree of cooperation with the unions, but their efforts were nullified by the leaders of heavy industry, who were determined to turn the clock back to 1913, as far as labour relations, welfare and wages went. Borchardt argues that this conflict was unbridgeable. On the one hand the employers had to cut production and wage costs to survive, while on the other the unions were duty-bound to defend the gains made in 1918–1919.

See Document 49

When the Grand Coalition was formed under the SPD chancellor, Hermann Müller (1876–1931), in 1928, the unions became more assertive. In the autumn of 1928 a strike over wages in the Ruhr and Rhine metal industry was settled by state arbitration, which awarded the workers a small increase. The employers ignored the award and locked out about 250,000 metalworkers for nearly 2 months in an attempt to curb accelerating wage demands and to destroy the state arbitration mechanism. A majority in the *Reichstag* supported the workers, who were given financial assistance by the state. Eventually the employers accepted a second arbitration, which awarded the employees a minimal shortening of the week and a 4 per cent wage increase. The failure of the employers to gain complete freedom to set their own wage structure persuaded the heavy industrialists that ultimately a more authoritarian government was needed, which would dismantle the welfare state and allow employers to discipline their workers. This was to determine the former's attitude in the economic and political crisis of 1930–1933 (see p. 227).

To recapture lost markets and to increase profits, industrialists sought to rationalize their plants. Surplus labour was ruthlessly combed out and new technology was introduced, especially in the mining industry where by 1929 one miner in four had lost his job. This led to a steadily increasing pool of structural unemployment, which did not disappear even in the brief spells of economic expansion that occurred in 1925 and 1927–1928. To protect markets and to avoid price undercutting by rivals, the large industries also continued their pre-war policy of creating cartels (see p. 108), which for investment relied heavily on the government for funds.

Relative industrial stagnation was paralleled by the worldwide agricultural depression, which hit both the east Elbian landowners and the smaller farmers a devastating blow in 1928, and led to a steep fall in grain prices. Already before the depression the great estates in the east were caught in a 'scissors crisis': to sell their goods on the world market they needed to modernize, yet despite receiving state aid (*Osthilfe*) they were unable to do this, and consequently sank deeper into debt. After 1928, only about 50 per cent of the farms in the west and 33 per cent of those in the east were solvent. The agricultural slump affected not only the farmers but the whole of rural society. Anger in the countryside was directed both at the welfare policy of the state, which was perceived to be favouring the urban working classes and at its commercial policies, which in practice encouraged the import of foreign food in exchange for the opening up of export markets. In 1928 there were large-scale peasant protests in Schleswig-Holstein where public officials and buildings were attacked. In Oldenburg some 30,000 peasants demonstrated with slogans such as 'From the Welfare State to the Work State'. This hostility was to be effectively exploited by the Nazi propaganda machine (see p. 230).

The structural weaknesses of the German economy were very visible during this brief period of stabilization. Essentially the battle to distribute the financial burdens imposed by the lost war and escalating cost of welfare payments fairly between employers and employees, pensioners and the state, and town and country could only be solved in a context of uninterrupted growth, which seemed impossible after 1929 with the onset of the recession.

Welfare, society and culture: the problems of modernization

The war, and the upheavals that came in its wake, accelerated the pace of change and the 'modernization' of German society. Even in times of prosperity and profound peace, the process can be painful and disorientating, but in the aftermath of a lost war and in the midst of deep-seated economic and political crises, the accelerating modernization of German society merely exacerbated the situation and provoked what Detlev Peukert calls the crisis of 'classical modernity'.

What is the theory of classical modernity?

'Modernization' is a vague and often subjective term. It was conceived initially by Max Weber, the German sociologist, and then elaborated on by American and German social scientists as a means of providing a systematic account of the development of industrial societies. As applied to German history, it has often used developments in western Europe and America as the yardstick for measuring German peculiarities and has tended to reinforce the concept of the *Sonderweg*. Peukert, in his influential study of the Weimar Republic, defines 'modernity' as 'consisting in the process of industrialization, that took off on a large scale around the middle of the nineteenth century, the urbanization that followed in the closing decades of the century and the social and cultural transformations that occurred as the nineteenth century was succeeded by the twentieth'.[10]

The welfare state

One of the characteristics of 'classical modernity', which was already visible in the Wilhelmine era, was the development of a welfare state. The welfare policy of the Weimar Republic 'represented a quantum leap in the evolution of the welfare state in Germany'.[11] The constitution guaranteed a comprehensive welfare system as one of the basic rights of the German population. Inevitably these ambitious, all-embracing targets for meeting the citizens' welfare needs in turn engendered frictions and problems that are endemic to modern social policy. Increasingly there was the tendency for the 'nanny state' to emerge, as legislation subordinated the individual to what the official mind considered 'normal'. The welfare state also became ever more bureaucratic and expensive to run, with the corollary that taxation rose, and ultimately failed to deliver what it had so ambitiously promised in 1919.

Youth

The Weimar Republic, like other contemporary modern societies, also had its 'youth problem', which was a 'code name for the breakdown of traditional ties and social controls'.[12] Young people adapted more easily to city life and the new Americanized urban culture. For the Weimar politicians and bureaucrats, the key to solving the 'youth problem' was essentially control. The Reich Youth Welfare Law of 1922 established both a welfare service for dealing with 'deviants' and a youth service whose task was to encourage parents to give their children an upbringing which would ensure both physical and social fitness. While the Republic had considerable success in setting up youth clubs and organizations, it was unable to earn the loyalty and respect of many of the younger generation. It was seen, to quote Joseph Goebbels (see p. 238), as an 'old men's republic' paralysed by bureaucratic red tape,[13] and was assailed by the youth movements on both the left and the right. These were relatively small in

The Weimar constitution and welfare

Article 119 guaranteed 'the maintenance of the purity and health of the family'; Article 155 expressed a commitment to social housing schemes, and Article 165 to co-determination by means of works councils; Articles 161–163 committed the Reich to expanding its social insurance scheme and Article 163 contained the ambitious claim that 'Every German shall be given the opportunity to earn his living through productive work. If no suitable opportunity for work can be found, the means necessary for his livelihood will be provided.'

numbers, but did much to propagate the cult of the new youth, which was free of 'bourgeois hypocrisy' and to pioneer new lifestyles. There were, too, the *wilde Cliquen*, which were made up of rebellious, nonconformist, mainly young working-class males who, like their successors in the 1930s and 1950s (see pp. 264–265, 339 and 348) alarmed the middle-class establishment by deliberately ignoring social norms and rules. The contempt of many of the young for the Republic was exacerbated by youth unemployment, particularly in the years 1930–1933. Paradoxically, the Weimar Republic 'gave young people a new prominence, but at the same time threatened them with marginalization'.[14]

Wilde Cliquen: wild gangs

See Document 54

Women

Women were given formal equality by the Weimar Republic. They voted for the first time in a national election in January 1919 and nearly 10 per cent of the deputies in the National Assembly were female. However, as in Britain, they had little impact on economic, fiscal and foreign policy, which was still a male preserve. Regardless of party orientation, they tended to concentrate on issues, such as social reform and welfare, which were more immediately pertinent to the family, society and the problems facing women in their daily activity.[15] The overall number of women working in Germany in 1925 was 35.6 per cent as compared to 31.2 per cent in 1907, yet this total masked a decline of women at work in domestic service and on the land, and an increase in female white-collar workers and industrial workers. In higher education the proportion of women students studying at university rose to 16 per cent in the winter of 1931–1932.

The popular image of the new German woman, which appeared in magazines, newspapers, advertisements and films, was far from reality. According to Peukert[16] it was arguably a male projection which focused largely on the young, single, female, office workers, earning their money by day in the typing pools and spending the night dancing the Charleston or watching **UFA** and Hollywood films. Yet Kathleen Canning points out that 'these images … endlessly reproducible … also had the power to shape and inform habits and desires'.[17] Inevitably this image attracted a considerable backlash. Some of the more conservative observers of both sexes attributed the decline in the population to 'the "boundless egoism"

UFA: *Universum Film Aktiengesellschaft –* Universal Film Company, whose origins go back to the military film units of 1916

of women who were betraying their natural vocation and striving for greater personal freedom and independence'.[18] Yet in reality the roles of women did not change very much. Both left and right still believed that a woman's real place was at home with her family. It had, however, become acceptable that, until marriage, women should enjoy an 'intermediary stage of personal independence'.[19] Unless married to farmers, restaurateurs or shopkeepers, the assumption was still that women would, after a few years of independence, stop working, marry, stay at home and dedicate themselves to house and family. The emergence of the nuclear family with an average of two children, as a result of improved and cheaper contraception and the increase in 'domestic mechanization', did not necessarily make women's work any easier. Smaller families and the simplification of housework merely meant that women had more time to devote to the often exhausting task of managing their families.

The decline in the birth-rate led to a considerable debate about population policy. On the one hand there were those who fulminated about *Völkertod*, the dying out of the population, and the harmful effects of contraception and abortions, while others, including Social Democrats, advocated a selective population policy, which involved the rearing of healthy babies and children. How this was to be done was debatable. The mildly left-wing Professor Alfred Grotjahn (1869–1931) advocated, for instance, sterilization of 'unsuitable mothers'.[20] There was, however, a consensus that the quality of the German race needed to be improved, and in 1926 the Prussian Ministry of Welfare set up marriage advice centres, whose task was to examine and advise on the 'racial hygiene' of engaged couples.

Despite the exaggerated publicity about the modern young woman, who worked and allegedly led a hedonistic life, the image of the mother and dedicated wife still remained supreme. By 1930, for instance, the American concept of Mother's Day had become widely accepted. There was general agreement that women in the final analysis would have to be 'dutiful, selfless, conciliatory members of an idealized *Volksgemeinschaft*'.[21]

**Volksgemein-
schaft:** 'people's
community'

The old and the new Germany

As in the 1950s, **'Americanism'** became a 'catchword for untrammelled modernity',[22] which involved efficiency, rationality and above all prosperity through mass production and consumerism (see p. 339). To many, Americanism was also a means of escaping the bitter feuds, class divisions and self-destruction of the old continent. During the short period of fragile prosperity between 1925 and 1929, Weimar took on some of the characteristics of American society. Mass consumption of high-tech goods such as cars, telephones and radios began to increase. The new 40-hour week and statutory holidays created the context for the development of mass leisure. Boxing, cycle races, football, and the like, all attracted vast audiences, which the development of the radio enabled millions to follow. Similarly, the growth of the cinemas and the popularity of dance halls facilitated mass participation.

Americanism:
it could also be
argued that what
many contempo-
raries took for
'Americanism' in
fact had its roots in
European, particu-
larly German, social
and economic
developments.

It was above all the great cities which were in the vanguard of modernism. Under the influence of the Bauhaus architects, new avant-garde suburbs as well as large public buildings were constructed. The big cities, particularly Berlin, which by 1920 was the third largest city in the world after New York and London, became 'the quintessential modern habitat',[23] where all the restraints of convention and small, stifling communities could be ignored. Yet because of this the city also came to symbolize isolation, alienation and rootlessness, particularly to the traditionalists and the rural population.

A municipal renaissance?

In the same way that historians like Geoff Eley and Margaret Anderson have revised the picture of Imperial Germany as a repressive and authoritarian state by looking more closely at local history (see p. 122) Benn Liebermann[24] has shown that during the stabilization era (1925–1929) the German cities underwent a considerable renaissance. The mayors backed by a cross-party majority were able to attract foreign investment and complete impressive building programmes, modernize the utilities, such as water and gas supplies, and build exhibition halls and airports. The financing of this led inevitably to intense distributional conflicts both with the government in Berlin and industry, which argued that the money would be better spent on raising industrial productivity rather than on urban aggrandizement.[25]

Over the course of the decade the accelerating modernization process inevitably began to erode the old social political groupings of the Empire. Before 1914 the Social Democratic movement was seen as a state within a state with its own 'Kaiser' – **August Bebel** (1840–1913). Although its clubs and institutions continued to proliferate after 1919, the formation of the KPD divided and weakened the workers' movement and attracted a growing number of younger workers, as did the Nazi SA after 1930. Like the SPD, Catholicism remained a political and social force. Its heartland was in the small towns and rural communities in southern Germany and the industrial areas of the Rhineland, but the ending of official discrimination against Catholicism and the rise of more secular attitudes freed liberated Catholics to vote for parties other than the Centre Party. By 1933, except in Bavaria, only 40 per cent of all Catholics in Germany voted for the Centre. The *Mittelstand*, too, was becoming fragmented. The small shopkeepers, self-employed craftsmen and, above all, the peasantry were hit hard by the convulsions of 1914–1923 and felt their existence challenged by urbanism, department stores, organized labour and the cartels. The white-collar workers, on the other hand, were, as Peukert has put it, 'largely a *tabula rasa* on which the effects of the process of modernization were being particularly vividly imprinted'.[26] They were at home in the big city and benefited from mass consumerism, but once their prospects for upward mobility were destroyed by the great economic crisis of 1929–1933, many began to turn to the Nazi Party.

August Bebel: one of the founders of the SPD and subsequent leader of the party until 1913

Tabula rasa: blank page

See Document 54

The Jews and the ethnic minorities

By Article 113 of its constitution the Weimar Republic was committed to respecting the rights of minorities. Thus the state itself did not discriminate against the Jews, the Poles or any of the other small number of minorities within its frontiers, although the Roma and Sinti fared less well.

The Germans Jews were predominantly urban, middle-class and professional, and played a prominent role in Weimar culture and, to a lesser extent, in politics. Increasingly they were becoming assimilated into the German population, a fact which accounted for the overall decline in the numbers of the Jewish community in Germany between 1919 and 1933. An exception to this trend were the *Ostjuden*, who came in as migrant workers from the ghettos of eastern Europe. Inevitably their alien appearance and vulnerability fuelled anti-Semitic attacks and prejudice. In the *Scheunenviertel*, the eastern European Jewish quarter in Berlin, a crowd of 30,000 people attacked the Jews in November 1923. Up to a point the incident anticipated *Reichskristallnacht* on 9–10 November 1938 (see p. 262), but the crucial difference was that in 1923 the police cleared the mobs from the streets. The established Jewish community also suffered attacks from such anti-Semitic organizations as the Pan-German League and the Nazi Party, which called for the disenfranchisement and expulsion of the Jews, while anti-Semitic prejudice was rife in the universities, the DNVP and the Centre Party.

The post-war plebiscites had cut down on the number of minorities within the Reich, but along the Polish and Danish borders there were still pockets of Poles and Danes in Reich territory. Altogether there were nearly 900,000 Poles in Germany, but many of these, particularly in the Ruhr, were well on the way to being assimilated. Polish immigration into Germany during the Weimar Republic almost dried up, although the great estates in the east still needed to recruit seasonal labour from Poland. The Poles were not popular, but the government was bound by Article 113 of the Weimar constitution to allow the establishment of Polish schools in the Ruhr and the eastern borderlands. The Roma and Sinti, however, continued to experience continued official discrimination because they were seen as nothing more than a host of itinerant beggars. Wherever possible they were corralled into specially appointed campsites, and in Prussia, Hessen and Bavaria those over the age of 16 could be sent to the workhouse if they could not prove that they had a regular job.

Scheunenviertel: The incident was similar to, but on a larger scale than, the riots in Neustettin, 1881 and Xanten, 1891 (see p. 117).

Weimar culture

Weimar culture, which was heavily subsidized by the state, became the symbol of what we understand by 'modernity'. Through art, architecture, music and literature it sought to explore every aspect of modern life. The roots of much of it, of course, went back to before the war. **Expressionism** in painting, literature and theatre, modern architecture, as well as psychoanalysis and the physics of relativity had all made important breakthroughs before 1914 (see pp. 118–119), but it was only in the 1920s that they really began to affect the public's consciousness and attitudes. In every sphere of the arts there was the desire to experiment and start afresh. As Gordon Craig has so succinctly put it, 'the great caesura of war gaped between them and a past whose institutions, traditions and values had been smashed beyond repair'.[27]

Expressionist theatre was didactic and, through stark stage sets and a variety of new techniques such as film strips and newspaper montage, 'the gospel of social revolution'[28] was propagated. Reinhard Goering (1887–1936) in *Seeschlacht* (*Sea Battle*) and Fritz von Unruh (1885–1970) in *Heinrich aus Andernach* (*Henry from Andernach*), for instance, urged an end to war and nationalism, while other dramatists like Ernst Toller (1893–1939) and Georg Kaiser (1878–1945) worked for the liberation of the masses from poverty and capitalism. In music, Paul Hindemith (1895–1963) composed string quartets and songs based on expressionist poetry and jazz, and Arnold Schoenberg (1874–1951) pioneered the 12-tone scale and atonal music. On a more popular level, Kurt Weill (1900–1950) wrote the music for Brecht's (1898–1956) *Dreigroschenoper* (*The Threepenny Opera*) and *Mahagonny*. In the mid-1920s the *Neue Sachlichkeit*, or New Objectivity Movement, was launched by writers such as Joseph Roth (1894–1939), Hermann Kesten (1900–1996) and Erich Kästner (1899–1974) and painters like Otto Dix (1891–1969) and Georg Grosz (1893–1959). Their aim was not only to expose the hypocrisies and frailties of the time, but also to come to terms with the express-train tempo of modern life. Visually and in the sphere of design the greatest force for modernity was the *Bauhaus*, which was established in 1919 by Walther Gropius (1855–1933) in Weimar with the aim of setting up a new school of art, architecture and design to 'break down the arrogant barrier between craftsman and artist', in order to bring about a new unity between architecture and art and to 'conceive the new building of the future'. In cooperation with skilled craftsmen and expressionist painters, such as Lyonel Feininger (1871–1956) and Paul Klee (1879–1940), the Bauhaus revolutionized the design of everything from cutlery, china and lamps to new housing estates in Germany.

The great majority of artists and writers felt a profound alienation from the Republic and were bitterly critical of the compromises that men like Ebert and Stresemann had to make to stabilize the political situation. Ernst Toller's play *Hoppla Wir Leben* (*Whoops, We Live!*) portrays, for instance, a revolutionary who suffers a breakdown and goes into an asylum for 8 years. On his release he discovers that the worst of the old regime has survived and his old comrades have surrendered their ideals. The Republic was also attacked in often similar language by the writers of the radical right. Moeller van den Bruck (1876–1925) urged the replacement of decadent capitalist liberalism by a regime, which he did not describe in detail but called the 'Third Reich'. His ideas were enthusiastically received by right-wing radicals, and inspired Spengler to produce

> Expressionism is the term used to describe developments in German literature, art, theatre, film and music during the period 1909–1925. It analyses the world subjectively through the eyes of the artist and seeks through distortion and exaggeration to conjure up emotions and evoke thought.

> See Document 55

his *Decline of the West*. Oswald Spengler (1880–1936) and Moeller van den Bruck influenced a whole generation of radical conservative writers like Ernst Jünger (1895–1998), who ennobled war and the experience of combat in his novels and despised the pacifism of the new Republic.

Party politics, 1924–1929

Has the instability of Weimar politics from 1924 to 1929 been exaggerated? Within a European context Weimar's experiences were not unique. In France, for instance, and Italy before Mussolini's dictatorship, cabinets were equally short-lived. As McElligott points out, there were also strong continuities in German politics during this half decade. The six cabinets headed by Hans Luther and Wilhelm Marx, for instance, all pursued 'an almost seamless domestic and foreign policy'. Not surprisingly McElligott comes to the conclusion that 'Weimar's parliamentary system was quite stable in spite of the superficial changes signaled by cabinet reshuffles and the odd spat in the *Reichstag*'.[29] One wonders whether this is not an example of the revisionist pendulum swinging too far the other way! It is undeniable that during this period the parliamentary and party system functioned 'more or less adequately', but during 1930–1933 its intrinsic structural weaknesses were exposed and eventually proved fatal to the body politic. To understand these weaknesses is justification for an analysis of political developments 1924–1929, even though they were not *necessarily* 'a one-way street, leading inevitably to political crisis and the collapse of democracy'.[30]

Structural weaknesses?

Key party abbreviations used in this section:

BVP: Bavarian People's Party (Catholic)

DDP: German Democratic Party (liberal)

DNVP: German National People's Party (nationalist)

DVP: German People's Party (liberal)

SPD: Social Democratic Party (socialist)

USPD: Independent Social Democratic Party (socialist)

See Document 49

The possibility of constructing a secure coalition, which could command a majority in the *Reichstag*, rested effectively on either forming a grand coalition stretching from the SPD to the DVP or on a Centre, DVP and DNVP bloc. The problem, however, was that disagreements on economic and social questions between the SPD and the bourgeois parties made the former difficult to sustain, while foreign-policy differences bedevilled relations between the DNVP and its two major potential coalition partners. This instability was compounded by divisions within the parties. Frequently the backbenchers would not support the political line taken by their leaders in the cabinet, which led to a situation which Gustav Stolper (1888–1947), a member of the DDP, described as creating a 'coalition of ministers, not a coalition of parties ... there are no government parties, only opposition parties'.[31]

The parties, which had never had to share governmental responsibility in Imperial Germany, had difficulties in coming to terms with their new role in a parliamentary democracy. The SPD made an attempt to become a more broad-based people's party with its Görlitz Programme of 1921, but this was effectively abandoned when it reunited with the USPD a year later, and in 1925 it reverted to an essentially **Marxist position**, as defined by its Heidelberg Programme. Thus, until it re-entered government in 1928, it offered its support to the bourgeois coalitions only on particular issues, one of these being Stresemann's foreign policy. The DNVP was similarly split between ideology and pragmatism. It hated parliamentary democracy, yet twice between 1925 and 1927 it briefly joined a coalition so that it could gain a bigger share of the economic spoils, but in 1928, with the election of Hugenberg (1865–1951) as party leader, it returned to its opposition to the democratic system.

The most consistent supporters of the Weimar system were the Centre and Liberal parties. The Centre was a pivotal force in every government from 1919 to 1931, but towards the end of the 1920s it began to move to the right, which made cooperation with the SPD all the more difficult. The former Liberal parties, the DDP and DVP, on the other hand, in the 6 years up to 1930 suffered an increasing erosion of their core support as a result of the rise of the special-interest and regional parties such as the Reich party of the German Middle Class and the Revalorization and Construction Party. In the election of May 1924 these parties gained well over 8 per cent of the vote, while the Nazis won 6 per cent. In the second election of 1924 the Nazi vote collapsed to 3 per cent, but the middle-class voters did not return *en masse* to their traditional parties. On the contrary, throughout the second half of the 1920s 'the DDP and DVP were confronted by a bewildering array of special interest parties, each competing for a segment of the already splintered middle-class vote'. In the 1928 election the special-interest parties attracted 14 per cent of the vote, which overtook the combined total of the DDP and DVP, and nearly equalled the DNVP's share of the vote. As yet the middle-class vote was not going to the Nazis, but there is no doubt that the destabilization of traditional middle-class voting patterns facilitated the rise of the NSDAP after 1928. Childers stresses that 'if the ultimate collapse of the Weimar party system is to be analyzed effectively, that analysis must begin not with the severe economic contractions of the early thirties but with the inflation and stabilization crises of the mid-twenties'.[32]

The deep divisions between the parties, the rise of the new interest groups and a system of proportional representation that allowed even the smallest party representation led to a long string of short-lived and unstable coalition governments. A brief factual analysis of these is necessary to help explain the fragility of parliamentary democracy in Germany, and how by 1930 there was an increasing desire for stability, even if this meant a more authoritarian government.

From Marx to Müller, 1923–1929

After Stresemann's resignation on 23 November 1923 a fragile Centre–Liberal administration was formed by the Centre leader, **Wilhelm Marx**. It continued to maintain the state of emergency declared by Stresemann (see p. 203) until March 1924 when the *Reichstag*'s refusal to approve its

Marxist position: a belief in the inevitability of class conflict and the collapse of capitalism

prolongation led to Marx's resignation and elections in May. These, held while the impact of the Ruhr crisis and hyperinflation were still fresh in the memory of the voters, significantly weakened the DDP, DVP and the SPD, while strengthening both the extreme right and extreme left. Marx's best option now was to create a Centre, DVP and DNVP coalition, but in the end he had to settle for another minority administration, as the DNVP was still formally opposed to the ratification of the Dawes Plan, which was the government's overriding priority. Because of the constitutional implications of the plan for the ownership of the state railways (see p. 208), Marx needed a two-thirds majority to ratify it. He had the backing of the SPD, but still needed the support of at least some DNVP deputies. After immense pressure not only from the government but also from such right-wing pressure groups as the Reich Association of German Industry and the *Landbund* (Land League), which was anxious to see the adoption of the plan and the subsequent flow of American money into Germany, the DNVP leadership reluctantly agreed to allow its members a free vote, and the plan was approved. Marx then hoped to strengthen his government by bringing the DNVP into the coalition, but was unable to overcome the reluctance of the DDP and considerable elements in his own party to work with it. In an attempt to create a more cooperative *Reichstag*, he once again requested its dissolution and fresh elections.

The election of 7 December 1924 was held in a calmer political and economic atmosphere. Thanks to the acceptance of the Dawes Plan, the German economy was beginning to revive. The extreme right and left vote declined, and the SPD again became the largest party in the *Reichstag*. It was possible either to form a grand coalition with the SPD or a bourgeois bloc stretching from the Centre to the DNVP. The latter alternative was the option preferred by Stresemann and the DVP, who felt that the DNVP would be easier to work with over fiscal policy than the SPD. To facilitate this, Stresemann made it clear that Marx would have to resign. President Ebert then appointed Hans Luther (1879–1962), the former non-party finance minister and mayor of Essen, to form an 'above party' cabinet in which members of the DNVP, DVP, Centre Party and BVP could serve without formally committing their parties to support it. Within a year, however, it broke up when the DNVP refused to vote in October 1925 for the Locarno Treaties, and Luther resigned in December.

After nearly 8 weeks of negotiations, Luther formed his second government on 19 January 1926, based this time on the Centre, DVP and DDP. An alternative to this would have been a grand coalition based on the parties which had voted for the Locarno Treaties – the SPD, Centre, DVP, DDP and BVP, but this foundered once again on the DVP's refusal to work with the SPD and the latter's reluctance to enter government. The SPD was unwilling to enter government both because it feared that the KPD would exploit its cooperation with the bourgeois parties at a time of rising unemployment and also because it was disillusioned with its last time in government in the Stresemann administration of August to

Hindenburg's election to the presidency in April 1925

Ebert died in February 1925, shortly before his extended time as president was due to finish. The president was elected directly by the people. In the first ballot the winner needed an absolute majority, in the second a simple majority was sufficient. In the first ballot in March there were seven candidates: Karl Jarres (1874–1951), who was jointly supported by both DNVP and DVP, won 10.4 million votes, the SPD Otto Braun (1872–1955) won 7.8 million and Wilhelm Marx (Centre) came third with 3.9 million. In the second ballot the Weimar parties rallied behind Marx, which forced the right to look for a popular figure in the great wartime hero, Hindenburg. On April 26 he won by a small majority of 900,000, largely because he attracted BVP voters, while the working-class vote was split by the KPD. Politically Hindenburg's election was a serious blow for the Republic. Although he respected the letter of the constitution, his presidency marked a slow but definite shift towards presidential power. His general aim was to exclude the SPD from government, if at all possible, whils including the DNVP.

November 1923 (see p. 204). A new factor operating against extending a government leftwards was the election of Hindenburg as president in April 1925, which effectively ensured that the influence of the president would now be mobilized, where possible, against the inclusion of the SPD in a coalition.

In May 1926 Luther's second cabinet collapsed as a result of the defeat by a combination of the left-wing parties and the DDP of the 'flag decree', which would have allowed German embassies abroad to fly the old imperial flag. Any immediate reconstruction of a more right-wing governing coalition to include the DNVP was blocked by the DNVP's implacable opposition to Germany joining the League of Nations, while a more left-wing coalition was also impossible because the SPD supported, together with the KPD, the proposal for a **referendum** on the question of expropriating the former royal houses of the German states. This was strongly opposed by the bourgeois parties, although they were unable to block it. Consequently, as a stop gap, virtually the same cabinet was resurrected within days, with only a very few changes under the chancellorship of Marx, on the assumption that once Germany joined the League and the referendum on the princes' estates was held, these issues would be solved and the way would be clear for either the SPD or DNVP to join the coalition.

The referendum took place on 20 June 1926 and was rejected, but voting support for the left-wing parties rose by 3.5 million compared to the previous election of December 1924.

In November Marx attempted to strengthen his government by cooperating more closely with the SPD, even though this met with suspicion from the DVP. Despite its hostility to the government's **defence policy**, the SPD was ready to join a grand coalition, but only if the Marx cabinet first resigned. When the cabinet refused, the SPD retaliated by moving a successful vote of no confidence on 17 December against the government, which ensured its resignation. The DNVP also voted against the government, as they hoped that its defeat would open up the way for their participation in a more right-wing administration. During the next 2 weeks

Defence policy: the SPD was highly critical of the *Reichswehr*'s relations with the Red Army, which was enabling it to test weapons secretly in the USSR.

General Schleicher, 1882–1934: served on the General Staff during the Great War and was political adviser to General Groener during the revolution of 1918. He then worked under General von Seeckt at the Ministry of Defence, where he played a leading role in planning German rearmament. By 1929, as a result of his close friendship with Hindenburg, he had become a major influence in the Republic.

intensive interparty negotiations took place. Hindenburg, working through **General Schleicher**, put pressure on the Centre Party to reject proposals for a grand coalition, and instead to work with the DNVP and DVP to form a government. If this proved impossible, Schleicher advised Hindenburg to go ahead and 'appoint a government in which he had confidence without consulting the parties or paying attention to their wishes', and then 'with the order for dissolution ready to hand, give the government every constitutional opportunity to get a majority in parliament'.[33] Here then was a dress rehearsal for the presidential interventions in 1930–1933 which are explored in the next chapter. This time, however, the Centre and the BVP agreed to a coalition with the DVP and DNVP, as the DNVP had come round to accept Locarno and Germany's membership of the League.

This fragile alliance managed to survive for a year, since foreign-policy issues did not become acute and the DNVP was ready to make some limited concessions over the introduction of unemployment insurance. But by the end of 1927 it was again becoming difficult to reconcile the contradictory interests of the coalition parties. In February 1928, for instance, as a result of opposition led by the DVP, the Centre Party's Schools Bill, which would have allowed denominational schools in states where they had previously not existed, was defeated. The Centre withdrew from the coalition and demanded a dissolution of the *Reichstag* and fresh elections.

See Document 49

The subsequent elections led to a swing to the left as well as a flow of votes from the DNVP, the Centre, the DDP and DVP to the new 'interest parties'. As the SPD had emerged greatly strengthened from the elections, and was ready to enter government, Hindenburg could not avoid entrusting Hermann Müller (1876–1931), the chairman of the parliamentary party, with the formation of a new administration. Since there were influential groups in both the Centre and the DVP, which did not want a grand coalition, Müller initially formed a 'cabinet of personalities' and only in January 1929 did this formally become the Grand Coalition backed by the SPD, Centre, DDP and DVP. The main task facing the Müller Cabinet was to negotiate the Young Plan and the Allied evacuation of the Rhineland. Once the Nationalists' **referendum campaign** was defeated the coalition's unity was exhausted. Its break-up in March 1930, which was to have such catastrophic consequences, is dealt with in the next chapter.

Referendum campaign: An alliance of Nationalists and Nazis was able to secure sufficient support to force the government to submit the Young Plan to a referendum. On 29 December only 13.8 per cent of the population voted against it.

Conclusion

In his masterful study of German history, 1866–1945 Gordon Craig wrote that the middle years of the Republic 'were marked by foreign success and domestic failure'.[34] Few would argue with this assessment of Stresemann's success in improving Franco-German relations and beginning the process of revising the Versailles settlement. On the other hand is it accurate to dismiss this period as 'domestic failure'? On a national basis it is hard to disagree with Kolb's assessment that the political stabilization of the Weimar Republic from 1924 to 1929 was at best 'fragile and superficial'.[35] It was disliked by significant sections of the population, and was attacked by the both the right and the extreme left. The breakneck pace of modernization and artistic experimentation which according to one historian made Germany 'a laboratory of the apocalypse',[36] disturbed and alienated significant groups. To the avant-garde artists and many young people these very groups made Germany a bourgeois, conventional 'old man's republic'.

Economically, the Weimar Republic was burdened by the economic legacy of a lost war and by the heavy costs of running a welfare state. To maintain these payments the economy would have to enjoy a long period of sustained growth, but to make any appreciable cuts in them would alienate the working classes and provoke a major political crisis. Partly as a result of the system of proportional representation, which maximized the impact of the small parties, but also because of the division in the left-wing vote between the KPD and the SPD, and the inability of the larger parties to work together in a coalition, the Weimar system failed to deliver a stable government.

On the other hand, as a corrective to this pessimistic picture, there was a bedrock of support for the Republic. To mark the tenth anniversary of its foundation 'hundreds of thousands of people turned out to mark the occasion in Berlin while the provinces reported similar crowds'.[37] It is also important to remember that Prussia, a state comprising three-fifths of the Reich, was ruled by a stable SPD, Centre and DDP coalition, which Otto Braun (1872–1955), its minister-president, called the 'guarantor of the continued existence of the German Republic'.[38]

11 The Change of Regime: The Collapse of Weimar and the Formation and Consolidation of the Third Reich, 1930–1934

TIMELINE

1930	30 March	Brüning, Reich chancellor
	16 July	*Reichstag* dissolved
	14 September	*Reichstag* elections. NSDAP: 107 seats
1931	February	Unemployment nearly five million
	March	Customs union plan announced – later vetoed by France
	11 May	Failure of Austrian *Kreditanstalt*
	6 July	Hoover moratorium
	13 July	Failure of *Darmstädter und Nationalbank*
	11 October	Harzburg front
1932	March–April	Presidential elections: Hindenburg re-elected
	13 April	Prohibition of SA and SS
	1 June	Von Papen, chancellor
	20 July	Prussian government suspended
	31 July	*Reichstag* elections: NSDAP: 230 seats
	13 August	Hindenburg refused to appoint Hitler chancellor
	6 November	*Reichstag* elections: NSDAP loses 34 seats
	4 December	General von Schleicher, chancellor
1933	30 January	Hitler, chancellor
	1 February	Dissolution of the *Reichstag*
	27 February	*Reichstag* fire
	28 February	The Decree for the Protection of People and State
	5 March	*Reichstag* elections: NSDAP: 288 seats
	23 March	Enabling Act passed
	31 March	First law for the coordination of the federal states
	2 May	Trade unions dissolved
	14 July	NSDAP declared sole legal political party
	20 July	Concordat with Catholic Church
	29 September	Reich Entailed Farm Law
	1 December	Law to ensure unity of party and state
1934	30 June	'Night of the Long Knives'. Röhm murdered
	20 July	SS established as an independent force under Himmler
	2 August	Death of Hindenburg. Hitler, president and chancellor

Introduction: problems, issues and questions

In 1955 Karl-Dietrich Erdmann observed that 'all research into the history of the Weimar Republic is necessarily governed, whether expressly or otherwise, by the question as to the causes of its collapse'.[1] In view of the horrors that Hitler unleashed upon the world, it is still hard not to avoid this perspective. The breakdown of the Weimar Republic and the seizure of power by Hitler was not just a change of regime but a revolution that was to destroy the German Empire and drag Europe down with it. Given the legacy of the authoritarian Wilhelmine elite, the lost war and the indecisive revolution of 1918–1919, not to mention hyperinflation and then the Great Depression, which Robert Boyce has called the 'third global catastrophe'[2] of the 20th century (the two world wars being the other two), it is no mystery why the Weimar Republic was so unpopular and vulnerable, but was it inevitable that it should be replaced by the **Third Reich** at a point when support for the Nazi Party appeared to be ebbing?

Third Reich: The first Reich was the Holy Roman Empire and the second the Empire created in 1871.

Economic, social, global and constitutional factors combined to create the context in which Hitler took over power, but how important were the failures and actions of individuals? Was it, for instance, inevitable that the Grand Coalition should have collapsed in March 1930, or that Gregor Strasser should have obeyed Hitler's veto to join Schleicher's cabinet in December 1932? Similarly what would have happened if Hindenburg had not at last agreed to appoint Hitler as chancellor? Even when Hitler became chancellor it was arguably not too late to stop the triumph of Nazism. Why was the Enabling Act not defeated in the *Reichstag* and why did the Röhm crisis in 1934 not lead to the rallying of the still considerable anti-Nazi forces?

The depression and the fall of the Müller government

The Wall Street Crash in October 1929 marked the onset of the world depression, which hit Germany particularly hard because its economy depended on short-term credits from America. Over the next 3 years the impact of the slump was devastating. By 1932 the production of capital goods had sunk to half its 1913 level, wages dropped to 87 per cent of their 1928 level, and unemployment rose to 5.1 million by September 1932. Inevitably, a depression on this scale affected every section of the economy, and a frightening loss of security was evident in every area of German society. Unemployment hit the age group 18–30 particularly hard, and by 1933 some of these had been unemployed for as long as 5 years. Many sought relief from this debilitating experience by joining the paramilitary organizations of either the right or the left – the SA, the SPD's *Reichsbanner* or the KPD's *Rotfront*.

See Document 54

Already by the end of 1929 the Grand Coalition was beginning to unravel. SPD backbenchers had voted against their own chancellor in protest against a cabinet decision to build a battle cruiser. In December 1929 Chancellor Müller had great difficulty in securing support for an emergency budget covering the state's deficit. Once the referendum opposing the Young Plan had been defeated the differences in the cabinet over financing the unemployment **insurance system** came to a head. The SPD argued that there should be no cut in benefits, while the DVP called for reductions. At the same time, German industry was beginning a concerted campaign against the whole principle of social welfare, the costs of which were already spiralling as a result of the onset of the depression.

Insurance system: by the German insurance law of July 1927, all workers were entitled to financial relief as long as they were willing to work and were unemployed through no fault of their own. Insurance contributions were limited to 3 per cent of wages and contributed equally by employer and employee. Financially, it was calculated, this would be sufficient to provide relief for about 800,000, with reserves for a further 600,000.

A compromise was offered by the Centre Party, which would have delayed a decision on the crucial issue of reform until the autumn, but under the influence of the trade unions this was rejected by the SPD, and the cabinet decided to resign on 27 March. Later, Rudolf Hilferding (1877–1941), the left-wing SPD deputy, bitterly criticized the trade unions and SPD backbenchers for being 'ready to let German democracy and the German Republic go to the devil … over the question of thirty pfennigs for the unemployed.'[3] In hindsight he had a point, as the demise of the Grand Coalition fatally weakened German democracy, but nevertheless at stake for the SPD was the emotive issue of whether or not unemployment benefits should be cut.

The number of unemployed (millions), January 1929–1933

1929	2.850
1930	3.218
1931	4.887
1932	6.042
1933	6.014

Adapted from B. Gebhardt, Handbuch der Source: deutschen Geschichte, vol. 4, ed., K. D. Erdmann, Stuttgart, Union Verlag, 1959, p. 352.

When Müller resigned, Hindenburg seized the chance to appoint Heinrich Brüning (1885–1970), the pro-monarchist war veteran and right-wing leader of the Centre Party in the *Reichstag*. Hindenburg and his advisers, particularly General Schleicher, the head of the Ministerial Bureau in the Defence Ministry, had been waiting to replace Müller with a more authoritarian and 'anti-Marxist' chancellor (see p. 224). He had already in January 1930 discussed with Count Westarp (1864–1945), the chairman of the DNVP parliamentary party, the possibility of appointing a **presidential cabinet.**

Presidential cabinet: a cabinet appointed by the president and independent of the *Reichstag*

The first Brüning cabinet, March–September 1930

Brüning's role in the destruction of the Republic is a matter of considerable controversy. Contemporaries were divided as to whether his chancellorship marked, in the words of Arthur Rosenberg, the 'death of the Weimar Republic', or whether, on the contrary, Brüning represented its last hope. Friedrich Meinecke, for instance, observed in 1946 that 'the path to the abyss' only began with Brüning's fall.[4] Similar debates continue to reverberate. Werner Conze[5] echoed Meinecke with his arguments that Brüning was intending to create a presidential constitution (along the lines, perhaps, of the later French Fifth Republic), which had been made inevitable by the collapse of coalition politics, and that only *after* his dismissal did Germany's slide towards dictatorship accelerate.

Bracher, however, both in his classic study on *The Dissolution of the Republic* and in later works, does not hesitate to attribute considerable blame to Brüning for the dissolution of the Republic. He stresses that 'Brüning's solution occurred at a time when parliamentary majorities were still possible'. Hans Mommsen is equally critical, even though he gives full weight to the structural complexities facing Brüning, and unequivocally argues that '[b]reaking the spirit of the constitution and replacing it with formal legalism was his doing'.[6] Brüning's recent biographer, William Patch rejects the Mommsen–Bracher thesis and argues trenchantly that 'his fall not his appointment marked the crucial turning point of the Weimar Republic'.[7]

Until the late 1970s there was a widespread consensus that Brüning's savage deflationary policy was avoidable, and, whatever his political aims, this greatly facilitated the rise of the Nazi Party. Yet Knut Borchardt has questioned this orthodoxy and argued that, as there was no realistic alternative to deflation, 'we can only study this tragedy and … abstain from engaging in over-presumptuous criticisms'.[8] In his memoirs, which Patch characterizes as 'petulant and self-righteous' Brüning claimed that he was a revisionist who was determined to end reparation payments and achieve military equality with the Entente Powers. This, however, may well have represented a later rationalization of what seemed to contemporaries an increasingly confused set of policies.[9]

See Document 58

Brüning's first cabinet formed on 28 March was supported by the Centre, the DDP and DVP. From the start he made it clear that if his government were defeated, he would request a dissolution of the *Reichstag* and govern with emergency decrees. His first finance bill achieved a narrow majority, but the second one, involving increased taxes, deflationary cuts in welfare expenditure and 'an emergency contribution' from those on fixed incomes, was defeated in July. When further attempts to promulgate it by resorting to Article 48 were rejected as unconstitutional by the *Reichstag*, it was promptly dissolved and a general election was held on 14 September. This was a decision of 'breathtaking irresponsibility',[10] which allowed the Nazi Party to become a major political force, and began, to quote Gerhard Schulz, 'the permanent violation of the constitutional system by the dictatorial power of the *Reichspräsident*'.[11]

See Document 47

Hitler and the Nazi Party, 1925–1930: the emergence of a new revolutionary force

When Hitler was released from prison in December 1924, he had learnt from the failure of the Munich *putsch* (see p. 205) that for the foreseeable future he would have to campaign constitutionally and achieve regime change through what he was later to call a 'legal revolution'.

See Document 56

With the lifting of the ban on the Nazi Party in Bavaria in January 1925, he rapidly rebuilt the party with himself in the position of **charismatic** leader. The *Führer* cult (see p. 247) helped integrate the oddly-sorted groups with conflicting interests, which composed the party, into

Charismatic leader: one who can inspire his followers with fanatical loyalty

Cadre: a core unit, which can serve later as a basis for mass expansion

Gauleiter: regional Nazi Leader in charge of a Gau (province)

Bolshevism: for the first time in Russian history Jews became prominent in public life during the Bolshevik Revolution. Hence to its opponents, the Whites, the revolution was often seen as Jewish-inspired.

See Document 57

some sort of coherent whole. Over the next 4 years the essential nature of the party was determined until its dissolution in 1945. The organization of the NSDAP became institutionalized through party bureaucrats in Munich, such as Rudolf Hess (1894–1987), who protected Hitler's charismatic image without posing any threat to his power. Hitler only intervened in issues that involved his supreme authority. The NSDAP was controlled from its party offices in Munich, and each level was subordinate to the one above it. On a national basis the party was divided into 35 *Gaue*, or regions, each controlled by a **Gauleiter**. Below these were the local branches, which were run by a **cadre** of activists. This seemingly logical pattern was threatened, however, by the determination, which was encouraged by Hitler, of the organizations affiliated to the party, such as, for example, the SA, the Hitler Youth and the Nazi Teachers' Association, to see themselves as responsible to *him* alone rather than being firmly integrated into the party system.

Hitler never officially revised the party's 1920 programme (see p. 205), but in practice he toned down its economic radicalism to win over new supporters. A better guide to his first principles can be found in *Mein Kampf*, even though it is not a precise blueprint for the future. Page after page shows that for Hitler the world was a battlefield where the 'Aryan' races clashed with the agents of world Jewry. His identification of the Jews with Russian **Bolshevism**, was far from original, but had, to quote Ernst Nolte, an 'explosive political effect',[12] and enabled his ideas to reach a wider middle-class public, which was deeply alarmed by the prospect of a communist revolution in Germany. Hitler's whole programme for the regeneration of Germany depended on creating a racially pure state, which would be demographically strengthened by the colonization of western Russia by German farmers.

While the party's core supporters remained the *Mittelstand*, which had been impoverished by the war and above all by the inflation, Detlef Mühlberger has shown that its membership during this period was 'remarkably heterogeneous in social terms'.[13] Up to 1927 the Nazi Party, following the example of Italian Fascism, attempted to dominate the cities, but in the winter of 1927–1928 Hitler abandoned the Urban Plan and began to campaign more intensively in the countryside. Despite his determination not to alter the 1920 programme, he moderated the emphasis on land confiscation in Point 17. This policy change was too late to help the Nazi Party much in the 1928 elections, but its potential effectiveness was illustrated by the fact that in some rural areas in north-west Germany, such as Schleswig-Holstein, the Nazis gained over 10 per cent of the vote.

In the electoral campaign of September 1930 the Nazi Party exploited the growing insecurity of the voters with consummate skill. Its main theme was that only Hitler could unite the people, whom parliamentary democracy had demoralized and split into competing egotistical interest groups, into a new national community. Whole regions were saturated with Nazi canvassers and electoral meetings, while Hitler himself held major speeches in the large cities. The results on 14 September were 'a political earthquake',[14] when the NSDAP increased its seats from 12 to 107, and became the second largest party in the *Reichstag*. The communists vote also increased dramatically, and they now had 77 seats instead of 54.

See Documents 47, 49 and 59

The second Brüning cabinet, September 1930–May 1932

Brüning at first hoped to gain the passive support of the NSDAP for his government in the *Reichstag*, and even proposed that 'in all *Land* [state] parliaments where it was arithmetically possible, the NSDAP and the Centre might combine to form a government',[15] but Hitler rejected this as he was unwilling to call off his strident demands for the immediate cancellation of reparations. Brüning was equally unsuccessful with the DNVP, but in the end was saved by the SPD, which agreed to 'tolerate' his cabinet, partly to keep Hitler from the chancellorship, but also to keep intact its coalition with the Centre in Prussia. In the eyes of the KPD this only confirmed that the SPD had sold out to the class enemy. As long as he enjoyed both the toleration of the SPD and the support of Hindenburg, Brüning's cabinet could survive, but whether he intended it or not, over the next 2 years parliamentary democracy in Germany was progressively weakened. The number of emergency decrees rose from five in 1930 to 66 in 1932, and Brüning increasingly bypassed the *Reichstag* either by consulting party and pressure group leaders directly or by using the *Reichsrat* as a substitute for the legislature, as had been the case in the war (see p. 176).

Where did the Nazi votes come from?

In 1930 6.5 million or 18.3 per cent of the electorate voted for the Nazis and this increased to 37.3 per cent in July 1932. The sharp increase in the electoral turnout in 1930 and 1932 and the large number of first-time voters, who came onto the electoral roll between May 1928 and July 1932, benefited the Nazis. Mass unemployment, Hitler's pledges to create work, and the glamour of the SA attracted many young, male voters. The Nazi vote was further increased by voters moving over from the smaller, middle-class single-interest parties (see p. 221). By 1930 the NSDAP had constructed a web of middle-class organizations, which were able to attract peasants, self-employed businessmen, clerical workers, students, and women, as well as many members of the professions. Although statistics indicate that the NSDAP did best in the predominantly Protestant and rural districts of northern Germany, and was not as effective in the Catholic areas and cities, it did nevertheless attract votes from all sections of society. As Jürgen Falter has shown,[16] about 40 per cent of Nazi voters were workers, as were 60 per cent of the SA. In contrast to the SPD, which became increasingly associated with Brüning's deflationary policy, the Nazis promised to provide work-creation projects and offered the prospect of creating a new classless national community.

His priority was to use the misery of the Depression to persuade the Western powers to scrap reparations. At the same time, he was hoping to lay the foundations for a future economic recovery by cutting back on welfare costs. To appease the right, he also backed plans for a **customs union** with Austria, which, he argued, would give Germany 'an adequate natural area of living space'. Inevitably this provoked sharp protests from France, and when Germany was plunged into a major banking crisis in July 1931 (see below), the French vetoed every proposal for an emergency loan until Germany not only renounced the customs union but also gave up attempts to revise reparations for at least 5 years. Brüning responded by threatening to suspend reparation payments until further notice. This threat, which caused a massive flight of capital from Germany and the severity of the banking crisis persuaded the American president, Herbert Hoover (1874–1964), to force the French into agreeing to declare a moratorium on reparation payments for a year. At great cost, Brüning was now near to achieving one of his main aims. He was able to convince a committee of financial experts specially convened under the provisions of the Young Plan that Germany would not be able to make any payments, even after the expiry of the moratorium. The committee then suggested that both reparations and inter-Allied debts should be cancelled, a proposal that was effectively adopted at the Lausanne Conference in June 1932.

> **Customs union:**
> The issue was referred to the International Court at the Hague and by a one vote majority in September declared a violation of Versailles.

Brüning was not able to exploit this dearly bought success, as he was dismissed from office by Hindenburg on 29 May 1932, when, as he claimed, he was 'just one hundred metres from his goal'.[17] Why then was he so abruptly removed? Certainly a key reason was that the depth and intensity of the depression inevitably caused his government to lose popular support. His deflationary policies of reducing the salaries of the civil servants, freezing wage levels and reducing unemployment payments alienated both the *Mittelstand* and the workers. These policies were so unpopular that Brüning became known as the 'Hunger Chancellor' and increased support for both the Nazis and Communists. When he travelled by train, the window blinds of his carriage were permanently drawn to stop crowds catching sight of him and hurling missiles.[18] Although by temperament conservative and a monarchist, his continued cooperation with the SPD and quasi-constitutional regime alienated him from the DNVP, which in October 1931 had held a joint protest rally with the Nazi Party at Bad Harzburg to demonstrate its hostility to the government. A few days later Brüning was only saved by SPD votes from losing a vote of no confidence in the *Reichstag*. This dependence on the SPD also alienated the Ruhr industrialists, and it was significant that in January 1932 Hitler was invited to speak to their representatives at the Industry Club in Düsseldorf.

Brüning could survive as long as he had Hindenburg's backing, but this too was beginning to be eroded. He lost much of his trust when he was unable to gain a majority in the *Reichstag* for a constitutional amendment prolonging Hindenburg's term in office without another presidential election. Ironically, in this election Hindenburg emerged as the candidate of the constitutional parties and was opposed in the second ballot by Hitler

---

The banking crisis of July 1931

The banking crisis was triggered by the failure of the *Kreditanstalt* in Vienna in July 1931. The German banks, which had since the inflation of 1923 only small capital reserves, were immediately put under pressure by their customers, who, alarmed by the repercussions of the collapse of the *Kreditanstalt*, started withdrawing their deposits. On 13 July the *Darmstädter und Nationalbank* (DANAT) had to stop all payments. On 14 and 15 July all the other German banks also closed, and when they reopened, customers could only withdraw small sums. The government was forced to come to the rescue with a sum of one billion marks.

---

as the representative of the nationalist right, who gained 36.8 per cent of the vote. By the spring of 1932 Hindenburg was being advised by General Schleicher to drop Brüning, on the grounds that the latter's dependence on the SPD alienated the very groups his administration was supposed to protect.

The immediate causes of Brüning's dismissal were the government's ban on the SA of 13 April 1932 as a result of growing evidence that it was planning a *coup d'état* against the state, and its proposals for dividing up the bankrupt estates in the east for peasant settlement. These were immediately pounced on by the east Elbian landowners as 'agrarian bolshevism'. Schleicher, who had secretly negotiated with **Ernst Röhm** the leader of the SA, an agreement that in the event of war the SA would come under the command of the *Reichswehr*, argued that the SA ban would deprive the *Reichswehr* of a potential military reserve force. In reality, however, he was working to prepare the way for Hitler's membership of a nationalist coalition led by Franz von Papen, a right-wing member of the Centre Party in the Prussian *Landtag*, which would replace the Republic with an authoritarian regime backed by the *Reichswehr*. Hitler responded to these overtures with caution, as he was determined not to enter a coalition in a subordinate position. He was convinced that the Nazis were capable of winning an overall majority in an election and consequently initially agreed to support Papen, provided that the SA ban was lifted and a general election was held within weeks. Hindenburg and Schleicher accepted these conditions and on 29 May Brüning was dismissed and **von Papen** was appointed chancellor.

Ernst Röhm, 1887–1934: Former staff officer in the *Reichswehr*; participated in the Munich *putsch*, head of SA, 1930–1934; murdered 2 July 1934.

Franz von Papen, 1879–1969: General Staff, 1911 and then military attaché in Washington; elected to Prussian *Landtag*, 1919; chancellor, 1931; vice-chancellor 1933–1934; later ambassador to Austria and Turkey.

The von Papen and Schleicher cabinets, June 1932– January 1933

The election took place on 31 July and resulted in the Nazi Party gaining 230 seats, but it was still well short of an overall majority, even though it was the largest party in the *Reichstag*. Papen himself could only rely on the 37 members of the DNVP. Hitler demanded the right to form a new

The *coup d'état* against Prussia

The SPD–Centre government was deposed on 20 July. The chancellor assumed the post of minister-president, while a Reich commissioner took over the Ministry of the Interior. The *coup d'état* crippled the SPD, and deprived them of a vital source of support. The Prussian police now came under the direct control of the Reich. Why did the SPD not offer any resistance against this illegal act? The odds were stacked against them: the *Reichswehr* was ready to intervene; with huge numbers unemployed there was little chance of a general strike succeeding; and the two left-wing parties were bitterly divided. The KPD viewed the SPD as 'social fascists' who had backed Brüning and were their main 'class' enemy, as they were ready to cooperate with the bourgeois parties rather than overthrow the system. The consequence of the coup was gravely to weaken the SPD.

government, but suffered a major political setback on 13 August, when Hindenburg only offered him the vice-chancellorship in the cabinet. Papen, who had already deposed the Prussian government in July, had ambitious plans for dissolving the *Reichstag* and delaying elections until he had drawn up a new constitution which, with a restricted franchise and a non-elected upper chamber, would drastically reduce the powers of the legislature. However, the timing of his plans went wrong when he was compelled on 12 September to dissolve the *Reichstag* prematurely after an overwhelming vote of no confidence in his government. At first he was determined not to set a date for a new election, but retreated when the Centre and the NSDAP threatened to use Article 59 to indict him for violating the constitution.

The elections of 6 November were another blow for the Nazis. As a result of increasing disenchantment with Hitler, who appeared to be unable to win power and implement his electoral promises, the Nazis actually lost two million voters and their number of seats fell to 196, while the Communists increased their seats to 100. Even this setback did not persuade Hitler to serve in a Papen cabinet in a subordinate role. Initially Papen was ready to seek presidential authority to use the army to dissolve the *Reichstag*, suppress the parties and then have a new authoritarian constitution endorsed, either through a plebiscite or a specially elected national assembly. Schleicher, who was now minister of defence, opposed this course as he feared that it would lead to civil war. As an alternative he was convinced that he could win over Hitler, or at the very least persuade **Gregor Strasser** and some 60 Nazi deputies to back the government. Hindenburg was initially ready to back Papen, but when Schleicher made it clear to him that the *Reichswehr* did not support the chancellor, he dismissed him and appointed Schleicher himself chancellor on 2 December.

The following day Schleicher offered Strasser the posts of vice-chancellor and minister-president of Prussia. This plunged the Nazi Party into crisis. Hitler immediately vetoed Schleicher's proposal. Strasser

Gregor Strasser, 1892–1934: came from a lower middle-class background in Bavaria. He joined the Nazi Party in 1922 and believed passionately in a 'German or national socialism'. In 1928 he played a key role in improving the party's organization. He was murdered in the 'Night of the Long Knives' (see p. 240).

resigned in protest, and Hitler was only able to prevent a split in the party by appealing to the loyalty of the *Reichstag* deputies, *Gauleiter* and regional inspectors to their *Führer*. While the Nazi Party was in turmoil, Schleicher attempted to persuade both the SPD and the trade unions to support his government through a package of economic reforms and work-creation projects. This alarmed both the industrialists and the east Elbian landowners and made them more ready to contemplate an alliance with the Nazis.

Papen, smarting at being outmanoeuvred by Schleicher, was anxious to do a deal with Hitler, and as early as 10 December, had put out feelers via the Cologne banker, Kurt von Schröder (see p. 205), with whom Hitler was also in contact. On 4 January Schröder arranged a meeting between Hitler and Papen. Initially Hitler appeared to be ready to accept office in a Papen cabinet, provided that he controlled the defence and interior ministries. Over the next 2 weeks Hitler's position was strengthened by the electoral success in the state election of Lippe, where the NSDAP won 39.5 per cent of the vote, and by the increasing difficulties facing the government. Schleicher had failed to win over either the SPD or the unions and also had infuriated the east Elbian landowners by not increasing tariff duties on imported food. In mid-January Hindenburg finally came round to instructing Papen 'personally and in strict confidence'[19] to explore the possibility of forming a government with the Nazis. On 28 January Schleicher resigned after Hindenburg neither gave him permission to dissolve the *Reichstag* nor granted his request for unlimited emergency powers. Hitler was now able successfully to demand the chancellorship for himself and the ministries of the interior in both the Republic and Prussia for the Nazi lawyer **Wilhelm Frick** and **Hermann Göring** respectively. Papen believed that by appointing reliable conservative figures to the other nine posts, he would be able to contain Hitler and the other two Nazis in the cabinet. On the evening of 28 January this arrangement was accepted by Hindenburg and the new Hitler cabinet was sworn in on 30 January.

That evening throughout Germany there were immense parades of uniformed party members cheered on by enthusiastic well-wishers. The evening did not, however, belong entirely to the Nazis. Many of the enthusiastic bystanders were cheering the culmination of a 'nationalist' uprising rather than a Nazi revolution, while the huge SPD rally just the day before in Berlin showed clearly that the Nazis did not speak for the whole nation.[20]

Could Hitler's appointment as chancellor have been avoided? Support for the Nazi Party was, to quote Michael Burleigh, 'a mile wide, but beyond a hard-core of fanatics, only an inch deep', and by the autumn of 1932 was to use Dietrich Orlow's graphic words already on the way to 'the rubbish pile of history'.[21] Yet his appointment did have a certain political logic about it: the Weimar Republic was irreparably damaged by 1932 and the traditional elites were not strong enough to set up an authoritarian regime themselves. If they were to seize power, they had no alternative

Wilhelm Frick, (1877–1946): Nazi lawyer and member of the Reichstag; Minister of the Interior, 1933–1943; Protector of Bohemia and Moravia, 1943–1945; executed 1946.

Hermann Göring, 1893–1946: fighter pilot in the First World War; joined Nazis in 1923; Prussian Minister of Interior, 1933; C. in C. *Luftwaffe*, 1935; head of Four Year Plan, 1936; committed suicide, 1946.

but to work with Hitler. The electoral reverses that the NSDAP had suffered in November also encouraged them to hope that the Nazis could be more easily exploited as lobby fodder.

The failure to contain Hitler, March 1933–August 1934

Historically the 30 January is seen as the date of the Nazi 'seizure of power', but this date 'represents only the beginning of the comprehensive conquest of power'. In the much quoted words of Alan Bullock, he 'did not seize power; he was jobbed into office by backstairs intrigue'.[22] Given the overwhelming non-Nazi majority in the cabinet, Papen's rash boast that within 2 months 'we will have pushed Hitler so far into a corner that he'll squeak' is perhaps understandable[23], but it did, of course, show no understanding of the dynamism of the Nazi movement and Hitler's own determination to outflank his conservative 'minders'.

The election of 5 March 1933

Hitler's immediate aim, shared by his cabinet, was to eliminate the remaining powers of the *Reichstag*. He thus turned down the offer of a pact with the Centre Party, which would have given him a majority in the *Reichstag*, and gained the cabinet's consent for yet another election. The only opposition was from Alfred Hugenberg (1865–1951), the leader of the DNVP and the new minister of economics, who supported a dissolution but feared the increased power that an election might give Hitler. In the subsequent campaign Hitler cleverly exploited the nation's desire for unity and recovery, and stressed the total failure of the 'November parties' by implication associating his allies in the cabinet with them. He cleverly reassured those who feared the revolutionary potential of the Nazis by pledging to protect 'Christianity as the basis of our morality and the family as the nucleus of our nation and state'. He also promised both to assist agriculture and to launch 'a massive and comprehensive attack on unemployment'.[24]

See Document 47

Exploiting the scope that Article 48 gave the chancellor the government in early February granted itself the necessary powers to ban political meetings and opposition newspapers. The abolition of the Prussian government also ensured that Hermann Göring, as Prussian Minister of the Interior, could control the Prussian police and reinforce them with auxiliary SA men. It was, however, the *Reichstag* fire that provided Hitler with an ideal chance both to exploit the fears of a communist uprising, which the Nazis had so assiduously spread, and immediately to promulgate the Decree for the Protection of People and State. The decree gave Hitler enormous powers and has been described as 'a kind of *coup d'état*'.[25] The central government was now able arbitrarily to order the arrest of individuals, censor the post and have private houses searched, and dismiss *Land* governments if they refused to implement the

The *Reichstag* fire: The fire was so opportune that contemporaries were convinced that the Nazis started it, but it is probable that the former Dutch Communist, Marinus van der Lubbe, was to blame.

necessary 'measures for the restoration of public security'. Yet when the German people voted on 5 March 1933, the Nazis won only 43.9 per cent of their votes, and to claim a majority in the *Reichstag* had to rely on their alliance with the DNVP, which was supported by a mere 8 per cent of the electorate.

The Enabling Act

The election results released a new burst of revolutionary and terrorist activities which amounted to a **'revolution from below'**. The SA became, in effect, a revolutionary force, which dealt not only with the Communists, but also destroyed both potential and actual political opposition to the Hitler government. This wave of violence that swept through Germany was not, however, without its dangers for Hitler. It constantly threatened to spiral out of control and alienate both Hitler's coalition partners and the president, whose support at this stage was still vital. Hitler thus made repeated appeals, which were not totally successful, to end the gratuitous violence against individuals and particularly the 'obstruction or disturbance of business life'.[26] To reassure his coalition partners, Hitler invited the Crown Prince, the military establishment of the *ancien régime* and the president to a brilliantly orchestrated ceremony at the Garrison Church in Potsdam where he pledged allegiance to the traditions and values of the past and skilfully reawakened memories of the unity of August 1914. As the descriptions of the pageantry against the stirring background of military music and tolling church bells was broadcast to the nation, 'the images of unity were made available for national consumption'.[27]

Two days later the newly elected *Reichstag* (sitting in the Kroll Opera House) debated the Enabling Bill, the intention of which was to transfer full legislative and executive powers to the chancellor for a 4-year period. Initially it was drafted on the basis of previous Weimar emergency laws, but its scope was dramatically widened by the introduction of clauses which gave the cabinet full powers to introduce budgets and to change the constitution independently of the *Reichstag*. Since this involved a change in the constitution, the government had first to secure a two-thirds majority. Although the majority of the KPD deputies and 12 of the SPD members had already been arrested, the approval of the bill was only made possible when the Centre Party, reassured by the Concordat signed with the Papacy on 14 July in which Hitler promised to protect the rights and privileges of the Catholic Church, and believing that it would also be able to influence Hitler 'from the inside', as it had successive Weimar administrations since 1919, decided to vote for the bill. Hitler sought to reassure the bourgeois parties that the *Reichstag* and *Reichsrat*, the presidency, and the *Länder* would not be permanently weakened, but also made it quite clear that if he did not gain the necessary majority, he was nevertheless 'prepared to go ahead in face of the refusal and the hostilities which will result from that refusal'.[28] The Opera House was encircled by the **SS**, while inside the SA lined the corridors.

Revolution from below: a revolution that is driven by the grassroots of the party rather than being dictated from above

SS: *Schutzstaffeln* (guard unit) founded originally in 1925 to protect leading Nazis.

The bill was passed by 444 votes to 94 with only the SPD opposing it. The Enabling Act was of crucial importance as it preserved the façade of the legal revolution and removed any doubts the civil service or the judiciary had as to the legality of the Nazi takeover.

Gleichschaltung and the creation of the one-party state

The Enabling Act decisively strengthened Hitler's position in the cabinet because the signature of the president was no longer required for decrees or legislation. As early as 22 April, according to Joseph Goebbels, 'the Führer's authority in the Cabinet is absolute'.[29] Empowered by the Enabling Act, strengthened by the SA and enjoying considerable support from public opinion, Hitler was able, through the process of coordination or ***Gleichschaltung*** to create a one-party centralized Reich by early 1934.

Gleichschaltung: originally an electrical term meaning synchronization

The states lost what remained of their traditional independence. Through a mixture of revolutionary pressure from below and coercion from above, their legislatures were brought into line with the new National Socialist regime, a process which had already started before the Enabling Act was passed. In those states which the Nazis did not already control, the police forces were initially taken over by newly appointed commissioners, then the assemblies were reconstituted to reflect the ratio of the parties in the *Reichstag*, and finally Reich governors, who were usually the local *Gauleiter*, were appointed with the necessary powers to dismiss uncooperative ministers and to draw up their own legislative programmes. In the Prussian provinces *Gauleiter* were also appointed *Oberpräsidenten* (senior administrative officials). The states' assemblies were dissolved in January 1934. The state governments survived but were subordinated to the Reich Ministry of the Interior. (see p. 244).

In the course of the summer of 1933 all parties, associations and private armies were either abolished or taken over by the Nazis. On 2 May the SA and SS occupied trade union offices throughout Germany, and from then on all workers were enrolled in the new German Labour Front (DAF). On 22 June the SPD was banned, while the Law against the New Formation of Parties of 14 July confirmed the dissolution of the political parties and made the Nazi Party the only legal party in Germany. Employers' associations were amalgamated and formed into the Reich Chamber of German Industry, and in January 1934 the Reich Economic Chamber was set up, but within this businessmen were able to manage their own affairs and were not subordinated to party zealots. Nazi direction of education, the media and culture was quickly achieved. **Goebbels**, as Minister of Propaganda, controlled broadcasting and censured a uniform news coverage in the press. In September 1933 the Reich Chamber of Culture was created. All 'intellectual workers' were compelled to join. Teaching organizations were also affiliated to the National Socialist Teachers' Organization.

Joseph Goebbels, 1897–1945: journalist, *Gauleiter* of Berlin, 1926–1928; from 1928 onwards in charge of party propaganda; March 1933–1945 Minister for Popular Enlightenment and Propaganda; July 1944 Reich Trustee for total war; 1 May 1945 committed suicide.

The Churches

For the time being the Churches managed to maintain their independence. The Concordat signed between the Vatican and the German government appeared to more than compensate for the dissolution of the Centre Party; it was guaranteed not only religious freedom, the right to administer itself, appoint its own clergy, but also the continued existence of Catholic confessional schools.

Initially Hitler attempted to group the Protestant Churches into one Reich Church under an elected Reich bishop, in order to facilitate their political subordination, but these attempts drew him into a 'minefield of intermingled religion and politics'.[30] The election of his nominee, Bishop Otto Müller (1883–1945), an ex-military chaplain and fanatical Nazi, was met with strong opposition within the Protestant Churches, spearheaded by Martin Niemöller (1892–1984). Initially Müller responded by intimidation which led to Niemöller setting up the Confessing Church in October 1934. Eventually Hitler withdrew his support for Müller and created a Ministry of Church Affairs, but this too failed to coordinate the Protestant Churches. These were now divided into three main groups: the 'German Christians' under Müller, the Confessional Church and the mainstream Church establishment, which attempted to cooperate with the Nazis while safeguarding its independence.

The defeat of the 'second revolution'

By July of 1933, far from being pushed into a corner, Hitler had created a single-party monopoly and a centralized governmental dictatorship. Yet the ambiguities and apparent compromises of the 'legal revolution' of 1933 still left Papen and Hindenburg in office, and the 'conservative bearers of state',[31] the bureaucratic, military and big business elites, intact. Hitler needed their help if he was going to revive the economy and rearm Germany, but they were, however, increasingly resented by the SA and the radical wing of the party, which had hoped that the seizure of power would entail a clean break with the *ancien régime*. Hitler's most dangerous critic was Ernst Röhm, who, as chief of staff of the SA, controlled a potentially revolutionary force of some two and a half million men.

See Document 60

Once Hitler had declared an end to the 'legal revolution' in July 1933, the SA increasingly became an 'embarrassing legacy of the years of struggle'.[32] Röhm still hoped for a second and more radical Nazi revolution, which would achieve the more socialist aspects of the Nazi programme. Above all he wanted to turn the SA into the basis for a new mass army. It was this that threatened the *Reichswehr*'s role and led to its growing rivalry with the SA. Hitler had already shown that he wished to retain the *Reichswehr*, when in January 1934 he decided in principle on the reintroduction of traditional military conscription. However, what made the problem increasingly urgent by the spring of 1934 was the imminent question of the succession to the presidency, which was posed by Hindenburg's ill health and great age. It was more than likely that the generals would attempt to block Hitler's own ambitions to succeed him if they perceived the SA still to be threatening their role in rebuilding Germany's armed forces. For Hitler there was a real danger that the army and the conservative elites might, after Hindenburg's death, demand a monarchist restoration, which was their last chance of imposing some control on the Nazi regime. There were already reservations in national-conservative circles about having brought Hitler to power, and the hope that a crisis over the SA might enable them to establish an authoritarian government under their own control. Edgar Jung, a leading right-wing intellectual and Papen's speech writer, observed: 'We are partly responsible that this fellow has come to power [and] we must get rid of him again'.[33] However, as long as Hitler could control the SA, the *Reichswehr* would not support a restoration, as both General von Blomberg (1878–1946), the defence minister, and General Freiherr von Fritsch (1880–1939), the new commander-in-chief of the army, as well as many junior officers, were convinced that Hitler was the right man to rearm Germany.

From March 1934 onwards Hitler, egged on by Göring, Himmler and Hess, who desired to eliminate a dangerous rival to their own ambitions within the party, 'moved erratically and with spells of doubt and indecision towards a showdown with the SA'.[34] On 17 June Hitler received a sharp rebuke from Papen in a sensational speech delivered at Marburg University. The latter warned against the consequences of a second revolution and went on to criticize the growing *Führer* cult. 'Never again in the Third Reich', as Ian Kershaw has observed, 'was such striking criticism at the heart of the regime to come from such a prominent figure'.[35] When Hitler visited the president at his estate at Neudeck on 21 June, he was left in no doubt about the threat facing him, as he was informed by Blomberg that if he failed to control the SA, Hindenburg would hand over power to the army.

Consequently, if his regime was to survive, Hitler now had little choice but to destroy Röhm, but he was also determined to eliminate his leading critics on the right as well. In what subsequently became known as the 'Night of the Long Knives' (30 June–1 July 1934) not only the SA leaders, but the two conservative monarchists in Papen's office, Herbert von Bose and Edgar Jung, as well as other political enemies of Hitler, including General Schleicher and Gregor Strasser, were all murdered. Police files indicate that at least 85 people were liquidated, while according to the 'white book', which was published in Paris by German émigrés, the number was as high as 401.

Following the elimination of Röhm, Hitler was able to consolidate his power without difficulty. Papen was dismissed and was lucky to escape with his life. When Hindenburg died on 1 August, there was no opposition from the army to Hitler combining the offices of chancellor and president – a step which was confirmed by plebiscite on 19 August. As head of state, Hitler became the supreme commander of the armed forces, which now swore an oath of loyalty to him. He had survived a crisis which could have led to civil war and the end of the Nazi regime and he had succeeded in eliminating the threat from the SA without becoming the prisoner of the conservative elites.

Conclusion

Bracher argued that a 'combination of inevitability and chance'[36] led to the Nazi dictatorship. The Weimar Republic, beset by deep-seated structural, political and economic problems was losing its political legitimacy in the eyes of a large number of Germans by late 1929. Hindenburg and his advisers were already weighing up the possibility of returning to a more authoritarian structure based on the Bismarckian constitution. In that sense it was possible that the Weimar Republic would in any event have been replaced with a more authoritarian regime. The onset of the world depression in 1929 and the rise of the Nazi Party as a mass movement of protest injected a new dynamic into German politics and made the dissolution of the Republic much more likely. It offered the possibility of a realignment of the forces on the right and held out the prospect to the Nationalist–Conservative right of mass backing for their plans for an authoritarian presidential regime. Over the period 1930–1932 a *de facto* presidential regime was set up and the Prussian government, the bastion of social democracy, destroyed. When it was initially appointed, the Hitler government seemed, as Papen later claimed, to be merely a logical development of the politics of the previous 3 years. In that sense it had an air of inevitability about it, but the Nazi Party was essentially a fragile party of protest and appeared already to be in decline in January 1933. Chance, luck and personalities played into Hitler's hands.

12 The Third Reich: Domestic Policies, 1933–1939

TIMELINE

1935	15 September	Nuremberg laws
1936	17 June	Himmler appointed head of German police
	18 October	Decree on the Execution of the Four Year Plan
1937	30 January	Enabling Act extended for a further 4 years
	14 March	Papal encyclical, *Mit brennender Sorge.*
	26 November	Schacht resigned as economics minister
1938	4 February	Ribbentrop appointed foreign minister; dismissal of Fritsch and Hitler assumed command of armed forces
	5 February	Last meeting of the Reich cabinet
	7–8 November	*Reichskristallnacht*
1939	21 January	Schacht dismissed from presidency of the *Reichsbank*
	25 March	Hitler Youth membership compulsory for all Germans aged between 10 and 18
	27 August	Food rationing started

Introduction: problems, issues and questions

Attempts to explain the nature of National Socialism or Nazism began as soon as it became a major force in the 1930s and have continued ever since, which has resulted in an academic literature 'beyond the scope even of specialists'.[1] Contemporaries puzzled over whether it was a form of fascism, socialism or revolutionary nationalism, while Rauschning (1887–1982), the former Nazi President of the Danzig Senate, perceived Nazism to be a 'revolutionary power whose creed was action for action's sake and whose tactics were the destruction and undermining of all that is in the existing order'.[2] During the Second World War western historians and propagandists, such as Rohan, Butler in their attempts to explain Nazism put forward an early version of the *Sonderweg* theory to the effect that there was a line of continuity in German history which stretched from 'Luther to Hitler'.[3] In reaction to this sweeping condemnation, conservative German historians, like Gerhardt Ritter, argued after 1945 that Nazism could only be understood within the general European crisis triggered by the First World War and the global depression of 1929–1933.[4]

Inevitably the outbreak of the Cold War influenced the historical debate on Nazism. In the GDR and the communist world the arguments of Georgi Dimitrov (1882–1949), the General Secretary of the Commintern, first made in 1935, that Nazism was 'the open terrorist dictatorship of the most reactionary and chauvinist and most imperialist elements of finance capital'[5] remained valid. In the West, Nazism was now perceived to be a variant of totalitarianism, and according to Carl Friedrich, the

German émigré political scientist in the US, it had much in common with Soviet communism – 'a total ideology, a single mass party, a terroristic secret police, a monopoly of mass communications … and a centrally planned economy'.[6]

In the 1960s a dramatic new approach to the origins and history of the Third Reich was signalled by the emergence of the Structuralist School (see p. 122). Its leading historians, Hans Mommsen, Martin Broszat and Tim Mason challenged the traditional view of an all-powerful Hitler and put emphasis on a structural analysis of the Third Reich. They argued that Hitler was often the prisoner of forces which he may have unleashed but could not totally control. This approach inevitably played down the traditional role of the individual and met with fierce resistance from the Intentionalists, who see Hitler and his aims as central to the study of the Third Reich.[7] These arguments can at least partially be reconciled by the concept of 'working toward the *Führer*': (see p. 247) Hitler was the charismatic leader, who inspired and empowered his subordinates to fulfil his aims even though he did not pursue a 'hands-on' policy.

Auschwitz, the Holocaust and genocidal war have made it very difficult for historians to 'historicize', or normalize, the Hitler regime and assess dispassionately the social and economic impact of the Hitler years on German history after 1945. Dan Diner, a leading critic of historicization has argued that 'Auschwitz is a no man's-land of understanding, a black box of explanation, a vacuum of extra historiographic interpretation'.[8] Yet the task of historians is to try to understand and explain even the most evil and inexplicable of actions. Attempts to come to terms with the Third Reich and somehow to put it into context led to the *Historikerstreit* or historians' dispute of 1985, where Ernst Nolte argued that the Holocaust should be seen within the context of both Stalin's and **Pol Pot's** purges and genocides.[9] This led to a major public debate in West Germany in the course of which Michael Stürmer lamented that excessive concentration on the Third Reich had effectively made earlier German history inaccessible to those born after 1945. These arguments were, however, seen by others as attempts to relativize or even minimize the atrocities of the Third Reich. Jürgen Habermas, the sociologist, for example, uncompromisingly stressed that 'a commitment to universal constitutional principles rooted in conviction has only been feasible in the cultural nation of the Germans after and through Auschwitz'.[10]

In 1989 with the fall of the Berlin Wall (see p. 378) the perception that the defeat of Nazism in 1945 had terminated the history of a united Germany changed. As Saul Friedländer observed, reunification had 'given back natural continuity to German history'.[11] Over the last two decades or so historians have moved on from the structuralist–intentionalist debates to exploring such questions as the modernity of the Third Reich, its social and economic legacy to the Federal Republic and how individual Germans responded to the *Volksgemeinschaft* (see p. 254). As Detlev Peukert has

Auschwitz concentration camp: was built near Oswiecim in Polish Upper Silesia. About one million European Jews were gassed there, and after the war its name came to symbolize Nazi terror and brutality.

Pol Pot, (1995–1998): The Khmer Rouge leader was responsible for some two million deaths in Cambodia, 1975–1979.

reminded us, the paradoxical association of the concepts of 'normality and modernity' with 'fascist barbarism' in the Third Reich raises fundamental questions about the 'pathologies and seismic fractures within modernity itself, and about the implicit destructive tendencies of industrial class society'.[12]

The political structure of the Third Reich

The Third Reich was a polycratic regime ultimately subordinated to Hitler, but characterized by rival hierarchies and centres of power as well the lack of a clear command structure. It is possible to distinguish the following distinct centres of power, although there was some overlap between them:

- the central government with its traditional ministries and civil service;
- the emergence of the SS state under Himmler by the end of the 1930s;
- the single-party monopoly of the Nazi Party;
- the charismatic dictatorship of Hitler.

Central government

When Hitler came to power he had no detailed plans for creating a specifically Nazi state as such. Nevertheless he was determined to have a pliant state that would enable him to implement his aims of territorial expansion, mobilization of the population and ultimately the racial re-ordering of Europe. His approach was pragmatic. As long as he faced no opposition he was happy to leave intact much of the existing personnel and structure, but he was also ready to create new hybrid party-state organizations to achieve specific tasks.

Although the Reich cabinet became increasingly less relevant after the passing of the Enabling Act, right up to the winter of 1937–1938 seven important ministries of state were still in the hands of Conservative–Nationalist ministers. Only in December 1935 did General Blomberg, the war minister, for instance, permit his civil servants to join the NSDAP, and Frick, the Nazi minister of the interior, was equally anxious to exclude the party from meddling in his ministry. The bureaucracy escaped a radical restructuring, although, by the Law for the Restoration of the Professional Civil Service, it was purged of potential enemies to the regime and of Jews, unless they were war veterans. It was not until February 1939 that party membership became an essential condition for any new entrant. Overall, the weakening of the traditional federal structure of the Reich strengthened the central ministries, but the individual state governments remained and became 'caught up in the dynamics of Nazi polycracy' and learnt to appeal to the *Führer* over the head of central ministries. Cultural particularism as opposed to political federalism was welcomed as a sign of 'tribal consciousness' and was an important part of Nazi propaganda.[13]

Parallel to, but virtually independent of, the traditional ministries, there grew up a series of hybrid Reich organizations, which combined both party and state responsibilities. Their leaders were prominent Nazis, who were responsible to the *Führer*. Fritz Todt (1891–1942), Hitler's road-building expert, was given the necessary powers to implement the *Autobahn* programme. As Inspector General for German Roads, his office formed 'an element of direct *Führer* authority ... alongside the normal state government and administration.'[14] Another characteristic of the Nazi government was the accumulation of ministries and influential positions by individual Nazi leaders. In May 1933 Göring, for example, was appointed Reich Aviation Minister, while still retaining the Prussian Minister-Presidency and Ministry of the Interior. Then in 1936 he was put in charge of the new Four Year Plan (see p. 252).

The SS state

Heinrich Himmler, by building up the SS into a 'state within a state', created an independent sphere of authority, which was accountable theoretically only to Hitler. This sprawling SS empire was the most important of the new **Supreme Reich authorities**, and, like so many National Socialist organizations, created a large number of new offices which, in Broszat's words, 'tended repeatedly to generate new positions having a "direct" relationship with Hitler and to encourage these in turn to strive for a separate existence, like some permanent process of cell division.'[15]

The SS had been formed in 1925 as a small force to protect the leading Nazis. Under Himmler, who became its head in 1929, it took charge of the party's intelligence and espionage section. As a reward for its loyalty to Hitler in 1934 during the confrontation with Röhm it was made independent of the SA and given responsibility for running the concentration camps, for which task the notorious Death's Head Units (*Totenkopfverbände*) were formed. In February 1936, despite opposition from Frick, Himmler was effectively given control over the political police, the *Gestapo*, and was able to fuse it with the SD, the Security Service of the SS. His appointment as Chief of the German Police in June 1936 enabled him to command both the SS and the Reich police forces. Himmler's power potential was further increased by the formation of a small number of armed regiments, the *Waffen-SS*, based on the SS squads which had operated together with the SA as a 'revolutionary strike force' in the early months of the takeover of power.

The party

In the spring of 1933 the role of the NSDAP in the new Nazi Germany was far from clear. Röhm and many of the *alte Kämpfer* passionately

Supreme Reich authorities: authorities directly responsible to Hitler rather than to a department of state

Heinrich Himmler, 1900–1945: Briefly a poultry farmer; took part in the Munich *putsch*; 1929 head of SS; by 1936 had consolidated his grip on the German police; 1939 Commissar for the Consolidation of German Nationhood; minister of Interior, 1943; committed suicide, 1945.

Alte Kämpfer: Nazi veterans who joined the party before 1923

believed it should spearhead a radical social and political revolution (see p. 239), but this view was not shared by Goebbels, Göring, Himmler and Frick, who had created for themselves formidable empires and did not relish competition from the party. Whether the NSDAP should become a cadre party, which would train the future leaders of the regime, or merely a large depoliticized mass movement, that could be used both to mobilize the masses and for propaganda purposes, was also a matter of debate. In the summer of 1933 Hitler had played with the idea of creating a National Socialist Senate along the lines of the Fascist Grand Council in Italy, but he rapidly dropped the idea for fear that it might undermine his own position. In July 1933 he cryptically stated that the 'party had now become the state' and that all power lay with the Reich government. Its role in practice, as Hitler made clear at the *Gauleiter* conference on 2 February, was to carry out propaganda activities and indoctrination on behalf of the government's measures and in general 'to support the government in every way'. Yet Hitler also needed it to counter-balance the bureaucracy and thus he could not allow the party to decline into a mere propaganda organization. At Nuremberg in September 1935 he reminded the civil service that 'whatever can be solved by the state will be solved through the state, but any problem which the state through its essential character is unable to solve will be solved by means of the movement'.[16]

In general, until 1938 party influence within the government remained relatively weak. While in some ministries there was a personal union of party and state, Nazi ministers, especially Wilhelm Frick at the Ministry of the Interior, often objected vigorously to party attempts to interfere in their departments. As long as the wishes of the *Führer*, as far as they could be ascertained, were not ignored, it was usually possible to contain the party's meddling, and civil servants quickly learnt to see 'the party as a rival but not necessarily as an invincible one', and party and state appeared to settle down to an 'uneasy coexistence'.[17]

Yet in the winter of 1937–1938 Nazi influence began to increase. Ribbentrop was appointed to the Foreign Ministry specifically to weaken the influence of the career diplomats. In February 1938 the independence of the military was also seriously impaired when Hitler sacked both General Fritsch (1880–1939), the Commander-in-Chief, for allegations that he was a homosexual, and the Defence Minister, Blomberg, for marrying a former prostitute. The Defence Ministry was replaced by the new High Command of German Armed Forces (OKW), which was directly responsible to Hitler. The *Anschluss* of Austria and then the annexation of the Sudetenland and Bohemia (see p 270) also strengthened the influence of the party, as the newly appointed commissioners were able to implement Nazi policy without any of the interference from the judiciary or the bureaucracy which they had experienced in the **old Reich**.

Old Reich:
The Reich of 1933–37 before the addition of the later Nazi conquests.

The role of Hitler

Only Hitler could mediate between the mass of competing agencies of which the Third Reich was composed. Theoretically Hitler was omnipotent. As *Führer* he was the supreme legislator, supreme administrator and supreme judge, as well as being the leader of the Party, the Army and the People. The cabinet seldom met after 1934, the *Reichstag* was a rubber stamp and Hitler had combined the presidency with the chancellorship. Paradoxically, however, Hitler did not play a significant part in the day-to-day running of the government. Edward Petersen described him as a 'remote umpire handing down decisions from on high',[18] but even this arguably exaggerates his role in government. He disliked making decisions and usually preferred to let events take their course rather than intervene. At most he might announce vague declarations of intent which did not transmute into clear directives. Often his ministers had no communication with him at all, especially when he was in his isolated chalet in the Berghof in Bavaria. Thus officials frequently had little option but to interpret Hitler's intentions themselves, often drawing contradictory conclusions. Werner Willikens (1893–1961), the state secretary in the Prussian Agriculture Ministry, accurately described this Byzantine process of interpreting Hitler's will as 'working towards the *Führer*'.

While historians agree that the administration of the Third Reich was chaotic and deeply divided by personal and institutional rivalries, the reasons for this are still sharply debated. The intentionalists argue that Hitler *intentionally* employed a policy of divide and rule to protect his own position, while structuralists insist that this chaos was the *result* of Hitler's unstable, charismatic rule and the situation it created rather than his *intention*.[19] Was this chaos at the centre of the Nazi regime a sign that Hitler was really a 'weak dictator'? In Hans Mommsen's frequently quoted words, Hitler was 'reluctant to take decisions, often uncertain, concerned only to maintain his own prestige and personal authority, and strongly subject to the influence of his environment – in fact, in many ways, a weak dictator'.[20] There is, however, little evidence that Hitler ever desired a different system. On the contrary, his charisma depended on distancing himself from the mundane day-to-day decisions of government. In reality, of course, although Hitler was theoretically omnipotent, he was not immune to the pressure from events. Party members, for instance, put him under pressure at times to intensify the persecution of the Jews (see p. 261), and there were also, of course, difficult economic problems, such as the worsening balance of payments deficits. On the other hand, by 1938 he had broken most potential centres of opposition to his regime. In determining foreign policy and rearmament, in which he was particularly interested, he had been able successfully to implement his policies. The Third Reich was not shaped 'simply by warring groups'. Hitler unmistakably moved it 'towards war expansion and racial annihilation'.[21] Arguably, his 'weakness', if that is really the right word, lay in the fundamental instability of the regime he had created.

See Documents 61 and 62

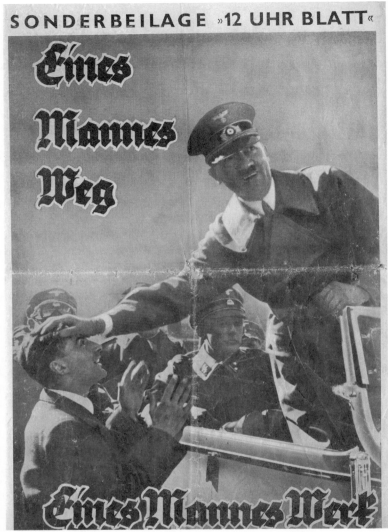

6 'The charismatic Führer'. The front page of the supplement to *12 Uhr Blatt* celebrating Hitler's 50th birthday, 20 April 1939

Sonderbeilage 12 Uhr Blatt, 20 April 1939, front page

The economy

In January 1933 the Hitler government was confronted with formidable economic problems. The German economy was practically bankrupt and the official unemployment rate was well over six million, and in reality possibly as high as eight or nine million. Industrial production had declined to the levels of the 1890s, the volume of German trade had sunk by 50 per cent, and agriculture was burdened with debt and was uncompetitive internationally. If the Nazi regime was to survive, it had to honour its pledges drastically to reduce unemployment and revive industrial production.

Reviving the economy and reducing unemployment

The new government, in the words of the Ministry of Labour, applied 'a multitude of inter-related measures'.[22] to revive the economy and cut employment, some of which were policies which Papen and Schleicher had cautiously begun to experiment with. Immediate action to bring down unemployment was taken. As many young people as possible were removed from the labour market and were employed temporarily by such organizations as the Voluntary Labour Service or the Land Service, and by 1935, with the reintroduction of conscription, a million young men were annually absorbed for 2 years by the *Reichswehr*. The length of the working week was also cut, and many women were squeezed out of the labour market with the carrot of the marriage loan, which was only available to newly married couples on condition that the wife stayed at home. The Law for Reducing Unemployment pumped a billion *Reichsmarks* into public works schemes such as road and canal building. Government subsidies were also provided for house construction and the renovation of dilapidated buildings. The motor industry was aided by tax concessions, which dramatically improved sales and helped the component industries. Its expansion was further encouraged by the Autobahn programme for 7000 kilometres of motorway. Arguably the motor industry did more than any other industry to drag Germany out of recession.[23]

Hitler and the business community

At the same time Hitler took great care to assure the business community that there would be no 'wild experiments'.[24] **Hjalmar Schacht**, the *Reichsbank* president, was given responsibility for ensuring that job creation schemes did not lead to inflation, a task that was made easier by the dissolution of the trade unions and fixing of wage rates at 1932 levels. While employers' associations did not completely escape coordination (see p. 238), businessmen were given considerable leeway to manage their own affairs. Also, despite all the earlier rhetoric, few concessions were made to the *Mittelstand*'s demands for abolishing the department stores or controlling the great trusts. On the contrary, 'the fighting organizations of the industrial middle classes' were dissolved and the steady growth in cartels proceeded unchecked. Helped by the upturn in the economic cycle, Nazi efforts to revive the economy were remarkably successful. By the summer of 1934 unemployment had come down to 2.5 million, although it then stubbornly remained stuck at that level until conscription and rearmament caused its decline to accelerate in 1936, and by 1938 virtually full employment was achieved.

Hjalmar Schacht, 1877–1970: 1923–1930 President of the *Reichsbank* 1934–1939; economics minister, 1934–1937; involved in the plot of 20 July to kill Hitler; tried at Nuremburg Tribunal but acquitted, 1946.

See Document 60

7   Examples of how the *Volksgemeinschaft* and the achievements of full employment were sold to the workers. These pictures form a page in the 12 *Uhr Blatt Sonderbeilage* (Special Edition) marking Hitler's 50th birthday 20 April 1939. Top left the caption in headlines reads: 'German workers, do you remember?' The captions under the pictures top left to right: '1939 so marched millions – 1929 so stood millions' (the notice on the figure top right states: 'Work of any sort accepted'. Middle row left to right: '1 May 1929 – 1 May 1939'; '1929 holiday without money – 1939 relaxing at sea'; Bottom left to right: '1929 "a crust of bread please" – 1939 nobody goes cold and hungry'. Bottom right (left to right): 'children in backyards 1929 – children in the fresh air and sunshine'; '1929 work in filth, 1939 work in beauty'.

Agriculture

By 1932 German agriculture was in a desperate situation and the plight of the peasantry rivalled that of the industrial workers. Initially Alfred Hugenberg, the Minister for Food and Economics, increased tariffs on selected food imports and declared a moratorium on peasant debts until October 1933, but his successor Richard-Walther Darré (1895–1953) embarked on a radical reorganization of German agriculture. In the autumn of 1933 the Reich Food Estate was set up, which assumed responsibility for all aspects of food production and marketing. Initially a combination of higher tariffs, tax cuts, favourable interest rates and guaranteed prices helped boost the agrarian economy. In 1938–1939 productivity was 25 per cent higher than 10 years earlier, and Germany was 83 per cent self-sufficient. On the other hand, by 1935 price controls on food began to operate against the agricultural interest. Since they were intended to stop rises in the cost of living, they prevented farmers from profiting from the growing demand for foodstuffs and consequently, the profit margins of agriculture remained relatively low (see p. 257).

The economics of rearmament and the Four Year Plan, 1933–1936

In order to finance rearmament at the same time as huge work-creation projects were being implemented, in the summer of 1933 Schacht devized the brilliant device of '*Mefo* bills', which were of crucial assistance in initially raising the necessary funds. Government agencies paid industries, which received military contracts, with credit notes, or '*Mefo* bills'. These were issued by four large private companies and two government ministries under the name of the *Metall-Forschungs AG* (Metal Research Co., abbreviated to *Mefo*). On receipt of the *Mefo* bills the *Reichsbank* paid cash, and so ensured that companies were promptly reimbursed. As the bills were valid for a 5-year period, the government also raised large sums of money by offering them at 4 per cent per annum on the bond market and also by forcing the banks to invest 30 per cent of their deposits in them.

Yet, even so, the progress of German rearmament was constantly threatened by recurring balance of payments crises as the revival of the economy led to a rapid rise in imports. By June 1934 the Reichsbank's currency holdings were reduced to less than 100 million *Reichsmarks*, which was hardly enough to finance a week's imports. According to Adam Tooze between 'March and September the Nazi regime suffered the closest thing to a comprehensive socio-economic crisis in its entire twelve year history'.[25] To pay for the imports needed for rearmament, Schacht, who became economics minister in 1934, introduced the New Plan, which set up strict controls for the government regulation of imports and currency exchange. He also managed to negotiate a series of bilateral trade agreements with the Balkan and South American states by which German purchases were paid for in *Reichsmarks*. These in turn were used by these countries to purchase German goods and to invest in the construction of plants, which would later produce goods required for the German war economy. His efforts, however, had only minimal success and the gathering pace of rearmament and economic recovery continued to suck in an ever-growing volume of imports. In December when the Defence Ministry demanded the doubling of copper imports, Schacht argued that the necessary foreign exchange to pay for this did not exist and that from now on rearmament would have to be paid for by increasing the volume of exports.

Hitler refused to allow economic arguments to slow down the rearmament programme. First of all in April 1936 he began to marginalize Schacht by appointing Göring commissioner of raw materials and currency, and then in August, in a memorandum which is 'one of the basic documents of the Third Reich',[26] launched the Four Year Plan, the execution of which was Göring's responsibility. By increasing production and encouraging the use of substitutes for imported raw materials, its aim was to make Germany as independent as possible of imports and to be ready for war by 1940. Richard Overy argues that it marked 'the point at which the armed forces' conception of recovery of defensive strength gave way to Hitler's conception of large-scale preparations for aggressive imperialism over which the armed forces were to have less and less say'.[27] To Hitler the conquest of *lebensraum* was the vital prerequisite for a sustainable economic recovery. Without it Germany would be merely 'a medium sized workshop economy, entirely dependent on imported food' and the goodwill of France, Britain and the US.[28] During the winter of 1936–1937 Göring effectively took over responsibility for rearmament from the Ministries of Economics and Defence, forcing Schacht to resign in November.

In 1959 the American historian Burton Klein drawing on statistics produced by the US Strategic Bombing Survey of September 1945 challenged the accepted view that Germany had been preparing for total war, and argued that, despite the Four Year Plan, the 'scale of Germany's economic mobilization for war was quite modest'. He pointed out that consumer goods output had in fact increased by over 30 per cent

How the Four Year Plan worked

The core of the Four Year Plan was to increase production in synthetic rubber, fuel oil and iron ore. Large plants were built for the production of synthetic rubber and oil, and the *Reichswerke*, the Hermann Göring Steelworks, were constructed at Watenstedt-Salzgitter to exploit local low-grade ores. In 1938 it took over the running of the major Austrian iron, steel and machinery companies, and, 6 months later, the Škoda works in the Sudetenland. While massive increases in production were achieved, the Plan failed to meet its targets, particularly in synthetic fuel, and consequently imports continued to be a drain on Germany's currency reserves.

between 1936 and 1939. A. J. P. Taylor pounced on this to support his claim that Hitler had no plans for a major war, while Alan Milward insisted that he envisaged only a series of brief *Blitzkriege* that would not overstrain the German economy.[29] The Klein–Milward thesis became something of a 'new orthodoxy' but first Richard Overy and then Adam Tooze effectively challenged its assumptions. Overy has conclusively showed that the Four Year Plan really was 'a decisive step towards preparing Germany for total mobilization', which provided the vital economic base for the later expansion of the armaments industries. Overall, according to Overy, 'consumption as a share of national income declined from 71 per cent in 1928 to 58 per cent in 1938' and between 1936 and 1939 armaments and preparations for war absorbed over 60 per cent of all capital investments made. This is not to say that Hitler would not have welcomed a brief war, but in May 1939, as he warned his generals, 'the government must ... also prepare for a war of from ten to fifteen years' duration'.[30]

A growing economic crisis?

Rearmament at this pace did, of course, create economic problems. There were production bottlenecks and inter-service rivalry for scarce resources, as well as labour shortages and a constant lack of sufficient foreign exchange to pay for imports. The threat of inflation increased as the banknote circulation trebled between 1933 and 1939. Tim Mason has argued that Hitler was forced into war in 1939 'because of domestic pressures and constraints which were economic in origin and also expressed themselves in acute social and political tension'.[31] The German economy certainly faced problems, but the situation in the summer of 1939 was more under control than it had been a few months earlier. Walther Funk (1890–1960), who succeeded Schacht as economics minister in November 1937, had launched the New Finance Plan, by which businesses with state armaments contracts would receive 40 per cent of their payments in tax certificates, a certain proportion of which could only be cashed in after 3 years. Labour shortages were being met by recruiting foreign workers from southern and central Europe, the introduction of labour conscription, and large-scale industrial retraining programmes. By 1939 the German economy was second only to America's and less vulnerable to global pressures than either the French or British. Not surprisingly, Overy insists that '"crisis" is an inappropriate characterization of the German economy in the months before the war', an assessment supported by Tooze.[32]

Yet there were signs of growing inflationary trends and an increasing shortage of resources with which to meet the escalating demands of the rearmament programme. Although it was the diplomatic rather than economic factors that determined the actual outbreak of the war in 1939, it is nevertheless argued by Kershaw that 'the mounting economic problems fed into the military and strategic pressures for expansion'.[33]

The *Volksgemeinschaft*

The Nazi *Volksgemeinschaft*, or 'People's Community', consciously drew on popular nostalgia for the 'spirit of 1914', which had both enthused and united the Germans at the beginning of the Great War (see p. 167). It mobilized millions of the population almost as if a war was actually being fought. Eight million volunteers joined the Reich Air Defence League, while thousands filled local positions in the SA, Hitler Youth and the Reich Labour Front. At least a million party members and volunteers as well as the Hitler Youth participated annually in the Winter Relief Campaigns (*Winterhilfswerk*), which raised millions of marks for 'racially worthy but impoverished Germans' and culminated in the 'Day of National Solidarity' on the first Saturday in December.[34] For Hitler the ultimate aim of the *Volksgemeinschaft* was to inculcate a new mentality and ethos into the German people that would turn it into a 'fighting community' ready for war. Crucial to this new community were the Nazi and Social Darwinist concepts of racial purity and perpetual struggle.

Radio, film and the arts: fostering the spirit of the *Volksgemeinschaft*

The Propaganda Ministry under Goebbels was set up on 13 March 1933 'to transform the very spirit itself to the extent that people and things are brought into a new relationship with one another'.[35] In achieving this, the new medium of the radio as well as the cinema played a major role. Regional radio stations, which had previously been under the control of the states, were amalgamated into the Reich Radio Company, whose director liaised closely with Goebbels. Cheap radios were mass-produced and great efforts were made by specially appointed local radio wardens to encourage the Germans to buy them and to tune in to the programmes. Initially Nazi strategy was 'to transmit live as many Nazi ceremonies and Hitler speeches as possible'.[36] By 1935 the emphasis switched to programmes reporting on everyday life across the Reich. A remarkable success was the **Wunschkonzert**, to which some 80 per cent of the population listened. It turned the Germans into 'one big family' presided over by the 'radio uncle' Hans Goedecke.[37] Party ceremonies and national celebrations were also filmed and shown repeatedly in the local cinemas. Goebbels recognized the importance of light and largely apolitical popular entertainment such as comedies, thrillers, love stories and musicals. Individuals were also encouraged to take their own snapshots of historic events so that they could record and therefore participate in 'history in the making'. The Propaganda Ministry devised strict guidelines for all the arts, as it was vital that the public should be fed a suitable cultural diet which did not undermine the *Volksgemeinschaft*. The arts became in the ministry's words 'a public exercise' subject to

Wunschkonzert: Musical request programme

'police supervision' and state guidance.[38] A similar approach ensured that 'degenerate' modern art was replaced by suitable pastoral scenes or depictions of great battles, and so on.

Education

In July 1933 when Hitler declared the end of the 'legal revolution' (see p. 239), he stressed that the new task was to educate the people. The aim was to unite all the people behind a single revolutionary ideal – the creation of the racial state, which would protect its people from Jews and 'racial undesirables'. Ultimately this racial state would assume the responsibility of reorganizing Europe along racial lines and creating *Lebensraum* in the east.

Although the traditional structure of the German educational system remained intact, educational syllabuses in both schools and universities were changed to reflect the demands of Nazi ideology. In schools the curriculum was revised to give more teaching time to history, biology and German as the three subjects which lent themselves to exploitation by Nazi propaganda, and in September 1933 a new subject, 'racial science', was introduced as a compulsory element in the timetable. Physical education both in schools and universities became compulsory. Its crucial role can be seen by Hitler's comment that 'the racial state' must concentrate 'not on the pumping in of empty knowledge but on the development of healthy bodies'.[39]

The Nazis created a small number of special schools and institutions which were entrusted with the task of producing the future elite of Germany. By 1939, 21 **Napolas**, ten Adolf Hitler schools and four **Ordensburgen** had been set up. These institutions were supposed to educate a new Nazi elite, but the *Napolas* attracted very few members of the professional classes, who continued to regard the grammar schools and universities as the best way to influential and well-paid careers. Ultimately, students from the *Napolas* were to go to the *Ordensburgen*, which were intended to be finishing schools for the future Nazi elite.

Napolas: National Political Educational Establishments

Ordensburgen: the castles constructed by the medieval order of the Teutonic Knights

The Hitler Youth

The most effective instrument for influencing young people was the Hitler Youth. By 1936, 60 per cent of all young people in Germany were members, and increasing pressure on the Catholic Church led to the dissolution of its own youth organizations in 1939, the year in which service in the Hitler Youth became compulsory. Its activities and sense of belonging undoubtedly attracted many young people. Christa Wolf (1929–2011), who was later one of East Germany's leading authors, recalled in a semi-autobiographical novel how at first it seemed to offer 'the promise of a loftier life'.[40]

Between the ages of 10 and 14, boys belonged to the *Jungvolk* and from 14 to 18 to the Hitler Youth, where their time was taken up by a mixture of sport, war games and indoctrination. For girls of 10–14 there was the *Jungmädel* and then from 14–18 the *Bund deutscher Mädchen* (German Girls' League), where the emphasis was on physical fitness and the teaching of traditional female domestic skills. To quote Klaudia Koonz, they 'prepared girls for a lifetime in the second sex'.[41] By the late 1930s the Hitler Youth had become a large bureaucratic organization. Compulsory membership also meant that it had to absorb numerous bored and resentful teenagers. Peukert argues that by the second half of the 1930s it was 'facing a growing crisis' (see pp. 264–265).[42] In the war it suffered from the absence of a large number of youth leaders who were called up, but it remained the key organization for indoctrinating youth into the *Volksgemeinschaft*.

Women and the family

Were women the 'victims of National Socialism', as Gisela Bock argues? There was certainly 'structural discrimination in politics, society and the economy against women', while 'racially inferior' women were forcibly sterilized, and probably at least 4500 died as a consequence. However, Claudia Koonz points out that, by creating a pleasurable and relaxing family life for Nazi officials and party members, many women contributed to the stability of the Nazi system and were therefore, like their husbands, perpetrators of Nazi crimes or at least of 'complicity' in them.[43] The primary importance of women to the Nazis was their role as child bearers and homemakers. To train women for motherhood and marriage, the regime set up two women's organizations, the National Socialist Womanhood and the German Women's Enterprise (DFW). Initially it attempted to persuade young women to leave work by making motherhood an attractive financial alternative by offering loans, tax-relief schemes and family allowances (see p. 249). However, the government did accept that women would continue to work in industry once the economy recovered. A women's section was formed within the German Labour Front in July 1934 under Gertrud Scholtz-Klink (1902–1999), and women were recruited to work in many of the new plants which were built under the Four Year Plan. By May 1939, 12.7 million women were in employment and comprised 37 per cent of the German workforce. Increasingly, women also joined the professions in greater numbers, even though in 1933 they had been dismissed from the higher ranks of the civil service, and medical and legal professions. For instance, the total of female doctors actually increased from 5 per cent in 1930 to 7.6 per cent in 1939. The *Völkische Beobachter* conceded in 1937 that 'today we can no longer do without the woman doctor, lawyer, economist and teacher in our professional life'.[44]

See Document 63

The Nazi concept of the family was contradictory. On the one hand the family was the 'germ cell' of the nation, yet as a small oasis of privacy it was also subject to some distrust by the regime. Parental control over children was threatened by the government's racial laws and eugenic policies and by the growing pressure for children to join the Hitler Youth. According to Claudia Koonz, Nazi family policy was 'deeply revolutionary because it aimed at the creation of a family unit that was not a defence against public invasion as much as the gateway to intervention'.[45]

In reality the Nazi priority was not so much the family as the procreation of healthy 'Aryan' children. Hitler himself observed that 'it must be considered reprehensible conduct to refrain from giving healthy children to the nation'.[46] This led both to banning abortion in May 1933 and to some improvement in the status of unmarried mothers, even though public opinion and the party itself were conservative on this issue. The unmarried mother's greatest defender was Himmler, who argued that she should be 'raised to her proper place in the community, since she is during and after her pregnancy, not a married or an unmarried woman but a mother'.[47] As long as single-parent children were 'racially and hereditarily valuable', he was ready to protect them through a 'legal guardianship'. He opened the **Lebensborn** homes for pregnant and nursing mothers whose children had been fathered by SS men and 'other racially valuable' Germans.

> **Lebensborn:** Spring of Life

The peasantry

The German peasantry had a key role in the *Volksgemeinschaft*. Not only was it to grow as much food as possible to thwart any future blockade, but along the eastern frontiers new **farming settlements** were to form 'a living wall against the Slavs pressing forward'[48] as one Nazi commentator put it. Above all the peasantry was also seen by the Nazi regime as the 'blood spring' of the *Volksgemeinschaft*. It was therefore important to preserve its way of life and stop the flight to the cities. The Reich Food Estate (see p. 251) initially guaranteed farmers financial security and the Reich Entailed Farm Law of September 1933 gave the small-scale farmers security of tenure by declaring that farms between 7.5 and 125 hectares were to remain the permanent property of the original owners, At the same time there was a drive to promote the peasant's image as a key member of the *Volksgemeinschaft* by reviving old traditions, some of which were entirely bogus. In September 1933 the Propaganda Ministry organized the first of the national harvest festivals. 700,000 peasants were addressed by Hitler at the Bückerberg, near Hameln, and the whole nation was connected to the ceremony through the radio.[49] Through propaganda in the rural vocational schools and even the primary schools the rural population were introduced to such topics as *lebensraum* and racial hygiene. Despite this propaganda, once the economy started to expand, the government could not halt the renewed flight from the land. The rural population reacted to poor housing, bad pay and the gruelling nature of unmechanized farm work by migrating to the cities. Consequently, the pace of urbanization and modernization speeded up and Germany, despite Nazi rhetoric about rural life, increasingly continued to develop into an advanced industrial society.

> **Farming settlements:** Only 328 hectares of land settlement were created by 1938 as a result of opposition from the Junkers and the army, which argued that large estates were vital for producing rye and potatoes.

The workers

Peter Fritzsche observed that National Socialist efforts to win over the workers were 'the ultimate test of the people's community'.[50] Only when they were successfully absorbed into the *Volksgemeinschaft* would it be truly inclusive. Socialists and particularly Communists had an ideology which psychologically prepared them to oppose Nazism. However they were assailed from two directions. Not only was their organizational structure destroyed, but they were also the target of a seductive Nazi propaganda campaign. The Nazis claimed that they alone understood the concerns of the working classes. In his address on 1 May 1937 Hitler stressed that National Socialism had 'broken with a world of prejudices' and created equality between the 'workers of the brain and fist'.[51] Hitler argued that he had liberated the workers from their unpatriotic Marxist leaders and had given them a more respected place in society. They were returning to ideals of the 'spirit of 1914'.

The workers were corralled into the Labour Front (see p. 238), while their employers were officially called 'plant leaders'. Elected Councils of Trust were set up in all factories where there were more than 20 workers, but, after 1935, elections were abruptly discontinued because the workers were electing what the regime considered to be politically 'unreliable' candidates. Theoretically these councils could take an employer to a Court of Social Honour as long as they had the support of the local labour trustee, an official appointed by the Ministry of Labour, but this rarely happened. Between 1934 and 1936 there were only 616 cases out of a workforce of well over 20 million.

See Documents 64 and 65

Politically the Labour Front could not afford to be just an instrument of control. It also had to be seen to be putting into operation what Hitler called 'socialism of the deed'. To achieve this it set up two organizations, which owed much to the experiments in welfare capitalism in the 1920s. The first one, the 'Beauty of Work' scheme, headed by **Albert Speer**, attempted to persuade employers to make their factories a more humane environment by improving the lighting and installing swimming baths, showers and canteens. By 1939 nearly 70,000 companies had agreed to implement these improvements. The second one, the Front's leisure organization, 'Strength Through Joy' (KDF), was primarily – as its head, Robert Ley, observed – an attempt to dispel boredom, as from it 'sprang stupid, heretical, yes, in the end criminal ideas'.[52] It organized concerts and plays for the workers and arranged a number of subsidized cruises or holidays in the German countryside. By 1938 both the hotel industry and much of the passenger traffic of the **Reichsbahn** were becoming economically dependent on the KDF's holiday plans. In many ways its mass tourism marked 'the modernisation of leisure'.[53]

One of the most popular policies of the KDF was the **Volkswagen** (VW) project. The work started on building the VW in the summer of 1938. The workers were offered a savings scheme which in theory would eventually enable them to purchase the car. However, unlike conventional

Albert Speer, 1905–1981: joined NSDAP 1931 and became 'party architect'; 1942–1945 armaments minister; sentenced to 20 years imprisonment 1946

Reichsbahn: the national railways

Volkswagen: people's car

hire-purchase agreements, the VW would only be delivered after the final payment had been made. By 1940, 300,000 people had already signed up to the scheme although the war halted production and the cars were never produced. This according to Hartmut Berghof is an example of National Socialism's promise of a better future for the German people – eventually! It 'propagated a combination of sacrifice and wealth creation'. The real rewards would come only with the creation of *Lebensraum* and the racial re-ordering of Europe.[54]

Full employment, which the political scientist Franz Neumann (1900–1954) called Hitler's 'sole gift to the masses',[55] gave the workers a growing economic power which they were beginning to exploit. In 1936 absentee-ism and go-slows increased, and a series of lightning strikes compelled the regime to take steps to control the situation. Workers who broke their contracts with their employers to move on to fresh jobs were threatened with the confiscation of their work books, without which they could not be employed. In June 1938, in an effort to stop employers from poaching labour from each other, the Trustees of Labour were given the power to determine uniform wage levels in key industries. Labour conscription was also introduced, which could channel workers towards particular industries. Ultimately, as a final deterrent, there loomed the terror of the *Gestapo* and 'the camps of education for work', which were almost as brutal as the concentration camps. None of these measures stopped wages from rising in the armaments industries, where the workers, either individually or in small groups, managed to exploit the novel situation of full employment by gaining concessions from the employers, which Detlev Peukert called a 'sort of "do-it-yourself" wage system'.[56]

How integrated were the workers into the *Volksgemeinschaft*? Were they incarcerated 'in a great convict prison', to quote the former SPD trade union leader, Wilhelm Leuschner (1888–1944),[57] or did they in fact share at least some of the values of the *Volksgemeinschaft*? While a working-class culture did manage to survive in the Third Reich, Nazi values nevertheless had some impact on it. Younger workers, for whom the Hitler Youth had provided new chances, took advantage of retrain-ing possibilities and transferred to more skilled jobs. Material benefits like longer holidays and low heating and lighting costs certainly appeased the workers, but many, like almost all their compatriots, also could not help admiring Hitler for his foreign policy successes.[58] As oral history projects have revealed, in the immediate post-war period of turmoil many workers looked back nostalgically on the years 1934–1939 as a period of 'work, adequate nourishment, KDF and the absence of disarray'.[59]

See Document 65

Race and eugenics

The *Volksgemeinschaft* was to be composed of a racially homogeneous 'Aryan' people, whose health and racial purity were at all costs to be pre-served. A series of laws increasingly discriminated against those Germans

Left-wing opposition to the Nazi regime

Until the 1970s the history of worker opposition to Nazism 'followed the pattern of the respective political camps during the Cold War'.[60] In the GDR the East Germans exaggerated the importance of the Communist opposition and dismissed the SPD as traitors, while in the FRG there was virtually a conspiracy of silence about the role of the Communist underground, which only began to change in the 1970s with the emergence of 'everyday-life studies' in west German historiography. The SPD was forced to establish its party headquarters first in Prague and then in Paris, from where it managed to smuggle illegal literature across the frontiers. The Communists were more successful than the SPD in developing an underground movement, which the *Gestapo* was never able completely to eliminate. In 1935 they were ordered by Stalin to negotiate a united front with the SPD against Fascism, but years of mistrust and hostility between the two parties was impossible to overcome. The KPD remained a tool of the Kremlin, and with the signature of the Nazi–Soviet Pact in August 1939 (see p. 270), it was given the contradictory instructions of supporting Hitler's foreign policy, while opposing his domestic policy. In reaction to the divisions between the KPD and SPD, several smaller left-wing groups emerged, which aimed to unify the left in Germany and avoid the divisions of the Weimar years. The *Roter Stosstrupp* (Red Assault Party), for instance, hoped to create a new socialist society once the Third Reich had collapsed, while *Neu Beginnen* (New Start) believed that only by close cooperation between the best elements in the KPD and SPD could Hitler be opposed effectively and a democratic socialist society be built after the war. These groups fared no better than the SPD and were virtually wiped out by the mid-1930s.[61]

who were judged to be of 'lesser racial value', banning them, for instance, from receiving any of the financial privileges given to those with large families, and, after October 1935, all prospective marriage partners had to have a fitness certificate. As the Nazis believed that criminal and 'asocial' behaviour as well as sexual deviancy, under which they also classed homosexuality, were determined by genetic factors, they were convinced that individuals suffering from these perceived 'disorders' had to be sterilized for the good of society. The law of November 1933 against dangerous habitual criminals, for example, introduced the principle of compulsory castration for certain types of sexual offenders, and increasingly both punishment and the treatment of prison inmates were determined by biological–racial criteria.

Euthanasia was a logical development of this policy. At first, beginning in the winter of 1938–1939, it was practised on children with 'congenital deformities', and then a few months later in considerable secrecy it was extended to adults. It was, however, temporarily halted when it became public knowledge and was condemned by the Catholic Archbishop of Münster, Clemens von Galen (1878–1946), in August 1941. It soon recommenced and was widened to embrace foreign workers judged to be suffering from incurable physical illnesses, racially 'inferior' babies of eastern European women working in the Reich, terminally-sick inmates from the German prisons and sometimes even *Wehrmacht* soldiers suffering from incurable shellshock.

Wehrmacht: The *Reichswehr* changed its name to the *Wehrmacht* in 1935.

The non-Jewish racial minorities

The sterilization laws were extended to cover the small number of mixed race children fathered by French African soldiers during the Rhineland occupation (see p. 193). The Nazi regime inherited from the Weimar Republic a legacy of hostile policies towards the Sinti and Roma. In 1935 the SS financed a research unit in the Ministry of Health, which decided that 90 per cent of the Sinti and Roma were of mixed race, and were therefore likely to be of a criminal and **'asocial'** predisposition, and should as a consequence be sterilized. In September 1939 Himmler started to deport the 30,000 gypsies in the Reich to occupied Poland. Initially only a small number were transported, but from December 1942 onwards the programme gathered pace and by 1945 only a few hundred had escaped being sent to Auschwitz.

'Asocial': term used to describe people, such as tramps and the homeless, who did not conform to accepted social non-Jewish racial minorities.

Unlike the Weimar Republic, the Third Reich was not committed by a constitution to guaranteeing civil rights to its Slav minorities. Initially, however, the fear of retaliation against German minorities in Poland and Czechoslovakia compelled the Nazi government to adopt a relatively tolerant policy towards the Poles and the Sorbs, a people of Slav descent who lived along the Silesian-Saxon borderlands. Once Czechoslovakia was dismembered and Poland occupied (see pp. 270 and 271), both the leaders of the Sorb and of the Polish communities were arrested and sent to concentration camps. Himmler intended to move the Sorbs to occupied Poland, as he viewed them as 'the same racial and human type'[62] as the Poles, but his energies were absorbed by dealing with the far larger number of Jews (see p. 273), and he was never able to implement these plans.

See Document 48

The Jews

When Hitler first came to power, he did not issue any policy directives on the Jewish question. Initially, independent action by the SA against individual Jews and their property, which threatened to damage his government's reputation internationally, forced Hitler to attempt to channel the violence into a boycott of Jewish shops on 1 April, but this was rapidly halted when it was sharply criticized both at home and abroad. Hitler then sought to appease the party by expelling the Jews from the Civil Service, the universities and journalism. Over the next 2 years economic and political realities forced the Nazi government to discourage overt racial violence against the Jewish community, but in the summer of 1935 Hitler again responded to fresh acts of anti-Semitic violence by attempting to placate party activists. On 15 September he announced at Nuremberg the notorious 'Law for the Protection of German Blood', forbidding marriage or sexual intercourse between Jews and German gentiles, and

The intentionalist–structuralist debate on Nazi policy towards the Jews

Over the last decades the historical debate on Nazi Jewish policy has been influenced by the arguments between the 'intentionalists' and 'structuralists'. The intentionalists, particularly Lucy Dawidowicz, Klaus Hildebrand and Karl Dietrich Bracher, argue that Hitler from the beginning *intended* the mass murder of the Jews, even though he could not implement this straightaway. Structuralist scholars, such as Martin Broszat, Hans Mommsen and Karl Schleunes, while not disputing Hitler's anti-Semitism, locate the ultimate cause of the Holocaust in the disjointed and chaotic way in which Nazi Germany was governed. They argue that the bureaucracy and the Nazi leaders competed with each other in formulating anti-Semitic policies, which led to ever more radical policies being implemented. Understandably, the intentionalists are highly critical of what they regard as attempts to depersonalize the responsibility of what ultimately led to the Holocaust. Dawidowicz, indeed, regards such an approach as initiating a new 'cycle of apologetics' in German history.[63] Both positions have 'a number of merits and demerits'.[64] Nazi Jewish policy was 'evolutionary rather than programmatic'[65] in the 1930s, but Hitler's views on the Jews and the racial state cannot be ignored as they were to prove decisive in the sanctioning the Holocaust (see p. 230).

See Documents 57 and 66
the Reich Citizenship Law, which deprived Jews of their German citizenship. However, both laws disappointed many of the Nazi zealots, who suspected that Hitler had accepted advice from his civil servants rather than from the party.

By the spring of 1938 the party activists were again demanding ever more radical measures against the Jews, while Göring, as commissioner of the Four Year Plan was urging their rapid economic expropriation. The triumphalist mood caused by the *Anschluss* of Austria and the growing threat of war with Czechoslovakia also contributed to the clamour for further action against the Jews. A whole raft of anti-Semitic decrees were promulgated, which involved not only measures forcing Jews to adopt specifically Jewish forenames but also having their wealth and property registered as a preliminary for expropriation by the state.

The turning point in the treatment of the Jews was the *Reichskristallnacht* riots of November 1938. The immediate cause of this pogrom was the assassination of Ernst von Rath (1909–1938), a junior diplomat in the German embassy in Paris, by Herschl Grynszpan (1921–1942), a 17-year-old student, whose parents, together with 17,000 other Jews of Polish descent, had recently been expelled from Germany. As the Polish government refused to admit them, they were forced to camp on the no man's land between the Polish and German frontiers. Goebbels, apparently with the tacit approval of Hitler, organized 'spontaneous' attacks on synagogues and Jewish-owned businesses. Some 25 million marks' worth of damage was done and probably as many as a hundred Jews were killed, while nearly 30,000 were interned in concentration camps.

The Jews were made to pay a collective fine of 1.25 billion marks. Individual Jews were forced out of jobs in the retail trade, skilled labour and management. In April 1939 the remainder of their wealth was seized, and they were banned from public places, such as theatres and beaches. The small number of Jewish children who were still pupils in state schools were expelled. Reinhard Heydrich (1904–1942), the chief of the security police and the SD, was given responsibility for organizing the emigration of the remaining 214,000 Jews in Germany, but paradoxically Göring's ruthless expropriation policies had made Jewish emigration more difficult to achieve, since foreign states were reluctant to accept refugees without any financial means of support.

Although, on 12 November 1938, Hitler had, it seems, informed Göring both verbally through his chief of staff, **Martin Bormann**, and by phone that 'the Jewish question [should] be now once and for all coordinated and solved one way or another',[66] he did not publicly associate himself with the series of anti-Semitic policies initiated in the aftermath of *Reichskristallnacht*. Twice, however, in January 1939 he was quite clear about the future fate of the Jews. He told the Czech foreign minister of his intention to 'destroy the Jews', and soon afterwards made his chilling prophecy in the Reichstag that the outbreak of war would lead to the 'annihilation of the Jewish race in Europe'.[67]

The intentionalists interpret these threats as evidence of Hitler's ultimate aims, but the structuralists remain unconvinced. They warn historians against taking Hitler's words too literally. Hans Mommsen, for example, argues that Hitler 'considered the "Jewish question" from a visionary political perspective that did not reflect the real situation',[68] and is convinced that Hitler was invoking a ritual hatred of the Jews, rather than spelling out precise plans for their murder. While these horrific threats were not a blueprint for the Holocaust, it is difficult not to see them as expressions of intent, however vague they might be, that the Jews should be removed from Germany one way or other. As Lucy Dawidowicz pointed out about one of Hitler's earlier speeches, 'in the post-Auschwitz world' his words carry a 'staggering freight'.[69]

> **Martun Borman**
> 1900–1945: served in World War I and the Freikorps; joined Nazi party in 1927. After 1933 served as Hess' deputy and in 1941 director of the Party Chancellery.

See Document 66

The limits of loyalty to the *Volksgemeinschaft*

The Germans, particularly younger Germans, who were conditioned by the Hitler Youth, were put under huge pressure to identify with the *Volksgemeinschaft*. It offered, as we have seen, a new inclusivity for 'Aryan' Germans, but the fate of those who were excluded on racial or health grounds was increasingly clear to see. Inevitably each individual approached National Socialism differently, some motivated by fear, dissent, opportunism, or indeed laziness and indifference, others by 'varying degrees of **ideological conviction**'.[70]

Although only a relatively small number of outstandingly courageous Germans joined the active opposition (see pp. 284–286), there were a great many more who rejected certain elements of National Socialism and indulged in relatively minor acts of civil disobedience such as refusing to give the 'Heil Hitler' salute or hanging out a church banner rather than a swastika flag on a saint's day. In the 'Bavaria Project' on 'Resistance and Persecution in Bavaria' historians have shown how grassroots opposition in fact 'block[ed] or partially restrict[ed] Nazism's societal penetration'.[71] This analysis has led to the use of the controversial concept of *Resistenz*, a medical term, which in this context means immunity to Nazi ideology. It helps the historian understand that grey area between resistance to and acceptance of the regime in which so many Germans existed. Two examples of this phenomenon are explored below:

Ideological conviction: according to *Gestapo* statistics, in 1939 there were 27,367 German political prisoners.

The Churches

This concept of *Resistenz* is particularly useful when assessing the attitude of the Churches towards the *Volksgemeinschaft*. Potentially the Churches had both the organization and the ideology to oppose the Third Reich, but they could not in practice divorce themselves from the climate of the times. Most priests, like their parishioners, approved of much of Hitler's foreign policy and anti-Bolshevism, while among both the clergy and laity in the Catholic and Protestant Churches, despite many honourable exceptions, there was, to say the least, no root-and-branch opposition to the regime's anti-Semitism. Pope Pius's condemnation of Hitler's violations of the Concordat and his racial policy in the encyclical of 1937, *With Burning Concern*, was an exception to the general policy of tolerating the regime.

Encyclical: papal letter sent to all Roman Catholic bishops

Only in matters that affected their independence or when they enjoyed overwhelming public support were the Churches ready seriously to oppose Hitler (see p. 239). Archbishop Galen's campaign against euthanasia in August 1941 was effective in criticizing the regime precisely because it enjoyed public support. As institutions, it was inevitable that both the Catholic and Protestant Churches should react cautiously, as they had to be responsive to public opinion, the political situation and above all think of their own self-preservation.

The swing movement and the *Edelweiss* pirates

The concept of *Resistenz* is again helpful in understanding the relationship of youth subcultures to the Nazi regime.[72] The activities of the 'swing movement' in the late 1930s, which was popular among students, were apolitical but the liking of its adherents for jazz, American dances like the jitterbug, American and British fashions, and above all their acceptance of Jews and half-Jews in their groups challenged the social norms of the *Volksgemeinschaft* and led Himmler to threaten their 'ringleaders' with incarceration in the concentrations camps. The 'Edelweiss Pirates', groups of young teenage workers, which were located mainly in the Ruhr and Rhineland cities, emerged at the same time as a reaction against regimentation in the Hitler Youth and the factories, and were for the most part also apolitical. Their activities were limited to boycotting, as far as possible, Hitler Youth activities, but some groups did physically attack Hitler Youth patrols, and during the war distribute Communist leaflets or Allied propaganda sheets, which they had found during their excursions to the countryside (see p. 285).

Conclusion

In January 1933 the new Hitler government was greeted with a widespread feeling that it was, as Golo Mann remarked, 'historically right',[73] and that its time had come. The majority of Germans were ready to make allowances in the spring of 1933 for what they assumed to be at the time the casual and short-lived brutalities of the SA, provided Hitler could deliver on his promises to create a new deal and provide work. His attempts to create an inclusive nation, where membership was defined by race rather than class, has been brilliantly characterized by Schoenbaum as a 'verbal social revolution'.[74] Nazi propaganda put great emphasis on the equality of all ethnic Germans. In many ways this was an illusion as big business, the Junkers and the bourgeoisie still survived. Nevertheless, Hitler did manage to create a feeling of hope and an element of moderate prosperity. Of course, this was underpinned by terror against dissidents and Jews, and had only been achieved by the destruction of the **pluralist state**. Overall, the public perception of Hitler was that he had restored 'law and order' to Germany and was the architect of a great national revival and 'economic miracle'.

Yet the paradox of the Third Reich was that behind the facade of efficiency and unity it was what Franz Neumann, called a 'Behemoth' or 'a non-state, a chaos, a situation of lawlessness, disorder and anarchy'.[75] What was it that prevented its collapse from internal contradictions and conflicting agencies? Certainly the SS and the *Gestapo* played a vital role in protecting the regime, but then so did the long line of Hitler's foreign policy successes up to 1941, which are explored in the next chapter. In 1940 after the fall of France Hitler was probably the most popular chancellor Germany has ever had! As long as the Third Reich was seen as the agent of national renewal and future prosperity, it enjoyed at least the benefit of doubt from the majority of Germans.

Pluralist state: a state in which there are different groups – in fact a diversity of forces

13 *Expansion, War and Defeat*

Introduction: problems, issues and questions

Between 1933 and 1941 Hitler achieved a success that would have satisfied even the insatiable appetites of the German Fatherland Party (see p. 180) but then in the snow before Moscow his luck began to falter. From 1942 onwards Germany was locked into a total war. Was this essentially a racial war for *Lebensraum* long planned by Hitler, as the intentionalists of the **programme school** argue, or an undesired consequence of the Polish crisis? A. J. P. Taylor has argued that Hitler had no particular foreign policy before 1939 and was just pursuing a pragmatic policy of making Germany 'the greatest power in Europe from her natural weight'.[1] Hans Mommsen, too, has doubts about whether his foreign policy really consisted of unchanging priorities and is convinced that, like his anti-Semitic policy, it was determined more by 'structural' factors such as economic pressures, opportunism and expectations from within the Nazi Party.[2] In reality, however, these views are not contradictory if one adopts Alan Bullock's argument made as far back as 1967 that it combined 'consistency of aim with complete opportunism in methods and tactics'.[3] Certainly in the short term Hitler's foreign policy was contradictory and opportunist, but, his obsession with the need for *Lebensraum* in western Russia is a constant thread that runs through his speeches to generals, officials, businessmen and journalists. Essentially, as has been seen in the preceding chapter domestic policy in the Third Reich was ultimately geared for *Lebensraum* and genocide. Consequently as Jonathan Wright has pointed out it is arguable that 'the distinction between domestic and foreign policy ... is a false one'.[4]

> **Programme school:** intentionalist historians who argue that Hitler had a very definite programme firstly involving the defeat of France and then of the Britain and the USA. Andreas Hillgruber and Klaus Hildebrand are the main protagonists of this argument.

How much popular support was there for Hitler's foreign policy? It is quite clear that there was powerful backing for overthrowing the Versailles settlement, but public opinion became more anxious when the danger of war approached in 1938–1939. The string of victories that followed up the summer of 1940 were met with ecstatic enthusiasm. After the autumn of 1941 it was essentially the fear of defeat and above all of Bolshevism that kept the German people fighting. A more difficult question to answer is to what extent did the Germans support, the genocidal war in the east against the Poles, Russians and the Jews and Hitler's aims of re-drawing the map of Europe along racial lines.

The road to war, 1933–1939

During his first 3 years in power Hitler had to tread carefully. It was obvious, as a senior official in the Foreign Office told him, that 'in judging the situation we should never overlook the fact that no kind of rearmament in the next few years could give us military security ... we shall for a long time yet be hopelessly inferior to France'.[5] Thus Hitler's room for manoeuvre was initially very limited. Nevertheless he did take several initiatives during the period 1933–1935. Germany withdrew from the League of Nations in October 1933 and in January 1934 signed a 10-year non-aggression pact with Poland, which breached the French alliance system in eastern Europe. Hitler also gave tacit backing to the attempted coup by Austrian Nazis in Vienna in July 1934. In March 1935 he took a considerable risk, when he announced the introduction of conscription. This led to a meeting of the British, Italian and French heads of government at Stresa, who issued a joint statement confirming their determination to maintain the peace settlements. Hitler was, however, easily able to break up the unity of the 'Stresa Front', when Britain, without consulting either Italy or France, accepted his offer of a bilateral naval pact, which limited the German navy to 35 per cent of the Royal Navy.

Mussolini's attack on Abyssinia in October 1935 and the Anglo-French decision to support the League of Nations and impose sanctions on Italy gave Hitler the opportunity to remilitarize the Rhineland. To avoid isolation and possible defeat, Mussolini had little option but to assure him of Italian support for this move. Using the pretext of the ratification of the Franco-Soviet treaty of 27 February 1936, which was a response to the German introduction of conscription, Hitler ordered the reoccupation of the Rhineland with a weak military force, despite the reservations of his generals and diplomats. His gamble paid off as neither France nor Britain intervened. It robbed France of its main strategic advantage over Germany and showed with painful clarity that neither Britain nor France was ready to defend the Locarno settlement and the Treaty of Versailles.

Although Germany's military weakness prevented Hitler from taking any major initiatives for the next 2 years, he gave limited military assistance to General Franco (1892–1975), the Spanish Nationalist leader, in his uprising against the Republican government. This was partly because Hitler feared a Communist takeover in Spain, but the civil war in Spain also helped divert the attention of the great powers from Germany and central Europe. It is 'a good example of Hitler reacting to a development he had not foreseen'.[6] The German–Italian October Protocols, or the Rome–Berlin axis as Mussolini called them, and the **Anti-Comintern Pact** of November 1936 with Japan, which Italy joined a year later, were two further propaganda coups that pointed in the direction of a 'new globe spanning alliance'[7] which threatened the democracies in every theatre, even though the agreements lacked any diplomatic substance.

By the end of 1937 Germany's military and diplomatic position had improved dramatically. At a meeting at the Reich chancellery on 5 November attended by his military chiefs, Hermann Göring and Constantin von Neurath (1873–1956), the foreign minister, Hitler reviewed foreign policy options for the next 7 years. He informed the assembled generals and ministers that Germany's 'problem of space' had to be solved by 1943–1945, but that if the right opportunities, such as a political crisis in France or an Italian–French war, presented themselves, Czechoslovakia could be destroyed as early as 1938. The memorandum of the meeting was used by the prosecution during the Nuremberg war crimes trials in 1946 (see p. 293) to show that Hitler had a precise blueprint for war. Taylor, however, in 1961 'stirred up a hornets nest' by arguing that it was 'for the most part 'day dreaming unrelated to what followed in real life' and the meeting was essentially concerned with the allocation of raw materials rather than foreign policy.[8] While historians agree that the memorandum was hardly a blueprint for action and failed to mention the

Anti-Comintern Pact: This was aimed against the Comintern – the Communist International set up by Lenin in 1919.

see Document 67

crucial question of war against the USSR, the consensus of research still favours William Carr's views that Hitler was warning his generals that 'a more adventurous and dangerous policy was imminent'.[9] Significantly on 22 November the decision was taken to increase the production of Germany's raw iron to the 'limit of capacity'[10], and on 7 December General Jodl (1890–1946) drew up plans for an offensive rather than defensive war against Czechoslovakia.

The opportunities to annex Austria and then to destroy Czechoslovakia arose both more quickly and in a different form from that foreseen in Hitler's exposition of 5 November. It was Schuschnigg (1897–1977), the Austrian chancellor, who was the unwitting catalyst for the *Anschluss*. In an attempt in February to reach some agreement that would have controlled the activities of the Austrian Nazis, he provided Hitler with an opportunity to dictate a series of conditions which would have turned Austria into a German satellite. It was then Schuschnigg's attempt on 9 March to regain a measure of independence by asking his countrymen to vote in a referendum for a 'free and German, independent and social, Christian and united Austria' that pushed Hitler 3 days later into sending troops across the frontier. Faced with an enthusiastic reception from the crowd at Linz, Hitler quickly abandoned his original idea of appointing a satellite government under the Austrian Nazi, Seyss-Inquart, and instead incorporated Austria into the Reich.

See Map 7

The *Anschluss* was a 'watershed for Hitler and the Third Reich'.[11] French and British passivity convinced him that his plans for creating a Greater German Reich were now within his grasp, but before he could do that, he would have to liquidate Czechoslovakia, whose strategic position, well-equipped army and efficient armaments industry made it a considerable threat to Germany's southern flank. Its potential strength, however, was undermined by ethnic tensions between the Czechs and Slovaks, and the existence of three million Sudeten Germans who wished to join the Reich. Two weeks after the *Anschluss* Hitler instructed Henlein (1898–1945), the Sudeten German leader, to formulate demands for Sudeten self-government, which in reality could not be granted without breaking up the Czechoslovak state. In May the Prague government, mistaking German manoeuvres near the borders for preparations for an invasion, completely surprised Hitler by ordering a partial mobilization. In response to British, French and Russian protests, Hitler proclaimed his innocence, but the incident confirmed his suspicions of Czechoslovakia, and led him to set 1 October as the deadline for 'smashing' it. For the rest of the summer Hitler continued both to encourage Sudeten separatism and to stir up similar demands among the Hungarian and Polish minorities in Czechoslovakia so that Poland and Hungary would support its destruction.

On 12 September Hitler's demand for immediate self-determination for the Sudeten Germans triggered a major international crisis which led to escalating unrest in the Sudetenland and to the intervention of Neville Chamberlain (1869–1940), the British prime minister, who flew to see Hitler three times between 15 and 29 September. First of all at

Berchtesgaden on 15 September Hitler initially agreed to Chamberlain's proposals for sending an international commission to the Sudetenland to arrange for ceding to Germany all areas which contained a German population of over 50 per cent. By the time Chamberlain had secured French and Czech agreement to this and returned for the second conference at Bad Godesberg on 22 September, Hitler had changed his mind and now demanded the immediate German occupation of the Sudetenland, which the following day he only reluctantly postponed to 1 October. What motivated this unexpected rejection? The weight of evidence suggests that Hitler was ready for war. He calculated that Prague would reject his terms and be abandoned by the Western powers, who would give Germany a free hand to destroy the state. But in the face of partial British and French mobilization and the lack of enthusiasm of his generals and Mussolini for war, 'the unthinkable happened'[12]: Hitler accepted Mussolini's offer of mediation and on 29 September at the Munich Conference agreed to an international guarantee of rump Czechoslovakia while German forces would be permitted to occupy the Sudetenland in

See Map 7

stages between 1 and 10 October 1938.

Paradoxically for Hitler the conference was a diplomatic defeat, which cheated him of Czechoslovakia and also provided evidence that Britain, despite its willingness to appease, would not allow Germany a completely free hand in eastern Europe. Consequently on 21 October 1938 he ordered the army to draw up new plans for the destruction of Czechoslovakia. His chance came when the tensions between the Slovaks and the Czechs, which he had done so much to provoke, came to a head in March 1939. He was able to force the Czech President, Hacha (1872–1945), to agree to the German occupation of Prague and the creation of an independent Slovakia, which effectively became a German protectorate.

The occupation of Prague, which was followed shortly afterwards by the annexation of Memel, led to the Anglo-French guarantee of Poland in March 1939. As German diplomatic attempts over the course of the winter to persuade Poland to agree to the restoration of Danzig and the Corridor to German rule in return for eventual gains in the Ukraine had failed, the guarantee convinced Hitler that he would have to destroy Poland, and perhaps fight Britain and France as well, if he were to continue with his expansionary policy. As early as 3 April, orders were issued to the army to prepare for an invasion of Poland by 1 September at the latest.

Both the Western powers and Germany, recognizing that the key to the coming conflict lay in Moscow, began negotiations with Stalin. The subsequent Nazi–Soviet Non-Aggression Treaty of 23 August was an enormous success for Hitler, as it secured Stalin's benevolent neutrality in return for territorial concessions in eastern Europe and deprived Britain and France of the only alliance which could have stopped Poland's defeat. When the Western powers unexpectedly responded to this treaty by ratifying their treaties of guarantee with Poland, and Mussolini made clear that Italy would not enter the war, Hitler temporarily 'lost his nerve',[13] postponed the attack and attempted to separate Britain and Poland by offering Britain an alliance and a guarantee of its empire. Once this failed, Germany invaded Poland on 1 September and France and Britain declared war on Germany on the 3rd. Taylor, stirring up another 'hornets nest' argues that the war began because Hitler launched 'on 29 August a diplomatic manoeuvre aimed at persuading the British to force the Poles to make concessions which he ought to have launched on 28 August'.[14] Possibly, given more time, he might have separated Britain and Poland, but he did not want a compromise settlement with the Poles. At most he was hoping to manoeuvre them into a position where their 'stubbornness' could be blamed for causing the war.

The defeat and occupation of Poland

Poland's fate was sealed in little over a month. Anglo-French military passivity enabled the *Wehrmach*t rapidly to defeat the Polish forces. In many ways the war was a rehearsal for the later Russian campaign. Seven *Einsatzgruppen*, totalling 2700 men were assigned to the German armies to deal with 'elements hostile to the Reich and Germany'. In practice this meant Jews and Polish partisans. In September alone some 16,000 people had been killed by these *Einsatzgruppen*.[15] On 17 September Soviet troops occupied eastern Poland in accordance with the secret protocol accompanying the Nazi–Soviet Pact. Initially Hitler considered creating a small Polish satellite state in the hope that this would persuade Britain and France to make peace. When the Allies rejected this, Germany annexed some 94,000 square kilometres with a population of about ten million. The remainder of Poland, now named the General Government, was put under direct German control and administered by **Hans Frank**.

In the annexed areas Himmler, who had been appointed head of the newly formed Reich Commission for the Strengthening of the German Race (RKFVD), was given the task of repatriating the **Volksdeutsche** to German territory and of eliminating the 'influence of such alien parts of the population as constitute a danger to the Reich and the German community'. In the course of the winter 1939–1940 a full-scale Germanization policy was launched in Posnań and Pomorze. In the first half of December, nearly 90,000 Poles, Sinti, Roma and Jews were arrested in Posnań, forced into cattle trucks and sent over the frontier into the General Government. Himmler began to categorize the remainder of the population in the annexed areas according to racial criteria.

In Poland the most radical elements of National Socialism were able to carry out what they interpreted to be the *Führer*'s will without any of the moral and legal constraints that still existed in the Reich. The Government General was described by Hans Frank as the 'the first colonial region of the German nation' where the interests of German culture must

Einsatzgruppen:
special task forces consisting of the SS, SD and the police

Hans Frank, (1900–1946):
Head of the NSDAP's legal office, then justice minister in Bavaria and in 1934 the Reich Minister Without Portfolio.

Volksdeutsche:
ethnic Germans living outside the Reich in Poland and elsewhere

prevail'. At the end of October, in Lublin, his deputy, Arthur Seyss-Inquart (1892–1946), explained to German occupation personnel and local *Volksdeutsche* that the Polish intelligentsia and elite were, like the Jews, to be destroyed. This was no idle threat. In Lublin, from the end of October until early February, the population was terrorized by a series of manhunts, and hundreds of prisoners were delivered daily to the state prison in the castle where many were shot. One Catholic priest, who escaped to Rome in January 1940, observed that 'The Germans systematically destroyed Catholicism and Polish traditions with atheistic hatred'.[16] Altogether the conquest of Poland placed two to three million Jews into Hitler's power. Initially in the winter of 1939–1940 the RKVD's plan was to create a massive Jewish reservation in the Lublin area, but this was repeatedly shelved as it could not be carried out simultaneously with the influx of the *Volksdeutsche* from the Baltic States and Volhynia, who were given priority.[17]

In the autumn of 1939, the mass of the German Army was moved westwards in preparation for the advance into France. The men left behind were, for the most part, comparatively elderly reservists, often sickened by the atrocities they witnessed on a daily basis. They were ordered not to talk about such incidents, but according to a report in the Danish newspaper, the *Politiken* on 4 February 1940: 'they do so all the same, and when one hears what these soldiers have to report … one well understands that they feel the urge to confess, to shake free from the impressions they carry about with them'. The Polish Father General of the Jesuits, Father Ledóchowski (1866–1942), confirmed this when he told the British Ambassador to the Vatican in January that 'he had heard of German soldiers who had returned from Poland and expressed their horror of what they had perpetrated'. The Vatican also received reports at Christmas of Bavarian troops going to Confession given by Polish priests, who were themselves being persecuted by the *Gestapo*.[18] How much of this percolated through to the Germans in the Reich? Patriotism, victory and the *Führer* cult all 'encouraged people to overlook the incipient genocide in Poland'.[19] Much was also made of the **Bromberg 'massacre'** as evidence of Polish 'depravity' and 'untrustworthiness'.

Bromberg 'massacre': On 3 September the *Volksdeutsche*, anticipating the arrival of German troops, attempted to seize power in Bromberg, but were pre-empted by Polish troops who killed about 1000 *Volksdeutsche*. This number was greatly inflated by German propaganda.

From the defeat of France to the invasion of Russia, June 1940–June 1941

On 10 May the German offensive opened in western Europe. Within weeks France was suing for an armistice, and British troops had been driven from the continent.

Germany now controlled most of the Continent of Europe from the Pyrenees to the borders of Soviet-occupied Poland. In Norway and Holland the Germans appointed *Reichskommissars*, while in Denmark the existing government was left intact. Northern France and Belgium were run by German military governments, as they were in the front line in the war against Britain, but the rest of France was administered from Vichy by its own quasi-Fascist regime under Marshal Pétain (1856–1951). Alsace and Lorraine were re-annexed (see p. 192) and amalgamated with the Baden and Saarpfalz *Gaue*. Apart from the eventual removal of the Jews the Nazi regime did not 'aim to drastically transform the racial composition of these countries'.[20] More important was the need to exploit their economies for Germany's war effort. Initially there was some attempt to disguise German intentions under the veneer of idealistic talk about a united anti-Bolshevik Europe, in which, according to Otto Dietrich, Germany's press chief, there would be 'equal chances for all'.[21] The reality of course was different. Labour conscription was imposed and the economies of the occupied states were controlled from Berlin.

The resettlement question unsolved

Throughout the summer of 1940 the problems caused in the annexed territories in Poland by the resettlement of the *Volksdeutsche* and the deportation of the Jews and Poles remained insoluble. However, briefly with the fall of France it had seemed that the European Jews could be settled in the French colony of Madagascar, but this had to be shelved once it was clear that as long as Britain remained a belligerent the Royal Navy would continue to control the Indian Ocean. Consequently the RKFVD persisted with only limited success in its attempts to concentrate the Polish Jews in ghettos in occupied Poland. Although this caused immense logistical problems, as it coincided with the military build-up for the invasion of Russia, Hitler refused to stop the deportation programme and rejected any suggestion that the Jews in the newly annexed territory should be employed in the war industries in Germany. Similar problems emerged in the west. In July 1940 the deportation began of Roma, Sinti, 'asocials', criminals, the mentally ill and irreconcilable French nationalists from Alsace and Lorraine into Vichy France, as well as some 6504 German Jews from Baden, but French objections at the Wiesbaden Armistice Commission halted any further flows. As Christopher Browning has succinctly observed, 'the greater the frustration [over resettlement], the lower the threshold to systematic mass murder'.[22]

Plans for resettling Jews in Madagascar and Siberia

Plans for 'resettlement' in Madagascar, or later in Siberia, were not really an alternative to extermination. As Hermann Graml has pointed out, the Nazi authorities assumed that the great majority of Jews would die in Madagascar from disease, and consequently mass murder would be 'given the appearance of a natural process'.[23] It is significant that Philipp Bouhler (1899–1945), who had been in charge of the euthanasia programme in Germany (see p. 260), was the designated governor of Madagascar.

The decision to invade Russia

Hitler had assumed that after the fall of France Britain would terminate hostilities. When it did not, he considered a number of options ranging from invasion to military collaboration with Nationalist Spain and Vichy France and the construction of a global alliance with Italy, Japan and the USSR against the British Empire. His real priority, however, was the destruction of the USSR. Already by August 1940 a growing number of troops were being sent eastwards, and on 18 December he made the crucial decision to attack Russia in the spring of 1941. Hitler tried to convince his generals that the defeat of the Soviet Union would also lead to the defeat of Britain, but if Britain's defeat had really been his first priority, he would surely have concentrated on the naval war and on attacking Britain in the Mediterranean with adequate forces. It is therefore more accurate to say that the defeat of Britain was only a 'subsidiary aim of the Russian offensive'.[24] While Stalin had exploited the Nazi–Soviet Pact to strengthen the Russian position in eastern Europe, he was still supplying Germany with raw materials and food, and there was no evidence that he was planning war in the near future. The decision to attack Russia at that juncture can only be understood in the context of Nazi ideology. Hitler's belief in his mission to destroy Bolshevism and to provide *Lebensraum* for the expansion of the German race was the real reason for the invasion. As he said in a discussion with his commanders on 9 January 1941 'the giant space of Russia holds immeasurable riches'.[25] He had planned the operation carefully, and, as Bullock emphasizes, 'of all decisions it is the one which most clearly bears his own personal stamp, the culmination (as he saw it) of his career'.[26]

On 30 March he outlined what war against the USSR would involve. It was a 'conflict between two ideologies'. Bolshevism was quite simply 'an antisocial criminality' and a 'huge danger for the future'. Consequently a key task of the army was 'the annihilation of Bolshevik commissars and the communist intelligentsia'. In preparation for the Russian campaign, four SS *Einsatzgruppen*, each numbering between 500 and 1000 men, were formed to prepare the way for 'the political and administrative organization' of the occupied areas. In practice this meant, as one of their number later testified at Nuremberg, 'putting to death all racially and politically undesirable elements among the prisoners' – Soviet officials, gypsies, Jews and the so-called 'second class Asiatics'.[27]

Greece: In October 1940 an Italian attack on Greece was repulsed. In January British forces had landed in Greece to protect her from an anticipated German intervention aimed to assist the Italians.

Operation Barbarossa

Barbarossa was launched on 22 June 1941 after German forces had first pushed the British out of **Greece** and overthrown the anglophile administration in Yugoslavia. It marked *the* turning point in the history of the Third Reich. It was a war for racial empire culminating in genocide and the Holocaust. At home in Germany it led to increased radicalization and the mobilization of the population and the economy for total war.

Initially the German offensive was brilliantly successful, but once it was halted before Moscow in December 1941, the Germans faced the prospect of a long-drawn-out war on two fronts.

See Document 68

On 7 December the war became global when Japan attacked the US fleet in Pearl Harbor and Germany in turn declared war on the US. Hitler had been warned by Fritz Todt that the war would be unwinnable once the USA became a belligerent, but he gambled on the Japanese preventing the US from assisting Britain.[28] In the early summer of 1942 the German advance was renewed and by July had reached the Caucasus. Briefly there seemed to be a prospect that the *Wehrmacht* would achieve total victory, but such hopes were snuffed out at Stalingrad where the Sixth Army surrendered on 2 February 1943 and later in July in the epic tank battle at Kursk, which ended in a Soviet victory.

The war of ethnic annihilation

As Peter Longerich has stressed 'from the outset the war against the Soviet Union was conceived as a campaign of racial domination and **annihilation**'.[29] Quite apart from the execution of 'Jewish Bolsheviks', the creation of *Lebensraum* and the economic exploitation of the countryside would inevitably lead to the deaths of millions of people through starvation – a rough estimate by the Reich Ministry of Food was some 30 million. In May 1941 the Agricultural section of the Economic Organization East, which had been set up to exploit the Soviet economy predicted that 'many tens of millions [of Russians] … will become surplus to requirement and will have to die or emigrate to Siberia'.[30] Russian troops were often shot by the *Wehrmacht* as soon as they surrendered, while millions of those who went into prisoner-of-war cages starved to death. A year later this policy was reversed when Russian POWs were increasingly sent to Germany to work in the factories (see p. 282).

When the USSR was invaded, three large new territories, Bialystok, Ostland and Ukraine, were formed and placed under German control. Ultimately Hitler's intention was to build up a German population of 250 million in western Russia over the course of about 80 years, while Himmler had similar ambitions for resettling the whole of Poland with Germans. Shortly after the invasion, the RKVD began work on the General Plan East, which envisaged within 25 years an initial settlement of the Ukraine and Volga regions with a series of frontier marches or settlements populated by SS war veterans. A start was made in the Hegewald in the Ukraine and at Zamosce in Poland, but the defeat at Stalingrad put a stop to any further settlements.

Annihilation: between 140,000 and 580,000 Soviet officials or 'Bolsheviks' were shot. By 1943 about 2.2 million Soviet Jews were also murdered. The lot of the majority of Russian prisoners of war was equally horrific. They were imprisoned in camps behind the front and fed with minimal rations. By 1945 57.5 per cent had died in captivity.

The Holocaust

The resettlement of millions of people according to racial criteria and the systematic attempts to eliminate the Russian and Polish elites was the context in which the **Holocaust**, the liquidation of nearly six million Jews,

Holocaust: the dictionary definition of which is 'a sacrifice totally consumed by fire or a burnt offering', implies, in Michael Marrus's words, 'an urge not only to distinguish this massacre from all others, but also to register the ethereal quality of this terrible episode, its removal from customary discourse's

took place. To the two to three million Jews who fell into Nazi hands after the conquest of Poland, were added a further three million Jews in Russia and half a million in the occupied territory in western Europe. The horror of the Holocaust does, of course, render it a particularly difficult subject for dispassionate historical analysis. The structuralist view that it was the result of muddle and improvisation, rather than a consequence of clear planning, is criticized by Lucy Dawidowicz as a 'mechanistic interpretation' of Nazi Germany, which eliminates personal blame.[31]

The invasion of Soviet Russia in June 1941 was a turning point in Nazi policy towards the Jews. It was a war of extermination against 'Jewish Bolshevism' in which by the spring of 1942 well over a million Jews, who were not members of the Communist Party, had been murdered. Just to quote one example: In September 1941 at Babi Yar 33,751 Jews from Kiev were massacred. These massacres marked a new and more deadly threshold in Nazi policy. The structuralists argue that it was the successful Red Army counter-attack in December 1941 which was the crucial factor leading to the Holocaust.[32] Not only did the continuation of the war rule out Siberia as a possible area for Jewish 'resettlement', but it created severe logistical problems in Poland and occupied Russia, which would be further exacerbated by bringing more Jews into the area. This is why Broszat argues that the Holocaust was a '"way out" of a blind alley into which the National Socialists had manoeuvred themselves'.[33] The intentionalists respond that this interpretation reduces the Holocaust to an accidental consequence of the military situation in eastern Europe. Dawidowicz, for example, argues that Hitler 'implemented his plan in stages, seizing whatever opportunities offered themselves to advance its execution'.[34] In many ways Christopher Browning endorses this view when he writes that 'in the long evolution of Nazi Jewish policy to the Final solution, Hitler had been of course not only "champion and spokesman" but also the necessary and pivotal decision maker'.[35] At the very least, it must have been obvious to senior Nazis and their officials that Hitler supported such policies. Arguably, this was sufficient to inspire them to 'work towards the *Führer*' and ensure that his wishes would be carried out.

See Document 62

Already by August 1941 in the German-occupied areas a transition was taking place from murdering male Jews of military age to 'cleansing' whole swathes of the country of the Jewish population.[36] In the autumn the decision was also made to begin the construction of the extermination camps at Sobibor and Belzec, while in Auschwitz experiments were made with the poison gas, Zyklon B. The deportation of the Jews from German-occupied Europe had also started. Between 15 October and 9 November some 25,000 Jews from the **Greater German Reich** were sent to Lodz and another 34 transports to Riga took place over the next 3 months. By late 1941 there were so many schemes being worked on for the ultimate extermination of the Jews that it is more than likely that 'a green light was coming from the highest level'.[37]

Greater German Reich: the Reich expanded by its annexations, 1938–1940

In January 1942, at the Wannsee Conference in Berlin, plans were drawn up for rounding up the Jews throughout Europe and conscripting them into labour gangs in eastern Europe, where it was assumed that 'a large number will drop out through natural elimination'. The remainder would then be 'dealt with accordingly'.[38] Despite the euphemisms, 'the genocidal implications were totally and unmistakably clear'.[39] Appended to the minutes was also a list of Jews from every country in Europe, including neutral Southern Ireland and undefeated Britain, who were ultimately to be deported. The Reich's *Judenpolitik* was now to be extended to every country under German control. The extermination programme was accelerated in the spring and summer of 1942. In the 12 months from March 1942 to March 1943 some 80 per cent of the victims of the Holocaust were murdered in what Christopher Browning has called a veritable '*Blitzkrieg* against the Jews'.[40] By 1945 nearly six million Jews had been murdered.

See Documents 57 and 66

The German people and the Holocaust

The murder of the Jews in Poland was by 1942 an 'open secret'.[41] The deportation of the remaining Jews from the Reich, 1942–1943, could not be hidden and rumours of what was occurring behind the lines in the USSR and the death camps in Poland were spread widely by soldiers on leave, railway personnel and German officials and their families in occupied territory. What was the reaction of the German people? Daniel Goldhagen argues, to quote the title of his book, that the Germans were 'Willing Executioners', and that both they and Hitler were 'of one mind' about the Jews. Hitler merely 'unshackled' this 'pre-existing, pent up' anti-Semitism to 'perpetrate' the Holocaust.[42] Certainly anti-Semitism was a force in German society on the *Völkisch* and populist right before 1933 (see pp. 119–120), as it was in France and many other European countries. Many conservatives, some of whom were later to join the Kreisau Circle and the 20 July resistance movement were, as Hans Mommsen has pointed out, openly anti-Semitic. Initially in 1933 'the mounting violence of the SA and the Nazi Party against the Jews was a matter of regret for conservatives, but they portrayed this as mere teething troubles that would soon fade'. Eventually they were appalled by the massacres in Russia and the death camps, but this 'as a general rule' was 'a minor factor' in their 'decision to commit high treason'.[43] Nazi racial propaganda and negative stereotyping probably had most impact on the cohorts passing through the Hitler Youth. On the other hand Ian Kershaw writing on public opinion in Bavaria during the Third Reich came to the conclusion that 'dynamic Jew haters were certainly a small percentage of the population but active friends of Jews formed an even smaller proportion',[44] an assessment supported by several other historians. Of course there were examples of kindness and sympathy to individual Jews. In Berlin, for instance, some 5000 Jews were hidden from the authorities until 1945, but the majority of the Germans were more preoccupied by the nightly air raids and their own struggle for survival.

A more difficult question to answer is the motivation of those actually caught up in perpetrating genocide in eastern Europe. Was it a dogged acceptance of 'duty' or were they 'willing executioners'? Christopher Browning in his *Ordinary Men*, a study of the work of Reserve Police Battalion 101, shows that while there were 'eager killers' and a small group of 'non shooters', who were exempted from the shooting 'if they did not feel up to it', the majority simply pressed on with their murderous task 'without ever risking the onus of confronting authority'. Increasingly Browning argues that 'they felt more pity for themselves because of the unpleasant work they had been assigned than they did for their dehumanized victims'.[45]

The attitude of the Churches

Criticism by the Churches of Nazi racial policies continued for the most part to be muted (see p. 264). In 1941, when Jews were already being deported to Poland and murdered in Russia, the Catholic Church was careful to complain only about the fate of 'non-Aryan' Catholics or of Jews married to Catholics. The Confessing Church was equally careful, although in October 1943 it did address a pastoral letter to all its congregations, in which it unambiguously announced that 'terms like "eradication", "liquidation" or "unfit to live" are not known in the law of God'. On the other hand, many individual Protestant and Catholic priests, such as **Dietrich Bonhoeffer** and **Alfred Delp**, felt no such inhibitions and did not hesitate to condemn Hitler for his genocidal policies, as is testified by the death of several hundred clergy in Buchenwald.

Dietrich Bonhoeffer, 1906–1945: a Protestant pastor and member of the Confessing Church. He was arrested in 1943 and hanged in April 1945. **Alfred Delp,** 1900–1945: a Jesuit, who was a member of the Kreisau Circle (see p. 285) and was arrested in July 1944 and hanged after torture in February 1945.

After the war the Americans calculated that 300–400 Protestant clergy died, while the number of Catholics was 800, although some of these would have come from the annexed Polish territories (see p. 280).

The increasing influence of the party and the SS

From June 1941 until November 1944 Hitler was rarely in Berlin and was isolated from all contacts in his headquarters in East Prussia and the Ukraine. As supreme commander of the army, he took on an immense workload, leaving him little time for matters affecting the home front. The Reich government became ever more dysfunctional, despite repeated attempts by ministers to create an effective executive. The Ministerial Council for the Defence of the Reich, which was set up in August 1939, ceased to meet after November 1939, and Hitler consistently opposed the emergence of any committee with real executive powers that might eventually be used to challenge him. He vetoed attempts by Heinrich Lammers (1869–1962), the head of the Reich Chancellery, to reintroduce regular cabinet meetings and even disapproved of ministers meeting unofficially. Decisions could still be achieved by going straight to Hitler, but increasingly access was controlled by Martin Bormann, the chief of the party chancellery at the *Führer* headquarters. Essentially the regime was incapable of being reformed, as, to quote Ian Kershaw, it 'was both the inexorable product of Hitler's personalized rule and the guarantee of his power'.[46]

As with the French revolutionaries in 1791–1792 (see pp. 12–13), the war was seen by many of the party activists to be 'a great school of public virtue' in which the restrictive compromises of 1933 could at last be swept away. Both the SS and the party made considerable inroads into the authority of the state. The SS threatened to develop into a 'collateral state', which could undermine and dissolve the existing state institutions.[47] As commissioner for consolidating German nationhood (RKFDV), Himmler was given responsibility for the resettlement of ethnic Germans and eliminating 'the harmful influences of such alien parts of the population as constitute a danger to the Reich and the German community'[48] in the occupied and incorporated territories. He also accumulated key military and civil positions: Reich minister of the interior in 1943, commander of the reserve army in 1944, and then in quick succession commander-in-chief of the Rhine army group in December 1944 and of the Vistula army group in January 1945. Yet paradoxically, while his power grew in the Reich, his influence on Hitler was undermined by Bormann at the *Führer* headquarters. The control of the concentration camps enabled the SS to use prison labour in its industrial undertakings, which in 1944 consisted of about 150 firms ranging from quarrying to the manufacture of armaments and textiles. The SS also controlled a military force of some 35 divisions, the *Waffen-SS*.

The war increased the party's responsibilities at every level. On it fell the task of maintaining the morale of the civilian population. The *Gauleiter* were appointed Reich defence commissioners in September 1939, and in the event of an emergency, such as an invasion, were to take complete charge of the civil authorities within their *Gaue*. These became the key administrative units within the Reich, on which the citizen's militia, the *Volkssturm*, was based when it was created in the autumn of 1944. In the occupied and newly annexed territories in the east the party was able to assert its authority. The new *Gaue* were not encumbered with the administrative legacies of the pre-1933 period, which in the old Reich forced the party administrators to share power with the traditional bureaucracy. In new territories the Reich commissioners were first and foremost party functionaries, whose task was not to create an efficient administration but to carry out the ideology of the Nazi movement.

The war also sharpened the party's ambition to achieve the ideological and anti-Christian revolution which had been denied it in the 1930s. Supported by Bormann who, in a circular in June 1941 to the *Gauleiter*, bluntly stated that Christianity was incompatible with National Socialism, a vicious campaign was launched by the NSDAP against the Churches. Christian publications were seized, while the welfare activities of the Catholic nuns were now carried out by 'the brown sisters', a Nazi organization, and feast days, which were traditionally celebrated as holidays, were simply moved to the nearest Sunday, so as to avoid any interruption in the war effort. Confronted by popular opposition, particularly from the Catholics, Hitler stopped the campaign within the old Reich, but

See Map 7

in the newly annexed territories it continued unchecked. In the *Reichsgau* Wartheland which had been annexed from Poland for example, 94 per cent of the churches in the dioceses of Posen–Gnesen were closed down and 11 per cent of the clergy murdered. As Kershaw has observed, this 'clearly showed the face of the future',[49] and, if Germany had emerged from the war victorious, the Churches would almost certainly have faced renewed persecution.

In many other spheres the war also enabled the party to extend its social, cultural and political influence. The evacuation of city children to the countryside, where they were without their parents, to escape the Allied bombing raids increased both the responsibilities of the Hitler Youth leaders and their opportunities for exposing children to Nazi ideology. What remained of the independence of the judiciary was fatally undermined when in April 1942 a *Reichstag* 'resolution' gave Hitler complete power to remove from office 'judges, who clearly fail to recognize the mood of the hour'.[50] This now enabled the party to interfere directly in the legal process. After Stalingrad, Nazi influence within the army also increased. By the end of 1943 party officials took part in the selection and training of new officers, and after the 20 July plot (see p. 286) the Nazi salute replaced the traditional military salute. Goebbels set up a special post office box address, to which any soldier in the ranks could write if he felt that his officers were not sufficiently loyal to the regime.

The war economy

German war economy: In 1940, for instance, Germany spent about $6000 million on armaments, while Britain spent only $3500 million; yet the latter managed to produce over 50 per cent more aircraft, 100 per cent more vehicles and nearly as many tanks as did Germany.

When Allied economic experts analysed the records of the **German war economy** in 1945, it seemed to them that the German economy had not been mobilized for a total war until 1942. These findings, as has been noted (see p. 252), led to the *Blitzkrieg* thesis. This was according to Alan Milward a 'system of warfare best suited to the character and institutions of Hitler's Germany',[51] since it did not involve full mobilization of all economic resources, which would have strained the loyalties of the civilian population, as it did in the latter stages of the Great War (see p. 173–175). Much emphasis has been placed on the fact that Britain in 1940 and 1941 outperformed Germany in the mass production of weapons, but Richard Overy has convincingly argued that this was not because of a lack of German investment but rather because of structural problems in the German war economy. The timing of the outbreak of the war had wrong-footed Hitler, since much of the initial spending on rearmament had been invested in military infrastructure projects, such as barracks and airfields, rather than weapons. Many of the smaller and medium-sized German armament firms were reluctant to introduce modern, mass-production techniques, while the *Reichswehr* preferred quality rather than quantity of armaments, all of which considerably slowed up the tempo of production.

Albert Speer and the total war economy

By the winter of 1941 it was clear that these problems could only be overcome through mass production and rationalization of the war economy. A start had been made by Fritz Todt but he was killed in a plane crash in February 1942. His successor as armaments minister was Albert Speer, the party architect, who had the decisive advantage of having direct access to Hitler. He could thus override objections from the armed forces simply by appealing to Hitler. Over the next 2 years he was to achieve a 'production miracle'.[52] In April 1942 the Central Planning Board, 'the true war cabinet of the German economy'[53], was set up, which allocated the supply of raw materials to each sector of the economy. Speer was even able to take away from the armed forces their fiercely protected right to design their own weapons. He also encouraged industrialists to apply new scientific management techniques, to rationalize production, maximize plant capacities and standardize designs. Employers were helped in this process by the employment of foreign workers and POWs who were subject to harsh discipline and could not oppose the new production methods, as some German workers still attempted to do. Armament factories were put under control of the SS, and engineers and managers involved in design and production were 'to knock down anybody who blocks your way'.[54]

In 1943 Speer also produced plans for integrating the French economy more closely with the German. In exchange for the ending of labour conscription and deportation to German factories for French workers, France would produce consumer goods for the German market, thereby allowing German factories to concentrate completely on war production. The plan, however, was vetoed by Fritz Sauckel (1894–1946), the plenipotentiary for labour mobilization. Although Speer achieved an impressive increase in armaments production, which, despite the Allied bombing campaign, peaked in 1943–1944, he was nevertheless, to quote Gordon Craig, 'denied the right to go beyond the limit of what rationalization could accomplish'.[55] His efforts were undermined by the autonomy of both the *Gauleiter* and the SS, whose economic resources he was unable to exploit (see p. 279). In the end, too, the Allied strategic bombing campaign also disrupted production by interrupting supplies, forcing factories to evacuate and demoralizing the workers.

The labour problem

Although, in September 1939, females already composed 37.4 per cent of the total labour force, the Reich Labour Ministry in the spring of 1940 urged the introduction of comprehensive female conscription, but the unpopularity of this measure both at home and with married soldiers on the front caused the party leadership to have second thoughts. Initially, Polish labour and then, after the defeat of France in June 1940, French prisoners of war were made available for German industry and agriculture. Proposals to use Russian workers were at first opposed by many

Nazis, including Himmler, for both racial and security reasons, but Speer, with the support of Hitler, overcame these objections. The party was reassured by the appointment of Fritz Sauckel (1894–1946), a trusted and loyal Nazi, who was commissioner for the military district of Kassel, to the post of plenipotentiary for labour mobilization. His task involved both organizing the large-scale recruitment of foreign labour into Germany, and then ensuring that this workforce was effectively exploited and disciplined.

8   A heavily stamped leave pass for a Dutch electrical worker travelling from Berlin to Amsterdam. This indicates the relatively favourable conditions under which western as opposed to eastern European and Italian workers (after 1943) were employed in the Third Reich during the Second World War

In response to the ever-increasing demand for German troops on the eastern front, which inevitably ensured that many workers needed at home were called up, Hitler announced at the end of January 1943 that all males between 16 and 65, who were not in the armed forces, and all females between 17 and 45 were to register for war work. In fact, only about 900,000 women were called up as mothers with young children, and wives of the self-employed, were exempt. Reich commissioners were given the power to close all non-essential trades and businesses and allocate their workers to the war industries. This spelt ruin for the small independent artisans, who had in 1933 been among Hitler's most enthusiastic supporters. The employers of the large armament industries, however, preferred foreign workers, whom they could discipline and often ruthlessly exploit. By the end of 1944 there were over seven million foreign workers in Germany. The West European workers, particularly the Dutch, Flemish-speaking Belgians and the French, were treated comparatively well, but the Poles, the Russians and the **Italians** operated in conditions which were little better than slave labour. German society, with a workforce increasingly stratified by race, began to show, in Ulrich Herbert's words, the characteristics of a 'quasi-colonial social order'.[56] Michael Burleigh and Wolfgang Wippermann have argued that the huge influx of foreign labour 'made the German working class more or less passive accomplices in Nazi racial policy',[57] as it became ever more closely involved in the whole machinery of surveillance and repression in the factories. In general the majority of German workers, preoccupied with their own problems, showed little concern for the fate of the foreign workers. As Ulrich Herbert has observed, 'the foreigners were simply there, as much part of wartime life as ration cards or air raid shelters … Their own privileged position as Germans *vis-à-vis* these workers was likewise nothing exceptional, certainly no cause for misgiving'.[58]

> **Italians:** Once Italy had defected from the Axis side in September 1943, the Germans occupied most of Italy and effectively treated it as a conquered country.

The struggle for survival: the German people, 1942–1945

Up to 1944 the German population received adequate rations – an '*Existenzminimum*', below which living standards were not allowed to fall. Basic food rations were between 7 and 15 per cent above the minimum calorific standard. Workers in heavy industry received generous food allowances, which often provided better diets than they had experienced in peacetime. Soldiers' families received special ration coupons for food and rent. As Goebbels noted in his diary, 'before Germany starved, it would be the turn of a number of other peoples'.[59] Nevertheless, the longer the war lasted the greater the burden that fell on the home front, particularly on women, many of whom had both to work and look after their families in the absence of their husbands in the armed forces. This inevitably changed their lives by giving them a new responsibility and independence and often produced acute tension when their husbands returned on leave hoping to find their home life untouched by war.

See Documents 69

Loneliness, separation from their husbands and children, if they were evacuated, and, the ever-present threat of death from the bombs also led to a greater sexual promiscuity.

The war also intensified the burden on the peasantry, who became increasingly alienated from the Nazi regime. In practice, despite the Nazi propaganda about blood and soil (see p. 257), their interests were being sacrificed to the urban majority. The peasantry was burdened with endless regulations and red tape aimed at setting sowing and harvesting targets, their horses were requisitioned and sons called up. Their wives were particularly severely hit by the war. In the words of a military report from Nuremberg in 1942, 'a peasant wife whose husband is at the front ... has not a single quiet minute from 4 in the morning until 9 at night'.[60] Many farms did, of course, have Polish or French workers, but they too could create problems, especially when fraternization with Germans, which was strictly forbidden, took place.

The longer the war lasted, the more German society increasingly resembled a 'kind of kicked-in anthill'.[61] As early as 1940, perhaps as many as two million children were moved out from the cities in the north and the west. As the bombing intensified in 1943–1944 a further nine million women, children and elderly men were moved or fled to the countryside, where mass migration on this scale caused severe problems. Many urban refugees disliked what they considered the tedium of rural life, and, as the *Regierungspräsident* of Upper Bavaria observed, while 'a majority of the local women are working ... the evacuees just try to make life for themselves as comfortable as possible'.[62]

In 1944 refugees from eastern Germany started to join the evacuees. In the autumn of 1944 Soviet troops entered East Prussia. An indication of what awaited many east Germans was seen in the raping, mutilation and murdering of women and children in the small East Prussian village of Nemmersdorf. To avoid this horrendous fate, about five million civilians from East Prussia, the Warthegau, Danzig, Pomerania, Silesia and eastern Brandenburg from October 1944 to January 1945 'trekked' into the interior of the Reich. In 1969 an analysis by the Federal Archives in Bonn came to the conclusion that at least 600,000 of these refugees died and a further 2.2 million cases were 'unresolved'.[63]

The White Rose group: based in Munich and led by Professor Kurt Huber (1893–1943), and five Munich students, among whom Hans (1918–1943) and Sophie Scholl (1921–1943) played a key role. In 1942–1943 they distributed anti-Nazi leaflets in Munich, calling for the overthrow of the Nazi regime, which were aimed at the professional middle classes and their fellow students. In February 1943 they were arrested, tried and executed.

The German opposition, 1939–1945

Unlike resistance movements in occupied Europe the German opposition had to operate among a population which accepted Nazism with varying degrees of enthusiasm or resignation. Both the research of Father Alfred Delp and the former SPD politician Julius Leber (1891–1945) showed that the majority of industrial workers were 'relatively loyal' in their support of the regime.[64] Unlike 1918, there were no unions or socialist parties, and the cohesion of the workforce had been diluted by the conscription of so many workers and their replacement by women, foreign slave labourers and teenagers. The SPD's opposition networks within the Reich had been destroyed (see p. 260), but some of the Communists' survived. Yet they were unable to expand them beyond their original party cadres, and in reality posed little threat to the regime. The younger generation with a few obvious exceptions such as the **White Rose group** and the **'Edelweiss Pirates'** were conditioned by the indoctrination of the Hitler Youth. Neither was there much support among what Mommsen calls the 'broad middle class': businessmen, industrialists, skilled tradesmen and members of the liberal professions were for the most part conspicuous by their absence from the opposition.

The Conservative elites and the Kreisau Circle

It was the Conservative–Nationalist opposition that provided the most effective resistance to Hitler, as it could work within the system, especially through the *Wehrmacht*, to destroy Nazism. Its members were prominent individuals or 'notables', such as Erwin Planck (1893–1945), Papen's former state secretary, Carl Goerdeler (1884–1945), price commissioner, 1934–1935, and Lord Mayor of Leipzig, and General Beck (1880–1944), army chief of staff until 1938. Initially the notables had supported or at least tolerated Hitler, but the Sudeten crisis (see p. 270) led many of them to conclude that he would plunge Germany into a war that it could not win. In the summer of 1938 plans were drawn up by Erich Kordt (1903–1969), chief of the ministerial bureau in the Foreign Office, and Generals Beck, Witzleben (1881–1944) and Oster (1887–1945) to have Hitler arrested, martial law declared and elections called for a constituent assembly, but the Munich agreement destroyed what, to say the least, was 'a most promising attempt to overthrow Hitler'.[65] In the autumn of 1939 another plan for assassinating Hitler by placing a bomb in the Reich chancellery was halted at the last minute, when he cancelled a meeting at the chancellery. Ironically a few weeks later a lone assassin, **Georg Elser**, nearly succeeded where the army failed.

With the formation of the Kreisau Circle in 1941, the non-Communist opposition in Germany for the first time had a forum where it could discuss plans for the future of post-war Germany across the political divide. The circle, which was composed of Social Democrats, both Protestant and Catholic priests, civil servants and *Wehrmacht* officers, met at Kreisau, the Silesian estate of **Count Helmuth James von Moltke** and became the 'think tank' of the opposition until it was broken up by the *Gestapo* in January 1944.

20 July 1944

There were cells of opposition in both the Army Group Centre on the Russian front and in **General Olbricht's** headquarters in Berlin which in 1943 planned a series of assassination attempts against Hitler, but each one, as a consequence of 'a barely credible succession of trivial

---

Edelweiss Pirates: In Cologne-Ehrenfeld in 1944 an 'Edelweiss Pirates' gang worked closely with an underground group which assisted *Wehrmacht* deserters, escaped prisoners of war and foreign workers. It attacked military installations and even managed to kill the head of the Cologne *Gestapo* before it was broken up.

Georg Elser, (1903–1945): former communist and committed Christian managed to place a bomb behind a pillar in the *Bürgerbräukeller*, but Hitler was only saved because bad weather delayed his arrival. He died in Sachsenhausen concentration camp.

Count Helmuth James von Moltke: 1907–1945: was the grand-nephew of Field Marshal Helmuth von Moltke (see p. 77). His mother was an English South African. He had studied law in Britain and practised in Berlin.

General Olbricht 1888–1944: Chief of Staff of the home army

How reactionary was the conservative opposition?

It should come as no surprise that the foreign policy of the Conservative–National opposition automatically assumed that Germany should retain most of what it had acquired up to October 1939. Hermann Graml has argued that it was based on 'seductive visions of a German Reich of medieval proportions' and Prussian and conservative in character.[66] In a memorandum in January 1941 Goerdeler proposed the return of Germany's colonies and the creation of a confederation of free European states under German leadership. The Kreisau Circle was more committed to a European federation with a European parliament and cabinet. The domestic policies of the Conservative opposition, as Ian Kershaw has pointed out, 'were essentially oligarchic and authoritarian, resting heavily on corporatist and neo-conservative notions advanced in the Weimar Republic, envisaging self-governing communities, limited electoral rights and the renewal of Christian values'.[67]

Colonel Claus von Stauffenberg, 1907–1944: wounded in Africa and appointed staff officer in Berlin in 1943. Executed within hours of the 20 July plot failing.

Colonel Brandt was a staff officer present at the conference on 20 July.

incidents',[68] failed. In early 1944 Operation *Valkyrie*, a plan both to assassinate Hitler and stage a military *coup d'état* by mobilizing the reserve army, was drawn up by **Colonel Claus Schenk von Stauffenberg**. After Hitler's assassination, martial law would be declared, a provisional government including Conservative, Centre, Social Democrat and non-party representatives formed, and peace negotiations immediately opened with the West. Stauffenberg's appointment as chief of staff to General Fromm, the commander-in-chief of the home army, gave him access to Hitler's headquarters, where, after two unsuccessful attempts on 6 and 15 July, he was able to plant a bomb on July 20.

The tragic consequences of 20 July 1944 are well known. In a sense the coup failed because '**Colonel Brandt** kicked Stauffenberg's briefcase to the wrong side of the oak support of the conference table',[69] but the plotters also left 'too many loose ends … dangling'.[70] They failed to put the communications centre at the *Führer* headquarters out of action, seize the radio stations in Berlin and arrest party and SS leaders. As soon as it became known that Hitler was still alive, the conspirators lost the initiative, and the armies both in Germany and France refused to cooperate. The consequences of its failure was the elimination of most of the German opposition, as Hitler ordered the arrest of more than 7000 people, 5000 of whom were executed by April 1945.

The end of the Third Reich

Although the 20 July events shook the regime 'its pillars … were left not only standing, but buttressed'.[71] The popular reaction to the plot was relief that Hitler had survived and anger at the treachery of the army. It strengthened his grip on Germany and enabled Goebbels' propaganda machine to drum up support for a final 'backs-to-the-wall effort'.[72] Party fanatics redoubled their efforts to realize the National Socialist revolution.

The end of the war was already in sight by the autumn of 1944. The Western Allies had landed in Normandy in June and most of the Balkans had fallen to the Red Army. Oil supplies had been drastically reduced and transport facilities disrupted throughout the Reich by Allied bombing raids. The Allied advance into the German-occupied territories and the increasing reluctance of the neutral states to export raw materials to Germany also exacerbated the acute economic difficulties and shortages on the home front. Yet the regime managed to survive until Hitler's death on 30 April 1945, by which time the Red Army was in Berlin and the Western Allies had crossed the Rhine and Elbe. Why was this? Kershaw argues in his recent study, *The End*, that apart from a residue of popular backing, terror, the greatly increased power of the party and the 'Bormann-Goebbels-Himmler-Speer quadrumvirate' the real reason was the way the 'charismatic *Führer* regime was structured'.[73] Party leaders, both great and small, *Gauleiter*, army officers and the generals in the wake of 20 July all 'worked towards the *Führer*', whose wish was to continue the struggle until the end.

Post script: the Dönitz episode

As his successor, Hitler had nominated Admiral Dönitz (1891–1980) president of the Reich with Goebbels as his chancellor and Bormann as party minister. Both Göring and Himmler were passed over because they had been rash enough to take **independent action** on the assumption that Hitler was already dead or incapacitated. Goebbels and Bormann immediately attempted to negotiate a ceasefire with the Soviets. When this failed, Goebbels and his wife committed suicide on 1 May after first killing their children, while **Bormann** was killed attempting to flee Berlin. Dönitz, who was in Schleswig-Holstein, meanwhile broadcast to the Reich the news that Hitler had died in combat 'at his post in the Reich Chancellery, while fighting to the last breath against Bolshevism'.[74] He intended to conclude a separate armistice with the Western powers, which would allow him to continue the war long enough on the eastern front to enable as many German troops as possible to retreat westwards and evade surrendering to the Soviet forces. He formed a Nazi–Nationalist cabinet and was determined to maintain an authoritarian state, purged of only the worst Nazi abuses. For a very short time Himmler was left in charge of security, but on 6 May he was dismissed and most of the SS officers were arrested by the *Wehrmacht*. He committed suicide on 23 May after being arrested by the British.

Dönitz avoided formally capitulating to the Allies until 8 May, which allowed nearly three million German troops to escape being taken prisoner by the Russians. The Third Reich survived for 2 more weeks, as Dönitz persuaded the British and American occupying forces that his administration was still temporarily needed to help with the growing problems of hunger, disease, refugees and the threat of Communism, but his position became increasingly untenable, as he wished to preserve 'the

independent action: Himmler asked the Swedes to mediate with the Western Allies, while Göring sent Hitler a telegram on 23 April that, if not informed to the contrary by 10 p.m. that evening, he would act according the edict of 29 June 1941, which nominated him Hitler's successor.

Bormann: for a long time it was thought that he had escaped, but his skeleton was unearthed on a building site in 1972.

most beautiful and best that National Socialism has given us – the unity of the racial community'. He also openly criticized the denazification policies of the Western Allies for destroying those 'quiet, decent citizens', who stood between Germany and Communism.[75] On 23 May 1945 he and his cabinet were at last arrested, and on 5 June the Allies became the sovereign rulers of occupied Germany.

Conclusion

The restructuring of Europe along racial lines through genocidal war was the ultimate aim of the Third Reich. The occupation policies in Poland, Russia, the concentration camps and the Holocaust were its consequences. In 1941 Major-General von Tresckow (1901–1944) observed to a fellow officer that guilt would fall on the Germans for a hundred years 'and not just Hitler alone, but on you and me, your wife and mine, your children and my children, the woman crossing the road now and the boy playing with a ball over there'.[76] Few Germans would now deny this and for the most part their willing and honest atonement for these atrocities is one of the main themes of the rest of this book. This is the moral legacy of the Third Reich, but Hitler did, of course, also leave Germany and indeed much of the European Continent shattered and divided – Hitler was the true 'architect' of 'German disunity' 1949–1990.[77] Yet, as we shall see, in some areas the Third Reich left a more positive legacy to the post 1949 Federal Republic of Germany. Richard Overy has shown that the impressive post-war expansion of the car industry had its root in the Third Reich, while Michael Roseman stresses that some policies such as 'the modernization of leisure' and health care for small children, mothers and workers set precedents for the development of mass tourism and the post-war welfare state.[78]

Part Four

*Partition and Reunification,
1945–1990*

14 *Occupation and Division, 1945–1949*

Introduction: problems, issues and questions

With the total defeat of the Third Reich the wartime allies now had the opportunity to reform Germany and eliminate for ever the factors that had given rise to Nazism. Ambitious reforms were drawn up but 20 years later they were criticized by historians in the Federal Republic of Germany for their failure to carry out a root-and-branch purge of Nazi personnel in the administration. How justified was this criticism? Was it really possible to eliminate every former party member from public life? Was it not more important to change the context of German politics and society so that the values that gave rise to Nazism were no longer relevant? Arguably the Cold War through the partition of Germany did more to change Germany than any Allied reform. It achieved in the Western zones the creation of a liberal, tolerant German state, but was this at the cost of substituting in the Soviet Zone one dictatorship for another?

Post-war Europe

In 1945 Europe was a much diminished continent. Its great powerhouse, Germany, was a shattered wreck, its cities reduced to ruins, its roads clogged with refugees and much of its population subsisting on only the

See documents 70 and 71

291

**Marxist
Leninism:** the
communist
doctrine based on
the teachings of
Marx and Lenin.
This advocated
revolution, the
creation of the
dictatorship of the
proletariat and ulti-
mately the creation
of an egalitarian
communist society.

**Free trade
capitalism:** an
economic system
dependent on the
investment of
private capital and
free access to
global markets

See Maps 8 and 9

**Henry J.
Morgenthau** was
the US treasury
secretary,
1934–1945

most basic rations (see p. 298–299). Eastern Europe, which had been
liberated by the Red Army, was now firmly within the Soviet sphere of
influence with Communists playing a key role in the new post-war
regimes in Poland, Bulgaria, Romania, Czechoslovakia and Hungary.
Western Europe was the mirror image of the east: the USA and Britain,
which had played the key part in its liberation, ensured that power in the
new post-war regimes rested with liberal democratic and essentially anti-
Communist regimes. Both France and Britain were empires in decline
facing terminal threats to their colonial possessions from nationalism
aided by communism. Europe was now dominated by the two great
powers: USSR and USA, both of which had diametrically opposed ideologies, which they were convinced were the key to progress, justice and
prosperity: the former, **Marxist Leninism** and the latter political liberalism combined with **free trade capitalism**. The history of Europe was to
be determined by the rivalry, hostility and in the end coexistence and
compromise between these two superpowers.

The great powers and the future of Germany

Germany surrendered unconditionally on 8 May and, with the demise of
the Dönitz regime 2 weeks later (see p. 287), government effectively
passed into the hands of the Allied commanders-in-chief. Germany was
divided into the four zones agreed upon at the Yalta Conference in
February 1945 and each occupying power was also allotted a zone in
Berlin but, beyond that, Britain, France, the USA and the USSR had no
clear plans for the future of the former Reich. The British and Americans
had wavered between the extremes of the **Morgenthau** Plan which would
have reduced Germany to a deindustrialized backwater, and a cautious
acceptance of a future Germany based on a loose federal constitution.
Stalin too had initially agreed that the Allies should eliminate 'forever'
Germany's 'ability to function as a single state,'[1] but by the spring of 1945
he had accepted the possibility of a united but disarmed and neutral
Germany. Whether he believed that it would be communist is not clear,
but the USSR's most immediate aim was for reparations to rebuild its
shattered economy. At this stage it was the French who were the most
determined opponents of German unity, and their overriding aim was to
create an independent Rhineland and a Ruhr under international control.
Whatever shape the future Germany would be, it had been agreed at Yalta
that Poland would be compensated for the land lost to the Soviet Union
by the Nazi–Soviet Pact in 1939 by the annexation of German territory
on its western borders.

By the time the time Allies met at Potsdam, they could only paper over
the growing differences between themselves on how Germany should be
treated. Although there was a consensus on the need to enforce the 'four
ds' – denazification, demilitarization, decartelization and democratization, there was no real agreement on how this should in practice be
carried out. The Allies accepted the eventual restoration of a united, but

decentralized Germany, but 'for the time being' there was to be no German government, although central departments or ministries were to be set up for finance, transport, communications, foreign trade and industry. The allies confirmed that Germany should ultimately pay reparations of $20 billion, half of which should go to Russia, but failed to come to an agreement on how, and over what length of time this should be paid. A compromise was accepted which would enable the USSR and the Western powers to extract reparations from their own zones, although Britain and America would allocate 10 per cent of these to the USSR, and a further 15 per cent in exchange for food and raw materials from the Soviet Zone. The failure to devise an overall reparation policy did not bode well for the future of Germany. Molotov, the Soviet foreign minister, was quick to ask what, 'if reparations were not treated as a whole ... would happen to overall treatment of economic matters?'[2] Britain and America protested strongly over the delineation of Poland's western frontiers where, contrary to their wishes but with Soviet support, the Poles had annexed German territory right up to the western branch of the river Neisse, rather than to the eastern branch as had initially been agreed to. By July large-scale expulsions of Germans from Silesia and the Oder-Neisse region were already taking place.

See Map 8

See Documents 71 and 72

Germany under military government, 1945–1947

The four allied commanders on the Control Council in Berlin were supposed to apply the Potsdam guidelines to their joint administration of Germany but, as their governments increasingly could not agree on the country's future, each occupying power began to implement the Potsdam agreements in its own way and to reform German institutions and society according to its own standards.

Denazification and re-education

Twenty-two Nazi leaders, 12 of whom were sentenced to death, were tried by the international military tribunal at Nuremberg for conspiracy against peace and crimes against humanity. At a lower level in each zone, denazification was implemented with varying degrees of thoroughness. The Russians, convinced that Nazism was a product of German capitalism, removed not only Nazi officials, teachers and industrialists but also changed the whole economic structure of their zone. Thus the estates of big landowners, which were seen as breeding grounds for reactionaries, were broken up and the larger factories nationalized. The Americans pursued denazification initially with a fanatical zeal, and by December 1945 had arrested nearly double the number detained by the British.

Denazification, however, rapidly encountered major problems throughout Germany, as administrative and managerial personnel were removed from key positions and often replaced with incompetents. After a major coalmining disaster in the Ruhr in 1946, for instance, the British decided to tolerate ex-Nazis in key management posts as long as they could produce the coal. In October 1946 the Control Council divided the Germans into five categories ranging from major offenders to non-offenders and handed over the responsibility for their denazification to German tribunals working under Allied supervision Although this was a necessary step towards restoring self-government in Germany, the ruling by the German courts that all Germans seeking employment in official positions should have written statements confirmed by oath (affidavits) attesting to their good character was all too easily abused. As the Cold War intensified, denazification became an irrelevance and by early 1948 the four occupying powers had each declared the process to be at an end.

See Document 73

9 A German soldier returning to Berlin from a Yugoslav prisoner-of-war camp, June 1946

Presse- und Informationsamt der Bundesregierung, no. 111569

As the Potsdam Agreement had decreed that all traces of militarism and National Socialism were to be eliminated in order to prepare the way for the development of democracy, denazification was accompanied by ambitious attempts to reform the German education system. Nazi teachers were purged, old textbooks withdrawn and new teachers hastily trained. Again it was in the Russian Zone that the most radical reforms were implemented. Comprehensive schooling was introduced, although for the time being a selective sixth form was preserved for those going on to higher education, and universities were forced to practise positive discrimination in favour of the children of workers and peasants. The Western powers on the other hand failed to change the basic structure of the German education system, and both universities and the *Gymnasien* (grammar schools) managed to survive the occupation virtually unscathed.

Democratization and decentralization

The occupying powers were committed by the Potsdam Agreement both to decentralizing the political structure of Germany and to making local government more democratic. The Allied decision to break up Prussia in February 1947 allowed the non-Prussian states in western Germany at last to escape Prussian domination and cleared the way for the creation of a more balanced federal system. In the British Zone three new states, Schleswig-Holstein, Lower Saxony and North Rhine-Westphalia were created out of the former Prussian territory. The boundaries of the French and American Zones had been drawn up without regard to the historic borders of the south German states. Most of Bavaria was included in the American Zone, but the Zone's western regions, as one American official observed, were 'made up of such an assortment of legs, arms, fingers, ears and other stray pieces of dismembered body that one could hardly believe one's eyesight'.[3] Out of these **fragments** the Americans created Hesse and Württemberg-Baden, while the French, faced with a similar problem, joined together Baden and Württemberg-Hohenzollern. The Russian zone was divided into five states: Saxony, Mecklenburg, Saxony-Anhalt, Thuringia and Brandenburg.

Fragments: Only in 1952 was the state of Baden-Württemberg created

Each power had a different approach to reconstructing the German local government system. The British created a Central Economic Office, which was run by German officials subject to military government instructions, and treated their zone as a unified whole. The French, on the other hand, who wished to encourage separatism and hoped eventually to annex the Saar, had no coordinating body above the *Land* level. Both the French and the British believed, however, that political power should be conceded only gradually from the bottom upwards to the Germans, and it was not until the autumn of 1946 that municipal elections were held in both zones. The Americans, inspired by their own political traditions of federalism, rapidly restored the states governments in their zone. By the end of 1946 democratically elected states legislatures had met in Munich,

Wiesbaden and Stuttgart, but it was only in May 1947 that similar elections were held in the British and French Zones. The Russians set up governments in their states as early as July 1945, but they also formed what could have been the nucleus of either a central German or a Soviet zonal administration when they created 11 central zonal 'ministries. These, however, had only symbolic value, as according to an American observer, they 'had only fragmentary information'[4] about the economic situation in the provinces and had no power to influence them.

The re-emergence of political parties

The Russians allowed the formation of German political parties in their zone as early as June 1945, probably hoping that they would be able to use them as a means of projecting their own influence throughout Germany. The Americans hastily followed suit in August, the British a month later and the French not until December 1945. In all four zones similar party groupings emerged, consisting of the Communists (KPD), the Socialists (SPD), the Christian Democrats and the Liberals (LDPD).

German Party leaders and activists were determined not to re-create the divisive politics of the Weimar Republic, which they believed had done much to let the Nazis seize power in 1933. They therefore attempted to make their parties as inclusive as possible. The Christian Democratic Union (CDU) together with its sister party the CSU in Bavaria aimed to appeal to both south German and Rhineland Catholics as well as north German Protestants. It was, as a French newspaper commented, 'socialist and radical in Berlin, clerical and conservative in Cologne, capitalist and reactionary in Hamburg and counter-revolutionary and particularist in Munich.'[5] Its political opponents believed that it would collapse under the weight of these contradictions but they underestimated the political skills of **Konrad Adenauer**, who, after being dismissed by the British at the age of 70 from the post of *Oberbürgermeister* of Cologne, rapidly emerged as the most powerful man in the CDU. He was a pragmatist, who believed that party programmes were essentially 'instruments' for winning elections. Although he himself was convinced that 'with the word socialism we win five people and twenty run away',[6] he agreed in 1947 to compromise with the Christian–Socialist wing of the CDU and accept the Ahlen Programme, which advocated the nationalization of heavy industry and the major banks. This prevented a divisive row with Jakob Kaiser (1888–1961), the leader of the CDU in the Soviet Zone, who saw the party as a bridge between East and West, and enabled Adenauer to concentrate his efforts on building up the party's organization in the Western zones. With the intensification of the Cold War and Kaiser's flight to the West in December 1947, Adenauer was able to steer the CDU away from socialism in the direction of the market economy (see p. 332).

Despite its poor showing in 1932, liberalism as a political force also revived spontaneously in 1945. It appealed to those who disliked the CDU's close links with the Catholic Church, but who wanted a capitalist

Konrad Adenauer,
(1876–1967): Lord Mayor of Cologne, 1917–1933 and 1945; after the 20 July conspiracy briefly arrested, although innocent of involvement; chairman of CDU in British Zone, 1946–1949; President of Parliamentary Council, 1949; Chancellor of the FRG, 1949–1963; Chairman of the CDU, 1950–1966.

rather than a socialist economy. In 1947 a united Liberal party, the DDP, was founded at Eisenach under the joint chairmanship of Theodor Heuss (1884–1963) and Wilhelm Külz (1875–1948), the Liberal leaders in the Western and Soviet zones respectively. The DDP collapsed, however, when Külz supported the German People's Congress, which was convened by the East German Socialist Unity Party in Berlin in December 1947 (see p. 305) to oppose moves towards forming a West German state. The Liberal rump in West Germany then set up the broadly based Free Democratic Party (FDP) under the chairmanship of Heuss, which appealed to both supporters of the old right-wing National Liberal Party and the more left-wing Democratic party.

Initially the mood among the workers in both the Soviet and Western zones was to create one inclusive working-class party, but Stalin at first rejected this, hoping that the KPD would by itself be able to dominate the anti-Fascist bloc of parties in the Soviet Zone, which consisted of the CDU, KPD, SPD and the Liberals. By the autumn this policy was failing. The KPD and its leaders were seen as 'bullies and stooges'[7] of the Russians, and the SPD, as the larger party, represented a potential challenge to Soviet authority, especially with the emergence in the British Zone of **Kurt Schumacher** as its leader, who was bitterly hostile to cooperation with the Communists. Belatedly Stalin decided on the forced amalgamation of both parties. In February 1946, after several months of bribery and intimidation, the Central Executive of the SPD in the Soviet Zone voted for a new united party, the Socialist Unity Party of Germany, the SED, which was modelled on the Russian Communist Party.

The democratic credibility of the vote was implicitly challenged when **Wilhelm Pieck**, the chairman of the KPD, rashly agreed to submit the decision to a referendum of both SPD and KPD party members in Berlin on 31 March. In East Berlin the Russians were able to close down the polling stations half an hour after they had opened, but in Western zones of the city the voting continued and only 18 per cent of the SPD members approved of the amalgamation. This rejection was, however, qualified by a second vote. In response to the question of whether they supported 'an alliance ... which will guarantee continued cooperation and exclude fraternal strife', 62 per cent of the membership agreed. The SPD's amalgamation with the KPD in the Soviet Zone destroyed the claims of the SPD to be the strongest political party in Germany, and it was reduced to a rump party, with its electoral base in the industrialized areas in the British Zone.

Kurt Schumacher, (1895–1952): SPD member of the *Reichstag*, 1930–1933; interned in Dachau, 1933–1943; leader of the SPD, 1946–1952.

See Document 74

Wilhelm Pieck: (1876–1960): joined the KPD in 1919 and during the Third Reich was in exile in France and the USSR. He returned to Germany with the Red Army. From 1949 to 1960 president of the GDR.

The trade unions

At Potsdam the Germans were given the right to form trade unions, but the implementation of this was again left to the occupying powers. The Americans and the French encouraged the Germans to reconstruct the movement from the grassroots upwards, but it was in the more industrialized Soviet and British Zones that the future patterns of German trade unionism were to be created. The Russians backed the idea of a central-ized unitary trade union movement, because they hoped that the SED would be able to exploit it to exercise a decisive influence throughout Germany. Consequently the Free German Trade Union Association (FDGB) was formed in the Soviet Zone in February 1946 as a single trade union representing all German workers. In the British Zone trade union-ists at first also wanted a centralized organization, as it would avoid the divisions and weaknesses of the Weimar period. Hans Böckler (1875–1951), the future Chairman of the German Trade Unions Federation (DGB), put forward plans for a united general union, but the scheme was criticized by the military government and its British trade union advisers, who feared that this would both maximize Communist influence, and discourage members from actively participating. Böckler was persuaded to accept instead a scheme whereby independent unions were grouped together into an overall federation. In August 1947 the trade union move-ments in the American and British zones were fused, and were joined by those in the French Zone in December. At first there was considerable contact between trade unionists in the Western and Eastern zones but the onset of the Cold War made a united German trade union movement impossible to bring about.

The economy

As the Allies advanced into the Reich they witnessed scenes of 'indescrib-able, impenetrable chaos'.[8] To the west of Berlin nearly every town with a population of over 50,000 had been destroyed by British and American bombers. In Cologne, for instance, 72 per cent of the buildings were destroyed, while in Berlin the number was a high as 75 per cent. The railways had been paralysed by Allied bombing, and the main roads were blocked with long columns of refugees. It was no wonder that the Germans called it *Stunde null* (the year zero). Yet paradoxically, amid this destruction and misery, the preconditions for a German economic and political revival already existed. A surprising amount of industrial machinery had survived the bombing. In May 1945, compared to Britain, Germany still possessed double the number of machine tools. Even before the war had ended, in reaction to the stifling autarky of the Third Reich, some businessmen were also considering a return to a more liberal economy and had clandestinely made contact with free-market econo-mists such as Ludwig Erhard, the future economics minister of the FRG.

Initially in accordance with the Potsdam Agreement the Allies were committed to developing 'common policies' covering disarmament, decartelization, and land reform, and to maintaining a common currency and transport system as well as 'import and export programmes for Germany as a whole'. In reality the economies of the four zones were at first virtually sealed off from each other. The manufacturing industries in the Soviet Zone, for example, had no access to their markets in Western Germany and goods could only be exported to Western Europe if they were paid for in dollars, which no European country could afford. Coal

See Document 70

production in the Ruhr in 1946 was running at a third of its 1936 daily average, and Germany's main food-producing areas in the east – Pomerania and East and West Prussia, had been ceded to Poland. Food shortages were the single greatest cause of misery during the occupation, and it was not until the currency reform of 1948 (see p. 304) that rations approaching 2000 calories per day were available.

The *Reichsmark* currency, thanks to the ravages of wartime inflation, was almost valueless, and if the Allied powers had not continued the Third Reich's policy of freezing pay and prices, Germany would have been overwhelmed by hyperinflation. As long as the introduction of a new currency was delayed by Allied disagreements on the future of Germany, there were two distinct economies in Germany: one was 'the official economy, grinding along on the basis of rations, production plans and quotas',[9] while the other, the economy of barter or the **'black market'**, was the standard means by which individuals obtained food, and factories their raw materials.

Black market: illegal traffic in officially rationed or very scarce commodities

In March 1946 the four occupying powers published the 'Plan for Reparations and the Level of the Post-War German Economy', which aimed to limit post-war production to the level of 1932, but it was never implemented, since the Allies were unable to reach any agreement on the future of Germany as a political or economic entity. Both the Russians and French ruthlessly exploited their zones in the interests of their home economies. By 1949 the Russians had probably already extracted the $10 billion reparations they had claimed at Potsdam. The Soviet authorities siphoned off reparations from current production by converting factories which had previously been privately owned into SAGs (Soviet limited companies), which by the end of 1946 produced some 30 per cent of the zone's industrial output.

The four powers also failed to agree on a common policy for land reform and the restructuring of German industry. The most radical steps were undertaken in the Soviet Zone where by 1948 both the key industries had been nationalized and the large estates and farms divided up. The British Labour government also attempted to break up (decartelize) and then nationalize the component parts of the great industrial cartels in the Ruhr, but nationalization was halted by the formation of the Bizone (see p. 302) in January 1947, which gave America an effective veto over economic policy in the British Zone. The Americans were determined that decartelization should only take place within the overall context of a capitalist economy, and the whole problem was consequently left for a West German government to solve later (see p. 333).

By the end of 1947, in the absence of any effective central control, Germany was already divided into two distinct economic zones: the American-controlled, capitalist west and the Soviet-dominated, socialist east. There were some signs of economic recovery in the Anglo-American Bizone. Production climbed up to half the 1936 level and manufacturers were beginning to rebuild their plants, accumulating stocks of raw materials in preparation for an economic upturn. The Russians only began to develop a comprehensive economic strategy for the reconstruction of their zone in June 1947, when, in response to the Bizone, they set up the

German Economic Commission to administer the economy of their zone (see p. 303). To increase production, the Soviet Military Administration (SMAD) attempted to mobilize the workforce in their zone, and in October 1947 issued Order 234, which 'amounted to a full blown transfer of Soviet style labour relations to East Germany'.[10] Key factories were allocated special deliveries of food, and efforts were made to improve their working conditions by the introduction of welfare provisions such as crèches and medical clinics. People's Control Committees were set up to stop thefts on the factory floor, and workers were to be paid piece rates. Order 234 started, according to Jeffrey Kopstein, the crucial process in East Germany of 'refashioning the factory as a social and political as opposed to purely economic institution'[11] (see p. 347).

Was the occupation a missed opportunity for radical reform?

The question, as far as the Western zones were concerned, was a matter of heated discussion, particularly in the 1960s and 1970s. Lutz Niethammer has, for instance, shown that the number of ex-Nazis in the states administration in the American Zone was greater than the numbers of Nazi Party members employed in the equivalent area before the war. He argued that denazification was a superficial process that permitted a large number of ex-Nazis to regain their positions 'with a fresh white waistcoat'. There were similar arguments about the failure to change the education system. David Welch, for instance, speaks for many when he says that a major opportunity 'to break with the past was lost'. Other historians (E. Schmidt) regret the failed attempts to reform the civil service and the total and speedy abolition of cartels (Abelshauser).[12] It is all too true that many ex-Nazis did return to power and influence, but they did so in a society in which the appeal of Nazism had been shattered through defeat, and where as a result of the Nuremberg trials the history of Nazi atrocities had become well known. The failure to reform the universities certainly fuelled the student unrest of the 1960s (see p. 354), but they did not become the reserve of the nationalist right as they did during the Weimar Republic. The ambitious reform programmes of the Western powers, particularly the British were curtailed by the Cold War and the resulting swing to the bourgeois right throughout Western Europe in the early 1950s. In the Soviet Zone, on the other hand, there really was a fundamental social and political revolution.

The decision to set up a West German state and the Soviet response, 1946–May 1949

In the 1950s there was little doubt in the West that the blame for starting the Cold War and the partition of Germany lay squarely with the USSR. Yet an analysis of the events leading up to the division shows that the

10 Leaflet scattered on the West German side of the inner German border July 1967. It is informing the West German frontier guards that the commander of the southern border section of the frontier force (*Bundesgrenzschutz*), General Otto Dippelhofer (1909–1989), had been a member of the SS

Western powers 'repeatedly took initiatives to which Soviet measures came largely as a response'.[13] Of course it is true that events such as the ruthless suppression of opposition in Poland by the communists and the shotgun marriage of the SPD–KPD to create the SED bred an atmosphere of fear in the West, but it is, nevertheless, at least arguable that Western actions in light of the perceived Soviet threat precipitated the division of Germany.

The Bizone and the German Economic Commission, 1946–1947

The failure to agree on a joint reparation policy at the Potsdam Conference was already a step towards partition. In May 1946 the USSR refused to accept an inter-zonal import–export plan proposed by General Clay (1897–1978), the American military governor, as it would have involved waiting for the delivery of reparations until the German economy had recovered sufficiently to finance its own essential imports of food and raw materials. Clay responded by announcing that no further reparation deliveries would be made from the American Zone until German economic unity was restored. Shortly afterwards at the Paris Conference of Foreign Ministers in July James Byrnes, the American Secretary of State, repeated this message, but he also offered to integrate the American zone economically with the other three zones in an effort to bring about German economic unity on terms acceptable to Washington. Only the

British, faced with spending what was then the huge sum of $320 million per year on their zone, accepted.

On 6 September American policy on the future of Germany became clearer still when Byrnes announced at Stuttgart that there should be no delays to economic reconstruction and that more power should be handed over to the Germans to run their own affairs. The economic merger of the British and American Zones to form Bizonia on 1 January 1947 marked the beginning of economic and eventually political partition. Initially Britain and the US went out of their way to allay Soviet suspicions that it was a political entity in embryo. There was to be no central council and the Bizone's offices were located in five different cities. Only with the failure of the Moscow Foreign Ministers' Conference in April 1947 did it begin to acquire some of the characteristics of a provisional administration.

At the Moscow Foreign Ministers' Conference, March–April 1947, a key role was played by Ernest Bevin (1881–1951), the British foreign secretary, who was convinced that Stalin would only consent to a united Germany if he believed that the Communists would dominate it.[14] To continue with the pretence of four-power rule in Germany would simply prolong the economic and political deadlock and ensure that the escalating cost of feeding the Germans in the heavily industrialized British zone would fall on the British government at a time when Britain was virtually bankrupt. Bevin believed therefore that it was imperative to set up, as a temporary measure, an independent and economically self-supporting West German state. Bevin successfully persuaded the Americans to drop a proposal which would have enabled the Russians to receive reparations from the current production of coal and steel in the Ruhr, and focus instead on rebuilding the West German economy. The conference therefore ended without any effective decision on Germany's future.

In July Britain and the US agreed to permit the level of production within the Bizone to reach the levels achieved in 1936. The pretence was also dropped that the Bizone had no political importance. Its offices were now centralized at Frankfurt, and to these were added an Economic Council made up of 52 members who were chosen by the state assemblies, and an Executive Committee, composed of the directors of the Bizonal administrative agencies. This had the powers, subject to overall Anglo-American approval, to promulgate laws on economic matters and to ensure that they were carried out, as well as to appoint and remove the directors of the Bizonal economic agencies. The composition of the Economic Council reflected the composition of the state parliaments: the SPD and the CDU combined with its sister party in Bavaria, the Christian Social Union (CSU), were each given 20 seats. The remaining 12 seats were distributed among the smaller parties, most of which, with the exception of the KPD, were more inclined towards the CDU than the SPD. A glimpse of the politics of the future West German state can already be seen in the struggle over the appointments of the senior officials who would run the five administrative offices of the Bizone.

When the SPD group failed to secure its preferred candidates, it retired into opposition, and the council's business was carried out by the other parties led by the CDU–CSU, the so-called Frankfurt Coalition. In retrospect the Bizone was, to quote the historian Theodor Eschenburg, the 'germ cell and prefiguration' of the future federal republic of Germany.[15]

The formation of the Economic Council and the streamlining of the Bizonal administration confirmed Soviet suspicions that the Bizone was a political as well as economic entity. Stalin began therefore to strengthen the Soviet Zone by setting up the German Economic Commission in June 1947. Its task was to coordinate economic policy and, with the assistance of the SMAD, to draw up a zonal economic plan. The Commission was composed of the heads of the zone's ministries, the chairmen of the zonal federation of the trade unions (FDGB) and the farmers' association (VdgB), both of which were controlled by the SED. As with the Bizone, it can in retrospect be called the 'germ cell' of a future German state – the GDR, although the Russians played down its political and economic significance by emphasizing that it was firmly under control of the Soviet military government.

The Marshall Plan, the OEEC and the Cominform

While the emergence of Bizonia anticipated the creation of a West German state, the Marshall Plan created the international context in which the new state would eventually have to function. On 5 June 1947 the American Secretary of State, George Marshall, announced the European Recovery Programme (ERP) or Marshall Plan, which offered economic aid to Europe, provided the recipient states agreed on a common programme and a liberal free trade system. While this offer was enthusiastically accepted by the Western European nations, Stalin saw this as further evidence of Washington's efforts to create an American-dominated, capitalist, West European block. In September he set up the Cominform, the Communist Information Bureau, which would coordinate the policies and tactics of the communist parties throughout Europe. The Cominform was welcomed by the SED, which was only too aware that the economic misery within the Soviet Zone made the Marshall Plan potentially attractive to the East Germans. In April 1948 the Organization for European Economic Cooperation was set up by the Western European states to distribute the ERP funds, and both Bizonia and the French zone were represented on it.

Steps towards the creation of a West German state

When the next foreign ministers' conference met in London in November, 'partition seem[ed] to be in the air',[16] as General Robertson, the British military governor, observed. The conference ended in deadlock. The USSR accused the Western Allies of breaking the Potsdam Agreement, while the latter rejected proposals from Moscow for setting up a central German government on the grounds that this would merely facilitate the spread of communism throughout Germany. As soon as the conference broke up, Bevin and Marshall in bilateral discussions decided that, in the absence of any agreement with the Soviets on a single German currency, the Western Zones would have to be given a new currency. More importantly, the decision was taken to create over the coming year what would in effect be a West German state based on the Bizone, which would now be expanded to include the French Zone. Bevin also stressed that the option for genuinely free elections for an all-German government should still be left open by the Western powers. He hoped that this offer would ensure that 'that any **irredentist** German movement should be based on the west rather than the east'. In other words, a democratic West Germany would, he hoped, ultimately act as a 'magnet' to attract the Soviet Zone, rather than the other way round.[17]

To work out how to implement these decisions, Britain, France, the USA and the Benelux states conferred in London from February to early June. A note of urgency was given to the proceedings by the **Communist seizure of power in Czechoslovakia** at the end of February. French cooperation was assured by an Anglo-American endorsement of the formation of a customs union between France and the Saar in April 1948. On 2 June plans were announced for setting up a West German state. The West Germans were authorized to convene a constituent assembly or 'Parliamentary Council' whose members would be selected by the state parliaments. On 20 June a new currency, the *Deutschmark*, was introduced into Bizonia and the French Zone, and 3 days later into West Berlin. In itself this was a major step towards an independent West Germany.

Irredentist: demanding the restoration to a country of land originally belonging to it

Communist seizure of power in Czechoslovakia: The Czech Communists used their control of the trade unions and police on 22 February to seize power in Prague. Elections were held on 30 May on the basis of a single National Front list, which committed all the parties to supporting a manifesto approved by Moscow.

Currency reform in the Western zones and the Soviet zone, June 1948

1 In the West

- The *Deutschmark* (DM) was introduced to replace the *Reichsmark*. Every West German was immediately allowed to change 40 marks at a 1:1 rate and then 2 months later they could exchange a further 20. Businesses were given an allowance of 60 DM per worker towards their wage costs.
- Wages, salaries, pensions and share dividends were protected and converted into DM at the rate of 1:1. The tough measures aimed at cutting down the volume of notes in circulation hurt the small saver as opposed to owners of shares or real estate. Those who had money on deposit in the banks had to exchange the old currency for the new at a ratio of 100 *Reichsmarks* to DM 6.50.
- The banks were granted generous deposits of DM which enabled them to extend credit to business and industry.
- The Western Allies protected the new currency by making the *Bank Deutscher Länder* into an independent central bank with responsibility for managing the currency. They also laid down that public authorities must not run up debts unless they were covered by current income.

2 **In the East**

The introduction of the *Ostmark* (the East German Mark) on 23 June penalized the remaining independent industrialists and businessmen in the Soviet Zone. Their financial assets were converted at a rate varying from 3 to 10 *Reichsmarks* to 1 *Ostmark*, while the financial assets of the state-owned factories (VEBs), *Land* governments, trade unions and the SED was converted at the rate of 1:1. Effectively the currency reform was exploited by the Russians to ensure a partial confiscation of all investments and savings still in the private sector.

The German People's Congresses for Unity and Just Peace

To counter the decision to create a West German state, the Russians tried to play on the many reservations which West Germans inevitably had about the impending partition of their country. Walther Ulbricht, the First Secretary of the SED, called two German People's Congresses (*Volkscongresse*) for Unity and Just Peace. Their task was to mobilize public opinion right across Germany against partition. The first congress met in early December 1947 in Berlin. Roughly a third of those attending came from the West, but they were mainly delegates from the KPD strongholds in the Ruhr. In March 1948 the second congress met and set out to evoke the revolutionary spirit of 1848 (see Chapter 3). It elected a German People's Council (*Volksrat*) of 400 delegates to prepare for a referendum on German unity and to draw up an all-German constitution, which could also serve temporarily as the basis for an East German constitution, should it be impossible to thwart the Anglo-American plans for an independent West Germany. In May Wilhelm Pieck told the party's leadership cadres that once a West German state was created, the Soviet Zone would inevitably have to 'develop its own independent state structure'. It was immaterial whether the Western powers 'tore Germany apart … a month earlier or a month later. The important thing was to be prepared for every eventuality.'[18]

The Berlin Blockade, June 1948–May 1949

On 23 June the Russians responded to the currency reform in the West by introducing the new *Ostmark* in the Soviet Zone. Ostensibly to stop their zone from being inundated with devalued *Reichsmarks*, they imposed a blockade on West Berlin during the night of 23–24 June, which was to last until 12 May 1949. In reality, of course, this was an attempt to stop the creation of a West German state. The rail and road links to the West were cut and the supply of electricity from East Berlin to the Western sectors was halted. The blockade rapidly became a struggle which America and its allies could not afford to lose if their plans for the construction of a West German state were to be realized. The immediate response of the Western Allies was the airlift which, contrary to expectations, managed to supply West Berlin with food and fuel

See Map 9

throughout the relatively mild winter of 1948–1949. Unsure that the airlift would succeed, the Western Allies initially discussed with the Russians in August 1948 the option of allowing the *Ostmark* to become the sole currency for the whole of Berlin, subject only to the control of a four-power financial commission, but the talks broke down once it became obvious that Moscow's primary aim was to drive the Western powers from Berlin and to force them to abandon their plans for a West German state. Consequently, in spite of efforts by the United Nations to mediate, the blockade continued until 9 May 1949, when Stalin, realizing that it had failed, called it off. For Soviet policy its consequences were a disaster: it not only facilitated the integration of the Western Zones into an American-dominated Western Europe but it also ensured that the Western part of Berlin would eventually become an economic, political and social outpost of West Germany.

The birth of the two Germanies

The constitutions for the two German states were drawn up against the threatening background of the Berlin crisis. The East and West German political elites had in common a 'deep distrust of the common man'.[19] In the West this took the form of creating a complex constitutional system of checks and balances, which would ensure stability and consensus. In the East, despite references to the power of the 'people', it took the form of creating a one-party dictatorship. Neither set of politicians were free agents, as their constitutions had to be approved of by their respective occupying powers. The West German politicians were, however, in a stronger position than their counterparts in the SED, as there was a broad consensus both on the left and on the right in support of a democratic constitution, and they were skilfully able to exploit the differences between Britain, France and America to achieve concessions. The SED leaders, on the other hand, were dependent on Stalin for their survival, and it was always possible that a change of policy in Moscow could still consign their constitution, and indeed state, to the dustbin.

Carlo Schmid, 1896–1979: lawyer, later judge; 1940–1944, bureaucrat in the German military administration in France and Belgium; 1945–1947, head of the German administration in Württemberg-Hohenzollern under the French; 1947 joined the SPD and was elected to its executive. As son of a French mother, an ardent supporter of Franco-German reconciliation.

The Federal Republic

The first draft of the constitution was drawn up by a committee of constitutional experts and then analysed in depth by the Parliamentary Council, which was elected by the *Länder* parliaments. The CDU–CSU and the SPD each had 27 seats, but on social and economic questions the former could count on the backing of the five Liberals (FDP) and the smaller parties, while the SPD could only sometimes rely on the support of the two KPD members. The SPD made a serious tactical mistake when it decided to accept Adenauer's nomination as president of the Parliamentary Council in return for allowing its own **Carlo Schmid** to chair the main committee. Adenauer was able to exploit this position to turn himself into a national figure, which was to be much to his advantage in the election campaign of August 1949 (see p. 308).

In Peter Pulzer's words, the founding fathers of the Bonn constitution (the Basic Law) were 'burnt children who knew what fire was like. Their vision was one of disaster-avoidance, not a new heaven and a new earth'.[20] The Basic Law was a 'hybrid' or 'mixture of Weimar traditionalism and a determination to reform'.[21] The Parliamentary Council inevitably drew on the Weimar model (see p. 191), but it was also determined to improve it. The intention of Article 67, for example, was to prevent a repetition of the unstable coalition governments of the Weimar period by laying down that a chancellor could only be forced to resign if there was already a majority in the lower house (***Bundestag***) for his successor. Similarly, according to Article 68 the president could only call an election before the statutory end of a parliament, provided the *Bundestag* after 21 days had failed to choose a new chancellor. There were to be no referenda, except on local matters, and the president was not to be directly elected by the people but chosen by the Federal Convention, a body made up of an equal number of *Bundestag* and state representatives (Article 54). In the first 19 articles of the constitution, basic human rights such as freedom of conscience and speech and the right to property were guaranteed, and provision was made for setting up a federal constitutional court to interpret the constitution. The Basic Law was essentially a compromise and, unlike the Weimar constitution, did not seek to define the future socio-economic shape of the state. Article 6, which committed the state to protecting 'marriage and family', was welcomed by the Churches, but no special protection was afforded to denominational schools, while the trade unions were disappointed that there was no mention of co-determination or nationalization of key industries (see p. 334). One of the most controversial issues debated by the Parliamentary Council was the powers of the *Bundesrat,* the upper house. Neither Adenauer nor the SPD wanted a strong *Bundesrat* which would be able to veto bills coming up from the *Bundestag.* On the other hand, the CDU did not want an upper house in which the majority of delegations would be appointed by the predominantly SPD state governments. In the end a compromise was reached whereby the state were represented in the *Bundesrat* by delegates selected by the state governments on the basis of their population. As most of the smaller states were SPD-controlled, this would ensure that they would be balanced by the larger, predominantly CDU–CSU states like Bavaria.

When the Parliamentary Council presented the final draft of the Basic Law to the military governors for their approval, changes were demanded in two areas: initially at any rate, West Berlin was not to be part of the federation, and the federal nature of the constitution was to be reinforced by giving the state greater fiscal powers. On 8 May the Parliamentary Council finally approved the amended Basic Law and 2 days later it decided that the provisional seat of government should be Bonn. With the exception of Bavaria, the state legislatures ratified the Basic Law, but

Bundestag: literally means the federal assembly. The term *Bund* (federation) was used to stress the decentralized structure of the new FRG.

See Document 75
and Map 8

even the Bavarians were arguably 'whisper[ing] "yes" in the same breath as shouting "no"',[22] as they consented in a second vote to accept the law as long as two-thirds of the states had already approved it.

The date for the general election was fixed for 14 August. Fifty per cent of the deputies were to be elected by a direct constituency vote, while the rest were to be selected from party lists compiled on the basis of the states. There was also a 'barrier clause' under which a party had to win 5 per cent of the total votes in order to win any seats in the *Bundestag*. The campaign was dominated by Schumacher and Adenauer, who made the main theme of his campaign a veritable crusade against the SPD's plans for creating a Socialist economy. He was helped by his alliance with Erhard, the economics director of the Bizone, whose social market economic policies (see p. 332) were apparently beginning to show some signs of success. Adenauer also benefited from Schumacher's ill-judged attack on the Catholic Church as the 'fifth occupying power', which inevitably irritated many Catholic voters. The CDU–CSU with 139 seats just managed to beat the SPD, which won 131 seats, while the FDP gained 52. When the *Bundestag* met in September, Adenauer was elected the first chancellor of the Federal Republic (FRG), supported by an FDP–CDU–CSU coalition. Many of his party would have preferred a grand coalition with the SPD, but Schumacher's insistence that he would only consider it if the SPD controlled the Economics Ministry effectively ruled that option out.

The German Democratic Republic

For Stalin the division of Germany was a major defeat. Not only would partition make it much more difficult for the USSR to influence German politics at national level, but it would also ensure that the massive economic potential of the Ruhr would be harnessed by the Western powers. Therefore as long as there was still the chance of a restoration of four-power control and the eventual creation of a neutral German state potentially friendly to the USSR, the Russians were reluctant to set up an independent East German state. Once it became obvious that the Berlin blockade had failed, Stalin cautiously allowed the SED to draw up plans for a separate East German state as long as they did not exclude the possibility of German unity. This caution was not shared by the SED leadership, which wanted sole control of a Communist East German state. During the spring and summer of 1949 the SED leadership pursued a dual policy. On the one hand it created an all-German National Front based on the People's Congress movement (see p. 305), which in deference to Stalin's policy would enable the SED to pose as the 'champion of national unity' in contrast to the 'splitters' in the West. On the other hand it worked to persuade the Soviet occupying authorities to allow the party greater political independence, which they hoped would 'lift the burden of guilt by association – for the rape, plunder, repression and economic exploitation by Soviet forces',[23] which had acted to the party's detriment since 1945.

The People's Council (*Volksrat*), which had been elected by the Congress for Unity and Just Peace (see p. 305) approved in March 1949 the constitution of the future German Democratic Republic (GDR). Although on paper its constitution appeared to be not so different from the Basic Law, in reality it was a 'make-believe constitution',[24] which attempted to camouflage a one-party dictatorship. Its citizens were theoretically guaranteed the fundamental democratic rights of freedom of speech and freedom of the press, and the right to strike and even to emigrate. Superficially the parliament was not dissimilar to the model adopted in the FRG. The *Volkskammer* (People's Chamber) was to be elected for 4 years under a system of proportional representation, while the upper house, the Chamber of States, was a watered-down version of the *Bundesrat*. In May, elections for a third People's Congress were held. The voters were presented with a single list of candidates representing the mass organizations (trade unions, etc.) and the **bloc parties**, which included the Soviet Zone Christian Democrats (CDUD) and the Liberal Democrats (LDPD). The leaders of these parties still believed that by forming an electoral bloc with the SED they would act as a bridge to their sister parties in the FRG. The voters were also asked whether they were 'for or against German unity and a just peace treaty'. This was, as they knew, in reality an appeal to support the creation of an East German state. Despite a massive propaganda campaign and considerable manipulation of the voting results, it was impossible to hide the fact that a third of the electorate had voted against the proposals, which was enough to convince the SED leadership that elections to the *Volkskammer* needed to be delayed for at least a year.

Stalin did not give his final consent to setting up the East German state until the outcome of the August elections in West Germany had made it clear that no compromise was possible with the Western powers. On 7 October the People's Congress proclaimed the formation of the German Democratic Republic (GDR) as 'a powerful bulwark in the struggle for the accomplishment of the National Front of Democratic Germany'.[25] SMAD was replaced by the Soviet Control Commission, and most of its responsibilities were transferred to the GDR. For the time being the People's Council became the provisional parliament, and a government headed by Otto Grotewohl, the former chairman of the central Council of the SPD, and **Walther Ulbricht**, who as party secretary of the SED wielded the real power, was formed on 12 October. Although Stalin might still have entertained the possibility of sacrificing the GDR for the reunification of a neutral Germany, Gerhart Eisler (1897–1968), the director of the information department of the Economic Commission remarked prophetically at a meeting on 4 October that 'once we have set up a government, we will never give it up, neither through elections or other methods'. Ulbricht then added 'A few still have not understood this.'[26]

Bloc parties: In July 1945 SMAD created the anti-Fascist bloc of parties in the Soviet zone. By 1948 it was composed of the CDUD, LDPD, DBD (Farmers Party), NDPD (National Democratic Party of Germany) and SED.

Otto Grotewohl, (1894–1964): SPD deputy, 1925–1933; active in the SPD underground, 1933–1938; Chairman of the Central Council of the SPD, 1945–1946 ; Minister-President of GDR, 1949–1964.

Walther Ulbricht, (1893–1973): KPD member of *Reichstag*, 1928–1933; Secretary of the KPD's Politburo in exile in Moscow, 1933–1945; co-founder of the National Committee for a Free Germany, 1943; General Secretary/First secretary of the SED, 1946–1971; Chairman of GDR's State Council, 1960–1963.

Conclusion

The defeat of the German Reich in 1945 led, as in 1806–1807 (see p. 15), to massive territorial changes in Germany. The historic state of Prussia lost its eastern territories, and in 1947 was dissolved. The influence of the east Elbian Junker landowners had been finally eliminated by the death of many of the traditional officer class on the Eastern Front and the liquidation of their estates, and often their families too, by the advancing Red Army. At Potsdam the wartime allies accepted a united, although territorially diminished, Germany. However, lack of agreement above all about reparations and the economy led to its partition. For Stalin the creation of the FRG was a major defeat, which left the Ruhr and the greater part of Germany in the hands of the Western Allies. The GDR has been described by Willy Loth as Stalin's 'unwanted child',[27] since its creation was essentially a response to the policies of the Western Allies. Whether partition could have been avoided is open to debate. Perhaps some sort of neutral Germany could have emerged, but the Western Allies were not alone in distrusting Stalin's motives. The record of raping and pillage committed by the Red Army in 1945 was, in the eyes of the West Germans, a major deterrent to risking a neutral Germany, which might be vulnerable to Soviet pressure. These fears were evident when the minister-presidents of the states in the four zones of occupation met in Munich in June 1947 to discuss national unity. The conference rapidly ended in stalemate as the East Germans proposed a centralized model of government, while their West German colleagues rejected it on the grounds that it would lead to Soviet domination.

15 The Cold War and the Two Germanies, 1950–1988

TIMELINE

1949	22 November	Petersberg Treaty
1950	25 June	Outbreak of Korean War
	9 August	FRG constitution extended to West Berlin
	8 September	GDR joined Comecon
1951	15 April	European Coal and Steel Community replaced Ruhr Authority
1952	10 March	Stalin's note proposing a united but neutral Germany
	26 May	General Treaty signed in Bonn
	27 May	EDC Treaty signed in Paris
1953	5 March	Stalin's death
	16–18 June	Strikes and disturbances in GDR
1954	26 February	Basic Law amended to permit creation of *Bundeswehr*
	31 August	French Assembly rejects EDC
	19–23 October	London Conference
1955	5 May	FRG became a sovereign state
	9 May	FRG joined NATO
	14 May	Warsaw Pact set up
	9–13 September	Adenauer's Moscow visit
	20 September	USSR recognized GDR's sovereignty
	22 September	Hallstein Doctrine announced
1956	23 October–4 November	Hungarian uprising crushed
1957	25 March	Treaty of Rome signed creating EEC
1958	27 November	Khrushchev issued Berlin ultimatum
1961	13 August	Border between East and West Berlin closed. Start of construction of Berlin Wall
1963	22 January	The Élysée Treaty
1968	21 August	Warsaw Pact intervened in Czechoslovakia
1970	19 March	Stoph–Brandt meeting at Erfurt
	12 August	FRG–USSR Treaty signed in Moscow
	7 December	FRG–Polish Treaty signed
1971	3 September	Four-Power agreement on Berlin
1972	21 December	Basic Treaty signed between FRG and GDR
1973	11 December	Prague Treaty between FRG and Czechoslovakia
1975	1 August	Helsinki Declaration
1979	14 December	NATO's 'twin-track' decision
1980	13 December	Martial law declared in Poland
1985	11 March	Gorbachev, General Secretary of Communist party of USSR
1987	7–11 September	Honecker's visit to FRG

Introduction: problems, issues and questions

The two German states were the products of the Cold War. The Federal Republic traced its origins to the Bismarckian Empire and, until Willy Brandt's *Ostpolitik*, claimed the former German territory beyond the Oder–Neisse line, while the GDR argued that, unlike its rival in the West, it had made a true break with the past. As a result of the 'popular revolution', which purged the Soviet Zone of Nazism in the immediate post-war years, it alone could claim the moral high ground and represent the new Germany. Its historical mission, or so it proclaimed, was to create a united Marxist German workers' state purged of both capitalism and remnants.

In the early 1950s both the GDR and FRG were *de facto* protectorates of the occupying powers. In West Germany the **Occupation Statute**, which the new West German state had to sign with its former occupiers in 1949, gave the Allied high commissioners extensive rights to control foreign policy, approve domestic legislation and intervene whenever they felt that these rights might be threatened. Similarly in the GDR, the Soviet Control Commission was in reality a 'parallel government'[1] which was possessed of even wider powers. Both states were integrated at varying speeds into the opposing economic, political and military systems of their occupiers. The Cold War and the division of Europe created the parameters within which the two states conducted their foreign policies and attempted to come to terms with the consequences of the lost war.

Did this situation ensure that the FRG remained a satellite of the USA, and the GDR of the USSR until the end of the Cold War, or did both states in fact wield considerable influence within their rival blocs? What were their aims? Did each desire to reunite Germany in its own image or was self-preservation the real priority of each state? Certainly the construction of the Berlin Wall was clearly a defensive act, but how can the *Ostpolitik* pursued by Willy Brandt and his successors be understood? Was its main thrust essentially to appease the GDR and to mitigate the consequences of partition or did it in reality have the more subtle agenda of undermining the whole regime?

Occupation Statute: In 1949 the new West German government had to accept the Occupation Statute, by which the former Western occupying powers retained far-reaching powers to determine the foreign and economic policy of the FRG. In an emergency they also had the right to take over full powers to protect their troops stationed in West Germany.

Adenauer and Western integration, 1949–1954

For Adenauer Western integration was the 'great hope of the 1950s'[2] because it offered the dual prospect of close cooperation with the Western European democracies and security within an Atlantic community dominated by the USA. In time it would also become a means for revising the Occupation Statute and securing greater independence for the FRG. Integration was also supported by Washington and its allies, for whom it was not only the means for containing Soviet Russia, but also a way of preventing the re-emergence of a strong, belligerent Germany.

Adenauer cleverly exploited the situation created by the Cold War to achieve an ever-closer integration of the FRG into Western Europe. His first foreign policy success came with the Petersberg Agreement in November 1949. This permitted the FRG 'to re-enter the international sphere'[3] by joining the recently created Council of Europe and the OEEC (see p. 303) as an independent state, to open consulates in other countries and to have a seat on the board of the **International Authority of the Ruhr**. Adenauer had already floated ideas for joint Franco-German ownership of the Ruhr, and was therefore receptive to Schuman's plan for the pooling of the European coal and steel industries under supranational control to create a European Coal and Steel Community (ECSC), which would replace the International Authority of the Ruhr. He understood only too well that this plan was also a means for ensuring that France retained more influence over the Ruhr than its economic strength warranted, yet to him these concessions were worth making. By preventing Franco-German economic rivalry, the ECSC treaty of 18 April 1951 broke the long tradition of Franco-German hostility, and 'fulfilled many of the functions of a peace treaty'[4] between the two powers.

> **The International Authority of the Ruhr** had been set up in 1948 to control the production and export of the Ruhr's coal, coke and steel.

Adenauer also believed that European integration could solve the difficult question of German rearmament. As early as the spring of 1950, he was urging the creation of an armed security police and a West German military component to 'an international legion'.[5] The outbreak of the Korean War in June led to increasing demands for a West German defence contribution. The French responded with the proposal for a European Defence Community (the Pleven Plan or EDC) in which West German troops would be firmly subordinated to a European Defence Commission. Adenauer immediately grasped that he could use German rearmament as a means of persuading the Western powers to abolish the Occupation Statute and grant sovereignty to the FRG.

In May 1952 both the EDC Treaty and the General Treaty were signed. By the latter agreement the Western powers consented to abolish the Occupation Statute and recognize the sovereignty of the Federal Republic. They also pledged to work for a reunified, democratic Germany modelled on the existing FRG and anchored firmly in the growing Western European community. As the Western powers still maintained their rights to negotiate, at some future date, a peace treaty with a united Germany, the question of the eastern frontiers was left open. This complex web of treaties completely unravelled when France refused to ratify the EDC Treaty on 30 August 1954. By guaranteeing to keep the size of the West German army to what had been agreed in the EDC Treaty and by voluntarily renouncing nuclear weapons, Adenauer ensured that a new General Treaty was rapidly negotiated in October. France, weakened by its defeat in Indochina, did not oppose the FRG's entry into NATO in May 1955. The Western Allies repeated their commitment to work towards a united federal Germany integrated into the European community, but until that happened units of their troops would still be based in the FRG, and Berlin would remain under four-power control.

See Map 9

Hans-Peter Schwarz has argued that the 1955 treaties compare favourably with the Vienna Settlement of 1815 (see pp. 25–27). A new, stable West European state system had been created, which was to survive virtually unchanged up to 1990, but this success was paid for by Germany. Although, in theory, the door was kept open for reunification, in practice the integration of the FRG into NATO, the ECSC and the Council of Europe made this unity impossible to achieve in the foreseeable future. To use Klessmann's phrase, Western integration intensified 'the reactive mechanism'[6] of the Cold War, which led to the GDR's ever-deeper integration into the Soviet bloc. This was the danger Kurt Schumacher was referring to when he committed the SPD in 1950 to opposing any agreement that did not 'leave open and even strengthen the possibilities of German unity'.[7] Adenauer's *Westpolitik* had the support of most West Germans, but it was, in Hermann Graml's words, 'constantly subjected to furious detailed criticism and anxious attempts to apply the brakes,'[8] because it cemented the division of Germany into two states.

See Document 76

Soviet efforts to halt the FRG's integration into the West

Moscow and the GDR tried to exploit this fear of the consequences of Western integration to halt West German rearmament. From the autumn of 1950 through to the spring of 1952 the Russians and the GDR leadership proposed a series of initiatives aimed at achieving a united but neutral Germany. How far these initiatives were genuine offers or just attempts to slow down Western integration and to destabilize the Adenauer regime is a matter of heated historical debate. The most controversial of these initiatives was launched by Stalin in March 1952 when he proposed an independent Germany and free national elections supervised by a commission of the four former occupying powers. Germany would have to accept permanent neutrality, but would be spared reparations and be free to form any government its people voted for. It would even be allowed to have a small army. In Hans-Peter Schwarz's words a 'certain mythology'[9] grew up around the history of this note, as it did with 'the stab in the back' myth of 1918 (see p. 194). There was a strong body of West German opinion, led by Schumacher, Jakob Kaiser, the minister for all German affairs, who had been the leader of the CDUD in the Soviet Zone but had fled to the West in 1947, and Paul Sethe, the influential editor of the *Frankfurter Allgemeine* newspaper, that was convinced that Adenauer should have been more responsive to Stalin's initiative. This view has been supported more recently by Rolf Steininger and Willy Loth, although rejected strongly by other historians such as Hans-Peter Schwarz and Gerhard Wettig.[10] Neither Adenauer nor the Western powers, however, were ready to jeopardize all that had so far been achieved in integrating the FRG economically and militarily into the West. Adenauer was also sceptical as to whether Stalin would risk the potential domino effect which self-determination for the GDR would have on the other Soviet satellites in eastern Europe. Consequently the Soviet initiative was never seriously taken up.

The GDR and German unity

The GDR **Politburo** was divided over how unity could be achieved. In the autumn of 1950 Ulbricht, who could only envisage German unity if it resulted in the creation of a Stalinist Germany, was isolated, while Otto Grotwohl, supported by other 'liberals' like Rudolph Herrnstadt (1903–1968), editor of the GDR paper *Neues Deutschland* and Anton Ackermann, state secretary in the GDR Foreign Ministry, were ready to explore different roads to unity. Herrnstadt even told the Central Committee of the SED in October that his colleagues should not think that 'the coming unified democratic Germany would simply be an enlarged copy of the present GDR'.[11]

After Stalin's death in March 1953, the question of German unity was again raised by Winston Churchill, who proposed a four-power summit to discuss the question, while Lavrentii Beria (1899–1953), the deputy Soviet prime minister, was actually considering abandoning the GDR to the West for $10 billion, provided that it resulted in a neutral and peaceful, reunited Germany. However, the riots in East Germany in June (see pp. 343–345) and Beria's subsequent fall, as well as American and West German reluctance to open the Pandora's box of German unity, just at a time when the consolidation of Western Europe was taking place, ensured that the Big Four summit did not take place until July 1955 in Geneva. By this time the Federal Republic had been recognized as a sovereign state and joined NATO, while the GDR's membership of the new Warsaw Pact, which had been created to counter NATO, was imminent. Khrushchev effectively ruled out unification by observing that Russia would not tolerate any threat to the 'political and social achievements' of the GDR, and 2 months later recognized its sovereignty but he agreed to end the military occupation of Austria provided it remained neutral.

> **The Politburo** or Political Bureau was the executive committee of the SED, which was modelled on the Politburo of the USSR.

The FRG as a European power, 1955–1958

Relations with the Western powers

Adenauer's foreign policy was based on Western integration, the core of which was Franco-German cooperation and a close alliance with the USA. He viewed the 1957 Treaty of Rome, which set up the EEC, as an event which was equal in importance to the unification of Germany in 1871. His American and European policies worked well as long as the Americans were ready to commit a large number of troops to Europe and make no concessions to the USSR about the status of the GDR or Berlin. Once America started in 1957 to adopt a more flexible policy towards the USSR and consider cutting its garrison in Germany, Adenauer drew closer to France. The incipient Franco-German *entente* survived the coming to power of General de Gaulle in 1958, and strengthened during the acute crisis over Berlin, 1959–1961, even though both statesmen had fundamentally different visions of Europe, as de Gaulle wanted only a very loose confederation of states completely independent of America. Their complex political relationship has been characterized as a 'masked conflict' or a 'senile friendship based on a misunderstanding'.[12]

Relations with the GDR and the USSR

In September 1955 Adenauer visited Moscow and agreed to the exchange of ambassadors in return for the repatriation of the remaining German prisoners of war. He was, however, determined that this should not lead to a diplomatic recognition of the GDR, and thus announced in the *Bundestag* on 22 September what became known as the **Hallstein Doctrine**. He stated that Bonn would treat the recognition of the GDR of any state other than the USSR as an unfriendly act which would result in the termination of diplomatic relations. Financial assistance and development aid for the new states in Asia and Africa was also made strictly dependent on their non-recognition of East Germany. However, the longer the division of Germany lasted, the more this policy began to be seen as a quixotic attempt to 'overcome the status quo by ignoring it'.[13] It cut the GDR off from the Western and developing worlds, but at the price of further integrating it into the Soviet bloc. By 1957, officials like Herbert Blankenhorn (1904–1991), the FRG's representative to NATO, and Karl Pfleiderer (1899–1957), the West German ambassador to Yugoslavia, were beginning to anticipate the thinking of 10 years later (see p. 319) and argue that the recognition of the GDR and closer economic links with the other satellite states would 'slowly draw them step by step into the direction of the West and as a consequence towards liberty'.[14]

Hallstein Doctrine: This was named after Professor Hallstein, the state secretary in the Bonn Foreign Ministry, 1951–1957.

The Berlin crisis, 1958–1961

The main challenge to the existence of the GDR stemmed from the 'miraculous' economic recovery of the FRG (see p. 333). The bright lights and prosperity of West Germany inevitably attracted many of the GDR's younger and more ambitious citizens through the still-open frontier in Berlin – a situation which both the West German and American governments did everything to encourage. Between 1945 and 1961 altogether about one-sixth of the whole East German population had fled westwards through the hole in the Iron Curtain in Berlin. A dramatic improvement in the standard of living in the GDR would stem this exodus, but to achieve this it was first of all necessary to stop the brain drain of skilled workers and professionals to the FRG via the open frontier of West Berlin. To achieve this would, however, entail forcing the Western Allies to change the status of West Berlin. Khrushchev

(1894–1971), the first secretary of the Soviet Communist Party, was at first cautious when urged by the East Germans to do this, but by the autumn of 1958 he was increasingly confident that the USSR was strong enough to force the USA into revising the status of West Berlin and even possibly into signing peace treaties with the two German states. By putting pressure on West Berlin, he believed he could easily squeeze concessions from the Western Allies without the risk of war. As he crudely observed, 'Berlin is the testicles of the West … every time I want to make the West scream I squeeze on Berlin.'[15]

The second **Berlin crisis** began on 10 November 1958, when Khrushchev called for a peace treaty with the two German states. On 27 November he issued a 6-month ultimatum, demanding the demilitarization of West Berlin, the withdrawal of Western troops, and its change of status into a 'free city'. If the Western Allies refused to sign a peace treaty with the two German states, Khrushchev threatened to conclude a peace treaty with the GDR alone and to recognize its sovereignty over East Berlin, which was still nominally under four-power control. This would enable it to control access to West Berlin and interfere with traffic using the corridors from the FRG. The Western Allies would thus have to deal with East German rather than Russian officials, and so in effect be compelled to recognize the GDR, which would shatter the Hallstein Doctrine.

Although the Western Allies rejected the ultimatum, they agreed that a foreign ministers' conference should meet in Geneva in the summer of 1959. Adenauer viewed with growing alarm London's and Washington's evident desire for compromise, and in an attempt to avert damaging concessions, launched the **Globke Plan**, which combined proposals for both a provisional and a comprehensive solution to the German problem. The deepening crisis, however, ensured that neither this plan nor a revised version of it in 1960 were ever discussed. At Geneva no agreement was secured and over the next 2 years Khrushchev successfully kept up the pressure. Officially the Western powers continued to demand free all-German elections, but plans for creating a nuclear-free zone in Central Europe, recognizing Poland's western frontiers and the GDR, were also seriously considered. Adenauer, meanwhile, was desperate to stop any of these plans from reducing the FRG to a neutral, third-class state, but, in May 1960 when the Paris conference was due to open, he had no idea what President Eisenhower (1890–1969) and Harold Macmillan (1894–1986), the British prime minister, might be about to propose. It was therefore, for him at least, 'a gift from heaven',[16] when Khrushchev used the shooting down of an American **U2 spy plane** over Russia as an excuse to walk out of the summit meeting, and wait until a new American president was elected in the autumn.

Until the autumn of 1960 it was Khrushchev who orchestrated the Berlin crisis, and Ulbricht was only a minor player, but, faced with the flood of refugees to the West in 1960–1961, Ulbricht began to press Khrushchev to sign a separate peace treaty with the GDR, at one point

The first **Berlin crisis** was 1948–1949. See pp. 305–306.

U2 spy plane: On 5 May 1960 a Soviet anti-aircraft missile shot down an American U2 spy plane over the Urals.

The Globke Plan: According to this plan drawn up by Hans Globke (1898–1973), the state secretary in the chancellery, the FRG and GDR would recognize each other's sovereignty, and Berlin would become a free city. A referendum on unification would be held within 5 years, and if there was a majority for reunification, free elections would follow for a parliament representing a united Germany.

sharply commenting: 'You only *talk* about a peace treaty, but don't *do* anything about it.'[17] Although John F. Kennedy (1917–1963), the new American president who had been elected in November 1960, was tougher than Khrushchev had expected, Washington's response did indicate a possible solution to the Berlin problem. While Kennedy strengthened American forces in Europe, he also urged negotiation on the whole German question and pointedly stressed in a television broadcast on 25 July 1961 that the West was mainly interested in free access to West Berlin rather than to Berlin as a whole. Hitherto Khrushchev had rejected the possibility of closing off the East Berlin frontier, as he had aimed at detaching West Berlin from the FRG rather than cutting it off from East Germany. However, the growing unrest in the GDR caused by the forced collectivization of agriculture (see p. 346), which in turn increased the number of refugees to the West, persuaded him to agree to Ulbricht's demands for closing off East Berlin from the West. This decision was confirmed at a meeting of the Warsaw Pact states in Moscow on 3–5 August 1961, and in the early morning of 13 August the operation was efficiently and swiftly carried out.

See Document 77 and Map 9

The construction of the Berlin Wall marked a turning point in the German question:

- The United States and its allies, by tolerating it, in effect acknowledged the GDR's right to exist.
- The Wall both consolidated the GDR and ensured that the Soviet Union retained responsibility for maintaining international access to West Berlin.
- The existence of the GDR was assured for the foreseeable future, and ultimately there would be little option for Bonn but to recognize it and seek, in the words of Egon Bahr (1922–2015), the SPD politician and father of *Ostpolitik*, 'change through rapprochement'.[18]

Ostpolitik: the 'eastern' policy of the FRG towards the GDR and the Eastern Bloc after 1969

Détente: a state of lessened tension or growing relaxation between two states

The desire of Britain and America for a **détente** with the USSR, which was obvious throughout the Berlin crisis, persuaded Adenauer to strengthen his links with Gaullist France. He consequently supported de Gaulle's dramatic veto of Britain's application to join the EEC in January 1963, and on 23 January signed the Franco-German Treaty of Friendship (Élysée Treaty). When this treaty was debated in the *Bundestag*, a preamble was added which emphasized that it did not mark a hostile shift in the FRG's foreign policy towards Britain and America. Nevertheless, Adenauer's pro-French policy marked the beginning of bitter divisions in the CDU–CSU between the Atlanticists, like Ludwig Erhard and Gerhard Schröder (1910–1989), who looked primarily to Washington and wanted Britain in the EEC, and the Gaullists like Franz Joseph Strauss (see p. 337) and Adenauer himself, who now looked to Paris and ultimately wanted an integrated Western Europe independent of the USA.

11　The Berlin Wall being constructed at the Harzer Strasse, 18 August 1961

Presse- und Informationsamt der Bundesregierung, no. 60479

The development of *Ostpolitik*, 1963–1969

The Berlin crisis of 1958–1961 had made it clear that the United States accepted the status quo and was ready to give a greater priority to a détente in Europe than to German unification. The West Germans, as Willy Brandt was later to put it, 'lost certain illusions that had outlived the hopes underlying them'.[19] Thus gradually during the 1960s Bonn began the slow and painful process of jettisoning the Hallstein Doctrine and rethinking its policy towards the GDR and the Soviet bloc.

The first tentative signs of a new approach from Bonn were visible as early as June 1962, when the Adenauer government tried unsuccessfully to use the decision to renew inter-German trade and the granting of credits to force the GDR to allow West Berliners access to East Berlin. In December 1963, Willy Brandt, as mayor of West Berlin, seized the initiative and negotiated directly with East Berlin. By agreeing to refer to it as the 'GDR capital', he secured for 18 days the right of West Berliners to visit their relatives across the Wall. Later these arrangements were extended to cover public holidays up to Whitsun 1966. They were a good example of the policy of 'small steps',[20] which

Brandt had been urging Bonn to take in order to alleviate the plight of the East Germans.

Ostpolitik began to take a more definite shape when the Grand Coalition under Kurt Kiesinger was formed in December 1966, with Willy Brandt as foreign secretary (see p. 353). In his first few months in power, Kiesinger made several statements defining the scope of the new policy. The old references to the East zone from the Adenauer era were replaced by the more cryptic references to 'the other part of Germany', and he stressed that by encouraging 'human, economic and cultural relations' he wished 'to bridge the gulfs and not deepen them'.[21] In April 1967 Kiesinger presented the GDR with several practical proposals for improving inter-German trade, communications and contacts between relatives cut off by the division of Germany. This was supplemented by an open letter from the SPD to the 7th Party Congress of the SED suggesting talks between the two parties.

Willy Brandt, 1913–1992

During the Third Reich Brandt worked in the SPD resistance movement in Norway. He returned to Berlin in 1946. From 1957 to 1966 he was mayor of West Berlin. He was a charismatic figure and was compared to America's John F. Kennedy. He led the SPD election campaigns of 1961 and 1965, but failed to win sufficient seats to put his party in power. In 1966, when the SPD joined the Grand Coalition, he became foreign minister and began to work towards a better understanding with the GDR. In 1969 he became chancellor and was able to pursue a more vigorous policy of *Ostpolitik*.

See Document 78

Soviet intervention in Czechoslovakia in August 1968: Warsaw Pact troops invaded Czechoslovakia to replace the Dubcek government, whose reforms were undermining the Eastern bloc. In November Brezhnev defended the invasion by stressing that any threat to socialism in a Warsaw Pact country was a threat to all its allies.

At first these initiatives were brushed aside by the SED. Ulbricht went out of his way to dismiss compromise and to argue that unity was only possible between two socialist Germanies. However, to avoid isolation in the Soviet bloc, where there was a considerable desire for détente, the GDR had to go through the motions of following up Bonn's proposals. In May, Willi Stoph (1914–1999), the prime minister, demanded the opening up of normal diplomatic relations between the two states. When Kiesinger replied by suggesting setting up a joint committee of officials to make proposals for facilitating contacts between the populations of the two states, he immediately met 'a wall of maximum demands' in a second letter which insisted upon the recognition of West Berlin as 'a separate political entity', as well as a treaty between the 'two sovereign German states'.[22]

The 'Prague Spring', the liberalization process initiated by Alexander Dubcek in Czechoslovakia, was perceived by East Berlin as an object lesson on the dangers of making too many domestic concessions. In West Germany, on the other hand, **Soviet intervention in Czechoslovakia in August 1968** and then the promulgation of the Brezhnev Doctrine were seen by many on the right wing of the CDU–CSU to prove the bankruptcy of *Ostpolitik* and led to demands for a return to the Cold War policies of the Adenauer days. Brandt, however, refused to discontinue *Ostpolitik* and argued that the USSR would be ready to make concessions now that it had firmly re-established its control in Eastern Europe.

After his election victory of September 1969 (see p. 356), Brandt was in a position to implement *Ostpolitik* more fully. Together with his foreign minister, Walther Scheel (1919–), the party chairman of the FDP, he embarked upon negotiating a complex set of interlocking treaties which were to mark a major turning point in relations between Bonn and Moscow and between the two Germanies themselves. On one level Brandt's policy was primarily a matter of coming to terms with the realities of 1945, or as he put it in his famous television speech from Moscow in August 1970, 'the political situation as it exists in Europe'.[23] This, of course, involved the *de facto* recognition of the East German regime, although his whole strategy, by defusing the tense situation between the two states, was also aimed at leaving the door ajar for future unification.

See Document 78

Ostpolitik was not conducted in a vacuum. Brandt was anxious to reassure the Western powers that he had no intention of reviving the *Rapallopolitik* of the Weimar Republic (see p. 202) and was thus adamant that the FRG did not intended to weaken 'its Adenauerian anchoring in the West'.[24] He told Brezhnev repeatedly that Bonn was committed to membership of NATO and the European Community. In the course of 1970–1972 five sets of intricate and interdependent agreements were negotiated. The FRG concluded bilateral treaties with the USSR, Poland, Czechoslovakia and the GDR, and also the four-power agreement on Berlin was signed.

The Moscow, Warsaw and Prague Treaties, 1970–1973

The key to a successful *Ostpolitik* lay in an improvement in relations between Bonn and Moscow. The FRG's signature of the Nuclear **Non-Proliferation Treaty** in November 1969, its readiness to increase technological and economic links with Russia and its willingness to participate in a European security conference, which Moscow hoped would confirm its post-war hegemony in Eastern Europe, were all preliminary concessions made with that aim in mind. Against a background of fierce opposition from the CDU press, the Moscow Treaty, which was 'the foundation stone of *Ostpolitik*',[25] was signed on 12 August by Brandt and Brezhnev. Both the USSR and the FRG declared that they had no territorial claims against any other state. The FRG recognized the 'non-violability' of Poland's western frontier and of its frontier with the GDR. In a second part of the treaty the FRG committed itself to negotiating treaties with Poland, the GDR and Czechoslovakia. While Bonn still did not officially recognize the GDR, it agreed to abandon the Hallstein Doctrine and accept that both Germanies would eventually become members of the United Nations.

The Russians had in effect gained West German recognition of their eastern European empire, yet this recognition was not unconditional. The

The Non-Proliferation Treaty, which aimed to prevent the further spread of nuclear weapons, was signed by the USA and the USSR in July 1968.

West Germans also presented Brezhnev with a 'letter on German unity' which stressed the FRG's right to work towards a state of peace in Europe in which 'the German people regains its unity in free self-determination'.[26] Similarly, the term 'inviolable' – as applied to the Oder–Neisse line and the inner German frontier – rather than the preferred Soviet word 'immutable', arguably kept the door open for a later peaceful revision of the frontiers. Finally, the ratification of the treaty was made dependent on a four-power agreement over Berlin.

Negotiations with the Poles ran parallel to the Moscow talks, but were loaded with a greater emotional freight. The Poles were uneasy that their frontiers were in effect recognized over their heads by the FRG and the USSR in the Moscow negotiations. There were, too, disagreements about the legality of the expulsion of the Germans from Upper Silesia and elsewhere in 1945 (see p. 293), and about the number of ethnic Germans still in Poland. Nevertheless, by December 1970 the negotiations were at last completed. Both states recognized that they had no territorial demands on each other and that the Oder–Neisse line was 'inviolable'. Trade and financial assistance from Bonn was to be increased, while the ethnic Germans still within Poland were to be allowed to emigrate to the FRG. When Brandt flew into Warsaw to sign the treaty, he visited the site of the former ghetto and, as a gesture of atonement for Germany's wartime crimes, went down on his knees in front of the memorial to the Jews who had been murdered there by the Nazis. This deeply symbolic act was viewed with mixed feelings at home, as indeed was the whole Warsaw Treaty, since it was felt that Brandt had ceded too much for too little, particularly when it later became clear that the Poles were only issuing a limited number of exit visas to the ethnic Germans.

The negotiations between the FRG and Czechoslovakia started in October 1970 but dragged on until June 1973 when the Treaty of Prague was signed, although it took the *Bundestag* another year to ratify it. Besides guaranteeing existing frontiers and renouncing the use of force, it also made the Munich Treaty of 1938 (see p. 270) 'void' whilst safeguarding the retrospective validity, as far as it concerned such matters as marriages or wills, of German law in the Sudetenland during the period 1938–1945. Czechoslovakia also agreed to allow the emigration of any Czechs with German citizenship – some 10,000 in all.

Four-power negotiations over Berlin, 1970–1971

The quadripartite Berlin negotiations in effect made the Western Allies the 'guarantors of *Ostpolitik*'.[27] This involvement of the Western powers strengthened Brandt's negotiating position *vis-à-vis* both the Russians and the East Germans. It also reassured NATO that *Ostpolitik* would not lead to a weakening of the FRG's links with the West and a return to the *Rapallopolitik* of the 1920s. In February 1970, in response to an earlier Western note of August 1969 requesting discussions on the thorny problem of access to West Berlin the Russians agreed to quadripartite

See Map 9

discussions on Berlin. The Western Allies wanted a settlement, underwritten by the USSR, which would finally confirm West Berlin's links with the FRG and guarantee its freedom of access to the West. At first the Russians were anxious to avoid making too many concessions, but their desire for a general European security conference and their reluctance to alienate President Nixon (1913–1994), at a time when he was planning to visit **China**, made them more ready to make concessions over Berlin. The agreement, signed on 3 September 1971, was a 'milestone in the history of divided Berlin and divided Germany'.[28] The Soviets conceded three vital principles:

See Map 9

China: Beijing was highly critical of the Soviet policy of détente and relations had deteriorated to the point where armed clashes had occurred along the Sino-Soviet border.

- unimpeded traffic between West Berlin and the FRG;
- the recognition of West Berlin's ties with the FRG;
- the right for West Berliners to visit East Berlin 'under conditions comparable to those applying to other persons entering these areas'.[29]

In return, the Western powers agreed that the Western sectors of Berlin were not legally part of the FRG (even if in practice they had been since West Berlin adopted the Basic Law in 1950), and that consequently Bonn should avoid holding provocative federal ceremonies, such as the election of the president of the FRG, there.

The Basic Treaty

A settlement with the GDR was the 'last and most important part of the *Ostpolitik* treaties',[30] and could only be achieved after the Moscow Treaty and the quadripartite agreement on Berlin. Brandt offered the GDR 'negotiations at government level' in his first formal policy statement to the new *Bundestag* on 28 October 1969. The leadership of the SED was divided in its approach. Ulbricht was now more inclined to explore the possibilities of a rapprochement with Brandt than the rest of the Politburo, and was, as he said in Moscow in August 1970, quite convinced that a treaty with the FRG was 'a means to move forwards large numbers of Social Democratic members' who 'are supporters of capitalism, but also against the Vietnam War'.[31] Erich Honecker, who was being groomed to take over from Ulbricht (see p. 368), and Stoph were more cautious and were acutely aware of the possible threat to the stability of the GDR of an open-ended agreement with Bonn. Even Brezhnev, despite his desire for a general European détente, was fearful that inter-German relations might take on a momentum of their own and wrench East Germany out of the Soviet orbit. Thus the initial contacts between the two German states were characterized by extreme caution on the side of the GDR. Nevertheless, in March 1970, as a result of Soviet pressure, Stoph invited Brandt to Erfurt. The meeting showed the potential dangers of *Ostpolitik* for the GDR as the immense enthusiasm of the crowds for Willy Brandt threatened to escalate out of the control of the police and gave the FRG an easy propaganda victory. Stoph insisted rigidly on full diplomatic recognition of the GDR by the FRG. Although Brandt could not concede this, he did tell Stoph that '[n]o one must try to subject the other to overweening influence. I have not come here to demand the liquidation of any ties of the GDR or of any social order'.[32] Nevertheless, despite this concession, the only agreed joint statement the two heads of state could make was the mutual declaration that 'war would never again originate from German soil'. Two months later Stoph and Brandt again met at Kassel just inside the West German border. As the East German delegation had been firmly instructed by Brezhnev to avoid the question of inter-German ties, and to concentrate on scoring propaganda points, the talks were inconclusive and both sides agreed to a pause for reflection before further meetings. In July Brezhnev stressed in discussions with Honecker the solid advantages of the treaty with the FRG for the GDR in that '[i]ts frontiers, its existence will be confirmed for all the world to see'. Nevertheless, he warned him that Brandt was aiming at the 'Social Democratisation' of the GDR and added: 'It ... must not come to a process of rapprochement between the FRG and the GDR ... Concentrate everything on the all-sided strengthening of the GDR, as you call it.'[33]

12   Willy Brandt on his knees before the memorial to the Warsaw Ghetto, Warsaw, 7 December 1970

Presse- und Informationsamt der Bundesregierung, no. 33028

The negotiations between the two German states started in November 1970. Initially little progress was made, but the deadlock was broken once the draft of the Four-Power Berlin Treaty was in place in September 1971. For it to be completed and signed, a series of technical agreements on transit traffic, the rights of West Berliners to visit East Berlin and postal communications had to be negotiated and included in the treaty. Once this was achieved, the two states moved on to negotiate the crucial Basic Treaty, which was only signed in December 1972. In it the FRG recognized the GDR as an equal and sovereign state. It was, however, stressed that the FRG still considered the people of the GDR to have a common German citizenship and, in a 'Letter concerning German unity' which it presented to East Berlin, it repeated its determination to work for German reunification. Despite intense opposition from the CDU (see p. 358), the Basic Treaty was ratified in May 1973. The existence of the two Germanies now seemed to be a permanent international fact, and both states joined the United Nations in 1973.

Ostpolitik in practice, 1973–1988

In May 1974 the two German states set up what the FRG insisted on calling 'permanent representations' in each other's capitals. Pointedly, the West German representative, Günter Gaus (1929–2004), reported back to the chancellor, while his East German opposite number, Michael Kohl, formally reported like any other diplomat to the GDR foreign minister. As Chancellor Helmut Kohl was to observe 10 years later, the task of *Ostpolitik* was an attempt 'to ease the painful consequences of the division of our fatherland [and] to strengthen the consciousness of belonging together among all Germans, to preserve what unites and to create new commonalities between them'.[34] Up to the autumn of 1989 most West Germans believed that the inner German frontier would survive for generations. Bonn thus exploited every contact and exchange, whether financial, political, social or sporting, with the GDR to create a whole web of close links or 'interdependences'. On the other hand, Bonn stopped well short of destabilizing the GDR, as it feared that this would trigger Russian intervention and end the benign consequences of *Ostpolitik*. The East German regime reacted defensively to this 'aggression in felt slippers',[35] as Otto Winzer (1902–1975), its foreign minister, had so perceptively phrased it as early as 1963, by attempting to fence itself off from the West. It declared itself to be a separate 'socialist nation' permanently allied to the USSR. West German visitors were reported on by the security police, transit routes were strictly controlled and the case histories of the East Germans who applied to travel to the West were investigated with particular care.

Viewed from Bonn, could *Ostpolitik* be called a success? It certainly had, in the words of a *Bundestag resolution* of 1987, 'directly useful results for the people'.[36] Transit links between East and West Germany were modernized with the help of West German subsidies, postal deliveries were improved and telephone calls from the FRG to the GDR climbed from half a million in 1969 to 40 million in 1988. Similarly, personal visits from West to East rose from one million a year in 1969 to eight million in the mid-1970s. Each visitor had to pay the sum of 13 Deutschmarks a day, which was doubled in October 1980. At the total cost of some 3.5 million Deutschmarks Bonn was also able to buy the freedom of 34,000 political prisoners and facilitate the reuniting of some 250,000 families.

For the GDR the main advantages of *Ostpolitik* were economic. The steady flow of Deutschmarks eastwards was supplemented by generous credits, which enabled the GDR to import vital industrial goods from West Germany. In 1983–1984 bank loans of nearly two billion Deutschmarks were negotiated by Franz Joseph Strauss, which saved the GDR from a possibly terminal economic crisis, and did much to restore its economic credibility. Altogether, from 1972 to 1989, some 14 billion Deutschmarks were transferred at state level from Bonn to the GDR. Inevitably this led to a growing financial dependency on West Germany. The two key East German financial link men with Bonn, Alexander Schalk-Golodkowski (1932–) and Gerhard Schürer, were convinced by 1988 that only some sort of confederation with the FRG could save the GDR from bankruptcy. This would appear to vindicate *Ostpolitik* and helps to explain the collapse of the GDR in 1989, but these credits were not used by Bonn primarily as a tool to bring down the regime. Rather they were a means to stabilize it and to prevent a dramatic collapse, which might lead to a repetition of the traumatic events of 1953 or 1961 and the end of *Ostpolitik*. Certainly up to 1988–1989 the assumption was that the Brezhnev doctrine still applied and that Russia would intervene to stop the disintegration of the GDR. Nevertheless, some concessions were demanded for this great flow of credit. In 1984, for example, Strauss extracted from the GDR further alleviations on inter-German travel, and the dismantling of minefields and automatic shooting devices along the frontier.

Chancellor Helmut Schmidt (see p. 360) consciously used *Ostpolitik*, as he wrote later in his memoirs, 'to increase the self-respect of Erich Honecker, Ulbricht's successor, in the international context and reduce the inferiority complexes of the GDR leadership'.[37] Once the CDU–CSU returned to power, Kohl continued this policy. In September 1987 Honecker paid a highly successful state visit to Bonn and right up to 1989 a regular stream of FRG politicians visited East Berlin and were photographed shaking Honecker's hand. One or two critical voices argued that the FRG had allowed the GDR to gain the initiative in *Ostpolitik*, but the consensus of opinion in the governing coalition, the bureaucracy and the SPD was that only 'stabilization' would give the GDR the self-confidence to liberalize.

The FRG between East and West

By the mid-1970s the FRG was, as Schmidt observed, 'in the eyes of the world de facto economically the second world power of the West'[38] and was the fourth largest contributor to the budget of the United Nations. As a major power the FRG faced a potentially serious dilemma. On the one hand it was enmeshed in NATO and the European Community, while on the other it was committed through *Ostpolitik* to a policy of détente with the USSR, the GDR and the other Russian satellites. Any serious East–West confrontation would destroy *Ostpolitik* and force Bonn back to the rigidities of the Adenauer era. Schmidt and his foreign minister, **Hans-Dietrich Genscher**, consequently worked hard to encourage détente and East–West links through NATO, **the EC**, the United Nations, the G7 and the many other international organizations that existed in the 1970s.

At the Conference on Security and Cooperation, which met at Helsinki, 1973–1975, Genscher and Schmidt in alliance with Henry Kissinger, the American secretary of state, managed to defeat the USSR's intention of negotiating what would in effect have been a peace treaty permanently guaranteeing the status quo in Eastern Europe. However, they did enthusiastically support the commitment to human rights and the vague-sounding provisions for peaceful cooperation in a variety of areas such as science, the environment, trade and energy which were incorporated in the Helsinki Final Act, as they saw these as the building blocks of détente.

By 1977 the FRG's delicate balance between Western integration and *Ostpolitik* began to come under severe pressure when it became evident that Russia had embarked on a large-scale programme for building a new generation of middle-range nuclear missiles, the SS-20s, which were a direct threat to Western Europe. Schmidt played a key role in convincing the NATO leaders in 1979 to adopt the controversial 'two track proposal', which he hoped would salvage the policy of détente by committing NATO to deploying, as a counter to the SS-20s, intermediate Pershing II and cruise missiles in Europe in 1983, only if reductions could not first be satisfactorily negotiated with Moscow. However, as a result of the **Soviet invasion of Afghanistan** in December 1979 and then the eruption of the Solidarity movement in Poland in August 1980, no such agreement was possible.

What the West German political establishment now feared most appeared to be about to happen: namely that hostility between the two superpowers would make *Ostpolitik* unworkable. In increasingly desperate attempts by Bonn to escape from this dilemma, *Ostpolitik* began to degenerate into an open appeasement of Moscow and the Eastern European regimes. Bonn did not join London and Washington in criticizing the Russian invasion of Afghanistan or the Polish government's reaction to **Solidarity**. Indeed no less a person than Willy Brandt actually condemned Solidarity for threatening the stability of the Polish regime. When martial law was declared by the Polish government in Poland in December 1981, Schmidt again went out of his way to avoid censuring it. He was unwilling to sacrifice what had already been achieved in *Ostpolitik* for the sake of the Poles. Nevertheless, he did ask Honecker to use his influence in Moscow to moderate Soviet policy arguing that 'in truth ... both German states have great weight ... we have a right to throw this weight into the scales'.[39] Ultimately the FRG was left with no option but

Hans-Dietrich Genscher, (1927–): leader of the FDP, 1974–1985, and foreign minister, 1974–1992.

EC: The EEC fused with the ECSC and EURATOM to form the EC (European Community) in May 1967. The G7 or Group of Seven was composed of the seven states with the world's leading economies.

Soviet invasion of Afghanistan: Brezhnev sent 100,000 troops into Afghanistan to defend a Marxist regime, which had recently seized power.

Solidarity: In August 1980, strikes organized by the Solidarity movement paralysed the Danzig shipyards and then spread throughout Poland giving rise to the fear that Soviet troops would invade to crush it.

to deploy the Pershing and cruise missiles in November 1983, although Kohl, Schmidt's successor, took great care to minimize the impact of this action on *Ostpolitik*.

The foreign policy of the GDR, 1973–1987

See Document 79

By 1984 132 states had recognized the GDR's sovereignty. Legal recognition enabled it to play a role in international politics through UNESCO and the UN where in the early 1980s it served for a 2-year spell as a non-permanent member of the Security Council. It also participated in the Helsinki Conference in 1975 as a fully independent state and signed the Final Act, which was something of a Trojan horse, as it encouraged dissidents within the GDR to demand greater civil rights (see p. 371). As an ally of the USSR, the GDR began to play an increasingly influential role in advising and assisting the revolutionary Marxist parties emerging in the African states of Angola, Ethiopia, Mozambique and Guinea-Bissau in the 1970s. In return for economic concessions, the GDR provided military and technical experts. By 1980 some 2700 East German military personnel were serving in Africa. The GDR also sent food and equipment to North Vietnam and field hospitals for Russian troops to Afghanistan.

Despite the growing dependence of the GDR on financial credits from Bonn for Honecker membership of the Warsaw Pact and close cooperation with Moscow remained the bedrock of the GDR's foreign policy. In October 1975, for instance, it signed a 25-year treaty of friendship, cooperation and mutual assistance with the USSR, and in 1980–1981 Honecker was a strong advocate of military intervention in Poland to crush the Solidarity movement. Yet, like Schmidt and Kohl, he also attempted to insulate inter-German relations from the effects of growing Russian–American tension, and he kept open the lines of communication with Bonn, even though Moscow vetoed his plans for a summit with Kohl until 1987.

Conclusion

The legacy of Hitler's war tore the German Reich apart. In the new confrontation between Communism and capitalism, the front line in Europe ran through Germany. The partition of Germany favoured the Western powers. On the one side the FRG contained the great industrial complex of the Ruhr and two-thirds of the population of post-war Germany, while on the other the GDR was a small rump cut off from its economic links with the West, and faced with the wrenching task of reorienting its economy towards the East. The basic parameters of the FRG's foreign policy were set in the Adenauer era. Integration into a Western bloc protected by American military strength would not only provide a reliable defence against the USSR but would also create a prosperity, which in time would drag the GDR out of the Soviet axis.

The policy of the GDR was a mirror image of that of the FRG. To defeat the magnet-like pull of the FRG and to stand any chance of appealing over the head of the Bonn government to the German people as a whole, it had to create a dynamic economy which would give the GDR a legitimacy it otherwise lacked. The only way the GDR could break out of the vicious circle caused by the flight of its skilled workers westwards into the FRG was to persuade Khrushchev to have the frontier with West Berlin sealed off. Once this occurred in August 1961, the GDR gained a certain immunity from the pull of the West. The period of détente, or 'the long peace',[40] which in essence was based on an overestimation by the West of the power and durability of the Soviet bloc, led to the abandonment of the Hallstein Doctrine and the decision by Kiesinger and Brandt to bring about what Egon Bahr (1922) called 'change through rapprochement'[41] with the help of *Ostpolitik*.

The signature of the Basic Treaty was a turning point in the relations between the two Germanies. Within their respective blocs both the FRG and the GDR played increasingly important economic, military and political roles. The FRG never tried, as did the Weimar Republic, to balance between Russia and the West. Through NATO and the EC it was clearly anchored in the West, even if its chancellors worked hard to persuade Washington and the other Western capitals to keep open their lines of communication with the East. Neither did *Ostpolitik* end the Franco-German axis within the EC. On the contrary, it deepened and took on 'the character of a well-established marriage in which quarrels would be expected but not taken as disastrous'.[42] Nothing, however, had changed the essential vulnerability of the GDR, whose very existence in the last resort still depended on the USSR's readiness to maintain it as a state as the events of 1989–1990 were to show (see p. 377), even though most West Germans up to the autumn of 1989 still believed that the inner German frontier would survive for generations. In the end both Adenauer's magnet theory and *Ostpolitik* were vindicated by events.

16 *Domestic Developments in the Two German States, 1949–1963*

TIMELINE

1950	8 February	Ministry for State Security (*Stasi*) set up in GDR
	25 June	Outbreak of Korean War
	9 August	FRG Constitution extended to West Berlin
	15 October	*Volkskammer* elections
1951	1 December	First Five Year Plan launched in GDR
1952	May	Equalization of Burdens Act
	9–12 July	Second SED Congress
	23 July	States dissolved in GDR
1953	5 March	Stalin's death
	26 May	10 per cent increase in work norms in GDR
	16–18 June	Strikes and disturbances in GDR
	6 September	FRG election: Adenauer retained power
1954	1 January	USSR ended reparation payments from GDR
	26 February	Basic Law amended to permit creation of *Bundeswehr*
1955	5 May	FRG became a sovereign state
1956	18 January	National People's Army formed in GDR
	December	*Bundeswehr* Conscription Law passed by *Bundestag*
1957	15 September	CDU–CSU win outright majority in general election
1958	9 January	Second Five Year Plan in GDR
	28 May	Rationing ended for meat and sugar in GDR
1959	1 October	Seven Year Plan replaced Five Year Plan
	13–15 November	Godesberg Programme adopted
1960	January	Collectivization of remaining independent farms in GDR
1961	13 August	Border between East and West Berlin closed
	17 September	Adenauer retained power in FRG election with greatly reduced support
1962	October	*Spiegel* affair: Strauss resigned
1963	25 June	'New Economic System' started in GDR
	15 October	Erhard, Chancellor

Introduction: problems, issues and questions

Both German states shared a common heritage and had been part of a united Germany. Both had the difficult task of coming to terms with their Nazi past and were confronted with the challenge of integrating the expellees from the east, reviving their economies and reshaping their welfare system. Their responses to these challenges, however, were so different that Hartmut Kaelble observed that 'apart from the language and the history up to 1945'[1] the two Germanies had very little in common by 1990. How far had this process reached by 1963? Did the GDR before the building of the Berlin Wall manage to establish its own identity and legitimacy as a German state or was it rather the FRG that established itself more effectively as the heir to the Bismarckian

Empire and the Weimar Republic? If the FRG can be described as a conservative 'restoration state', can the GDR best be characterized as a workers' state?

The FRG

Adenauer's initial survival, 1949–1953

By the mid-1950s West Germany had made such an impressive recovery that Adenauer was already being proclaimed a statesman of European and indeed world stature. Yet in the winter of 1949–1950 the FRG was beset with apparently intractable economic problems and the failure of his government seemed imminent. It was by no means clear that Adenauer possessed sufficient power to govern effectively. The Occupation Statute (see p. 312) ensured that ultimate responsibility for foreign policy, security, the export trade and the Ruhr still lay with the Western Allies. The increased powers of the states whose minister-presidents were, as Hinrich Kopf, the minister of Lower Saxony, observed, determined not 'to sing the Horst-Wessel song and to say yes,'[2] appeared to be a formidable brake on a strong central government. The situation in the *Bundestag* initially also seemed uncomfortably similar to that in the Reichstag during the Weimar Republic. Despite the electoral law prohibiting parties from claiming seats in the *Bundestag* unless they had won at least 5 per cent of the total votes cast, there were still 12 parties represented in parliament. Some of these, like the BP (Bavarian Party) or the SSW (South Schleswig Voters' League), represented regional or group interests or were parties of protest. The CDU itself was a fragile structure which could easily have fractured, and it was only in 1950 that its leadership began to build up an effective national party organization. There was, too, the challenge of how to integrate the 9.5 million refugees and expellees from the former territories in the east, which was 'ticking like a time bomb in the framework of the fledgling state.'[3]

How then did Adenauer manage to survive and consolidate the FRG so effectively? There are a number of factors which help explain this. He was able to attract support from a diverse cross section of West Germans: Catholics and Protestants who wished to rebuild Germany as a Christian community; the supporters of the social market economy; many younger voters and politicians who embraced European integration; and finally those, many of whom were expellees, who hated the USSR and still hoped for the return of the eastern territories. He also possessed a superb political machine in the chancellor's office which was run by Hans Globke. This carefully monitored developments within the party and vetted senior appointments to the civil service in order to ensure that only politically reliable men occupied the key posts. He was assisted by the failure of the SPD under Kurt Schumacher, whose bitter criticism of the market economy alienated many potential supporters. Schumacher gambled on

Hans Globke, 1898–1973, had drafted the Nuremberg race laws of 1935 and became state secretary in the West German chancellery, 1953–1963.

its collapse, but once its success and durability became clear, the SPD had nothing to offer. Above all, Adenauer was helped by the Cold War, which ensured that the Western powers urgently needed the support of the FRG. Soviet military intervention in the GDR to quell the riots of June 1953 (see p. 344) increased the distrust of the USSR in the FRG and acted as an endorsement of Adenauer's policy of Western integration. In 1953 a combination of these factors helped Adenauer win a decisive electoral victory, which showed that neither Western integration nor the social market economy could easily be reversed.

See Document 80

The social market economy and the 'economic miracle'

In the 1950s economic growth in the FRG was outstanding, yet in the winter of 1949–1950 there were few signs of this development. After the short inflationary boom in the second part of 1948 triggered by the currency reform (see p. 304) and Erhard's decision to lift price controls, the economy cooled in the winter of 1948–1949. Industrial production grew again by an overall 24 per cent in the following year, but in the winter of 1949–1950 economic recovery faltered. Unemployment was over two million, prices were rising and industry faced serious bottlenecks in supply. It seemed as if Erhard's aim of creating a free-market economy had already failed. Criticism was growing not only in the SPD and the unions but also within Adenauer's cabinet and among the Allied high commissioners. Although Erhard did announce a small work-creation programme, he refused to be panicked into emergency measures, and his approach initially seemed to be vindicated when the outbreak of the Korean War in June 1950 led to a sharp rise in industrial production. Yet by early 1951 the economy was faced with a serious balance of payments deficit caused by the cost of imported raw materials. Ironically, Erhard was put under pressure by the Americans, the champions of the free market, to control raw materials to ensure that heavy industry would have priority. The SPD assumed that the market economy had failed, but Erhard skilfully avoided state intervention by delegating to the industrialists the task of allocating raw materials through their own associations to the manufacturing industries. By the autumn of 1951 the global economic boom caused by the Korean War began to work in favour of the FRG. There was a huge demand for machine tools, steel and high-tech exports, which West German industry was in a strong position to meet.

Ludwig Erhard and the social market economy

The social market economy became the 'brand name'[4] for the economic system of West Germany. It was seen as a 'third way' between a completely free market and a state-controlled socialist economy, which increasingly existed in the GDR. The concept originated in the

1930s and its aim, in A.J. Nicholl's words, was 'to wed free price mechanism and market competition to a socially responsible policy'.[5] The state had to enforce fair competition, prohibit the formation of cartels and stimulate the economy when necessary. Initially as economics director of the Bizone and then as economics minister under Adenauer, Erhard attempted to put these ideas into practice. Inevitably he had to make many compromises. In agriculture, for instance, its principles were never applied, as Adenauer, for reasons of social cohesion and electoral politics, continued a policy of subsidies and protection, which was virtually unchanged since the Third Reich. Similarly it was not until 1957 that anti-cartel legislation was introduced.

As Richard Overy has observed, the German economic miracle was 'not a miracle in the sense that defied explanation'[6]. Liberalization of world trade, coupled with the cheap price of raw materials and a tight monetary policy carried out by the Federal Central Bank, *Die Bank Deutschen Länder*, ensured that manufacturers made their profits in the export market rather than at home. The FRG was spared the burden of **reparations** and, unlike its competitors, the FRG was also initially spared the huge expense of rearmament, although from 1952 onwards the government began to put aside money in a contingency fund in preparation for setting up the new West German army (see p. 335). Although the funds allotted to the FRG by the Marshall Plan were relatively modest, they did help buy vital equipment and expand the capacity of the iron and coal industries. Arguably the plan's real significance was the stability and confidence it provided by indicating the degree of American commitment to Western European reconstruction and defence against communism. Above all the German workforce was skilled and well-educated, and constantly boosted by the flow of predominantly young and highly-skilled refugees from the GDR. Between 1950 and 1962 some 3.6 million people had fled from the GDR to the FRG. To quote Alan Kramer, it was 'not the Marshall Plan and its contribution of $1.5 billion spread over 4 years, but Stalin's – and Stalinism's – annual gift of DM 2.6 billion worth of trained labour that provided the greatest capital input to the West German economy'.[7]

Die Bank Deutschen Länder was renamed the *Bundesbank* in 1957.

Reparations: Although, unlike the Weimar Republic, the FRG was spared reparation payments, in 1952 Adenauer agreed to repay the Marshall Plan credits and the pre-war loans raised under the Dawes Plan (see p. 208). Israel was also awarded a sum of DM 3 billion.

The first half of the 1950s was a golden age for the West German economy. It enjoyed a rapid and sustained growth. In 1955 the gross domestic product grew by 12 per cent. In the spring of 1956 inflation rose to 2 per cent, and the central bank increased the discount rate, much to the irritation of Adenauer, who feared that it might damage his chances of being re-elected in 1957. In 1958 there was a small recession in which the GDP rose by a mere 4.4 per cent. The bank then eased its monetary controls and 1960 witnessed another boom year in which the economy grew by an annual rate of 8.6 per cent. Only gradually in the early 1960s could it be seen that 'the miracle years of growth had passed'.[8]

The spectacular economic achievements of the social market economy did much to defuse labour unrest, but social peace was also a

13   A German family enjoying the fruits of the economic miracle, November 1960

Presse- und Informationsamt der Bundesregierung, no. 9077/4

precondition of its success. In the early 1950s there was considerable potential for labour unrest as profit margins far outstripped wages. In 1951 over a million working days were lost in strikes, but the actual wage claims were moderate and did not erode industrial profits, which continued to be reinvested in modernization projects. One reason for this relative moderation was that Adenauer, when confronted by the threat of strikes in the Ruhr, conceded, against the wishes of the FDP and many in his own party, the principle of **co-determination** to the iron, steel and coal unions. In 1952 the Works Constitution Law was passed, which extended workers' consultative councils throughout industry. This did not go as far as the workers wanted, but within the context of rising prosperity the councils did create a framework for relatively peaceful labour relations. With the exception of a 3-week engineering strike in Bavaria in 1954 the first really significant wage push occurred in 1960, by which time the population was becoming more accustomed to prosperity.

> **Co-determination (Mitbestimmung):** a system that aims to create harmonious relations between employers and employees by setting up a series of collaborative institutions

Social integration

The economic recovery made it easier to integrate the expellees and defuse their growing bitterness, the potential dangers of which were shown in 1950 when the 'Bloc of Expellees and Disenfranchised', whose three leaders were all former Nazis, won 23.4 per cent of the vote in Schleswig-Holstein. The most immediate need of not only the expellees but also the majority of Germans was housing. As a result of the war, about 25 per cent of the housing stock had been destroyed. The Construction Law of April 1950 permitted central government to make generous grants to the cities and the states for large-scale building projects, and by 1957 well over four million dwelling units had been built.

See Documents 70

To ensure that the financial consequences of defeat were more fairly shared, the Adenauer cabinet proposed in 1952 the Equalization of Burdens bill. Its intention was to compensate the expellees and those who had lost all their property as a result of the war at the expense of those who had been more fortunate. The SPD hoped for what would effectively be a 'second Basic Law' (see p. 307) as Erich Ollenhauer (1901–1963), Schumacher's successor, expressed it, which would create a more just and equal society, while the CDU and FDP tried to minimize its implications for private property. Eventually a compromise was achieved, which played a major part in satisfying and integrating the expellees and other financial causalities of the war into the new West German state.

The apparently unstoppable rise in GDP also enabled Adenauer to reform the provisions for old-age pensions in 1957. Instead of adopting a system modelled on the principle of the social market economy, which would have encouraged individuals to take out private pensions, Adenauer introduced index-linked state pensions accompanied by a large one-off rise of 60–75 per cent which was naturally very popular and contributed to his victory in the 1957 General Election.

Equalization of Burdens Act, 1953

Klessmann calls this the 'greatest tax on wealth in the history of Germany'[9]:

There was to be a levy on 50 per cent of the wealth of all real assets, that is, land, buildings and capital goods, within West German territory, as measured by the values current on 21 June 1948. The tax would be paid over 30 years and would be redistributed in the form of grants and pensions to the recipients after their claims had been carefully sifted by special committees. However, as the value of property and land had increased rapidly in the 1950s and 1960s as a consequence of economic growth and inflation, 'an originally daring venture became a quite marginal affair'.[10] Nevertheless, by 1978 110.4 billion Deutschmarks had been redistributed.

The *Bundeswehr*: a citizen's army

Historically army–state relations have been one of the most intractable problems in German political history. Initially, when the scheme for a new West German army as part of the European Defence Community was drawn up under the Pleven Plan in 1952 (see p. 313), public opinion was sceptical, and the SPD opposition would almost certainly have prevented Adenauer from obtaining the necessary two-thirds majority to amend the Basic Law to permit its creation. The protracted delay caused by the French failure to ratify the plan enabled the government not only to win round public opinion, but also to consider how the new army should best be integrated into a democratic German society. The German soldier was no longer to be an automaton obeying orders instantly, but rather a 'citizen in uniform' who was to think for himself and willingly defend the democratic values of his society. A cross-party majority in the *Bundestag* also insisted on appointing a parliamentary special commissioner with the right to investigate military affairs and a personnel advisory committee to review the appointment of senior officers. The necessary changes to the Basic Law were made in March 1956 with the support of most of the SPD. Unlike the *Reichswehr* in the Weimar Republic, the *Bundeswehr* as an institution was completely integrated into the democratic state and played only a marginal role in its politics.

Triumph and decline: the Adenauer regime, 1953–1963

In 1957, after 4 more years of increasing prosperity, the CDU–CSU won an absolute majority of 50.2 per cent of the vote. The chancellor, with his call for no experiments, had caught the mood of the time. At the age of 81 Adenauer was at the height of his political power, but gradually over the next 4 years his formidable political skills began to desert him, and his own party, the FDP and the West German people became increasingly impatient for his retirement. An early indication of how the Adenauer regime might eventually come to an end was afforded by the crisis in the governing coalition in the winter of 1955–1956. The FDP split and the majority led by Thomas Dehler (1897–1967), who was critical of Adenauer's rigid policy towards the USSR and the GDR, withdrew from the coalition, and began to consider working with the SPD. This did indeed happen in North Rhine-Westphalia where a break-away group of the FDP began to work with the SPD and succeeded in destroying the FDP-CDU ruling coalition. In Hans-Peter Schwarz's view, 'irrevocable forces were let loose by this event … which ventured into new directions, and gained a majority in the late 1960s'.[11]

Adenauer was essentially an authoritarian figure cast in a Bismarckian mould, impatient of parliament and the states. By the end of the 1950s this cavalier attitude began to alienate public opinion. In 1959, for example, he considered becoming president of the FRG when Theodor Heuss (1884–1963) retired, believing that it would enable him still to dominate politics. When he discovered that the constitution would not permit this, he rapidly backtracked and pushed the nondescript agriculture minister, Heinrich Lübke (1894–1972), into the post.

By the late 1950s, for the first time since 1952, Adenauer faced the challenge of an effective and modernized SPD. In reaction to its defeat in 1957, the party at last came to terms with the Adenauer–Erhard political revolution. In the Godesberg Programme of 1959 it embraced much of

Erhard's philosophy. In a famous formula coined by Professor Schiller (1911–1995) (see p. 354), the SPD would aim for 'as much competition as possible' with 'as much planning as necessary'.[12] In June 1960 the party moved on to embrace Western integration and NATO, and in August it chose Willy Brandt, the young and charismatic Mayor of West Berlin as the chancellor candidate to challenge Adenauer.

The 1961 election campaign was dominated by the closure of the frontier between East and West Berlin on 13 August. Adenauer made a serious mistake when he appeared to play down this momentous event and delayed his visit to West Berlin until 22 August. This allowed Brandt to accuse him of indifference towards West Berlin and indeed the whole question of German unity. Nevertheless, despite losing their overall majority in the election, the CDU–CSU still retained 46 per cent of the vote, while the SPD increased its percentage by only 4.4 per cent. It was the FDP which did best by increasing its share of the poll from 7.7 per cent to 12.8 per cent, which enabled it to hold the balance between the CDU and SPD. Adenauer managed to negotiate a coalition with the FDP and survive for 2 more years, but he had first to appease Ludwig Erhard, the leading contender for his position, by promising that he would step down before the next election and fend off the demand by Erich Mende (1916–1998), the leader of the FDP, for his immediate resignation by holding exploratory talks with the SPD on the possibility of forming a grand coalition without the Liberals.

> See Documents 77 and 80

The event that finally made retirement inevitable was the *Spiegel* affair. In October 1962 **Der Spiegel**, the news magazine, published a confidential report on the inefficiencies of the *Bundeswehr*. The minister of defence, Franz-Josef Straus, who, as a high-profile politician, was frequently criticized by *Der Spiegel*, was persuaded by his civil servants that the article was treasonable and that the editors, Rudolf Augstein (1923–2002) and Conrad Ahlers (1922–1980), should be arrested. This heavy-handed reaction, with police raids in the middle of the night, awakened memories of the Third Reich and provoked considerable public opposition. The press was highly critical, the intelligentsia strongly supported Augstein and there were student demonstrations and sit-ins at several universities. Adenauer badly misjudged the situation when he launched a bitter attack against Augstein in the *Bundestag* on 7 November, claiming that the country faced an 'abyss of treason'.

> **Der Spiegel**, which was launched in 1947, was a news magazine modelled on the American Time magazine. It had a circulation of over half a million and a readership of five million.

> See Document 81

Franz-Josef Strauss, 1915–1988

Strauss was one of the most controversial figures in West German politics. His father was a butcher, but Franz-Josef's intellectual brilliance won him a place at the *Maximilianeum* in Munich, a special school for gifted students. After a brief period as a prisoner of war, he played an increasingly important part in post-war Bavarian politics and was a founder member of the CSU. In 1948 he was elected to the Economic Council of the Bizone and in 1949 to the *Bundestag*. After serving as minister for special tasks and nuclear energy, he was appointed defence minister in 1957. After his resignation in 1962 he returned to office as finance minister in 1966 in the Grand Coalition (see p. 354), but he never succeeded in becoming chancellor of the FRG because his nationalism and his apparently extreme anti-Communism frightened off the majority of electors in a period of détente and *Ostpolitik*. He was chairman of the CSU, 1961–1988.

Adenauer could probably have ridden out the storm if the Free Democrats had not resigned from the cabinet in protest against the failure of the Defence Ministry to consult the FDP Minister of Justice, Wolfgang Stammberger (1920–1982), before acting against Augstein. Adenauer once again began negotiations with the SPD for a grand coalition. This had its effect and brought the FDP back into government, subject to two conditions: Strauss would have to resign and Adenauer himself would have to retire by October 1963.

The *Spiegel* affair was a major event in modern German political history. For the first time a government had been compelled constitutionally to concede defeat over the question of civil liberties. Adenauer never recovered from this setback. His popularity dropped dramatically, and in March 1963 the CDU lost the Rhineland-Palatinate *Land* election. At last, on 22 April, he recognized Erhard as his successor and he resigned 6 months later. He did, however, retain the chairmanship of the CDU, a position which he used unsparingly to criticize Erhard.

FRG: reconstruction or modernization?

The Adenauer era was full of paradoxes. On the one hand it witnessed accelerated economic and social change, which created an upwardly mobile society. Farming, for instance, was mechanized and lost half its workforce by 1960. On the other hand the 1950s also witnessed the survival of many of the pre-war elites in the Churches, the universities and big business. The one elite that was destroyed by the war was the old Prussian ruling class (see p. 310), whose traditional place in the bureaucracy was filled mostly by southern and western German middle-class officials.

The role of women illustrates the uneasy balance between change and restoration that epitomizes the Adenauer period. Women had played a vital role as both breadwinners and mothers in the immediate post-war period when so many men were still POWs. They were granted full equality in the Basic Law and the government was committed to amend the anachronistic Wilhelmine Civil Code by 1953, but in practice the cabinet was in no hurry to carry out this pledge. By the early 1950s it was clear that the immediate post-war period had not irreversibly transformed the position of women. Indeed, according to the revised Civil Service Law of 1950 the government had the power to dismiss women from state employment, provided that their husbands earned sufficient money to support the family. Only slowly under pressure from the Federal Court did the situation begin to change, but the expectation was still 'that a woman should marry, raise a family and build her life around the private sphere'.[13] Yet, paradoxically, as a result of the war there were a large number of single women who had no marriage prospects and therefore had to develop a new and independent lifestyle. 'Unwittingly', as Eva Kolinsky observed, 'the non-married women of the lost generation were trailblazers of change'.[14]

See Document 82

The degree to which West German society became 'Americanized' in the 1950s is debatable. Ralph Willett sees the occupation as 'the prologue to a more developed Americanization. Chewing gum and Lucky Strikes whose packaging alone symbolized the beautiful new world of modernity, were harbingers of McDonalds, corporation skyscrapers and nuclear missiles'.[15] Yet initially most West Germans were still constrained by a shortage of money, long working hours and poor living conditions. Only towards the end of the decade did a real breakthrough take place into the 'consumer age', when the West Germans began to spend on cars, new furniture and holidays, and to follow American fashion styles.

Popular attitudes in the FRG in the early 1950s also reveal a 'striking and elusive mixture of restoration and new tones and accents'.[16] On the one hand, society was characterized by a studded indifference to politics, a pessimistic view of the future and a strong desire to lead a private life – the *ohne mich* **attitude**. Hitler was still quite widely admired and many Germans rejected the responsibility of their country for the war. There was also a deep cultural conservativism, which was strengthened by the leading role of the Catholic Church. This led to tighter film censorship and in the early 1950s to the production of *Heimat* films, which propagated the message that the Germans themselves were also the victims of Nazism. The emergence of rock and roll and *die Halbstarken*, or teddy boys, whom some journalists compared to the SA, triggered a major cultural battle about what Uta Poiger has called 'the complicated process of reconstructing Germanness'.[17] This led to the paradox that while the West German conservative elites supported the integration of the FRG into a Western world dominated by the USA, they were scornful of popular American culture.

> **Ohne mich literally** means 'without me' and summed up the wish of many Germans in the 1950s not to become involved in politics.

On the other hand, there was a refreshingly new openness and desire for social harmony. Among the population there was considerable demand for foreign films, recipes and literature. Hemingway, for example, was one of the most popular authors in Germany in the early 1950s. The Adenauer era was a period of psychological and spiritual reconstruction. The West Germans wished to adapt to a modern and more liberal society the message and experience of the Nazi *Volksgemeinschaft*, which had preached, even if it did not always practise, social equality (see p. 265). Ironically, so Mark Rosen argues, the Germans pursued a 'reverse *Sonderweg*'[18] in the 1950s, as a more modern and classless society than their Western European neighbours.

The GDR, 1949–1961

Democratic centralism: the dictatorship of the SED

The model for the SED, the ruling party of the GDR, was the Communist Party of the Soviet Union. Just before its first party conference in January 1949 it set up that 'classic model of the executive committee of the Communist Party, the Politburo',[19] on which sat **four former Communists and three former Social Democrats**. Under the chairmanship of Ulbricht a small secretariat was also formed both to prepare the agenda of the Politburo and to ensure that its decisions were carried out after they had been given what was usually an automatic endorsement by the Central Committee, which was composed of 80 members elected at the party congress. These three organs were able to control the party, the mass organizations, such as the trade unions, and the Free German Youth Movement, as well as the state bureaucracy. A pyramid-like structure was thus created in which the chain of command ran from the top to the bottom and extended right across the GDR so that all subordinate party committees and groups at whatever level received their orders from the committee immediately above them.

The government of the GDR had been formed on 12 October 1949. Theoretically it was a coalition under Otto Grotewohl in which the SED shared power with the CDUD and LDPD, but the five key posts of the Interior, Education, Planning, Justice and Industry were firmly in the hands of the SED. Optimistically the two bourgeois parties believed that they would win the coming election with a landslide, but under Soviet pressure they agreed to delay it for a year, which enabled the SED to consolidate its position. In the hysterical atmosphere produced by the outbreak of the Korean War, witch-hunts were carried out by the Party Control Commission against alleged **'Titoists'** and other dissident socialists. It rapidly became more dangerous to be a former member of the SPD than a Nazi. The authority of the state was strengthened by the creation in December 1949 of the Supreme Court and the Department of Public Prosecutions and in February 1950 the formation by the Ministry of State Security of the *Stasi*, which was accountable to the Politburo. Its duty was to detect all internal opposition to the SED regime and to spy intensively on the population of the GDR.

Through a process reminiscent of the Nazi *Gleichschaltung* in the years 1933–1934 (see p. 238) the SED was able to turn the mass organizations and the bourgeois parties into 'conveyor belts' for the transmission of SED policy. Pressure was also exerted on the two bourgeois bloc parties, the CDUD and LDPD, to purge their more dissident elements. By the autumn of 1950 they joined the National Front, an inclusive organization which had been set up by the *Volkskongress* movement (see p. 305) to act as a comprehensive all-German organization representing all the parties and organizations interested in national unity – albeit a unity on the SED's terms. The Front was entrusted with drawing up the single unified

The Communists were Pieck, Ulbricht, Merker and Dahlem and the former SPD members were Grotewohl, Meier and Friedrich Ebert, the son of the former president of the Weimar Republic.

See Document 74

'Titoists': In 1947 Joseph Tito, the Yugoslav Communist dictator, refused to tow the party line from Moscow and pursued an independent foreign policy.

14   Parade of the Free German Youth (FDJ), Berlin, 4 July 1952

Press- und Informationsamt der Bundesregierung, no. 892/32

lists of candidates all offering the same policies which were to be presented to the voters in the elections on 15 October. The election was the final stage of what Willy Loth has called 'a *coup d'état*'[20] against the constitution of the GDR. The party claimed that 99.72 per cent of the voters had voted for the unity list. The dominant position of the SED was camouflaged by the composition of the elected *Volkskammer*. It won outright only 25 per cent of the vote, but thanks to the 30 per cent gained by the mass organizations and a further 7.5 per cent each secured by the Peasants' Party (DBD) and the National Democratic Party of Germany (NDPD), which were both led by ex-Communists, there was never any chance of the two bourgeois parties being in a position to veto policy. In 1952 the powers of 'democratic centralism' were further strengthened when all five of the states in the GDR were abolished and replaced by 14 regions (*Bezirke*).

Building a socialist economy, 1948–1952

Economic recovery was delayed both by the Stalinist policies of the SED and by the continued Russian demands for reparations. As late as 1950 some 25 per cent of the industrial goods produced in the GDR went to the USSR as reparations. Since the GDR was cut off from Western investment and the supplies of Ruhr coal and steel on which its industries were dependent before the war, it was forced into a search for domestic raw materials which at times, according to Rainer Karlsch, reached the 'irrational'.[21] The Cold War inevitably tightened the GDR's economic links with the Soviet bloc. In September 1950 it joined **Comecon**, and by 1951 76 per cent of its trade was with the Socialist bloc.

Comecon: The Council for Mutual Economic Aid had been set up in Moscow in 1949 in response to the OEEC.

By splitting up the larger farms, post-war land reform in the Soviet zone had seriously weakened the agricultural sector (see p. 299). Yields continued to be hit by a lack of fertilizers, and an acute shortage of livestock led to shortages in milk, cheese and meat. Inevitably these shortages drastically depressed the standard of living and the productivity of its workers. In 1950 wages had sunk to 71 per cent of their 1936 level, while meat and fat consumption were a mere 50 per cent of their 1934–1938 level. Both to consolidate its position and to plan production targets, investment and distribution, the government needed to control the economy. By 1950 it was well on the way to doing this. The **VEBs**, together with the **SAGs**, accounted for some 76 per cent of the total industrial production, while the banking and insurance sectors were completely in the state's hands. Independent retail trade faced fierce competition from the **HOs**, and both the surviving larger farms and independent artisans were harried by punitive taxation. Production targets were ambitious. The Five Year Plan, which was based on the Soviet model, was launched in 1950, and aimed at doubling the output of 1936, while living standards were 'to exceed significantly the pre-war level'.[22] Its main targets were the metallurgical and machine-building sectors, which were to expand by 153.6 per cent and 114.8 per cent respectively.

VEB: *Volkseigener Betrieb* or nationalized enterprise; **SAG:** *Sowjetischer Aktiengesellschaft* or Soviet limited company, which produced goods for the USSR as part of East Germany's reparations, 1946–1953

HO: *Staatliche Handelsorganisation* (state trade organizations), ran a whole range of shops.

In reality these targets could only be met by neglecting the consumer industries and keeping wages at a permanently low level. Butter, milk and sugar were still rationed. Pensions were kept to a minimum and the house-building programme remained at a markedly more modest level than in the *Bundesrepublik*. The expellees, too, were given far less generous compensation than those in the FRG. The workers were alternatively repressed and bribed by the party. Co-determination 'in the managing of the economy' was, so they were told, realized 'through the democratic organs of the state'.[23] Only if they exceeded the production norms set for their plant were they awarded bonuses. Following the Russian example, **the activist movement** was introduced in 1948, and Adolf Hennecke (1905–1975), a 43-year-old coal miner from Zwickau, was carefully coached to exceed his norm of coal mined during one shift by at least 250 per cent. When he achieved this by 387 per cent, he was turned into a popular hero.

The activist movement: In the 1930s the Stakhanov movement in the USSR aimed at raising the production of labour. The feats of Alexei Stakhanov, who, under especially favourable conditions, achieved spectacular production results, were used to justify raising the production targets of the other workers.

The Five Year Plan initially achieved some impressive successes in the production of iron, steel and chemicals. Raw steel production was, for example, already double that of 1936, and on the basis of these statistics at its party conference in July 1952 the SED leadership decided, despite Soviet reservations, to accelerate the planned construction of Socialism and to overcome the 'last traces of capitalist thought'.[24] The speed with which Ulbricht moved must be seen in the context of the international situation. The future of the GDR, as the Stalin note of March 1952

The expellees in the GDR

The three and a quarter million expellees from the German eastern territories formed a diverse group of skilled artisans, agricultural labourers and even former members of the Prussian landed gentry. By the law of 8 September 1950 they were given some financial assistance to buy tools and household furniture and promised priority in housing, but after that the state assumed that the increasing demand for labour and the expansion of heavy industry would integrate them into the GDR. The term 'worker–settler' was dropped, and the expellee problem was officially deemed to have been solved.

(see p. 314) indicated, was by no means assured. Ulbricht hoped that the socialization of the GDR along Stalinist lines would make reunification impossible except on the SED's terms. Klaus Schroeder has described this policy as 'a disguised opposition to the keeping open of the German question by the Soviet Union'.[25]

See Document 83

17 June 1953: riot or popular revolt?

By 1953 Ulbricht had managed to unite almost the whole of the East German people against his regime by the ruthlessness with which he had attempted to impose a Soviet pattern of socialism on a highly developed, capitalist, industrial society. The farmers resented the low prices they received for their crops and the fines they were forced to pay if they were late with their food deliveries. The remaining independent businessmen and artisans were also worried about whether their livelihoods would be nationalized by the state. The workers, too, resented the low wages, high taxation and rising food prices which were necessary to pay for the creation of the new armed frontier force. Tension was further heightened by the arrest of the leading politicians in the bloc parties, the LDPD and CDUD. Not surprisingly, the number of refugees fleeing to the West, despite the construction of a five-mile-deep restricted zone along the frontier, increased to almost half a million in the first 6 months of 1953. In February 1953 the situation was so charged that the bishops of the Evangelical Church in the GDR warned the government to take note 'of the distress which threatened to lead to a catastrophe of major proportions'.[26]

After Stalin's death in March 1953, Ulbricht came under pressure from the **new Soviet leadership**, which desired a détente with the West, to modify his policies. In early June the SED leaders were summoned to Moscow and told that unless they halted all moves towards collectivization, encouraged independent businessmen and stopped the persecution of the Churches, there would be a 'catastrophe'.[27] As Willy Loth argues,[28] Soviet policy needs to be seen within the context of Beria's proposals for the future of the GDR (see p. 315). The Russians, however, had omitted to make one vital change: they did not order Ulbricht to cancel his May directive increasing the work norms for the workers by 10 per cent.

New Soviet leadership: There was no immediate heir to Stalin. The key members of the new Soviet leadership were Malenkov, Bulganin, Beria and Khrushchev, who by 1957 became the dominant leader.

See Document 83 Ulbricht's refusal to rescind this led to growing unrest. On 16 June a demonstration of building workers marched first to the trade union headquarters and then to the House of Ministries to demand the abolition of the norms. Failing to obtain instant concessions, the workers began to call for a general strike and the production of more consumer goods, the restoration of works councils and the lifting of the ban on the SPD. In the meantime a wave of spontaneous and uncoordinated strikes and demonstrations had erupted across the whole of the GDR. There was intense anger directed at the regime. Crowds collected outside prisons and state and party offices and called for the resignation of the government, but only in Görlitz and Bitterfeld were efforts made to set up democratic local governments. Elsewhere there were no plans to control radio stations and transport networks or to seize arms. By 18 June, Soviet military intervention and the immediate withdrawal of the work norms restored order, although sporadic strikes, protests and demonstrations fanned by American radio transmissions from West Berlin continued for the next few weeks.

The nature of the events of 16–17 June

The events of 16–17 June were interpreted very differently in the two Germanies. In the GDR they were seen by the SED as a Fascist *putsch* manipulated by the West, while in the FRG the riots were regarded as a popular uprising against Stalinist tyranny. In 1965 Arnulf Baring modified this latter view by arguing that the revolt went through three brief phases:

- Initially it was a demand for lower work quotas and food prices.
- On the afternoon of 17 June it was 'transformed into a popular revolt'.
- This rapidly petered out, not so much as a result of Soviet intervention but because of a lack of leaders and a programme.

Christoph Klessmann argues that it was 'undoubtedly a workers' uprising'. On the other hand it was also partly, as Armin Mitter and Stefan Wolle stress, a forerunner of the events of 1989 (see pp. 375–379).[29] There were demands for lifting the frontier, free elections and the resignation of the government. Yet both these explanations are simplifications of complex events. The GDR was a deeply fractured society, and many of those who demonstrated on 16 and 17 June had their own separate agendas. More recently Gareth Pritchard[30] has argued that it was a complex mixture of factors: a recrudescence of Nazism, a youth revolt, a struggle for Westernization, and a violent but last spasm of the German socialist tradition.

The quelling of the riots by Soviet troops illustrated only too clearly that 'the power of the SED rested on Russian bayonets'.[31] The SED party leadership was determined to prevent a repetition of these traumatic events. It immediately arrested some six thousand people, who were held in conditions reminiscent of 'the torture chambers of the SA … during the Hitler period',[32] and thousands were purged from the SED, the trade unions and the bloc parties. The *Stasi* was reformed and put more effectively under the control of the party, and had from then on to compile daily reports, which would be processed by information groups in each regional administration (*Bezirksverwaltung*). Under Soviet supervision, the police and the **paramilitary plant defence groups** were re-equipped and made more effective. However, the Russians also insisted on the regime making considerable concessions: pensions were increased, more consumer goods were to be produced and food prices lowered. As a gesture of goodwill, the USSR also agreed to return the last 33 SAGs to German ownership.

Paramilitary plant defence groups: factory defence groups composed of local workers

Beria was made the scapegoat for the course of events in the GDR.

Ulbricht's survival against the odds, 1953–1957

Any chances of radical change in the aftermath of these events was, however, destroyed when Ulbricht managed to rout his critics in the Politburo. On 7 July 1953 he had only two supporters, Erich Honecker (see p. 369) and Hermann Matern (1893–1971), but the majority were unwilling to strike without explicit Kremlin backing, which after **Beria's fall** on 29 June was not given. It was indeed 'a turning point at which GDR history failed to turn'.[33] On 18 July Wilhelm Zaisser (1893–1958), Rudolph Herenstadt (1903–1968) and Max Fechner (1892–1973), who had dared to defend the workers' right to strike, were expelled from the Central Committee. At the 4th Party Congress Ulbricht was re-elected first secretary, and in the national election of October 1954 he was able once again to present the voters with a single list of candidates. In the new government 20 of the 28 ministers belonged to the SED. Both Ulbricht and the party, it seemed, had recovered from the events of June 1953.

Poznań uprisings: In June 1956 Polish factory workers in Posen rioted in protest against their working conditions, and the revolt had to be crushed by armed force.

Hungarian revolt: In the summer of 1956 the new Communist leadership in Hungary began to make political concessions. By the autumn these had led to an ever-growing demand for more democratization. By the end of October Hungary was threatening to pull out of the Warsaw Pact. To stop this, Russian troops were sent in on 4 November to restore a pro-Soviet regime.

Two years later Ulbricht faced another challenge when Khrushchev's dramatic revelation of Stalin's crimes at the 20th party congress in Moscow in February 1956 plunged the Communist world into crisis. Within the GDR this caused growing criticism of the SED's leadership. There was considerable support for **the uprising in Poznań in June**. In August and September a series of strikes broke out in the GDR. The Hungarian uprising at the end of October led to further unrest in the large industrial cities and the universities. As one miner in Saxony observed, it seemed that 'a small spark would be sufficient to begin an uprising amongst us'.[34] Nevertheless, a repetition of 17 June was avoided partly by political and economic concessions such as a shortening of the working day and the release of 20,000 political prisoners, but also by the effective deployment of factory defence forces. The brutal defeat of the **Hungarian revolt** by Soviet troops in November also acted as a powerful deterrent to the population of the GDR.

The events of 1956 were 'a flashpoint that failed to ignite'.[35] There had been plans in Moscow to replace Ulbricht with a more moderate figure, a **'German Gomulka'**, who would adopt a reformist programme. In early 1956 Karl Schirdewan (1907–1998) was actually being groomed by Moscow as Ulbricht's replacement, but the revolts in Poland and Hungary distracted the Soviet leadership at the critical moment, and simultaneously Ulbricht's value to the USSR was greatly increased by the loyalty of

'German Gomulka': Wladyslaw Gomulka had been dismissed from power by Stalin in 1948 but was brought back as first secretary of the Polish Communist Party as the only politician who could placate the Polish people.

the GDR during these crises. This reprieve gave him the necessary freedom to defeat his reformist rivals. One group led by Wolfgang Harich (1923–1995) was arrested in early 1957 and, by skilfully exploiting the divisions among his other opponents, Ulbricht managed to make a clean sweep of the rest by the summer of 1958.

Failure to catch up with the FRG and the construction of the Berlin Wall

By 1955 the standard of living in the GDR was the highest in the Comecon. Wages had risen rapidly since 1953, yet the availability of food and consumer goods still lagged far behind the FRG. With the launch of the second Five Year Plan in 1958, Ulbricht stated that the 'main economic task' was to overtake the FRG 'within a few years ... in per capita consumption of all important food items and consumer goods'.[36] The GDR had little option, as he expressed it, but 'to square off'[37] against the FRG. Only by rivalling the FRG's prosperity could it defeat the magnet-like pull of its economy and effectively challenge the Hallstein Doctrine (see p. 316).

Initially it seemed as if Ulbricht's gamble would succeed. In 1958–1959 the GDR's economy grew by almost 12 per cent per annum. In 1959, to coordinate the GDR's economy more closely with the other Comecon states, the second Five Year Plan was replaced by a Seven Year Plan with an emphasis on energy, chemicals and electrical engineering. By 1965 industrial production was planned to have increased by 188 per cent and consumer production by 177 per cent. In December 1959, in order to lay the basis for a more efficient agricultural sector which could out-produce the FRG, the decision was also taken to complete the process of collectivization.

However, these targets were, as Christoph Klessmann has put it, 'aiming for the stars'.[38] High labour costs in the GDR, poor-quality work, the lack of foreign exchange and the domination by the Western powers of the global economy all indicated that the GDR would fall ever further behind the FRG. The immediate economic impact of collectivization was disastrous. There were severe teething troubles: yields plummeted and serious shortages in bread, butter and meat were reported. There was consequently a huge increase in the number of refugees fleeing westwards through the open frontier in Berlin. In 1960 199,000 fled, and in the 6 months up to June 1961 a further 103,000. By June 1961 the *Stasi* was also reporting increasing unrest in the factories. Ulbricht, however, refused to make any concessions. Possibly, as Dietrich Staritz and Christoph Klessmann have argued, he was consciously intending to exploit the mounting economic crisis to push Khrushchev into agreeing to close the inner Berlin frontier, but it is more likely that the party accelerated the pace of collectivization because socialization in the countryside was proceeding more slowly than in the rest of the economy – at the end of 1959 only 43 per cent of the agricultural sector was collectivized.

Collectivization: the replacement of private farms by cooperatives and state-run farms

The torrent of refugees did, however, make the Berlin Wall inevitable, if the GDR was not to collapse. Once permission was given for the closure of the frontier at the meeting of the Warsaw Pact states on 3–5 August 1961 Erich Honecker, the minister in charge of security, carried out operations efficiently and swiftly in the early hours of 13 August. At first much of 'the anti-Fascist protective wall' consisted of barbed wire, but this was quickly replaced by a more permanent concrete structure, the notorious Berlin Wall. Although it was bitterly resented in the GDR, the security forces prevented any widespread protests. This day, 13 August, was a major turning point in the history of the GDR and the party loyalists came to regard it as the 'secret foundation day of the GDR'.[39]

The socialist '*Volksgemeinschaft*'

The SED was determined to build a new workers' and peasants' state in which capitalism, the 'seedbed' of Fascism, would for ever be eliminated from East German society. There was no partial restoration of the old order as in the FRG. Instead 'almost the whole of the old society'[40] was deconstructed over the decade 1950–1960. Only in the Church and the medical profession did the traditional bourgeoisie manage to retain its influence.

The key posts in both party and state were occupied by former KPD members, who had gained their political experience in the Weimar Republic. Below them a new elite had hastily to be trained, among the generation of workers' and peasants' children who had joined the Free German Youth (FDJ) in 1945, to fill the posts in the mass organizations, the schools and the nationalized industries. Shaped by their experiences in the Hitler Youth and traumatized by the end of the war, 'a minority, although probably a large minority'[41] accepted the offer of re-education at special workers' and peasants' faculties and 'bonded' enthusiastically with the new regime to build what they hoped would be a modern, classless industrial society.

What was the nature of this new German state they created? Klessmann has described it as 'a contradiction-ridden socialist experiment conceived as an alternative to the FRG and accepted as such by a small loyal minority'.[42] Unlike Poland, Hungary or the other Eastern European states, it was not a nation state. It was only a fragment of a nation and locked into permanent competition with the other German state, the FRG. Claus Offe has argued that the GDR possessed only an economic identity and represented 'a pure ... form of a socialist economic society'.[43] The factory became the context for socializing the adult population. It provided routine medical care, and organized cultural and social activities and even shopping facilities. Legally women enjoyed complete equality with men in this new workers' and peasants' state. By the Law on the Protection of the Mother and the Child in 1950 it was clearly stated that 'Marriage does not lead to any restrictions or narrowing down of a woman's rights.'[44] Through the provision of factory crèches and after-school supervision of children, women were actively encouraged to work. In reality, however, most women occupied the lowest-paid and unskilled jobs, as they lacked the right qualifications. They suffered under 'the bondage of a double burden'[45] because they still had the role of looking after the children and the home.

Education, literature, art and the mass media were all employed in helping to create a new working-class and socialist mass identity. Schools and universities became institutions primarily concerned with producing a steady supply of qualified workers, technicians and managers for industry and agriculture, and with the indoctrination of their students into Marxism–Leninism. In 1959 a single, comprehensive, ten-class higher school with a uniform curriculum was introduced, in which science and technical subjects played the major part. The universities were set similar goals and their staff was subjected to close supervision. The main inspiration for the arts and literature was socialist realism. Cultural activities were controlled by the state and were viewed as 'a force of production that would help to raise labour productivity'.[46] Jazz and much of Western literature and modern art were dismissed, as they had been in the Third Reich, as both decadent and irrelevant.

Opposition and dissent

Although some of the GDR's policies were beneficial, such as the provision of full employment and assistance for working women, nevertheless, 'a lot of people', as Mary Fulbrook has observed, 'did not like the GDR'.[47] The riots of 16–17 June 1953 were the most dramatic example of opposition to SED rule until September–October 1989, but there was a considerable amount of low-key **Resistenz** to party policies right up to 1989, particularly from workers, who disliked the intrusive nature of party demands. There was grumbling about pay levels, working conditions and production quotas, which sometimes led to brief strikes. Former SPD members, older people, who could not accept the division of Germany, and members of the traditional professions, particularly doctors, formed 'pockets of immunity to the Party'.[48] In the rural areas in the 1950s there were still some remnants of Nazism. Swastikas and graffiti were sometimes scrawled on walls, but, more often than not, this was the work of school students, and was rather the desire to shock the authorities than evidence of a Nazi revival.

Resistenz is best translated as 'immunity' to an ideology (see p. 264).

Like the FRG, the GDR also had its youth problem. There were occasional political protests particularly at the universities during the Hungarian revolt of 1956. East German youth was also influenced by American fashions in clothing, music and films. In the late 1950s rock and roll fan clubs sprang up, and there were disturbances in East Berlin and the other larger cities. Idolization of Elvis Presley went hand in hand with what one *Stasi* report described as 'depraved ravings against leading comrades'.[49]

It was, however, the Protestant Church that provided the most effective opposition to the totalitarian claims of SED Germany, as it possessed a coherent anti-Marxist philosophy. It represented an alien body in the GDR, and, as in the Third Reich, was capable of considerable *Resistenz* to the regime (see p. 264). The Protestant Church was not, however, a united monolithic body, but a group of eight loosely connected regional Churches, some of which had close links with the Protestant Churches in West Germany. It was, therefore, subject to constant harassment from the regime. Although Ulbricht's initial confrontation with the Church, in which he attempted to destroy its youth organizations, was halted as a result of Soviet pressure in June 1953 (see p. 329), the SED nevertheless continued to try to marginalize the Church's influence: in 1954 it introduced the *Jugendweihe*, as an alternative to confirmation, and put considerable pressure on parents to participate. It also sought to divide the pro-Western and strongly anti-GDR supporters of Otto Dibelius (1888–1967), one of the founders of the Confessing Church in 1934 and the Bishop of Berlin Brandenburg, from those pastors who were more prepared to compromise with the regime.

In 1958 the intensifying Cold War enabled the SED to weaken the links of East German Protestants with their brethren in the West. When the West German Evangelical Church decided to provide military chaplains for the *Bundeswehr*, the East German Churches had little option but to distance themselves from the decision. In July 1958 this led to a truce between Church and state. On the one hand the party managed to negotiate an agreement whereby the Church consented to 'respect the development towards socialism and contribute to the peaceful construction of the life of the community', but on the other hand, in return for this concession, the state had to concede that 'every citizen enjoys full freedom of belief and conscience'.[50] This enabled the Church to continue both to provide a rival ideology to Communism and to run a wide range of social organizations that were not under the SED's control. Ultimately, in the 1980s, these were to play an important part in the downfall of the regime (see p. 377).

> In 1948 the Confessing Church, which had been created in 1934 to resist Hitler's attempts to create a German Nazi Church, was replaced by the United German Evangelical Church, which included both East and West German members.

> *Jugendweihe* was the secular, socialist version of the Christian ceremony of confirmation. It marked the coming to maturity of young people in a socialist community.

Conclusion: the two Germanies: a comparison

Between 1949 and 1961 Germany was increasingly divided into two states integrated into mutually hostile blocs. On the one side, to quote T. A. Schwartz, 'the FRG in its early years of existence was effectively a part of the American political, economic and military system, more like a state such as California or Illinois than an independent nation',[51] while, on the other, the GDR became ever more closely enmeshed in a socialist Eastern Europe dominated by the USSR. Thus two different and competing systems grew up. The 1950s was a decade of reconstruction for both Germanies. In the FRG this took the form of an export-orientated social market economy within the overall framework of Western integration and liberal democracy, but in the GDR it was a time of enforced socialism and massive state investment in heavy industry carried out according to the Soviet pattern within the context of Comecon and the Warsaw Pact.

The experiences of the German people in the two states rapidly diverged. In the GDR the Churches were marginalized and at times persecuted, while in the FRG the Roman Catholic Church, in particular, exercised considerable influence through the CDU on both the government and the people. In the GDR there was legal equality for women, who were urgently needed in the workforce, even though in practice this equality was not a reality, but not even this theoretical legal equality had been achieved in West Germany, where married women were still encouraged to devote themselves exclusively to the family. In both states traditional rural life was revolutionized: farming was mechanized in the West and the numbers working on the land halved by 1960; in the East, collectivization swept away the independent small farmer. The experiences of the middle and professional classes could not have been more contrasting. In the FRG, a dynamic, upwardly mobile society was created and the bourgeois elites survived in business, law, the teaching professions and local government, while, in the GDR, only in medicine and the Church did the pre-war bourgeoisie enjoy a significant presence.

17 The Decades of Challenge: The Two Germanies, 1963–1988

Introduction: problems, issues, questions

For both Germanies the 1960s were a decade of considerable change, which some historians argue amounted to 'a second foundation' or 'refoundation'[1] of the two states. While both states, in almost a 'looking glass symmetry',[2] relaxed the dogmas and orthodoxies of the 1950s, are such terms as 'refoundation' perhaps an exaggeration? In the GDR the construction of the Berlin Wall created a situation where the whole population was in effect under 'house arrest'.[3] It no longer had the option of flight to the West and thus had grudgingly to come to terms with the party and state as best it could. Ulbricht, now assured of the survival of the GDR, was able to introduce a series of reforms which partially modernized its economic, legal and social structure. Did this then amount to the 'golden age' of the GDR? And to what extent were these effective in bridging the massive economic differences between the two German states?

In the FRG there was a similar process of modernization. The legal code was liberalized and the welfare state expanded, but starting with the *Spiegel* affair of 1962 (see p. 337) there was also what has been described as a 'cultural and political revolution'.[4] The decade witnessed a rapid growth in political activism, agitation and public debate, which challenged the 'collective amnesia'[5] of the 1950s. To what extent did this succeed in making the FRG a more liberal and tolerant state by the 1980s? In the GDR, given the ubiquity of the *Stasi*, political protest was isolated and uncoordinated. Nevertheless, by the 1980s there were, as in the FRG, environmentalist, civil rights and homosexual self-help groups. How effective were these in changing the political culture of the GDR and ultimately bringing about its demise?

A turning point in the history of both states was the dramatic hike in oil prices by OPEC in 1973 and the inflationary crisis caused in part by America's inability to balance her budget in the wake of the Vietnam War. To survive, industrial economies were faced with a decade of 'wrenching re-orientation'.[6] The FRG was strong enough to adapt to the challenging demands of the global economy, while the long-term failure of the GDR – and indeed of the whole of Comecon – to restructure and to adapt its industries was ultimately to be one of the most crucial reasons for its collapse in 1989–1990. Why was the GDR unable to respond more effectively to this crisis?

The FRG, 1963–1989

The Erhard government

Arguably by 1963 the FRG was a secure, prosperous and democratic state integrated into Western Europe. Yet in the eyes of many, especially in the generation which came of age in the early 1960s in the FRG, West German democracy was still on probation. Its stability was yet to be challenged by the combination of a major economic and political crisis. In the mid-1960s, however, it did have to face its 'first acid test',[7] when growing economic problems coincided with the end of 17 years of predominantly CDU–CSU rule and the emergence of strident political extremism on both the far right and far left.

Although in retrospect the Erhard coalition is seen as a brief postscript to the long Adenauer era, initially there seemed to be no reason why it should collapse so rapidly. Economic growth improved sharply in 1964, and in the election of September 1965 the CDU–CSU won 47.6 per cent of the vote, which was its second most impressive victory since 1949. In his first policy statement to the new *Bundestag*, Erhard dramatically announced that the post-war era was 'at an end'. He ambitiously attempted to launch a new programme for a 'shaped' or 'fully formed' society (*formierte Gesellschaft*) that would build on the achievements of the social market economy, yet at the same time persuade pressure groups such as the trade unions and professional and industrial associations to moderate their sectional interests and cooperate with each other for the common good of society. This concept made little impact, even though it did pinpoint one of the main problems of contemporary democracy.

Of far more immediate concern to both the government and the people was the state of the economy. By early 1966 inflation was creeping up to a rate of 4 per cent per annum and public spending had been increasing more than government revenues since 1961. By 1965 the budget deficit had risen to 1.4 per cent of the GDP. Wages, too, had been increasing more rapidly than labour productivity. Not surprisingly, after the election the government's first priority was to fight inflation by squeezing domestic demand. The *Bundesbank* did this so effectively that it slowed down the domestic economy to the point of recession. Politically the consequences of this for Erhard were disastrous. His reputation for economic invincibility was severely damaged and in July 1966 the CDU lost the Rhineland–Westphalian state election. The coalition was also divided on how to deal with the budget deficit. The CDU–CSU proposed extra taxes, while the FDP wanted cuts in expenditure. The last straw for the FDP was Erhard's failure to persuade the Americans to accept cuts in Bonn's financial contributions towards the cost of stationing US troops in West Germany. The FDP's resignation from the coalition on 27 October led to Erhard's replacement as leader of the CDU–CSU by **Kurt Kiesinger**, who then rapidly negotiated a coalition with the SPD to the exclusion of the FDP.

Kurt Kiesinger, (1904–1988): joined the Nazi Party in 1933; elected to the *Bundestag*, 1949–1958, after which he became minister–president of Baden-Württemberg; Chancellor, 1966–1969.

The Grand Coalition, 1966–1969

The formation of the Grand Coalition marked a controversial period in the politics of the FRG. It gave the SPD the chance to gain political credibility and finally break with the Schumacher legacy of opposition by accepting the responsibilities of government, while the CDU saw membership as a chance to consolidate its position and remove the stranglehold of the Liberals on government. To many West Germans the Grand Coalition communicated a reassuring sense of unity in the face of the growing problems confronting the FRG, but others, particularly students and the left-wing intelligentsia, were appalled by the fact that the only parliamentary opposition to the new government was provided by the small FDP. To them it seemed as if the FRG was teetering on the edge of becoming a one-party state. The writer, Günter Grass (1927–2015), warned that 'the youth of our country will turn to left and right wing extremism'.[8]

The Grand Coalition became a target for extremism, but it did not cause this extremism by itself. On the right the rise of the National Democratic Party of Germany (**NPD**), which bitterly criticized 'the so called pluralist society' and campaigned for a strong, nationalist Germany independent of NATO and the West, was primarily a product of the recession. On the left some of the more radical members of the Social Democratic Students Federation set up in December 1966 'the extra-parliamentary opposition' (APO) in reaction to the formation of the Grand Coalition. Ever since the *Spiegel* affair there had been a growth in

The NPD: (*Nationaldemokratische Partei Deutschlands*) was formed in 1964, but was already in decline by the late 1960s.

left-wing political activism, agitation and public debate that had challenged the political amnesia of the 1950s, but arguably the real motor for student unrest was the overcrowded, outdated and authoritarian nature of the German universities, which had hardly changed since the late 19th century. The unrest developed into 'the greatest trauma of the entire history of the Federal Republic',[9] and reached its peak at Easter 1968 when **Rudi Dutschke**, a leading member of APO, was shot and wounded by a right-wing assassin. This led to the most serious rioting in Germany since 1932, with demonstrations in 27 cities.

It was against this background, which could so easily have led to an authoritarian backlash, that the government pursued its policies for stabilizing the economy, updating the constitutional structure of the state and beginning the difficult process of rethinking the FRG's foreign policy (see p. 320). All in all it is fair to say that 'the Grand Coalition managed to set Germany back on track in the most difficult circumstances'.[10] The economics minister, the SPD Karl Schiller, and the CSU finance minister, Strauss, although temperamentally very different, formed a strong team which was able to restore confidence in the economy. In June 1967, when the recession was at its trough, the *Bundestag* passed the Stabilization Law which set up a legal framework to enable the government to steer the economy in times of slump by raising credits, altering income and business taxes, and building up reserve funds for public investment. These measures, which were inspired by the determination to avoid a repetition of the economic crisis of 1930–1933, were widely praised as the '"Magna Carta" of **Keynesianism** in a market economy', although criticized by others as 'corporate gradualism'.[11] They did, however, restore confidence. By 1969 the GDP grew by 5.6 per cent and inflation dropped to 1.5 per cent.

Rudi Dutschke,
1940–1979: initially made his name in a Berlin group called Subversive Action, which organized several demonstrations against the Vietnam War and the state visit of the Shah of Iran, 1966.

See Document 58

Keynesianism:
the economic theory based on the work of the British economist, John Maynard Keynes, who advocated state investment and public works at times of economic recession (demand management) to avoid unemployment

The cultural revolution

Politically this was led by the three Hamburg-based papers: *Der Spiegel, Die Zeit* and *Der Stern*. They enthusiastically backed *Ostpolitik* and were increasingly anti-American and more sympathetic towards the USSR. The majority of the literary and academic intelligentsia moved sharply to the left and became highly critical of the *Bundesrepublik* and of conservative institutions generally. This mood was fuelled by such works as Fritz Fischer's *Griff Nach der Weltmacht* (see p. 164), Rolf Hochhuth's play **Der Stellvretreter,** (*The Deputy*) which virtually accused Pope Pius XII of complicity in the Holocaust, and Karl Jaspers's **Wohin treibt die Bundesrepublik?** (*The Future of Germany*) Jaspers argued vehemently that the FRG was about to develop into an authoritarian regime. The Eichmann trial of 1960 in Israel and the Auschwitz trial of 1963–1965 of 16 former SS men and one prisoner overseer in Frankfurt refocused attention on Nazi crimes at a time when Ludwig Erhard and Franz-Josef Strauss were attempting to declare the end of the post-war era. Until the early 1980s the left dominated the political debate, and it was scarcely 'respectable' for any educated person to vote for the CDU!

The Grand Coalition's commitment to more intervention in the economy inevitably involved some encroachment by the central government on the financial powers of the states. In June 1967 Article 109 of the Basic Law was changed so that the states governments would be forced to take account of the condition of the national economy as a whole when planning their budgets. Two years later further changes were made to the Basic Law, facilitating financial cooperation between the states and central government in such areas as higher education, agriculture and structural improvements to the regional economy. These reforms inevitably strengthened the power of the central government, but the constitutional position of the states in the *Bundesrat* still made it difficult for Bonn to coerce them against their will.

Another constitutional measure of importance was the enactment of the Emergency Laws. In 1949 when the Basic Law was drawn up (see p. 307), these powers were still exercised by the high commissioners of the occupying powers. Clearly the Basic Law needed to be amended so that the FRG could protect itself in the event of war or civil unrest. Inevitably, the very concept of an Emergency Law awoke old memories and fears of the notorious Article 48 of the Weimar Constitution (see p. 191), which had helped Hitler to power. A campaign group was set up called 'Emergency of Democracy' which gained support not only from the APO, but also from a considerable number of FDP and SPD voters. Nevertheless, in spite of strident opposition, the law was passed in May 1968 and provision was made for an elected committee of 22 *Bundestag* members and one representative from each state in the *Bundesrat* to have the power to issue decrees if two-thirds of the committee agreed that parliament could no longer function effectively.

See Document 47

There was also discussion between the SPD and CDU–CSU about dropping proportional representation and creating a first-past-the-post voting system similar to the British system. The initial attractions of this to them was that it would deny the small Liberal party the role of kingmaker in the formation of governments and thus enable a single party to gain a sufficiently large majority to form a stable government by itself. When a public opinion survey in January 1968 showed that the CDU–CSU would gain a large majority through this electoral system, the SPD quickly changed its mind.

By 1969 cracks were beginning to appear in the coalition. Voting for the new president (speaker) of the *Bundestag* in February and then for the federal president was divided along party lines. Willy Brandt, the SPD's chancellor candidate (see p. 320), despite the cautious attitude of many of his colleagues, decided in September, before the general election, to go for the option of an SPD–FDP coalition. The election was by no means a foregone conclusion. Kiesinger was more popular than Brandt, but the SPD did have some important advantages. Schiller made much of the success of his economic policy, and showed that the SPD could be trusted with the economy, while Brandt and Gustav Heinemann, who had been elected federal president, managed to mobilize nearly all but the most extreme left-wing intellectuals, journalists and opinion-formers behind the SPD. In a hard-fought election campaign, the SPD and FDP won between them 48.5 per cent (the FDP only 5.8 per cent) of the vote, while the CDU–CSU gained 46.1 per cent. Brandt and Walther Scheel (1919–), the leader of the FDP, then managed to convince their parties of the viability of a social–liberal coalition, and on 21 October 1969 Brandt was elected chancellor by the *Bundestag* with a narrow majority of two.

Gustav Heinemann, 1899–1976: a president of his times

Heinemann initially served in the Adenauer cabinet, 1949–1950, as minister of the interior, but resigned in 1950 and then withdrew from the CDU in protest against rearmament and Adenauer's policy of Western integration, which to him appeared to rule out the possibility of German reunification. He moved over to the SPD in 1957 and in 1966 became minister of justice. From 1969 to 1974 he was the president of the FRG. His political outlook was formed when he was a member of the Confessing Church (see p. 239) and he was convinced that the FRG should conduct a dialogue with the GDR and Eastern Europe. As president he also advocated tolerance and understanding of the views of the New Left and APO.

Willy Brandt as chancellor, 1969–1974

The first Brandt administration

See Document 80

The SPD–FDP coalition enabled Brandt in October 1969 to become the first SPD chancellor since 1930. Brandt's rhetoric and charismatic style of leadership awakened expectations which he was unable to satisfy, except in the area of *Ostpolitik*. In his first speech as chancellor in the *Bundestag* he declared confidently 'we do not stand at the end of our democracy. We are only at the beginning', and then he made his famous invocation 'to dare more democracy'.[12] He announced a whole range of prospective reforms in taxation, welfare and law, all aimed at creating a fairer and more democratic society. Over the next 4 years he succeeded in expanding the provisions of the welfare state:

- The Pension Reform Act of 1972 made the rights to a pension less dependent on past financial contributions.
- The effectiveness of Health and Accident Insurance was improved, and family and unemployment allowances raised.
- The criminal law was modernized and made more humane.
- In particular, efforts were made to remove the inferior status of women. Abortion was made easier to obtain, although it was not until 1977 that the concept of guilt in divorce was swept away and replaced by the term 'irreparable breakdown'.

- Some attempt was made to reform the educational system. In 1971 the Educational Support Law provided grants for students from the lower income groups and after prolonged controversy some of the states introduced comprehensive schools.
- Equally controversial were the SPD's attempts to expand the role of workers' councils originally set up by the Adenauer government (see p. 334). These were bitterly contested and only in 1979 after a decision by the Federal Constitutional Court did the law take effect. Supervisory bodies were set up in companies with more than 200 employees composed of equal numbers of employers' and employees' representatives. In the case of deadlock the chairman, who was elected by the shareholders and owners had the casting vote.
- Censorship was relaxed, as were laws against homosexuality.

Inevitably these welfare measures and social reforms drove up government spending at the very time when inflationary pressures, largely caused by the dramatic weakening of the American dollar and the collapse of the fixed exchange rates created by the Bretton Woods Agreement in 1944 (see p. 359), were increasing, and needed to be countered by cuts in both personal and public expenditure. The strong *Deutschmark*, which in the opinion of most economists was ripe for revaluation, tempted speculators to change millions of American dollars into West German marks. This enabled banks to grant loans to individuals and businesses on easy terms, which only further fuelled inflation. Both Finance Minister Möller (1903–1985) and his successor, Karl Schiller, urged spending cuts, which were stubbornly opposed by the left wing of the SPD and the powerful and ambitious minister of defence, Helmut Schmidt (see p. 360). It was only when Schiller resigned in June 1972 that Schmidt, who then took over the combined Ministry of Finance and Economics, ruthlessly pushed through the very cuts he had opposed earlier.

Terrorism

The wave of terrorism that swept through the FRG from 1970 to 1972 forced the government in one crucial area to revert to authoritarian policies more reminiscent of the Adenauer era at the height of the Cold War than the new era of democracy announced by Brandt in 1969. There were in 1971 some 392 extreme left-wing organizations with a total membership of 67,000, ranging from the reconstituted **Communist Party** (now known as the DKP-German Communist Party) to groups of urban terrorists, who represented the hard core of the radical student movement of the 1960s. The most well known of these was the Baader-Meinhof Group. Its aim was, through arson and assassination of state officials, particularly judges, to inspire 'the intimidated masses'[13] to liberate themselves from capitalist oppression. The potential danger for Brandt in all this lay in the increasing polarization of public opinion on the issue of urban terrorism. At a time when he was in the midst of negotiations over

Communist Party: the KPD (Communist Party of Germany) was banned in 1956. See also Document 84

Ostpolitik (see p. 321), he could not afford to be accused of being soft on terrorism. He therefore carefully distanced his party from the extreme left, and in January 1972, together with the minister-presidents of the states, issued the so-called 'extremist directive', which reminded the authorities responsible for recruiting state employees that loyalty to the Basic Law was essential. Secret surveillance of the terrorists was authorized and a reorganization and coordination of the *Länder* police forces carried out. These measures were vindicated when Ulrike Meinhof (1934–1976) and Andreas Baader (1943–1977) were arrested in June 1972 after bomb attacks on the offices of Springer Press in Hamburg and on the headquarters of the American army in Heidelberg. In September, terrorism returned to the FRG when the Olympic Games in Munich were the scene of an Arab terrorist attack which killed 11 Israelis and one German policeman.

A vote of 'constructive no confidence': a vote of no confidence which actually designated a successor to the chancellor (see p. 307)

The election of November 1972 and Brandt's second administration

Brandt's *Ostpolitik* came in for fierce criticism at home, and thus the 'extremist directive' must be seen as partly a response to the criticism of those like Gerhard Schröder (see p. 386), who accused the Brandt–Scheel government of a 'fatal drift to the Left'.[14] Brandt's government only survived **the vote of constructive no confidence** in April 1972 on its *Ostpolitik*, which was tabled by the CDU–CSU, by a mere two votes. These, it later emerged, were won over by bribery. Three weeks after the Basic Treaty was ratified in May 1973, Bavaria applied unsuccessfully to the **Federal Constitutional Court** to have it declared incompatible with the Basic Law of 1949. By the summer of 1972 defections from both the SPD and FDP had eroded the government's slender majority in the *Bundestag*. The SPD's difficulties were further increased by a severe defeat in the Baden-Württemberg *Land* election. Nevertheless, while the SPD itself was unpopular, Brandt and *Ostpolitik* were not. Thus he was ready to risk a general election which would in effect become a referendum on his handling of *Ostpolitik*.

Federal constitutional Court: Unlike the Weimar constitution (see p. 307) there was no provision for referenda on national issues. Instead, the only way of challenging a government decision was the cumbersome route of going to the Federal Constitutional Court in Karlsruhe.

Through 'a somewhat dubious manoeuvre'[15] he managed to contrive to lose a vote of no confidence in the *Bundestag* in September, which opened the way up for an **election on 19 November**. Brandt fought a quasi-presidential campaign in which, as one of his biographers observed, he 'reached new heights of charismatic leadership'.[16] The SPD gained three million new votes, the majority coming from first-time voters, and achieved the greatest victory in its history.

Election of 19 November: According to the constitution, elections were normally held at fixed intervals. However, as a result of his defeat both the opposition and the governing coalition recommended to the president that there should be fresh elections.

Despite this success, Brandt failed to dominate his second administration. Immediately after his electoral victory he underwent an operation for laryngitis. In his absence Schmidt and Herbert Wehner (1906–1990), the deputy party chairman, appointed the new cabinet without consulting him. When Brandt came out of hospital, he became increasingly remote and indecisive. Within the SPD, divisions between the right and left intensified. At the party conference in March 1973 the left, which drew its support mainly from the Young Socialists, the SPD youth movement, strengthened its grip on the party directorate, where it won 28 of the 34 seats.

Brandt's problems were compounded by the continued speculative conversion of billions of dollars into *Deutschmarks*. From January to March 1973 the West German money supply was swamped by the inflow of 27.8 billion dollars. Only when the *Deutschmark* left the **Bretton Woods system** in March and its relation to the dollar was left to the market, was the *Bundesbank* able to implement a tight counter-inflationary policy. In October the effectiveness of this policy was destroyed by the decision of the Arab states, organized in **OPEC**, to triple the price of oil in the winter of 1973–1974. Consequently, the FRG had to spend some 17 billion more marks on oil imports in 1974 than in 1973, thereby giving further impetus to inflation. The situation was exacerbated by trade-union militancy. In January 1974, for instance, the union of public employees went on strike, forcing the states to negotiate an 11 per cent wages increase. By the spring of 1974 the economists were forecasting 8 per cent inflation and high unemployment.

Just at the very time when decisive leadership was required, it was becoming obvious to the electorate that Brandt could not provide it. Consequently the SPD rapidly began to lose support. In March it even lost control of Hamburg, a traditionally left-wing stronghold. The final straw for Brandt was the revelation that his personal assistant, Günter Guillaume (1927–1995), was an East German agent and a member of the *Stasi*. In the marked absence of any support from the leading members of his party he resigned and was replaced by the ambitious Schmidt.

> **Bretton Woods system:** In 1944 at Bretton Woods, USA, 44 states agreed to the creation of fixed rates of exchange between currencies after the war. In 1949 the *Deutschmark* accepted the Bretton Woods system.

> **OPEC (Organization of the Petroleum Exporting Countries),** as a consequence of the Yom Kippur war of October 1973, which ended in an Arab defeat, dramatically increased the price of oil.

The Schmidt era, 1974–1982

Schmidt was a very different man from Brandt. He was an abrasive realist who often spoke contemptuously of the more utopian ideas of the left wing of his party. He was essentially a man of action or *Macher*, as he was called. To the silent majority in the FRG his decisiveness was a welcome change to Brandt's dithering, but within the SPD his pragmatism was to lead to serious problems. Between 1969 and 1972 the membership of the SPD had increased by 22.5 per cent, a considerable percentage of which had initially been members of the APO. The social composition of these new members was predominantly middle-class and their politics were significantly more radical than the traditional blue-collar supporters of the SPD. Thus increasingly in the contentious areas of the economy and defence Schmidt's policies were subjected to a growing volume of criticism from them. By 1980, as Peter Pulzer observed, 'in many respects the West German divide between Left and Right now ran not between the parties but down the middle of the SPD'.[17]

See Document 85

Helmut Schmidt, 1918–

At the end of the war Schmidt joined the SPD in Hamburg and in 1953, after holding various posts in the city's government, was voted into the *Bundestag*, where he became an expert on defence and security matters. He was also a major proponent of modernization within the SPD and influenced the Godesberg Programme of 1959 (see p. 336). After a spell back in local government in Hamburg, he returned to the *Bundestag* in 1965 and was appointed leader of the SPD parliamentary group, 1967–1969. He was defence minister, 1969–1972 and finance minister, 1972–1974. As chancellor, 1974–1982, he emerged as a pragmatic but forceful leader who did much to strengthen West Germany's international reputation.

Economic problems

The most difficult problem facing Schmidt right up to his resignation in 1982 was the economic consequences of the oil price rises. By 1975 unemployment had increased to one million and the GDP fallen by 1.6 per cent. The left wing of the SPD wanted the government to spend its way out of the recession, but Schmidt cautiously pursued a policy of moderate expenditure cuts and reductions in tax concessions. He was determined that the FRG should pay for the increased price of oil through exports and thus was strongly opposed to protectionism in the Western world. To prevent this he adopted a three-pronged strategy. He threw the formidable weight of the FRG behind successive measures for achieving exchange-rate stability. In 1978, together with the French President, Giscard d'Estaing, he took the lead in devising the European Monetary System in which members of the EC would coordinate their monetary and fiscal systems. He also worked hard to strengthen such international economic institutions as the **International Monetary Fund** and the **World Bank** and played a key part in the economic summits of the G7 (see p. 327). Under Schmidt it was quite clear, to quote Lothar Kettenacker, that 'West Germany was no longer the proverbial political dwarf and economic giant, but a fully accepted player on the global field.'[18]

By 1978 the West German economy appeared to be well on the way to recovery. At the Bonn Economic Summit, Schmidt agreed that the FRG should act as a locomotive for the world economy and reflate its economy by the equivalent of 1 per cent of the GNP, provided that the Americans brought their own inflation under control. In the short term these measures seemed to work. In 1979 the GDP grew to 4.2 per cent and unemployment fell to below a million, but OPEC's second drastic price hike in the aftermath of the **Iranian revolution in 1979–1980** caused the price of oil to rise by 45 per cent for two consecutive years and plunged the FRG back into recession by late 1980.

Despite these recurring economic crises, throughout this period the majority of the population grew steadily wealthier. Wages increased while the working week shrank and holiday entitlement grew. Mass tourism, as one sociologist observed, by encouraging 'spontaneity, mobility, the

The International Monetary Fund and the **World Bank** were set up at the Bretton Woods Conference in 1944.

Iranian revolution in 1979–1980: the overthrow of the Shah of Persia and his replacement by Ayatollah Khomeni

capacity for enjoyment and an interest in new experiences replaced the old values of order, thrift and self-discipline associated with the work ethic'.[19] Only in the 1980s when unemployment rose to over two million did the FRG become a 'two-thirds society',[20] a phrase used to describe the existence of an intractable rump of unemployed who were effectively excluded from the consumer society. Overrepresented in this underclass were the foreign workers living in Germany, who numbered some 4.5 million by 1981.

Party politics, 1974–1982

Schmidt remained in office during this period only by virtue of a difficult balancing act between an ever more leftwards-inclined SPD and an increasingly more conservative FDP. Walther Scheel, who had been elected federal president in May 1974, was replaced by the more right-wing Hans-Dietrich Genscher (1927–), a friend of the new leader of the CDU, Helmut Kohl. Genscher would have preferred to work with the CDU, but for the time being the hostility of Strauss's CSU to the whole concept of *Ostpolitik* made this an impossibility. The situation was exacerbated by demands on the left of the SPD for economic reflation, while the FDP urged financial retrenchment and moved towards a more **monetarist** approach to the economy. In March 1976 it was uncertain whether the FDP would remain in the coalition. In Lower Saxony, for example, it was already negotiating a coalition with the CDU. For the time being, however, Schmidt was saved by the divisions within the CDU–CSU. Kohl was ready to accept *Ostpolitik* and work with the FDP, but Strauss and Hans Filbinger (1913–2007), the CDU minister-president of Baden-Württemberg, were still bitterly opposed to it and saw the FDP as 'the stirrup holder for the Social Democrats'.[21] In the *Bundestag* elections of October 1976 the distrust of Strauss among northern CDU voters and the FDP was a powerful factor which brought about the narrow CDU–CSU defeat. The Schmidt–Genscher coalition just managed to survive with a two-vote majority.

> **Monetarism** was a shift away from the Keynesian priorities of reducing unemployment to the belief that it was the government's main duty to control inflation and balance the budget.

Foreign workers in the FRG

The West German government only began to import foreign workers on a large scale once immigration from the GDR dried up. Whereas before 1914 Germany had looked to Eastern Europe for a source of extra labour (see p. 114), as a result of the Cold War employers were now forced to recruit in Greece, Turkey, Italy, North Africa, Spain and Portugal. In the early 1960s the government signed a number of labour-importation treaties with these states. During the rest of the decade immigration rose dramatically. By 1973 there were 2,595,000 foreign workers in the FRG, the majority of whom came from Turkey. As with the Poles some 80 years earlier, these workers were imported into West Germany 'as fodder to fuel economic growth'.[22] They were to come to Germany as '*Gastarbeiter*' (guest workers) and were not eligible for German citizenship.

During the recession of 1973 the West German government banned all further recruitment, but the number of foreigners nevertheless continued to increase, largely as a result of the immigration of dependents. Gradually the migrant workers developed 'mature ethnic groupings resembling the Polish community in the Ruhr before the First World War'[23] with their own newspapers and cultural clubs. The Turks and other Muslims also set up their own mosques. In 1987 Duisburg, for instance, had 30 mosques, while in the early 1990s 1200 Muslim parishes had been created in the whole of reunified Germany.

Most of the German population was ambivalent about the *Gastarbeiter*. Right into the 1970s there was relatively little social contact between the host community and the immigrants, and by the 1980s immigrants were becoming targets for the small racist groups that were beginning to emerge. On the other hand, a degree of assimilation had also taken place. In 1990 some 9.6 per cent of all marriages in Germany were 'mixed'.

See Document 80

Schmidt's decisive but pragmatic leadership was another reason why the SPD–FDP coalition managed to struggle on until 1982. His genius for crisis management was fully displayed in 1977 when he refused to capitulate to blackmail by the 'Red Army Group' in the Mogadishu incident (see below). Schmidt's handling of this crisis enhanced his appeal to the electorate, but, as the 1980 election approached, he was again helped by the divisions in the CDU–CSU and the rivalry between Strauss and Kohl, which culminated in Strauss replacing Kohl as chancellor candidate. In the election campaign Strauss almost certainly 'frightened away more voters than he attracted'[24] and, consequently, while the CDU lost 4 per cent of its vote, the SDP's share remained stable and the FDP gained 10.6 per cent, its best result since 1961. The defeat of the CDU finally ended Strauss's hope of the chancellorship, and Kohl once again took over the leadership of the party.

Schmidt's position, however, remained precarious. Much of his party opposed the monetarist policy of the economics minister, the FDP Count Otto Lamsdorff, while the left wing of the SPD was implacably hostile to his twin-track policy on nuclear missiles (see p. 327). Politically the SPD also faced a growing challenge when the hundreds of citizen-initiative groups, which had sprung up during the 1970s to campaign against the government on such environmental issues as the building of nuclear power stations or airport runways, finally coalesced into a general umbrella organization known as the Green Party in 1980. They now had the potential to attract many of the middle-class voters who had voted for the SPD in 1969 and 1972. By the summer of 1982 the FDP was beginning to move towards a coalition with Kohl. In a pre-emptive strike, Schmidt forced the FDP to resign from the coalition on 17 September. His hopes of a dissolution of parliament and a general election were dashed when, on 1 October, Kohl won a vote of constructive no confidence in the *Bundestag* and was able to form a coalition with Genscher. A surprise SPD victory in the Hesse elections in late September had persuaded both Genscher and Kohl not to run the risk of holding an early election which might see the return of the SPD, supported, perhaps, by the Greens.

Schmidt and the Mogadishu incident

After assassinating the federal attorney-general and the director of the Dresdner Bank, the 'Red Army Group' kidnapped Hans-Martin Schleyer (1915–1977), the president of the Federal Association of German Industry, and demanded, in exchange for his release, the freeing of 11 terrorists from prison. Schmidt personally took control of the situation and insisted that there could be no deal. His resolution was tested on 13 October 1977 when an Arab terrorist group in close contact with the 'Red Army Group' hijacked a Lufthansa Boeing 737. After murdering the pilot in Aden, they flew the plane on to Mogadishu in Somalia. Schmidt rejected an exchange of the passengers for the terrorists and, after receiving permission from the Somali government, dispatched a force of elite West German border guards who successfully rescued the passengers on 17 October. Although this decisive action did not prevent the murder of the unfortunate Schleyer, it was nevertheless a severe defeat for the terrorists, which strengthened rather than weakened public confidence in the democratic institutions of the FRG.

A conservative counter-revolution?: The Kohl–Genscher governments, 1982–1989

In his inaugural speech to the *Bundestag*, Kohl promised a rigorous economic programme of cuts, deregulation and encouragement to entrepreneurs. More ambiguously, he also stressed the need for 'spiritual moral change'[25] which was interpreted by some observers to mean a return to the ideas of the Adenauer era. He did, after all, declare himself to be Adenauer's spiritual grandson. In reality, however, he was a cautious and pragmatic chancellor, who did much to preserve the legacy of his predecessors.

Kohl's immediate task on becoming chancellor was to consolidate his own position. Like Brandt in 1972 he engineered the loss of a no-confidence vote to force an early election in March 1983, which he fought on the basis of a programme for economic stabilization and the implementation of NATO's twin-track decision. The continuation of *Ostpolitik* was guaranteed by the inclusion of the FDP in the coalition. The SPD was in no position to defeat Kohl. Although its new chancellor candidate, Hans Jochen Vogel (1926–), was a moderate in the mould of Schmidt, his party was badly split on the issue of missile deployment in the FRG, and, by ruling out a coalition with the Greens, he had rejected in advance the only route whereby the SPD could at that stage have returned to power. Predictably, the election was a disaster for the SPD, whose share of the vote declined to the level of 1959. The CDU, on the other hand, gained its best result since 1957, while the FDP just cleared the 5 per cent hurdle with a mere 6.5 per cent of the vote. The Greens managed to win sufficient votes to gain representation in the *Bundestag* for the first time.

See Document 80

Helmut Kohl, 1930–

Born the son of a custom's official in Ludwigshafen in the Rhineland, he was a co-founder of the conservative youth movement *Junge Union* in 1946, and he joined the CDU youth wing in 1947. He worked for some years in industry, and was elected to the *Landtag* of the Rhineland-Palatinate in 1959. Ten years later he became the state's minister-president. In 1973 Kohl was elected chairman of the federal CDU and in 1976 was the chancellor candidate in the national election. Although in 1980 Strauss replaced him as chancellor candidate, he retained the chairmanship of the CDU, and thus was in a strong position to form a government in 1982. Kohl presided over the reunification of Germany in 1990 and remained chancellor until 1998.

The government was only moderately successful in its attempt to return to the principles of the social market economy. It introduced a programme for tax cuts phased over 7 years and tried to keep annual budget increases down to 3 per cent, but nevertheless it could not prevent a rise in welfare spending and industrial subsidies. Confronted with mass unemployment, it enacted measures to make the labour market more flexible, and to encourage retraining and early retirement, but in 1987 the number out of work was still over 2.2 million. In 1983 the economy had started to recover. With the collapse in oil prices in the mid-1980s the terms of global trade began once more to favour the FRG. Inflation fell from 6.2 per cent in 1981 to 0.6 per cent in 1986. For the next 5 years the FRG was able to build a large trade surplus which was annually worth more than 5 per cent of the GDP. It was this economic power that was to facilitate German unity in 1989–1990 (see Chapter 18).

The stubborn persistence of unemployment, which remained at over two million for most of the decade, undoubtedly damaged the mid-term popularity of the government. In addition, Kohl's competence as party leader was put in question by the continued bitter feuding between Strauss and the FDP. Within the CSU itself there were internal divisions caused both by Strauss's arrogant leadership and his extraordinary volte-face over *Ostpolitik* when, after years of hostility to *Ostpolitik* and Communism, he was instrumental in negotiating financial credits to the GDR (see p. 326). Two CSU members split off in 1983 to form the new right-wing Republican Party, which in 1989 achieved considerable success in the West Berlin *Land* elections. Both the FDP and the CDU were also deeply involved in the **'party donations affair'**. As chairman of the CDU, Kohl was inevitably caught up in the ramifications of this scandal, although he was not legally culpable. In the eyes of many voters the Bitburg affair also raised serious questions about his judgement. Kohl had planned to stage a symbolic gesture of reconciliation on the 40th anniversary of the end of the Second World War in a small military cemetery at

'Party donations affair': Over a long period of time considerable financial donations from industry had been made secretly and illegally to all three political parties. In 1984 the FDP finance minister, Count Lambsdorff, resigned when it was discovered that he had exempted the Flick Corporation from large tax payments after financial donations had been made to the FDP.

Bitburg during President Reagan's state visit to Germany. When it was discovered that SS troops were buried there, Kohl, despite considerable international pressure, stubbornly persisted with the ceremony.

The debate on German national identity and the Nazi past

The Bitburg affair needs to be understood within the context of the debates on German identity and the German past, particularly the Holocaust. In the late 1970s and early 1980s a consensus was emerging that the FRG did not owe total loyalty to the USA, and had interests of its own which it was legitimate to pursue. Accompanying this growing self-confidence was the recurring question about the responsibility of the German people for the Holocaust. The debate erupted again when Kohl stated on a visit to Israel in January 1984 that by the 'grace of late birth'[26] his generation was not directly guilty. The 40th anniversary of the end of the Second World War fuelled the debate further, and in 1985–1987 it became the focus of a major and often bitter historical debate (*Historikerstreit*) (see p. 243). Andreas Hillgruber in two essays appeared to compare the consequences and suffering of the destruction of the Reich in 1944–1945 with the Holocaust, while Ernst Nolte, in an even more controversial article in the *Frankfurter Allgemeine Zeitung*, which was entitled 'A Past that Will Not Go Away', argued that the **massacre** of the Armenians by the Turks in 1915 and the Kulaks by the Soviets in 1929 were as iniquitous as the Holocaust and that consequently the Germans should not be accused of a unique crime.

Both historians were accused by the left of moral relativism and trivialization of the Holocaust.[27] Many on the left, such as the social philosopher, Jürgen Habermas, and Rudolf Augstein, the editor of the *Spiegel*, were convinced that these arguments were part of a conservative counter-revolution.

In the state *elections* the SPD was able to exploit the unpopularity of the government, but when it came to the General Election of January 1987 it was again defeated. It attempted in vain to *attract* the Green vote by committing itself to the 'ecologization of production and consumption',[28] but this merely exposed it to taunts from the CDU of being opposed to progress. The ruling coalition's campaign, however, was again seriously weakened by bitter infighting between the CSU and FDP. The vote of the CDU–CSU fell back to 44.3 per cent while the FDP rose to 9.1 per cent.

The party splits in the governing coalition deepened over the next 2 years. Right at the beginning of the new parliament there were bitter disagreements over the legislative programme for the new parliament, and 15 members of the coalition withheld their vote when Kohl was elected chancellor by the *Bundestag*. In the state elections the CDU–CSU suffered a series of devastating defeats which accumulatively weakened Kohl's authority in Bonn. By the autumn of 1989 it seemed that Kohl's days as chancellor were numbered, but he was 'thrown a much needed lifeline'[29] by the collapse of the GDR.

See Document 80

Massacres: In 1915 and 1916 the Turks had massacred and deported the majority of the Armenian population in Asia Minor. In 1929, during the collectivization programme, Stalin deported the expropriated Kulaks (independent farmers) to Siberia, where a large number died.

15   Top: GDR Stamps celebrating in April 1966 the 20th anniversary of the forced amalgamation of the KPD and SPD to create the SED Bottom: receipt of a fine incurred by the author in August 1972 for travelling from Potsdam to the centre of East Berlin without the necessary official permission from the GDR authorities.

The GDR, 1961–1989

Partial modernization, 1961–1970

As for the Federal Republic, the 1960s were a watershed for the GDR. Ulbricht was convinced in 1961 that the closing of the inter-German border gave the GDR for the first time a chance to compete equally with the FRG. His aim, he stated, 'was to improve the material and cultural living conditions of our people, so that we clearly prove our superiority over West Germany and also over other capitalist countries'.[30] To achieve this, however, he had radically to modernize the cumbersome economic and planning structure of the 1950s. Thus he and the new, more technocratically minded members of the Politburo, like Erich Apel (1917–1965) and Günter Mittag (1926–1994), enthusiastically embraced the ideas of Yevsei Lieberman (1897–1981) the Russian economist, who advocated both ceding more independence to management and the introduction of the principle of profitability. To implement this, the 'New Economic System' for planning and managing the economy was announced in July 1963. A key position was held by the 82 Associations of Nationalized Enterprises (VEB) which were given considerable latitude in carrying out proposals put forward by the National Planning Commission. Significantly, workers' wages were linked to profits in an attempt to boost production.

The New Economic System depended on the support, or at least cooperation, of the population. Thus there had to be a considerable change of emphasis in the control techniques practised by the party, and, to achieve this, Ulbricht underwent something of a metamorphosis into a 'liberal'. Rather than the overt use of terror there was a more subtle attempt to win over the population or at least neutralize discontent. These reforms, of course, stopped well short of allowing any genuine democracy to develop. Wolfgang Berger, one of the economic reformers of the 1960s, recalled in 1992 that their 'aim was ... to develop and improve the existing mechanisms, to stress the democratic in democratic centralism'.[31] The mass organizations did however, undergo a degree of liberalization. The Trade Union Federation (FDGB) was encouraged to defend more actively the interests of the workers, even though it was never allowed to develop into an independent trade union movement, as all the key positions in the union still lay in the hands of the SED. There was also a more sensitive attempt to appeal to young people. The Free German Youth (FDJ) temporarily lost its monopoly as a youth organization, and had, for a time, to compete with the unions and student clubs to attract young East Germans.

The constitutional and legal structure of the GDR was also partially modernized. The new legal code significantly liberalized the old Prussian legal system, which had remained the basis of East German law in many areas. On the other hand, the definition of crimes against the state was widened to include 'anti-state agitation', which was so loosely defined that it could be applied to almost any criticism of the regime. Increasingly the SED based its power on what Peter Ludz has called a form of 'consultative authoritarianism'[32] rather than Stalinist terror. In the local elections of October 1965, for instance, voters were allowed to reject individual candidates on the single list, although in practice only two candidates failed to be elected. There was also an element of public consultation when the new constitution was drafted, which in its final form was submitted to a referendum in April 1968. Freedom of conscience and religion were theoretically conceded as were many other civil rights, but the position of the

SED as the ruling party was confirmed and thus declarations on the freedom of the media and on parliamentary sovereignty were mere travesties of the truth.

By the end of the decade it was clear that Ulbricht's gamble had failed. The hostile reaction of the population to the invasion of Czechoslovakia by Warsaw Pact troops in August 1968 (see pp. 320–321), in which the GDR played a limited supporting role, revealed that under the surface there was still a deep resentment of the regime that the largely cosmetic social and political reforms had not obliterated. There were refusals in factories to sign party petitions backing the invasion, while in some towns groups of youths staged illegal gatherings and chanted such slogans as 'We want our freedom'.[33] In places the West German flag was flown; elsewhere Nazi songs were sung and at one FDJ campsite near Rostock a picture of Hitler was displayed.

See Document 86

Neither was there much chance that an East German economic miracle might mollify the population. The New Economic System had been only partially successful: initially production did increase, the living standards of the population rose and more consumer goods became available, but by 1969 East German productivity was again falling in comparison with that of the FRG. In a desperate attempt to reverse this trend, Ulbricht and the economic reformers invested vast sums, which had not originally been budgeted for, in introducing automation into the metalworking industries. This merely led to cuts in the consumer goods available for the population and reinforced popular discontent. Within the Politburo, Honecker managed to mobilize sufficient support to compel Ulbricht in September 1970 to abandon the New Economic System. The association of similar reforms in Czechoslovakia with political liberalization persuaded Brezhnev and 'conservatives' in the GDR like Honecker to veto any further economic liberalization. Ulbricht remained in office as a mere figurehead and had impotently to stand aside while a more modest Five Year Plan was drafted. In April 1971 he was ordered to resign by Brezhnev, who was irritated by his insistence that the highly developed nature of German socialism made the GDR the equal of the USSR. Two months later Honecker, who replaced him, abandoned his reforms completely. Ulbricht lingered on as 'honorary chairman of the SED' until his death on 1 August 1973.

Could Ulbricht's economic reforms have saved the GDR? Charles Maier[34] argues that if they had remained in place they would have 'eventually unleashed forces for pluralism', and would also have enabled the GDR to develop a much more flexible economy, which could have withstood more effectively the shocks of the oil price rises in the 1970s and early 1980s. Honecker's economic policy failed catastrophically in 1989, but this does not mean that the continuation of Ulbricht's New Economic System would necessarily have saved the GDR. It was, after all, visibly failing in 1968–1970. Harold James[35] has pointed out that in Hungary and Poland experimentation with semi-liberal economic policies did continue, but failed to prevent economic collapse. The GDR had a stronger economy than both those states, but even so it was also severely handicapped by deficient raw material reserves, an acute shortage of foreign exchange with which to purchase Western technology and its economic dependence on Russia. An inevitable consequence of this weakness was the mediocre quality of its industrial research, caused by poor equipment and low budgets.

The Unity of Social and Economic Policy, 1971–1989

Honecker replaced the New Economic System with the much more cautious concept of the Unity of Social and Economic Policy. Central decision-making and controls were reintroduced without any serious attempt to analyse the underlying economic problems. Rising economic production was to finance social reform. In reality this meant that an expensive social welfare policy was to be pursued at the cost of industrial investment, which might ultimately have produced goods that could have been internationally competitive. Retrospectively Gerhard Schürer (1921–2010), the head of the Planning Commission, believed that this decision to subsidize overgenerous welfare provision was the fatal flaw in the GDR's economic policy. In 1991 he observed that 'that was when the switches were set. From then on the train travelled millimeter by millimeter in the wrong direction. It travelled away from the realities of the GDR'.[36] Social expenditure rose by 90 per cent between 1971 and 1979, while national income increased by just 46 per cent.

Erich Honecker, 1912–1994

Honecker was born in the Saar as the son of a miner. He joined the Communist youth organization in 1926 and, after attending a course in Moscow, became one of its leaders in 1930. He was arrested by the Nazis in 1935 and only freed in 1945. He was put in charge of building up the Free Communist Youth (FDJ) until 1955, and then, after a further year in the USSR, he returned to become minister for security. In this role he was responsible for planning and building the Berlin Wall in 1961. In the 1960s he was the 'crown prince' to Ulbricht, whom he replaced in 1971. When the GDR collapsed, legal proceedings were started against him, but in 1993 they were halted on the grounds of his ill health and he was allowed to join his wife in Chile.

Honecker's retreat to the orthodox policies of centralized planning ensured that a top-heavy system of bureaucratic control prevented the East German economy from reacting quickly to the economic challenges of the 1970s – the destabilization of the international monetary system and the dramatic rise in oil prices. Nor was the flexibility of East German industry helped by the socialization of the remaining small, independent enterprises. Errors and missed opportunities, as Charles Maier has commented, 'accumulated throughout that decade and emerged spectacularly during the 1980s'.[37] In January 1980 a belated attempt was made to streamline East German industry when the main branches of industry were organized into *Kombinate* (combines), which embraced all the main factories in a particular industrial sector, but these, too, were in their turn subjected to the dead weight of bureaucracy, as their decisions were closely scrutinized by a Workers' and Peasants' Inspectorate.

The GDR's economy like West Germany's was severely hit by the sudden rise in the prices of oil and raw materials in 1973. Although the USSR did not immediately charge market prices for its oil exports to the Comecon states, the rapid rise in world prices for hydrocarbons and chemicals inevitably led to a worsening of the GDR's balance of payments, since the price of imports rose more steeply than the price of exports. Over the period 1972–1975, for example, import prices rose by 34 per cent, whereas export prices increased by only 17 per cent. In turn, this sharp deterioration in the terms of trade led to the GDR increasing its foreign debt, particularly with the Western states. Honecker's failure to achieve solvency was to be one of the main reasons for the collapse of the GDR in 1989. As early as November 1973, he responded to pessimistic forecasts about the growth of debt over the next seven year period by ordering, ostrich-like, all further work on such projections to cease. Again in May 1978 the Council of Ministers blocked attempts by the State Planning Commission to get to grips with the balance of payments problem on the grounds that it would irreparably damage the Unity of Economic and Social Policy. West German loans in 1983 and 1984 (see p. 326) temporarily saved the GDR from bankruptcy, but by November 1987 the debt to the West had risen to 38.5 billion **Valuta marks**. The financial situation was made much worse in the early 1980s by the failure of an ambitious attempt to develop a viable computer industry, which had cost the GDR nearly 14 billion marks. The economic outlook was so grim that it is not surprising that in September 1987 the *Stasi* was reporting that economic problems and shortages were discrediting the regime.[38]

Valuta mark: the currency used for foreign trade by the GDR, which was roughly equivalent to the *Deutschmark* in value

The 'niche society'

While Honecker's economic policy proved in the long term to be fatal for the GDR, it did enable him for a time to neutralize opposition and create a social peace of sorts. Günter Gaus (1929–2004), the first West German permanent representative in East Berlin, coined the concept of the GDR as a 'niche society' where people withdrew into private retreats, such as the family, circles of friends or the pursuit of hobbies, 'so that a good man with his family and among friends can water his potted flowers, wash his car, play skat, have conversations, celebrate holidays'.[39] The corollary of this was that party control of the public sphere was at least grudgingly tolerated.

The concept of a 'niche society' was immediately seized upon by the West and became an overworked cliché used to explain the apparent acceptance of the regime by the population. The *Stasi* files show that in reality 'the evidence of workers unrest and the splutterings of revolt is far greater than ever imagined'.[40] Mary Fulbrook indeed questions whether there was ever 'a "golden age" in the GDR when the subordinate masses were genuinely content to leave politics to a well-meaning but powerful elite'.[41] However, for a time Honecker did in the early to mid-1970s create at least the illusion of stability and an acceptance of the regime by the population. By the 1970s almost the whole population participated in the mass party organizations. Diplomatic recognition by the West made the GDR an international fact of life. The vast majority of East Germans had little option but grudgingly to come to terms with the party. Acceptance of the regime was, of course, also assisted by Honecker's social reforms, a greater toleration initially towards writers, artists and intellectuals, and the production of more consumer goods, such as fridges, washing machines and cars. The strength of the regime seemed confirmed in March 1978 when the Protestant Churches again recognized that they had to work within a socialist society and in return received a 'precarious and partial negotiated autonomy (see p. 349)'.[42]

Honecker's cultural policy

Up to the mid-1970s there was something of a honeymoon with the cultural intelligentsia. The novelist, Ulrich Plenzdorf (1934–2007), was able to write, for instance, about 'a socialist drop-out'[43] who suffered from having to fulfil industrial norms and pressures to conform. There was also a spate of books about the difficulties experienced by women in the GDR. However, in 1976 the honeymoon came to an abrupt end when the folk singer Wolf Biermann (1936–) was deprived of his passport whils on a tour in the FRG.

Growing opposition

Some of the factors that gave the regime this illusion of permanence began by the end of the 1970s to develop the potential for undermining it. *Ostpolitik* and the implications for human rights of the Helsinki Accords (see p. 327) increased popular demand for closer contact with the West and a more liberal regime. The March agreement of 1978 had sought to exploit the Church 'as an indirect means of controlling dissent'.[44] Thus, astonishingly frank discussions could take place, provided that they occurred on Church premises and within the context of a gathering or prayer meeting presided over by a priest who, it was understood, would keep a tight control of the situation and ensure discretion.

See Documents 78 and 79

In the late 1970s and early 1980s under the protection of the Church it was perhaps inevitable that incipient political activism should take root. Initially a network of small peace groups grew up. These were critical both of NATO's deployment of missiles in West Germany and of the GDR's introduction of military education into the school curriculum, as

Gorbachev: In 1985 Mikhail Gorbachev as general secretary of the USSR was determined to reform the Soviet economy. To do this he realized that the financial drain caused by the arms race and the war in Afghanistan would have to be stopped and that both Soviet society and the economy would have to be modernized. He therefore pursed the policies of *perestroika* (restructuring the economy) and of *glasnost* (more openness in politics) and sought to end the Cold War.

Olaf Palme peace march: This was an international march or demonstration in memory of the Swedish prime minister, Olaf Palme, who was assassinated on 28 February 1986.

Luxemburg–Liebknecht parade: This was held in honour of Rosa Luxemburg and Karl Liebknecht, who were murdered by *Freikorps* troops in January 1919 (see p. 189).

well as of the Soviet invasion of Afghanistan. In June 1985, at the Peace Workshop in East Berlin, the possibility of setting up a GDR-wide seminar on human rights was first mooted, and in the autumn two campaign groups were founded: *Gegenstimmen* (Counter-voices) and *Initiative Frieden und Menschenrechte* (Initiative for Peace and Human Rights). The latter group functioned independently of the Church and attempted to exploit **Gorbachev**'s more liberal approach to put pressure on Honecker for change.

In 1986 the Peace Workshop attracted some 1300 participants and was banned the following year by the *Stasi*. The mid-1980s also saw the rise of the environmentalist movement for which the disaster at the Russian nuclear power station in Chernobyl in 1986 acted as a catalyst. The *Stasi* managed with some success to sow dissension among the environmentalists and split the movement, but the subsequent burgeoning of small groups in fact only served to fuel public debate.

In 1987 there briefly seemed to be some hope that the GDR would follow **Gorbachev's** example and embark upon a policy of liberalization. Before his state visit to West Germany, Honecker allowed a dramatic increase in the issue of visas for those who wished to see relatives and friends in the FRG. The celebrations marking the 750th anniversary of the foundation of Berlin also deliberately fostered 'the view of the GDR as a forward-looking, progressive and increasingly tolerant society'.[45] On the **Olaf Palme peace march** of September 1987, for example, the unofficial peace movements were allowed to participate alongside official representatives of the GDR. Yet by the late autumn there were signs that the government was reverting to a policy of confrontation. In November 1987 the *Stasi* raided the Environmental Library in Berlin, seized the printing presses and made several arrests. In January 1988 large numbers of demonstrators who sought to infiltrate the annual **Luxemburg–Liebknecht parade** were also arrested. Over the next 12 months Honecker continued to clamp down on all expressions of dissident views. He even censored the Soviet magazine *Sputnik*, as it was uncomfortably full of Gorbachev's ideas on *perestroika* and *glasnost*. He failed, however, to stamp out the activities of the dissidents. In May 1989, for example, dissident groups monitored the local elections and exposed the massive vote rigging in favour of the SED.

Up to this point the great mass of the population still remained quiescent, but in the course of the summer of 1989, with the opening of the Hungarian frontiers to Austria this was to change.

Conclusion: a tale of two Germanies

Despite gloomy predictions in the early 1960s that the West Germans were merely 'fair weather democrats',[46] the constitution of the FRG relatively easily withstood the minor recession of 1966–1967, the student riots of 1968, the subsequent outbreak of terrorism and the major economic crises caused by the steep rise in oil prices in 1973 and 1979.

Indeed, with the development of numerous citizen initiatives and the Green movement at the end of the 1970s the FRG was arguably well on the way to becoming a more participatory democracy. The pessimistic forecast of Karl Jaspers (see p. 354) could not have been further from the truth.

Behind the barrier of the Wall the GDR was able to achieve a stability of sorts. Ulbricht, hitherto 'the keeper of the holy grail of Marxism–Leninism',[47] began to dismantle the rigidly centralized economic structure of the Stalinist economy and to create a more flexible economy in which the profit motive acted as an important spur. Eventually these reforms would have 'unleashed forces for pluralism',[48] which would in all probability have destabilized the GDR politically. In that sense Honecker's return to orthodoxy, coupled with more generous welfare policies, was at least a short-term act of preservation, even though in the longer term it prevented the East German economy from responding more flexibly to the new post-Keynesian demands of the world economy after 1973.

The collapse of the GDR in 1989 has inevitably focused the attention of contemporary historians on its obvious structural weaknesses, yet arguably a more challenging area of research is the 'astonishing fact' that the GDR 'none the less existed for 40 years'.[49] Some historians see its history as a 'Decline and Fall in Stages' (to quote the title of Mitter and Wolle's book – *Untergang auf Raten*)[50] from 1953 onwards, but this interpretation ignores the fact that there was in fact 'a rise ... from the baseline of 1953 to a period of comparative tranquility in the early 1970s'.[51] Only from the mid-1970s onwards was this gradually undermined by economic problems and the 'increasing permeability of the GDR towards the West'[52] as a consequence of *Ostpolitik* and the Helsinki Agreements. In the end, however, it was the weakening of Russia's will to hold the GDR that signalled its demise, as will be shown in the next chapter.

18 *Reunification and Its Aftermath, 1989–2013*

Introduction: problems, issues and questions

However inevitable it might seem in retrospect, the collapse of the GDR was not foreseen in Moscow, Bonn or any other Western capital. Was this essentially because German unification was not, as proponents of *Ostpolitik* had envisaged, a gradual knitting together of the two states taking perhaps decades but rather a sudden 'hurtling and hurling together sanctioned by great power negotiations'?[1] Without the radical political and economic changes that swept through Eastern Europe in the late 1980s, German unity would surely have been inconceivable. Russia, weakened by military stalemate in Afghanistan and the flare-up of ethnic conflicts within its borders, and virtually bankrupt, was no longer in a position to enforce the Brezhnev Doctrine (see p. 320). Gorbachev thus had little option but to wind up the Cold War, seek Western credits and try to rejuvenate the Soviet economy by the partial introduction of market principles. By early autumn 1989 both Poland and Hungary had virtually ceased to be members of the Soviet bloc. Was it Russian weakness alone that made the GDR unviable? With the creation of the Berlin Republic a new chapter in German history began, but what did this really mean in the 1990s? With Kohl still in power was the Berlin Republic simply the old Bonn Republic writ large? Given the economic situation in the former GDR, can it be argued that there were in fact still two Germanies way into the 21st century? Perhaps it was only with the formation of the Schröder and Merkel governments and the economic tempests of the years 2008–2012 that the new chapter really started.

The collapse of the GDR

To survive the enormous changes sweeping through Eastern Europe in the late summer and autumn of 1989, the GDR needed to win the loyalty of its own people. Whils there was some support among intellectuals for an independent and more democratic East German state which could pioneer a 'third way', avoiding both capitalism and the post-Stalinist dictatorship of the SED, events were to show in 1990 that the overwhelming desire of the population was for unity with the FRG as the surest way of guaranteeing security, the rule of law and (so it was hoped) prosperity. Throughout 1988–1989 West Germany had continued to exercise its magnet-like attraction on the East Germans. In 1988 nearly two and a half million GDR citizens received visas to visit the FRG, and in the period from November 1988 to September 1989 over 86,000 requests for permanent emigration were granted. Not surprisingly then, it was the emigration issue that was to be the catalyst for the terminal crisis of the GDR.

On 2 May 1989 Hungary began to dismantle the barbed wire along its frontiers with Austria, thereby providing a potential escape route to the West. Toward the end of July thousands of East Germans travelled to Hungary, ostensibly on holiday. By 7 August, 200 had broken into the gardens of the West German embassy in Budapest and were camping there in an attempt to force Bonn to intervene on their behalf with the Hungarian and Austrian authorities and so facilitate their emigration to Austria and thence to the FRG. On 11 September the Austrians agreed to accept them, and they began to pour across the frontier. In the meantime more GDR refugees similarly besieged the West German mission in East Berlin and the embassies in Prague and Warsaw. By early September, 3500 East Germans were encamped in the embassy grounds in Prague.

Developments in Poland and Hungary, 1988–1989

As early as January 1989 the Polish Communist party decided to recognize the Solidarity movement (see p. 327), which had been officially banned in the autumn of 1982. This concession, which was not opposed by Gorbachev, led to the 'round table' negotiations between the government, the Church and Solidarity, which were influential in speeding up the pace of change throughout the Eastern bloc. It was agreed that Solidarity could contest the elections of June 1989, although the Communist party still reserved 60 per cent of the seats in the lower house. In August, however, as a result of the growing popularity of Solidarity, which won most of the seats available to it, a new Solidarity-led government was formed, in which the Communists had only two members. Significantly, Gorbachev made it clear that the USSR would not intervene to prop up an unpopular Communist regime. In Hungary modernizing Communists seized control of the party in early 1989 and committed it to recognizing the emerging non-Communist parties and to removing the fortifications and alarm systems along the Austrian border. As early as March 1989 Gorbachev declared that he would not interfere in Hungarian domestic politics. In June 'round table' talks began between the government and the opposition groups. In October a new temporary democratic constitution was adopted and free parliamentary elections were held in March and April 1990.

Unwilling to force a confrontation on the eve of the celebration of the 40th anniversary of the founding of the GDR, Honecker responded to pressure from the West German and Czech governments to grant them exit visas to the West, but he insisted that they would have to travel back through the GDR to West Germany in sealed trains, after which the Czech–GDR frontier would be closed. There was no chance of keeping these events secret from the rest of the population of the GDR whose televisions were nightly turned on to news programmes from the West German television stations. Once the route the trains were taking to the West German frontier became known, large crowds attempted to storm Dresden station in the hope of somehow boarding them. For the first time since 1961, the crippling prospect of mass emigration again faced the GDR government.

This much-publicized exodus was a turning point for the protest movement within the GDR. Paradoxically, the sudden opportunity to emigrate prompted the formation of new and stronger opposition movements among those who were determined to stay and press for democratic reforms at home. The government's hesitant and unsure handling of the crisis had lifted the 'taboo on open debate; private grumbles could no longer be isolated, ignored, denied'.[2] There was the sudden perception that protest really might effect change. In the vanguard of this were small reform groups, which over the previous few years had been meeting under the protection of the Evangelical Church (see p. 371). In the early autumn of 1989 they began to reorganize themselves into political organizations such as the *New Forum, The Social Democratic Initiative, Democracy Now* and *Democratic Awakening*, and work for political change.

The crisis escalated significantly on 24 September when a mass demonstration took place at Leipzig. Since 1982 there had been regular Monday evening services in the **Nikolaikirche** dedicated to praying for peace. When these resumed in early September 1989 at the time of the annual international Leipzig trade fair, they attracted increasingly large numbers. On 25 September tens of thousands of demonstrators paraded peacefully through the city singing protest songs and shouting out such slogans as 'We are the people' and 'We are staying here' (implying that they would push for reform at home rather than escape to the FRG). In retrospect it can be seen that the 'fate of the East German regime was decided on the Leipzig Ring'[3] on four successive Monday evenings between 25 September and 16 October. Although there were clashes between the police and demonstrators, particularly on 2 October, the crucial factor was that the regime did not dare use force on a large scale to clear the streets, as the Chinese had in **Tiananmen Square** earlier in the year. Once the police permitted the Leipzig demonstrators to march into the inner city on 9 October they set a precedent that was followed all over the GDR in the coming weeks.

Nikolaikirche: St Nicholas's Church

Tiananmen Square: On 4 June 1989 Chinese troops forcibly cleared Tiananmen Square of protesters and pro-democracy activists.

The reasons for non-intervention are complex. The demonstrators were disciplined and non-violent, and the Politburo was deeply divided about what approach to take and unsure of the loyalty of the factory defence groups and the young conscript policemen. Above all, in the climate of reform initiated by Gorbachev, it is doubtful whether any such intervention would have been successful. When Gorbachev visited East Berlin on 6–7 October to celebrate the 40th anniversary of the GDR, he pointedly supported reform, remarking cryptically that 'life punishes late comers'.

On 17 and 18 October the frustration in the Politburo with Honecker's stubborn refusal to reform and come to grips with the crisis sweeping the GDR led to a 'palace revolution' and his replacement by Egon Krenz (1937–), the former head of security and youth affairs. The Krenz regime, which lasted for barely a month, was nothing but a short interregnum. He grandly announced a policy of change or *Wende*, but in reality his concessions were all designed to protect the SED's monopoly of power. There were, for instance, to be elections on the basis of the existing constitution, which of course could only result in confirming the leading role of the SED. At local level, however, the SED leaders were already beginning to negotiate with Church leaders.

In the absence of any effective restraints by the police or the army, the crowds of demonstrators in the cities continued to grow. On 4 November half a million congregated in Alexanderplatz in East Berlin to demand further reform and the right to travel. Two days later a proposal was made by the Krenz government to issue permits for travel on up to 30 days a year, but this was rejected by the *Volkskammer* as insufficient. On 9 November a more sweeping concession was made, which gave to all GDR citizens with a passport the right to an exit visa valid for any frontier crossing including Berlin. Initially this was supposed to take effect from the morning of 10 November, but it was announced prematurely to a press conference on the evening of the 9 November, and at 11 p.m. the border guards facing a crowd of 20,000 opened up the crossing points. The breaching of the Berlin Wall became the symbol of the revolutions that ended Communist power in Eastern Europe, even though Krenz hoped that it would be an act of damage limitation and win back support for the government and party. His hopes were proved wrong. All over the GDR local party leaders came under attack and were forced to resign. Those who remained were forced onto the defensive by the revelations of party incompetence and corruption.

On 13 November the *Volkskammer*, which was still dominated by the SED, charged Hans Modrow (1928–), the Dresden party secretary, with the formation of a new government. Modrow, who had never been trusted by Honecker, was seen as a reformer and modernizer. Although, in his opening speech to the *Volkskammer*, he recognized the role of the people in the 'democratic renewal' of the GDR, the government was still unelected and dominated by the SED. Consequently, it was unable to appease the new opposition groups, and even within the *Volkskammer* the old bloc parties, the CDUD and LDPD (see p. 340) began to reconstitute themselves as genuine democratic parties.

To contain the revolution, the Modrow government agreed on 22 November to an initiative first put forward by the Church for a dialogue with the opposition groups. The model taken was the Polish 'round table' meetings where Solidarity delegates had negotiated with the Warsaw government. Between 7 December and 12 March 1990 there were 16 (East German) 'round table' meetings, which, in the absence of elections, 'became the repository of whatever legitimacy existed'.[4] At the first meeting Modrow conceded that free elections should take place on 6 May 1990.

In January the major bone of contention between the government and opposition groups was the future of the former Ministry for State Security, the *Stasi*, which in December had undergone a metamorphosis into the Office for National Security. Modrow believed it still had a role in defending the state from subversion from within, while the opposition groups were adamant that it should be dissolved. Faced with the threatened resignation of the bloc parties from his government and the boycott of the 'round table' meetings by the opposition groups, he agreed on 11 January to its dissolution. Two days later the authority of his

government received another blow when a protest demonstration escalated out of control. Angry crowds invaded the old *Stasi* headquarters in
the *Normannenstrasse* and began to ransack the files. They could only be
restrained by the personal intervention of Modrow and the leaders of the
New Forum.

By mid-January Modrow was faced with problems on all sides:

- Heavy emigration westwards showed no signs of stopping.
- Morale within the SED was rapidly collapsing.
- Within the *Volkskammer* the bloc parties were reluctant to be associ-
  ated with the SED or, as it was now called, the Party of Democratic
  Socialism (PDS).

Once he agreed to advance the date for the election from 6 May to
18 March 1990, Modrow was able in early February to construct a 'government of national responsibility' which included the main opposition
parties and groups. The March elections, which reduced the PDS vote to
16.4 per cent and gave the CDUD 40.8 per cent of the vote, marked the end
of Communism in the GDR and made unification a virtual certainty. As
Konrad Jarausch observed, 'the overwhelming vote for quick union with

16 The Berlin Wall, 10 November 1989, after its opening the evening before
Presse- und Informationsamt der Bundesregierung, no. 1131364/EN

the Federal Republic provided irrefutable domestic and international legitimation for the unification drive'.[5]

Reunification: Kohl seizes the initiative

In the autumn of 1989 the Kohl government in Bonn had no idea that the gathering crisis in the GDR was terminal. At the end of October Kohl wished Krenz 'success' with his reforms and, very much in the tradition of *Ostpolitik*, declared that Bonn wanted 'a calm sensible development'. This measured response was, however, overtaken by the sheer pace of change in the GDR. The growing demand for unity, the flood of refugees westwards and the visible disintegration of the GDR ultimately forced Kohl into pursuing a more active policy for German unity. Still, even by 28 November in his 10-point programme he was envisaging a confederate structure that would only slowly and in the distant future lead to full unity. Then, just before Christmas, he visited the GDR where the enthusiastic reaction of the crowd in Dresden left him in little doubt of the strength of feeling for national unity.

Under pressure from public opinion and the accelerating disintegration of the GDR, Modrow, too, moved closer to advocating unity. On 1 February, in a document entitled 'For Germany, one Fatherland', he conceded that the 'union of the two German states [was] moving onto the agenda'.[6] He then went on to outline plans for an economic, currency and transport union, which would gradually evolve by way of a confederation into a united neutral German federation. Kohl rejected the proposal for neutrality outright because the continued membership of Germany in NATO was essential to win the support of the Western powers for unification, and he was now ready to force the pace of both political and economic currency union. The success of the East German CDU in the election of 18 March and the formulation of a coalition government led by the CDU leader **Lothar de Maizière** made the realization of Kohl's plans much easier. By the end of April the two German leaders agreed in principle on a monetary and economic union to begin on 1 July.

It was crucial to gain the agreement of the USSR, America and Germany's main Western European allies, Britain and France, to German unity. However, only Russia and America had the power to stop it. Thus the real negotiations were between Bonn, Moscow and Washington. At first Gorbachev was opposed to the liquidation of the GDR, and in December 1989 he told his Central Committee that he would 'see to it that no harm comes to the GDR'. Yet by the end of January his support for it was ebbing rapidly. On 10 February he informed Kohl in Moscow that the Germans themselves should decide on the question of German unity, although he was still reluctant to agree to a united Germany's membership of NATO. Nevertheless, the way to unity now seemed clear. At Ottawa 4 days later, President Bush also gave the green light and outlined a formula for proceeding with the negotiations, the Two-Plus-Four talks,

Lothar de Maizière, (1940–): joined the CDUD as a young man, but refused any party job until November 1989. As a lawyer, he made a speciality of defending Christians who were in trouble with the GDR authorities, although the *Spiegel* was later to accuse him of being a *Stasi* informer.

which would bring together both the two Germanies and the four former occupying powers, who still had residual rights in Berlin. In a series of negotiations in Bonn, Berlin and Paris in the summer of 1990, German unity was brokered, and on 12 September the Two-Plus-Four Treaty was signed in Moscow. It was in effect a peace treaty legally ending the Second World War. It terminated the remaining rights of the former occupying powers in Germany and committed Germany to recognizing the Oder-Neisse border with Poland. Residual Russian opposition to German unity and the membership of a united Germany in NATO had been overcome by generous West German loans, which Gorbachev hoped would facilitate the modernization of the Russian economy. 'This was', as Garton Ash has observed, '*Realpolitik* in a highly civilized form with the telephone and cheque book instead of blood and iron, but it was *Realpolitik* all the same.'[7] Any incipient opposition in the West, particularly in London and Paris, was stilled by Kohl's insistence on the new united Germany's membership of NATO and the incorporation of East Germany into the European Community.

From April to October the de Maizière government presided over the liquidation of the GDR. Parallel to the Two-Plus-Four talks, the two Germanies negotiated the terms of their reunification. The State Treaty on Monetary, Social and Economic Union was concluded on 18 May. The introduction of the *Deutschmark* at midnight on 1 July was the third major German monetary reform of the 20th century, but unlike those of 1923/1924 or 1948 (see pp. 203 and 304), the monetary assets of those affected were strengthened rather than sacrificed:

- wages and pensions were converted at the rate of one East mark to one DM;
- savings above 4000 marks for those between 14 and 59 years old were converted at the rate of 50 pfennigs to one East mark;
- for citizens over the age of 59 this limit was raised to 6000 East marks.

Negotiations for political unity began on 6 July. The negotiators faced the challenge of reconciling two mutually hostile political cultures. Although de Maizière and his spokesman in the negotiations, Günter Krause (1953–), tried hard to argue that the new unified Germany should be a genuine mix of both the former GDR and the FRG, in practice the overwhelming power of Bonn ensured that essentially the treaty, which was signed on 31 August 1990, incorporated the GDR into the FRG. In Article 23 of the Basic Law, which had been used to integrate the **Saar** territories into the FRG in 1957, there was a simple mechanism for unity. It provided for the automatic extension of the Basic Law to any other regions of Germany joining the FRG. The political structure of the new Germany was 'simply the Federal republic writ large'.[8] Thus the former states in the GDR were to be reconstituted and given representation in the *Bundesrat*, while 144 new members representing the East Germans would take up their seats in the *Bundestag* in Bonn. At midnight on

Saar: It had been intended in 1948 that the Saar would remain an autonomous territory economically fused to France, but when the population voted for union with the GDR in 1955, the French raised no objections to it becoming the eighth *Land* of the FRG. See also Document 87.

2 October 1990 a united Germany came into existence. On 2 December 1990 a reunited Germany went to the polls and overwhelmingly supported the CDU–FDP coalition.

Kohl: the First Chancellor of the Berlin Republic, 1990–1998

The return to Berlin

A key decision to confront the first government of united Germany was whether to move the seat of government back to Berlin. The unification treaty had named Berlin the capital but had left the final decision to the newly elected *Bundestag*. The parliamentary debate was inevitably influenced by the whole question of German national identity and history and whether Germany was essentially an Eastern or Western European state. Did reunification mean that the Germany of 1871 or 1919 had been restored, or in reality had little changed since the pre-*Wende* period as the country still remained a member of NATO and the **EC/EU**? If this was so, it could be argued that it was preferable for the government to remain in Bonn, which had been for the last 40 years the capital of Germany's most successful democracy, rather than move to Berlin, a city haunted by the ghosts of Germany's past. On the other hand it was pointed out that the East German states had no historic link to Bonn and that the FRG's Basic Law of 1949 (see p. 307) had designated Berlin as the capital of a future reunited Germany. After a debate of several hours the *Bundestag* in June 1991 chose Berlin by a close vote of 338 for to 320 against. Although the losers attempted legally to challenge the decision, in the summer of 1999 the *Bundestag* and the Federal Government moved to Berlin. Bonn, however became a federal town and several ministries, most notably the Defence Ministry, remained there.

Die Wende: literally turning point or change from a divided to a united Germany in 1990

EC/EU: The EC changed its name to the European Union or EU when the Maastricht Treaty came into force in 1993.

The economic legacy of unification, 1990–1998

In the heady days of the summer of 1990 it was assumed that unification would be quick and painless and that the East German states would rapidly undergo an economic miracle, as West Germany had done in the early 1950s (see p. 333). However the reality was very different. An opinion poll, which was taken in the summer of 1991 showed that a large majority on each side believed that 'only since unification has it become evident how different Eastern and Western Germany are'.[9] The West Germans began to resent the economic burdens imposed by reunification, while the East Germans saw themselves as only second-class citizens. Unification had not produced in the former GDR a land of milk and honey overnight. It became increasingly clear that a much longer time than originally envisaged would be necessary to integrate East Germany economically and to some extent politically into the FRG. There are hardly any precedents for the situation which faced post-unification

Germany except perhaps, as Rolf Steininger has argued, the situation in the United States at the end of the Civil War.[10]

It was above all economic difficulties that hindered a smooth fusion of the two Germanies. The hastily negotiated state treaty which began to operate on 1 July 1990 sought to merge two fundamentally different economic systems – a **semi-autarchic**, centrally planned socialist economy on the one hand with a capitalist, free-trading global economy on the other. The treaty laid down that the former GDR had to accept:

Semi-autarchic:
semi-self-sufficient

- the relevant economic, social and labour laws;
- a monetary and banking system regulated by the *Bundesbank;*
- a currency union of 1:1 for all wage earners and current financial transactions;
- the break-up and privatization of the state monopolies (*Kombinate*) by the ***Treuhandanstalt*** (THA), which was set up in June 1990.

Treuhandanstalt:
state holding trust

The economy of the old GDR was granted no interim period before being confronted by the full rigour of West German and EC/EU competition. Not surprisingly, the effect of this was devastating. By 1992 whole swathes of East Germany were virtually deindustrialized, and it had become an area of long-term structural unemployment resembling the *Mezzogiorno* (Southern Italy). Could this have been avoided? The speed of unification was, of course, determined by political considerations. Among the economists there were a few who believed that the 'shock therapy' of immediate unification would work wonders, but the majority were more cautious and were in favour of a more gradual process of economic integration, with parallel currencies based on a realistic exchange rate. In retrospect it is clear that the government made a series of false calculations. It set the exchange rate for the East mark against the DM at too high a rate, which resulted in making most of the former GDR's production uneconomic. Wage harmonization with West Germany in 1996 dealt a mortal blow to profitability because, as a result of the lower productivity in the East, wage costs soared to over 70 per cent above those in the West. East German industrial concerns were also initially disposed of far too quickly by the THA at knock-down prices and before they had a chance to rationalize and to be made profitable. Inevitably, the collapse of the East German economy led to widespread bitterness against the Kohl government. In the spring of 1991, when three million East Germans were either on short time or unemployed, in Leipzig and other major cities there were large demonstrations directed against the government. This led to an immediate massive increase in subsidies, grants and financial assistance for retraining.

From mid-1992 to January 1993 East Germany suffered a further disastrous double-dip slump. By the time the upturn started in late 1994, the remaining industries in East Germany supplied only 12 per cent of local demand compared to 70 per cent in 1989, and unemployment affected 25 per cent of the workforce. The output of the service industries was now

50 per cent higher than that of the manufacturing sector. However, along-side the old rust heaps of obsolescent heavy industry there was a modest growth in new high-tech industries. Siemens, for instance, built a 2.4 billion DM microchip plant in Dresden, while Opel and Volkswagen opened new plants in the former GDR. Above all, the construction industry, assisted by 33 billion Deutschmarks' worth of tax allowances, did much to kick-start East German economic growth during the period 1994–1996. East Germany was again particularly hard hit by the downturn in the economy between 1997 and 1998. The slowdown was exacerbated by the ending of building subsidies. Overall growth was also significantly lower than that in the West. Thus East Germany by the end of the century remained a poor relation to the core states of the old FRG, and dependent on tax breaks and grants to fuel economic expansion.

Economically, reunification was a heavy burden for the West Germans and led to the development of a dual economy in the new Germany. Briefly it seemed that unification would cost the West Germans very little, and in the December 1990 election Kohl promised that taxes would not be increased. However, the temporary boom it triggered in the West rapidly led to inflationary overheating, which caused the *Bundesbank* sharply to raise its interest rates to an all-time high, which did much to deepen the recession of 1992–1993. Belatedly Kohl then imposed 'one-off' surcharges of 7.5 per cent on each individual's tax bill in 1991–1992 and again in January 1995. This went only a fraction of the way to funding the huge costs of regional assistance to the East. Christopher Flockton has calculated that in 1993 alone DM 235 billion were transferred to the former GDR.[11] Inevitably this added an immense burden to the FRG's public finances and in 1994 its debt was equivalent to 58 per cent of its GDP and had overshot the **Maastricht guidelines** by a massive 60 per cent in 1995.

Maastricht guidelines: agreed upon at Maastricht in 1990 for the convergence of the core EU economies in preparation for the single euro currency.

The depth of the recession of 1992–1993 led to an agonizing reappraisal of the German economy. On the one hand it had performed impressively at the end of the 1980s, while on the other it was burdened by the highest production costs in the world, the shortest working week and a raft of restrictive environmental legislation. Free-market economists advocated privatization, the cutting of red tape and a whole range of other measures aimed at making the German economy more competitive. Under pressure from the EC/EU, steps were taken to privatize the railways, Lufthansa and the *Bundespost*. German industry also did much to reduce wage and production costs in 1992–1993. The fact that the export industries helped drag Germany out of recession in 1993–1994 indicated that considerable progress was made in regaining international competitiveness, but then growth again slowed with the recession of 1995–1996 and the onset of a prolonged period of economic stagnation in 1998.

The Maastricht Treaty and the preparations for introducing the single currency also made structural reforms in the German economy even more urgent. In January 1996 the Kohl government introduced the '50-Point Plan' and then in April its 'Programme for Growth'. These set out plans to reform the tax, pension and health systems and remove a considerable amount of red tape, but much of his programme was either modified by or rejected by the SPD-dominated *Bundesrat*.

Politics, 1991–1998

German reunification certainly shook the party structure of the old FRG, but in the 1990s it did not fundamentally alter it. The two large federal parties, the SPD and CDU–CSU, remained dominant, although in 1998 the Greens replaced the FDP as the pivotal party which could make or break coalitions. In 1990 both the CDU and FDP linked up with their GDR counterparts, the former bloc parties which had since November 1989 once again become democratic parties. In the election of December 1990 the CDU became temporarily the largest party in the East, while the FDP won more voters there than in the West. In January 1990, the SPD was refounded in the GDR after merging with the GDR's Social Democratic Party (SDP), which had been formed in October. In the December 1990 elections the SPD polled only 33.5 per cent in Germany as a whole and 23.6 per cent of the votes in the new states largely because the SDP had been sympathetic to Modrow's failed attempts to create a third way in the GDR between old-style socialism and West German capitalism. The West German Greens who were the only party not to merge with their Eastern counterparts before the 1990 elections failed to clear the five percent hurdle and so gained no seats. Only in 1993 did a united Green alliance emerge: 'Alliance '90/The Greens'. The PDS (formerly the SED), helped by the fact that the 5 per cent electoral law (see p. 307) was applied separately to East and West Germany, managed to win a base of 17 seats in the *Bundestag*, and succeeded in preserving at an electoral presence in the newly reconstituted states in east Germany. Kohl was able to capitalize on his success in unifying Germany to win an impressive electoral victory. For similar reasons the FDP, by concentrating on Genscher's role in unification, was able to win its largest share of the vote since 1949. See Document 87

Support for both government parties rapidly began to evaporate with the escalating problems in eastern Germany and the downturn in the economy in 1991–1992. The massive increase in asylum seekers entering Germany in 1991–1992 also led to criticism of the government, and a marked increase in racial incidents. Right across the new states, CDU support declined to the 20 per cent level, and the revival of the far-right Republican Party (see p. 364) chalked up significant successes in the Baden-Württemberg regional elections in 1992. Kohl was 'down but not out'[12] by early 1994. In the October election he made a surprising comeback partly because of the upturn in the economy and his success in amending the constitution so as to make the entry of asylum seekers more difficult. The CDU–CSU lost ground in the new states but managed to hold its core support in the old FRG. While the SPD made some gains in the East, it was the PDS that won most of the protest votes, and in the West the Greens, now part of Alliance 90, made a strong recovery. Kohl was able to form a coalition with the FDP and, despite the SPD's control of the *Bundesrat*, his government was able to make some progress in simplifying the tax system and lowering tax rates for businesses.

The Red–Green coalitions, 1998–2005

The 1998 election initially appeared to be 'a watershed event'.[13] For the first time in the history of the Federal Republic a government was comprehensively defeated in the polls and forced immediately to resign. The CDU/CSU lost heavily in the new states and overall gained only 35.1 per cent of the votes, which was their worst result since 1949, while the SPD with its best result since 1972 won 40.9 per cent and attracted the majority of working-class votes in the East. The parties of the extreme right had a negligible impact and failed to surmount the 5 per cent hurdle to gain seats in the Bundestag. The Greens overtook the FDP as the third largest party, and the PDS with 5.1 per cent of the votes just managed to get into the *Bundestag*. The economic downturn and rising unemployment did, of course, benefit the SPD, but there was also a widespread desire to break with the past and eject the 'eternal chancellor', Helmut Kohl. The German voter wanted a new type of politics, which Schröder seemed more likely to provide. Schröder was a disciple of the British prime minister, Tony Blair (1953–), and was a modernizer, who with his calls for a 'new centre' attempted to wean the SPD away from its socialist traditions and to make it more appealing to CDU voters as well as the young, many of whom had already been deeply disillusioned with politics.

Gerhard Schröder, 1944–

As the son of a war widow, Schröder grew up in relative poverty. He studied law as a mature student and made a name for himself by defending Horst Mahler and other RAF terrorists (see p. 357). He was federal chairman of the Young Socialists, 1978–1980, and was then elected to the Bundestag. From 1990–1994 he was a successful minister-president of a Red–Green coalition in Lower Saxony, but he failed to become his party's chancellor candidate in 1993. It was not until 1998 that he was successful. As chancellor he took great pains to cultivate his image and appeared on popular TV programmes, and, like Tony Blair, deliberately used slang and clichés to connect with the voters. Allegedly he claimed that to govern Germany he only needed the support of the tabloid paper, die *Bild Zeitung*, and the television stations.

Schröder negotiated a coalition with the Greens. Its leader in the *Bundestag*, Joshka Fischer, who had been a former student radical and member of the APO (see p. 353), was appointed foreign minister, while Oskar Lafontaine, the chairman of the SPD, occupied the key post of minister of finance. As with Tony Blair's administration in Britain, the new government marked not just a generational change but also a change in political and social culture. Initially, however, the government was seriously weakened by the clash between Schröder's politics of the 'new centre' and Lafontaine's determination to implement more traditional SPD policies. The Government embarked on a programme that owed more to Keynesianism and traditional SPD politics than the 'new centre'. Large sections of Kohl's pension reforms were repealed, child benefits were increased, medical coverage payments cut and the bottom rate of income tax lowered to the detriment of the middle classes. An 'eco tax' was imposed on mineral oil and an orderly phasing out of nuclear power by 2020 was planned. The immigration process was simplified and the children of immigrants were given dual citizenship.

However, in the absence of any marked improvement in the economy and the very evident tension between Schröder and Lafontaine, public opinion began to turn rightwards again. In Hesse the February 1999 elections resulted in a defeat of the Red–Green coalition and a new CDU–FDP government. In light of this Schröder rapidly began to jettison his left-wing programme, which led to the resignation of Oskar Lafontaine in March. In June Schröder published a joint paper with Tony Blair without any involvement of his own party, the SPD, entitled 'The Way Forward for Europe's Social Democracy'. Essentially this involved 'Thatcherism with a human face'.[14] Budgets were to be balanced, there was to be no redistributive taxation, but on the other hand efforts were to be made to bring about greater social egalitarianism and equality of opportunity as well as closer cooperation between the state and private industry.

Inevitably this policy of the 'new centre' was met with sharp criticism from the left wing of the SPD. When Schröder, for instance, announced plans to restructure the government's welfare policy, the Young Socialists declared it 'a declaration of intellectual bankruptcy'.[15] The government's difficulties were further compounded by catastrophic results in the **European elections** and five state elections. Yet in the winter of 1999–2000 his popularity began to rise again. This was partly a consequence of his ability to appease his party critics by making timely but relatively small concessions and by the fact that the CDU was thrown into chaos by the ongoing **party donations scandal** (see p. 364), which closely involved Kohl. In the Schleswig-Holstein regional elections in February 2000 the SPD actually increased its vote.

The SPD's recovery was also helped by Schröder's ability to appeal to the German electorate. He was a major asset to his party despite the doubts about him held by many of its core voters. After the departure of Lafontaine, Schröder also attempted to get to grips with Germany's economic problems. Income tax was cut, the pension system was reformed and plans were drawn up for balancing the budget by 2006. An agreement was also concluded on compensation for victims of the forced labour policies of the Nazi era (see p. 282). It was also the Red–Green coalition which gave the go-ahead for the construction of the Holocaust memorial in Berlin and legalized civil partnerships for homosexuals.

Yet in the spring of 2002 the CDU was recovering from the effects of the Party donations scandal and becoming a more formidable electoral opponent. Angela Merkel (see below), having condemned Kohl's for his

European elections: Elections to the European Parliament held every 5 years

Party donations scandal: Kohl admitted to receiving large amounts of money secretly from businessmen and industrialists throughout the 1990s.

role in this affair in an article in *die Zeit* in December 1999, was elected the CDU chairwoman in April 2000. In January 2002 she bowed to internal party pressure and gave way to Edmund Stoiber (1941–), the leader of the CSU, who become the chancellor candidate to challenge Schröder. Right up to August 2002 the defeat of the Red–Green coalition by the CDU–CSU seemed a forgone conclusion. Its main problem was the sluggish state of the German economy. In 1998 Schröder could blame this on the Kohl administration, but in 2002 he had to campaign on the record of his own administration. However, Stoiber's wooden style was no match for Schröder's personal popularity as his quick response to those who had suffered in the **disastrous floods** in August in central Germany showed. More importantly his refusal to allow Germany to be dragged by America into a war with Iraq, which was already being contemplated in Washington, touched a chord with the electorate, whereas the CDU/CSU were split over whether to support President Bush. Thus it was no surprise that by the end of August the government coalition had regained the initiative and was able to retain power after the election of 2002 with a reduced majority of just nine.

In August 2002 after torrential rain the Elbe overflowed and flooded Dresden and the surrounding countryside.

Angela Merkel, 1954–

Angela Dorothea Merkel (née Kasner) is the daughter of a teacher and a Lutheran pastor, who after completing his studies in Hamburg returned to the GDR in 1954 to take charge of a parish in Berlin Brandenburg shortly after the birth of Angela. Inevitably Angela Merkel grew up in the restrictive and hostile atmosphere of the communist GDR. As the daughter of a priest she was regarded with suspicion by the authorities and in order to complete her studies at school and go on to university she had to avoid controversy and as far as possible conform. Hence she joined **the Ernst Thälmann** Young Pioneers and the FDJ youth movement. She studied Physics at Leipzig University and then worked at the Institute of Physical Chemistry of the Academy of Sciences in East Berlin. By the autumn of 1989 she was active in the organization for Democratic Change and became in effect a press spokesperson for its chairman. Following the election of March 1990, she became a press representative for de Maizière's brief caretaker government (see p. 380). After unification she went on to become ministerial adviser in the Federal Press and Information Office and entered the *Bundestag* as the CDU deputy for Mecklenburg-Vorpommern. Kohl then appointed her Federal Minister for Women and Youth and in 1994 Minister for the Environment. In 1998 she became the general secretary of the CDU and played a key role in forcing Kohl's resignation after the party donations scandal (see above). Her position within the CDU was greatly strengthened by Edmund Stoiber's failure to win the election of 2002. In 2005 she won the first of her three elections victories, and by 2013 was the most powerful politician in Germany.

Schröder's second government, 2002–2005

Ernst Thälmann, (1886–1944): leader of the KPD during the Weimar Republic

The economic and political problems faced by the new Red–Green administration were so formidable that in the immediate aftermath of the election many political observers were already questioning whether the coalition would survive for any length of time. In September 1998 the number of unemployed in Germany was 3.97 million and 4 years later it had only declined to 3.94 million. Germany's increasingly serious economic position was compared, admittedly with some exaggeration, by Graf Lambsdorff, the former FDP economics minister, to the 'British sickness' of the 1970s.[16]

Before the election, in an attempt to create a consensus for further reform, Schröder had set up two commissions chaired by non-partisan experts: the Commission for the Reduction of Unemployment under the chairmanship of Dr Peter Hartz (1941–), Labour Director on the Board of Management of *Volkswagen*, and the Commission for the Financial Sustainability of the Social Security Systems under the pensions expert, Professor Bert Rürup (1943–). Their advice was incorporated in the Agenda 2010, which was announced in the *Bundestag* in March 2003. It marked in the words of one economic historian 'a serious willingness to redefine the German market economy'[17] and to make it more globally competitive. Labour mobility was encouraged by reducing full unemployment benefits to a period of 12 months and by cuts in public assistance. Hiring of workers by small firms was made easier by relaxing the employment protection laws – a policy pursued by Kohl but reversed by the first Schröder government. Apart from a job creation scheme supporting about 100,000 long-term unemployed, relatively little was done to help the eastern states.

Given his small majority in the Bundestag and the CDU/CSU majority in the Bundesrat, Schröder made slow progress in realizing Agenda 2010. In early 2005 the government's popularity was badly damaged by the 'Visa Affair' when it emerged that the German consular authorities in Kiev were issuing visas for the FRG too laxly. After a string of electoral defeats in the states culminating in a humiliating reverse in North Rhine-Westphalia, Schröder and the new SPD chairman Franz Münterfering (1940–) decided to bring forward the date for a general election to Autumn 2005. To achieve this, a vote of no confidence was engineered in the *Bundestag* in July, which the government lost by 151 votes to 296. Schröder again showed his brilliance as a popular politician in the subsequent electoral campaign by rallying support for the SPD and seriously threatening Angela Merkel's impressive lead in the opinion polls. In the election itself the SPD emerged just four seats behind the CDU/CSU. Despite Schröder's initial reluctance to give up the Chancellorship, a grand CDU/CSU–SPD coalition was formed under Merkel's leadership, and on 23 November he resigned his seat in the *Bundestag*. Two SPD politicians, Frank-Walter Steinmeyer (1956–) and Peer Steinbrück (1947–), became foreign minister and the finance minister respectively.

The Grand Coalition 2005–2009

In March 2006 Merkel announced the Eight Point Programme, which set out her government's intentions to reform the relations between the states and the federal government, balance the national budget, cut the bureaucracy, lower the tax burden on industry and liberalize the labour market as well introducing family-friendly legislation and reforming the health service. In this she achieved only very limited success partly because of the opposition from her coalition partners, the SPD, but also because from August 2007 onwards Germany was engulfed in the worst economic and banking crisis since the early 1930s. Nevertheless Merkel did make some progress. By 2008 she had significantly lowered the deficit, raised the statutory retirement age from 65 to 67 and opened up new child care centres. By raising VAT to 19 per cent and reducing expenditure on education, she also managed to lessen the tax burden on German businesses.

However, the major challenge facing the Grand Coalition was the global banking crisis. The first intimation of this in Germany was the threatened collapse of the IKB *Deutsche Industriebank* AG in August 2007. The bank had incurred huge losses after investing heavily in securities tied to the US housing market, which had crashed when property prices had reached unsustainable levels. Merkel responded by sanctioning a bailout package for the IKB, and it initially seemed that the US

Subprime crisis:
the financial crisis
in the USA caused
by over generous
granting of mort-
gages to those
who could not
repay them

subprime crisis had not harmed the German economy as a whole. In September 2008 after the collapse of the New York-based Lehman Brothers Holdings Inc., the fourth biggest investment bank in Wall Street, it was clear that Germany was not, after all, immune to the crisis. Germany's second biggest property lender, Hypo Real Estate Holding AG of Munich, was on the brink of collapse, and there was a real danger that Germany's financial system would fail as the flow of credit dried up. Clearly the bank needed an urgent bailout package, but Merkel was determined that the banks themselves should contribute to the 35 billion euros this would cost. To achieve this she conducted a policy of brinkmanship, which could easily have gone wrong and might well have resulted in the biggest bank failure since 1931, but in the event she successfully managed to persuade the other banks to contribute 8.5 billion.

The banking crisis was far from ended. On 5 October 2008 to stop panic withdrawals the government was forced to issue a guarantee on bank deposits. Later on that month it set up a 480 billion-euro bank rescue fund to stabilize the banking system. This was followed by an economic stimulus of 50 billion euros to be topped up to 85 billion in 2009. The government was forced drastically to revise its economic growth targets and abandon its intention to balance the budget by 2011. Later Merkel was to remark that 'after 2008, in certain areas the minimum unit became the billion, and that was something we just hadn't experienced before'.[18]

The ferocity of the banking crisis initially damaged the standing of the CDU/CSU and benefited the SPD, but Merkel's determination to punish the bankers for their role in the crisis and regain control of the state's finances boosted her popularity. Bonuses were barred at those German banks which were receiving aid financed from the taxpayer, and a cap was set on executive pay. In 2009 legislation was passed to force the federal government and the states to balance their budgets. The state's deficit was now not to exceed 0.35 per cent of the GDP.

The election of September 2009 was fought against the forbidding backcloth of the economic crisis. Germany was in the midst of its worst slump since 1929–1933 (see p. 227), and the economy had contracted by 3.7 per cent in the first quarter of 2009. Merkel's handling of the crisis did, however, win respect among the electorate, and enabled her to marginalize her SPD cabinet colleagues Steinmeier and Steinbrück, but her personal ratings were in contrast to her party's unpopularity. In the election in September 2009 the CDU/CSU gained only 33.8 per cent of the vote, its lowest share of the vote since 1949, but it was outdone by the SPD, which received a mere 23 per cent of the vote, its worst result since March 1933. The smaller parties did proportionately better: the FDP, **die Linke** and Alliance '90 (The Greens) all achieved the best result in their history, but nearly 30 per cent of the electorate boycotted the election. The election results nevertheless made possible a CDU/CSU–FDP coalition under Merkel as chancellor.

Die Linke: created in 2007 through the amalgamation of the PDS and the WASG (The 'Labour and Social justice – the Electoral Alternative' Party)

Merkel's second government and the financial crisis, 2009–2013

The event that defined Angela Merkel's second government was the eruption of the euro crisis, which for a time threatened the very existence of the single currency. By the spring of 2010 the economies of Ireland, Portugal, Greece and Spain were on the brink of bankruptcy owing to years of chronic overspending and indebtedness. In the subsequent bailouts, Germany as the eurozone's largest economy was called upon to play the leading part. In May the European Financial Stability Facility (EFSF) was set up. Out of the 500 billion-euro fund, which was topped up by a further 150 billion from the International Monetary Fund (IMF), Germany alone contributed 123 billion euros. Merkel was determined to use the crisis to instil financial discipline into the eurozone. She pointedly remarked that 'it is almost like a battle of politics against the markets and politics must win primacy … I am determined to win the battle'.[19]

At Deauville in October 2010 Merkel gained French support for plans to make changes in the EU Treaty to reinforce budget discipline in the member states and to create a permanent rescue fund, **the European Stability Mechanism**. A year later at Brussels the EU states with the exception of Britain and Czech Republic agreed to incorporate this proposal in their own constitutions. By the autumn of 2012 the worst of the sovereign debt crisis appeared to be over. The European Central Bank's declaration that it was 'ready to do whatever it takes' to preserve the euro, apparent Greek willingness to accept drastic economies and Merkel's assurance that she would after all not allow Greece to be pushed out of the euro, calmed the financial markets and gave the euro a reprieve. However the Greek crisis itself remained acute and it was far from clear over the next 3 years whether Greece would be able to stay in the eurozone.

The European Stability Mechanism: was set up in Luxembourg on 27 September 2012.

See Document 88

Initially German assumption of the greatest share for the Greek and European bailout fund met with considerable criticism from the electorate and in particular from the *Bildzeitung*, which demanded that Greece should be ejected from the euro. In May 2010 the CDU/CSU lost control of North Rhine-Westphalia and consequently lost their majority in the *Bundesrat*. Merkel's popularity continued to decline for the rest of 2010 and much of the following year. In October 2010 she incensed the Greens by reversing Schröder's decision to phase out nuclear power by 2020. Yet she performed a spectacular U-turn when an earthquake and tsunami ruptured a nuclear reactor at Fukushima in Japan and rapidly returned to Schröder's original decision. To the Greens the reversal smacked of opportunism, and on 26 March 2011 a quarter of a million people demonstrated throughout Germany and called for an end to nuclear power. The following day the CDU lost Baden-Württemberg to a Green–SPD alliance – the Greens took a record 24.2 per cent of the votes. In one opinion poll 70 per cent of the respondents were convinced that her U-turn was merely dictated by political opportunism.

Throughout 2011 the CDU/CSU continued to lose support, and the FDP, its coalition partner, suffered even worse. Yet by the end of the year Merkel's ratings were improving. The voters were impressed by her determination to push the EU governments towards budgetary restraint and her handling of the sovereign debt crisis in Greece, Portugal and Spain. She was also helped by the resilience of the German economy. Thanks to the competitive exchange rate of the euro and the cumulative effect of years of reforms (see above) aiming to make the German economy more efficient and cost effective, the German export trade pulled Germany out of recession. In 2010 there was a 14.2 per cent rise in exports. To offset the declining euro area German firms increased sales to China and the US. In the first 11 months of 2012 Germany registered a 10 per cent increase in exports outside the euro area. The German stock market index, the DAX, rose 29 per cent that year – its best record since 2003.[20] Yet this growth spurt was to taper off by the end of 2014.

By the end of 2012 Merkel was re-elected CDU chairwoman with 98 per cent of the votes cast, and nationally across Germany she had become effectively a presidential figure, whose appeal was far greater than her party's. In the elections in September 2013 the CDU/CSU gained their best result since 1990 but, with the failure of the FDP to clear the 5 per cent hurdle and gain any seats in the Bundestag, Merkel despite her victory had little option but to form another Grand Coalition with the SDP. It was to face in 2015 a renewed euro crisis and the immense challenge posed by migrants and refugees from Syria and elsewhere.

German foreign policy in a changed world, 1990–2005

Unlike 1871 Germany was reunited in 1990 peacefully at the cost of no other state's territorial integrity. Nor did reunification trigger a blaze of triumphalism. Essentially the priorities of the new Germany's foreign policy still lay with NATO and the EC–EU. As it had done over the preceding four decades, European integration remained, 'an integral part of the FRG's *raison d'état*'.[21] In modern Germany, power is still equated with economic strength and prosperity rather than the size of its armed forces. Nevertheless, the end of the Cold War had radically changed the context in which the FRG conducted its foreign policy. Europe was no longer divided into two apparently stable blocs, as it was for much of the Cold War. Germany now in the 1990s bordered a zone of potential instability and chaos and was faced, like her Western allies, with a very different international and security environment:

- Russia still remained a great power, but with an ageing nuclear arsenal, while many of the former Soviet states, which had broken away from the old USSR, were politically unstable and themselves possessed nuclear weapons.
- The ethnic–national conflicts between the states in ex-Yugoslavia threatened to destabilize the Balkans and send further waves of asylum seekers to Germany.
- Germany, like the rest of the developed world, was also threatened by state-sponsored terrorism and the flood of economic immigrants from Africa and Asia.

Rather than acting unilaterally, the German government's response to these dangers was to support and develop a dense network of overlapping multilateral institutions: NATO, the Council of Europe, **the Council of Baltic Sea Cooperation**, the **Schengen Group** and the European Union. NATO remained the bedrock of Germany's foreign policy, and its government pressed hard to extend it eastwards. For instance in 1991 a US–German initiative for regular consultations between NATO, Russia, and the Baltic and Eastern European states was accepted at the NATO summit in Rome. To defuse its neighbours' residual fears of a united Germany, the German government has also constantly stressed the importance of widening and deepening the European Union. At Maastricht not only did it agree to a monetary union with a common currency, the euro, which came into force in January 2002, but also to a common foreign and security policy. Thus, in cooperation with France, Germany became the prime mover in creating the Eurocorps, a small multinational task force of 35,000 troops. Kohl also sought to build a bridge between the defence roles of NATO and the EU by creating 'a combined joint defence force' under the **Western European Union** but within NATO. With strong German support, accession negotiations to the EU began not only with the Eastern European states, Bulgaria, Estonia, Latvia, Lithuania, Poland, the Czech Republic, Romania, Slovakia and Hungary but also with Cyprus and Malta, all of which joined in 2002. Schröder favoured the admission of Turkey into the EU arguing that it was a bridge between East and West, but this was later opposed by Merkel, who was ready to offer Turkey a 'privileged partnership' as opposed to full EU

The Council of Baltic Sea Cooperation: set up in 1992. To it belong all the Nordic and Baltic states.

Shengen Group: seven EU states decided in 1995 to end all frontier controls.

The Western European Union: established in 1954.

membership. At root she felt that Turkey did not belong in an essentially European and Christian community.

As the most powerful state at the heart of Europe, Germany inevitably struggled to reconcile potentially contradictory agendas. The special relationship with Paris at times conflicted with its traditionally close relations with Washington, while the desire to extend the EU to the Eastern European states was a potential cause of friction with Russia. To square the circle, the German government sought both to create a multilateral framework for its foreign policy, and, within this, to construct a series of 'smaller diplomatic groupings which fall into an "institutional grey zone" between unilateralism and mutilateralism'.[22] On the one hand Germany tried to develop the Organization for Security and Cooperation in Europe which, in its original form, was set up after the 1975 Helsinki Conference (see p. 327) to act as a forum for discussing pan-European problems with the eastern states. On the other hand Germany joined a number of much smaller groupings such as the five-power Contact Group to coordinate policy in the Balkans, and also agreed with Denmark and Poland to form a joint army corps.

In the post-Cold War world, Germany has also had to face up to demands for its participation in peace-keeping missions, which have involved increasing military commitments. The *Bundeswehr* was prevented from playing a part in the **Gulf War of 1991** both by the strength of public opinion and by the Basic Law which prevented the deployment of German troops outside the NATO area. In July 1994 the Constitutional Court removed this restriction, stipulating, however, that German forces could only be used within the context of a peace-keeping multilateral organization. This then made possible the sending of a contingent of German troops to Somalia, the dispatch of ground troops to Bosnia, participation in the war in Kosovo in 1999, and in 2002 assisting British and American forces in Afghanistan. Opposition within the Red–Green coalition was overcome by the argument of the foreign minister, Joschka Fischer, that 'it took a foreign army to free Auschwitz'.[23] Nevertheless, Fischer was adamant that troops should be used only if diplomatic efforts for a settlement had been exhausted. This same caution was visible when Schröder refused to join the USA, Britain, Poland and Australia in **the Iraq War of March–April 2003**. This policy, temporarily at least, ruptured the traditional German 'special relationship' with Washington.

The foreign policy of the Merkel governments, 2005–2013

In opposition Merkel had supported the Iraq War, but she initially offended President Bush by comparing the **Guantanamo Bay** internment camp to a concentration camp. However, this did not seriously damage German–US relations. In 2007 she agreed to increase the number of German troops in Afghanistan, although they were still not to enter into combat, and consented to set up a transatlantic EU–US forum to lower trade barriers and

Gulf War of 1991: fought in response to Iraq's occupation of Kuwait in August 1990

Iraq War of March–April 2003: an allied coalition led by the US invaded Iraq in the belief that it possessed 'weapons of mass destruction'

Guantanamo Bay: set up by the US in 2002 to hold and to interrogate prisoners captured in Afghanistan and elsewhere

develop common financial regulations. After an appeal from Israeli Prime Minister Ehud Olmert (1945–), Merkel also agreed to the participation of German troops in the UN peace-keeping force in South Lebanon. In March 2008 Merkel was the first foreign head of government to address the Knesset, the Israeli parliament, where she declared that the security of the Israeli state was one of Germany's national priorities.

Nevertheless, as with all German administrations since Adenauer, European integration remained the real priority of German foreign policy. As President of the EU Council between 1 January and 30 June 2007 she ensured that the draft EU constitutional treaty, despite being rejected by referenda in France, Ireland and Holland, was salvaged and after some cosmetic changes was duly signed in Lisbon in 2008. The sub-prime crisis in 2008 and then the sovereign debt crisis in Greece and Southern Europe (see above) confirmed Merkel's belief in the supreme importance of the EU for the future of Europe and Germany. Building on what had been the Federal Republic's position since its inception she gave complete priority to European unity, arguing that if the 'euro fails, then Europe fails'. To her the only effective way to defend the euro was 'more Europe and not less Europe'.[24]

Germany as the most powerful economy in Europe had no option but to take on the leadership of Europe. Initially Merkel was able to operate through the traditional Franco-German duopoly. Her close working relationship with President Sarkozy after the Deauville conference (see above) of October 2010 was dubbed by the press 'Merkozy'. Yet, given France's ailing economy, it was an unequal partnership, which was weakened still further by the election of François Hollande in May 2012. The economic crises also led to the emergence of further differences between Washington and Berlin. President Obama was critical of Merkel's initial caution and emphasis on deficit reduction, arguing that Germany should use its overwhelming financial force to halt the crisis. Merkel on the other hand was highly critical of US bankers and the American policy of 'quantitative easing', which she argued led to inflation.

'Merkozy': an amalgamation of the names Merkel and [President] Sarkozy coined by the German media

Quantitative easing: increasing the money supply by the central bank's purchase of financial assets from commercial banks and private institutions to stimulate the economy

By 2012 Germany had indeed become Europe's regional hegemon, but under the Merkel government it was still a cautious and risk-averse power. In March 2011, for instance, when the UN Security Council voted for a no-fly zone in Libya to protect the rebels from Quaddafi's troops, Germany did not join Britain, France and the US to enforce this, arguing that the outcome of the intervention was uncertain and that it did not want to behave like a great power. Commenting on this the *Economist* called Germany 'the unadventurous eagle'![25]

Conclusion: the Berlin Republic

With reunification and then the symbolic move of the government to the former capital of Berlin in September 1999, the long post-war period in German history was well and truly at an end. Although in 1990 there was considerable anxiety among Germany's neighbours about the political consequences of German reunification, the new Berlin Republic, far from dominating Europe, suffered initially from a series of major economic problems resulting not only from unification but an increasing overregulation of the labour market and the economy. The subprime crisis and then the protracted euro crisis, however, forced Germany to assume the leadership of Europe, but it was a leadership very different from that aspired to by Bismarck, the Kaiser or Hitler. It was not military power that mattered in Berlin, but rather financial rectitude among the nations participating in the euro. Despite emerging as the undisputed regional hegemon in Europe, there has been little evidence of aggressive German nationalism. The new Germany remains one of the most pacifist nations in Europe and intensely distrustful even of apparently just wars against dictators as obviously evil as Saddam Hussein of Iraq or Quaddafi in Libya. Politically the Germans of the early 21st century are profoundly different from their forebears of a hundred years earlier.

Part Five
Assessment

19 *Is There a German Sonderweg?*

Given the disastrous developments in German history in the first part of the 20th century, which engulfed the world in two major wars and culminated in genocide and the Holocaust, it is not surprising that both German and non-German historians alike are preoccupied by the question of what went wrong in the course of German history. When and why did Germany embark on the fatal *Sonderweg* which led to the horrors of the Third Reich and Auschwitz?

Up to a point all states and cultures have their own defining characteristics which make them unique. Unlike the British Isles, the Iberian or Italian Peninsulas or even France, Germany lacks any clear-cut geographical borders. The survival of the Holy Roman Empire gave German civilization a certain universalism, which inspired nationalists like Friedrich Jahn in the early 19th century to argue that a future German state should include the Dutch, the Flemings, the Danes and the Swiss, as well as the Austrians and the Prussians. In practice, however, the international situation has always determined at any given moment what shape the great German core of Europe should take. It was Napoleon and the French revolutionary wars which destroyed the Holy Roman Empire. Similarly it was the balance of forces in Europe in 1815 and the fears of revolutionary nationalism, which still left Austria as one of the great powers and led to the creation in 1815 of that '*Zwitterding*' (hermaphrodite), the German Confederation, to quote Karl Marx.

Could the Confederation have evolved into a *grossdeutsch* German federal state? In its early years the odds were against this happening. The formation of a German state was against the interests of Austria as a great European power with territories in Italy, in eastern Europe and along the Adriatic. The creation of the middle-sized states, the 'third Germany', also added a further barrier to the formation of a united German state. However, if the 1848 revolts really had led to the collapse of the Austrian Empire, some sort of federal *Grossdeutschland* would probably have emerged, but the Austrian revival in the winter of 1848–1849 ensured that, as far as national unity went, 1848 was a 'turning point that did not turn'. Yet the attempt to realize a Prussian-dominated *Kleindeutschland* through the Radowitz Plan and the successful opposition to this by Austria and the South German states was a dress rehearsal for the dramatic events that led to the creation of Prussian Germany in 1866–1871.

To the great majority of historians between 1871 and 1914 both in the Empire and abroad, it seemed that Germany, far from pursuing a *Sonderweg* in 1870, had at last become a nation state and had joined the mainstream of European development. Only after 1945 or maybe even after 1960, was the nature of the Bismarckian Reich seen as increasingly reactionary and diverging from the Western liberal model. To structuralist historians like Hans-Ulrich Wehler and Wolfgang Mommsen, the unstable Bonapartist system created by Bismarck, which was aimed at protecting the Prussian monarchy and the conservative elites, prevented the political modernization of the German state, and consequently impelled Germany on its *Sonderweg*. While Bismarck did create a constitution that could not easily accommodate change, it is not easy to argue that the Second Reich as a whole was reactionary. In many areas it was an exemplary modern society with, for example, excellent education, welfare and legal systems.

For Germany, as indeed for Europe, the First World War was the catastrophe that opened the way up for both the Bolshevik revolution and the rise of Fascism. To what extent was Germany responsible for that catastrophe? While there were certainly nationalist and ultra-conservative advocates of a short preventive war to restore the popularity of the Bismarckian settlement, it was Bethmann Hollweg's assessment of the threatening international situation that led him into the fatal decision to support Austria. Given the extraordinary success of the German economy and its justified claims to be a world power, strained relations with its neighbours were from time to time unavoidable, but German policy, partly through its own incoherence, provoked the formation of hostile blocs against it. These alliances would in time, however, have loosened and perhaps even have unravelled. In retrospect it can all too easily be argued that Germany's mistakes were to overrate the Russian threat, to put too much emphasis on the need for a colonial empire and to alienate Britain by building a battle fleet for use in the North Sea, but to many, though not all, Germans, this was not apparent at the time.

The impact of the war was a disaster for Germany. Despite the initial *Burgfrieden* it was deeply divisive and the longer it lasted the more economically ruinous it became. Defeat led to democratization and accelerated modernization, but within the worst possible context. The bitter struggle with France over the execution of the treaty prolonged the immediate post-war dislocation until 1924. If the Weimar Republic had enjoyed a fraction of the economic prosperity and political stability of the *Bundesrepublik* in the 1950s, it would slowly have been able to reconcile and integrate its domestic enemies into a more democratic society.

Hitler was able to rise to power within the context of the political, economic and social crisis of the early 1930s. The Nazi combination of *völkisch*, authoritarian and nationalist ideas provided a solution for both the dispossessed middle classes and the traditional elites. It promised both 'restoration' and a 'new deal' without destroying the actual structure of society in the way Bolshevism had in Russia. Nazism was a charismatic and pseudo-religious movement which, as Peuckert has stressed, was 'the combined outcome of the experience of crisis, the yearning for security and the desire for aggression, all merged into a breathless dynamism that latched on to whatever was the next immediate event: the next election campaign, the next mass demonstration, the next brawl'.[1]

By far the most difficult task facing historians is to explain convincingly how Hitler's unstable charismatic dictatorship was able to establish such a grip on Germany. It helps here to remember Martin Broszat's[2] advice that history should not always be studied backwards. Obviously many of those who at first supported Hitler could not foresee how the Third Reich would develop. The aims of both the elites and the majority of the German people overlapped with the initial stages of Nazi policy. Hitler's destruction of the Treaty of Versailles and provision of full employment were achievements which had overwhelming popular backing. The Nazi 'economic miracle' and, up to a point, the *Volksgemeinschaft* appeased the working classes, despite longer working hours and wage controls. The atomization of society through the destruction of the trade unions, pressure groups and the political parties as well as the terror apparatus of the *Gestapo* and SS also made opposition on any large scale very difficult to achieve.

Hitler's legacy to Germany was its occupation by the four victorious powers and then its division into two mutually hostile states in the subsequent Cold War. Once again it was outside forces that imposed a new order on Germany. Western Germany under the protection of the USA became a prosperous liberal state, while East Germany became integrated into the Soviet system. With the building of the Berlin Wall and Bonn's abandonment of the Hallstein Doctrine for *Ostpolitik* this division seemed permanent. As a consequence of the 'cultural revolution' of the 1960s and 1970s West Germany evolved into an open-minded social democratic society, which ceaselessly reproached itself for the crimes of the Nazi past and the Holocaust. In the GDR a certain degree of stability also appeared to have been achieved in the 1970s, but by 1989 changes in the international balance of power again paved the way for the reorganization of Germany. Once it was clear that the USSR lacked both the strength and the will to prop up East Germany, reunification became possible in 1990.

In both London and Paris it was feared that the new united Germany would, as in the past, be a colossus dominating Europe, but its first decade of existence did not witness any triumphalism or flexing of muscles. On the contrary, initially the German economy faced major problems in both absorbing the GDR and in rising to the challenge of globalization. With Kohl in power until 1998 the Berlin Republic appeared to be the Bonn Republic writ large. It still favoured European integration and was deeply reluctant to participate in military ventures unless their peace-keeping purposes were self-evident. Even with the election of the Red–Green coalition in 1998 and the coming to power of the radical student generation of 1968 little seemed to change. It was the tsunami of financial and economic crises which swept over Europe from 2008 to 2012 that really marked the coming of age of the Berlin Republic. Through sheer financial pressure Germany was forced to take the lead in saving the euro, from collapse and to emerge as the regional hegemon in Europe. In November 2011 the Polish Foreign Minister, Radek Sikorski (1963–) in a speech to the German Council of Foreign Relations in Berlin stated that 'I fear German power less than German inactivity. You have become Europe's indispensable nation'.[3] Such a speech coming from a representative of a nation that had suffered terribly under the Third Reich surely indicates Germany's radical break with her militarist and undemocratic past. If Germany is still pursuing a *Sonderweg*, it is, as Mark Rosen[4] has observed, a 'reverse *Sonderweg*', which makes Germany, in spite of all its blemishes, in so many ways a more liberal, peaceful and open state than many of its neighbours.

See Document 88

Part Six
Documents

1 Growing opposition to the French, 1793

Professor Bartholomäus Fischenich expresses his increasing dislike of the French in a letter to the poet and playwright, Friedrich von Schiller, March 1793.

If the French advance further and reach here (Bonn), then I shall probably go away for I am most dissatisfied with the way they are behaving and would not be able to refrain from saying so publicly. I cannot bear it that they should propagate their ideas by force and that they should be unfaithful to their own principles. They inveigh against compulsion in matters of religion and yet they use armed force to make their citizens take oaths of loyalty and they propagate their liberty with fire and the sword.

Source: T. C. W. Blanning, *The French Revolution in Germany: Occupation and Resistance in the Rhineland, 1792–1802*, Oxford, Oxford University Press, 1983, p. 264.

2 An extract from Fichte's lecture to the German nation

Fichte delivered these lectures (Reden) *in the amphitheatre of the Berlin Academy, where they were enthusiastically received in the winter of 1807–1808 just after the French had reduced Prussia to a rump state. In this extract Fichte argues that the Germans can only triumph over their enemies – and provide a beacon of hope to Europe – by staying true to their native genius and philosophy.*

It depends on you whether you will be … the end of an unworthy race … or the beginning … of a new age glorious beyond your dreams … remember that you are the last in whose power this great transformation lies.

Since affairs stand thus you will not overcome them with material weapons; your spirit alone must rise against them. The greater fate is yours to found the empire of the spirit and of reason and to destroy crude physical force as the ruler of the world. …

The old world with its splendor and greatness as well as its defects has sunk. … If that which has been expressed in these *Reden* is true, then of all peoples you are the one in whom the germ of human perfection most clearly lies and to whom the vanguard in its development has been assigned. If this quality in you is ruined, all hope of salvation for the entire human race in the depths of its evil will be destroyed. … There is no alternative; if you sink, entire humanity sinks with you, devoid of hope of future resurrection.

Source: E. N. Anderson, *Nationalism and the Cultural Crisis in Prussia, 1806–1815*, New York, Octagon Books, 1976, p. 59.

3 Karl Freiherr vom-und-zum Stein's assessment of the constitution of the German Confederation, 24 June 1815

Optimistically he hoped that pressure from the princes and public opinion would in time modify it.

Every man who loves his fatherland and who wishes it good fortune and fame is called on to investigate whether the contents of this document meet the expectations of the nation. ...

One can only expect so defective a constitution to have a very weak influence on the public well-being of Germany and one must hope that the despotic clauses of the constitution, which several meetings of the German leaders were unable to delete, will in time through public opinion, the freedom of the press and the example of several princes, especially in Prussia, who wish to grant their subjects a wise and beneficent constitution, be repealed.

Source: E. Huber, *Dokumente zur Deutschen Verfassungstheorie, vol. 1, 1803–1850*, Stuttgart, Kohlhammer, 1961, p. 562. (Translated by the author.)

4 Arminius Riemann's speech at the Wartburg Festival, 1817

Riemann was a member of the Burschenschaft *in Jena. His speech is shot through with bitter disillusionment about how the realization of German unity had been frustrated. Only Archduke Charles of Weimar had carried out his promise to grant a constitution by 1817.*

Four long years have flowed by since [the battle of Leipzig]; the German people had built up lovely hopes. THEY HAVE ALL BEEN FRUSTRATED. Everything has turned out differently from what we expected. Much that is great and splendid, that could and should have happened, has not taken place; many holy and noble feelings have been treated with mockery and derision. Of all the Princes of Germany, only one has honoured his given word, that one in whose free land we are celebrating the festival of the Battle.

Source: H. Schulze, *The Course of German Nationalism: From Frederick the Great to Bismarck, 1763–1867*, Cambridge, Cambridge University Press, 1991, p. 122. (Translated by Sarah Hanbury-Tenison.)

5 An extract from Karl Follen's *Fundamental Concepts for a German Reich Constitution*

Karl Follen was a lawyer and lecturer at Jena University and the most radical of the early nationalists. To his group belonged Karl Sand, the assassin of Kotzebue.

1 The Germans are a people, that is, they have the same physical and spiritual characteristics; to this can be added the same language, the

same historical memories, the same religion. To the German people belong: the Swiss, the inhabitants of Alsace and the Friesians, etc.

2 ... To preserve and foster this national unity the tribes are for ever unified in a single whole.

3 The Reich is a union of all Germans ... Germans see in their people their humanity and in their fatherland, their earth.

4 All Germans have the same rights. Nowhere do privileges exist. Their rights and laws are established by a majority after all have voted. All the power of the bureaucracy rests on the people's sole sovereign power. ...

5 Through elected representatives the people exercise legislative power.

6 Schooling is organized on a national basis; it ensures that all classes in the state receive the same education and that the division between townsman and peasant disappears.

Source: R. Müller, W. Hardtwig and H. Hinze (eds), *Deutsche Geschichte in Quellen und Darstellungen*, vol. 7, 1815–1817, Stuttgart, Reclam, 1997, pp. 247–249. (Translated by the author.)

6 Friedrich von Gentz defends the Karlsbad Decrees

Friedrich von Gentz (1764–1832) was one of Metternich's key advisers. In this extract he welcomes the decisions of the German ministers, who after a 6 month conference announced the Karlsbad Decrees.

It is already clear from the facts (which have until now been only revealed piecemeal, and are surely not exhausted) about the whole sequence of disturbances, that an exceptionally large number of unruly heads, part seducers and part seduced, have participated in the extravagant plans for a radical transformation of Germany, according to first one, then another idiotic model. This would certainly not have been the case if the last few years had not witnessed the prevalence of opinion that Germany viewed as an integral state and in her federal condition, basically only exists in name, has no real means of supporting herself, is liable any day to disintegrate and, in a word, is a blank slate on which anyone can write and sketch anything that the genius of caprice (which is called Freedom) might suggest. It is above all through the latest Federal Decrees, but especially through the establishment of this Commission that this madness, although not quite eradicated, has yet been visibly shattered.

Source: H. Schulze, *The Course of German Nationalism. From Frederick the Great to Bismarck, 1763–1867*, Cambridge, Cambridge University Press, 1991, p. 124. (Translated by Sarah Hanbury-Tenison.)

7 The Hambach Festival

Johann Wirth, the editor of Die Tribune, *appeals at the* Hambacher Fest, *27 May 1832, for an alliance of patriots to spread the gospel of nationalism and unity.*

[If only] the purest, most able, and courageous patriots could agree ... if only twenty such men, bound together by a common cause and led by a man they trusted … tirelessly pursued their mission … then the great work must succeed and the forces of treason would sink into the dust before the power of patriotic love and the omnipotence of public opinion.

Source: J. Sheehan, *German History, 1770–1886*, Oxford, Oxford University Press, 1987, p. 611.

8 Bavaria and the Confederation

The British ambassador in Frankfurt, Thomas Cartwright, sent this dispatch to the Foreign Office in London on 25 June 1832, an extract of which is published below.

Bavaria and the constitutional states have been unwilling to recognize in the Diet the arbitrary right of interfering beyond a given point in their internal affairs, and Austria will not be mending matters by carrying through the Diet by a simple majority a string of resolutions to increase that arbitrary power which those states already view with jealousy. If she does resort to such a course, the dissenting states will assuredly not feel themselves bound by articles to which they refuse to accede. … The Diet therefore will not find affairs advanced one iota by the adoption of any measures to which Bavaria and the other constitutional states are not parties; on the contrary the difficulties of its actual position will only be aggravated.

Source: G. S. Warner, *Bavaria in the German Confederation*, London, Fairleigh Dickenson/London University Press, 1977, pp. 234–235.

9 The problems of inner German trade

The Union of Merchants in a petition drawn up by the political economist, Friedrich List (1789–1846), in 1819 complained about the large numbers of customs barriers.

[They] cripple trade and produce the same effect as ligatures which prevent the free circulation of the blood. The merchants trading between Hamburg and Austria, or Berlin and Switzerland must traverse ten states, must learn ten customs tariffs, must pay ten successive transit dues. Anyone who is so unfortunate as to live on the boundary line between three or four states spends his days among hostile tax gathers and customs house officials. He is a man without a country.

Source: W. O. Henderson, *The Zollverein*, Cambridge, Cambridge University Press, 1939, p. 23.

10 Agreement between the Prussian and the Bavarian-Württemberg customs unions

Friedrich von Motz, the Prussian minister of finance, explains the significance of the commercial treaty between the Prussian Customs Union and the Bavarian-Württemberg Union in a circular note sent to the Prussian ministries in Europe on 18 August 1829.

It is not a customs union such as that formerly made between Bavaria and Württemberg and later between Prussia and Hesse-Darmstadt. It is characterized not so much by the establishment of a common tariff organization as by close cooperation in administering and collecting customs duties. ... It is a commercial treaty but of a far more comprehensive nature than any other of its kind. ... The states, which have signed the treaty have agreed first to secure uniformity in customs administration, secondly, to treat in the same way as their own produce that imported from the territory of another party to the agreement, and thirdly, to place each other's subjects on the same footing as their own as regards the carrying on of business and also to make all communications and other facilities for trade and commerce reciprocally available and to make use of them as cheaply as possible. An attempt has been made to remove, as far as trade and commerce are concerned, the frontiers dividing the various states from each other. In so far as this object has not been completely attained by the present treaty, efforts will be made to approach ever more closely to it at the annual conferences which it has been agreed to hold.

Source: W. O. Henderson, *The Zollverein*, Cambridge, Cambridge University Press, 1939, pp. 90–91.

11 Austria and the renegotiation of the *Zollverein*, 1851–1852

An extract from an undated and unsigned memorandum from winter 1851–1852 in the Vienna Haushof und Staatsarchiv.

This Customs union is a matter of life and death to Austria. She will push it forward with greater energy than anything else and will not blench even at concessions on the purely political field in order to promote it.

Source: H. Böhme, (ed.), *The Foundation of the German Empire*, Oxford, Oxford University Press, 1971, p. 70.

12 Impoverishment of the weavers in Silesia

Wilhelm Wolf, who later worked with Marx and Engels, described the plight of the weavers in Silesia in the early 1840s.

Devoid of all means the weaver had to buy his yarn from the manufacturer and then supply him with the finished cotton. As the yarn was bought by payment in the form of an advance on his wares the weaver was in the hands of the manufacturer ... I have often met these poor during the winter, in terrible weather, hungry and freezing, carrying their finished cotton many miles to the manufacturer. At home wife and children were waiting for the return of the father; for a day and a half they had eaten nothing other than potato soup. The weaver was shocked by the low offer made for his product, but there was no mercy ... he took what was offered to him and returned full of despair to his family.

Source: H. W. Koch, *A History of Prussia*, London, Longman, 1978, p. 230.

13 A negative view of the 1848 revolutions

A. J. P. Taylor wrote The Course of German History *at the end of the Second World War. His negative view of the consequences of the 1848 revolutions reflects the period it was written in.*

1848 was the decisive year of German, and so of European, history: it recapitulated Germany's past and anticipated Germany's future. Echoes of the Holy Roman Empire merged into a prelude of the Nazi 'New Order'; the doctrines of Rousseau and the doctrines of Marx, the shade of Luther and the shadow of Hitler jostled each other in bewildering succession. Never has there been a revolution so inspired by a limitless faith; never has a revolution so discredited the power of ideas in its result. The success of the revolution discredited conservative ideas; and the failure of the revolution discredited liberal ideas. After it, nothing remained but the idea of Force, and this idea stood at the helm of German history from then on. For the first time since 1521, the German people stepped on to the centre of the German stage only to miss their cues once more. German history reached its turning point and failed to turn. This was the fateful essence of 1848.

Source: A. J. P. Taylor, *The Course of German History*, London, Methuen, (paperback edition) 1961, p. 69.

14 The demands of the peasantry

In 1850 a correspondent made the following observation in the German periodical Die Gegenwart.

On the subject of ancient rights, the peasants have inherited a very communist conception of forest property. They don't need sermons on modern theories of property to come up with the idea that property should be generally distributed. When the popular movement broke out in 1848, and this idea immediately went through the whole of the Nassau peasantry, it was based *far less on revolutionary than on conservative inclinations*; they wanted to reestablish a convention which has existed since ancient times with respect to the wood, and if need be, to extend it to cover a number of other things too.

Source: W. Siemann, *The German Revolution of 1848–49*, New York, St. Martin's Press, 1998. p. 182.

15 The reaction to the riots in Berlin of 18–19 March 1848

The report of the Landrat *of the Calau* Kreis *in Brandenburg to the* Ober-präsident *of the Potsdam Province, 31 March 1848.*

The absence of any post from Berlin on 19 March created the greatest stress amongst the people here in Calau and the vicinity … as there was no doubt that in Berlin the most serious events must have taken place. On the evening of the 19th more precise information became available from local inhabitants who had left Berlin on the morning of the 19th, and there was great consternation as a result of the lamentably bloody clash between the army and the citizens [of Berlin]. … The excitement died down, however, when the proclamation of his Majesty the King became known and the people trusted him absolutely. On the 21st both here and in Vetschau gatherings were organized to express sympathy for the wounded and for the relatives of those killed in Berlin. A large number of the inhabitants of Calau went to Berlin in order to attend the funeral of the fallen. On the 22nd memorial services were held in Calau and Lub-benau and on the 25th in Senftenburg, where – in Senftenburg – officials and citizens in formal address met in front of the *Rathaus* and accompanied by school students, teachers and the clergy processed into the church with a flag with the German colours [black red yellow]. After the service they moved to the market place where from a platform appropriate speeches were held and a collection made for the widows and orphans of those who fell in Berlin on 18 and 19 March. Then the meeting broke up peacefully. … To be prepared for all possible occurrences in Calau for the protection of people and property a *Bürgerwehr* (home guard) has been formed and its leaders elected. At the moment it is not carrying out patrol and guard duties, as this is at present unnecessary. Only drill is taking place.

Source: G. Falk (ed.), *Die Revolution, 1848–49 in Brandenburg. Eine Quellenversammlung*, Frankfurt am Main and Berlin, Lang, 1998, pp. 89–90. (Translated by the author.)

16 An extract from Wilhelm Jordan's speech on 24 July 1848

Wilhelm Jordan, a delegate from East Prussia, who had begun his career as a radical liberal, made this speech in the Frankfurt parliament in response to a proposal by 16 left-wing delegates to recognize the independence of Poland.

I say that the policy that is presented to us: Give Poland her freedom whatever it might cost, is a short sighted, self-forgetting policy, a policy of weakness, a policy of fear, a policy of cowardliness. It is high time for us, finally, to wake up out of that bemused self-forgetfulness, in which we enthuse about all the other nationalities, while we ourselves still lie in shameful bondage and are trampled upon by the whole world – to wake up to a healthy national egoism [*Volksegoismus*] in order to state clearly what the well-being and honour of the fatherland requires. …

If we wish to be absolutely honest, then we must not only give Posen back, but half Germany. …

The superiority of the German tribes over the Slavonic peoples, with the possible exception of the Russians is a fact, which must strike every unbiased observer. Against such – I would like to say – natural historical facts, a decree in harmony with cosmopolitan justice won't get anywhere. That is a proposition, which is as real for us as the globe itself (laughter from the left and centre).

Source: R. Müller, W. Hardtwig and H. Hinze (eds), *Deutsche Geschichte in Quellen und Darstellungen*, vol. 7, Stuttgart, Reclam, 1997, pp. 298–299. (Translated by the author.)

17 The situation in October 1848

Heinrich B. Oppenheim (1819–1880), *the editor of* Die Reform, *wrote perceptively in this radical paper on 5 October.*

The Frankfurt central state is floating in the air, and the basis of our reality, the place of our choice for our battles lies elsewhere. As certain as it is that German unity is to be founded only on and by freedom, just as certain is it that the victory or failure of democracy will be decided in the individual states and – as most recent events have shown clearly enough, in the German states of the first rank, in their capitals, in Vienna or Berlin. Dynasties do not fall before paper storms that have been flung at Frankfurt – but they waver before the hammer blows of social democracy in Berlin and Vienna. If Prussia goes backward, German freedom is lost, but if democracy is victorious in Berlin, it is victorious for all Germany.

Source: J. Davis Randers-Pehrson (ed.), *Germans and the Revolution of 1848–1849*, New York and Washington, Peter Lang, 1999, p. 427.

18 King Frederick William rejects the imperial crown

In a letter dated 13 December 1848 the king informs his friend Count Bunsen, the Prussian ambassador in Berne, who had advised him to accept it, why this was impossible.

You say (literally as Herr von Gagern said to me on 26 and 27 of last month): 'You want consent of the princes; well and good, you shall have it'.

But my dearest friend, therein lies the rub: I want neither the Princes' consent to THE election, nor THE throne. Do you understand the words I have marked?

I will cast light over them for you as briefly and brightly as possible. The crown is actually no crown. The crown which a Hohenzollern could accept IF the circumstances COULD make this possible, is not one which an Assembly, which, although constituted by princely consent is riddled with the seeds of revolution, MAKES … , but one which bears God's mark, which makes HIM on whom it is set after being anointed with holy Chrism, 'by the Grace of God', because and how it made more than thirty-four princes into Kings of the Germans by the Grace of God and always keeps company with the last ones of that ancient line. The crown which the Ottonians, the Hohenstaufens and the Habsburgs have worn, a Hohenstaufen can of course wear; it honours him superabundantly with the glitter of a thousand years. The one, however, which you unfortunately mean, dishonours superabundantly with its carrion reek of the 1848 revolution, the absurdest, the stupidest and the worst, if not, God be praised, also the most evil thing of this century.

Source: H. Schulze, *The Course of German Nationalism. From Frederick the Great to Bismarck, 1763–1867*, Cambridge, Cambridge University Press, 1991 pp. 139–140. (Translated by Sarah Hanbury-Tenison.)

19 Bismarck gives his support to the Olmütz proclamation

Bismarck spoke in support of the proclamation in the upper house of the Prussian Landtag, *3 December 1850.*

What kind of a war is this? Not an expedition of isolated regiments to Schleswig or Baden, not a military promenade through troubled provinces, but a major war against two of the three great continental powers, whilst the third mobilizes on our frontier, eager for conquest and well aware that in Cologne there is treasure to be found that could end the French revolution and give their rulers the French Imperial crown. … Why do large states go to war nowadays? The only sound basis for a large state, and this is what distinguishes it from a small state, is state egoism and not romanticism, and it is not worthy of a great state to fight for something that is not in its own interest. Show me therefore, Gentlemen, an objective worthy of war, and I will agree with you.

Source: W. Medlicott and D. Coveney (eds), *Bismarck and Europe*, London, Arnold, 1971, pp. 16–17.

20 Hans-Ulrich Wehler on Bismarck's Bonapartism

For a comparative typology of forms of political rule, which can accommodate the constitutional reality of Imperial Germany, the concept of Bonapartism is particularly useful. Its explanatory value in illuminating the social function of political authority is to be found in its peculiar combination of charismatic plebiscitary and traditionalist elements, all of which were also clearly in evidence in Germany. Deriving from the regime of Napoleon III … Bonapartism is best understood as an authoritarian government which first appeared in a relatively early phase of industrialization when the pre-industrial elites were still able to demonstrate their strength; the bourgeoisie was making rapid advances, while simultaneously threatened below by the workers movement – foreshadowed by the 'red spectre' of the revolutionary years of 1848 to 1849. … The bourgeoisie was being strongly moved by fear of social upheaval into accommodating itself with the forces of tradition. … In the light of such a specific constellation of forces, often viewed as an open-ended state of suspension, extraordinary opportunities could open up for a charismatic politician to carry out a policy of stabilization on behalf of the ruling classes by the use of certain devices appropriate to the times.

Source: H.-U. Wehler, *The German Empire, 1871–1918*, Leamington Spa and Dover, NH, Berg, 1985, p. 57.

21 The link between the economy and national unity

The Bremer Handelsblatt *was one of the more prominent liberal newspapers in north Germany, and, in a leading article on 11 July 1857, it stressed the imperative of economic unity.*

Whoever looks at the situation without prejudice and fear will recognize immediately the intimate connection, especially in Germany, of the national political problem, this Alpha and Omega of German politics. The commerce and transportation of a country have in spite of the egoism among individuals a common aspect. They demand one law, one defence abroad. This need has been satisfied in all other countries which we may mention, but not in Germany. A common code of commercial law is now slowly struggling to life; a common legislation is a pious wish, and abroad we all enjoy the same right, defencelessness.

Source: E. N. Anderson, *The Social and Political Conflict in Prussia, 1858–1864*, Nebraska, University of Nebraska Press, 1954, p. 149.

22 Bismarck predicts war with Austria

As the Prussian minister in Frankfurt, Bismarck was able to follow Austrian policy closely. In April 1856 he sent the following assessment to Otto von Manteuffel, the Prussian prime minister and foreign minister, and Leopold von Gerlach.

Because of the policy of Vienna, Germany is clearly too small for us both; as long as an honourable arrangement concerning the influence of each cannot be included and carried out, we will both plough the same furrow, and Austria will remain the only state to whom we can lose or from whom we can permanently gain. … For a thousand years intermittently – and since Charles V, every century – German dualism has regularly adjusted the reciprocal relations [of the powers] by a thorough internal war; and in this century also no other means can set the clock of evolution at the right hour. ... In the not too distant future we shall have to fight for our existence against Austria ... and it is not within our power to avoid that, since the course of events in Germany has no other solution.

Source: G. Craig, *The Politics of The Prussian Army, 1640–1945*, Oxford, Oxford University Press, 1955, p. 160.

23 Bismarck's 'blood and iron' speech

On 29 September 1862 Bismarck addressed the Budget Commission of the Prussian Landtag.

Germany does not look to Prussia's liberalism, but to its power: Bavaria, Württemberg, Baden can indulge in liberalism, but no one will expect them to undertake Prussia's role; Prussia must gather and consolidate her strength in readiness for the favourable moment, which has already been missed several times; Prussia's boundaries according to the Vienna treaties are not favourable to a healthy political life; not by means of speeches and majority verdicts will the great decisions be made – that was the great mistake of 1848 and 1849 – but by iron and blood.

Source: Medlicott and Coveney, Bismarck and Europe, St. Martin's Press, London, 1973, pp. 30–31.

24 The Treaty of Prague, 23 August 1886

Article I. [Proclaims a new era of peace and friendship between Prussia and Austria]
Article II. [Austria agreed to concede Venetia to Italy.]
Article III. [All prisoners of war to be freed as soon as possible.]
Article IV. His Majesty the Emperor of Austria acknowledges the dissolution of the Germanic Confederation, as hitherto constituted, and gives his consent to a new organization of Germany without the participation of the Imperial Austrian state. His Majesty likewise promises to recognize the more restricted Federal relations, which His Majesty the King of Prussia will establish to the north of the line of the Main; and he declares his concurrence in the formation of an Association of German States situated to the south of that line, whose national connection with the North German Confederation is reserved for further arrangement between the parties, and which will have an independent national existence.
Article V. His Majesty the Emperor of Austria transfers to His Majesty the King of Prussia all the rights, which he acquired by the Vienna Treaty of Peace of 30 October 1864 over the Duchies of Holstein and Schleswig, with the condition that the populations of the Northern Districts of Schleswig shall be ceded to Denmark if, by a free vote they express a wish to be united to Denmark.

Article XI. His Majesty the Emperor of Austria undertakes to pay His Majesty of Prussia the sum of 40,000,000 Prussian Thalers, to cover part of the expenses, which Prussia has been put to by the war.

Source: E. Hertslet, *The Map of Europe by Treaty*, vol. 3, London, Butterworth's, 1875–1891, pp. 1720–1726.

25 Heinrich von Treitschke on German unity, December 1870

Heinrich von Treitschke (1834–96), historian and National Liberal delegate in the Reichstag, *was critical of the concessions that Bismarck had to make to Bavarian particularism in November 1870, but conceded that there was no alternative.*

(7 December 1870). … We have never had any illusions that the inclusion of the south at the present moment would be anything but the greatest sacrifice that the north has ever made for the German cause. … But such a cornucopia of particularistic concessions as are contained in the treaty with Bavaria exceeds our worst fears. …

It cost me a bitter struggle before I recognized that in spite of all this, the *Reichstag* has no mandate to reject the Bavarian treaty. Our justified resentment must yield to a higher duty, to the faith that we must keep with our south German compatriots. …

If the noble ideas of the war prevail in peacetime too, the German state can exist and grow despite its loose institutions.

Source: W. M. Simon, *Germany in the Age of Bismarck*, London, Allen and Unwin, 1968, p. 139.

26 The experience of workers in the Empire –

1) *The following is an extract from a letter written by Max Lotz (1876–?), a coalminer in the Ruhr, to Adolf Levenstein, a factory foreman and amateur sociologist. Lotz was the illegitimate son of a Jewish tenor and a variety show actress. Here Lotz complains about how his employer, who in this case is the Prussian state as he works in a nationalized mine, has increased its demands on its employees.*

Every car holds fourteen bushels, so I may state that the Prussian state has the honour (along with Haniel, Stinnes, Thyssen and accomplices) of having introduced the largest cars anywhere in the Ruhr area. In fact in recent weeks they have tried (and as I write this, they have almost completely accomplished it) to force on us a whole new line of cars, which, according to our calculations, hold five to six shovelfuls more than the old size. Of course the piecework rate for both kinds of cars is the same, so we don't have much good to say about the new cars.

Source: A. Kelly (ed.), *The German Worker*, Berkeley, CA and London, University of California Press, 1987, p. 330.

2) *Doris Vierbeck (1869–?) worked as a cook in a wealthy Hamburg household. She came to Hamburg from rural Holstein in 1888.*

If the bell rang once, it was for me, twice was for the maid; and three short rings meant the manservant was wanted. When they rang for me, I was allowed first to ask at the speaking tube what they wanted; the maid and the manservant had to rush right upstairs, and often just for a trifle. At the speaking tube I had to say, 'what do you wish?' That's what the ladies wanted. If there was no answer, I had to run upstairs. Now frequently I had something on the stove that couldn't be left for long. At the very least I had to take it off to make sure it wouldn't boil over or burn because the conferences upstairs could drag on. But this took too long for the ladies, so they rang loud and long, and when possible a third time, before I got upstairs. 'My God, where have you been?' – that was the usual beginning. My apologies were not accepted. 'Empty excuses' they called them. It often happened that they'd send me many times a day for no reason at all. Then they'd say scornfully as I left, 'see how fast you can get away!' And so they drove us pointlessly to exhaustion.

Sources: A. Kelly (ed.), *The German Worker*, Berkeley, CA and London, University of California Press, 1987, p. 140.

27 The Jewish question

Walther Rathenau, the son of Emil Rathenau, the founder of the electrical company, AEG, was, as a Jew, acutely sensitive to the atmosphere of anti-Semitism in Germany at the turn of the century. He wrote in an article in Die Zukunft, *30 March 1897, about the Jewish question in Germany by which he meant the position of the Jews in Germany.*

[It] buzzes through the classrooms and university lecture halls; it runs through the streets and examines the names of the shops; it makes a noise in the office and giggles down the back stairs; it nests in the seats of the railway carriages and presides over the bars; it swaggers on the parade ground and knocks on the doors of the courts.

Source: Höre, Israel, *Die Zukunft*, 6 June 1897, p. 455 (translated by the author).

28 William II's views on art

When opening the Siegesallee (Victory Avenue) in Berlin in 1901, the Kaiser delivered the following attack on modern art.

Sculpture has remained, in large part unsullied by the so called modern trends and tendencies, and still holds the commanding heights. Preserve it thus. … Art that disregards the laws and limits I have described is no longer art; it is factory work, trade. … Whoever … departs from the laws of beauty, and from the feeling for aesthetic harmony that each man senses within his own breast ... is sinning against the original well springs of art. ... If, as so often happens nowadays, art merely makes misery look more loathsome than it is already, then it is sinning against the German people.

Source: W. Mommsen, *Imperial Germany, 1867–1918,* London, Arnold, 1995, p. 132.

29 A Protestant, nationalist view of the *Kulturkampf*

In 1874 the liberal, Protestant historian, Heinrich von Sybel supported the Kulturkampf *as a political necessity.*

A party with branches all over Europe, strongly disciplined and unconditionally subject to orders of the Pope, has been doing everything it can for six years to prevent the advance of Prussia and the unity of Germany. Immediately after the German victory the German members of this party constituted themselves into a parliamentary party in order, as their manifestos openly proclaimed, to defend the interests of the Pope, this same Pope whose servants and agents everywhere are fighting with passionate bitterness against the German cause. ... It was politically wise to take little notice of this clerical hostility before the French army was defeated; but after France had been overwhelmed it was an urgent duty of the state to render the internal enemy of our national cause harmless. There has never been a juster defensive struggle.

Source: W. M. Simon, *Germany in the Age of Bismarck*, London, Allen and Unwin, 1968, pp. 171–172.

30 Extracts from the Anti-Socialist Law, 1878

1 Societies which aim at the overthrow of the existing political or social order through democratic, socialistic or communistic endeavours are to be prohibited.

This applies also to societies in which democratic, socialistic or communistic endeavours aiming at the overthrow of the existing political or social order are manifested in a manner dangerous to the public peace, and particularly to the harmony among the classes of the population.
   Associations of every kind are the same as societies ...
4 The police are empowered:
1 To attend all sessions and meetings of [a] society.
2 To call and conduct membership assemblies.
3 To inspect the books, papers and cash assets, as well as to demand information about the affairs of [a] society.
4 To forbid the carrying out of resolutions which are apt to further the endeavours in 1, paragraph 2.
5 To transfer to qualified persons the duties of the officers or other leading organs of society. To take charge and manage funds ...

6 Whoever knowingly, or after public notice is given, acts in contravention of these regulations, or of the decisions based thereon, is to be punished by a fine not exceeding one thousand marks, or with arrest or imprisonment not exceeding six months.

Source: V. L. Lidtke, *The Outlawed Party – Social Democracy in Germany, 1878–1890*, Princeton, NJ, Princeton University Press, 1966, pp. 339–348.

31 Kaiser Wilhelm II's approach to politics

In his memoirs the former Chancellor Hohenlohe recorded the following discussion about the German navy with the Kaiser in March 1897.

He enumerated the ships we have and the ones we would need in order to survive a war … he would have to find the means, and if the *Reichstag* didn't approve this, he would nevertheless carry on building and present the *Reichstag* with the bill later. Public opinion didn't concern him. He knew that people didn't love him, and cursed him; but that wouldn't deter him. I then reminded the Emperor of the difference between Prussia and the Empire; said that in Prussia he had old rights which continued to exist, so far as the Prussian constitution had not limited [them]. In the Empire the Emperor had only the rights which the *Reichstag* conceded to him. The Emperor interjected 'the Emperor hardly has any rights', which I attempted to refute. Besides this was quite unimportant, said H.M: the South German democratic states didn't worry him. He had 18 army corps and would make short work of the South Germans.

Source: I. Porter and I. Armour, *Imperial Germany, 1890–1918*, London, Longman, 1991, pp. 72–73.

32 The Pan-German League

This was founded in 1894 with the intention of protecting German interests throughout the world. Its aims were expressed in its handbook.

1 The Pan-German League strives for the invigoration of German national feeling, especially the awakening and cultivation of the consciousness of racial and cultural belonging of all sections of the German people.
2 This task means that the Pan-German League undertakes:

   a) the preservation of German nationality in Europe and beyond and its support in areas where it is threatened;
   b) a solution to the cultural, educational and school questions in favour of German nationals;
   c) to fight with all its might, whatever hinders our national development;

d) an energetic policy for German interests throughout the world, especially a continuation of German colonialism towards practical results.

Source: P. Panayi, *Ethnic Minorities in Nineteenth and Twentieth Century Germany*, Longman, Harlow, 2000, p. 79.

33 A report of an interview with the Kaiser in the *Daily Telegraph*, 27 October 1908

While staying at Colonel Stuart Wortley's house in England, the Kaiser informed his host of all he had allegedly done for Britain. Stuart Wortley used this as a basis for an interview with the Kaiser, which was published in the Daily Telegraph *after it had been sent to Berlin for approval. Bülow failed to read it and to realize the anger it would cause in Germany.*

In your Black Week, when disaster followed disaster, I received a letter from my revered grandmother, which showed that her health and peace of mind were being undermined by grief and anxiety. Instantly I wrote her a sympathetic answer, but I did more than that! I told my *aides-de-camp* to draw up the most accurate statement in their power of the numbers and positions of both armies, as they stood at that period. I worked on these figures to the best of my ability, drawing up a plan of campaign, which I submitted to the criticism of my staff; then I sent it to England, where in Windsor Castle it awaits the impartial verdict of history. And let me remark on an extraordinary coincidence – my plan almost exactly corresponded with that which Lord Roberts ultimately adopted and carried through to the successful end. And now I ask you – is not this the behaviour of a man who wishes England well? Let England give a fair answer.

Source: E. Ludwig, *Kaiser Wilhelm II*, London and New York, Putnam's, 1926, p. 341.

34 Conservative foreboding

In January 1896 Arthur von Posadowsky-Wehner expressed the following fear.

Germany is becoming more and more an industrial state. Thereby that part of the population is strengthened upon which the Crown cannot depend – the population of the great towns and industrial districts, whereas the agricultural population provided the real support for the monarchy. If things went on as present, then the monarchy would either pass over to a republican system or, as in England, become a sort of sham monarchy.

Source: V. Berghahn, *Germany and the Approach of War in 1914*, London, Macmillan, 1973, p. 18.

35 Bismarck's 'nightmare' of an enemy coalition

Bismarck's Kissingen Memorandum of 15 June 1877 is a valuable guide to his diplomatic strategy and ceaseless efforts to hinder the formation of a hostile coalition against Germany.

A French newspaper said of me recently that I had a 'coalition nightmare'; this kind of nightmare will long (and perhaps always) be a legitimate one for a German minister. Coalitions can be formed against us, based on the western powers with the addition of Austria, even more dangerous perhaps on a Russo-Austrian-French basis; great intimacy between two of the last named powers would always offer the third of them a means of exerting very effective pressure on us. In our anxiety about these eventualities, I would regard as desirable results of the eastern crisis (not immediately, but in the course of years): 1. gravitation of Russian and Austrian interests and mutual rivalries towards the east; 2. Russia to be obliged to take up a strong defensive position in the East and on its coasts, and to need our alliance; 3. for England and Russia a satisfactory status quo, which would give them the same interests in keeping what they hold as we have; 4. separation of England, on account of Egypt and the Mediterranean, from France, which remains hostile to us; 5. relations between Russia and Austria which would make it difficult for them to launch against us the anti-German conspiracy to which centralist or clerical elements in Austria might be somewhat inclined.

Source: W. Medlicott and K. Coveney (eds), *Bismarck and Europe*, London, Arnold, 1971, pp. 102–103.

36 The Krüger telegram

This was drafted in early January by the German Foreign Office and represented an effort to tone down the Kaiser's warlike intentions.

I wish to express my sincere congratulations that you and your people without asking the help of friendly powers, have succeeded in restoring peace through your own actions against armed bands, which broke into your country as disturbers of the peace, and in preserving the independence of your country against attack from without.

Source: A. Palmer, *The Kaiser*, London, Weidenfeld and Nicolson, 1979, p. 77.

37 Hugo Stinnes's advice: the gradual approach

In 1911 Hugo Stinnes made the following observation to Heinrich Class, the leader of the Pan-German League.

Give us three or more years of peaceful progress, and Germany will be the undisputed master of Europe. The French are lagging behind us; they are a nation of small rentiers. And the English dislike hard work and lack the mettle for new ventures. Apart from them, there is no one in Europe to compete with us. Three or four years of peace, then, and I assure you that Germany will secretly come to dominate Europe

Source: W. J. Mommsen, *Imperial Germany, 1867–1918*, London, Arnold, 1995, p. 91.

38 Anglo-German naval rivalry

This extract is from a note compiled by an official in the Reich Navy Office in February 1900.

the enlargement of the British fleet cannot proceed at the same rate as ours because the size of their fleet requires considerably larger replacements. … The inferiority in tonnage which our battle fleet will continue to have *vis a vis* Britain's in 1920, shall be compensated for by particularly good training of our personnel and better tactical manoeuvrability of large battle formations.

Source: V. Berghahn, *Germany and the Approach of War in 1914*, London, Macmillan, 1973, p. 38.

39 Hazards of war

In October 1908 the Crown Prince was critical of Bülow's relatively accommodating attitude towards France in Morocco. Bülow made the following reply.

Unless our honor is engaged, we should always ask ourselves what is to be expected from a war. No war in Europe can bring us much. There would be nothing for us to gain in the conquest of any fresh Slav or French territory. If we annex small countries to the Empire we shall only strengthen those centrifugal elements which, alas, are never wanting in Germany.

In 1866 and 1870 there was a great prize to be won. Today that is no longer the case. Above all, we ought never to forget that nowadays no war can be declared unless a whole people is convinced that such a war is necessary and just. A war, lightly provoked, even it were fought successfully, would have a bad effect on the country; while if it ended in defeat it might entail the fall of the dynasty.

Source: D. Kaiser, 'Germany and the Origins of the First World War', *Journal of Modern History*, vol. 55, 1983, pp. 455–456.

40 Bethmann Hollweg and July 1914

As the chancellor's secretary, Kurt Riezler was in a position to understand his master's thinking during the crisis of July 1914. The following are extracts from his diary.

7 July 1914

The secret information which he [Bethmann] imparts to me conveys a disturbing picture. He regards the Anglo-Russian negotiations over a naval convention ... very seriously, last link in the chain. ...

The Chancellor talks of difficult decisions. Murder of Francis Ferdinand. Official Serbia involved. Austria wants to bestir herself. Message of Francis Joseph to the Emperor enquiring about *casus foederis*. Our old dilemma in every Austrian move in the Balkans. If we encourage them, they will say we pushed them into it; if we try to dissuade them, then we are supposed to have left them in the lurch. Then they turn to the western powers whose arms are open, and we lose our last halfway reliable ally. This time it's worse than 1912; for this time Austria is on the defensive against the subversive activities of Serbia and Russia. A move against Serbia can lead to world war. The Chancellor expects a war, however it turns out, to lead to an overthrow of the whole existing order. ... The future belongs to Russia, which grows and grows and weighs upon us like a heavier and heavier nightmare.

8 July 1914

If war comes from the East, so that we would come to Austria–Hungary's aid rather than Austria–Hungary coming to ours, we have a chance of winning it. If war does not come, if the Tsar does not want it or if an alarmed France advises peace, then we still have the prospect of manoeuvring the *Entente* apart over this move.

Source: I. Porter and I. Armour, *Imperial Germany*, London, Longman, 1991, pp. 99–100.

41 The Burgfrieden

On 4 August Hugo Haase, who was co-chairman of the SPD together with Friedrich Ebert, and was later to be a member of the USPD read the following statement on behalf of the SPD to the Reichstag.

We stand today before the brutal fact of war and the terrible threat of enemy invasion. The decision to be made is not whether to take sides for or against the war but rather on the means necessary for the defence of our country ... our heartiest best wishes go out to our brethren, irrespective of party affiliations, who are called to the colours. ... Much if not all would be lost to our people and its future independence in the event of a victory of Russian despotism. ... We therefore shall act in accordance with what we have already emphasized: we shall not abandon the fatherland in its hour of danger. ... We condemn ... every path of annexation.

Source: K. S. Pinson, *Modern Germany*, New York and London, Macmillan, 1966, p. 314.

42 *Mitteleuropa*

In the late August of 1914 war aims and programmes were drafted by industrialists, generals and government departments. On 28 August the Pan-German League drew up the following plan for a German-dominated Central Europe, which had a considerable input into Bethmann Hollweg's September Programme.

Central Europe ... together with those regions which the German Reich and Austria Hungary will win as a result of victory, will form a large economic area ... This core will gradually ... and without pressure from the core states bring about integration with the Netherlands, Switzerland, the three Scandinavian states, Finland, Italy, Romania and Bulgaria. If one includes the colonies and neighbouring territories of these states, an enormous economic area will come into existence, which will be able to defend and assert its economic independence against any other.

Source: F. Fischer, *Griff nach der Weltmacht*, Düsseldorf, Droste, 1964, p. 120. (Translated by the author.)

43 The peace resolution, 19 July 1917

On 19 July the Centre party, the Progressives and the MSP, which together possessed a majority passed the following resolutions:

As on 4 August 1914, the German people, on the threshold of the fourth year of the war, stand behind the words of the speech from the throne: 'we are not driven by a desire for conquest!' Germany took up arms only for the defence of its freedom and independence and for the preservation of its territorial integrity.

The *Reichstag* strives for a peace of understanding and lasting reconciliation of nations. Such a peace is not in keeping with forcible annexations of territory or forcible measures of political, economic or financial character.

The *Reichstag* also rejects all plans which would result in economic isolation and hostility among nations after the war. The freedom of the seas must be made secure. Only economic peace will prepare the ground for the friendly living together of the nations.

The *Reichstag* will actively support the creation of international judicial organizations.

So long as the enemy governments will not agree to such a peace ... the German people will stand together as one.

Source: K. S. Pinson, *Modern Germany*, New York and London, Macmillan, p. 334.

44 The deteriorating morale of the German army

Rudolph Binding, a staff officer, and later a writer, wrote the following in his diary on 28 March 1918 at the height of the German spring offensive on the Western Front.

Today the advance of our infantry suddenly stopped near Albert. Nobody could understand why. Our airmen had reported no enemy between Albert and Amiens. The enemy's guns were only firing now and again on the very edge of affairs. Our way seemed entirely clear. I jumped into a car with orders to find out what was causing the stoppage in front. ...

As soon as I got near [to Albert] I began to see curious sights. Strange figures, who looked very little like soldiers, and certainly showed no sign of advancing, were making their way back ... there were men driving cows before them on a line; others who carried a hen under one arm and a box of note papers under the other. Men carrying a bottle of wine under their arm and another open in their hand.

Source: J. Terraine, *The First World War*, London, Macmillan, 1984, p. 165.

45 Hindenburg concedes defeat

On 3 October 1918 Hindenburg wrote the following to the imperial chancellor even though some two weeks later he argued that Germany could hold the western front.

The Supreme Command continues to hold to its demand expressed on September 29 of this year that a request for an armistice should be sent to our enemies immediately. As a result of the collapse of the Macedonian Front, the consequent weakening of the reserves on our western front, and the impossibility of making good the very severe losses which we have suffered in the last few days, there is, as far as it is humanly possible to judge, no further chance of forcing a peace on the enemy. Our adversaries are continually bringing up fresh reserves.

Source: A. Rosenberg, *Imperial Germany. The Birth of the German Republic*, New York, Oxford University Press (paperback), 1970, p. 245.

46 The November revolution

The War Ministry sums up the situation in a report to the government dated 8 November 1918.

9 A.M. serious riots in Magdeburg
1 P.M. In Seventh Army Corps Reserve District rioting threatened
5 P.M. Halle and Leipzig Red. Evening: Düsseldorf, Halstein, Osnabrück, Lauenburg Red; Magdeburg, Stuttgart, Oldenburg, Brunswick and Cologne all Red
7.10 P.M. General Officer Commanding Eighteenth Army Corps Reserve at Frankfurt deposed.

Source: R. M. Watt, *The Kings Depart*, London, Weidenfeld and Nicolson, 1968, p. 186.

47 Article 48

The key emergency powers which enabled the issue of legislation by presidential decree were contained in paragraph 2 of the Weimar Constitution.

II. If a [state] *Land* does not fulfil the responsibilities assigned to it under the constitution or laws of the *Reich*, the *Reich* President can take the appropriate measures to restore law and order with the assistance of the armed forces.

In the event of a serious disturbance or threat to law and order, the *Reich* President may take the necessary measures for restoring law and order, intervening if necessary with armed forces. To achieve this he may temporarily suspend either completely or partially the basic rights in Articles 114, 115, 117, 118, 123, 124 and 153.

III. The *Reich* President is bound to report immediately to the *Reichstag* all measures taken under paragraphs 1 and 2 of this article. The measures are to be rescinded on the request of the *Reichstag*.

Source: W. Michalka and G. Niedhart, *Die Ungeliebte Republik. Dokumente zur Innen-und Aussenpolitik Weimars 1918–1933*, Munich, 1980, p. 62. (Translated by the author.)

48 The Germans on the wrong side of the new frontiers

A German government proclamation issued on the date of the coming into force of the Treaty of Versailles on 10 January 1920.

The unfavourable result of the war has surrendered us defenceless to the mercy of our adversaries, and imposes upon us great sacrifices under the name of peace. The hardest, however, which is forced upon us is the surrender of German districts in the east, west and north. Thousands of our fellow Germans must submit to the rule of foreign states without the possibility of asserting their right of self-determination.

... In this dark hour, let us appreciate the treasure which remains our common property, and which no outside power can take away from us.

Together we keep the language, which our mother taught us, together with the realm of thought, of speech, of ideas, in which the greatest minds of our people have striven to express the highest and noblest ideas of German civilization. By all the fibres of our being, by our love and by our whole life we remain united.

Everything that is in our power to preserve your mother tongue, your German individuality, the intimate spiritual connection with your home country will be done. Just as before, whenever we had a possibility to negotiate, we made it our secret task to preserve your vital national rights in spite of your separation. ...

For centuries it has been the fate of the German people that many Germans outside the German Empire had to submit to the rule of foreign powers. But wherever their colonies existed, even in the midst of foreign nations, they have retained their German individuality and the spiritual union with the mother country through the hardest times, and the power of their national civilization has sent its rays over vast expanses. Their work shall be an example to you for the difficult task which a hard fate imposes upon you.

Source: *Documents on British Foreign Policy*, First Series, vol. IX, London, HMSO, 1960, pp. 17–18.

49 National election results in the Weimar Republic in percentages

Date	NSDAP	DNVP	DVP	Centre/ BVP	DDP	SPD	USPD	KPD	Others
19.1.19	–	10.3	4.4	19.7	18.6	37.9	7.6	–	1.5
6.6.20	–	14.9	13.9	17.6	8.3	21.6	17.9	2.1	3.7
4.5.24	6.5	19.5	9.2	16.6	5.7	20.5	1.1	12.6	8.3
7.12.24	3.0	20.5	10.1	17.3	6.3	26.0	–	9.0	7.8
20.5.28	2.6	14.2	8.7	15.2	4.9	29.8	–	10.6	14.0
14.9.30	18.3	7.0	4.9	14.8	3.8	24.5	–	13.1	13.6
31.7.32	37.3	5.9	1.2	15.7	1.0	21.6	–	14.3	3.0
6.11.32	33.1	6.5	1.8	15.0	1.0	20.4	–	16.9	5.3
5.3.33	43.9	8.0	1.1	13.7	0.9	18.3	–	12.3	1.08

Based on T. Childers, 'Inflation, Stabilization and Political Realignment in Germany, 1924 to 1928', in G. D. Feldman et al. (eds), *The German Inflation Reconsidered*, Berlin, de Gruyter, 1982, p. 430.

50 Hitler in Munich in 1920

Hans Frank, a Nazi lawyer and later governor-general of German-occupied Poland, recalled the impression Hitler made on him when he first heard him speak in January 1920 in Munich.

I was strongly impressed straight away. It was totally different from what was otherwise to be heard in meetings. His method was completely clear and simple. He took the overwhelmingly dominant topic of the day, the Versailles *Diktat*, and posed the question of all questions: What now German people? What's the true situation? What alone is now possible? He spoke for over two-and-a-half hours, often interrupted by frenetic torrents of applause – and one could have listened to him for much, much longer. Everything came from the heart, and he struck a chord with all of us … He uttered what was in the consciousness of all those present and linked general experiences to clear understanding and the common wishes of those who were suffering and hoping for a programme. In the matter itself he was certainly not original … but he was the one called to act as spokesman of the people … He concealed nothing … of the horror, the distress, the despair facing Germany. But not only that. He showed a way, the only way left to ruined people in history, that of the grim new beginning from the most profound depths through courage, faith, readiness for action, hard work, and devotion to a great, shining, common goal … he placed before the Almighty in the most serious and solemn exhortation the salvation of the honour of the German soldier and worker as his life task … When he finished, the applause would not die down … From this evening onwards […] I was convinced that if one man could do it, Hitler alone would be capable of mastering Germany's fate.

Source: I. Kershaw, *Hitler, 1889–1936: Hubris*, London, Allen Lane, 1998, pp. 148–149.

51 Reaction to the Treaty of Versailles

1) *The German Chancellor, Gustav Bauer, accompanied the signature of the treaty with the following statement.*

Surrendering to superior force but without retracting its opinion regarding the unheard of injustice of the peace conditions, the government of the German Republic declares its readiness to accept and sign the peace conditions imposed by the Allied and Associated governments.

Source: G. Schutz, *Revolutions and Peace Treaties, 1917–1921*, London, Methuen, 1972, p. 189.

2) *The Pan-German* Deutsche Zeitung *published the following on its front page on 28 June.*

Vengeance! German nation! Today in the Hall of Mirrors of Versailles the disgraceful treaty is being signed. Do not forget it! In the place where, in the glorious year of 1871, the German empire in all its glory had its origin, today German honour is being carried to its grave. Do not forget it! The German people will, with unceasing labour, press forward to reconquer the place among the nations to which it is entitled. Then will come vengeance for the shame of 1919.

Source: K. S. Pinson, *Modern Germany*, New York and London, Macmillan, p. 398.

52 The impact of the inflation

Frieda Wunderlich, who was financially dependent on her salary as editor of Die Soziale Praxis, *indicates the devastating impact of hyperinflation.*

May I give you some recollection of my own situation at that time? As soon as I received my salary, I rushed out to buy the daily necessities. My daily salary, as editor of the periodical, *Sociale Praxis*, was just enough to buy one loaf of bread and a small piece of cheese or some oatmeal. On one occasion I had to refuse to give a lecture at a Berlin city college because I could not be assured that my fee would cover the subway fare to my classroom, and it was too far to walk. On another occasion, a private lesson I gave to the wife of a farmer was paid somewhat better – by one loaf of bread for the hour.

Source: J. Hiden, *The Weimar Republic*, London, Longman, 1974, p. 86.

53 Stresemann's strategy for revising the Treaty of Versailles

Stresemann wrote to the German ex-crown prince on 7 September 1925.

[T]here are three great tasks that confront German foreign policy in the more immediate future. In the first place the solution of the reparation question in a sense tolerable for Germany, and the assurance of peace, which is essential for the recovery of our strength. Secondly the protection of the Germans abroad, those 10 to 12 millions of our kindred who now live under a foreign yoke in foreign lands. The third great task is the readjustment of our eastern frontiers; the recovery of Danzig, the Polish frontier, and a correction of the frontier of Upper Silesia.

Source: E. Sutton (ed.), *Gustav Stresemann: His Diaries, Letters and Papers*, vol.3, Macmillan, London, 1939, p. 505.

54 An SA convert

A British tourist, Patrick Lee Fermor, met in 1933 a young German worker who had just left the KPD for the NSDAP.

[The walls of his room] were covered with flags, posters, slogans and emblems. His SA uniform hung neatly ironed on a hanger. He explained these cult objects with a fetishist zest, saving up till the last the centre-piece of his collection. It was an automatic pistol. ... When I said that it must be rather claustrophobic with all that stuff on the walls, he laughed and sat down on the bed, and said: 'Mensch! You should have seen it last year! You would have laughed! Then it was all red flags, stars, hammers and sickles, pictures of Lenin and Stalin and Workers of the World Unite! I used to punch the heads of anyone singing the Horst Wessel Lied! ... Then suddenly, when Hitler came to power, I understood it was all nonsense and lies. I realized Adolf was the man for me, All of a sudden!' 'Had a lot of people done the same, then?' [Fermor asked] 'Millions! I tell you, I was astonished how easily they all changed sides!'

Source: M. Burleigh, *The Third Reich*, London and Basingstoke, Macmillan, 2000, pp. 132–133.

55 Culture and modernity

H. Reiser made the following observation in a perceptive review in the periodical, Die Schöne Literatur.

But what if [artistic] form – that is, all known and familiar forms – has become a lie, because the present age, as a cultural epoch, has no form – creates no forms other than steel structures, machines and other technical marvels? What if the present age, both in its material externals and in spiritual, cultural and artistic terms, is itself a formless disintegrated mishmash – if it is as God-forsaken and futile as any age has ever been? … Who can doubt that a casualty of this age will want to vent his cries of despair? Anyone can read Mörike [the poet, 1804–75]. But in this age of cinema, radio and Stinnes, he will have to hoodwink himself if he is going to find Mörike the perfect answer. He will have to pretend that the express-train tempo of modern life is a post-chaise canter, that the stink of petrol is like rose petals, and that a stock exchange wizard has a fairy-tale heart of gold.

Source: D. Peukert, *The Weimar Republic: The Crisis of Classical Modernity*, Harmondsworth, Penguin, 1991, p. 168.

56 Working within the constitution

In September 1930 three young army officers stationed in Ulm were accused of working for the Nazi Party and so breaking military regulations which banned soldiers from supporting revolutionary parties. They were put on trial before the Supreme Court at Leipzig. When Hitler was called as a witness, he stressed how he aimed to achieve a 'legal' revolution.

The National Socialist movement will try to achieve its aim with constitutional means in the state. The constitution prescribes my methods, not the aim. In this constitutional way we shall try to gain decisive majorities in the legislative bodies so that the moment we succeed we can give the state the form that corresponds to our ideas.

The chairman of the court summed up the statement to the effect that the setting up of the Third Reich was being worked for in a constitutional way.

Source: J. Noakes and G. Pridham (eds), *Nazism 1919–1945*, vol. 1, *The Rise to Power, 1919–1934*, Exeter, Exeter University Press, 1998, p. 90.

57 Hitler on the Jews in *Mein Kampf*

To Hitler 'the Jew' was the most deadly enemy of 'the Aryan', and his ultimate intention was global domination. In Chapter 11 of Mein Kampf *Hitler argued that the Jews had found in Marxism the ideal weapon for destroying the German state.*

In the organized mass of Marxism he has found the weapon which lets him dispense with democracy and in its stead allows him to subjugate and govern the peoples with a dictatorial and brutal fist.

He worked systematically for revolutionization in a twofold sense: economic and political. Around peoples who offer too violent a resistance to attack from within he weaves a net of enemies, thanks to his international influence, incites them to war, and finally, if necessary, plants the flag of revolution on the very battlefields.

In economics he undermines the states until the social enterprises, which have become unprofitable are taken from the state and subjected to his financial control.

In the political field he refuses the state the means for its self-preservation, destroys the foundations of all national self maintenance and defence, destroys faith in the leadership, scoffs at its history and past, and drags everything that is truly great into the gutter.

Culturally he contaminates art, literature, the theatre, makes a mockery of natural feeling, overthrows all concepts of beauty and sublimity, of the noble and the good, and instead drags men down into the sphere of his own base nature.

... Now begins the great last revolution. In gaining political power the Jew casts off the few cloaks that he still wears. The democratic people's Jew becomes the blood Jew and tyrant over peoples. In a few years he tries to exterminate the national intelligentsia and by robbing the peoples of their natural leadership makes them ripe for the slave's lot of permanent subjugation.

The most frightful example of this kind is offered by Russia where he killed or starved about thirty million people with positively fanatical savagery, in part amid inhuman tortures, in order to give a gang of Jewish journalists and stock exchange bandits domination over a great people.

Source: Hitler, *Mein Kampf*, with an introduction by D. C. Watt, London, Hutchinson, 1974, pp. 295–296.

58 Could the impact of the Great Depression of 1930–1933 on Germany have been mitigated?

Knut Borchardt argued in a seminal study that in reality little could have been done to avert the economic course of events.

With the depression begins a new epoch in the history of capitalist or market economies. From this point so called *Globalsteuering* (macro-economic policy) became the duty of the state. In particular the goal of a high level of employment, not to say full employment, received practically the status of a constitutional requirement. This is one of the most important consequences of the Great Depression. ... But for the Germans, the consequences went even further. In their country there was something additional that allowed the economic crisis to become an event of exceptional significance: the collapse of the Weimar Republic and the rise to power of National Socialism. Among the answers to the question, 'How was this possible? How was Hitler possible?', it is usual to refer to the great depression.

In this regard, it is easy to see the question has often been posed as to whether the crisis could have been avoided if only politicians had more insight or more competence [Borchardt, however, rejects these arguments]. [...]

That an expansionary economic policy actually did assist the subsequent upturn after 1932 is explicable in part because a readjustment and especially a massive lowering of costs, actually did occur during the depression. Previously there had been no such solution to Germany's economic problem. For in Germany the real problem of the Great Depression was its pre-history and the subsequent restraints that followed from that pre-history. … We can only study this tragedy and we should abstain from engaging in over presumptuous criticism.

Source: K. Borchardt, *Perspectives on Modern German Economic History and Policy*, Cambridge, Cambridge University Press, 1991, pp. 143 and 161.

59 Hitler as Saviour

In his memoirs, Albert Speer recalls the hope and optimism that Hitler radiated in the dark days of 1930–1932. In 1931 Speer heard him speak for the first time.

Here it seemed to me was hope. Here were new ideals, a new understanding, new tasks. … The perils of Communism, which seemed inexorably on the way, could be checked, Hitler persuaded us, and instead of hopeless unemployment, Germany could move toward economic recovery. He had mentioned the Jewish problem only peripherally. But such remarks did not worry me, although I was not an anti-Semite; rather I had Jewish friends from my school days and university days, like virtually everyone else. … It must have been during these months that my mother saw an S.A. parade in the streets of Heidelberg. The sight of discipline in a time of chaos, the impression of energy in an atmosphere of universal hopelessness, seems to have won her over also.

Source: A. Speer, *Inside the Third Reich*, London, Weidenfeld and Nicolson, 1970, pp. 16–18.

60 Hitler's speech to the *Reichsstatthälter* (Reich Governors), 6 July 1933

It was vital to prevent interference by the party and the SA threatening economic recovery and alienating the army, big business and the bureaucracy. Hitler had no wish for a showdown with the old elites at this point, as this would only delay rearmament and economic recovery. Consequently he made the following speech to the Reichsstatthälter *on 6 July.*

The revolution is not a permanent state of affairs, and it must not be allowed to develop into such a state. The stream of revolution released must be guided into the safe channel of evolution … we must therefore not dismiss a businessman if he is a good businessman, even if he is not yet a National Socialist; and especially not if the National Socialist, who is to take his place knows nothing about business. In business, ability must be the only authoritative standard …

History will not judge us according to whether we have removed and imprisoned the largest number of economists, but according to whether we have succeeded in providing work. … The ideas of the programme do not oblige us to act like fools and upset everything, but to realize our trains of thought wisely and carefully. In the long run our political power will be all the more secure, the more we succeed in underpinning it economically. The *Reichsstatthälter* must therefore see to it that no organization or Party Offices assume the functions of government, dismiss individuals and make appointments to offices, to do which the Reich Government alone – and in regard to business the Reich Minister of Economics – is competent.

Source: N. Baynes (ed.), *Hitler's Speeches, 1922–39, vol. 1*, Oxford, Oxford University Press, 1942, pp. 865–866.

61 The difficulties of obtaining a decision from Hitler

Carl Schmitt, a leading constitutional lawyer, and the diplomat, Ernst von Weizsäcker, recalled after the war the difficulties of obtaining a decision from Hitler.

Ministers … might for months on end and even for years, have no opportunity of speaking to Hitler. … Ministerial skill consisted in making the most of a favourable hour or minute when Hitler made a decision, this often taking the form of a remark thrown out casually, which then went its way as an 'order of the Führer'.

Source: J. Noakes and G. Pridham (eds), *Nazism 1919–1945, vol. 2, State, Economy and Society, 1933–1939*, Exeter, Exeter University Press, 1984, p. 197.

62 Working towards the Führer

The state secretary in the Prussian Agricultural Ministry, Werner Willikens, in a speech on 21 February 1934 to representatives from the agricultural ministries in the federal states, advised them on the art of interpreting the will of the Führer when no precise guidelines were given by him.

Everyone with opportunity to observe it knows that the *Führer* can only with great difficulty order from above everything that he intends to carry out sooner or later. On the contrary, until now everyone has best worked in his place in the new Germany if, so to speak, he works towards the *Führer*. …

Very often, and in many places, it has been that individuals, already in previous years, have waited for commands and orders. Unfortunately, that will probably also be so in the future. Rather, however, it is the duty of every single person to attempt, in the spirit of the *Führer*, to work towards him. Anyone making mistakes, will come to notice it soon enough. But the one who works correctly towards the *Führer* along his lines and towards his aim will in future as previously have the finest reward of one day suddenly attaining legal confirmation of his work.

Source: J. Noakes and G. Pridham (eds), *Nazism 1919–1945*, vol. 2, *State, Economy and Society, 1933–1930*, p. 13.

63 The role of women in Nazi Germany

On 8 September 1934 Hitler summed up for the National Socialist Women's Section the Nazi view of the role of women in society.

If one says that man's world is the State, his struggle, his readiness to devote his powers to the service of the community, one might be tempted to say that the world of woman is a smaller world. For her world is her husband, her family, her children and her house. But where would the greater world be if there were no one to care for the small world? ... Providence has entrusted to women the cares of that world which is peculiarly her own. ...

Every child that a woman brings into the world is a battle, a battle waged for the existence of her people.

Source: N. Baynes (ed.), *Hitler's Speeches*, vol. 1, Oxford, Oxford University Press, 1942, pp. 528–529.

64 Social equality in the *Volksgemeinschaft*

In a speech made in Berlin on 1 May 1937 Hitler claimed to have created a new equality in Germany.

We in Germany have really broken with a world of prejudices. I leave myself out of account. I, too, am a child of the people; I do not trace my line from any castle: I come from the workshop. Neither was I a general: I was simply a soldier, as were millions of others. It is something wonderful that amongst us an unknown from the army of the millions of German people – of workers and of soldiers – could rise to be head of the Reich and of the nation. By my side stand Germans from all walks of life who today are amongst the leaders of the nation: men who once were workers on the land are now governing German states in the name of the Reich. ... It is true that men who came from the bourgeoisie and former aristocrats have their place in this Movement. But to us it matters nothing whence they come if only they can work to the profit of our people. That is the decisive test. We have not broken down classes in order to set new ones in their place: we have broken down classes to make way for the German people as a whole.

Source: N. Baynes (ed.), *Hitler's Speeches*, vol. 1, Oxford, Oxford University Press, 1942, pp. 620–621.

65 Recalling the Third Reich

The universities of Essen and Hagen in the 1980s conducted an oral history project on the Life, History and Social Culture of the Ruhr, 1930–1960. *It consisted of some two hundred interviews. Extracts from an interview with Ernst Bromberg, a retired fitter, are quoted below. Bromberg stressed that he had no time to participate in Nazi politics.*

Yes well obviously, if you were on piece work, you didn't have any time to make speeches, you got up in the morning when you had to, you didn't overstretch your break periods – because after all – the money was tempting. ... I didn't worry any more about the Nazis, put it that way, apart from my Labour Front contribution, I just didn't have anything to do with the Nazis, you know – anyway I was tied up with my Protestant clubs all week, you know. ... Nothing really changed there.

Source: Ulrich Herbert, 'Good Times, Bad Times: Memories of the Third Reich', in R. Bessel (ed.), *Life in the Third Reich*, Oxford, Oxford University Press. 1987, p. 99.

66 Hitler threatens the Jews with annihilation

In a speech to the Reichstag *on 30 January 1939 Hitler promised the annihilation of the Jews should war break out.*

Today I will once more be a prophet: If the international Jewish financiers in and outside Europe should succeed in plunging the nations into a world war, then the result will not be bolshevization of the earth and thus the victory of Jewry, but the annihilation of the Jewish race in Europe!

Source: N. Baynes (ed.), *Hitler's Speeches*, vol. 1, Oxford, Oxford University Press, 1942, p. 741.

67 The Hossbach Memorandum

Hitler summoned a meeting of his key ministers and service chiefs on 5 November 1937. He informed them that what he had to say was the product of intense deliberation and should be regarded as his 'last will and testament'. Five days later minutes of the meeting were compiled by Hitler's adjutant, Colonel Hossbach. In 1946 what survived from these minutes was accepted by the Nuremberg tribunal as a 'blueprint' of Hitler's intentions to wage war.

The aim of German policy was to make secure and to preserve the racial community and to enlarge it. It was therefore a question of space [*Lebensraum*]. ... The question for Germany was: Where could she achieve the greatest gain at the lowest cost? German policy had to reckon with two hate inspired antagonists, Britain and France, to whom a German colossus in the centre of Europe was a thorn in the flesh ... Germany's problem could only be solved by the use of force ... If the resort to force with its attendant risks is accepted ... there then remains still to be answered the questions 'When?' and 'How?' In this matter there were three contingencies to be dealt with:

Contingency 1: Period 1943–5

After that date only a change for the worse, from our point of view, could be expected [...] Our relative strength would decrease in relation to the rearmament which would then have been carried out by the rest of the world. If we did not act by 1943–5 any year could, owing to lack of reserves, produce the food crisis [...] and this must be regarded as a 'waning point of the regime'. [...] If the *Führer* was still living, it was his unalterable determination to solve Germany's problem of space by 1943–5 at the latest ...

Contingency 2

If internal strife in France should develop into such a domestic crisis as to absorb the French army completely and render it incapable of use for war against Germany, then the time for acting against the Czechs would have come.

Contingency 3

If France should be so embroiled in war with another state that she could not 'proceed' against Germany. For the improvement of our politico-military position our first objective, in the event of our being embroiled in war, must be to overthrow Czechoslovakia and Austria simultaneously in order to remove the threat to our flank in any possible operation against the West.

Source: *Documents on German Foreign Policy, Series D*, vol.1, London, HMSO, 1957–1966, pp. 29–38.

68 Hitler issues the order to prepare for war against the USSR, July 1941

General Halder recorded Hitler's assessment of the military and diplomatic situation at a military conference on 31 July 1940. To defeat Britain and keep America out of the war he argued, Russia would have to be invaded.

Führer:

(a) Stresses his scepticism regarding technical feasibility [of an invasion of Britain]; however satisfied with results produced by Navy.

(b) Emphasizes weather factor.

(c) Discusses enemy resources for counteraction.

(d) In the event that invasion does not take place, our action must be directed to eliminate all factors that let England hope for a change in the situation. To all intents and purposes the war is won. ... Submarine and air warfare may bring about a final decision, but this may be one or two years off. Britain's hope lies in Russia and the United States. If Russia drops out of the picture, America too is lost for Britain, because elimination of Russia would tremendously increase Japan's power in the Far East.

Russia is the Far Eastern sword of Britain and the United States pointed at Japan. …

With Russia smashed, Britain's last hope would be shattered. Germany will then be master of Europe and the Balkans. Decision: Russia's destruction must therefore be made part of this struggle. Spring 1941. The sooner Russia is crushed, the better. Attack achieves its purpose only if Russian state can be shattered to its roots with one blow … Holding part of the country alone will not do. Standing still for the following winter would be perilous. So it is better to wait a little longer but with resolute determination to eliminate Russia.

Source: J. Noakes and G. Pridham (eds), *Nazism 1919–1945,* vol. 3, *Foreign Policy, War and Extermination,* Exeter, Exeter University Press, 1991, p. 790.

69 The impact of the war on the family

By the autumn of 1943 the war was taking its toll on family life as the following extracts from an SD report of 18 November 1943 indicate.

Many women are also concerned that the stability of their marriages and the mutual understanding of their partners is beginning to suffer from the lengthy war. The separation which, with short breaks, has now been going on for years, the transformation in their circumstances through total war and in addition, the heavy demands which are nowadays made on every individual are changing people and filling their lives. When on leave, the front-line soldier often no longer shows any understanding for his family's domestic circumstances, which are governed by the war, and remains indifferent to the many daily cares of the home front. This often produces an increasing *distance between the married couple.* Thus wives often point out that having looked forward to being together again during their husband's leave, the occasion is spoilt by frequent rows caused by mutual tensions. That even happens in marriages which were previously models of harmony …

The *splitting up of families* without the possibility of making visits with all the accompanying problems is in the long run felt to be an intolerable burden both by men but in particular by women … Above all, the married men say that their family is the only compensation they have for their heavy work load. One shouldn't take away from them the only thing that makes life worth living. But the wives are no less subjected to a heavy mental burden because they want to live in their own homes, to look after them and to care for their husbands and children … the majority of the evacuated women and children are accommodated in small villages and rural parishes under the most primitive conditions. They have to cook in the same kitchens with their hosts, which often gives cause for conflict, since people look into each other's pots and get jealous if the other family has something better to eat. In a number of cases there can be no question of family life since sometimes not all children can be accommodated with their mother in the same house, and furthermore often the only living room that is available has to be shared with the host family.

Source: J. Noakes (ed.), *Nazism, 1919-1945*, vol. 4. *The German Home Front in World War II*, Exeter, Exeter University Press, 1998, pp. 360–362.

70 Western Germany in 1945

An extract from the diary of Sir William Strang, political adviser to the British military government, 1–6 July 1945.

Villages and small towns off the main roads quite intact: towns and villages at important communication points badly smashed. Larger centres like Münster or Osnabrück, half or three-quarters devastated; industrial cities like Dortmund almost totally in ruins, except round the outer fringes. The population more healthy looking, better dressed, and showing less sign of strain than one would have expected, even in the more heavily damaged urban areas. The official ration is low, but in the country it is at present supplemented from stocks and garden produce. The position in the large towns is difficult, and the workers certainly do not receive enough to sustain heavy labour. ... Roads still lead in and out of Dortmund (though it is like threading a maze to find one's way about them), and where those roads meet the life of the community continues to spring and begins to reorganize itself. I asked whether [the commander of the military government detachment at Dortmund] thought that Dortmund would ever be re-built. He said certainly, sooner or later. The city authorities were already thinking ahead and actively debating alternative schemes: he himself had been brought into consultation.

Source: Sir William Strang (political adviser to the military governor of the British Zone), *Diary of a Tour Through the British Zone, 1–6 July 1945*, National Archives, London, NA. FO 371 46933.

71 The situation in Breslau, July 1945

Father Paul Peikert, a Catholic priest, described the situation in Breslau under Soviet–Polish occupation in a letter to a colleague.

Already now 300 to 400 people die in Breslau a day, that is 10,000 to 12,000 people a month.

Now the same methods of extermination are applied to us as we applied to other peoples, only with the one outward appearance of humanity that the Russians and the Poles do not murder senselessly as did our *Waffen SS* and *Gestapo* in the occupied territory to the horror of the whole world. But if one considers the intention, it amounts to the same thing.

Source: S. Siebel-Achenbach, *Lower Silesia from Nazi Germany to Communist Poland, 1942–1949*, London, Macmillan, 1994, p. 127.

72 The political principles of the Potsdam Agreement, 2 August 1945

1 In accordance with the Agreement on Control Machinery in Germany, supreme authority in Germany is exercised, on instructions from their respective governments, by the Commanders-in-Chief of the armed forces of the United States of America, the United Kingdom, the Union of Soviet Socialist Republics, and the French Republic, each in his own zone of occupation, and also jointly, in matters affecting Germany as a whole, in their capacity as members of the Control Council. ...

2 So far as is practicable, there shall be uniformity of treatment of the German population throughout Germany.

3 The purposes of the occupation of Germany by which the Control Council shall be guided are:

I. The complete disarmament and demilitarization of Germany and the elimination or control of all German industry that could be used for military production ...

II. To convince the German people that they have suffered a total military defeat and that they cannot escape responsibility for what they have brought upon themselves, since their own ruthless warfare and the fanatical Nazi resistance have destroyed the German economy and made chaos and suffering inevitable.

III. To destroy the National Socialist Party and its affiliated and super-vised organization, to dissolve all Nazi institutions, to ensure that they are not revived in any form, and to prevent all Nazi and militarist activity or propaganda.

IV. To prepare for the eventual reconstruction of German political life on a democratic basis and for eventual peaceful co-operation in international life by Germany ...

9 The administration of affairs in Germany should be directed towards the decentralization of political structure and the development of local responsibility. To this end ...

IV. For the time being no central German government shall be established. Notwithstanding this, however, certain essential central German administrative departments headed by State Secretaries, shall be established, particularly in the fields of finance, transport, communications, foreign trade, and industry. Such departments will act under the direction of the Control Council.

Source: R. Morgan (ed.), *The Unsettled Peace*, London, BBC, 1974, pp. 63–64.

73 Denazification in the American Zone

General Clay, the military governor of the American Zone, in a communication to the War Department in Washington sums up the problems caused by large-scale denazification.

15 December 1946

On my return to Germany I find that as a result of my talk with the Laenderrat [sic] [Council of States] there has been a vigorous upswing in execution of the denazification program. However, it has become apparent that due to the large number of people chargeable under the law (estimated at approximately three million) the administrative difficulties will require at least two years and perhaps longer for full completion of the program. Obviously, political stability in Germany cannot be obtained fully until the program is completed. Therefore, it appears most desirable to reduce the numbers chargeable under the law, emphasizing that this reduction is to permit German administration to concentrate on the punishment of active Nazis who were or are in places of prominence in German life.

Source: J. E. Smith (ed.), *The Papers of General Lucius Clay: Germany, 1945–49*, vol. 1, Bloomington, Indiana University Press, 1974, p. 265.

74 The SED as a Marxist party

An extract from the resolution of the 1st party conference, 28 January 1949.

The characteristics of a party of the new type are:

The Marxist–Leninist party is the conscious vanguard of the working class. That is, it must be a workers' party which primarily has in its ranks the best elements of the working class, who are constantly heightening their class consciousness. The party can only fulfil its role as the vanguard of the proletariat if it has mastered Marxist–Leninist theory, which gives it insight into the laws of development of society. Therefore the first task in the development of the SED into a party of the new type is the political and ideological education of the membership and particularly of the office-bearers in the spirit of Marxism–Leninism.

The role of the party as vanguard of the working class is realized in the day-to-day strategic guidance of party activity. This makes it possible to direct all aspects of party activity in the areas of government, economy, and cultural life. To achieve this it is necessary to form a collective strategic party leadership by electing a Political Bureau (Politburo). ...

The Marxist–Leninist party is founded on the principle of democratic centralism. This means strictest adherence to the principle that leading bodies and officers are subject to election and that those elected are accountable to the membership. This internal party democracy is the basis for the tight party discipline which arises from members' socialist consciousness. Party resolutions are binding on all party members, particularly for those party members active in parliaments, governments, administrative bodies, and in the leadership of the mass organizations.

Democratic centralism means the development of criticism and self-criticism within the party and supervision to ensure that resolutions are rigorously carried out by the leadership and by members.

Toleration of factions and groupings within the party is not consistent with its Marxist–Leninist character.

Source: J. Thomanek and J. Mellis (eds), *Politics, Society and Government in the GDR: Basic Documents*, Oxford and New York, Berg, 1988, pp. 48–49.

75 The Basic Law, 23 May 1949

Preamble:

The German people in the *Länder* [states] of Baden, Bavaria, Bremen, Hamburg, Hesse, Lower Saxony, North-Rhine Westfalia, Rhineland-Palatinate, Schleswig-Holstein, Württemberg-Baden, and Württemberg-Hohenzollern, conscious of its responsibility before God and man, animated by the resolve to preserve its national and political unity, and to serve the peace of the world as an equal partner in a united Europe, desiring to give a new order to political life for a transitional period, has enacted, by virtue of its constituent power, this basic law of the FRG. It has also acted on behalf of those Germans to whom participation was denied.

The entire German people is called on to achieve by free self-determination the unity and freedom of Germany …

Article 20: (1) The FRG is a democratic and social federal state.

Article 21: (1) The parties participate in the shaping of the political will of the people. Their foundation is free, their inner structure must correspond to democratic principles, they have to account for the source of their funds in public.

Article 23: For the time being, this Basic Law applies in the territory of the *Länder* [mentioned above in the preamble]. In other parts of Germany, it shall be put into force on their accession. …

Article 116: (1) This Basic Law understands as German, except for other legal stipulations, whoever has German citizenship or whoever lived as a refugee or expellee of German ethnic origin or as his spouse or descendant on the territory of the German Empire on 31 December 1937.

Source: K. Jarausch and V. von Gransow (eds), *Uniting Germany. Documents and Debates*, Oxford and Providence, Berg, 1994, pp. 6–7.

76 Adenauer and Western integration

Sir Ivone Kirkpatrick, the permanent under-secretary of state at the Foreign Office in London, wrote an account of the following conversation with the West German ambassador, Herbert Blankenhorn, in December 1955.

The German ambassador told me yesterday that he wished to make a particularly confidential communication to me on this subject. I would recollect that I had told him on my return from Geneva that I had come to the conclusion that we might eventually have to be more elastic than the Americans were prepared to be and that we might have to move to a position in which we declared that, provided Germany was unified by means of free elections and provided that unified German Government had freedom in domestic and foreign affairs, we should sign any reasonable security treaty with the Russians.

The Ambassador told me that he had discussed this possibility very confidentially with the Chancellor. Dr Adenauer wished me to know that he would deprecate reaching this position. The bald reason was that Dr Adenauer had no confidence in the German people. He was terrified that when he disappeared from the scene a future German Government might do a deal with Russia at the German expense. Consequently he felt that the integration of Western Germany with the West was more important than the unification of Germany. He wished us to know that he would bend all his energies towards achieving this in the time which was left to him, and he hoped that we would do all in our power to sustain him in this task.

Source: R. Steininger, *The German Question, the Stalin Note of 1952 and the Problem of Reunification*, New York, Columbia University Press, 1990, pp. 118–119.

77 Adenauer's message to the East Germans

After the closing of the frontier in Berlin on 13 August 1961, Adenauer made a speech before a special session of the Bundestag *on 18 August.*

Let me finally say a few words to the inhabitants of the Eastern sector of Berlin and the Soviet zone of Germany. Your sorrow and suffering are our sorrow and suffering. In your particularly difficult situation you were able at least to derive some comfort from the thought that, if your lot should become quite unbearable, you could mend it by fleeing. Now it looks as if you had been deprived of this comfort, too. I request you with all my heart: do not abandon all hope of a better future for yourselves and your children. We are convinced that the Free World, and particularly we here, shall some day be successful in our efforts to obtain freedom for you. The right to self-determination will continue in its victorious march throughout the world and will not halt at the boundary of the Soviet zone. Believe me, the day will come when you will be united with us in freedom. We do not stand alone in the world; justice is on our side, and so are all the nations who love freedom.

Source: W. Heidelmeyer and V. von Gransow, *Documents on Berlin, 1943–63*, Munich, Oldenbourg Verlag, 1963, p. 288.

78 Willy Brandt on *Ostpolitik*

In January 1970 Brandt outlined in the Bundestag *the philosophy behind his foreign policy.*

Some 25 years after the unconditional surrender of the Hitler Reich the concept of the nation forms the tie in divided Germany. In the concept of the nation, historical reality and political will are combined. The word 'nation' encompasses and means more than common language and culture, more than state and social system. The word 'nation' is based on the continuous feeling of belonging together held by a people of a nation.

Nobody can deny the fact that in this sense there is and will be one German nation as far as we can think ahead. ... We must ... have a historical and political perspective ... if we confirm the demand for self-determination for the whole German people. History which has divided Germany through its own faults – at any rate not without its faults – will decide when and how this demand can be implemented. Yet as long as the Germans muster the political will not to abandon this demand the hope remains that later generations will live in one Germany in whose political system the Germans in their entirety can cooperate.

The national components will also have their place in a European peace settlement. We have, however, a long and tedious way to go to reach self-determination for the Germans. ... The length of this road must not prevent us from arriving at a regulated coexistence between the two states in Germany. ... What matters is the German contributions in an international situation in which, to quote President Nixon, a transition from confrontation to cooperation will occur.

Source: D. Bark and D. Gress, *A History of West Germany*, vol. 2, Oxford, Blackwell, 1993, p. 167.

79 *Ostpolitik* and the Helsinki Final Act viewed through East German eyes

The first secretary of the SED in the Schwerin district wrote to Honecker on 19 June 1978 about the attitude of the public to the whole process of détente with the West.

[It can be] sensed ... that many citizens have difficulty in the correct evaluation of the specifics of our policies in the interests of peace ... in this connection the influence of the class enemy is not without effect.

It is still clear that every step toward normal international legal relations between states leads to illusions with respect to the Federal Republic of Germany, for example, concerning travel there or other such matters.

Here we see that the enemy is still, despite all, using his manifold organizational influences to target citizens, at least as far as problems concerning holiday travel or a sense of nationalism – if only occasionally – is concerned.

Source: M. Fulbrook, *Anatomy of a Dictatorship*, Oxford, Oxford University Press, 1995 p. 146.

80 Election results, FRG, 1949–1987, Berlin Republic, 1990–2013

Year	CDU–CSU	SPD	FDP	KPD	DRP	Greens
1949	31.0	29.2	11.9	5.7	1.8	–
1953	45.2	28.8	9.5	2.2	1.1	–
1957	50.2	31.8	7.7	–	1.0	–
1961	45.3	36.2	12.8	–	0.8	–
					NPD	
1965	47.6	39.3	9.5		2.0	–
1969	46.1	39.3	5.8		4.3	–
1972	44.9	45.8	8.4		0.6	–
1976	48.6	42.6	7.9		0.3	–
1980	44.5	42.9	10.6		0.2	1.5
1983	48.8	38.2	6.9		0.2	5.6
1987	44.3	37.0	9.1		0.6	8.3
				PDS	Republicans	
1990	43.8	33.5	11.0	2.4	2.1	5.1
1994	41.4	36.4	6.9	4.4	1.9	7.2
1998	35.1	40.9	6.2	5.1	6.0	6.7
2002	38.5	38.5	7.4	4.0	1.0	8.6
2005	35.2	34.2	9.8	8.7	0.6	8.1
2009	33.8	23.0	14.6	11.9	0.4	10.7
2013	41.5	25.7	4.8	8.6	0.2	8.4

Source: *Statistisches Bundesamt*, Wiesbaden, Germany.

* In 2007 the PDS amalgamated with the WASG (labour and Social justice-the Electoral Alternative) to form a new party Die Linke, which fought the 2009 and 2013 elections.

81 The *Spiegel* affair

Sebastian Haffner, a leading West German journalist, made the following observation on the affair in the Süddeutsche Zeitung, *in November 1962.*

What is usually referred to as 'the accompanying circumstances of the *Spiegel* affair' is in reality the affair itself. The fateful question for Germany which is being raised at this time is not whether the *Spiegel* has – in some articles that may be weeks or months old – crossed the uncertain and flexible limit that distinguishes legitimate public information on defence matters from treason. Let the lawyers calmly decide that point for themselves. The question is whether the Federal Republic of Germany is still a free and constitutional democracy, or whether it has become possible to transform it overnight by some sort of *coup d'état* based on fear and arbitrary power.

Source: D. Bark and D. Gress, *A History of West Germany*, vol. 1, Oxford, Blackwell, 1991, p. 505.

82 The position of women in post-war Germany

Walther von Hollander writing in the woman's magazine, Constanza, *in 1948 describes the tensions between men and women in immediate post-war Germany.*

I know a great many women who try everything in their power to make sure that their husband does not notice the helpless and humiliating position in which he finds himself. In addition to the worries where the daily bread will come from and to the efforts of providing something resembling civilized living, women find the strength to encourage their husbands and to put up with his passivity and weakness. But the situation really becomes intolerable when the helpless man then acts like a domestic tyrant. A powerless tyrant – a disgusting type. And however many excuses one may find for his behaviour in the adverse circumstances of our times, his demands simply are too much for the woman who is already stretched beyond her physical and emotional strength.

Source: E. Kolinsky, *Women in Contemporary Germany. Life, Work and Politics* (2nd edn), Oxford and New York, Berg, 1991, pp. 29–30.

83 Soviet criticism of Ulbricht's policy, 2 June 1953

When Ulbricht, Oelssner and Grotewohl visited Moscow on 2 June they were given the following document by the Soviet Leadership.

The pursuit of a wrong political line in the German Democratic Republic has produced a most unsatisfactory political and economic situation. There are signs of bitter dissatisfaction – among broad masses of the population, including the workers, the farmers, and the intellectuals – with the political and economic policies of the GDR. The most conspicuous feature of this dissatisfaction is the mass flight of East German residents to West Germany. From January 1951 through April 1953, 447,000 people have fled alone. Working people make up a substantial number of the defectors. An analysis of the social composition of defectors reveals the following: 18,000 workers; 9,000 medium and small farmers, skilled workers, and retirees; 17,000 white-collar workers and intellectuals; and 24,000 housewives. It is striking that 2,718 members and candidates of the SED and 2,619 members of the FDJ were among the defectors to West Germany in the first four months of 1953.

It should be recognized that the main cause of this situation is the false course adopted during the Second Party Conference of the SED – and approved by the Central Committee of the Communist Party of the Soviet Union – accelerating the pace of the construction of socialism in East Germany, without the necessary domestic and foreign policy preconditions.

Source: V. Ingimundarson, 'Cold War Misperceptions: The Communist and Western Responses to the East German Refugee Crisis in 1953', *Journal of Contemporary History*, vol. 29, 1994, p. 473.

84 The Red Army Faction

Horst Mahler, founder of the Berlin Socialist Lawyers Collective and member of the RAF, was arrested in October 1972. When brought to trial, he made the following declaration to the court.

You charge me with conspiracy. … But you yourself, the gang of General Motors, Ford, Aramco, General Electric, ITT, Siemens, AEG, Flick, Quandt, BASF, Springer, Unilever, United Front, and certain others … are the most monstrous criminal association in history. To destroy this with all necessary and obtainable means is a necessity of life for more than 3 billion people. … The imperialist system, which presents hell on earth to ever increasing portions of humanity, may only be defeated by the action of armed people and not by incantations, moral appeals, and parliamentary trifling. The Red Army Faction has taken up the idea of arming the people.

Source: J. Becker, *Hitler's Children. The Story of the Baader-Meinhof Terrorist Gang*, London, Pickwick, 1989, p. 249.

85 The leftward drift of the SPD in the 1970s

In his book, People and Politics, *Willy Brandt described the changes taking place in the SPD in the 1970s.*

[The SPD's] membership was being restratified by a process of sociological change corresponding to the growth of the so-called service society. Its internal climate was also being modified by an influx of young and restless recruits. Within a single decade transformation and expansion had accounted for the remarkable fact that only one-third of the membership was 'old', while two-thirds were new recruits, very many of them academics and white-collar workers. The successful assimilation of this greatly altered body of support was not a foregone conclusion. Many feared – and others hoped – that a substantial left-wing group would diverge from the mainstream of the party.

Source: W. Brandt, *People and Politics*, Boston, Little, Brown and Co., 1978, p. 438.

86 Reaction of the population of the GDR to the invasion of Czechoslovakia by Warsaw Pact troops, August 1968

In early September the East German trade union movement, the FDGB, conducted a survey of public opinion, of which the following is an extract.

– increased daubing of swastikas, SS runes, graffiti in toilets, factories, on buildings and squares.

Mostly this graffiti consists of slogans such as 'long live Dubcek – freedom for Czechoslovakia

– Russians and Germans get out of Czechoslovakia – It is just like thirty years ago'. ...

– provocative expressions and incitements against our state, against the Soviet Union and leading personalities (particularly against Comrade Walter Ulbricht). For example four youths in the *Zentrum Warenhaus* Erfurt described Soviet soldiers as pigs and pig Russians.

Source: M. Fulbrook, *Anatomy of a Dictatorship. Inside the GDR, 1949–89*, Oxford, Oxford University Press, 1995, p. 197.

87 The decision on German unity

The Bundestag *welcomes the vote by the GDR* Volkskammer *to join the* FRG *on 23 August 1990.*

In a government declaration before the *Bundestag* on Thursday, Chancellor Helmut Kohl called the decision of the *Volkskammer* that the scope of the Basic Law be expanded to include the area of the GDR ... a 'memorable event in German history'. 'Today is a day of joy for all Germans. Wednesday 3 October 1990, will be a date of reunification. It will be a great day in the history of the people ...'.

Deputy SPD chairman, Oskar Lafontaine, also welcomed the *Volkskammer* resolution as representing a foundation upon which the people of East Germany would be able to live their lives in freedom. Lafontaine reminded listeners that political unification was a prerequisite for 'real unity' – namely, the establishment of uniform living standards throughout Germany. At the same time he referred to Carlo Schmidt's demand for a European nation, and spoke out for a new national concept that could be realized in a United States of Europe. ...

The Chancellor particularly acknowledged the contribution of his predecessor Konrad Adenauer, to the presently completed unification of Germany. What Adenauer described in his memoirs is finally being achieved, said Kohl.

Source: K. Jarausch and V. von Gransow (eds), *Uniting Germany. Documents and Debates, 1944–1993*, Oxford and Providence, Berg, 1994, pp. 180–181.

88 Germany: the benign hegemon

Radek Sikorski (1963–), the Polish foreign minister, in a speech to the German Council on Foreign Relations in Berlin on 28 November 2011 appealed to Germany to act decisively to save the Eurozone.

And I demand of Germany that, for your own sake and for ours, you help it [Europe] survive and prosper. You know full well that nobody else can do it. I will probably be the first Polish foreign minister in history to say so, but here it is: I fear German power less that I fear German inactivity. You have become Europe's indispensable nation. You may not fail to lead. Not dominate, but to lead in reform. Provided you include us in decision making, Poland will support you.

Source: A. Crawford and T. Czuczka, *Angela Merkel*, Wiley, Chichester, 2013, p. 166.

Notes and References

Chapter 1

1 N. Davies, *God's Playground*, vol. 2 (Oxford, Oxford University Press, 2005) p. vi.
2 T. Nipperdey, *Germany from Napoleon to Bismarck, 1800–1866* (Princeton, NJ, Princeton University Press, 1996) p. 1.
3 See H.-U. Wehler, *Deutsche Gesellschaftsgeschichte*, vol. 1 (Munich, Beck, 1987) pp. 544–545; T.C.W. Blanning, 'The French Revolution and the Modernization of Germany', *Central European History*, 22, 1989, pp. 110–120; M. Levinger, *Enlightened Nationalism* (Oxford, Oxford University Press, 2002) pp. 3–16 and W.M. Hagen, *Ordinary Prussians* (Cambridge, Cambridge University Press, 2002) pp. 1–6.
4 P.H. Wilson, *The Holy Roman Empire*, 2nd Edition (Basingstoke, Palgrave, 2011) p. 118.
5 J. Sheehan, *German History, 1770–1866* (Oxford, Oxford University Press, 1989) p. 14.
6 K.O.v. Aretin, *Das Alte Reich, 1648–1806* (Stuttgart, Klett-Cotta, 1993–1997) quoted in Wilson, *Holy Roman Empire*, p. 8.
7 Quoted in Wilson, *Holy Roman Empire*, p. 10.
8 Sheehan, *German History*, p. 23.
9 P.H. Wilson, *From Reich to Revolution, German History, 1558–1806* (Palgrave, 2004) p. 157.
10 Wilson, *Holy Roman Empire*, p. 63.
11 Ibid., p. 64.
12 Wilson, *From Reich to Revolution*, p. 320.
13 Ibid., p. 198.
14 See Hagen, *Ordinary Prussians*, p. 650ff. See also W. Hagen, *German History in Modern Times* (Cambridge, Cambridge University Press, 2012) pp. 45–51 for a more succinct summary.
15 A.J.P. Taylor, *The Course of German History* (London, Methuen, 1961) p. 3.
16 See Wilson, *Holy Roman Empire*, p. 104; G. Schmidt, *Geschichte des alten Reiches. Staat und Nation in der Frühen Neuzeit* (Munich, Beck, 1999); H.A. Winkler, *Germany, The Long Road West*, vol. 1 (Oxford, Oxford University Press, 2006); J. Whaley, 'Federal Habits: The Holy Roman Empire and the Continuity of German Federalism', in Maiken Umbach (ed.), *German Federalism, Past, Present Future* (Basingstoke, Palgrave, 2002), pp. 15–41.
17 Blanning, 'The French Revolution and Modernization of Germany', p. 126.
18 B. Simms, *The Struggle for Mastery in Germany* (London and Basingstoke, St. Martin's Press, 1998) p. 56.
19 See M. Rowe, *From Reich to State, 1780-1830* (Cambridge, Cambridge University Press, 2003) pp. 61–65 and, 'Resistance, Collaboration or Third Way? Response to Napoleonic Rule in Germany', in C.J. Esdaile (ed.), *Popular Resistance in the French Wars* (Basingstoke, Palgrave, 2005) pp. 67–90.
20 Sheehan, *German History*, p. 243.
21 See Wilson, *Holy Roman Empire*, p. 58.
22 J. Sperber, *Revolutionary Europe, 1780–1850* (Harlow, Longman, 2000) p. 163.
23 M. Levinger, *Enlightened Nationalism. The Transformation of Prussian Political Culture, 1806–1848* (Oxford, Oxford University Press, 2000) p. 42.
24 Ibid., p. 44.
25 For a discussion of this see Simms, *The Struggle for Mastery*, pp. 75–76 and Levinger, *Enlightened Nationalism, The Transformation of Prussian Political Culture, 1806–1848* pp. 4–5.
26 Sheehan, *German History*, p. 249.
27 See ibid., pp. 262–263 and K. Aaslestad and K. Hagemann, '1806 and Its Aftermath', *Central European History*, 39, 2006, pp. 547–579.

28   M. Rowe, 'France, Prussia or Germany? The Napoleonic War and Shifting Allegiances', *Central European History*, 39, 2006, pp. 611–640. See also Rowe, *From Reich to State* and T.C.W. Blanning, *The French Revolution in Germany: Occupation and Resistance in the Rhineland, 1792–1802* (New York, Oxford University Press, 1983).

29   Blanning, 'The French Revolution and Modernization of Germany', p. 124.

30   Rowe, *From Reich to State*, p. 201.

31   Levinger, *Enlightened Nationalism*, p. 63.

32   H. Schulze, *The Course of German Nationalism: From Frederick the Great to Bismarck, 1763–1867* (Cambridge, Cambridge University Press, 1991), p. 50.

33   Levinger, *Enlightened Nationalism*, p. 125.

34   P. Schroeder, *The Transformation of European Politics, 1763–1848* (Oxford, Oxford University Press, 1994) p. 352.

35   Rowe, *From Reich to State*, pp. 185–187 and also, 'The French Revolution, Napoleon and Nationalism in Europe', in J. Breuilly (ed.), *Oxford Handbook of the History of Nationalism in Europe* (Oxford, Oxford University Press, 2013) p. 140.

36   K. Hagen, 'Occupation, Mobilization and Politics', *Central European History*, 39, 2006, p. 593.

37   H.W. Koch, *A History of Prussia* (London, Longman, 1978) p. 198.

38   Michael Rowe, 'French Revolution, Napoleon and Nationalism in Europe', in *Oxford Handbook of the History of Nationalism in Europe* p. 141 and K. Hagemann, 'Occupation, Mobilization and Politics: The Anti-Napoleonic Wars in Prussian Experience, Memory and Historiography', *Central European History*, 39, 2006, pp. 594–603.

39   Rowe, *French Revolution*, p. 142.

40   Sheehan, *German History*, p. 386.

41   J. Whaley, 'The German Lands before 1815', in M. Fulbrook (ed.), *German History since 1800* (London, Arnold, 1997) p. 32.

42   Sheehan, *German History*, p. 320.

43   Rowe, 'France, Prussia or Germany? The Napoleonic War and Shifting Allegiances', pp. 638–639.

44   Schroeder, *The Transformation*, p. viii.

45   Ibid., p. 547. For the Polish–Saxon crisis see ibid., pp. 523–538.

46   Sperber, *Revolutionary Europe*, p. 220.

47   Schroeder, *The Transformation*, p. 546.

48   See Wilson, *Holy Roman Empire*, p. 118.

Chapter 2

1   W.D. Gruner, 'Die Deutschen Einzelstaaten und der deutsche Bund', in A. Kraus (ed.), *Land Reich, Stamm und Nation* (Munich, Beck, 1984), p. 20.

2   P.W. Schroeder quoted in Sheehan, *German History*, p. 410; W. Conze, *Staat und Gesellschaft im deutschen Vormärz 1815–1848* (Stuttgart, Klett, 1962); ibid.; E. Kraehe, 'The German Confederation and the Central European Order', in *American Historical Association Meeting* (American Historical Association, Washington, 1955).

3   See H.-U. Wehler, *Deutsche Gesellschaftsgeschichte*, vol. 2 *Von der reformära bis zur industriellen und politischen Doppelrevolution, 1815–1845/49* (Munich, Beck, 1996).

4   W.D. Gruner, *der deutsche Bund, 1815–1866* (Munich, Beck, 2012), pp. 9 and 29.

5   Schroeder, *The Transformation*, p. 508.

6   Levinger, *Enlightened Nationalism*, p. 142.

7   E.R. Huber, *Deutsche Verfassungsgeschichte*, vol. 1 (Stuttgart, Kohlhammer, 1957) p. 746.

8   Sheehan, *German History*, p. 409. See also ibid., pp. 408–409 for analysis of the Accords.

9   G.S. Werner, *Bavaria and the German Confederation, 1820–1848* (London, Associated University Press, 1977) p. 33.

10   Schroeder, *The Transformation*, p. 701.

11   Werner, *Bavaria*, p. 150.
12   C. Clark, 'Germany, 1815–1848: Restoration or Pre-March?', in Fulbrook (ed.), *German History since 1800*, p. 44.
13   See Simms, *Struggle for Mastery*, pp. 116–117.
14   Ibid., p. 115.
15   Nipperdey, *Germany from Napoleon to Bismarck*, p. 317.
16   W.O. Henderson, *The Zollverein* (Cambridge, Cambridge University Press, 1939) p. 53.
17   Ibid., p. 53.
18   H.-J. Voth, 'The Prussian Zollverein and the Bid for Economic Superiority', in P.G. Dwyer (ed.), *Modern Prussian History, 1830–1947* (Harlow, Pearson, 2001) p. 110.
19   H. Böhme, *Deutschlands Weg zur Grossmacht* (Cologne, Kiepenhauer und Witsch, 1966); Sheehan, *German History*, p. 503.
20   Nipperdey, *Germany from Napoleon to Bismarck*, p. 316.
21   Huber, *Deutsche Verfassungsgeschichte*, vol. 2, (1963) p. 298.
22   Wehler, *Deutsche Gesellschaftsgeschichte*, vol. 2, p. 131.
23   Gruner, *der deutsche Bund*, p. 60.
24   Werner, *Bavaria*, p. 60.
25   See Simms, *Struggle for Mastery*, pp. 160–162.
26   Werner, *Bavaria*, pp. 209–211.
27   Nipperdey, *Germany from Napoleon to Bismarck*, p. 281.
28   Levinger, *Enlightened Nationalism*, pp. 136–137.
29   Ibid., p. 146.
30   Rowe, *From Reich to State*, 270; Levinger, *Enlightened Nationalism*, p. 181.
31   Levinger, *Enlightened Nationalism*, pp. 199–200.
32   Nipperdey, *Germany from Napoleon to Bismarck*, p. 293.
33   Levinger, *Enlightened Nationalism*, p. 159.
34   Rowe, *From Reich to State*, p. 246.
35   Ibid., p. 280.
36   Ibid., p. 269.
37   Ibid., p. 259.
38   Ibid., p. 246.
39   Sperber, *Revolutionary Europe*, p. 388.
40   Simms, *Struggle for Mastery*, pp. 124–128.
41   L. Lee, 'Liberal Constitutionalism as Administrative Reform: The Baden Constitution of 1818', *Central European History*, 8/2, 1975, p. 112.
42   Sheehan, *German History*, p. 588.
43   Nipperdey, *Germany from Napoleon to Bismarck*, p. 254.
44   D. Langwiesche, *Liberalism in Germany* (Basingstoke, Palgrave, 1999) p. 2.
45   Ibid., p. 12.
46   Ibid., p. 6.
47   Ibid., p. 21.
48   Nipperdey, *Germany from Napoleon to Bismarck*, p. 344.
49   Levinger, *Enlightened Nationalism*, p. 123.
50   Levinger, ibid., p.159 and Wehler, *Deutsche Gesellschaftsgeschichte*, vol. 2, p. 397.
51   Langwiesche, *Liberalism in Germany*, p. 21.
52   Ibid., p. 25.
53   Wehler, *Deutsche Gesellschaftsgeschichte*, vol. 2, p. 412.
54   Nipperdey, *Germany from Napoleon to Bismarck*, p. 336.
55   Ibid., p. 340.
56   D. Blackbourn, *Germany 1780–1918* (London, Fontana, 1987), p. 107.
57   Sheehan, *German History*, p. 475ff.

58　Wehler, *Deutsche Gesellschaftsgeschichte*, vol. 2, pp. 133–134; W.G. Hoffmann, 'The Take-Off in Germany', in W. Rostow (ed.), *The Economics of Take-off into Sustained Growth* (London, Macmillan, 1974) pp. 95–118; H. Mottek, *Wirtschaftsgeschichte Deutschlands*, vol. 2 (East Berlin, Deutscher Verlag der Wissenschaft, 1978) pp. 56–58.

59　Henderson, *Zollverein*, p. 337.

60　Voth, 'Prussian Zollverein', p. 121. See also statistics on ibid. p. 115.

61　Sheehan, *German History*, p. 503.

62　See U. Frevert, *Women in German History. From Bourgeois Emancipation to Sexual Liberation* (Berg, Oxford, 1989) p. 71.

63　Blackbourn, *Germany 1780–1918*, p. 91. See also Clark, 'Germany, 1815–1848: Restoration or Pre-March?', pp. 38–60.

64　Blackbourn, *Germany 1780–1918*, p. 91.

Chapter 3

1　Taylor, *The Course of German History*, p. 69.

2　V. Valentin, *Geschichte der deutschen Revolution von 1848–1849*, 2 vols, New Edition (Hemsbach, Beltz, 1998).

3　See, for instance, W. Siemann, *The German Revolution of 1848–49* (London, Macmillan, 1998) pp. 218–23; Wehler, *Deutsche Gesellschaftsgeschichte*, vol. 2, p. 779; M. Rapport, *1848 – Year of Revolution* (Philadelphia, Basic Books, 2008) p. 400; Hans-Joachim Hahn, *The 1848 Revolutions in German-Speaking Europe* (Harlow, Pearson, 2001).

4　Sheehan, *German History*, p. 657.

5　Ibid., p. 636.

6　W. Carr, *Schleswig-Holstein, 1815–48* (Manchester, Manchester University Press, 1963) p. 255.

7　Wehler, *Deutsche Gesellschaftsgeschichte*, pp. 642–643 and 653.

8　See Rapport, *Year of Revolution*; Sperber, *Revolutionary Europe*, pp. 401ff.

9　Siemann, *German Revolution of 1848–49*, p. 57.

10　Sheehan, *German History*, p. 671.

11　Langwiesche, *Liberalism in Germany*, p. 20.

12　Ibid., p. 30.

13　Siemann, *German Revolution of 1848–49*, p. 76.

14　Sheehan, *German History*, p. 676.

15　Hahn, *1848 Revolutions*, p. 139.

16　Werner, *Bavaria*, p. 229.

17　Nipperdey, *Germany from Napoleon to Bismarck*, p. 547.

18　Siemann, *German Revolution of 1848–49*, p. 144.

19　Ibid., p. 146.

20　E. Barclay, 'Revolution and Counter-Revolution in Prussia, 1848-50', in Dwyer (ed.), *Modern Prussian History, 1830–1947*, p. 82.

21　M. Hewitson, *Nationalism in Germany, 1848–1866* (Basingstoke, Palgrave, 2010) p. 55.

22　Sheehan, *German History*, p. 691.

23　W. Carr, *History of Germany, 1815–1990* (London, Arnold, 1991) p. 64.

24　Sheehan, *German History*, p. 733.

25　See statistics in J. Breuilly, 'Revolution to Unification', in J. Breuilly (ed.), *19th-Century Germany* (London, Arnold, 2001) p. 140.

26　Sheehan, *German History*, p. 747.

27　J. Steinberg, *Bismarck* (Oxford, Oxford University Press, 2012) p. 122.

28　Koch, *A History of Prussia*, p. 245.

Chapter 4

1   C. Grant Robertson, *Bismarck* (London, Constable, 1918) p. 128.
2   H. Walser Smith, 'Nation and Nationalism', in J. Sperber (ed.), *Germany 1800–1870* (Oxford, Oxford University Press, 2004) p. 253.
3   J. Breuilly, *Austria, Prussia and Germany, 1806–1871* (Harlow, Pearson, 2002), p. 107.
4   Hewitson, *Nationalism in Germany, 1848–1866*, pp. 75–76.
5   Langwiesche, *Liberalism in Germany*, p. 76.
6   Nipperdey, *Germany from Napoleon to Bismarck*, p. 643.
7   O. Pflanze, *Bismarck and the Development of Germany*, vol. 1, 2nd Edition (Princeton, NJ, Princeton University Press, 1990) p. 168.
8   K.A. Lerman, *Bismarck* (Harlow, Longman, 2004) p. 33.
9   Steinberg, *Bismarck*, p. 5.
10 See Hewitson, *Nationalism in Germany, 1848-1866*, pp. 225–248.
11 See ibid., pp. 115–116 and 131–132 and N. Hope, *The Alternative to German Unification. The Anti-Prussian Party in Frankfurt, Nassau and the Two Hessen* (Wiesbaden, Frank Steiner Verlag, 1973).
12 Nipperdey, *Germany from Napoleon to Bismarck*, p. 627. See also D.G. Williamson, *Bismarck and Germany, 1862–1890*, 3rd Edition (Harlow, Pearson, 2011) pp. 26–27.
13 Hewitson, *Nationalism in Germany, 1848–1866*, p. 302.
14 Pflanze, *Bismarck and the Development of Germany*, vol. 1, p. 254.
15 F. Stern, *Gold and Iron: Bismarck, Bleichröder and the Building of the German Empire* (London, Allen and Unwin, 1977) p. 63 and Steinberg, *Bismarck*, p. 5.
16 L. Gall, *Bismarck, The White Revolutionary*, vol. 1, 1815–1871, London, Allen and Unwin, p. 258.
17 H.-W. Hahn, *Geschichte des Deutschen Zollvereins* (Göttingen, Vandenhoeck und Ruprecht, 1984) p. 179.
18 Nipperdey, *Germany from Napoleon to Bismarck*, p. 636.
19 Pflanze, *Bismarck and the Development of Germany*, vol. 1, p. 258.
20 Hewitson, *Nationalism in Germany, 1848–1866*, p. 258.
21 Sheehan, *German History*, p. 909.
22 See A. Bucholtz, *Moltke and the German Wars, 1864–1871* (Basingstoke, Palgrave, 2001) and G. Craig *The Battle of Königgrätz*, New Edition (Philadelphia, Penn Press, 2003).
23 Grant Robertson, *Bismarck*, p. 234 and Taylor, *Bismarck, The Man and the Statesman* (London, Arrow Books, 1961), p. 98.
24 Pflanze, *Bismarck and the Development of Germany*, vol. 1, p. 258.
25 Steinberg, *Bismarck*, p. 268.
26 Gall, *Bismarck, The White Revolutionary*, vol. 1, pp. 314–315.
27 Pflanze, *Bismarck and the Development of Germany*, vol. 1, p. 405.
28 G.A. Craig, *Germany, 1866–1945* (Oxford, Oxford University Press, 1978) p. 19.
29 W.E. Mosse, *European Powers and the German Question, 1848–71* (Cambridge University Press, 1958) p. 263.
30 S.W. Halperin, 'The Origins of the Franco-Prussian War Revisited: Bismarck and the Hohenzollern Candidature for the Spanish Throne', *Journal of Modern History*, 45, 1 1973, p. 85. See also Steinberg, *Bismarck*, p. 282.
31 Halperin, 'The Origins of the Franco-Prussian War Revisited', p. 91.
32 Eva Rosenhaft, 'Gender and Class in an Era of National Wars: Women and Service', in J. Sperber (ed.), *Germany 1800–1870* (Oxford, Oxford University Press, 2004) p. 231.
33 For a history of the war see M. Howard, *The Franco-Prussian War* (London, Rupert Hart Davis, 1962) and Bucholtz, *Moltke and the German Wars*.
34 Howard, *The Franco-Prussian War*, p. 388.

35   L. Gall, 'Das Problem Elsass-Lothringen', in T. Schieder and E. Deuerlein (eds), *Reichsgrundung, 1870–71* (Stuttgart, Seewald Verlag, 1970) p. 367.
36   T. Hamerow, *The Social Foundations of German Unification*, vol. 2 (Princeton, NJ, Princeton University Press, 1972) p. 417.

Chapter 5

1   Blackbourn, *Germany 1780–1918*, p. 313.
2   See discussion in J. Retallack, *Germany in the Age of Kaiser Wilhelm II* (Basingstoke, Palgrave, 1996) p. 67.
3   Hans Rosenberg, 'Political and Social Consequences of the Great Depression of 1873–1896 in Central Europe', in *Economic History Review*, 13, 1943, p. 64.
4   See Knut Borchardt, *Perspectives on Modern German Economic History and Policy* (Cambridge, Cambridge University Press, 1991) and also discussion in Retallack, *Germany in the Age of Kaiser Wilhelm II*, pp. 20–21.
5   H.-U. Wehler, *The German Empire, 1871–1918* (Leamington Spa and Dover, NH, Berg, 1985) p. 49.
6   B. Fairbairn, 'The Wilhelmine Regime and the Problem of Reform: German Debates about Modern Nation-States', in G. Eley and J. Retallack (eds), *Wilhelminism and Its Legacies* (New York/Oxford, Berghahn Books, 2003) p. 43.
7   Hagen, *German History in Modern Times*, p. 182.
8   V.R. Berghahn, *Imperial Germany, 1871–1914* (Providence, RI and Oxford, Berghahn Press, 1994) p. 77.
9   Blackbourn, *Germany 1780–1918*, p. 361.
10   D. Blackbourn and G. Eley, *The Peculiarities of German History* (Oxford, Oxford University Press, 1984) p. 269.
11   Retallack, *Germany in the Age of Kaiser Wilhelm II*, p. 101.
12   Ibid., pp. 101–102.
13   Blackbourn and Eley, *The Peculiarities of German History*, p. 223.
14   Ibid., p. 241.
15   Retallack, *Germany in the Age of Kaiser Wilhelm II*, p. 102.
16   See ibid., p. 95.
17   Nipperdey, *Germany from Napoleon to Bismarck*, p. 213.
18   Pflanze, *Bismarck and the Development of Germany*, vol. 3, p. 206.
19   P. Panayi, *Ethnic Minorities in Nineteenth and Twentieth Century Germany* (London, Pearson, 2000) p. 101.
20   Ibid., pp. 82 and 85.
21   W. Rathenau, 'Höre Israel', *Zukunft*, 6.3, 1897, p. 454.
22   Craig, *Germany, 1866–1945*, p. 215.
23   Quoted in Berghahn, *Imperial Germany, 1871–1914*, p. 133.
24   W. Mommsen, *Imperial Germany, 1867–1918: Politics, Culture and Society in an Authoritarian State* (London, Arnold, 1995) p. 132.
25   Ibid., p. 134.
26   Craig, *Germany, 1866–1945*, p. 36.
27   F. Stern, *The Politics of Cultural Despair*, Paperback Edition (Berkeley, Los Angeles, London, University of California Press, 1974) p. xv.
28   Blackbourn and Eley, *The Peculiarities of German History*, pp. 218–221.
29   Mommsen, *Imperial Germany*, p. 102.

Chapter 6

1 F. Meinecke, *The German Catastrophe* (Cambridge, MA, Harvard University Press, 1950) p. 13.
2 Quoted in Pflanze, *Bismarck and the Development of Germany*, vol. 1, Introduction and O. Pflanze, 'Bismarck and German Nationalism', *American Historical Review*, vol. 66, p. 566. See also A. Dorpalen, 'The German Historians and Bismarck', *Review of Politics*, 15, January 1953, pp. 53–67.
3 H.-U. Wehler, *German Empire*.
4 See Blackbourn and Eley, *Peculiarities of German History*, p. 204; G. Eley, 'Bismarckian Germany', in G. Martel (ed.), *Modern Germany Reconsidered, 1870–1945* (London, Routledge, 1992) p. 26; M. Anderson, *Practicing Democracy* (Princeton, NJ, Princeton University Press, 2000); Retallack, *Germany in the Age of Kaiser Wilhelm II*, pp. 8–15.
5 Mommsen, *Imperial Germany*, p. 34.
6 Steinberg, *Bismarck*, p. 474.
7 M. Seligmann and R.R. McLean, *Germany from Reich to Republic, 1871–1918* (London, Macmillan, 2000) pp. 17–18.
8 Ibid., p. 18.
9 Pflanze, *Bismarck and the Development of Germany*, vol. 2, p. 155.
10 Anderson, *Practicing Democracy*, p. 5.
11 Quoted in Wehler, *German Empire*, p. 53.
12 A good summary of his powers is given in C. Clark, *Kaiser Wilhelm II*, (London, Penguin, 2009) pp. 42–44.
13 Taylor, *Bismarck*, p. 160.
14 Gall, *Bismarck, The White Revolutionary*, vol. 2, p. 11.
15 M. Anderson, *Windthorst: A Political Biography* (Oxford, Oxford University Press, 1981) p. 197.
16 Steinberg, *Bismarck*, pp. 316–319.
17 Craig, *Germany, 1866–1945*, p. 71.
18 Blackbourn, *Germany 1780–1918*, p. 262.
19 Gall, *Bismarck, The White Revolutionary*, vol. 2, p. 64.
20 J. Sheehan, *German Liberalism in the Nineteenth Century* (London, Methuen, 1982) pp. 143–144.
21 Gall, *Bismarck, The White Revolutionary*, vol. 2, p. 85.
22 Anderson, *Windthorst*, p. 233.
23 Eley, 'Bismarckian Germany', p. 3; Böhme, *Deutschlands Weg*.
24 Quoted in Stern, *Gold and Iron*, p. 207.
25 E. Kraehe, 'Review Article on Otto Pflanze's Trilogy', *Central European History*, 23 (4), 1990, p. 376.
26 H.-U. Wehler, 'Bismarck's Imperialism, 1862–1890', *Past and Present*, 48, 1970, p. 147.
27 Pflanze, *Bismarck and the Development of Germany*, vol. 3, p. 350.
28 L. Abrahams, *Bismarck and the German Empire, 1871–1918* (Routledge, London and New York, 1996) p. 32.
29 Steinberg, *Bismarck*, p. 417.
30 Pflanze, *Bismarck and the Development of Germany*, vol. 3, p. 156.
31 Seligmann and McLean, *Germany from Reich to Republic*, p. 36.
32 See the discussion in Clark, *Kaiser Wilhelm II*, pp. 30–34.
33 Craig, *Germany, 1866–1945*, p. 79.
34 M. Stürmer quoted in Williamson, *Bismarck and Germany*, p. 113.
35 Quoted in Clark, *Kaiser Wilhelm II*, p. 76.
36 Anderson, *Practicing Democracy*, p. 191.
37 Wehler, *German Empire*, p. 62.
38 Clark, *Kaiser Wilhelm II*, pp. 78–80.
39 Seligmann and McLean, *Germany from Reich to Republic*, p. 78.

40   Craig, *Germany, 1866–1945*, p. 262.
41   Mommsen, *Imperial Germany*, p. 150; J. Röhl, *The Kaiser and His Court. Wilhelm II and the Government of Germany* (Cambridge, Cambridge University Press, 1994); K.A. Lerman, *The Chancellor as Courtier. Bernhard von Bülow and the Government of Germany, 1900–1909* (Cambridge, Cambridge University Press, 1990).
42   Seligmann and McLean, *Germany from Reich to Republic*, p. 93.
43   Clark, *Kaiser Wilhelm*, p. 100.
44   Fürst Chlodwig zu Hohenlohe -Schillingsfürst, *Denkwürdigkeiten*, vol. 2 (Stuttgart/Leipzig, Deutsche Verlagsanstalt) 1906, pp. 523.
45   Clark, *Kaiser Wilhelm*, p. 112.
46   Hohenlohe, *Denkwürdigkeiten*, vol. 2, p. 524.
47   Lerman, *The Chancellor as Courtier*, p. 25.
48   Quoted in Clark, *Kaiser Wilhelm*, pp. 124–125.
49   J.C.G. Röhl, 'The "Kingship Mechanism" and the Government of Germany', in J. Röhl, *Kaiser and His Court. Wilhelm II and the Government of Germany*, trans. T.F. Cole (Cambridge, Cambridge University Press, 1994) p. 116.
50   Mommsen, *Imperial Germany*, p. 151.
51   G. Eley, *Reshaping the German Right* (New Haven, CT and London, Yale University Press, 1980) p. 264.
52   Lerman, *The Chancellor as Courtier*, p. 208. See also Clark, *Kaiser Wilhelm*, pp. 147–149.
53   Eley, *Reshaping the German Right*, pp. 326–327.
54   K.H. Jarausch, *The Enigmatic Chancellor* (New Haven, CT and London, Yale University Press, 1973) p. 91.
55   Carr, *History of Germany, 1815–1990*, p. 185.
56   Clark, *Kaiser Wilhelm*, p. 162.
57   Wehler, *German Empire*, p. 62.
58   Steinberg, *Bismarck*, p. 479.
59   Walther Rathenau, *Tagebuch, 1907-1922*, (ed.), H. Pogge von Strandmann (Droste, Düsseldorf, 1967) p. 170.
60   Anderson, *Practicing Democracy*, p. 437; M. Rauh, *Die Parlamentarisierung des deutschen Reiches* (Düsseldorf, Droste, 1977); Blackbourn and Eley, *Peculiarities of German History*.

Chapter 7

1   W. Langer, *European Alliances and Alignments, 1871–1890*, 2nd Edition (New York, Knopf, 1962) pp. 503–504; B. Waller, *Bismarck*, 2nd Edition (Oxford, Blackwell, 1997), pp. 52–53. See also B. Waller, *Bismarck at the Crossroads* (London, Athlone Press, 1974) p. 254.
2   Gall, *Bismarck, The White Revolutionary*, vol. 2, pp. 40–41.
3   C. Clark, *The Sleepwalkers* (London, Penguin, 2013) p. 141.
4   I. Geiss, *German Foreign Policy, 1871–1914* (London, Routledge, 1976) p. 30.
5   Steinberg, *Bismarck*, p. 238.
6   See J. Stone and W. Baumgart, *The War Scare of 1875: Bismarck and Europe in the Mid-1970s* (Wiesbaden, Franz Steiner Verlag, 2010) for the argument that Bismarck was seeking to prevent a monarchist restoration in France, as this would facilitate a Franco-Russian rapprochement.
7   N. Rich, *Great Power Diplomacy, 1814–1914* (New York, McGraw-Hill, 1992) p. 227.
8   Craig, *Germany, 1866–1945*, p. 113.
9   Ibid., p. 114.
10   Böhme, *Deutschlands Weg*, p. 591; Gall, *Bismarck, The White Revolutionary*, vol. 2, p. 118.
11   W.N. Medlicott and D.K.Coveney (eds), *Bismarck and Europe* (London, Edward Arnold) p. 110.

12   A.J.P. Taylor, *The Struggle for Mastery in Europe, 1848–1918* (Oxford, Oxford University Press, 1954) p. 277.

13   M.E. Townsend, *The Rise and Fall of Germany's Colonial Empire* (New York, Macmillan, 1930) p. 160.

14   A.J.P. Taylor, *Germany's First Bid for Colonies* (London, Macmillan, 1938) p. 18 and *Struggle for Mastery*, p. 272.

15   Gall, *Bismarck, The White Revolutionary*, vol. 2, p. 141.

16   P. Kennedy, 'German Colonial Expansion: Has "the Manipulated Social Imperialism" Been Antedated?', *Past and Present*, 54, 1972, pp. 134–141.

17   Seligmann and McLean, *Germany from Reich to Republic*, p. 48.

18   See Wehler, 'Bismarck's Imperialism, 1862–1890', pp. 119–155.

19   Pflanze, *Bismarck and the Development of Germany*, vol. 3, p. 251.

20   J. Lowe, *The Great Powers, Imperialism and the German Problem, 1865–1925* (London, Routledge, 1994) p. 66.

21   Gall, *Bismarck, The White Revolutionary*, vol. 2, p. 153.

22   Langer, *European Alliances*, p. 425; Taylor, *Struggle for Mastery*, p. 318; Gall, *Bismarck, The White Revolutionary*, vol. 2, p. 153.

23   See Williamson, *Bismarck and Germany*, p. 104 and Gall, *Bismarck, The White Revolutionary*, vol. 2, p. 155.

24   Gall, *Bismarck, The White Revolutionary*, vol. 2, pp. 158–159.

25   Seligmann and McLean, *Germany from Reich to Republic*, p. 125.

26   See V. Berghahn, *Germany and the Approach of War in 1914* (London and Basingstoke, Macmillan, 1973); Wehler, *German Empire*; E. Kehr, *Economic Interest, Militarism and Foreign Policy of Imperial Germany*, trans. and ed. G. Craig (Berkeley, CA, University of California Press, 1977).

27   Lowe, *Great Powers*, p. 153.

28   M. Hewitson, *Germany and Causes of the First World War* (Oxford, Berg, 2004) p. 232.

29   D. Kaiser, 'Germany and the Origins of the First World War', *Journal of Modern History*, 55, 1983, p. 457.

30   Quoted in Taylor, *Struggle for Mastery*, p. 453.

31   D.C.B. Lieven, *Russia and the Origins of the First World War* (London, Macmillan, 1993) p. 37.

32   W. Mommsen, 'The Topos of Inevitable War in Germany in the Decade Before 1914', in V.R. Berghahn and M. Kitchen (eds), *Germany in the Age of Total War* (London, Croom Helm, 1981) p. 32.

33   Quoted in Seligmann and McLean, *Germany from Reich to Republic*, p. 144.

34   Röhl, *Kaiser and His Court*, p. 170.

35   Kaiser, 'Germany and the Origins of the First World War', p. 466.

36   Röhl, *Kaiser and His Court*, pp. 166 and 184–189.

37   Clark, *The Sleepwalkers*, p. 330.

38   Seligmann and McLean, *Germany from Reich to Republic*, p. 146.

39   Rich, *Great Power Diplomacy*, p. 442.

40   Clark, *The Sleepwalkers*, p. 413.

41   Berghahn, *Germany and the Approach of War in 1914*, pp. 191–192.

42   M. MacMillan, *The War That Ended Peace* (London, Profile Books, 2014) p. 523.

43   K. Jarausch, 'The Illusion of Limited War: Chancellor Bethmann Hollweg's Calculated Risk, July 1914', *Central European History*, vol. 2, 1969, pp. 48–76.

44   Clark, *The Sleepwalkers*, p. 419.

45   Ibid., p. 464.

46   Rich, *Great Power Diplomacy*, p. 452.

47   Clark, *The Sleepwalkers*, pp. 476 and 481.

48   MacMillan, *The War That Ended Peace*, p. 574.

49   D.E. Showalter, 'The Eastern Front and German Military Planning, 1871–1914: Some Observations', *East European Quarterly*, XV, 1981, p. 175; M. Trachtenberg, 'The Meaning of Mobilization in 1914', in S.E. Miller et al. (eds), *Military Strategy and the Origins of the First World War* (Princeton, NJ, Princeton University Press, 1991) pp. 215ff; A. Mombauer, 'Of War Plans and War Guilt: The Debate Surrounding the Schlieffen Plan', *Journal of Strategic Studies*, 28 (5), 2005, pp. 857–885. See also Seligmann and McLean, *Germany from Reich to Republic*, pp. 148–151.

50   MacMillan, *The War That Ended Peace*, p. 577.

51   Clark, *The Sleepwalkers*, p. 459.

52   The English editions are: F. Fischer, *Germany's Aims in the First World War* (London, Chatto and Windus, 1967) and F. Fischer, *War of Illusions: German Politics from 1911–1914* (London, Chatto and Windus, 1975).

53   See discussion in A. Mombauer, *The Origins of the First World War* (Harlow, Longman, 2002) pp. 176ff. See also G. Schöllgen, (ed.), *Escape into War? The Foreign Policy of Imperial Germany* (Oxford, Berg, 1990).

54   Niall Ferguson, *The Pity of War* (London, Penguin, 1999) p. 443.

55   Clark, *The Sleepwalkers*, pp. 560–561.

56   Paul W. Schroeder, 'World War 1 as Galloping Gertie', in D. Lee (ed.), *Outbreak of the First World War* (Lexington, D.C. Heath, 1975) p. 151.

57   Hewitson, *Germany and Causes of the First World War*, Chapter 9.

Chapter 8

1   J. Winter quoted in Ferguson, *The Pity of War*, p. 256.

2   See J. Kocka, *Facing Total War: German Society, 1914–1918* (Berg, Leamington Spa, 1984).

3   J. Winter, *Capital Cities at War* (Cambridge, Cambridge University Press, 1997) p. 10ff.

4   Ferguson, *The Pity of War*, p. 286.

5   See R. Chickering, *Imperial Germany and the Great War, 1914–1918* (Cambridge, Cambridge University Press, 1998) p. 16, Ferguson, The Pity of War, Chapter 7; Blackbourn, *Germany 1780–1918*, pp. 461–462.

6   Chickering, *Imperial Germany*, p. 17.

7   H. Herwig, *The First World War. Germany and Austria-Hungary* (London,Arnold, 1997), p. 67; Chickering, *Imperial Germany*, pp. 37–40 and also D. G. Williamson, 'Walther Rathenau and the KRA, August 1914-March 1915', *Zeitschrift für Unternehmensgeschichte*, 23, 1978, pp. 118–136.

8   Chickering, *Imperial Germany*, p. 39.

9   Ibid., p. 40.

10   Ferguson, *The Pity of War*, p. 279.

11   See J. Terraine, *The First World War* (London, Papermac, 1965) p. 97.

12   Chickering, *Imperial Germany*, p. 72 and Herwig, *The First World War*, p. 196.

13   G. Feldmann, *Army Industry and Labour* (Princeton, NJ, Princeton University, 1966).

14   Chickering, *Imperial Germany*, p. 103.

15   Ferguson, *The Pity of War*, p. 322.

16   Ibid., p. 329.

17   Mommsen, *Imperial Germany*, p. 224.

18   Chickering, *Imperial Germany*, p. 113.

19   Ibid., p. 120.

20   F. Fischer, *Griff nach der Weltmacht* (Düsseldorf, Droste, 1964) pp. 113–120; Jarausch, *Enigmatic Chancellor*, p. 198.

21   Clark, *Kaiser Wilhelm*, p. 310.

22   Chickering, *Imperial Germany*, p. 52; Herwig, *The First World War*, p. 147.

23   Herwig, *The First World War*, p. 147.

24   Chickering, *Imperial Germany*, p. 158.

25 Jarausch, *Enigmatic Chancellor*, p. 224.
26 Ferguson, *The Pity of War*, p. 286.
27 Herwig, *The First World War*, p. 283.
28 Clark, *Kaiser Wilhelm*, pp. 331–332 and 340.
29 Ferguson, *The Pity of War*, p. 311.
30 Herwig, *The First World War*, p. 283.
31 Ibid., p. 426.
32 E. Kolb, *The Weimar Republic* (London, Routledge, 1992) pp. 138–147.
33 G. Kennan, *The Decline of Bismarck's European Order* (Princeton, NJ, Princeton University Press, 1978) p. 3.

Chapter 9

1   K.D. Erdmann, in B. Gebhardt, *Handbuch der deutschen Geschichte*, vol. 4 (Stuttgart, Union Verlag, 1973) pp. 87–91; F.L. Carsten, *Revolution in Central Europe, 1918–19* (London, Wildwood House, 1972); S. Miller, *Die Bürde der Macht. Die deutsche Sozialdemokratie, 1918–1920* (Düsseldorf, Droste, 1978). This debate is explored in Kolb, *Weimar Republic*, pp. 138–147. For more recent views see also C. Fischer, 'A Very German Revolution? The Post-1918 Settlement Re-Evaluated', in *Bulletin* (London, German Historical Institute, November 2006) pp. 6–32; A. McElligott, 'Political Culture', in A. McElligott (ed.), *Weimar Germany* (Oxford, Oxford University Press, 2009) pp. 26–38 and C. Storer, *The Weimar Republic* (London, Tauris, 2013) pp. 27–56.
2   Feldman, *Army*, p. 523.
3   Kolb, *Weimar Republic*, p. 16.
4   Eley, *Reshaping the German Right*, p. 345.
5   Fischer, 'A Very German Revolution', p. 18.
6   McElligott, 'Political Culture', p. 30.
7   Quoted in Kolb, *Weimar Republic*, p. 30.
8   W. Elz, 'Foreign Policy', in McElligott (ed.), *Weimar Germany*, p. 30.
9   Mommsen, *Imperial Germany*, p. 253.
10 Fischer, 'A Very German Revolution', p. 19.
11 See Hagen Schulze in ibid., p. 21.
12 Kolb, *Weimar Republic*, p. 38.
13 Mommsen, *Imperial Germany*, p. 252.
14 Ferguson, *The Pity of War*, p. 424.
15 A. Tooze, *The Deluge* (London, Allen Lane, 2014) p. 8.
16 Ibid., p. 21.
17 P. Krüger, *Die Aussenpolitik der Republik von Weimar* (Darmstadt, Wissenschaftliche Buchgesellschaft, 1985) p. 91.
18 W.A. McDougall, *France's Rhineland Diplomacy, 1914–24* (Princeton, NJ, Princeton University Press, 1978) p. 138.
19 Quoted in D. Williamson, *The British in Germany, 1918–30* (New York and Oxford, Berg, 1991) p. 186.
20 See Tooze, *The Deluge*, p. 368.
21 Ferguson, *The Pity of War*, p. 411.
22 See Sally Marks, 'Reparations Re-Considered: A Reminder', *Central European History*, ii (4), December 1969, pp. 358–360 and C.S. Maier, *Recasting Bourgeois Europe; Stabilization in France, Germany and Italy in the Decade after World War I* (Princeton, NJ, Princeton University Press, 1975) pp. 241–242.
23 See Tooze, *The Deluge*, p. 371.
24 Ferguson, *The Pity of War*, p. 432.

25   C. Fink quoted in Williamson, *The British in Germany*, p. 151.

26   Tooze, *The Deluge*, p. 435.

27   Craig, *Germany, 1866–1945*, p. 451.

28   J. Wright, *Gustav Stresemann* (Oxford, Oxford University Press, 2002), p. 258.

29   Krüger, *Die Aussenpolitik der Republik von Weimar*, p. 227.

30   Mommsen, *Imperial Germany*, p. 231.

31   J. Hiden, *Republican and Fascist Germany* (Harlow, Longman, 1996) p. 43.

32   See Storer, *The Weimar Republic*, pp. 42–43.

Chapter 10

1   D. Peukert, *The Weimar Republic: The Crisis of Classical Modernity* (London, Allen Lane, 1991) p. 4.

2   McElligott, 'Political Culture', p. 4; Storer, *The Weimar Republic* pp. 199–205.

3   Tooze, *The Deluge*, p. 472.

4   Peukert, *Weimar*, p. 204. See also Wright, *Stresemann*, pp. 359–361.

5   Wright, *Stresemann*, p. 358.

6   Extract from Briand's speech to the Assembly of the League of Nations, *Proceedings of the Tenth Ordinary Session of the Assembly, Sixth Plenary Session*, Thursday, 5 September 1929, pp. 51–52.

7   Wright, *Stresemann*, p. 379.

8   See T. Childers, 'Inflation, Stabilization, and Political Realignment in Germany, 1924 to 1928', in G.D. Feldman, et al. (eds), *The German Inflation Reconsidered: A Preliminary Balance* (Berlin, de Gruyter, 1982) pp. 409–431.

9   Borchardt, *Perspectives* on Modern German History and Policy (Cambridge, Cambridge University Press, 1991), p. 171.

10   Peukert, *Weimar*, p. 82.

11   Ibid., p. 130.

12   Ibid., p. 89.

13   H. Mommsen, *From Weimar to Auschwitz, Essays in German History* (London, Polity Press, 1991) p. 36.

14   Peukert, *Weimar*, p. 95.

15   Kathleen Canning, 'Women and the Politics of Gender', in McElligott (ed.), *Weimar Germany*, p. 158.

16   Peukert, *Weimar*, p. 99.

17   Canning, 'Women', p. 164.

18   Frevert, *Women*, p. 186.

19   Ibid., p. 203.

20   Ibid., p. 188.

21   Ibid., p. 188.

22   Peukert, *Weimar*, p. 178.

23   Ibid., p. 181.

24   See B. Liebermann, *From Recovery to Catastrophe* (New York and Oxford, Berghahn, 1998).

25   See J. Bingham, 'The Urban Republic', in McElligott (ed.),*Weimar Germany*, pp. 127–145.

26   Peukert, *Weimar*, p. 157.

27   Craig, *Germany, 1866–1945*, p. 470.

28   Ibid., p. 472.

29   McElligott, 'Political Culture', pp. 38 and 37.

30   Both quotations in Kolb, *Weimar Republic*, p. 66.

31   R. Lepsius, 'From Fragmented Party Democracy to Government by Emergency Decree and National Socialist Takeover: Germany', in J. Linz and A. Stepan (eds), *The Breakdown of Democratic Regimes: Europe* (Baltimore and London, Johns Hopkins University Press, 1978) p. 44.

32   Childers, 'Inflation, Stabilization and Political Realignment', pp. 441 and 413.
33   Quoted in Kolb, *Weimar Republic*, p. 76.
34   Craig, *Germany, 1866–1945*, p. 470.
35   Quoted in Kolb, *Weimar Republic*, p. 66.
36   Storer, *The Weimar Republic*, p. 141.
37   Ibid., p. 79.
38   Hagen Schulze, 'Democratic Prussia in Weimar Germany, 1919–33', in P. Dwyer (ed.), *Modern Prussian History*, p. 214.

Chapter 11

1   Quoted in Kolb, *Weimar Republic*, p. 129.
2   R. Boyce, 'World War, World Depression: Some Economic Origins of the Second World War', in R. Boyce and E. Robertson (eds), *Paths to War* (London, Macmillan, 1989) p. 55.
3   Craig, *Germany 1866–1945*, pp. 532–533.
4   A. Rosenberg, *History of the German Republic* (London, Methuen, 1936) p. 306 and Meinecke, *The German Catastrophe*, p. 70.
5   W. Conze, 'Die Krise des Parteienstaates in Deutschland 1929/30', *Historische Zeitschrift*, 178, 1954, pp. 47–83.
6   K. Bracher, 'Democracy and Power Vacuum: The Problem of the Party State', in V.R. Berghahn and M. Kitchen (eds), *Germany in the Age of Total War*; Mommsen, *From Weimar to Auschwitz*, p. 140.
7   W.J. Patch, *Heinrich Brüning and the Dissolution of the Weimar Republic* (Cambridge, Cambridge University Press, 1998) p. 2.
8   Borchardt, *Perspectives*, p. 161.
9   H. Brüning, *Memoiren, 1914–1934* (Stuttgart, *Deutscher Verlagsanstalt*, 1970). Patch, *Heinrich Brüning*, p. 3.
10   I. Kershaw, *Hitler*, vol. 1 (London, Arnold, 1998) p. 324.
11   Quoted in Kolb, *Weimar Republic*, p. 113.
12   E. Nolte, *Three Faces of Fascism: Action Française, Italian Fascism, National Socialism* (New York, Mentor, 1969) p. 419.
13   D. Mühlberger, 'Rise of the NSDAP', in C. Leitz (ed.), *The Third Reich* (Oxford, Blackwell, 1999) p. 21.
14   Kershaw, *Hitler*, vol. 1, p. 333.
15   Quoted in Kolb, *Weimar Republic*, p. 113.
16   J.W. Falter, 'Die Wähler der NSDAP, 1928–1933: Sozialstruktur und parteipolitische Herkunft', in W. Michalka (ed.), *Die Nationalsozialistische Machtergreifung* (Padeborn and Munich, Schöning, 1984) pp. 47–59.
17   Quoted in McElligott, 'Political Culture', p. 39.
18   M. Burleigh, *The Third Reich: A New History* (London, Macmillan, 2000) p. 138.
19   Quoted in Kolb, *Weimar Republic*, p. 124.
20   P. Fritzsche, *Life and Death in the Third Reich* (Cambridge, MA and London, Harvard University Press, 2008) pp. 42–45.
21   Burleigh, *Third Reich*, p. 143; D. Orlow, *The History of the Nazi Party*, vol. 1, *1919–33* (Newton Abbot, David and Charles, 1971) p. 308.
22   A. Tyrell, 'Seizure and Consolidation of Power', in Leitz (ed.), *The Third Reich*, p. 33 and A. Bullock, *Hitler. A Study in Tyranny* (Harmondsworth, Penguin, 1962) p. 253.
23   Quoted in K. Bracher, *The German Dictatorship* (Harmondsworth, Penguin, 1973), p. 248.
24   Quoted in J. Noakes and G. Pridham (eds), *Nazism*, vol. 1 (Exeter, Exeter University Press, 1998) p. 132.

25   Ibid., p. 142.
26   Ibid., p. 150.
27   Fritzsche, *Life and Death in the Third Reich*, p. 44.
28   Quoted in Bullock, *Hitler*, p. 269.
29   M. Broszat, *The Hitler State* (London, Longman, 1981) p. 281.
30   Kershaw, *Hitler*, vol. 1, p. 489.
31   Broszat, *The Hitler State*, p. 262.
32   Bullock, *Hitler*, p. 286.
33   Kershaw, *Hitler*, vol. 1, p. 508.
34   Craig, *Germany 1866–1945*, p. 588.
35   Kershaw, *Hitler*, vol. 1, p. 510.
36   Bracher in Berghahn and Kitchen (eds), *Germany in the Age of Total War*, p. 190.

Chapter 12

1   For a discussion on interpreting Nazism see Ian Kershaw, *The Nazi Dictatorship: Problems and Perspectives*, 4th Edition (London, Bloomsbury, 2015); K. Hildebrand, *The Third Reich* (London, Routledge, 1991), p. 101.
2   H. Rauschning, T*he Revolution of Destruction* (London, Heinemann, 1939) p. 13.
3   R. Butler, *The Roots of National Socialism* (London, Faber and Faber, 1941).
4   Kershaw, *Nazi Dictatorship*, p. 6.
5   Ibid., p. 10.
6   C. Friedrich and Z. Brzezinski, *Totalitarian Dictatorship and Autocracy* (Cambridge, MA, Harvard University Press, 1956) p. 294.
7   The leading structuralists studies are Broszat, *The Hitler State*; T. Mason, 'Intention and Explanation: A Current Controversy About Interpretation in National Socialism', in G. Hirschfeld and L. Kettenacker (eds), *The Führer State: Myths and Realities* (Stuttgart and London, Kletta Cotta/German Historical Institute, 1981) pp. 23–42; H. Mommsen, 'National Socialism: Continuity and Change', in W. Laqueur (ed.), *Fascism* (Harmondsworth, Penguin, 1976) pp. 151–192 and ibid., 'Hitler's Position in the Nazi System', in H. Mommsen (ed.), *From Weimar to Auschwitz* (Oxford, Oxford University Press, 1991) pp. 163–188. The Intentionalist school is well represented by Andreas Hillgruber, *Hitlers Strategie, Politik und Kriegführung, 1940–1941* (Bernard and Graefe, Frankfurt am Main, 1965) and Hildebrand, *The Third Reich*.
8   Dan Diner quoted in P. Baldwin, *Reworking the Past* (Boston, MA, Beacon Press, 1990) p. 144.
9   E. Nolte, 'Between Myth and Revisionism? The Third Reich in the Perspective of the 1980s', in H.W. Koch (ed.), *Aspects of the Third Reich* (Basingstoke, Macmillan, 1985).
10   Quoted in Kershaw, *Nazi Dictatorship*, p. 199.
11   Ibid., p. 200.
12   D. Peukert, *Inside Nazi Germany* (Harmondsworth, Penguin, 1989) p. 16.
13   Introduction in M. Umbach, (ed.), *German Federalism, Past, Present and Future* (Basingstoke, Palgrave, 2002) pp. 9–10. See also J. Noakes, *Federalism in the Nazi State*, in ibid., M. Umbach, ed., *German Federalism* pp. 113–145.
14   Broszat, *Hitler State*, p. 266.
15   Ibid., p. 276.
16   Noakes and Pridham, *Nazism*, vol. 2, pp. 171, 234 and 237.
17   Orlow, *History of the Nazi Party*, vol. 2, pp. 135 and 193.
18   E. Petersen, *The Limits of Hitler's Power* (Oxford, Oxford University Press, 1969) p. 4. For an example of how a 'Hitler decision was reached' see C. Browning, 'Nazi Resettlement Policy and the Jewish Question', in C. Leitz (ed.), *The Third Reich* (Oxford, Blackwell, 1999) p. 291.
19   See Kershaw, *Nazi Dictatorship*, pp. 60–67.

20   Quoted in Hildebrand, *The Third Reich*, p. 137.
21   J. Wright, *Germany and the Origins of the Second World War* (Basingstoke, Palgrave, 2007) p. 11.
22   Quoted in R. Overy, *War and Economy in the Third Reich* (Oxford, Oxford University Press, 1995) p. 5.
23   Ibid., pp. 5 and 68–89.
24   Ibid., p. 56.
25   A. Tooze, *The Wages of Destruction* (London, Penguin Books, 2007) p. 69.
26   Noakes and Pridham, *Nazism*, vol. 2, p. 280.
27   Overy, *War and Economy*, p. 186.
28   Tooze, *The Wages of Destruction*, p. 169.
29   B.H. Klein, *Germany's Economic Preparations for War* (Cambridge, MA, Harvard University Press, 1959) p. 78; A.J.P. Taylor, *The Origins of the Second World War* (London, Hamish Hamilton, 1961) and A. Milward, *The German Economy at War* (London, Athlone Press, 1965).
30   Overy, *War and Economy*, pp. 185, 190 and 192. See also Tooze, *The Wages of Destruction*, p. 299.
31   Mason, 'Intention and Explanation', p. 39.
32   Overy, *War and Economy*, p. 223. See also Tooze, *The Wages of Destruction*, pp. 321–322.
33   Kershaw, *Hitler*, vol. 2, p. 163.
34   Fritzsche, *Life and Death in the Third Reich*, p. 51.
35   Quoted in Noakes and Pridham, *Nazism*, vol. 2, p. 397.
36   Fritzsche, *Life and Death in the Third Reich*, p. 61.
37   Ibid., pp. 70–71.
38   Quoted in Noakes and Pridham, *Nazism*, vol. 2, p. 397.
39   Quoted in Williamson, *The Third Reich*, 4th Edition (Harlow, Pearson, 2011) p. 58.
40   Quoted in C. Koonz, *Mothers in the Fatherland* (London, Cape, 1987) p. 193.
41   Ibid., p. 196.
42   Peukert, *Inside Nazi Germany*, p. 152.
43   A. von Saldern, 'Victims or Perpetrators? Controversies About the Role of Women in the Nazi State', in Leitz (ed.), *The Third Reich* (Oxford, Blackwell, 1999) pp. 210–213.
44   J.S. Stephenson, *Women in Nazi Society* (London, Croom Helm, 1975) p. 172.
45   Koonz, *Mothers in the Fatherland*, pp. 178 and 180.
46   Stephenson, *Women in Nazi Society*, p. 61.
47   Ibid., p. 64.
48   Farquharson, *The Plough and the Swastika* (London, Sage, 1976) p. 212.
49   Ibid., p. 204.
50   Fritzsche, *Life and Death in the Third Reich*, pp. 45–46.
51   Quoted in Noakes and Pridham, *Nazism*, vol. 3 (Exeter, University of Exeter, 1991) p. 1049.
52   Burleigh, *Third Reich*, p. 250.
53   See M. Roseman, 'National Socialism and Modernisation', in R. Bessel (ed.), *Fascist Italy and Nazi Germany: Comparisons and Contrasts* (Cambridge, Cambridge University Press, 1997) p. 210.
54   Introduction, H. Berghoff and U. Spiekermann (eds), *Decoding Modern Consumer Societies* (London/Basingstoke, Palgrave/Macmillan, 2012), p. 7.
55   F. Neumann, *Behemoth: The Structure and Practice of National Socialism* (Chicago, Ivan R. Dee, reprinted, 2009) p. 431.
56   Peukert, *Inside Nazi Germany*, p. 112.
57   Quoted in Overy, *War and Economy*, p. 224.
58   A. Lüdtke, 'The Appeal of Exterminating Others: German Workers and the Limits of Resistance', in Leitz (ed.), *The Third Reich*, p. 169.
59   Ulrich Herbert, 'Good Times, Bad Times; Memories of the Third Reich', in R. Bessel (ed.), *Life in the Third Reich* (Oxford, Oxford University Press, 1987) p. 97.
60   Lüdtke, 'The Appeal of Exterminating Others', p. 164.

61   H. Mommsen, 'German Society and Resistance Against Hitler', in Leitz (ed.), *The Third Reich*, p. 169.
62   Quoted in M. Burleigh and W. Wippermann, *The Racial State: Germany, 1933–45* (Cambridge, Cambridge University Press, 1991) p. 135.
63   L. Dawidowicz, *The War Against the Jews, 1941–45* (Harmondsworth, Penguin, 1986), p. xxvi; Hildebrand, *The Third Reich*; Bracher, *German Dictatorship*; M. Broszat, 'Hitler and the Genesis of the Final Solution', in H.W. Koch (ed.), *Aspects of the Third Reich* (London, Macmillan, 1985) pp. 390–429; H. Mommsen, 'The Realization of the Unthinkable: The "Final Solution" of the Jewish Question in the Third Reich', in G. Hirschfeld (ed.), *The Policies of Genocide* (London, Allen and Unwin, 1986) pp. 97–144; K.A. Schleunes, *The Twisted Road to Auschwitz* (London, Deutsch, 1972).
64   Burleigh and Wippermann, *The Racial State*, p. 135.
65   C. Browning, 'Nazi Resettlement Policy and the Search for a Solution to the Jewish Question, 1939–1941', in Leitz (ed.), *The Third Reich*, p. 281.
66   Quoted in Noakes and Pridham, *Nazism*, vol. 2, p. 588. See also S. Friedländer *Nazi Germany and the Jews, 1933–1945* (London, Phoenix, 2009) p. 116.
67   Dawidowicz, *War Against the Jews*, p. 142. And for the speech see Noakes and Pridham, *Nazism*, vol. 3, p. 1049.
68   Mommsen, 'Realization of the Unthinkable', p. 112.
69   Dawidowicz, *War Against the Jews*, p. 43.
70   Fritzsche, *Life and Death in the Third Reich*, p. 70.
71   Kershaw, *Nazi Dictatorship*, p. 159.
72   See Peukert, *Inside Nazi Germany*, Chapter 8.
73   Quoted in R. Gellateley, *The Gestapo and German Society* (Oxford, Oxford University Press, 1990) p. 12.
74   D. Schoenbaum, *Hitler's Social Revolution* (New York, Norton, reprinted, 1997) p. 52.
75   Neumann, *Behemoth*, p. 375.

Chapter 13

1   Taylor, *Origins of the Second World War*, p. 68.
2   H. Mommsen, 'National Socialism: Continuity and Change', in W. Laqueur (ed.), *Fascism: A Reader's Guide* (Harmondsworth, Penguin, 1979).
3   A. Bullock, 'Hitler and the Origins of the Second Word War', in E.M. Robertson (ed.), *The Origins of the Second World War* (London, Macmillan, 1971) p. 193.
4   Wright, *Germany and the Origins of the Second World War*, p. 4.
5   Noakes and Pridham, *Nazism*, vol. 3, p. 662.
6   Wright, *Germany and the Origins of the Second World War*, p. 79.
7   G. Weinberg, *The Foreign Policy of Hitler's Germany*, vol. 1 (Chicago and London, Chicago University Press, 1970) p. 348.
8   Wright, *Germany and the Origins of the Second World War*, p. 9.
     Taylor, *Origins of the Second World War*, p. 132.
9   W. Carr, *Arms, Autarky and Aggression* (London, Arnold, 1979) p. 128.
10   Tooze, *The Wages of Destruction*, p. 241.
11   Kershaw, *Hitler*, vol. 2, p. 83.
12   Ibid., p. 119.
13   Wright, *Germany and the Origins of the Second World War*, p. 143.
14   Taylor, *Origins of the Second World War*, p. 131.
15   P. Longerich, *The Holocaust* (Oxford, Oxford University Press, 2010) p. 144. For a detailed study of the German campaign in Poland see A.B. Rossino, *Hitler Strikes Poland* (Kansas, Kansas UP, 2003) and for the war itself D.G. Williamson, *Poland Betrayed: The Nazi-Soviet Invasions of 1939* (Barnsley, Pen and Sword, 2009).

16 See D. Williamson, *The Polish Underground* (Barnsley, Pen and Sword, 2012) pp. 16–17.

17 See Browning, 'Nazi Resettlement Policy and the Search for a Solution to the Jewish Question, 1939–1941', in Leitz (ed.), *The Third Reich*, pp. 287–289; Also C. Browning, *Origins of the Final Solution* (London, Arrow Books, 2005) Chapter 3.

18 Williamson, *The Polish Underground*, pp. 19–20.

19 Wright, *Germany and the Origins of the Second World War*, p. 155.

20 Browning, *Origins of the Final Solution*, p. 194.

21 G. Wright, *The Ordeal of Total War* (New York, Harper and Row, reprinted 1997 by Waveland Press, Illinois) p. 140.

22 Browning, 'Nazi Resettlement Policy', 'Nazi Resettlement Policy and the Search for a Solution to the Jewish Question, 1939–1941', in Leitz (ed.), *The Third Reich*, p. 293.

23 H. Graml, *Anti-semitism in the Third Reich* (Oxford, Blackwell, 1992) p. 82.

24 K. Hildebrand, *The Foreign Policy of the Third Reich* (*London, Batsford*, 1973) p. 17.

25 Wright, *Germany and the Origins of the Second World War*, p. 175.

26 Bullock, 'Hitler and the Origins', p. 218.

27 Quotations in Wright, *Germany and the Origins of the Second World War*, p. 176 and H. Bucheim et al., *Anatomy of the SS State* (London, Collins, 1968) p. 60.

28 Tooze, *The Wages of Destruction*, pp. 507–508.

29 Longerich, *The Holocaust*, p. 179.

30 Ibid., p. 181.

31 Dawidowicz, *War Against the Jews*, p. xxvi.

32 Broszat, 'Hitler and the Genesis of the Final Solution'; L. Kettenacker, 'Hitler's Final Solution and Its Rationalization', in Hirschfeld (ed.), *Policies of Genocide*, pp. 73–95; Mommsen, 'Realization of the Unthinkable', in ibid., pp. 97–144. For M. Marrus on the Holocaust see M.R. Marrus, 'The History of the Holocaust: A Survey of recent Literature' in *Journal of Modern History*, vol. 59 no.1, 1987, pp. 114–115

33 Broszat, 'Hitler and the Genesis of the Final Solution' in H.W. Koch, Aspects of the Third Reich, p. 405.

34 Dawidowicz, *War Against the Jews*, Introduction, p. xxxi.

35 Browning, *Origins of the Final Solution*, p. 428.

36 Longerich, *The Holocaust*, p. 207.

37 Noakes and Pridham, *Nazism*, vol. 3, p. 1136.

38 Ibid., p. 1131.

39 Browning, *Origins of the Final Solution*, p. 412.

40 C. Browning, *Ordinary Men* (London, Penguin, 2001) p. xiv.

41 R. Evans, *The Third Reich at War* (London, Penguin, 2009) p. 560.

42 D. Goldhagen, *Hitler's Willing Executioners* (London, Abacus, 1997) p. 443.

43 H. Mommsen, *Germans Against Hitler* (London and New York, Tauris, 2009) pp. 254 and 255.

44 Kershaw, *Nazi Dictatorship*, p. 159.

45 Browning, *Ordinary Men*, p. 215.

46 Kershaw, *Hitler*, vol. 2, p. 573.

47 J. Fest, *Hitler*, (Harmondsworth, Penguin) p. 180.

48 Broszat, *Hitler State*, p. 319.

49 Kershaw, *Hitler*, vol. 2, p. 428.

50 Quoted in Broszat, *Hitler State*, p. 341.

51 Milward, *German Economy*, p. 31.

52 Overy, *War and Economy*, p. 343.

53 Tooze, *The Wages of Destruction*, p. 560.

54 Ibid., p. 628.

55 Craig, *Germany 1866–1945*, p. 734.

56 U. Herbert, *Hitler's Foreign Workers* (Cambridge, Cambridge University Press, 1997) p. 189.

57 Burleigh and Wippermann, *The Racial State*, p. 235.

58   Herbert, *Hitler's Foreign Workers*, p. 396.
59   Tooze, *The Wages of Destruction*, p. 544.
60   Overy, *War and Economy*, p. 307.
61   P. Ayçoberry, *The Social History of the Third Reich* (New York, New Press, 1999) p. 231.
62   P. Erker, 'Landbevölkerung und Flüchtingszustrom', in M. Broszat, K.-D. Henke and H. Wolle (eds), *Von Stalingrad zur Währungsreform: Zur Sozialgeschichte des Umbruchs in Deutschland* (Munich, Oldenbourg Verlag, 1988) p. 377.
63   Ayçoberry, *Social History*, p. 231.
64   Mommsen, *Germans Against Hitler*, p. 36.
65   P. Hoffmann, *The History of the German Resistance* (London, MacDonald and Jane, 1977) p. 96.
66   H. Graml et al., *The German Resistance to Hitler* (Oxford, Blackwell, 1992) p. 21.
67   Kershaw, *Nazi Dictatorship*, p. 154.
68   H. Rothfels, *The German Opposition to Hitler* (London, Oswald Wolff, 1970) p. 78.
69   T. Prittie, *Germans Against Hitler* (London, Hutchinson, 1964) p. 248.
70   Kershaw, *Hitler*, vol. 2, p. 677.
71   I. Kershaw, *The End* (Penguin, London, 2011) p. 52.
72   Ibid., p. 53.
73   Ibid., p. 400.
74   Kershaw, *Hitler*, vol. 2, p. 832.
75   M. Kitchen, *Nazi Germany at War* (London, Longman, 1995) pp. 298 and 300.
76   Quoted in Burleigh, *Third Reich*, p. 707.
77   J.L. Gaddis, *We Know Now, Rethinking Cold War History* (Oxford, Oxford University Press, 1997) p. 115.
78   Overy, *War and Economy*, pp. 86–87 and see also Roseman, 'National Socialism and Modernisation', p. 210.

Chapter 14

1   N.M. Naimark, *The Russians in Germany; A History of the Soviet Zone of Occupation, 1945–1949* (Cambridge, MA, Harvard University Press, 1995) p. 9.
2   B. Kuklick, *American Policy and the Division of Germany* (Ithaca, NY, Cornell University, 1977) p. 157.
3   H. Zink, *The United States in Germany, 1944–55* (Westport, CT, Greenwood Press, 1974) p. 177.
4   Naimark, *Russians in Germany*, p. 45.
5   C. Klessmann, *Die Doppelte Staatsgründung* (Göttingen, Vandenhoeck and Ruprecht, 1988) p. 143.
6   Ibid., p. 145.
7   Naimark, *Russians in Germany*, p. 276.
8   R. Andreas-Friedrich, *Schauplatz Berlin: Tagebuchaufzeichnung, 1945 bis 1948* (Frankfurt am Main, Suhrkamp, 1984) p. 19.
9   A. Kramer, *The West German Economy* (Oxford and New York, Berg, 1991) p. 125.
10   J. Kopstein, *Economic Decline in East Germany, 1945–89* (Chapel Hill, NC and London, University of North Carolina Press, 1997) p. 23.
11   Ibid., p. 24.
12   L. Niethammer, *Die Mitläuferfabrik: Die Entnazifierung am Beispiel Bayerns* (East Berlin, Dietz Verlag, 1982) p. 13; D. Welch, 'Priming the Pump of German Democracy. British Re-Education Policy in Germany after the Second World War', in I.D. Turner (ed.), *Reconstruction in Postwar Germany* (Oxford and New York, Oxford University Press, 1989) pp. 215–238; E. Schmidt, *Die verhinderte Neuordnung, 1945–52* (Hamburg, Europäische Verlagsanstalt, 1970); W. Abelshauser, *Wirtschaftsgeschichte der Bundesrepublik* (Frankfurt am Main, Suhrkamp, 1983).

13 M. Fulbrook, *The Two Germanies, 1945–1990: Problems of Interpretation* (London, Macmillan, 1992) p. 14.
14 See J. Farquharson, "'The Essential Division". Britain and Germany and the Partition of Germany, 1945–49', *German History*, 9 (1), February 1990, pp. 23–45.
15 T. Eschenburg, *Jahre der Besetzung (1945–9)*, vol. 1, *Geschichte der Bundesrepublik Deutschland* (Stuttgart and Wiesbaden, Deutsche Verlags-Anstalt/Brockhaus, 1983) p. 419.
16 D. Williamson, *A Most Diplomatic General. The Life of Lord Robertson of Oakridge* (London, Brassey's, 1996) p. 114.
17 Ibid., p. 115.
18 S. Suckut, 'Zur Vorgeschichte der DDR-Gründung', in *Studien zur Deutschlandsfrage*, vol. 12 (Berlin, Duncker und Humblot, 1993) pp. 121–122.
19 P. Merkl, *The Origins of the West German Republic* (Oxford, Oxford University Press, 1963) p. 176.
20 P. Pulzer, *German Politics, 1945–1995* (Oxford, Oxford University Press, 1995) p. 47.
21 Eschenburg, *Jahre der Besetzung*, p. 511.
22 Merkl, *Origins of the West German Republic*, p. 160.
23 Naimark, *Russians in Germany*, p. 58.
24 Merkl, *Origins of the West German Republic*, p. 75.
25 Naimark, *Russians in Germany*, p. 59.
26 Suckut, 'Zur Vorgeschichte', p. 143.
27 W. Loth, *Stalin's Unwanted Child* (London, Macmillan, 1998).

Chapter 15

1 W. Otto, 'Deutsche Handlungsspielraum und sowjetischer Einfluss', in E. Scherstjanoi (ed.) *Protocoll des Kolloquiums. Die Gründung der DDR* (Berlin, Akademie Verlag, 1993) p. 144.
2 H.-P., Schwarz, *Konrad Adenauer. A German Politician and Statesman in a Period of War, Revolution and Reconstruction*, vol. 1 (Providence and Oxford, Berghahn, 1995) p. 459.
3 C. Adenauer, *Memoirs* (Weidenfeld and Nicolson, London, 1966) p. 221.
4 D. Bark and D. Gress, *History of West Germany*, vol. 1 (Oxford, Blackwell, 1989) p. 270.
5 Schwarz, *Adenauer*, vol. 1, p. 526.
6 Klessmann, *Die Doppelte Staatsgründung*, p. 177.
7 L.J. Erdinger, *Kurt Schumacher* (Stanford, CA, Stanford University Press, 1965) p. 172.
8 W. Benz, (ed.), *Die Bundesrepublik Deutschland*, vol. 1 (Frankfurt, Fischer, 1983) p. 355.
9 H.P. Schwarz, *die Ära Adenauer*, vol. 2, 1949–57 of *Geschichte der Bundesrepublik Deutschland*, Deutsche Verlags-Anstalt/Brockhaus, Stuttgart/Wiesbaden, 1981, p. 159.
10 Ibid.; R. Steininger, *The German Question, the Stalin Note of 1952 and the Problem of Reunification* (New York, Columbia University Press, 1990); G. Wettig, 'Stalin and German Reunification', *Historical Journal*, 37 (2), 1994, pp. 411–419.
11 P. Grieder, *Tension, Conflict and Opposition in the Leadership of the Socialist Unity Party, 1946–73*, Ph.D. thesis, University of Cambridge (no. d196726), 1995, p. 97 (published by Manchester UP, 1999).
12 C. Klessmann, *Zwei Nationen, eine Nation. Deutsche Geschichte, 1955–70* (Göttingen, Vandenhoeck and Ruprecht, 1988) p. 76.
13 Ibid., p. 85.
14 H-P. Schwarz, *Adenauer*, Konrad Adenauer vol. 2,: The Statesman, 1952-67 (Providence and Oxford, 1997) p. 299.
15 Gaddis, *We Know Now*, p. 140.
16 Klessmann, *Zwei Nationen*, p. 89.
17 Gaddis, *We Know Now*, p. 144.
18 Klessmann, *Zwei Nationen*, p. 93.
19 T. Garton Ash, *In Europe's Name. Germany and the Divided Continent* (London, Cape, 1993) p. 60.
20 B. Marshall, *Willy Brandt: A Political Biography* (London, Macmillan, 1997) p. 44.

21   Bark and Gress, *History of West Germany*, vol. 2, (Oxford, Blackwell, 1989) p. 98.
22   H. Jacobsen et al., *Drei Jahrzente Aussenpolitik der DDR* (Munich, Oldenbourg, 1979) pp. 432–433.
23   Garton Ash, *In Europe's Name*, p. 73.
24   Ibid., p. 79.
25   A.J. Nicholls, *The Bonn Republic* (London, Longman, 1997) p. 232.
26   Garton Ash, *In Europe's Name*, p. 71.
27   Marshall, *Willy Brandt*, p. 70.
28   Bark and Gress, *History of West Germany*, vol. 2, p. 194.
29   Ibid., p. 195.
30   Ibid., p. 215.
31   See Grieder, *Tension, Conflict and Opposition*, pp. 312–313.
32   Bark and Gress, *History of West Germany*, vol. 2, p. 178.
33   Garton Ash, *In Europe's Name*, p. 78.
34   Ibid., p. 137.
35   Ibid., p. 204.
36   Ibid., p. 139.
37   Ibid., p. 184.
38   Ibid., p. 87.
39   Ibid., p. 167.
40   J. Gaddis, *The Long Peace: Inquiries into the History of the Cold War* (New York and Oxford, Oxford University Press, 1987).
41   Garton Ash, *In Europe's Name*, p. 130.
42   Nicholls, *Bonn Republic*, p. 199.

Chapter 16

1   H. Kaelble, J. Kocka and H. Zwar (eds), *Sozialgeschichte der DDR* (Stuttgart, Klettcotta, 1994) p. 573.
2   H.P. Schwarz, *Die Ära Adenauer*, vol. 2, *Geschichte der Bundesrepublik Deutschland* (Stuttgart and Wiesbaden, Deutsche Verlags-Anstalt/Brockhaus, 1981, 1983) p. 178.
3   Ibid., p. 120.
4   H. Giesch, K.H. Paque and H. Schmieding, *The Fading Miracle* (Cambridge, Cambridge University Press, 1992) p. 31.
5   Nicholls, *Bonn Republic*, p. 60.
6   R. Overy, 'The Economy of the Federal Republic since 1949', in K. Larres and P. Panayi (eds), *The Federal Republic since 1949* (London, Longman, 1996) p. 34.
7   Kramer, *West German Economy*, p. 213.
8   Giesch, Paque and Schmieding, *Fading Miracle*, p. 141.
9   Klessmann, *Die Doppelte Staatsgründung*, p. 242.
10 Giesch, Paque and Schmieding, *Fading Miracle*, p. 80.
11 Schwarz, *Die Ära Adenauer*, vol. 2, p. 210.
12 Nicholls, *Bonn Republic*, p. 157.
13 E. Kolinsky, *Women in Contemporary Germany* (Oxford and New York, Berg, 1992), p. 79.
14 Ibid., p. 80.
15 R. Willett, *The Americanization of Germany* (London, Routledge, 1989) p. 132.
16 M. Roseman 'Reconstruction and Modernization', The Federal Republic and the Fifties, in *Bulletin*, vol. XIX (1) (London, German Historical Institute, May 1997), p. 11.
17 U. Poiger, 'Rebels Without a Cause', in R. Pommerin (ed.), *The American Impact on Postwar Germany* (Oxford and Providence, RI, Berghahn, 1995) p. 116.

18   Rosen, 'Reconstruction and Modernization', pp. 15–16.
19   D. Staritz, *Geschichte der DDR* (Frankfurt am Main, Suhrkamp, 1985) p. 52.
20   Loth, *Stalin's Unwanted Child*, p. 125.
21   Quoted in R.G. Stokes, 'Autarky, Ideology and Technological Lag: The Case of the East German Chemical Industry, 1945–64', *Central European History*, 208/1, 1995, p. 36.
22   McCauley, *GDR since 1945* (Basingstoke and London, 1985) p. 54.
23   Klessmann, *Die Doppelte Staatsgründung*, pp. 273–274.
24   Staritz, *Geschichte der DDR*, p. 77.
25   K. Schroeder, *Der SED – Staat* (Munich, Hauser, 1998) p. 116.
26   A. Mitter and S. Wolle, *Untergang auf Raten* (Munich, Bertelsmann Verlag, 1993) p. 45.
27   V. Ingimundarsan, 'Cold War Misperceptions: The Communist and Western Responses to the East German Refugee Crisis in 1953', *Journal of Contemporary History*, 29, 1994, p. 472.
28   Loth, *Stalin's Unwanted Child*, p. 155.
29   A. Baring, *Uprising in East Germany* (Ithaca, NY, Cornell University Press, 1972) pp. 73–76; Mitter and Wolle, *Untergang auf Raten*; Klessmann, *Die Doppelte Staatsgründung*, p. 277.
30   See G. Pritchard, *The Making of the GDR* (Manchester, Manchester University Press, 2000), pp. 217–220.
31   Mitter and Wolle, *Untergang auf Raten*, p. 162.
32   Ibid., p. 107.
33   Grieder, *Tension, Conflict and Opposition*, p. 136.
34   Mitter and Wolle, *Untergang auf Raten*, p. 256.
35   M. Fulbrook, *Anatomy of a Dictatorship. Inside the GDR, 1949–1989* (Oxford, Oxford University Press, 1995) p. 187.
36   Klessmann, *Zwei Nationen*, p. 309.
37   Kopstein, *Economic Decline*, p. 43.
38   Klessmann, *Zwei Nationen*, p. 310.
39   Staritz, *Geschichte der DDR*, p. 138.
40   Ibid., p. 77.
41   D. Wierling, 'The Hitler Youth Generation in the GDR: Insecurities, Ambitions and Dilemmas', in K. Jarausch (ed.), *Dictatorship as Experience* (New York and Oxford, Berghahn, 1999) p. 308.
42   C. Klessmann, 'Rethinking the Second German Dictatorship', in Jarausch (ed.), *Dictatorship as Experience*, p. 370.
43   Quoted in M. Kohli, 'Arbeit, Lebenslauf und soziale Differenzierung', in Kaelble, Kocka and Zwar (eds), *Sozialgeschichte der DDR*, p. 39.
44   Quoted in G. Edwards, *GDR Society and Social Institutions* (London, Macmillan, 1985) p. 13.
45   Ina Merkel, 'Leitbilder und Lebensweisen von Frauen', in Kaelble, Kocka and Zwar, *Sozialgeschichte der DDR*, p. 376.
46   McCauley, *GDR since 1945*, p. 58.
47   Fulbrook, *Anatomy of a Dictatorship*, p. 151.
48   Ibid., p. 161.
49   Ibid., p. 164.
50   Ibid., p. 101.
51   T.A. Schwartz, *America's Germany. John J. McCloy and the Federal Republic of Germany* (Cambridge, MA, Harvard University Press, 1991) p. 305.

Chapter 17

1   See Pulzer, *German Politics*, Chapter 4 and Staritz, *Geschichte der DDR*, p. 38.
2   C. Maier, *Dissolution. The Crisis of Communism and the End of East Germany* (Princeton, NJ, Princeton University Press, 1997) p. 89.

3   Fulbrook, *Two Germanies*, p. 19.
4   Bark and Gress, *History of West Germany*, vol. 2, p. 68.
5   Fulbrook, *Two Germanies*, p. 20.
6   Maier, *Dissolution*, p. 90.
7   L. Kettenacker, *Germany since 1945* (Oxford, Oxford University Press, 1997) p. 135.
8   Bark and Gress, *History of West Germany*, vol. 2, p. 73.
9   Nicholls, *Bonn Republic*, p. 193.
10   Kettenacker, *Germany*, p. 136.
11   Giesch, Paque and Schmieding, *Fading Miracle*, p. 148.
12   Marshall, *Willy Brandt*, p. 66.
13   Ibid., p. 79.
14   Ibid., p. 81.
15   Nicholls, *Bonn Republic*, p. 238.
16   Marshall, *Willy Brandt*, p. 82.
17   Pulzer, *German Politics*, p. 141.
18   Kettenacker, *Germany*, p. 147.
19   Nicholls, *Bonn Republic*, p. 185.
20   Kettenacker, *Germany*, p. 148.
22   Panayi, *Ethnic Minorities*, p. 219.
23   Ibid., p. 224.
21   Nicholls, *Bonn Republic*, p. 254.
24   Ibid., p. 273.
25   Larres and Panayi (eds), *The Federal Republic*, p. 123.
26   Quoted in Bark and Gress, *History of West Germany*, vol. 2, p. 424.
27   These are discussed in ibid., pp. 432–437; see also R. Evans, *In Hitler's Shadow* (London, Tauris, 1989) for a more detailed coverage.
28   M. Siekmeier and K. Larres, 'Domestic Political Developments II: 1969–90', in Larres and Panayi (eds), *The Federal Republic*, p. 132.
29   Ibid., p. 135.
30   J. Roesler, 'The Rise and Fall of the Planned Economy in the German Democratic Republic, 1945–89', *German History*, 9 (1), 1991, p. 55.
31   Grieder, *Tension, Conflict and Opposition*, p. 266.
32   Quoted in Klessmann, *Zwei Nationen*, p. 337.
33   Fulbrook, *Anatomy of a Dictatorship*, p. 195.
34   Maier, *Dissolution*, pp. 88–89.
35   H. James, 'The Landscape that Did Not Blossom', *Times Literary Supplement*, 13 June 1997, p. 5.
36   Quoted in Maier, *Dissolution*, p. 60.
37   Ibid., p. 81.
38   See ibid., pp. 59–107.
39   Ibid., p. 29.
40   Fulbrook, *Anatomy of a Dictatorship*, p. 155.
41   Ibid., p. 141.
42   Maier, *Dissolution*, p. 173.
43   McCauley, *GDR since 1945*, p. 185.
44   Fulbrook, *Anatomy of a Dictatorship*, p. 206.
45   Ibid., p. 235.
46   Fulbrook, *Two Germanies*, p. 73
47   Staritz, *Geschichte der DDR*, p. 195.
48   Maier, *Dissolution*, p. 89.
49   K.C. Lammers, 'The German Democratic Republic as History', *Contemporary European History*, 6 (3), 1997, p. 425.

50   Mitter and Wolle, *Untergang auf Raten*, Chapter 16.
51   Fulbrook, *Anatomy of a Dictatorship*, p. 172.
52   Ibid., p. 172.

Chapter 18

1   Garton Ash, *Europe's Name*, p. 343.
2   Fulbrook, *Anatomy of a Dictatorship*, p. 248.
3   Maier, *Dissolution*, p. 139.
4   Ibid., p. 177.
5   K. Jarausch, *The Rush to German Unity* (Oxford, Oxford University Press, 1994), p. 117.
6   J. Osmond et al., *German Reunification: A Reference Guide and Commentary* (London, Longman, 1992) p. 53.
7   Garton Ash, *In Europe's Name*, pp. 349 and 354.
8   W. Patterson and D. Southern, *Governing Germany* (Oxford, Blackwell, 1991) p. 11.
9   R. Steininger, 'The German Question, 1945–95', in K. Larres and Panayi (ed.), *Germany since Unification* (Basingstoke and London, Palgrave, 2001) p. 27.
10   Ibid., p. 29.
11   C. Flockton, 'The German Economy in the 1990s: On the Road to a Divided Polity', in ibid, p. 70.
12   W. Chandler, 'The German Party System since Unification', p. 95.
13   Introduction to 2nd Edition in ibid, p. xxxviii. See also M. Gehler, **Three Germanies**, (London, Reaktion Books, 2011) pp. 238–285
14   E. Wolfram, *Rot Grun an der Macht. Deutschland, 1998–2005* (Munich, Beck, 2013), p. 157.
15   C. Clemens, 'The Dynamics of Support in Chancellor-Democracy: Schröder and His SPD', in J. Sperling (ed.), *Germany at fifty-five* (Manchester, Manchester University Press, 2004) p. 268.
16   Quoted in *Die Zeit*, 26 September 2002, p. 6.
17   I. Collier, 'Can Schröder Do It? Prospects for Fundamental Reform of the German Economy and a Return to High Employment', in D. Conradt et al. (eds), *Precarious Victory* (New York/Oxford, Berghahn, 2005) p. 241. See also Gehler, *Three Germanies*, pp. 286–299.
18   A. Crawford and T. Czuczka, *Angela Merkel* (Chichester, Wiley Bloomberg, 2013) p. 52.
19   Ibid., p. 61.
20   Ibid., p. 117.
21   A. Hyde-Price, 'Germany's Security Policy Dilemmas: NATO, the WEU and the OSCE', in Larres (ed.), *Germany since Unification*, p. 212.
22   Introduction to 2nd Edition in Larres and Panayi (ed.), *Germany since Unification*, p. liii.
23   Ibid., p. lii.
24   Crawford and Czuczka, *Angela Merkel*, pp. 82 and 125.
25   Ibid., 106.

Chapter 19

1   Peukert, *Inside Nazi Germany*, p. 42.
2   Broszat, 'A Plea for the Historicization of National Socialism', in P. Baldwin, (ed.), *Reworking the Past: Hitler, the Holocaust and the Historians' Debate*, (Boston, MA, Beacon Press, 1990) pp. 77–87.
3   Crawford and Czuczka, *Angela Merkel*, p. 166.
4   See Chapter 16, note 23.

Bibliography

This bibliography is an introductory selection of books in English on German history, 1789 to the present.

Broad surveys covering the whole or the greater part of the period

W. Carr, *A History of Germany, 1815–1990*, London, Arnold, 4th edn, 1991, is well-written and, within its limits, a comprehensive study of virtually the whole period. M. Fulbrook, *A Concise History of Germany*, Cambridge, Cambridge University Press, 2004 is exactly what the title indicates: a brief history of Germany from the Early Middle Ages to the present. – (ed.), *German History since 1800*, London, Arnold, 1997 contains a series of interesting and stimulating essays by leading historians on various aspects of German history, many of which are reprinted in J. Breuilly (ed.), *19th Century Germany. Politics, Culture and Society, 1780–1918*, London, Arnold, 2001. F. B. Tipton, *A History of Modern Germany since 1815*, University of California Press, 2003 is a difficult but rewarding book, which goes beyond the traditional political and history to include economic, social and cultural history.

M. Kitchen, *A History of Modern Germany, 1800 to the Present*, Chichester, Wiley-Blackwell, 2011 is a more straightforward survey. H. Winkler, *The Long Road West, 1789–1990* (2 vols), Oxford, Oxford University Press, 2006 and 2007 is an up-to-date and magisterial study, which takes the view that while Germany was culturally part of the West, its history developed along very different lines. William Hagen, *German History in Modern Times*, Cambridge, Cambridge University Press, 2012 covers all aspects of Germany's development from the 17th century to 1990 in a series of perceptive but challenging essays, and also includes material on Austria. D. Blackbourn, *Germany 1780–1918*, London, Fontana, 1997 is a concise survey which is strong on social, economic and political history, as is V. R. Berghahn, *Modern Germany, Society, Economy and Politics in the Twentieth Century*, Cambridge, Cambridge University Press, 2nd edn, 1998. G. Craig, *Germany. 1866–1945*, Oxford, Oxford University Press, 1978 is a highly readable, but also scholarly study of the German Reich from its formation to its collapse and is particularly good on the arts. Knut Borchardt, *Perspectives on Modern German Economic History and Policy*, Cambridge, Cambridge University Press, 1991 contains a number of perceptive, even provocative, essays on the German economy in the 19th and 20th centuries.

International developments are covered by P. Schroeder, *The Transformation of European Politics, 1763–1848*, Oxford, Oxford University Press, 1994, which is by far the best study of this period. The next volume in this series, A. J. P. Taylor, *The Struggle for Mastery in Europe, 1848–1918*, Oxford, Oxford University Press, 1954, is inevitably dated, but it is still in print and above all, like all Taylor's works, intellectually provocative. J. Lowe, *The Great Powers and the German Problem, 1865–1925*, London, Routledge, 1994. N. Rich, *Great Power Diplomacy, 1814–1914*, Columbus, OH, McGraw-Hill, 1992 and K. Hildebrand, *German Foreign Policy from Bismarck to Adenauer*, London, Unwin Hyman, 1989, all offer a broad sweep of foreign policy, which enables the reader to put German foreign policy into a European context.

J. J. Sheehan, 'What is German History. Reflections on the Role of the *Nation* in German History and Historiography', *Journal of Modern History*, vol. 53, March 1981, pp. 1–23, is a brief but seminal article on the whole question of the German nation and German nationalism. P. Alter, *The German Question and Europe*, London, Arnold, 2000 and R. Rurup, *The Problems of Revolution in Germany, 1789–1989*, Oxford, Berg, 2000 are both concise and thoughtful studies of the 'German question' and nationalism.

Thematic works covering more than one period

The development of Prussia is covered concisely by H. W. Koch, *A History of Prussia*, London, Longman, 1978; P. G. Dwyer (ed.), *A Modern Prussian History, 1830–1947*, Harlow, Pearson, 2001 and C. Clark, *Iron Kingdom: The Rise and Downfall of Prussia, 1600–1947*, Cambridge, MA, Harvard University Press, 2006. For the army G. Craig, *The Politics of the Prussian Army, 1640–1945*, Oxford, Oxford University Press, 1955, is still well worth reading, as is G. Ritter's classic study, *The Sword and the Sceptre*, Miami, FL, University of Miami Press, 1969. The constitutional background is well covered by H. W. Koch, *A Constitutional History of Germany*, London, Longman, 1984. J. Sheehan, *German Liberalism in the Nineteenth Century*, London, Methuen, 1982 is still an invaluable guide to the development of German liberalism up to 1914, but a more up-to-date study is D. Langwiesche, *Liberalism in Germany*, Basingstoke, Palgrave, 1999 which follows developments beyond 1945, as is E. L. Evans, *German Centre Party 1870–1933: A Study in Political Catholicism*, Carbondale, IL, Southern Illinois University Press, 1981 for the Centre Party. For a survey of German conservativism see L.E. Jones and J.Retallack, (eds), Between Reform, Reaction and Resistance: Studies in the History of German Conservativism from 1789 to 1945, Berg, Providence, RI, Oxford, 1993. A. Milward and S. B. Saul, *The Development of the Economies of Continental Europe, 1850–1914*, London, Allen and Unwin, 1977 and C. Trebilcock, *The Industrialization of the Continental Powers, 1870–1914*, London, Longman, 1981 put the growth of the German economy within the European context, while M. Kitchen, *The Political Economy of Germany, 1815–1914*, London, Croom Helm, 1978 is a useful guide to developments in both agriculture and industry in the 19th century. For more recent studies see B. Scribner, S. Ogilvie and R. Overy (eds.), *Germany: A New Social and Economic History (1460 to the Present)*, London, Bloomsbury, 1996–2003.

Ute Frevert, *Women in German History*, Oxford, Berg, 1989 is an indispensable study for the history of women in Germany during this period. A good guide to the whole question of ethnic minorities in Germany is Panikos Panayi, *Ethnic Minorities in Nineteenth and Twentieth Century Germany*, Harlow, Pearson, 2000, while a comprehensive study of German nationalism is M. Hughes, *Nationalism and Society, Germany 1800–1945*, London, Arnold, 1988. Maiken Umbach (ed.), *German Federalism, Past, Present, Future*, Basingstoke, Palgrave, 2002 contains a series of articles on German federalism throughout the period covered by this book. W. Hagen, *Ordinary Prussians. Brandenburg Junkers 1500–1840*, Cambridge, Cambridge University Press, 2002 is a difficult book but a mine of detailed information about the peasantry and landlords in Brandenburg. A selection of primary sources can be found in J. C. G. Röhl (ed.), *From Bismarck to Hitler: The Problem of Continuity in German History*, London, Longman, 1970.

1789–1871

For a study of Prussia during the revolutionary era up to 1848 M. Levinger, *Enlightened Nationalism. The Transformation of Prussian Culture, 1806–1848*, Oxford, Oxford University Press, 2002 is essential reading. The best general books on the period are T. Nipperdey, *Germany from Napoleon to Bismarck*, Princeton, NJ, Princeton University Press, 1996 and J. Sheehan, *German History, 1770–1866*, Oxford, Oxford University Press, 1989, both of which are particularly strong on economic, social and cultural history. B. Simms, *The Struggle for Mastery in Germany, 1779–1850*, Palgrave, London and Basingstoke, 2011 is a briefer study, particularly helpful for Austro-Prussian relations. H. Schulze, *The Course of German Nationalism: From Frederick the Great to Bismarck 1763–1867* (trans. by S. Hanbury-Tenison), Cambridge, Cambridge University Press, 1991 is a useful collection of primary sources covering this period. J. Sperber (ed.), *Germany 1800–1870*, Oxford, Oxford University Press, 2004 is a collection of essays, one of the most interesting of which is Eva Rosenhaft, 'Gender and class in an era of national wars: women and service'. J. Sperber, *Revolutionary Europe, 1780–1850*, pp. 209–229 Harlow, Longman, 2000 helps place the events in Germany in their European context.

The impact of the French Revolution, 1789–1815

J. Gagliardo, *Holy Roman Empire as Idea and Reality, 1763–1806*, Bloomington, Indiana University Press, 1980 and P. H. Wilson, *The Holy Roman Empire*, Basingstoke, Palgrave, 2nd edn, 2011 are both indispensable for understanding the last years of the Holy Roman Empire. For the impact of the French Revolution on Germany the classic but now dated study of this period, G. P. Gouch, *Germany and the French Revolution*, reprinted Cass, London, 1965, is still useful and above all informative. M. Rowe, *From Reich to State, the Rhineland in the Revolutionary Age, 1780–1830*, Cambridge, Cambridge University Press, 2003 and C. J. Esdaile (ed.), *Popular Resistance in the French Wars*, Basingstoke, Palgrave, 2005 explore the questions of resistance, acceptance and collaboration in the Rhineland. T. C. W. Blanning, 'The French Revolution and The Modernization of Germany', *Central European History*, vol. 22, 1989, pp. 109–129; -, *The French Revolutionary Wars 1787–1802*, London, (Edward Arnold, London, 1996 and -, *French Revolution in Germany*: Occupation and Resistance in the Rhineland, 1792–1802, Oxford OUP, 1983 are all essential to an understanding of this complex period, as is B. Simms, *The Impact of Napoleon, 1797–1806*, Cambridge, Cambridge University Press, 1997. Important essays on the impact of the revolution on Germany are: K. Hagemann, 'Occupation, Mobilization, and Politics: The Anti-Napoleonic Wars in Prussian Experience, Memory and Historiography' and M. Rowe, 'France, Prussia or Germany? The Napoleonic Wars and Shifting Allegiances in the Rhineland' in *Central European History*, vol. 39, 2006, pp. 580–610 and pp. 610–640.

The restoration period, 1815–1848

The relations between the German states and the German Confederation are explored in D. Billinger, *Metternich and the German Question*, Newark, DE, University of Delaware Press, 1991. G. S. Werner, *Bavaria and the German Confederation, 1820–1848*, London, Associated University Press, 1977 is a specialized but readable analysis of the fiercely separatist German policies of Bavaria. W. Henderson, *The Zollverein*, Cambridge, Cambridge

University Press, first published in 1939, but republished by Cambridge University Press in paperback in 2013, is still the classic work on the *Zollverein* in English. H. J. Voth, 'The Prussian Zollverein and the bid for Economic Superiority', in P. G. Dwyer (ed.), *Modern Prussian History, 1830–1947*, London, Pearson, 2001, pp. 109–25 is a brief but more up-to-date study. L. Lee, 'Liberal Constitutionalism as Administrative Reform: The Baden Constitution of 1818', *Central European History*, vol. 8, no. 1, 1975 pp. 91–112 highlights developments in one of the more liberal south German states.

1848

J. Sperber, *The European Revolutions 1848–1851*, Cambridge, Cambridge University Press, 1994 places the German revolts in their European context, while W. Siemann, *The German Revolution of 1848–49*, Basingstoke and London, Macmillan, 1998 is arguably the best single-volume study of the revolutions in print. H. Hahn, *The 1848 Revolutions in German-Speaking Europe*, Harlow, Pearson, 2001 is also a clear and concise study of these complex events. From a liberal perspective E. Eyck, *The Frankfurt Parliament, 1848–49*, London, Macmillan, 1968 provides a very detailed treatment of the Frankfurt parliament. J. Davis Randers-Pehrsen, *Germans and the Revolution of 1848–49*, New York and Washington, Peter Lang, 1999 is also interesting and well worth reading. M. Hewitson, *Nationalism in Germany, 1848–1866*, Basingstoke, Palgrave, 2010 is essential reading for an understanding of how German nationalism developed.

The unification of Germany, 1851–1871

The political and economic background to unity is well covered in E. Anderson, *The Social and Political Conflict in Prussia, 1858–1864*, Lincoln, University of Nebraska Press, 1954 and T. Hamerow, *The Social Foundations of German Unification*, 2 vols, Princeton, NJ, Princeton University Press, 1969–72 (although these need to be supplemented by D. Langwiesche, *Liberalism in Germany* (see above) and M. Hewitson, *Nationalism in Germany* (see above)). The diplomacy of unification is analysed by W. Carr, *The Origins of the Wars of German Unification*, London, Longman, 1991 and W. E. Mosse, *The European Powers and the German Question, 1848–71*, Cambridge, Cambridge University Press, 1958. J. Breuilly analyses the development of German nationalism and the lead up to unification in *The Formation of the First German Nation State, 1800–1871*, Macmillan, London, 1996. His *Austria, Prussia and Germany, 1806–1871*, Pearson Harlow, 2002 is a short but concise guide to Austro-Prussian relations. A. Bucholz, *Moltke and the German Wars, 1864–71*, Basingstoke and London, Palgrave, 2001 is an illuminating study of Moltke's military genius and his conduct of the wars of unification, while D. Showalter, *The Wars of Unification*, London, Arnold, 2004 provides a useful guide to the three wars of unification. The Franco-Prussian war is covered by M. Howard, *The Franco-Prussian War*, London, Rupert Hart Davis, 1962 and S. W. Halperin, 'The Origins of the Franco–Prussian War Revisited: Bismarck and the Hohenzollern Candidature for the Spanish Throne', *Journal of Modern History*, vol. 45, no. 1, 1973, pp. 83–91. There are an enormous number of books devoted to the towering figure of Bismarck. The standard biographies in English are O. Pflanze, *Bismarck and the Development of Germany*, 3 vols, Princeton, NJ, Princeton University Press,

1990 and L. Gall, *Bismarck, and the German Empire*, 2 vols, London, Allen and Unwin, 1986. A. J. P. Taylor's *Bismarck. The Man and the Statesman*, London, Hamish Hamilton, 1955 is dated but remains a paradoxical and interesting work. E. Feuchtwanger *Bismarck*, London, Routledge, 2002 and K. L. Lerman, *Bismarck,* Harlow, Pearson, 2004 and J. Steinberg, Bismarck, Oxford, Oxford University Press, 2011 are recent biographies.

A brief guide through the complexities of the unification and the consolidation of the new Reich is D. G. Williamson, *Bismarck and Germany, 1862–1890*, Harlow, Longman, 3rd edn, 2011. H. Böhme, *Deutschlands Weg zur Grossmacht*, Cologne, Kiepenhauer und Witsch, 1966 is invaluable for the economic dimension to German unity, but for English language readers a very useful selection of the material which Böhme used for this book has been edited and translated: H. Böhme (ed.) (trans. by A. Ramm), *The Foundation of the German Empire*, Oxford, Oxford University Press, 1971. F. Stern, *Gold and Iron, Bleichröder and the Building of the German Empire*, London, Allen and Unwin, 1977 sheds light on the links between politics and high finance during the Bismarck period.

The German Empire, 1871–1918: broad surveys

Concise and informative is M. Seligmann and R. McLean, *Germany from Reich to Republic, 1871–1918*, Macmillan, Basingstoke and London, 2000 and L. Abrahams, *Bismarck and the German Empire, 1871–1918,* London and New York, Routledge, 1996 (reprinted 2006). H.-U. Wehler, *The German Empire, 1871*, Leamington Spa and Dover, NH, Berg Press, 1985 is the classic structural study of the empire, while W. J. Mommsen, *Imperial Germany, 1867–1918: Politics, Culture and Society in an Authoritarian State*, London, Arnold, 1995 contains a series of perceptive essays about how the Reich 'modernized' without becoming a constitutional liberal state. V. R. Berghahn, *Imperial Germany, 1871–1914*, Providence, RI and Oxford, Berghahn Press, 1994 is particularly strong on economic and social history; D. Blackbourn and G. Eley, *The Peculiarities of German History*, Oxford and New York, Oxford University Press, 1984 is a brilliant and by and large successful attempt to refute the *Sonderweg* theory, as is G. Eley, 'Bismarckian Germany', in G. Martel (ed.), *Modern Germany Reconsidered, 1870–1945*, London, Routledge, 1992, pp. 1–32. F. Stern, *The Politics of Cultural Despair*, Berkeley, Los Angeles, London, University of California Press, (paperback edition), 1974 is the classic analysis of cultural pessimism and the development of the *Völkisch* right.

M. Anderson, *Practicing Democracy. Elections and Political Culture in Imperial Germany*, Princeton, NJ, Princeton University Press, 2000 and J. Sperber, *The Kaiser's Voters. Electors and Elections in Imperial Germany*, Cambridge, Cambridge University Press, 1997 explore the functioning of universal franchise in the pre-war Reich. G. Schollgen (ed.), *Escape into War? The Foreign Policy of Imperial Germany*, Oxford, Berg, 1990 contains a series of interesting essays on aspects of German foreign policy, 1871–1914, and I. Geiss, *German Foreign Policy, 1871–1914*, London, Routledge, 1976 is still a useful survey.

The Empire under Bismarck 1871–1890

A. Green, Fatherlands: State Building and Nationhood in Nineteenth century Germany, Cambridge, Cambridge University Press, 2001 analyses the constitutional structure of the Bismarckian Empire. For an in-depth political study, albeit Bismarck centred, O. Pflanze, *Bismarck and the Development of Germany*, vols 2 and 3, (see above) is invaluable. M. L. Anderson, *Windthorst*, Oxford, Oxford University Press, 1981 is a helpful biography of the leader of the Centre Party. V. L. Lidtke, *The Outlawed Party – Social Democracy in Germany, 1878–1890*, Princeton, NJ, Princeton University Press, 1966 covers Bismarck's anti-socialist campaign. I. N. Lambi, *Free Trade and Protection in Germany, 1868–1879*, Wiesbaden, Steiner, 1963 is a useful account of the tariff debates in the 1870s, while H. Rosenberg, 'Political and Social Consequences of the Great Depression of 1873–1896 in Central Europe', *Economic History Review*, vol. 13, 1943, pp. 58–73 is inevitably dated, but is still a stimulating article. Bismarck is the hero in the classic W. L. Langer, *European Alliances, 1871–1890*, revised edn, New York, A. Knopf, 1951. G. F. Kennan, *The Decline of Bismarck's European Order*, Princeton, NJ, Princeton University Press, 1979 and B. Waller, *Bismarck at the Crossroads, the Restoration of German Foreign Policy after the Congress of Berlin*, London, Athlone Press, 1974 explore the complex last decade of Bismarck's diplomacy. M. E. Townsend, *The Rise and Fall of Germany's Colonial Empire*, New York, Macmillan, 1930 is still useful, but of course very dated. P. Kennedy, 'German Colonial Expansion: Has the "Manipulated Social Imperialism" Been Antedated?', *Past and Present*, vol. 54, 1972, pp. 131–141 is still a key introduction to Bismarck's colonial policy. H.-U. Wehler, 'Bismarck's Imperialism, 1862–1890', *Past and Present*, vol. 48, 1970, pp. 119–155 is a brilliant case for the social imperialism argument, while A. J. P. Taylor, *Germany's First Bid for Colonies*, London, Macmillan, 1938 argues that Bismarck was pursuing only diplomatic objectives. W. M. Simon (ed.), *Germany in the Age of Bismarck*, London, Allen and Unwin, 1968; T. B. S. Hamerow (ed.), *The Age of Bismarck. Documents and Interpretations*, New York, Harper Row, 1973 and W. N. Medlicott and D. K. Coveney (eds), *Bismarck and Europe*, London, Arnold, 1971 all provide relevant collections of the documents, the latter book concentrating solely on Bismarck's foreign policy. D. G. Williamson, *Bismarck and Germany*, Harlow, Longman, 1998 also contains a selection of documents.

Germany, 1890–1914

For William II's 'personal rule', key studies are: J. Röhl, *Germany Without Bismarck. The Crisis of Government in the Second Reich, 1890–1900*, London, Batsford, 1967; J. Röhl, *The Kaiser and his Court*, Cambridge, Cambridge University Press, 1994; J. Röhl and N. Sombart (eds), *Kaiser Wilhelm II, New Interpretations*, Cambridge, Cambridge University Press, 1982 and K. L. Lerman, *The Chancellor as Courtier, Bernhard von Bülow and the Government of Germany, 1900–1909*, Cambridge, Cambridge University Press, 1990 are key studies. Röhl is the doyen of Kaiser biographers. A three volume set of his *Wilhelm II* is published by Cambridge, Cambridge University Press, 2014, while a slimmed down version appeared at the same time, *Kaiser Wilhelm II A Concise Life*, Cambridge, Cambridge University Press, 2014. C. Clark, *Kaiser Wilhelm II*, London, Penguin, 2009 takes a more sympathetic view of Wilhelm II and fits him into his historical context. J. Retallack, *Germany in the Age of Kaiser Wilhelm II*, Macmillan, Basingstoke and London, 1996 and G. Eley and J. Retallack (eds), *Wilhelminism and Its Legacies*, New York/Oxford, Berghahn Books, 2003 are invaluable as an introduction to the historical debates and controversies on Wilhelmine Germany. I. Porter and I. Armour, *Imperial Germany, 1890–1918*, Harlow, Longman, 1991 is a good general account of the period (the latter also includes an interesting selection of documents), while K. Jarausch, *The Enigmatic Chancellor, Bethmann Hollweg and the Hubris of Imperial Germany*, New Haven, CT, 1973 is still the best study of Bethmann's chancellorship, 1909–14, G. Eley, *Reshaping the German Right*, Yale, New Haven and London, 1980 explores the development of the German Right and the impact of the new pressure groups.

Germany's uneasy relationship with Britain can be followed in M. Kennedy, *The Rise of Anglo-German Antagonism*, London, Allen and Unwin, 1980. A detailed but readable analysis of Germany's road to war can be found in V. R. Berghahn, *Germany and the Approach of War in 1914*, London and Basingstoke Macmillan, 1973 and F. Fischer, *War of Illusions: German Policies from 1911 to 1914*, London, Chatto and Windus, 1973. D. Kaiser, 'Germany and the Origins of the First World War', *Journal of Modern History*, vol. 55, 1983, pp. 442–474 contrasts the policies of Bülow and Bethmann Hollweg. An important essay also is W. Mommsen, 'The Topos of Inevitable War in Germany in the Decade before 1914', in V. R. Berghahn and M. Kitchen (eds), *Germany in the Age of Total War*, London, 1981. Schöllgen (ed.), *Escape into War? The Foreign Policy of Imperial Germany*, Oxford, Berg, 1990, M. Hewitson, *Germany and Causes of the First World War*, Oxford, Berg, 2004 and H. H. Herwig (ed.), *The Outbreak of World War I*, Boston and New York, Houghton Mifflin, 1997 provide a good introduction to the debate on the causes of the war. For the role of the Schlieffen Plan in German policy see in S. E. Miller et al. (eds), *Military Strategy and the Origins of the First World War*, Princeton, NJ, Princeton University Press, 1991 and A. Mombauer, 'Of War Plans and War Guilt: The Debate Surrounding the Schlieffen Plan', *Journal of Strategic Studies*, vol. 28, no. 5, 2005, pp. 857–885. The following explain German policy in the lead-up to the First World War and put it firmly in its European context: C. Clark, *The Sleepwalkers*, London, Penguin, 2013; M. Hewitson, *Germany and Causes of the First World War*, Berg, 2004; M. MacMillan, *The War That Ended Peace*, London, Profile Books, 2014; A. Mombauer, *The Origins of the First World War*, Harlow, Longman, 2002; Niall Ferguson, *The Pity of War*, London, Penguin, 1999 and Paul W. Schroeder, 'World War 1 as Galloping Gertie', in D. Lee (ed.), *Outbreak of the First World War,* Lexington, D.C. Heath, pp. 148–169. For a relevant selection of sources see I Geiss, *July 1914: The Outbreak of the First World War. Selected Documents*, New York, Norton, 1968.

1914–1918

By far the best overall studies are R. Chickering, *Imperial Germany and the Great War, 1914–1918*, Cambridge, Cambridge University Press, 1998; H. Herwig, *The First World War. Germany and Austria–Hungary,* London, Arnold, 1997 and J. Kocka, *Facing Total War: German Society, 1914–1918,* Leamington Spa, Berg, 1984. For a study of the German home front see the pioneering study, G. Feldman, *Army, Industry and Labour*, Princeton, NJ, Princeton University Press, 1966 (reprinted London, Bloomsbury, 2014). For comparative studies see Niall Ferguson, *The Pity of War* (see above), which has some excellent material on the German war economy and the home front and J. Winter (ed.), *Capital Cities at War: Paris, London, Berlin*, Cambridge, Cambridge University Press, 1997. Fritz Fischer's classic, *Germany's Aims in the First World War*, London, Chatto and Windus, 1967 is still essential reading. The Hindenburg Ludendorff semi-dictatorship is covered by M. Kitchen, *The Silent Dictatorship: The Politics of the German High Command, 1916–1918*, London, Batsford, 1976, and a more recent study, J. Lee, the Warlords, London, Weidenfeld and Nicolson 2005, the upheavals at the end of 1918 are well covered by A. G. Ryder, *The German Revolution of 1918: A Study of German Socialism in War and Revolt*, Cambridge, Cambridge University Press, 1967. For the naval mutinies see D. Horn, *The German Naval Mutinies of World War 1*, Rutgers, New Brunswick, 1969.

Books spanning 1919–1945

The majority of books focus either on the Weimar Republic or the Third Reich, but J. Hiden, *Republican and Fascist Germany*, Harlow, Longman, 1996, approaches the whole period from historiographic and thematic angles, and also has an excellent bibliography. H. Mommsen, *From Weimar to Auschwitz*, Princeton, NJ, Princeton University Press, 1991 in a series of essays traces the links between Weimar and the Third Reich.

The Weimar Republic

The revolutions of 1918–1919 are covered by F. L. Carsten, *Revolution in Central Europe*, London, Wildwood House, 1972, For more recent views see also C. Fischer, 'A Very German Revolution? The Post 1918 Settlement Re-Evaluated, *Bulletin*, London, German Historical Institute, pp. 6–32, November 2006. R. Bessel, *Germany After the First World War*, Oxford, Clarendon, 1993 is a study of the immediate post war years. There are numerous histories of the Weimar Republic: C. Storer, *The Weimar Republic*, London, Tauris, 2013; J. Hiden, *The Weimar Republic*, Harlow, Longman, 3rd edn, 1996; E. J. Feuchtwanger, *From Weimar to Hitler, 1918–33*, Basingstoke and London, Macmillan, 1993, and A. J. Nicholls, *Weimar and the Rise of Hitler*, Basingstoke and London, Macmillan, 1968. The best by a long way of the short, overall studies is E. Kolb, *The Weimar Republic*, London, Abingdon, Routledge, 2nd edn, 2005, as it has an invaluable section on 'Basic Problems and Trends of Research'. A. McElligott (ed.), *Weimar Germany*, Oxford, Oxford University Press, 2009 is a good introduction to modern research on the Weimar Republic as it contains essays on all aspects of its history. The essay by E. Canning, 'Women and the Politics of Gender' (pp. 146–174) is a good introduction to the position of women in the Weimar Republic. For this topic see also K. von Ankum (ed.), *Women in the Metropolis: Gender and Modernity in Weimar Culture*, Berkeley, University of California Press, 1997.

D. Peukert, *The Weimar Republic: The Crisis of Classical Modernity*, London, Allen Lane, 1991, is excellent on the social, economic and cultural background to the years 1919–1933. There is a large literature on Weimar culture. The classic is P. Gay, *Weimar Culture*, London, Secker and Warburg, 1968. More recent studies are in J. A. Williams (ed.), *Weimar Culture Revisited*, Basingstoke, Palgrave, 2011 An interesting but brief revisionist article on the problem of reparations is Sally Marks, 'Reparations Re-Considered: A Reminder', in *Central European History* V, no. 4 (Dec. 1969) pp. 356–365. M. Trachtenberg, *Reparation in World Politics: France and European Economic Diplomacy, 1916–1923*, New York, Columbia University Press, 1980, and B. Kent, *The Spoils of War. The Politics, Economics and Diplomacy of Reparations, 1918–32*, Oxford, Oxford University Press, 1989, are more weighty analyses. C. S. Maier, *Recasting Bourgeois Europe: Stabilization in France, Germany and Italy in the Decade after World War I*, Princeton, NJ, Princeton University Press, 1975, contains an interesting study of the German reparation and economic crisis, 1919–1923 and the partial stabilization after 1924. A. McDougall, *France's Rhineland Diplomacy, 1914–24*, Princeton, NJ, Princeton University Press, 1978 and D. G. Williamson, *The British in Germany, 1918–30*, New York and Oxford, Berg, 1992, provide useful background for Anglo-French policies on Germany. C. Fischer, *The Ruhr Crisis, 1923–1924*, Oxford, Oxford University Press, 2003 is an informative study of a vital turning point. A. Tooze, *The Deluge, the Great War and the Remaking of the Global Order, 1916–1931*, London, Allen Lane, 2014 is an important study of how World War 1 affected Europe, especially Germany, economically and paved the way for the emergence of the USA as a global power.

The impact of hyperinflation is covered by A. Fergusson, When *Money Dies: The Nightmare of the Weimar Hyper-inflation*, London, Old Street Publishing, 2010, E. E. Rowley, *Hyperinflation in Germany: Perceptions of a Process*, Aldershot, Scolar Press, 1994. T. Childers, 'Inflation, Stabilization and Political Realignment in Germany, 1924 to 1928', in G. D. Feldman et al. (eds), *The German Inflation Reconsidered: A Preliminary Balance*, Berlin, de Gruyter, 1982 analyses its political consequences, while K. Borchardt, *Perspectives on Modern German Economic History and Policy*, (see above) contains two important chapters on the Great Depression and the collapse of Weimar. R. Boyce, 'World War, World Depression: Some Economic Origins of the Second World War', in eds R. Boyce and E. Robertson, *Paths to War*, London, Macmillan, 1989 provides a concise global overview of the Depression and its consequences. W. Michalka, *German Foreign Policy, 1917–1933*, Leamington Spa, Berg, 1987 is a concise survey of foreign policy. J. Wright, *Gustav Stresemann*, Oxford, Oxford University Press, 2002 is an important biography of Stresemann, as is W. Patch, *Heinrich Brüning and the Dissolution of the Weimar Republic*, Cambridge, Cambridge University Press, 1998, of Brüning. D. Abraham, *The Collapse of the Weimar Republic. Political Economy and Crisis*, Princeton, NJ, Princeton University Press, 1981, and M. Broszat, *Hitler and the Collapse of Weimar Democracy*, Leamington Spa, Berg, 1987 cover the collapse of Weimar, while shorter studies can be found in K. Bracher, 'German Democracy and Power Vacuum: The Problem of the Party State', in V. B. Berghahn and M. Kitchen (eds), *Germany in the Age of Total War*, London, Croom Helm, 1981 and R. Lepsius, 'From Fragmented Party Democracy to Government by Emergency Decree and National Socialist Takeover: Germany', in J. Linz and A. Stepan (eds), *The Breakdown of Democratic Regimes*, Baltimore and London, Johns Hopkins University Press, 1978.

Hitler, Nazism and the Third Reich

There is an enormous bibliography on every aspect of the Third Reich.

An indispensable companion to Third Reich studies is the four-volume document collection by J. Noakes and G. Pridham, *Nazism, 1919–1945*, vol. 1, *The Rise to Power*, vol. 2, *State, Economy and Society, 1933–39*, vol. 3, *Foreign Policy, War and Racial Extermination*, vol. 4, *Germany at War: The Home Front, 1939–45*, Exeter, Exeter University Press, 1983–1998 (now reprinted by the Liverpool University Press, 2001).

I. Kershaw, *The Nazi Dictatorship, Problems and Perspectives*, London, Arnold, 1993 (4th Edition London, Bloomsbury, 2000) and K. Hildebrand, *The Third Reich*, London, Routledge, 1984 provide good guides to the complex historiographical problems involved in studying the Third Reich. M. Broszat, 'A Plea for the Historisation of National Socialism', in P. Baldwin (ed.), *Reworking the Past*, Boston, MA, Beacon Press, 1980 explores the problems of placing National Socialism's legacy and its place in the context of German history. Good, overall studies of the Third Reich are K. Bracher, *The German Dictatorship: The Origins, Structure and Consequences of National Socialism*, Harmondsworth, Penguin, 1973; N. Frei, *National Socialist Rule in Germany: The Führer State, 1933–45*, Oxford, Blackwell, 1993 and M. Burleigh, *The Third Reich: A New History*, London, Macmillan, 2001. The most comprehensive is R. J. Evans' three volume study, The *Coming of the Third Reich*, London, Penguin, 2004; *The Third Reich in Power*, London, Penguin, 2006 and the *Third Reich at War*, London,

Penguin, 2009. A brief introductory study is D. G. Williamson, *The Third Reich,* Harlow, Pearson, 4th edn, 2011. The essays in C. Leitz (ed.), *The Third Reich,* Oxford, Blackwell, 1999 are a a valuable guide to new perspectives on the Third Reich. There are a large number of Hitler biographies. A. Bullock, *Hitler. A Study in Tyranny,* Harmondsworth, Penguin, 1962, remains an important classic, but the best and most detailed biography is I. Kershaw, *Hitler* (vol. 1), *1889–1936: Hubris;* (vol. 2), *1936–1945: Nemesis,* London, Allen Lane, 1998–2000. A short but perceptive biography is N. Stone, *Hitler,* London, Hodder, 1980. L. Rees, *The Dark Charisma of Adolf Hitler,* London, Ebury Press, 2012 tackles the question of Hitler's ability to inspire and mesmerize supporters.

For structuralist studies of the Third Reich, M. Broszat, *The Hitler State. The Foundation and Development of the Internal Structure of the Third Reich,* London, Longman, 1981, is an indispensable study. T. Mason, 'Intention and Explanation: A Current Controversy About Interpretation in National Socialism', in G. Hirschfeld and L. Kettenacker (eds), *The Führer State: Myths and Realities,* Stuttgart and London, Klett-Cotta/German Historical Institute, 1981 and H. Mommsen, 'National Socialism: Continuity and Change' in W. Laqueur (ed.), *Fascism: A Reader's Guide,* Harmondsworth, Penguin, 1979 are further important structuralist analyses of the Nazi regime. D. Orlow, *The History of the Nazi Party* (2 vols), *1919–1945,* Newton Abbot, David & Charles, 1971–1973 is a thorough study of the role of the party (including the SS) throughout the Third Reich. The development of the SS state is analysed in H. Buchheim, M. Broszat and H.-A. Jacobsen, *Anatomy of the SS State,* London, Collins, 1968, and R. L. Koehl, *The Black Corps: The Structure and Power Struggles of the Nazi SS,* Madison, WI, University of Wisconsin Press, 1983 while R. Gellateley, *The Gestapo and German Society,* Oxford, Oxford University Press, 1987 is a study of how the Gestapo functioned and of the support it enjoyed from the German public. A more recent study of the Gestapo is F. McDonough, *The Gestapo: the Myth and Reality of Hitler's Secret Police,* London, Hodder, 2015, which is based on an analysis of Gestapo documens in Düsseldorf. P. Longerich, *Himmler,* Oxford, Oxford University Press, 2012 is the best biography of the head of the SS. E. N. Peterson, *The Limits of Hitler's Power,* Princeton, NJ, Princeton University Press, 1969 is dated but still relevant. For a study of Hitler as an integrative factor in the Third Reich, see I. Kershaw, *The Hitler Myth, Image and Reality in the Third Reich,* Oxford, Oxford University Press, 1987.

Authoritative studies on the Nazi economy are R. J. Overy, *War and Economy in the Third Reich,* Oxford, Oxford University Press, 1995 and A. Tooze, *The Wages of Destruction,* London, Penguin, 2007, but A. S. Milward, *The German Economy at War,* London, Athlone Press, 1965 is still worth reading. The best analysis of Nazi agricultural policy is J. Farquharson, *The Plough and the Swastika. The NSDAP and Agriculture in Germany, 1928–1945,* London, Sage, 1976. The impact of the war on rural society is explored in J. S. Stephenson, 'Nazism, Modern War and Rural Society in Württemberg, 1939–45', *Journal of Contemporary History,* vol. 32, no. 3, 1997, pp. 339–356. There are a large number of books on German society and the Volksgemeinschaft during the Third Reich. P. Fritzsche, *Life and Death in the Third Reich,* Cambridge, Harvard University Press, 2008 explores the degree of support it enjoyed. P. Ayçoberry, *The Social History of the Third Reich 1933–1939,* New York, The New Press, 1999 and R. A. Grünberger, *Social History of the Third Reich,* Harmondsworth, Penguin, 1974 provide useful overviews, while D. Schoenbaum's perceptive *Hitler's Social Revolution,* London, Weidenfeld & Nicolson, 1967 is a classic, which unfortunately only goes up to 1939. A. Lüdtke, 'The Appeal of Exterminating Others: German Workers and the Limits of Resistance', in C. Leitz (ed.), *The Third Reich, Oxford, Blackwell, 1999,* pp. 153–177 and Ulrich Herbert, 'Good Times, Bad Times; Memories of the Third

Reich', in R. Bessel (ed.), *Life in the Third Reich*, Oxford, Oxford University Press, 1987, are good introductions to the issue of the workers' attitude to Hitler and the *Volksgemeinschaft*. U. Herbert's *Hitler's Foreign Workers*, Cambridge, Cambridge University Press, 1997 is an interesting study of the role of foreign workers in the wartime economy and how they were treated by the Germans. J. S. Stephenson, *Women in German Society*, London, Croom Helm, 1975 and C. Koonz, *Mothers in the Fatherland. Women, the Family and Nazi Politics*, London, Jonathan Cape, 1987 are histories of the role of women in the Third Reich. A. von Saldern, 'Victims or Perpetrators? Controversies About the Role of Women in the Nazi State', in C. Leitz (ed.), *The Third Reich*, Oxford, Blackwell, 1999, pp. 209–227 is a brief but thought-provoking article. A. Peukert's *Inside Nazi Germany: Conformity, Opposition and Racism in Everyday Life*, Harmondsworth, Penguin, 1989, has some interesting chapters on youth and the workers. German Society during the war is covered by M. Kitchen, *Nazi Germany at War*, Longman, Harlow, 1995, and T. Charman, *The German Home Front 1939–1945*, London, Barrie and Jenkins, 1989. The most recent study is N. Stargardt, *The German War*, 1039–45, London, Bodley Head, 2015.

There is a huge literature on Nazi anti-Semitism and the Holocaust. S. Friedlander's two-volume study, *Nazi Germany and the Jews: the Years of Persecution, 1933–39* and *The Years of Extermination: Nazi Germany and the Jews, 1939–1945*, New York, Harper Collins 1997 and 2007 provide a comprehensive analysis of the whole period. *Nazi Germany and the Jews*, London, Phoenix, 2009 is an abridged version. D. Bankier, 'Hitler and the Policy-Making Process on the Jewish Question', *Holocaust and Genocide Studies*, vol. 3, no. I, 1988, pp. 1–20 and M. R. Marrus, 'The History of the Holocaust: A Survey of Recent Literature', *Journal of Modern History*, vol. 59, no. 1, 1987, pp. 114–160, are helpful introductions to the intentionalist/structuralist debate. M. Burleigh and W. Wippermann, *The Racial State: Germany 1933–45*, Cambridge, Cambridge University Press, 1991 is the best overall account of Hitler's racial and eugenic policies. K. A. Schleunes, *The Twisted Road to Auschwitz. Nazi Policy towards German Jews*, London, Deutsch, 1972, and H. Graml, *Anti-Semitism and its Origins in the Third Reich*, Oxford, Blackwell, 1992, analyse the complex events that led to the Holocaust. L. S. Dawidowicz, *The War against the Jews, 1933–45*, Harmondsworth, Penguin, (10th anniversary edn) 1986, trenchantly states the intentionalist case, while M. Broszat, 'Hitler and the Genesis of the Final Solution', in H. W. Koch (ed.), *Aspects of the Third Reich*, London and Basingstoke, Macmillan, 1985 pp. 390–429; H. Mommsen, 'The Realization of the Unthinkable: The "Final Solution" of the Jewish Question in the Third Reich' and L. Kettenacker, 'Hitler's Final Solution and its Rationalization', both in G. Hirschfield (ed.), *The Policies of Genocide*, London, Allen and Unwin, 1986, pp. 97–144 and 73–95 argue the structuralist point of view. D. J. Goldhagen, *Hitler's Willing Executioners. Ordinary Germans and the Holocaust*, New York, Abacus, 1997, rather simplistically considers the attitudes of the German people towards the persecution of the Jews. More nuanced studies are C. Browning, 'Nazi Resettlement Policy and the Search for a Solution to the Jewish Question, 1939–1941', in C. Leitz (ed.), *The Third Reich*, Oxford, Blackwell, 1999, pp. 279–299 and -, *Origins of the Final Solution*, London, Arrow Books, 2005. C. Browning, *Ordinary Men*, London, Penguin, 2001 is a study of the Reserve Police Battalion 101 and its role in the Final Solution. P. Longerich, *The Holocaust*, Oxford, Oxford University Press, 2010 is a scholarly study of Nazi extermination policies and the Holocaust.

J. Wright, *Germany and the Origins of the Second World War*, Basingstoke, Palgrave, 2007 is a recent survey of German foreign policy up to December 1941. The best study of German foreign policy in English up to 1939 is G. L. Weinberg, *The Foreign Policy of Hitler's Germany*, vol. 1, *Diplomatic Revolution in Europe, 1933–36*, vol. 2, *Starting World*

War II 1937–39, Chicago, University of Chicago Press, 1970–1980. W. Carr, *Arms, Autarky and Aggression*, London, Edward Arnold, 2nd edn, 1979 is a much shorter account of the years 1933–1939, while K. Hildebrand, *The Foreign Policy of the Third Reich*, London, Batsford, 1973 is a brief study of Nazi foreign policy up to 1945 from an intentionalist point of view. A. J. P. Taylor, *The Origins of the Second World War*, London, Hamish Hamilton, 1961 is still worth reading, as are A. Bullock, 'Hitler and the Origins of the Second World War' and T. Mason, 'Some Origins of the Second World War', in E. M. Robertson (ed.), *The Origins of the Second World War*, London, Macmillan, 1971. For Hitler's decision to attack Russia, see G. L. Weinberg, *Germany and the Soviet Union, 1939–41*, Leiden, Brill, 1954, R. Cecil, *Hitler's Decision to Invade Russia*, London, Davis-Poynter, 1975, and E. M. Robertson, 'Hitler Turns from the West to Russia, May–December, 1940', in R. Boyce and E. Robertson (eds), *Paths to War*, London, Macmillan, 1989. G. Roberts, *The Soviet Union and the Origins of the Second World War*, Basingstoke, Palgrave, 1995 draws on Soviet as well as German archival material. G. Wright, *The Ordeal of Total War, 1939–45*, New York, Harper & Row, 1968, N. Rich, *The Establishment of the New Order*, vol. 2, London, Deutsch, 1973–74 and M. Mazower, *Hitler's Empire*, London, Penguin, 2008 cover German policy in occupied Europe. A. Rossino, *Hitler Strikes Poland*, Lawrence, Kansas, Kansas University Press, 2003 and D. G. Williamson, *Poland Betrayed: The Nazi-Soviet invasions of 1939*, Barnsley, Pen and Sword, 2009 show that the Polish campaign was a prelude to genocide in the USSR two years later. For the Russian war see O. Bartov, *The Eastern Front, 1941– 1945: German Troops and the Barbarization of Warfare*, London, Macmillan, 1986. Overviews of the German resistance are provided by J. Fest, *Plotting Hitler's Death*, New York, Henry Holt, 1996; H. Rothfels, *The German Opposition to Hitler*, London, Oswald Wolff, 1973; T. Prittie, *Germans against Hitler*, London, Hutchinson, 1964; P. Hoffmann, *The History of the German Resistance in Germany*, Montreal, MacDonald and James, 3rd edn, 1996 and H. Graml et al., *The German Resistance to Hitler*, Cambridge, MA, Harvard University Press, revised edn, 1970. J. Conway, *The Nazi Persecution of the Churches, 1933–45*, London, Weidenfeld and Nicolson, 1967 concentrates on relations between the Nazi regime and the Church, while D. C. Clay (ed.), *Contending with Hitler. Varieties of German Resistance in the Third Reich*, Cambridge, MA, Harvard University Press, 1991 is a more comprehensive study, and I. Kershaw, *Popular Opinion and Popular Dissent in the Third Reich: Bavaria, 1933–45*, Oxford, Oxford University Press, 1983 explores the question of *Resistenz*. H. Mommsen, *Germans Against Hitler*, London/New York, Tauris, 2009 is a first rate study of the conservative nationalist opposition, the Kreisau Circle and the 20th July. The collapse and last months of the Third Reich is brilliantly analysed and explained in I. Kershaw, *The End*, London, Penguin, 2011.

For a good introduction to the question of modernization and the legacy of the Third Reich see M. Roseman, 'National Socialism and Modernisation', in R. Bessel (ed.), *Fascist Italy and Nazi Germany: Comparisons and Contrasts*, Cambridge, Cambridge University Press, 1997, pp. 197–229 and also H. Berghoff, 'Consumption Politics and Politicized Consumption', in ed. H. Berghof and U. Spiekermann (eds), *Decoding Modern Consumer Societies*, London/Basingstoke, Palgrave/Macmillan, 2012. An introductory article on the legacy of the Third Reich is H. James, 'The Preview of the Federal Republic', *Journal of Modern History*, vol. 63, March 1991, pp. 99–115, while H. Winkler, *The Long Shadow of the Reich Weighing upon German History* (the 2001 annual lecture), the German Historical Institute, London, 2002 discusses this over a longer period of time.

Germany, 1945–2000

General histories covering both Germanies

Informative and concise general histories on post-war Germany, which cover both the FRG and the GDR, are M. Fulbrook, *The Two Germanies, 1945–1990: Problems of Interpretation*, London and Basingstoke, Macmillan, 1992; L. Kettenacker, *Germany since 1945*, Oxford, Oxford University Press, 1997; P. Pulzer, *German Politics 1945–1995*, Oxford, Oxford University Press, 1995 and M. Gehler, *Three Germanies. West Germany, East Germany and the Berlin Republic*, London, Reaktion Books, 2011. D. G. Williamson, *Germany from Defeat to Partition, 1945–63*, Harlow, Pearson, 2001 covers the formative years of both states and also contains a selection of sources. P. Merkl, *The Origins of the West German Republic*, Oxford, Oxford University Press, 1963 is particularly good on the genesis of the FRG's constitution. How the two states dealt with their Nazi past is considered in G. Herf, *Divided Memory: The Nazi Past in the Two Germanys*, Cambridge, MA, Harvard University Press, 1997 and P. Biddiscombe, *The Denazification of Germany, 1945–50*, Tempus, 2007.

The occupation and division of Germany

R. Bessel, *Germany 1945: From War to Peace*, London, Simon and Schuster, 2009 describes the state of Germany in 1945. R. M. Douglas, *Orderly and Humane,*University Press, New Haven and London, 2012 is a scholarly study of the expulsion of the Germans after the Second World War. There are several books on the zonal policies of the occupying powers: J. Gimbel, *The American Occupation of Germany, 1945–49*, Stanford, CA, Stanford University Press, 1968; B. Kuklick, *American Policy and the Division of Germany*, Ithaca, NY, Cornell University Press, 1977; F. Willis, *The French in Germany, 1945–49*, Stanford, CA, Stanford University Press, 1962 and N. M. Naimark, *The Russians in Germany: A History of the Soviet Zone of Occupation, 1945–1949*, Cambridge, MA, Harvard University Press, 1995. British policy is covered by I. D. Turner (ed.), *Reconstruction in Post-War Germany*, Oxford and New York, Berg, 1989 and more briefly in the biography of the British military governor: D. G. Williamson, *A Most Diplomatic General. The Life of Lord Robertson of Oakridge*, London, Brassey's 1996. For the division of Germany, see W. Loth, *Stalin's Unwanted Child: The Soviet Union, the German Question and the Founding of the GDR*, London and Basingstoke, Macmillan, 1998; T. A. Schwartz, *America's Germany. John McCloy and the Federal Republic of Germany*, Cambridge, MA, Harvard University Press, 1991 and J. Farquharson, '"The Essential Division". Britain and the Partition of Germany 1945–1949' *German History*, vol. 9, no. 1, 1991, pp. 23–45. J. Gaddis, *We Know Now, Rethinking Cold War History*, Oxford, Oxford University Press, 1997 puts the division of Germany in the overall context of the Cold War. The debate about the Stalin note of March 1952 is covered in R. Steininger, *The German Question: The Stalin Note of 1952 and the Problem of Reunification*, New York, Columbia University Press, 1990 and G. Wettig, 'Stalin and German Reunification', *Historical Journal*, vol. 37, no. 2, 1994, pp. 411–419. F. Kemp, *Berlin 1961*, New York, Putnam, 2011 is a revisionist study of the Berlin Wall, which castigates Kennedy for weakly tolerating its construction. O. von Ruhm (ed.), *Documents on Germany under Occupation, 1944–55*, Oxford, Oxford University Press, 1955, is a useful collection of source materials on the occupation and the early years of the Cold War.

The FRG: from its origins to 1990

A. Glees, *Reinventing Germany. German Political Development since 1945*, Oxford and Washington, DC, Berg, 1996 and A. Nicholls, *The Bonn Republic*, London, Longman, 1997 are good introductions to the Bonn Republic up to 1990. A more detailed two-volume 'blockbuster' is D. Bark and D. Gress, *A History of West Germany*, vol. 1, *From Shadow to Substance, 1945–63*, vol. 2, *Democracy and its Discontents, 1963–1991*, Oxford, Blackwell, 2nd edn, 1991. The biographies and autobiographies of the major politicians are also important sources for understanding the history of the FRG. K. Adenauer, *Memoirs*, London, Weidenfeld and Nicolson, 1966, and the comprehensive two-volume biography, H.-P. Schwarz, *A German Politician and Statesman in a Period of War, Revolution and Reconstruction*, 2 vols (translated), Oxford and Providence, RI, Berghahn, 1995–1997 are key sources for the period 1945–1963. There is useful material, particularly on *Ostpolitik*, in B. Marshall, *Willy Brandt: A Political Biography*, Basingstoke and London, Macmillan, 1997, while L. J. Erdinger, *Kurt Schumacher*, Stanford, CA, Stanford University Press, 1965 is helpful for the early post-war years of the SPD. Economic developments up to 1955 are covered by A. Kramer, *The West German Economy*, Oxford and New York, Berg, 1995. H. Giesch, K. H. Paque and H. Schmieding, *The Fading Miracle*, Cambridge, Cambridge University Press, 1992 and R. Overy, 'The Economy of the Federal Republic since 1949', in K. Larres and P. Panikos (eds), *The Federal Republic since 1949*, Harlow, Longman, 1996, pp. 3–34, cover the developments up to 1990. An informative book on the new West German society is R. G. Moeller (ed.), *West Germany under Construction: Politics, Society and Culture in the Adenauer Era*, Ann Arbor, University of Michigan Press, 1997. The question of the Americanization of German society is discussed in R. Willett, *The Americanization of Germany*, London, Routledge, 1989, R. Pommerin (ed.), *The American Impact on Postwar Germany*, Oxford and Providence, RI, Berghahn, 1995 and M. Rosen, 'Reconstruction and Modernization. The Federal Republic and the Fifties', *Bulletin*, vol. XIX, no. 1, May 1997, pp. 5–16, London, German Historical Institute. C. C. Schweitzer (ed.), *Politics and Government in Germany, 1944–1994: Basic Documents*, Oxford and New York, Berg, 2nd edn, 1995 contains a useful collection of documents on politics in the FRG.

The GDR

The fall of the GDR in 1990 has inevitably made all the histories of East Germany written before that period out of date, as historians now have access to the East German archives. M. Fulbrook, *Anatomy of a Dictatorship. Inside the GDR, 1949–89*, Oxford, Oxford University Press, 1995 is one of the first books in English to use this new material and it has a useful chapter on the fall of the GDR. G. Pritchard, *The Making of the GDR*, Manchester, Manchester University Press, 2000 covers the early years of the Republic, while P. Grieder, *Tension, Conflict and Opposition in the Leadership of the Socialist Unity Party, 1946–73*, Manchester, Manchester University Press, 1999 covers the years up to 1973. Grieder's *The German Democratic Republic*, Basingstoke, Palgrave/Macmillan, 2012 is a concise survey of the GDR. Some older studies, such as M. McCauley, *The GDR since 1945*, Basingstoke and London, Macmillan, 1983; D. Childs, *The GDR: Moscow's German Ally*, London, Allen and Unwin, 1985 and G. Edwards, *GDR Society and Social Institutions*, London and Basingstoke, Macmillan, 1985 still remain useful for the political, social and economic aspects of the GDR. A. Baring, *Uprising in East Germany*, Ithaca, NY, Cornell University Press, repr. 1972 is well worth reading, but needs to be supplemented by post-1990 work, such as

V. Ingimundarsan, 'Cold War Misperceptions: The Communist and Western Responses to the East German Refugee Crisis in 1953', *Journal of Contemporary History*, vol. 29, 1994, pp. 463–481. K. J. Jarausch (ed.), *Dictatorship as Experience*, New York and Oxford, Berghahn, 1999 is an illuminating collection of essays on the socio-cultural history of the GDR, while J. Kopstein, *Economic Decline in East Germany, 1945–89*, Chapel Hill, NC, and London, University of North Carolina Press, 1997 is an interesting study of the GDR's economy. An unusual book on life in the GDR and the ever present threat of the Stasi is A. Funder, *Stasiland*, London, Granta, 2003. J. Thomaneck and J. Mellis, *Politics, Society and Government in the GDR: Basic Documents*, Oxford and New York, Berg, 1989 contains a selection of relevant primary sources.

The unification of Germany

Ostpolitik and unification are well covered in T. Garton Ash, *In Europe's Name. Germany and the Divided Continent*, London, Cape, 1993. K. Jarausch, *The Rush to German Unity*, Oxford, Oxford University Press, 1994 is a readable and comprehensive account of the events leading to unification, while C. Maier, *Dissolution. The Crisis of Communism and the End of East Germany*, Princeton, NJ, Princeton University Press, 1997 is particularly good on the economic collapse of the GDR. A helpful collection of primary sources on unification is K. Jarausch and V. von Gransow (eds), *Uniting Germany. Documents and Debates 1944–93*, Oxford and Providence, RI, Berghahn, 1994.

The Berlin Republic

As much of the history of the Berlin Republic is still contemporary, the bulk of studies on it are in the form of articles or monographs. K. Larres (ed.), *Germany Since Unification. The Development of the Berlin Republic*, London and Basingstoke, Palgrave, 2001; J. Sperling (ed.), *Germany at fifty-five*, Manchester, Manchester University Press, 2004 and M. Dennis and E. Kolinsky (eds), *United and Divided. Germany since 1990*, New York and Oxford, Berghahn, 2004 are informative collection of essays on the political, economic, military and diplomatic developments in the new Germany since 1990. D. P. Conradt, et al. (ed.), *Precarious Victory. The 2002 German Federal Election and its Aftermath* is an informative study of Schröder's victory in 2002. S. Kornelius, *Angela Merkel*, Richmond, Alma Books, 2013 and A. Crawford and T. Czuczka, *Angela Merkel: A Chancellorship Forged in Crisis*, Chichester, Bloomberg, 2013 are useful but inevitably unfinished biographies, which shed some light on Merkel and the financial crises of 2008–2012.

Online material

German History in Documents and Images (GHDI), an initiative of the German Historical Institute, Washington, is a comprehensive collection of primary source material with English translations. It consists of ten sections compiled by leading scholars in the field. It can be downloaded free of charge.

Glossary and Abbreviations

Anschluss:	The incorporation of Austria into Germany, 1938.
APO:	Extra-Parliamentary Opposition (*Ausserparlamentarische Opposition*). In December 1966 on the initiative of the radical student leader Rudi Dutschke, the APO was founded in opposition to the Grand Coalition. It had no formal structure and was closely connected to the Socialist Student Federation.
Aryan:	Originally a Hindu term meaning a member of the highest caste, which first appeared in Count Gobineau's (1816–1882) *Essay on the Inequality of the Races*. It was much used by the Nazis to denote ethnic Germans as opposed to Jews.
Blitzkrieg:	A lightning war, which would, to quote Hitler, 'defeat the enemy as quickly as lightning'.
Bloc parties:	In July 1945 the Russians created the anti-Fascist bloc of parties in the Soviet Zone. After April 1946 it was dominated by the SED (q.v.).
Bund:	The German Confederation, 1815–1866.
Bundesrat:	Federal Council or upper house of parliament in which the *Länder* (q.v.) are represented in the FRG (q.v.). It was also the name of the upper house in the Second Empire, where the states were represented according to their size and power. Thus Prussia had 17 votes, Bavaria, 6, Saxony and Württemberg 4 each, and the other states from 3 to 1 each.
Bundestag:	The lower house of parliament in the FRG (q.v.).
Bundeswehr:	The Federal Army of the FRG (q.v.).
Bureaucracy:	National and state administrations, the civil service.
CDU:	Christian Democratic Union (*Christlich Demokratische Union*).
CDUD:	German Christian Democratic Union in the GDR (q.v.) (*Christlich Demokratische Union Deutschlands*).
Centre party:	Founded by Ludwig Windthorst (1812–1891) to defend Catholic interests in united Germany. From 1893 to 1907 it was the key party in a Conservative–Centre coalition, and it joined or cooperated with every coalition government in the Weimar Republic up to 1932. It was disbanded in 1933.
Collectivization:	The replacement of private farms by LPGs (agricultural production co-operatives) in the GDR (q.v.) between 1952 and 1961.
Comecon:	The Council for Mutual Economic Assistance, which was set up by Stalin in response to the European Recovery Programme (Marshall Plan) and the OEEC. The GDR (q.v.) joined it in 1950.
CSU:	Christian Social Union in Bavaria (*Christlich–Soziale Union*). It is allied to the CDU (q.v.).
DAP:	German Workers' Party (*Deutsche Arbeiterpartei*).
DDP:	German Democratic Party (*Deutsche Demokratische Partei*).
DNVP:	German National People's Party (*Deutsch-nationale Volkspartei*).
DVP:	German People's Party (*Deutsche Volkspartei*).
EDC:	European Defence Community.

[E]EC:	[European] Economic Community of which the FRG (q.v.) was a founding member.
Entente, Anglo-French:	Originally an understanding reached by the two powers on colonial issues, but increasingly it became a focus for anti-German collaboration after the First Moroccan Crisis.
Entente, Triple:	The term applied to the collaboration between Britain, France and Russia, 1907–1917.
FDJ:	Free German Youth (*Freie Deutsche Jugend*). The youth movement in the GDR (q.v.), founded in 1946. In the 1980s, membership was about 2,300,000.
FDP:	Free Democratic Party (*Freie Demokratische Partei*).
FRG:	Federal Republic of Germany.
Führer:	Leader. The term adopted by Hitler to denote his absolute leadership over first the Nazi Party and then Germany as a whole.
Gau:	A regional division of the Nazi Party organization.
Gauleiter:	A regional Nazi Party leader in charge of a *Gau*.
GDP:	Gross domestic product.
GDR:	German Democratic Republic.
German Labour Front (*Deutsche Arbeitsfront*):	This was created in May 1933 and put under the control of Robert Ley to replace the trade unions.
Gleichschaltung:	Literally coordinating or streamlining; the process of putting everything under Nazi control.
Grossdeutschland:	A united Germany which includes the German-speaking regions of the Austrian Empire.
Holy Roman Empire:	Originally composed of the German and North Italian territories of Otto I who was crowned emperor by the Pope in 962. From 1273 onwards the Empire was increasingly dominated by the Habsburgs. It was dissolved in 1806 by Napoleon.
Intentionalists:	Historians who emphasize the importance of the *individual* and personal *intention* in history. For example, intentionalists, like Andreas Hillgruber, Klaus Hildebrand and Lucy Davidowicz, stress the *intentions* of Hitler and his key role in the formulation of policies, particularly the foreign and racial policies of the Third Reich (q.v. Structuralists).
Junker class:	A term used not always accurately to describe the great East Elbian Prussian landowners. The term originally came from *Jungherr* and denoted the sons of the nobility serving as officer cadets.
Kartell:	Cartel or manufacturer's group set up to control and regulate production. Also used to describe an alliance of parties in the Second Reich.
KDF:	Strength through Joy (*Kraft durch Freude*). The leisure organization of the German Labour Front (q.v.).
Kleindeutschland:	A united Germany without Austria and therefore dominated by Prussia.
Kolonialverein:	Colonial Society founded in 1887; it helped create the ideological framework in which German nationalism developed up to 1914. The society remained active during the Weimar period.

KPD:	The German Communist Party (*Kommistische Partei Deutschlands*). Founded in 1919 and banned in 1933; after working underground it was refounded in 1945, and amalgamated with the Soviet Zone SPD (q.v.) in 1946 to create the SED (q.v.).
Kulturkampf:	A struggle between cultures. A term used to describe Bismarck's conflict with the Catholic Church, 1871–1887.
Land:	An individual German state within united Germany. The Reich of 1871 had 25 federal states, the largest being Prussia which covered two-thirds of Germany (q.v. *Bundesrat*).
Landtag:	Chamber of deputies (or assembly) at the level of one of the individual German states.
Landwehr:	Set up in February 1813 to comprise all men not serving in the regular army. In 1815 the *Landwehr* was reorganized, so that in war it would amalgamate with the regular army, but in time of peace keep its character as a militia. Increasingly the liberals saw it, in Boyen's words, as 'the happy union of the warrior and civilian society'. Hence their dismay at von Roon's reforms in 1860, which reduced its size and downgraded its importance.
Lebensraum:	Literally, living space, which Hitler hoped to gain in Russia for an apparently overpopulated Germany. This was a key component of his foreign policy.
Mittelstand:	Literally 'middle estate'. It denoted what in Britain was called the 'lower middle class': peasants, small businessmen, self-employed artisans and white-collar office workers.
Modernization:	According to the German sociologist, Max Weber, and later German and American scholars, this involved first the emergence of a modern capitalist economy and bureaucracy and then a democratic national state (q.v. *Sonderweg*).
Moratorium:	A suspension of debt (or reparations) payment.
National Front of Democratic Germany:	Formed in 1949 in the GDR (q.v.) to campaign for a united democratic socialist Germany; in reality it was a front for Soviet control of the GDR.
Nationalism:	In the course of German history from the 18th century until the present, nationalism has taken on several different forms, ranging from a sense of linguistic and cultural identity to the more aggressive ambitions in the Second Empire to become a world power. Under the Nazis nationalism was one of the factors that led to the Holocaust and the extermination policies in eastern Europe.
Nationalverein:	The National Union founded in 1858 to agitate for the creation of a *Kleindeutschland* (q.v. Germany).
NATO:	North Atlantic Treaty Organization set up in 1949. The FRG (q.v.) joined in 1955.
NPD:	The right-wing National Democratic Party (*Nationaldemokratische Partei Deutschlands*) was formed in 1964.
NSDAP:	The National Socialist German Workers' Party (*Nationalsozialistische Deutsche Arbeiterpartei*). In February 1920 the small German Workers' Party changed its name to NSDAP. In July

	1921 Hitler was elected chairman. It was banned after the Munich *putsch* but refounded in 1925. On 14 July 1933 it was declared the only legal political party in Germany.
OPEC:	Organization of the Petroleum Exporting Countries.
Ostpolitik:	The eastern policy conducted by the FRG (q.v.) towards the GDR (q.v.).
Pan-Germans:	Those who believed in the unification of all Germans in Europe. Hence the Pan-German League believed that the 1871 frontiers were only the starting point for the future development of the German state.
PDS:	Party of Democratic Socialism (successor to the SED (q.v.)).
Politburo:	The Political Bureau of the SED (q.v.). It was based on the Russian model and was the key decision-making body in the GDR (q.v.).
Progressive Liberal Party (*Fortschrittspartei*):	Founded in 1861 and underwent several amalgamations with subsequent name changes until 1918, when most of its members joined the DDP (q.v.).
RAF:	Red Army Faction (*Rote Armee Fraktion*). A left-wing extremist group which carried out a campaign of violence in the FRG (q.v.) in the 1970s and 1980s.
Reich:	Literally Empire. The first Reich was the Holy Roman Empire (q.v.). The Second Reich was the united *Kleindeutschland* of 1871, while Hitler used the term Third Reich to describe the new Nazi Germany in 1933. The latter came into common usage with the publication of Moeller van den Bruck's book, *Germany's Third Reich* in 1923.
Reichsbank:	The German Central Bank, 1875–1945, responsible for currency issue.
Reichsrat:	The upper house of the German parliament in which the federal states were represented, 1919–1933. It was, unlike the *Bundesrat* (q.v.), which it replaced, in practice subordinated to the democratically elected *Reichstag* (q.v.).
Reichstag:	The lower house of the German parliament, 1871–1945.
Reichswehr:	The German army, 1919–1935. This was then replaced by the term *Wehrmacht*, which also included the air force and navy.
RKFDV:	Commission for the Consolidation of German Nationhood (*Reichskommissariat für die Festigung des Deutschen Volksstums*). This position gave Himmler responsibility for 'ethnic cleansing' in eastern Europe.
SA:	Nazi storm or assault troops (*Sturmabteilung*). The SA was originally founded in 1921 to protect party meetings. With the elimination of Röhm on 30 June 1934 it effectively lost its power to the SS (q.v.).
SAG:	Soviet limited company (*Sowjetische Aktiengesellschaft*). These were set up in the Soviet Zone in January 1946 to produce goods for the USSR as part of the German reparation programme.
SD:	Security Service of the SS (*Sicherheitsdienst*) (q.v.).
SED:	Socialist Unity Party of Germany (*Sozialistische Partei Deutschlands*).

Septennat: A septennial (i.e. lasting for 7 years) military budget.

SMAD: Soviet military administration in Germany.

Sonderweg: Literally, special path. Scholars such as Hans-Ulrich Wehler, using Britain and France as models, have argued that industrialization in Germany was not accompanied by social and political 'modernization' or democratization. Hence Germany took its 'special path'. This is disputed, particularly by D. Blackbourn and G. Eley.

SPD: The German Social Democratic Party (*Sozialdemokratische Partei Deutschlands*) was formed through the amalgamation of Ferdinand Lassalle's General German Workers' Union and August Bebel's Union of German Workers' Associations at the unity congress at Gotha in 1875. By 1912 the SPD was the largest party in Germany. It was dissolved by Hitler, but was reformed in 1945 (q.v. SED and USPD).

SS: Literally, protection squad (*Schutzstaffel*). It was founded in 1925 to protect the leading Nazis. It played a key role within the Nazi Party, when Himmler was put in charge of it in 1929, and then, after 1933, in Nazi Germany. When Himmler established control over the whole police and security systems within the Reich in 1936, its influence was greatly strengthened. Its control of the police and then the occupied territories enabled it to play a dominant role in formulating the racial policy of the Third Reich (q.v. *Waffen-SS*).

Stasi: State Security Police (*Staatssicherheitsdienst*) in the GDR (q.v.).

Structuralists: The name given to the school of historians, the most eminent members of which are H. and W. Mommsen, M. Broszat and H.-U. Wehler, who apply a structural analysis to modern German history. When dealing with the Third Reich, they play down the role of the individual and place more emphasis on the German elites and the polycratic nature of the regime (q.v. Intentionalists).

USPD: German Independent Social Democratic Party (*Unabhängige Sozialdemokratische Partei Deutschlands*).

Völkisch: This term can be translated as 'folkish', but there is no real equivalent in English. The *völkisch* ideology preached the creation and preservation of a traditional Germanic, national and above all racial community. It was anti-Semitic, as the Jews were perceived to be a threat to the traditional Germany, and it formed an important component of the ideology of the Nazi Party (q.v. nationalism).

Volksgemeinschaft: Literally, national community. This was to be created by unifying the population primarily on the basis of nationalism (q.v.) and race. By fusing nationalism with some elements of socialism, Hitler hoped to end class conflict and create a new national community.

Volkskammer: Lower house of the GDR parliament (q.v.).

Waffen-SS: Militarized or armed SS. A term first used in 1940. Three SS regiments were created after 1934, which formed the core of the *Waffen-SS* (q.v. SS).

Warsaw Pact: A military alliance of eastern European communist states set up by the USSR in 1955. The GDR joined in 1956 (q.v.).

Zollverein: The German Customs Union formed in 1833 with a membership of 18 states. By 1852 only the two Mecklenburgs, the Hansa cities and Holstein remained outside. The Austrian Empire, however, remained excluded.

Index